EL GRECO

First published in Spanish under the title
Doménikos Theotokópoulos El Greco, 1541-1614
by Ediciones Polígrafa, S. A.

Published in 1973 by The Viking Press, Inc.
625 Madison Avenue, New York, N. Y. 10022

Published simultaneously in Canada by
The Macmillan Company of Canada Limited

SNB 670-29083-1
Library of Congress catalog card number: 73-381

Printed and bound in Spain by La Polígrafa, S. A. - Balmes, 54 - Barcelona-7 Spain - Dep. Legal: B. 12.972 - 1973

DOMENIKOS THEOTOKOPOULOS

EL GRECO

1541-1614

BY

JOSÉ GUDIOL

TRANSLATED FROM THE SPANISH BY

KENNETH LYONS

A STUDIO BOOK

THE VIKING PRESS

NEW YORK

TABLE OF CONTENTS

PROLOGUE

This book is an endeavour to create a synthesis of all that is known today of Domenikos Theotokopoulos, to present reproductions of works that are unquestionably his or can be attributed to him with the greatest margin of accuracy, and to study the work of the great Cretan painter as a whole. The text is intended to constitute an analysis of his concept of painting, following the development of his style through its various stages and periods, and at the same time a compilation of all the known data on his life. Such works as are dated with chronological certainty have served as milestones for attributing possible dates to the non-dated works. This is not a complete catalogue of the works generally accepted as attributable to El Greco but we have endeavoured to include all those Grecos that we consider of real importance, the limitations of space imposed by a single volume having obliged us to leave out those exact or almost exact replicas that the painter carried out as part of his normal day's work. Nor have we included works done by his assistants – and still less the copies done by the painter's contemporaries. Though well aware that the definitive classification of these extremely important groups of canvases will still require an immense task of analysis on the part of future generations of art historians, we have not ventured to embark upon such a corpus, for every age must give its own vision of the works of the great artists of the past.

Let us now say something of the general characteristics of El Greco's work and development. In this painter we are confronted with the case of an artist of the very first rank whose work developed throughout the periods he spent in three very different artistic centres. First there was Crete, with his craftsman's work as the anonymous creator of icons; he was already a professional when he moved to Venice and, later, to Rome. His masters were the great Italian artists of the 16th century, the ones who opened up the way for modern painting. In a very few years El Greco, in spite of his humble origins, had reached as high a level as his teachers, achieving a revealing synthesis of his original personality.

At some unknown date he moved to Spain and he settled in Toledo in 1577, being then over thirty-five years old; in Toledo he established a studio with a team of assistants and there he died in 1614.

The circumstances of the time inevitably involved him in a bitter struggle, but his lack of success with Philip II spared him commitments which might possibly have circumscribed his liberty and the development of his art. The truth is that he created an absolutely new concept of painting, a concept, moreover, in which he was to have no real followers. Only he was capable of painting a "Greco". He passed from a first period still somewhat influenced by Italian models to a more analytical one, with geometrized forms. All accessories were eliminated from his pictures. Flesh tints, vast draperies, clouds and light through clouds were the only elements he employed to stir the emotions, with the occasional use of some landscape backgrounds, generally of the Escorial or Toledo. Though he had a profound interest in iconography and was a religious painter who followed faithfully the dictates of the counter-reformation, what really aroused his enthusiasm above all else was painting, i.e., pictorial quality for its own sake; and that is why his evolution is a constant ascent. Though capable, as he demonstrated, of painting in a perfectly realistic manner, his propensity for idealization led him to adopt a number of extremely personal procedures: elongation of the canon of the figures, attenuation of the faces, deformation of the foreshortening, flickering, flame-like rhythms and a predominantly vertical emphasis – to all of which should be added his constant inventiveness in the use of colour, handled with a boldness nobody else in his generation, or in the next, dared emulate. In his last phase, after the great "classic" pictures of his middle period, such as the world-famous *Burial of the Conde de Orgaz,* the deformation was no longer due to purely optical reasons but attained true expressionism, as may be seen in the *Fifth Seal,* the *Laocoön,* etc., without any falling-off in the quality of the works.

The great paradox consists in the fact that El Greco's style is quite easy to imitate. What cannot be imitated is the perfection of the results. His studio assistants and his own son, Jorge Manuel, imitated him with surprising ease, but they never attained to the same excellence. This, however, enabled him to organize a sort of mass production of quite a number of compositions, which were accepted as originals in his time and are still so accepted today.

As a result of this we have seen, in more recent times, the transition from imitations executed in good faith to what we might almost call systematic falsification. The forgers of El Greco's works have attained an incredible degree of skill in their trade and have succeeded in making both historians and collectors feel uneasy. It is to be hoped that research of ever greater depth, dwelling less upon the superficial aspects of what constitutes a "Greco", may gradually stem, once and for all, the execution and diffusion of such forgeries.

To come back to the artist himself, it seems clear that El Greco aroused the interest of the people of his time and succeeded in assimilating the mystic feeling of the Spain of Philip II; his lesser works, in particular, created a living climate in the imagery of the saints which evoked the devotion of Spaniards. Thanks to his studio mass production he managed to survive the great failures which marked his life in Spain, failures which, as often as not, came about in connection with his more important works. On the other hand, he had great and faithful admirers, from the Castilla brothers, who set him up in Toledo, to Dr. Angulo, who assisted him with advice and money throughout his difficult career. We can find witnesses to the esteem in which his painting was held in the most remarkable series of portraits which he painted towards the end of his life, at the same time as his important commissions and religious images. Velázquez possessed quite a collection of these portraits which, on his death, became part of Philip IV's collection. Palomino, speaking of Velázquez, says: "In his portraits he imitated Dominico Greco, for in his opinion that painter's heads could never be sufficiently extolled".

The eulogies devoted to the painter of the *Martyrdom of St. Maurice* reached their highest point in the impassioned sonnets of Fray Hortensio Paravicino, for which El Greco expressed his gratitude with one of his best portraits. And when he died he had sonnets dedicated to him by Luis de Góngora and Cristóbal de Mesa.

But Spain did not take long to forget El Greco. Only the most modest of painters endeavoured to keep his memory green with their unimaginative copies of his originals. The savants and the few writers on art of that time continued to refer to his work, but they generally did so rather coldly, as if simply fulfilling a rather tedious obligation.

The writers of the 18th and 19th centuries either pronounced unfavourable verdicts on his work or dismissed it with a handful of learned (and rather inexact) quotations, both approaches being equally harmful, despite the fact that there had been no decline in the general admiration for the *Burial of the Conde de Orgaz* and the *Espolio*. The more conscientious among these authors, men like Palomino (1724), Ponz (1772-94), Ceán Bermúdez (1800) and Stirling (1843), did not fail to express a certain admiration for some of his works, but the painter's genius was, on the whole, considered mere eccentricity in many cases.

Justi was one of the first to realize the enormous value of El Greco's concept of painting, but for this we have to wait until 1881. Justi was followed in his appreciation by the writers and artists of what is known in Spain as the "Generation of '98", who helped to prepare the way for a reassessment of this forgotten painter and to arouse and hold the admiration of scholars and experts on the occasion of the exhibition held in the Prado in 1902. This exhibition gave rise to Cossío's analytical studies, later expanded into his really extraordinary book, the first publication wholly devoted to El Greco (1908). After this seminal book was published studies of the Cretan painter became ever more numerous and enthusiastic. Among those figuring in our bibliography we might mention the works of Meier Graefe (1910), Barrès (1912), Kehrer (1914), Lafond and others. But it was Francisco de San Román, thanks to his scholarly and painstaking research in the archives of Toledo, who first established a documentary – and therefore reliable – basis for the complete study of El Greco, with works published between 1910 and 1934. In 1926 an extensive catalogue of El Greco's work was published by Mayer. Three years later Waterhouse brought out the first study of the painter's Italian period, a healthy reaction against the nonsensical muddle of Willumsen's book, published in 1927. The earlier work of El Greco was also studied by Pallucchini, who in 1937 revealed to the world the beautiful polyptych in the Galleria Estense. The first collection of reproductions worthy of El Greco's work was published by Goldscheider in 1938. All this paved the way for the three great modern works, those by Camón Aznar (1950), Soehner (1957-1960) and Wethey (1962), all of them indispensable for anyone interested in the great master's life, work, style, technique or working methods. In the course of the present text the reader will have occasion to see that it is principally on them that we base this work.

The author began the present study in Toledo, Ohio, where he spent the years 1940 and 1941 taking part in the important teaching programme of the Toledo Museum of Art, but its escalation into a book and the research involved in bringing this to fruition are of more recent date.

The author wishes to express here his gratitude for the very effective assistance received in the Toledo Museum of Art from its late and great director, Blake More Godwin. The research was carried out in the Instituto Amatller de Arte Hispánico, which made it possible to amass an extremely useful fund of bibliographical information and an incomparable collection of documentary photographs, apart from the opportunity of making frequent trips to study the originals. The author, therefore, also wishes to express his thanks to his collaborators in that institution, especially Juan Ainaud de Lasarte, Santiago Alcolea and Montserrat Blanch, and at the same time to helpful occasional consultants, among them the late Halldor Soehner and Martín Soria, and to his esteemed colleagues José Camón Aznar and Harold Wethey, both eminent Greco specialists. The author must also thank Francisco Javier Sánchez Cantón and Diego Angulo, who were directors of the Prado throughout all these years of work, and his good friend Javier de Salas, the present director of our great gallery, as well as María Elena Gómez Moreno, curator of the Greco Museum in Toledo. Indeed, this list of those who in one way or another helped to make this book possible should be much longer than it is.

Finally, the author must mention Juan-Eduardo Cirlot, who has been of inestimable assistance in the matter of certain stylistic analyses.

I

1541 - *c.* 1576

EL GRECO'S FAMILY — GIULIO CLOVIO'S LETTER AND MANCINI'S BIOGRAPHY — THE PROBLEM OF MAESTRO DOMENIKOS — WORKS PAINTED BY EL GRECO IN VENICE AND ROME — PORTRAITS PAINTED IN ITALY.

Domenikos Theotokopoulos, the man who was to go down in history under the name of El Greco, was born in Candia, the capital of Crete, in 1541. The date of his birth is known to us from two documents of 1606, documents included in the lawsuit brought in connection with the altarpieces of Illescas, in which the painter declares that he is sixty-five years old. Of his father, whose name was Jorghi, all we know is that he died some time before 1566. We know rather more, however, about the painter's elder brother, Manoussos, who in 1566 was given the post of tax collector in Candia by the ducal government in Venice; it should be remembered that the island of Crete had been a possession of the Venetian Republic since the thirteenth century. When El Greco's son was born in Toledo in 1578, he was given the name of Jorge Manuel, in deference to the custom of giving a grandson his grandfather's name. In this case he also received the name of his uncle, Manoussos, under whose shadow his father may well have begun his apprenticeship as a painter in Candia. All these data appear in an interesting study published by Constantino D. Mertzios on the transactions of the Greek notary Michael Maras, who worked in the capital of Crete between 1538 and 1578.

In these transactions we also find evidence of the painter's presence in Crete, for he appears as a witness to the sale of some house property on June 6th 1566, signing himself "Maistro Menegos Theotokopoulos Sgourafos". "Menegos" is the Venetian dialect form of Domenikos, while "Sgourafos" is the Greek form of the word "painter". Most historians are of the opinion that this signature in 1566 is evidence of nothing more than a chance visit by the painter to his native city, considering it certain that El Greco had already been living in Venice since at least as early as 1560. We think it better to leave this question unsettled, but we do incline to believe that El Greco's arrival in Venice took place in the summer of 1566. We have only indirect references to his residence in Venice, where the very numerous Greek colony lived in a cluster round the Orthodox church of San Giorgio dei Greci. The name of Domenikos Theotokopoulos does not appear in the records of this church, though this may possibly be due to the fact that the painter was brought up in the Roman faith.

Giulio Clovio's letter and Mancini's biography

To be accurate, the first specific information we have regarding El Greco's years in Italy comes from the providential letter written by Giulio Clovio to the Cardinal Alessandro Farnese and signed in Rome on November 16th of 1570, which reads in part as follows: "A young Candiote pupil of Titian's has arrived in Rome, a really excellent painter in my opinion. Among other things he has done a portrait of himself which has astonished all the painters in Rome. I should like to recommend him to the patronage of your Eminence, his only practical necessity being a room in the Palazzo Farnese for a short time, until he can find more suitable lodging. I should be grateful if your Eminence would accede to this and write to Count Ludovico, your steward, instructing him to provide this man with some room in the upper part of the palace. In this your Eminence would be performing a work of charity worthy of your Eminence and I should be much obliged to your Eminence. Kissing your hands in all reverence, I remain,

Your Eminence's most humble servant."

It will be recalled that Giulio Clovio, one of the greatest illuminators of manuscripts of his time, was a Greek of Croatian origin. He lived in the Palazzo Farnese from 1561 until his death in 1578. This letter does not mention the name of the "young Candiote pupil of Titian's" who, on his arrival in Rome, sought the support of a Greek artist well established in that city, but his identification as Domenikos Theotokopoulos is supported by the signed portrait of *Giulio Clovio (Fig. 32 - Cat. 25)* and by the fact that the inventory of the collection of Fulvio Orsini, librarian to Cardinal Farnese, includes seven paintings (among them the portrait of Clovio) "di mano d'un Grego scolare del Tiziano" and "del soprado Greco". We know, moreover, that two paintings from El Greco's Italian period, *Boy lighting a candle* in the Naples Museum and *Christ healing the blind man* in the Parma Museum, come from the Farnese collection *(Figs. 29 & 21 - Cat. 22 & 16),* all of which goes to prove that the Cardinal did in fact provide our painter with a lodging.

His stay in Rome, besides, would bring him into contact with Spaniards there. Through Fulvio Orsini he probably met Pedro Chacón, a canon of Toledo who lived for a long time in the Eternal City, collaborating on the reform of the church calendar, and Luis de Castilla, who was in Rome when El Greco was living there. Luis de Castilla was El Greco's first friend in Toledo and executor of his will in 1614. His brother, Diego de Castilla, who was Dean of the Chapter of Toledo Cathedral, was, as we shall see, the painter's first patron in Spain.

Another *point d'appui* for our knowledge of the earlier years of El Greco is the following biographical note, which is contained in a manuscript in the Vatican Library. Its author, Giulio Cesare Mancini, wrote it around the year 1619, i.e. five years after the painter's death. "During the pontificate of Pius V of blessed memory [1568-1572], there arrived in Rome . . . [a man] who was commonly known as El Greco. This man, who had studied in Venice, especially the works of Titian, had attained a high degree of excellence in his profession and in his way of practising it. From there he came to Rome at a time when there were not many men [painters], and none of them could paint works of the authority and freshness that characterized his. And these qualities grew even greater with the stimulus of private commissions, the result of one of which can be seen today in the collection of the lawyer Lancilloti, a work which some believe to be by Titian. At that time there was some talk of covering up some of the figures in Michelangelo's *Last Judgment,* which Pope Pius considered indecent, and [this painter] suddenly declared that if the whole work were destroyed he could paint it again chastely and decently and just as well as the original as regards good pictorial execution.

"Such was the indignation of all the painters and lovers of art that he found it expedient to remove to Spain, where, under Philip II, he painted many works of very good taste. But on the arrival in that country of Pellegrino Tibaldi, Federico Zuccaro and some Flemish painters, whose wiles and machinations helped them to the first places, he decided to leave the court and retire to . . . where he died at an advanced age, almost totally removed from the world of art. He was a man, nevertheless, who became, in the prime of his life, one of the best [painters] of his century."

Mancini's manuscript also makes a brief reference to the painter Lattanzio Bonastri, who is mentioned as having been El Greco's apprentice in Rome. The scanty and mediocre work of Bonastri, which is preserved in Siena, is not in the least reminiscent of the style of El Greco, though there is some similarity of anecdotal detail in his iconography.

Mancini's summary biography corroborates the letter from Clovio and El Greco's apprenticeship to Titian in Venice. It also reveals his high reputation for skill, since he is spoken of as superior to the other painters working in Rome during the time he spent in that city. And, in speaking of his removal to Spain, it indicates the importance of his failure to please Philip II thanks to the "wiles" of other foreign painters, the excellence of his copious work and his settling in a Spanish city —which is not named— where he died "at an advanced age, almost totally removed from the world of art". It should be observed that, though Mancini's knowledge of the essential facts was fairly exact, he was unable to give either El Greco's real name or the name of the city of Toledo in his text. Why should we not give credence to El Greco's boasting of what he could do if Pius V decided to destroy Michelangelo's fresco? If we grant this anecdote to be historically true, it is only logical to consider it, as Mancini does, one of the reasons for the painter's leaving Rome. And bearing in mind the fact that Pius V died in 1572, Mancini's assertion would mean that El Greco's sojourn in Rome lasted barely three years.

The problem of Maestro Domenikos

If it is true that the painter did not arrive in Venice until 1566, then his stay in that city would have been of approximately the same length. His Italian period being thus reduced to six years, it is much easier to understand his lack of any deep ties in that country and the ease with which he abandoned the formulas of Italian art —or quite a lot of them— when he was working out his personal manner in Spain. Nevertheless the impact of Venetian painting on the young painter from Candia, who had been trained in the routine techniques of a mere craftsman, must have been a very strong one.

It would be useless, in fact, to work out any hypothesis on the basis of such laconic documents. The works signed by El Greco in Italy, in spite of all the unexplained details, are much more explicit. But before we come to them there is one very difficult obstacle to be surmounted: the problem of the first works painted in Venice. Before going further we must confess that we have not come to any categorical conclusion in this respect. That is the great unknown factor that still affects all the studies published on El Greco, some of which admit the strangest attributions, some of which reject the most famous works in this group. The number of works attributed to El Greco in his first Venetian period has become a swift-growing tide, swollen by the combined efforts of extempore biographers, undemanding collectors, unscrupulous restorers and professional certificate-granters. It is almost always a case of paintings on small panels, from that still comparatively unknown world of the Veneto-Byzantine "Madonnieri". The discovery —after the publication of Cossío's book, which was the first analytical study of the work of El Greco— of three such paintings authentically signed seemed to clear up this problem, but such is not in fact the case, for these paintings present us with more doubts than certainties.

On all of these three works we find, in Greek capitals, the signature CHEÌR DOMÉNIKOU (Hand of Domenikos), which is indisputably authentic. They are a *St. Luke painting the Virgin (Fig. 1 - Cat. 1)* and an *Adoration of the Magi (Fig. 2 - Cat. 2)*, which are both in the Benaki Museum in Athens, and a small triptych in the Galleria Estense in Modena *(Figs. 5 & 6 - Cat. 3)*. Most art historians accepted them as original Grecos, and with this acceptance the problem of the Cretan painter's beginnings seemed to have been solved once and for all. The triptych, which comes from a collection formed in Venice towards the end of the eighteenth century, has six compositions of equal size: *Adam and Eve before the Eternal Father* and an *Annunciation,* on the outer surfaces of the doors; *The Adoration of the shepherds* and *The Baptism of Christ* on their inner side; an allegory of the glory of the Christian knight in the centre and, finally, a *View of Mount Sinai* on the back. It is this last composition that bears the signature. According to Pallucchini, the *Annunciation* derives from an engraving of a lost work by Titian, but this hypothesis is not accepted by Wethey. The *Adoration of the shepherds* is copied from an engraving by somebody who signs with the monogram I.B., after a painting by Titian. The composition in the centre is inspired by a woodcut, which was in turn the model for an engraving by Andrea Andreani in 1590. The view of Mount Sinai is based on a popular print that used to be sold to pilgrims at the monastery of St. Catherine on Mount Sinai itself.

The style of this triptych is one of fluid execution. On a greenish ground we find extensive sections treated with crimson, vivid yellow and scarlet. The details of the forms are determined with linear strokes in different tones, sometimes superimposing light on dark and forming a kind of vermicular network. This is the technique that characterizes the small paintings on panels, generally of a popular kind, produced by the "*Madonnieri*". The warm, strong tone of the narrative compositions contrasts with the almost monochrome treatment of the view of Mount Sinai painted on the back. Though the forms are rather soft, the work retains a slightly primitive quality. The most skilful feature of this triptych is, perhaps, the use of light and colour.

It is really difficult to agree that there is any unity of style between this triptych and the *Christ cleansing the Temple (Fig. 9 - Cat. 8),* a work signed by El Greco with his name and surname which we shall study later. It was Wethey who decided to destroy the unanimity of the historians by asserting that the painter of the Modena triptych was a certain Maestro Domenikos, a Greek "*Madonniero*" who worked in Venice.

It is a plausible theory enough, and certainly an attractive one, but it may perhaps be more prudent, pending fresh discoveries, to stick to the identification established by Mayer and Pallucchini. Nor can we fail to take into account the undeniable resemblance between the *Annunciation* of the triptych and the early works of El Greco on the same theme, to say nothing of the points of contact that exist between the central composition of the triptych and the *Adoration of the Name of Jesus (Fig. 38 - Cat. 29),* one of the first works El Greco was to paint in Spain. It is also true that there is some relationship between certain elements in the compositions of the triptych and some of El Greco's characteristic stylizations.

The *St. Luke* in the Benaki Museum, a panel acquired in 1956, does not seem to be the work of the painter of the triptych in Modena, being much more Byzantine and archaic in conception. Nor does the *Adoration* painted on canvas in the same museum, the third of these pictures signed CHEÌR DOMÉNIKOU, seem to have been executed either by the painter of the triptych or by the artist who painted the *St. Luke.* This would imply the existence of several painters called Domenico, which is not in the least unlikely —quite the contrary, in fact.

The problem becomes more complex with the appearance of a group of works that are technically related to the Modena triptych. The *Adoration of the shepherds,* a painting in oil on canvas in the Duke of Buccleuch's collection in England *(Fig. 3 - Cat. 4),* is a rather free copy of the same subject as in the triptych, but some of the characters —such as the central shepherd on the right— seem to approach the types that were to appear later in *Christ cleansing the Temple.* Another similar version, but smaller, is in the Broglio Collection in Paris *(Fig. 4 - Cat. 5).* A similar composition to the subject on the back of the Modena triptych is the *View of Mount Sinai* painted on a panel which was formerly in the Levi Collection in Venice *(Fig. 7 - Cat. 6).* Another work from the same group, representing *Christ in the house of Martha and Mary,* was formerly in the Brass Collection in Venice *(Fig. 8 - Cat. 7),* but it later passed from one collector to another and its present whereabouts is unknown. Here, too, the influence of Titian may be seen, but we would say that of all the group we are now considering this is the one that has most features in common with what was to be El Greco's style in later life, not only on account of the typology, but even in certain distortions. We have omitted from this group the series of works attributed to El Greco by Willumsen in his voluminous study of the painter's youth. Seldom, if ever, has the history of art reached such heights of error and confusion.

It is really difficult to arrive at any clear conclusions on the basis of such heterogeneous material. It is impossible to accept the whole of this group as the work of El Greco. But it is also rash, as we have already said, and at the same time too negative, to agree with Wethey in his sweeping elimination of all these paintings. Though we have no excessive faith in congresses and consensuses, we do think it might be possible to achieve some sort of basic criterion by bringing together in an exhibition of international scope as great a number as possible of the works that go to make up the group attributed to El Greco's beginnings in Venice.

Works painted by El Greco in Venice and Rome

Whatever the definitive decision of the historians may be with regard to the works we have just been considering, whichever of those among them will one day —by general consent— be considered to have been painted by the Domenikos who signed the Modena triptych, and whether this latter shall or shall not be identified beyond a doubt with Domenikos Theotokopoulos, what is really quite indisputable is that the very important group of panels and canvases that we are now about to deal with are the work of El Greco and were painted in Italy. Most of these paintings are signed with Greek capital letters. The unsigned ones are so very closely linked, in their subject-matter, technique and iconography, to those that bear the painter's signature that their inclusion in the catalogue of the original works of the great Cretan painter is now a matter of unanimity among art historians. The aforesaid signature appears in three forms: DOMÉNIKOS THEOTOKÓPOULOS EPOÍEI (made it), DOMÉNIKOS THEOTOKÓPOULOS KRÈS (Cretan) and DOMÉNIKOS THEOTOKÓPOULOS KRÈS EPOÍEI.

As we have already said, there is no certainty regarding either the exact date of El Greco's arrival in Venice or that of his removal from Rome. Some historians have proposed that his whole sojourn in

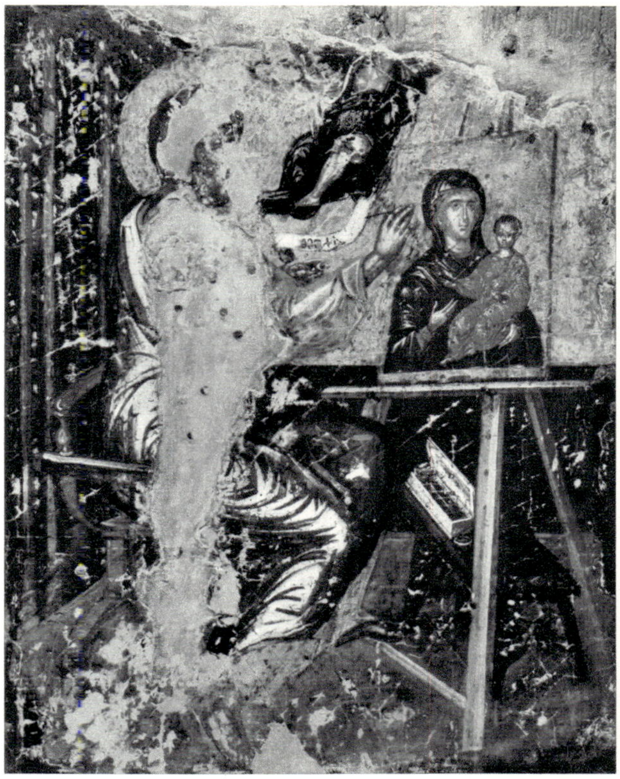

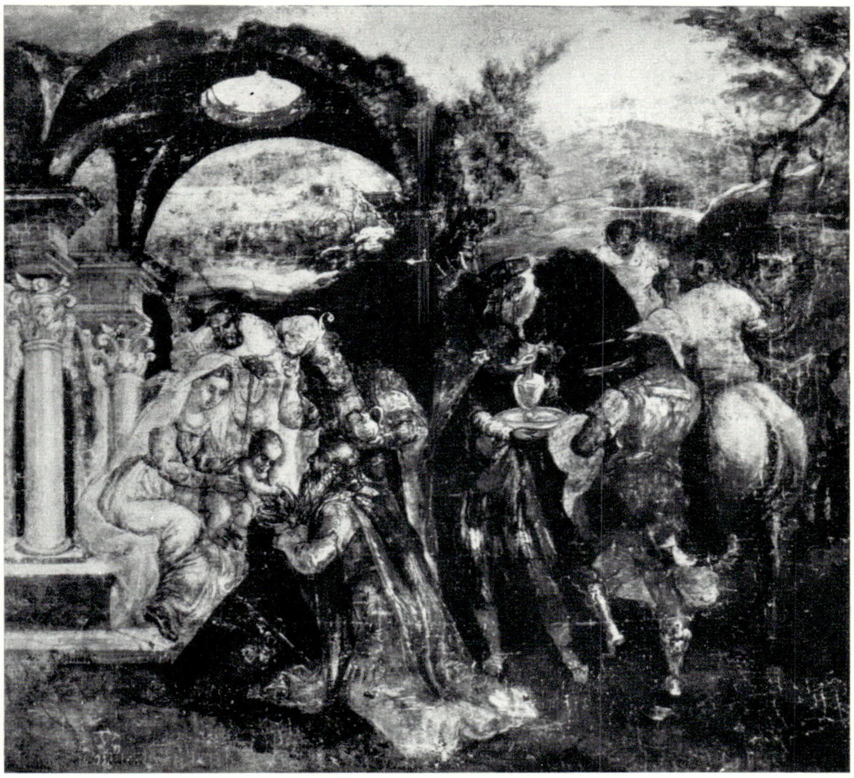

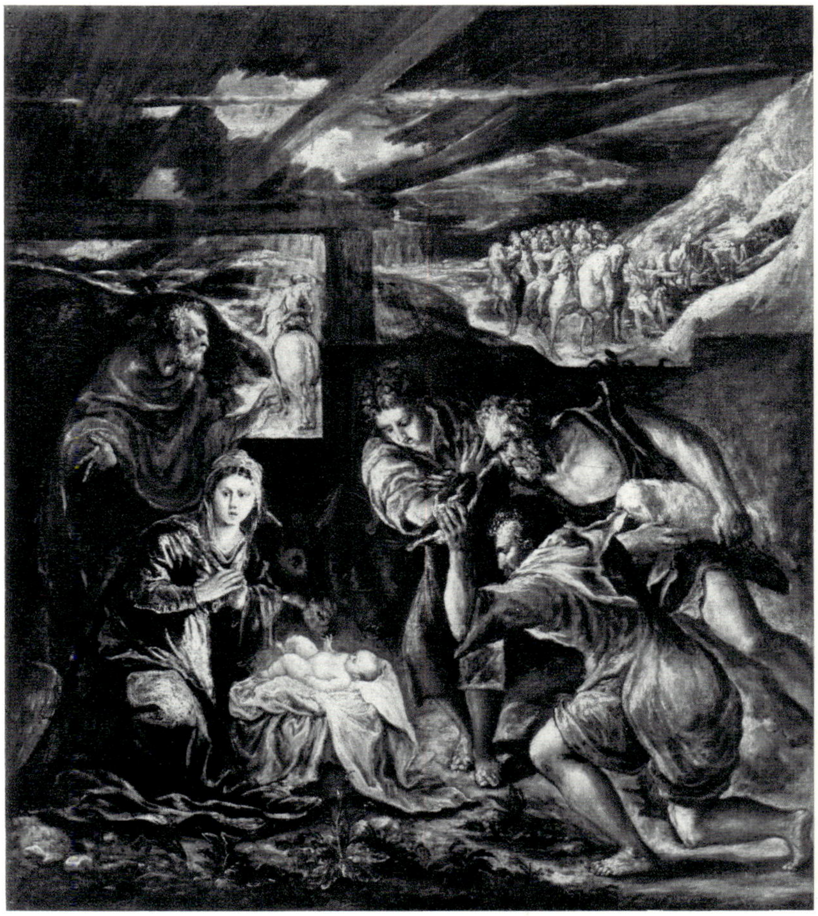

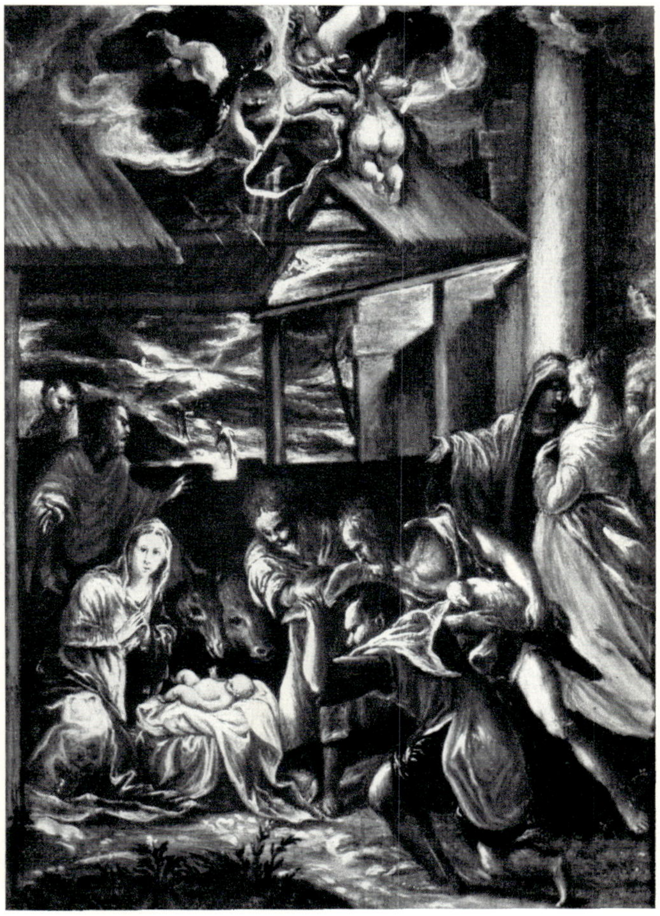

Fig. 1. St. Luke painting the Virgin. Panel signed CHEÌR DOMÉNIKOU. Athens, Benaki Museum. Cat. No. 1.
Fig. 2. The Adoration of the Magi. Canvas signed CHEÌR DOMÉNIKOU. Athens, Benaki Museum. Cat. No. 2.
Fig. 3. The Adoration of the shepherds. Kettering, Duke of Buccleuch Collection. Cat. No. 4.
Fig. 4. The Adoration of the shepherds. Paris, G. Broglio Collection. Cat. No. 5.

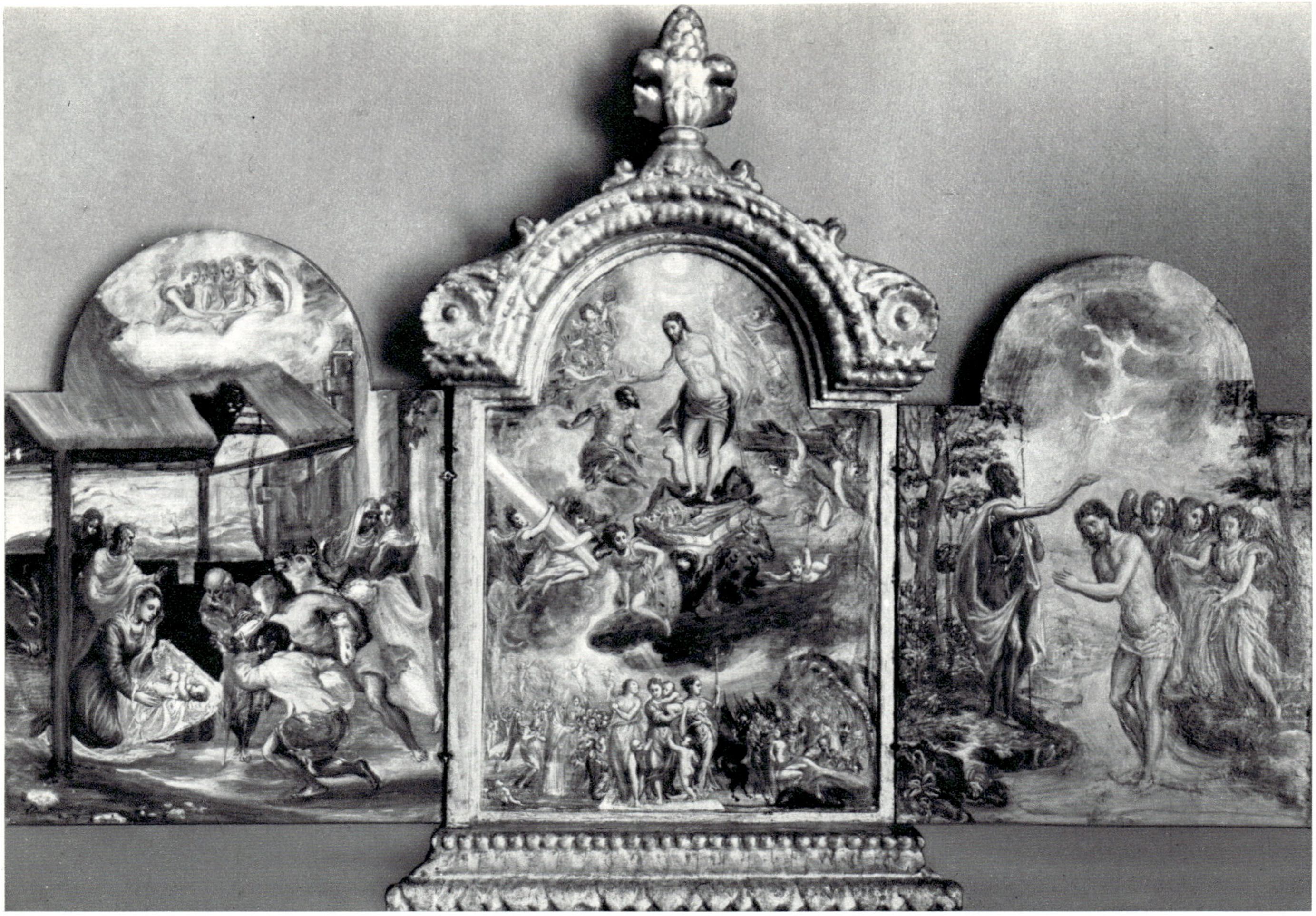

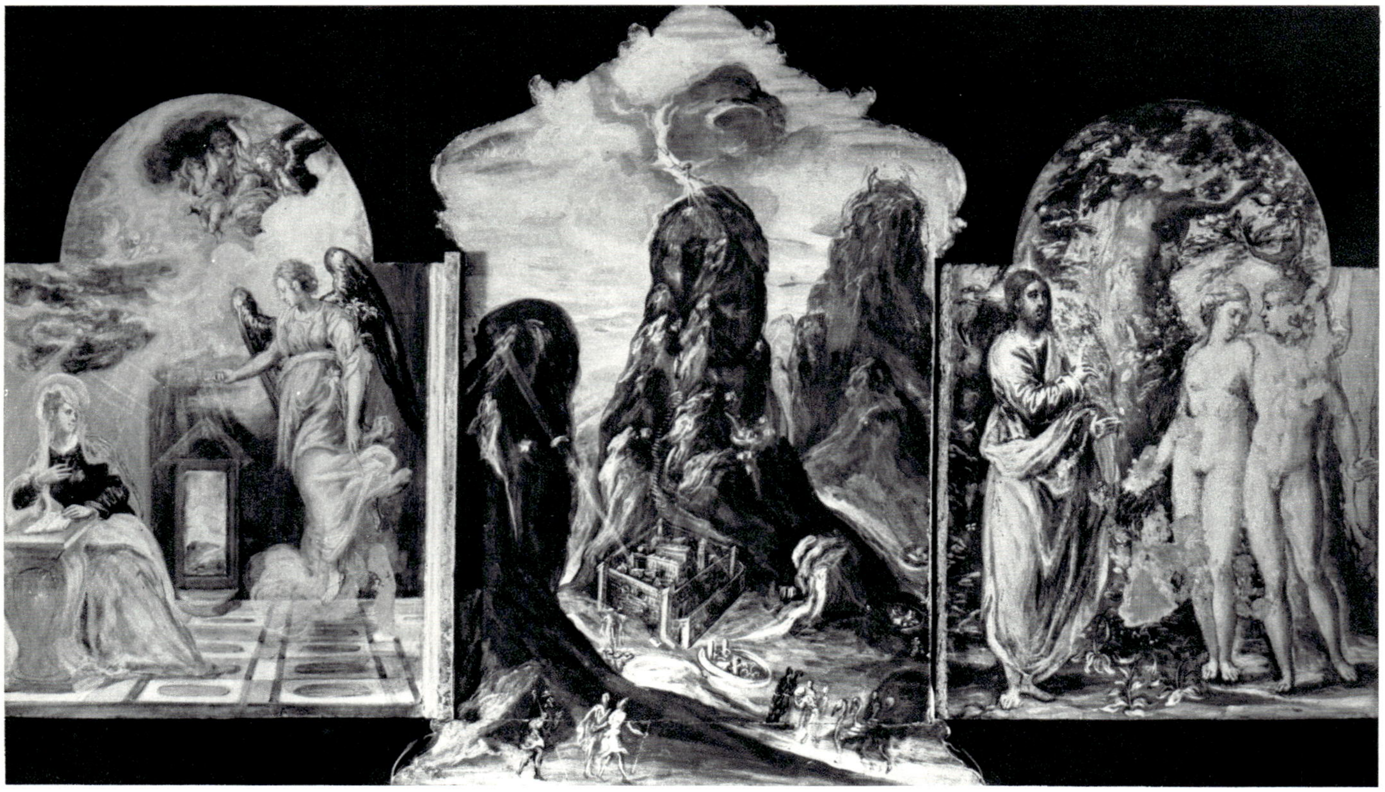

Figs. 5 & 6. Triptych. Signed CHEÌR DOMÉNIKOU. Modena, Galleria Estense. Cat. No. 3

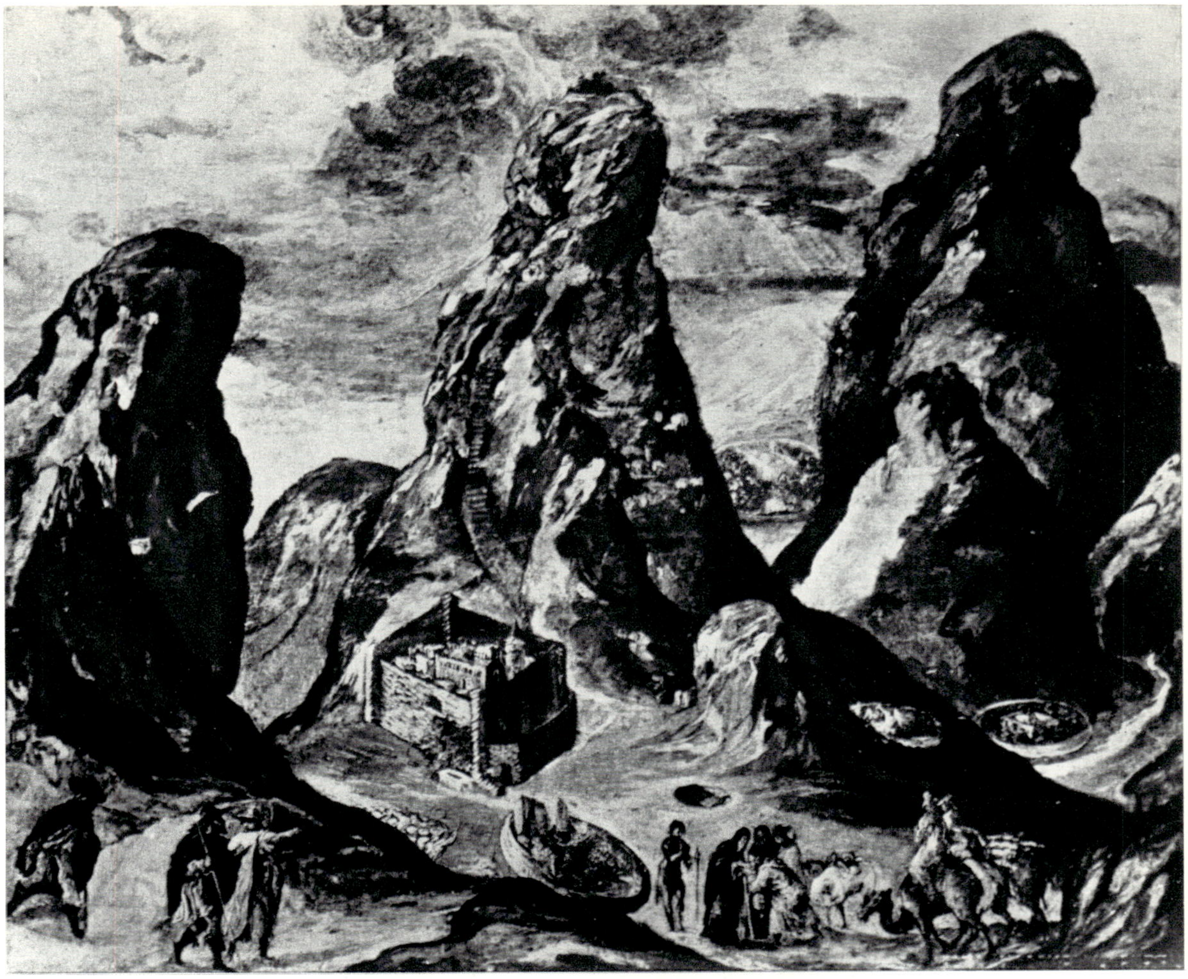

Fig. 7. View of Mount Sinai. Budapest, Baron Hatvany Collection. Cat. No. 6.

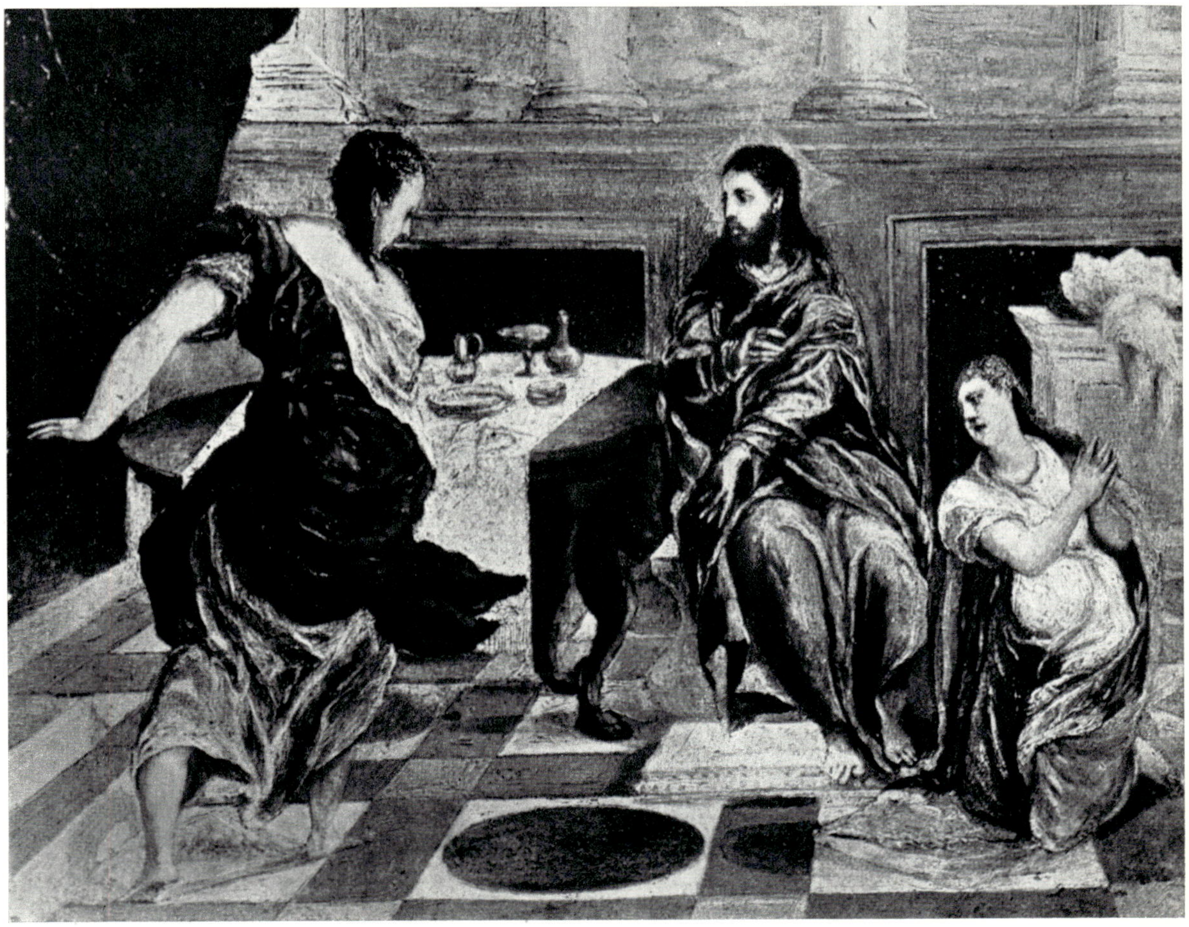

Fig. 8. Christ in the house of Martha and Mary. Formerly in the Brass Collection, Venice. Cat. No. 7.

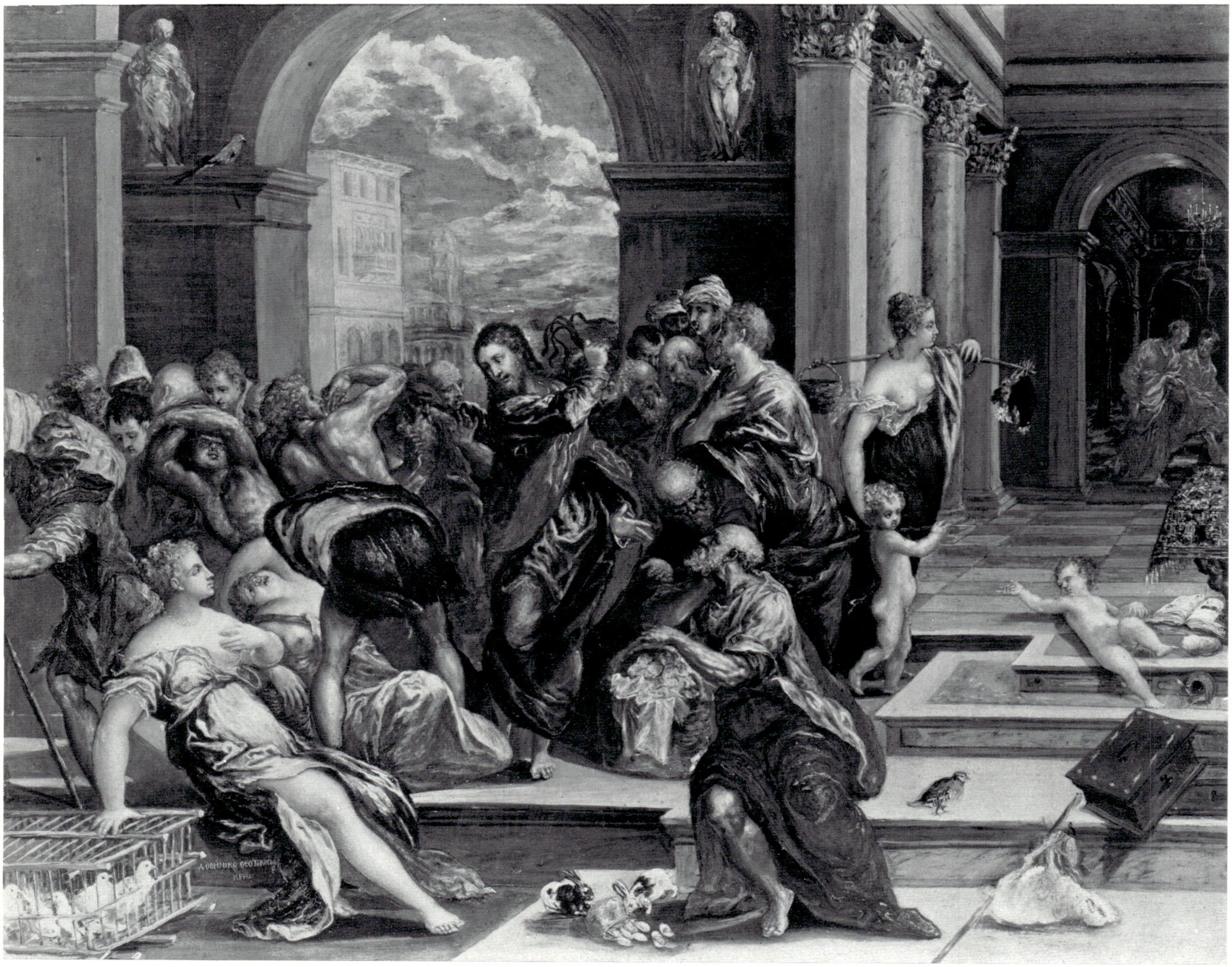

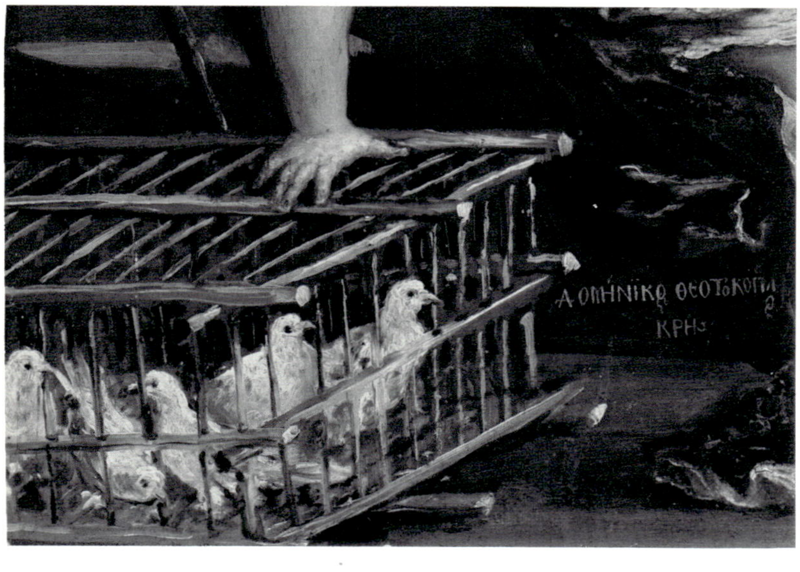

Figs. 9 & 10. Christ cleansing the Temple, before 1570. Washington, National Gallery. Cat. No. 8.

Italy should be divided into three periods, suggesting that he returned to Venice after having worked in Rome for four or five years. We ourselves prefer to abide by the simpler proposition of one stage in Venice and a later one in Rome, the dividing date being that of the letter from Giulio Clovio in 1570.

Although it is not necessarily the oldest of the works that go to make up the group we are about to study, we will begin this section with the famous *Christ cleansing the Temple (Fig. 9 - Cat. 8),* a small panel, now in the National Gallery in Washington, which is signed in Greek capitals. El Greco illustrated this passage from the Gospel of St. John by representing Christ striking out at a compact group of semi-naked men and women, who look more like refugees from one of Titian's Bacchanalia than peaceful vendors of caged pigeons, rabbits, chickens and eggs. The tumultuous scene is carefully planned and its actors, who are beautifully drawn, are evidently the result of direct studies from life. There is an abundance of foreshortening, generally well executed in accordance with the strictest canons of the later Venetian Renaissance, though the determination of the essential masses would seem to rely rather on colour than on the tonal values. The architectural background, which stands out against a blue sky, tends to unify the colours, being enlivened by the contrasting treatments of the ground, on which a transparent grey alternates with warm ochres and light blues. The principal colour in the clothing of the figures is a cobalt blue modelled in white, forming a kind of basic ground colour for the interplay of crimsons, greens, ochres and brownish tones, the whole being distributed in a disconcerting rhythm, though centered on the emphatic figure of Christ. His crimson-coloured robe dominates the whole composition chromatically, according to a hieratic system to which El Greco was to remain faithful all his life. The seated woman with the rather generous curves and Titian-like profile in the left foreground, the fallen girl (a copy of the classical figure of Niobe, which El Greco may have known through engravings) who appears behind this woman, the naked children on the right and the woman with the almost totally uncovered bosom who accompanies them, all provide centres of interest that contrast with the confused mass of the merchants.

We should also notice the skilled contrast between the rough structure of the draperies, full of ill-blended superimpositions, and the soft gradation of lights and shades in the modelling of the living elements. We have used the expression 'ill-blended', but we believe that this, which could be a defect, does not so much reveal ineptitude as the artist's fidelity to a long tradition: that of the Greek icon-painters from whose ranks he came. This *Cleansing* must have been one of the first works in which the painter showed that he was capable of freeing himself to a large extent —though still keeping some traces, as we have said— from the formulas he had used during his painting career in Candia. The preoccupation with line that is reflected in this technique was to disappear, but the independence of judgment which was, after all, what this formula represented, as against the meek copying of tactile qualities, was never to desert El Greco, who was to develop it, gradually but unremittingly, throughout his entire career.

Another anticipation of his later work may be found in the analysis of some of the foreshortenings and in his way of representing the nose from below, slightly distorting this feature in order to give it greater emphasis, as can be seen perfectly in the figure of the girl who has fallen and also in the man with the dark torso who is colliding with her. If we look attentively at two of the figures in the foreground, the woman sitting on the left and the old man with a sinewy arm who faces her, apparently listening to a companion who is leaning towards him (the grouping of the two heads is really excellent), we shall see that this painting undoubtedly belongs to a period of crisis. The figure of the woman expresses the teachings of Titian, with the new technique of blended modelling, though it still shows traces of the old procedures of the icon-painters; the figure of the merchant is carried out almost entirely by modelling in thin linear squiggles, reinforced by intense lights at the points of highest relief: foot, knee, muscles of the forearm, the shoulder covered by the grey cloth, etc. In the figures we may already see gestures that were to be typical of El Greco's work; in that of the man in blue, for instance, placing his hand on his breast to protest his good faith. Gesture was always to be one of El Greco's great resources, together with light, matter, form and rhythm, a resource that was to enable him to achieve that unique eloquence that distinguishes each and every one of his works.

The theme of the *Cleansing of the Temple* became an allegory of the counter-reformation, and as such it is represented on the reverse of several papal medals of the sixteenth century. It never really became very popular, however, undoubtedly because an angry Christ did not fit the traditional image of the Saviour. It is surprising, therefore, that El Greco should have dwelt on it throughout his career. Are we to see in this a psychological reflex on the part of the artist, a manifestation of his abhorrence of those who turned the temple (of religion or art) into a market-place? There are six signed versions of this theme extant, two painted in Italy and four in Spain, and all of them constitute basic milestones, as it were, to help us compare his changes in style and the evolution of his pictorial concept. Skipping some other works of undoubtedly earlier date, therefore, we will now study his second representation of the subject *(Fig. 12 - Cat 14).*

This picture, which is larger in size than the earlier one, is painted on canvas and was done after the artists's arrival in Rome, for it contains the portrait of Giulio Clovio. It is also signed in Greek capitals. A study of this painting will reveal the rapid progress El Greco had made. With a truly analytical spirit he gradually modified each of the elements. He simplified the scene of the action and gave it a greater appearance of reality; thus in the buildings that can be seen under the great entrance arch the Venetian influence is weakened by the addition of structures that come from the type of architecture then practised in Rome. He lifted the line of the horizon in order to create greater depth on the left, whereas on the right the horizon remains almost the same as in the first version. The columns flanking the arch eliminated the statues of Apollo and a female figure which appeared in the version carried out in Venice. The figure of Christ wielding the scourge, too, which owes much more to Titian than that in the earlier painting, stands out more naturally. The merchants form a much less chaotic mass, thanks to an evident improvement in the structure of each of the figures and a more suitable relationship between the tones. Surprising, too, is the change undergone by the figure of the woman selling chickens, in which the instability of the first version is accentuated, thus providing an interesting foretaste of what El Greco's figures were to be like in his Toledo period.

In general appearance the two versions of this theme are very different, on account of the radical change in the chiaroscuro effect of the masses. In this the teaching of Titian is plain to see. In reality, however, the principal cause of the change lies in the abandoning of the Byzantine formula in the representation of draperies. The vermicular strokes disappear and are succeeded by impressive masses which, within the limits of a conventional naturalism, make the structures clearer. Other causes of the greater clarity are the better distribution of the figures and the diminished intensity of line, together with a more monumental quality in the figures. It should not be forgotten that this monumental quality was a sign of advanced ideas at the time, for Late Gothic art took delight in prolixity of detail, a delight which is manifest even in the artists of the transitional period between the last stages of Gothic and Mannerism. That is why the first version seems more "primitive" than the second.

The great iconographic novelty of this second painting is to be found in the four personages painted bust-length in the right foreground, quite aloof from the Biblical scene and its agitated, dramatic character. Three of them are well-known: Titian, Michelangelo and Giulio Clovio. But the fourth, beardless and with a much younger air than his companions, is still of unknown identity. The most generally accepted identification of this figure is with Raphael, though it has also been suggested that it may represent Correggio or Sebastiano del Piombo, and there are even some who believe that this figure is a self-portrait.

In the first version we find a personal adaptation of the teachings of the Venetian masters of the time, while in the second this is merely a starting-point. The Titian-inspired character of the woman selling chickens has become more wholly El Greco's own, because by now he has succeeded in overcoming the conventionalism of typology. In El Greco, as we shall see later on, life had a profound influence on work, not only thanks to the technical lessons he learnt from his surroundings, nor yet as a reflection of the vicissitudes of existence (success and failure, pleasure and pain), but for two more important reasons: the slow maturing of his own conception of painting and his gradual invention of a typology and of a series of characteristic gestures which he created to give expression to his yearning for eloquence, and to satisfy a spirit at once mystical and aggressive.

In the working out of his own typology El Greco was gradually to abandon opulently-fleshed models in favour of more ascetic ones, replacing fair complexions and the hair that went with them by darker-hued skins. While living in Venice, he was indeed attracted for a time by that exuberance of flesh that was so much to the taste of Titian, Tintoretto and Veronese, but we can readily understand that he felt at home in Spain,

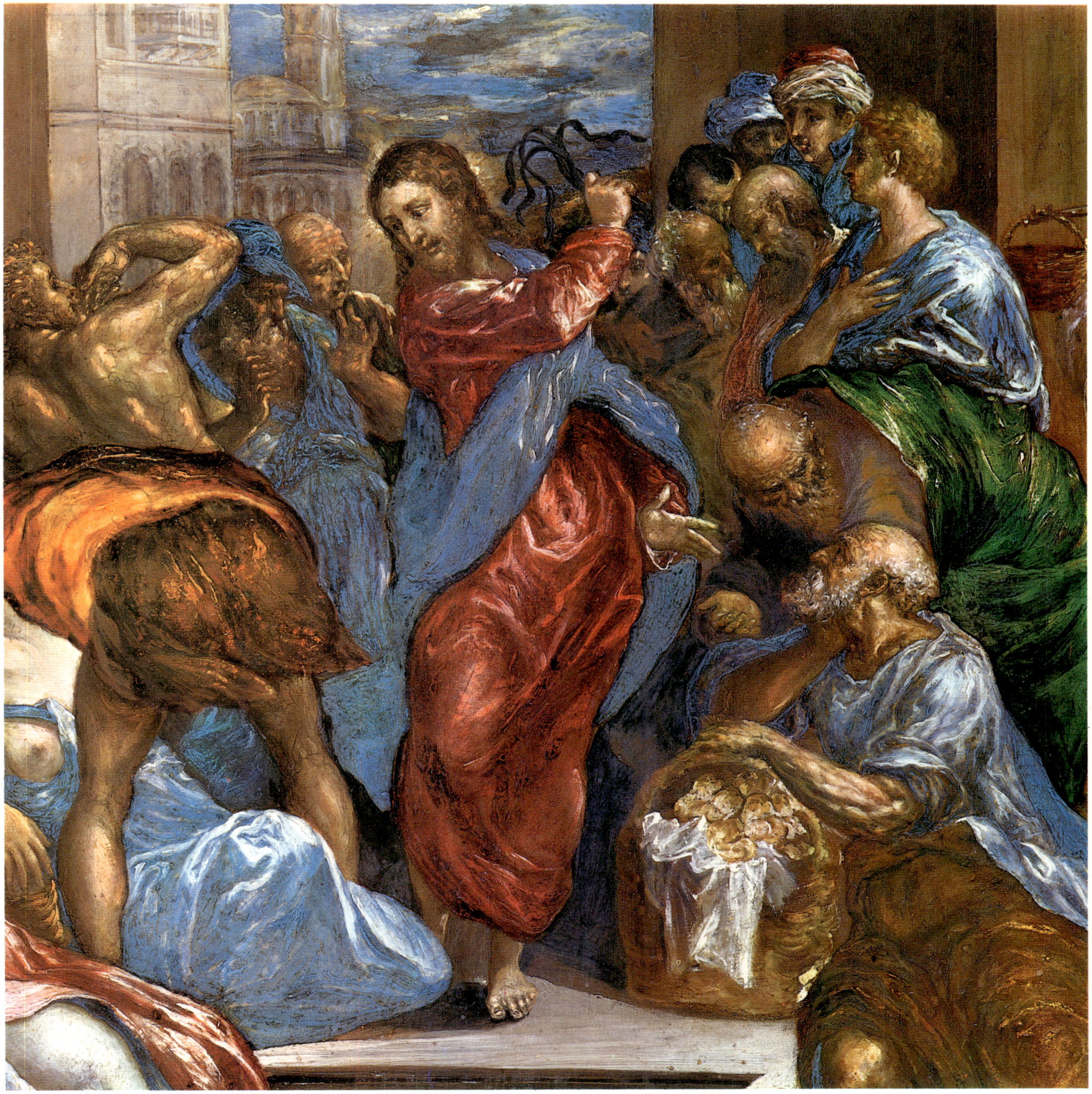

Fig. 11. Detail of figure 9.

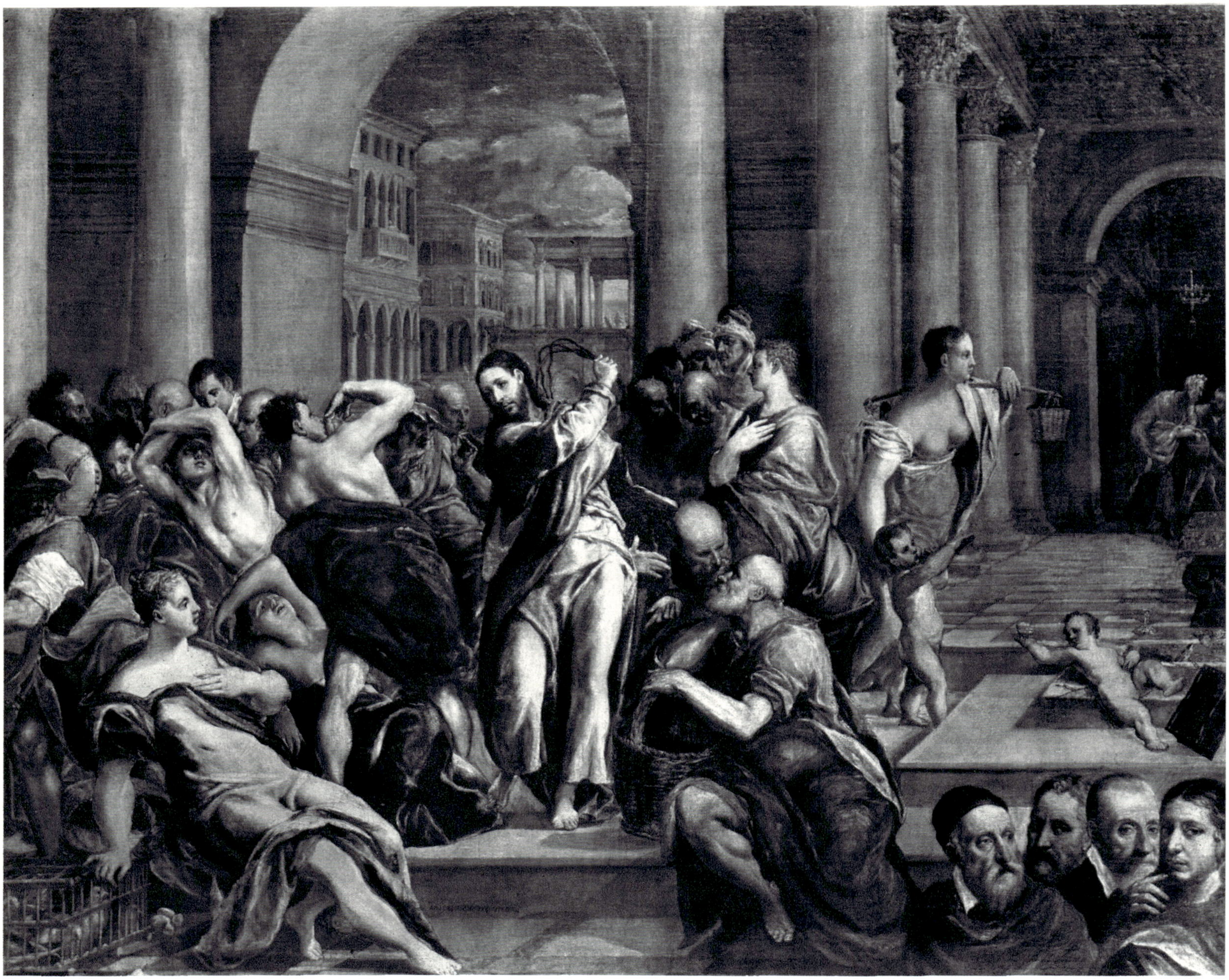

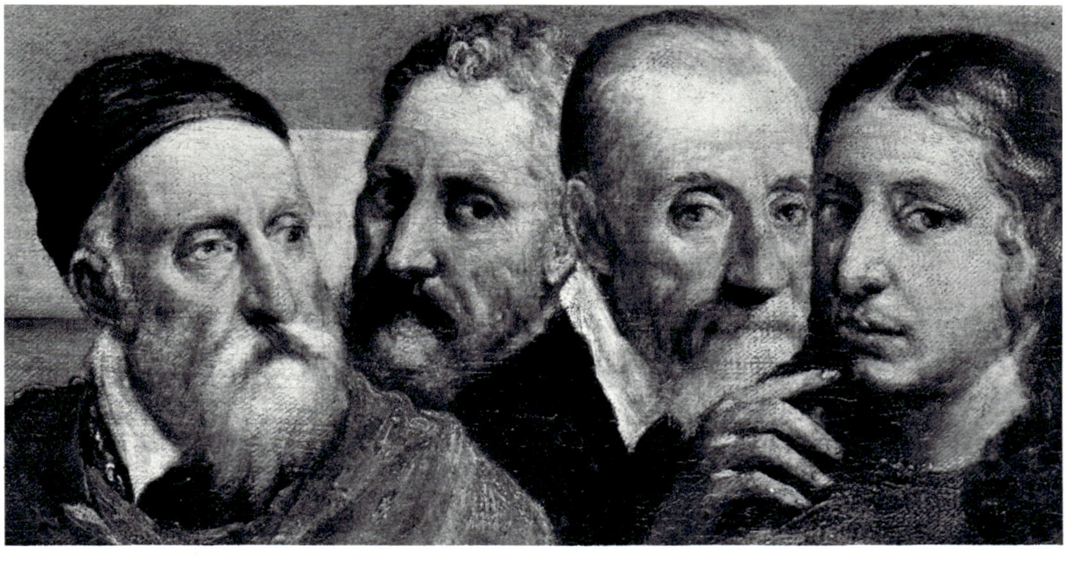

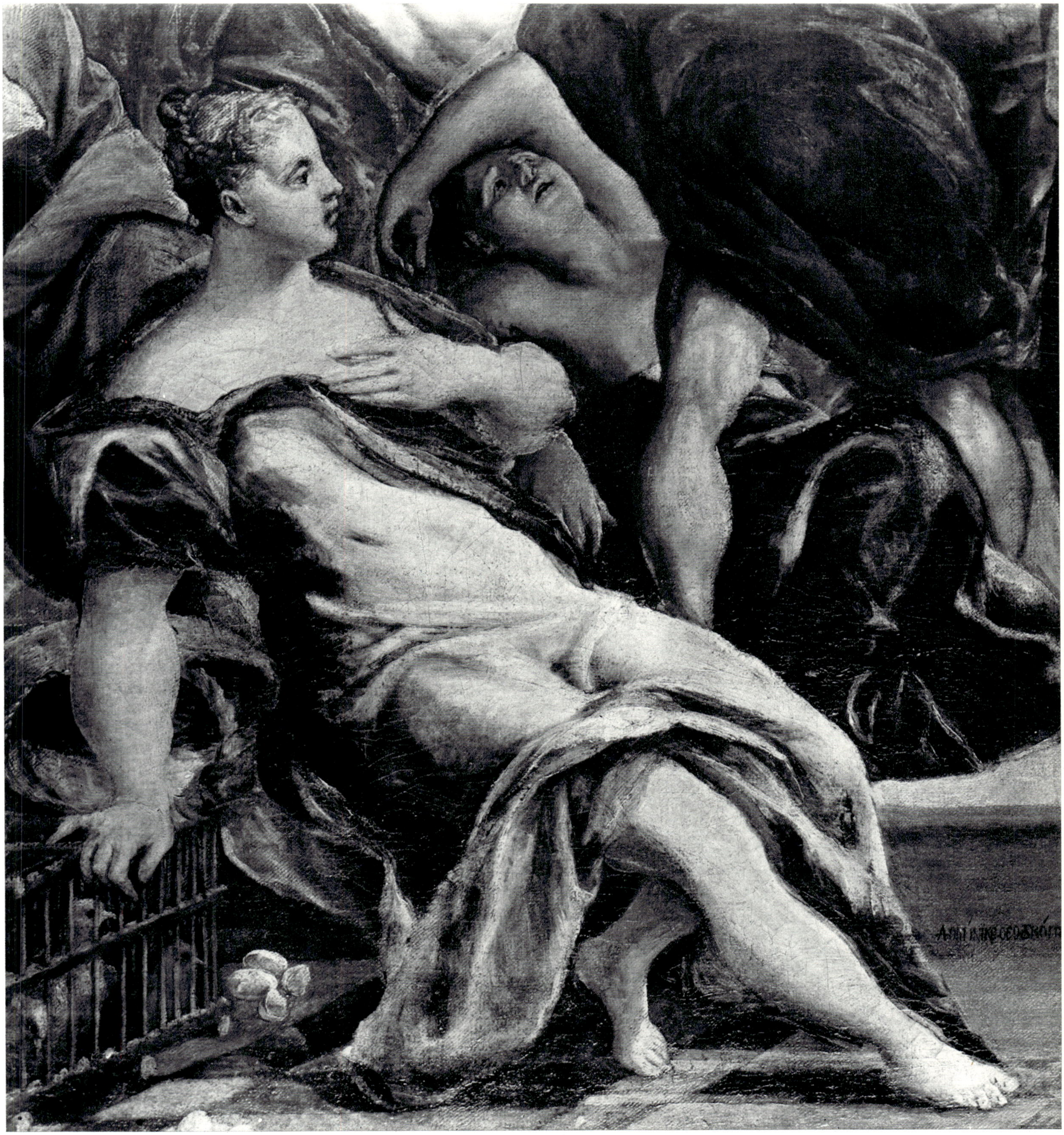

Figs. 12, 13 & 14. Christ cleansing the Temple, 1570-1575. Minneapolis, Institute of Arts. Cat. No. 14.

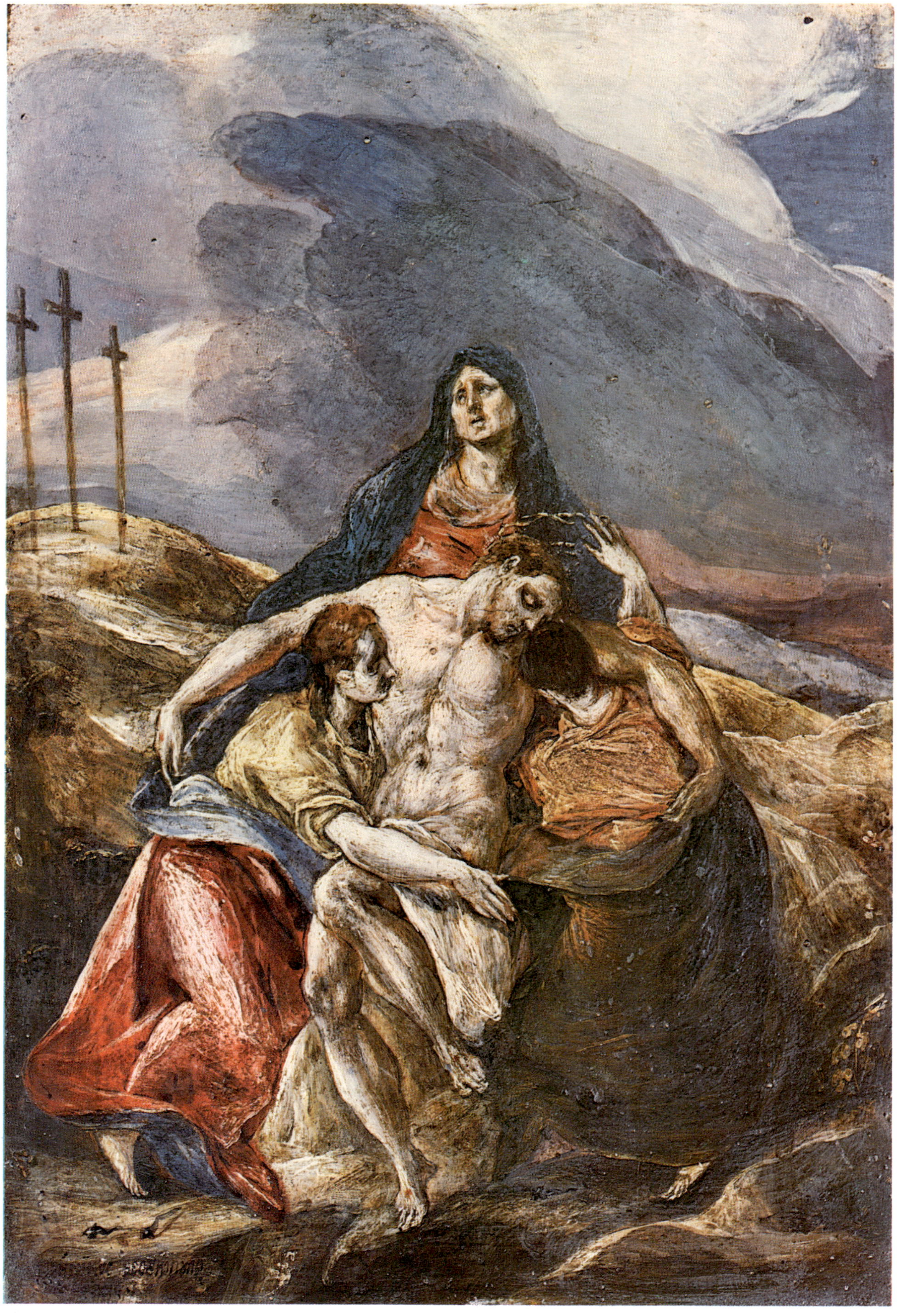

Fig. 15. Pietà, before 1570. Philadelphia, Johnson Collection. Cat. No. 9.

for there he found, instead of a second homeland, a reflection of his own home in Crete: a race that was predominantly dark, spare and nervous, a temperament prone to lyrical exaltation in its attitude to religion.

In this second version of the *Cleansing* we have a presentiment of the artist's later manner, just as in the first we saw the impact of the Venetian manner on the traditional technique of the Greek icon-painter. The advance in clarity of tone is an unmistakable sign of his broader understanding of plastic values. The hierarchical arrangement of the elements, too, is more logical in the second version than in the first. Later on we shall see El Greco, after his great intermediate period, once more playing with the chaotic without ever letting it overcome him, i.e., repudiating the remains of Italianism, remains which, however, never ceased to be absolutely necessary to his development, not only in cold, rational technique, but also in pure pictorial feeling. And the development of this feeling, closely bound up with his New Testament iconography, was to be the ultimate goal of his whole existence.

In the inventory of the property of Jorge Manuel Theotokopoulos, which was drawn up in 1621, we find under Number 24 a "*Cleansing of the Temple* measuring one and a third *varas* (about 3 ½ feet) in height by one and two thirds (about 4 ½ feet), or a little more". We are also told: "and it is the original". The reference is probably to this second version, the measurements of which coincide almost exactly with those in the inventory. The fact that an old —but bad— Spanish copy of it is still extant, a copy which includes the four portraits, seems to prove that this painting was taken to Spain by the artist. In the world of art-collecting it first appears, already attributed to El Greco, in the catalogue of paintings belonging to the Duke of Buckingham, printed in London in 1758, but drawn up in the seventeenth century.

Two versions are also known of the composition entitled *Pietà*. The first is painted on a panel, very small in size and signed with Greek capitals *(Fig. 15 - Cat. 9).* Its technique is the same, though perhaps slightly more Byzantine in feeling, as that of the *Christ cleansing the Temple* painted in Venice. We can still see in it the inheritance of the pictorial method based on the superimposition of linear strokes on masses of colour, which was used for giving modelling to the forms, especially in the draperies, landscape elements and skies.

The composition follows the Renaissance principle of the triangle, so noticeably marked out that we may suppose it to be the conscious intention of the painter. Together with obvious acquisitions from Italian technique and some persistence of the image-painting "primitivism" of the Greeks, however, we find in this painting evident signs of the heights to which the genius of El Greco was to attain. These signs are the bold contrast between the tight group of figures, which are linked together in a very original way, far removed from the conventionalism deriving from medieval formulas, and the bleak landscape in the background; the stronger colour, which is heightened by the intensity of the lights, as can be seen in the explicit introduction of white over the red of the figure on the left (most probably St. John the Evangelist); and, finally, the expressive rendering of forms, whether lyrical or dramatic, we can see in the clouds and in the attitude of the Virgin's head. All of this was to appear in his later period, transformed into something very different, but far removed, after all, from mere naturalistic interpretation, since it is based on a full appreciation of form, colour and handling for their own sake, independently of, though in intimate association with, the human motif they serve.

We believe that this work shows El Greco's potential at the age of twenty-five. It may be objected that at that age other artists of his genius had attained greater freedom in the use of their technique, but it should never be forgotten that at the beginning of his career he was probably much hampered by the enforced observance of an age-old craft, with all its limitations of concept, technique and spirit, and that it was only when he had become aware to some extent of his talent that he dared to take from the greatest masters of the Venice of his time —especially from Titian— the elements that were to enable him to become a good and skilful painter even at this early stage and later on, with the maturing of his personality in the following decade, one of the greatest painters the world has ever known and one, moreover, endowed with a personality and daring difficult to equal.

The second version of the *Pietà,* painted on canvas, has no signature, but its quality and character make it unquestionably El Greco's *(Fig. 16 - Cat. 15).* As is the case with the second version of the *Christ cleansing the Temple,* we can see that the technique is more completely influenced by Titian and the remains of the vermicular procedure have been almost entirely abandoned. The brush-stroke draws and models directly, in accordance with a system which is simpler yet remains naturalistic at the same time. We may also observe a change —compared with the first version of the *Pietà*— in the tonal scheme. The form, too, is broader and more monumental.

The composition, unlike that of the two canvases of the *Cleansing,* remains almost exactly the same in the two versions. The second seems to have been painted from a closer viewpoint, so that the figures become larger and the setting less important. But that is not all. The characters in this dramatic scene are linked together in the same way as in the first composition, and even the attitude of the Virgin is the same. The greatest differences —apart from the handling, but deriving from it— are to be found in the draperies. While the cloak that wraps the lower part of the disciple is darkened, as it were, in the first version by the shadows of its abundance of lines, in the second version this same fragment stands out clearly and makes a considerable contribution to the tonal balance of the whole. Arms and legs appear in the same position in the two versions, but their treatment differs, as is also the case with the *Cleansing.* The linear method that emphasized nerve and muscle gives way to a blended modelling, and thus gives greater softness to the flesh tints without any loss of strength in the form. In other words, the image is more synthetic and less analytical. The painter treated it first almost as if it were an engraving, but in the second version, using an already-created image as his starting-point, he tried to render the plastic values rather than a purely detailed definition of the iconographical elements. It would seem logical to attribute this second version of the *Pietà* to the early days of El Greco's Roman period.

The *St. Francis receiving the stigmata* in the Zuloaga Collection *(Fig. 17 - Cat. 10),* painted in oils on a panel and signed, is such a meticulously executed work that one might suppose it to be a sketch or model were it not for the existence of another composition, practically identical and also signed, in the Istituto Suor Orsola Benincasa, in Naples *(Cat. 11).* This latter was found in Italy. The first composition, on the contrary, comes from Toledo, and it was probably El Greco himself who brought it to Spain, for it was undoubtedly painted during his Italian period. In technique and pictorial conception, as is the case with the *Pietà* in Philadelphia, it shows the superimposition of Titian's influence on the primitive formula of the icon-painters. A breath of fantasy seems to have entered into the realism of the scene, which is executed in masterly impasto, with brush-strokes of a material that is at once dense and fluid. The saint is represented with dramatic rather than mystical emotion, a feature that was to be progressively modified in the later iconography of El Greco. The representation of the third dimension is perfect, which proves that as early as this —shortly before 1570— El Greco knew how to compose landscapes perfectly, alternating voids and solids in order to give the impression of movement and progressive distance, in accordance with the system established by the great Venetian painters of the Renaissance. The composition is very successful in the way in which all the elements of the landscape harmonize with the main figure and the rhythms determined by his attitude. The Naples version of this first composition in the brilliant Franciscan series created by El Greco is, as we have said, the same as the previous one in all essentials. On the back it bears the name of Monsignor Degli Oddi, member of an aristocratic family of Perugia.

The series attributed to El Greco's Venetian period continues with a little panel in oils representing *The Flight into Egypt (Fig. 18 - Cat. 12).* On the back it bears the monogram D.G.H., which indicates that it once belonged to Don Gaspar Méndez de Haro, nephew of the Count-Duke of Olivares and a great collector, who died when he was Viceroy of Naples. It figures in the inventory of his paintings drawn up in 1682, but attributed to Tintoretto. The work is unsigned, but we think it can very probably be attributed to El Greco. Painted in brilliant colours in a completely Venetian range, it shows the influence of Tintoretto, so often superimposed on that of Titian in El Greco's Italian period, which would explain its former attribution. Despite its small size, it has all the exuberance characteristic of the Venetians, though without entirely abandoning that touch of primitivism that is always to be found in the paintings of El Greco's first period. The composition is based on an asymmetric balance with the greater weight on the right, where we see the Virgin and Child riding on the ass, a traditional image of the flight into Egypt, near a clump of trees. The figures stand out against a sweeping panorama, with beautiful cloud effects, gently undulating land and a very simple foreground. In this work, as in the *St. Francis* studied above, there appears an interest in the landscape and in great empty spaces

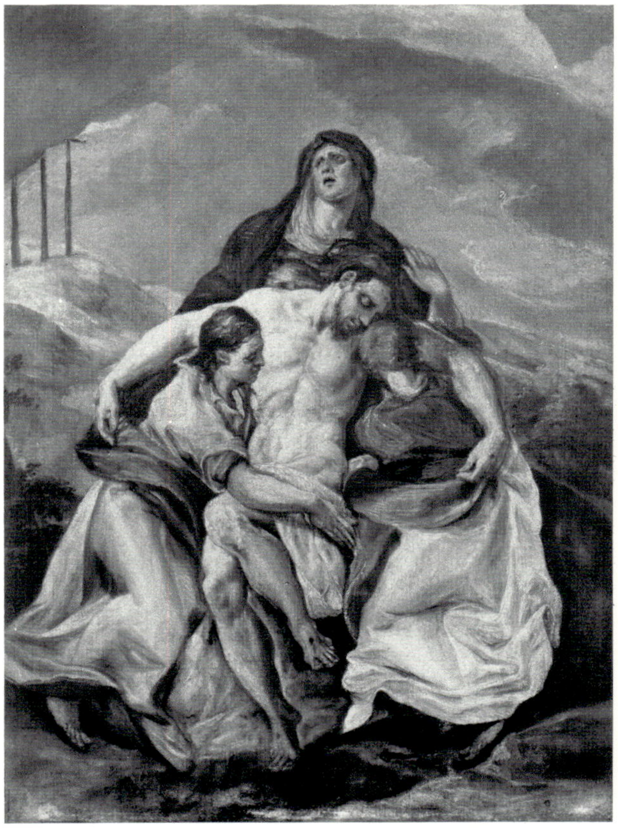

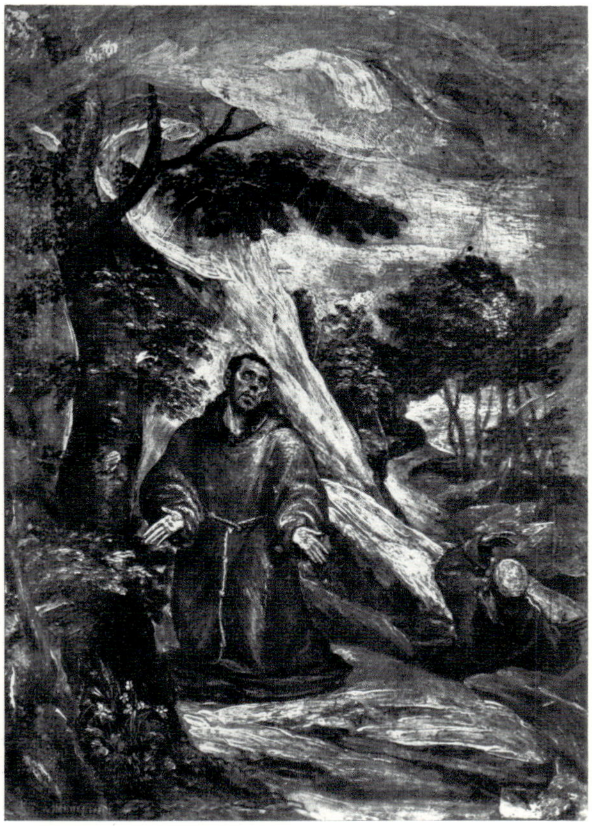

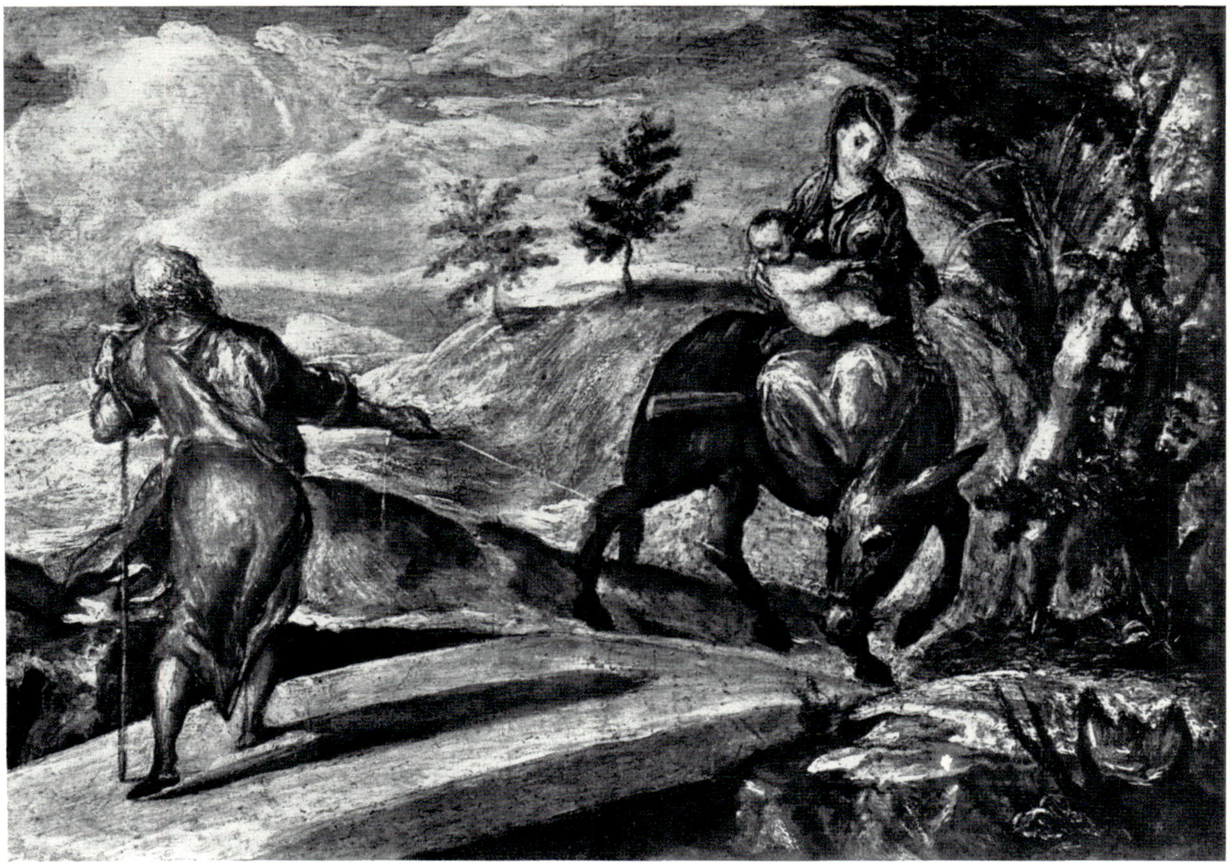

Fig. 16. Pietà, 1570-1575. New York, Hispanic Society. Cat. No. 15.

Fig. 17. St Francis receiving the stigmata, before 1570. Geneva, Antonio Zuloaga Collection. Cat. No. 10

Fig. 18. The Flight into Egypt, before 1570. Basle, Baron von Hirsch Collection. Cat. no. 12.

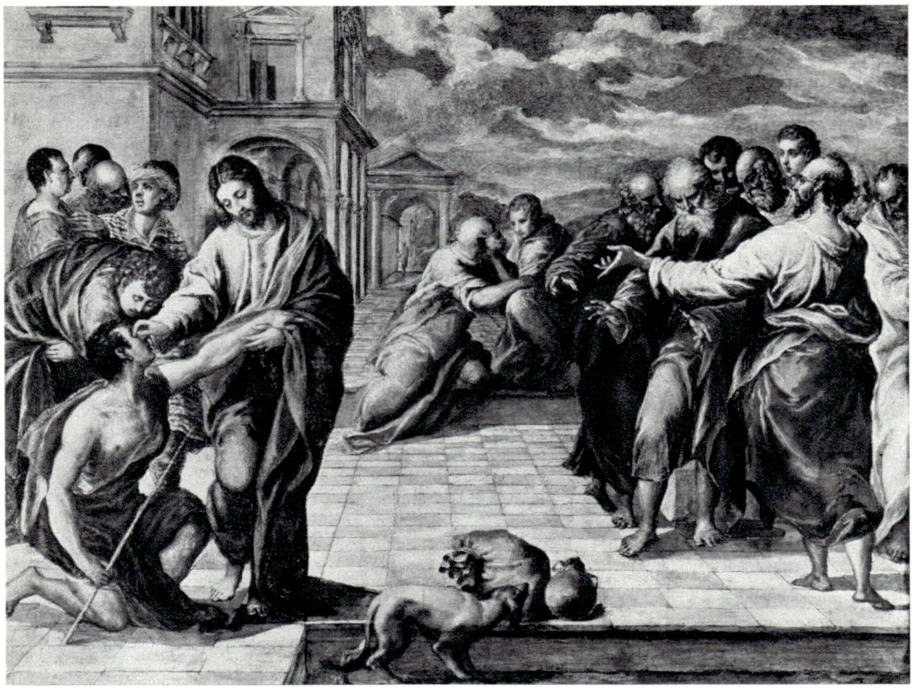

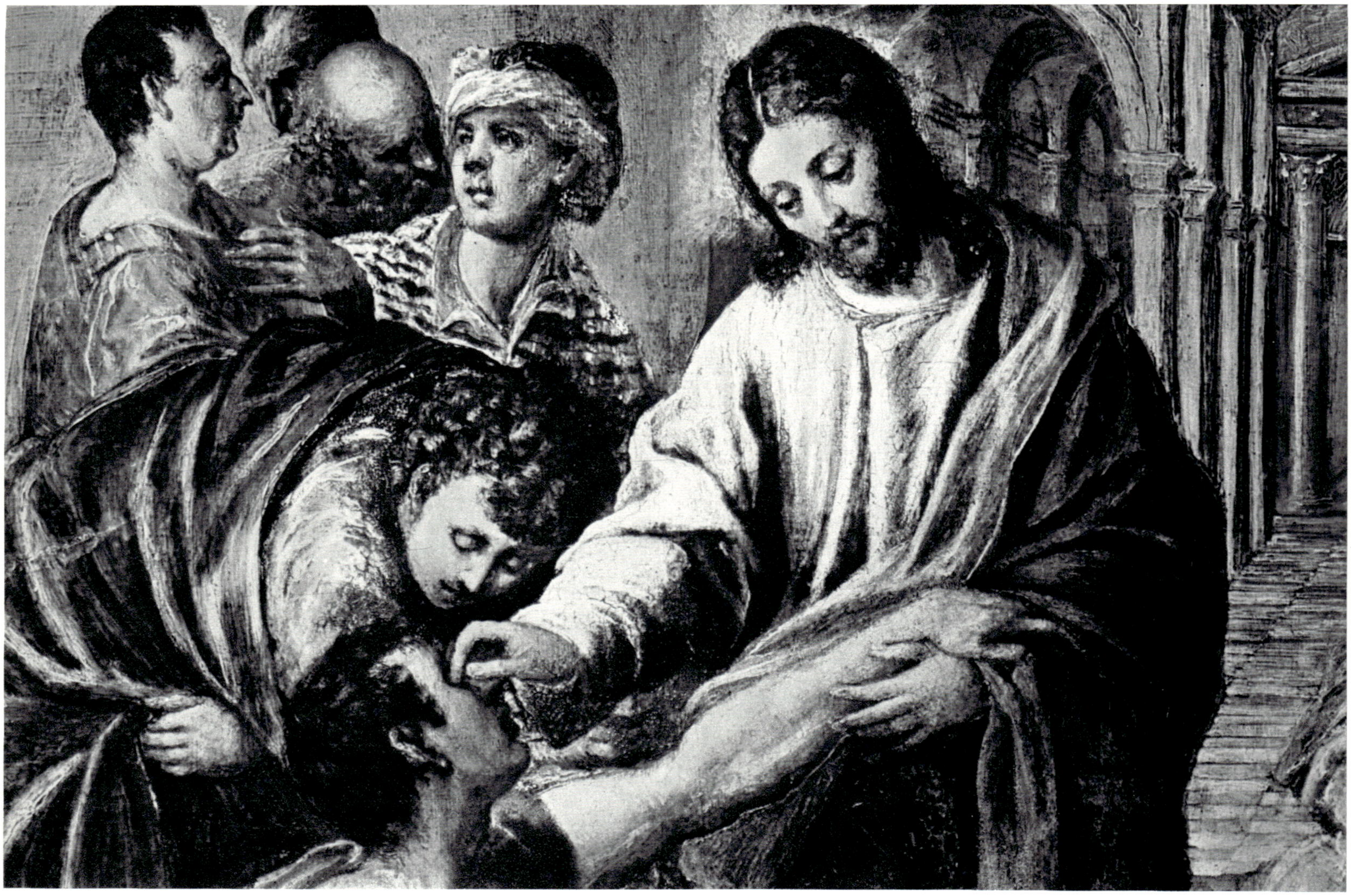

Figs. 19 & 20. Christ healing the blind man, before 1570. Dresden, Museum. Cat. No. 13.

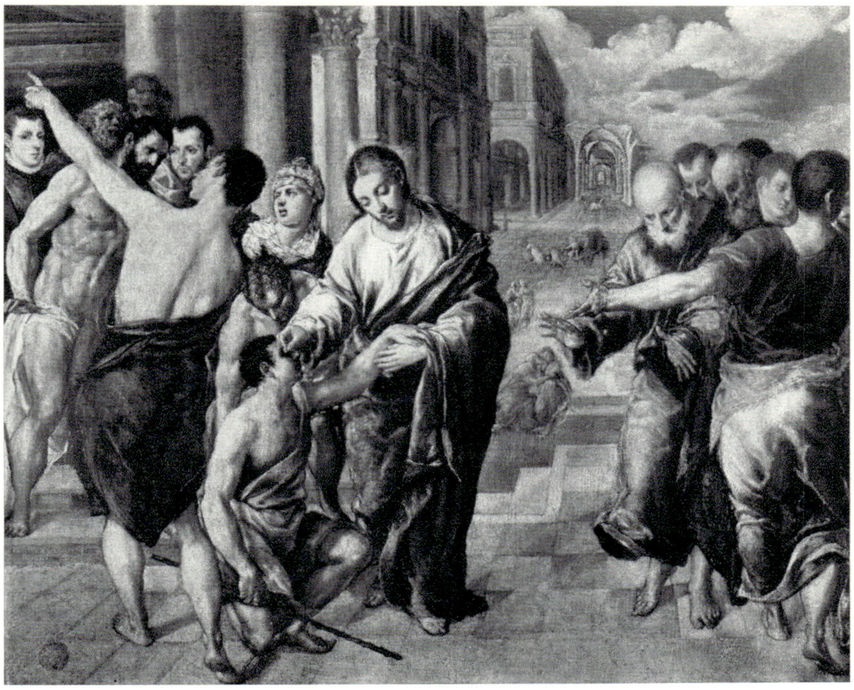

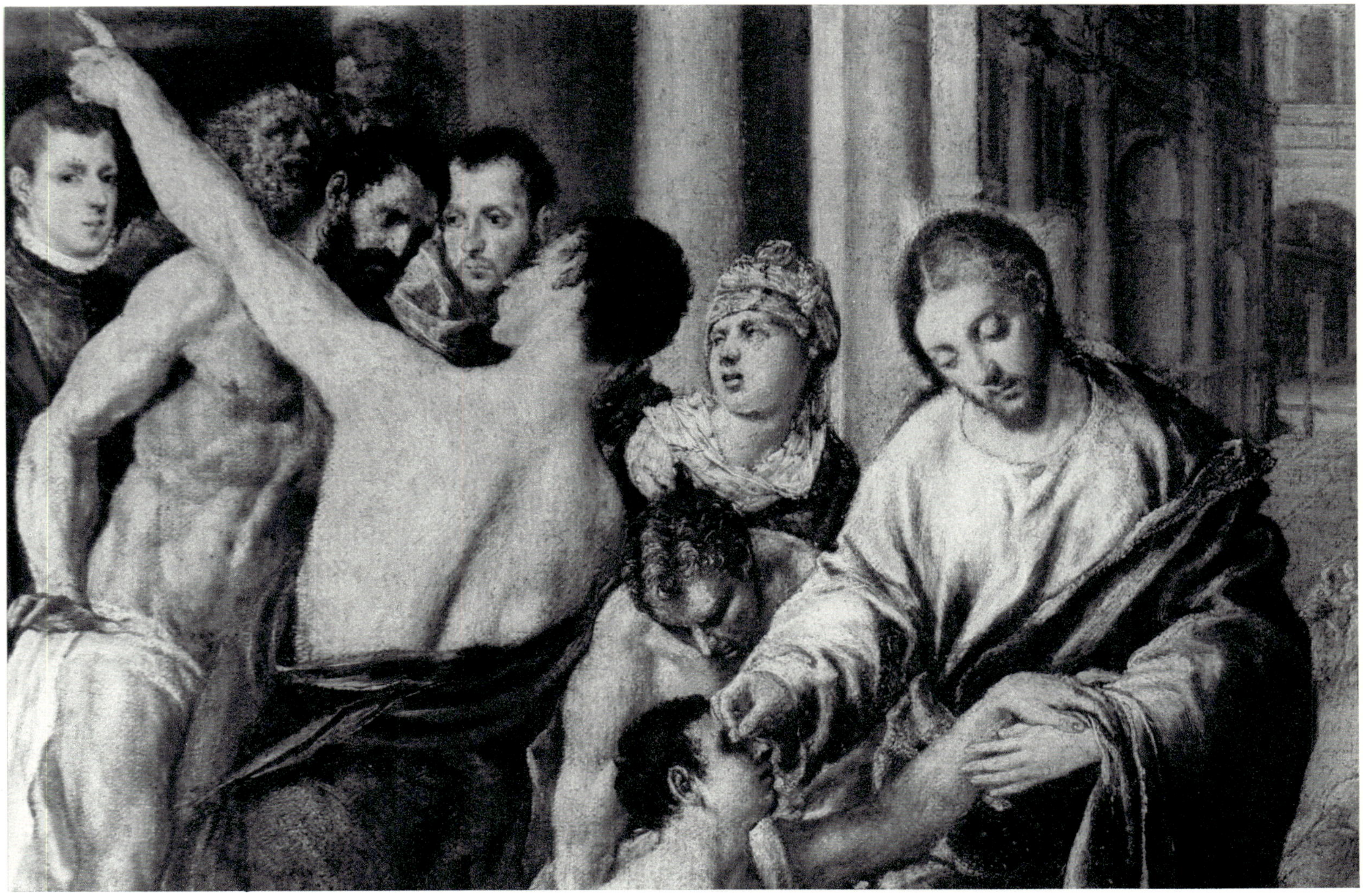

Figs. 21 & 22. Christ healing the blind man, 1570-1575. Parma, Museum. Cat. No. 16.

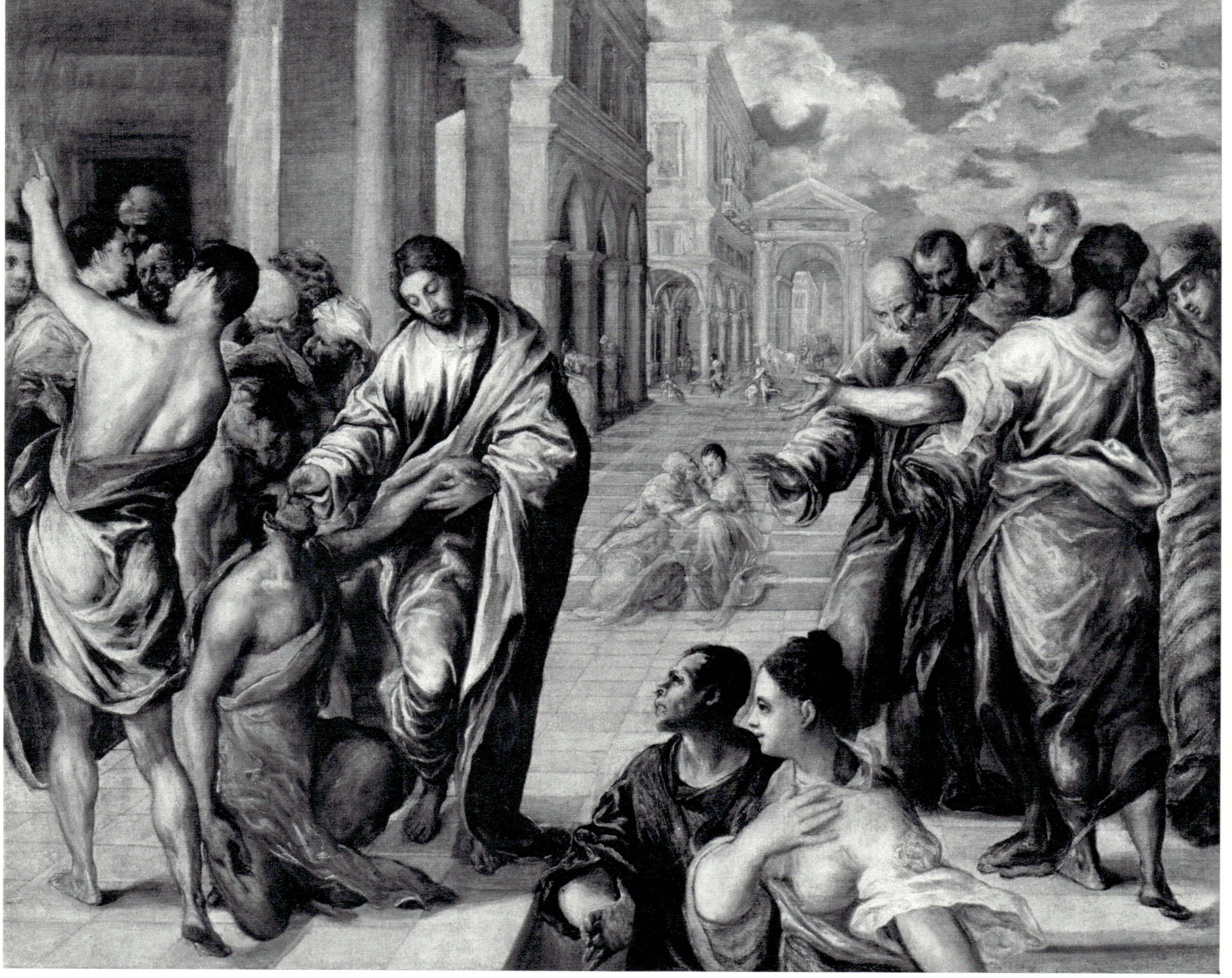

Fig. 23. Christ healing the blind man, 1570-1575. New York, Wrightsman Collection. Cat. No. 17.

that is not common in El Greco. The way in which the clothing is represented still has something of the "vermicular" method, above all in the figure of the Virgin, whose face, like that of the Child, is slightly but very exactly foreshortened.

Of the other subject painted by El Greco during his years in Italy —that of *Christ healing the blind man*— there are three signed versions extant. In all three the archaizing elements of the Veneto-Byzantine technique have disappeared. The one in the Dresden Pinakothek appears to be the oldest, being still of the Venetian period *(Fig. 19 - Cat. 13)*. It is executed in oil on a wooden panel and was acquired in Venice in 1741 for the King of Saxony's collection. At that time it was attributed to Leandro Bassano. But its similarity to the Parma version, which is signed by El Greco and which we are now about to study, confirms our attribution to the Cretan. As in the works of the Venetian school, El Greco adopts architectural backgrounds of a classical character, both to give splendour to his scene and to construct the space and perspective more clearly. He situates different elements at varying distances, i.e., in areas that gradually draw further away from the viewer in order to contribute to the sensation of a third dimension, a very important factor at that time and in that school. But the rhythmic intensity of the clouds and the gestures of the characters are of greater interest than the setting. On the left Christ is healing the blind man, who kneels on one knee. On the right various witnesses of the scene manifest, with that eloquent gesticulation which is one of El Greco's main resources, the impression it has had on them.

By and large, tre scene is as unnaturalistic as any Gothic composition, but a new conventionalism has taken the place of the previous one in the admirable way in which the bodies are depicted within the space that penetrates between them, enfolds them and turns the gestures of the figures into expressive factors on their own account. The group on the left is more static and, as only the busts of the figures can be seen, the painter's interest is focussed on the "dialogue" of the men. The painting is in the more advanced technique of El Greco's first period, so that it may be supposed that this work was carried out not long before 1570. A feature worth remarking is the way in which each group of figures is framed by architectural elements or set in free spaces, as is the case with the group on the right, so that everything may be unified in each area and contribute to the overall effect. Moreover, as in other works of this period, the balance is asymmetrical, a subtle compensation being sought among the volumes, spaces and movements. According to Wethey, this theme emerged soon after the counter-reformation as an allegory of the Church revealing the truth —an allegory that complements that of *Christ cleansing the Temple.*

What is considered to be the second version of this work, evidently cut down at either side, is of rather smaller size and is painted in oil on canvas. It is signed "DOMÉNIKOS THEOTOKÓPOULOS EPOÍEI" in Greek capitals and is now in the Parma Museum *(Fig. 21 - Cat. 16)*. It was probably painted in Rome, shortly after 1570, and in technique and colour recalls the second version of the *Cleansing of the Temple.* The identity of the young man in black who appears on the left, evidently a portrait, is unknown. The hypothesis that it may be the painter himself is still adhered to by some, but Miss Trapier has suggested the possibility of its being a portrait of the young Alessandro Farnese (1545-1592). As has been said, this painting figures in the 1680 inventory of the Palazzo del Giardino in Parma, which belonged to the Farnese family, but it is attributed to Veronese. It has the same scheme as the Dresden version, but with noticeable simplifications. The dog in the foreground has been eliminated; the groups have been painted from a closer viewpoint, so that they are more monumental in character; the figures of Christ and the blind man have been moved slightly towards the centre and, on the other hand, the perspective across the empty central space to the background is more animated, with a greater number of tiny figures nervously sketched in. There is a very noticeable change in the typology of the figures, who gain in humanity in accordance with the advance towards what was to be the art of the painter's mature years.

At this stage in his career El Greco's painting represents a struggle to exalt dynamic form above scenography, which he relegates to a secondary level. This is a factor of capital importance at this period, for all his later work was to accentuate this tendency to subordinate the backgrounds and settings to the figures, whether through the subject-matter and the feeling deriving from it or by means of the strength of the form in itself. Later this became a quality of texture in association with the tension of the volumes rather than a matter of surfaces. In this version he also gives a more important role to gesture, balancing the horizontally outstretched arm of the figure on the right with the one raised diagonally by a man, naked to the waist, standing to the left of the figure of Christ.

The third version of this composition, which is larger than the other two, is painted in oil on canvas *(Fig. 23 - Cat. 17).* It appeared in a London auction room in 1958, attributed to Veronese. Two evidently old copies of this last variant of *Christ healing the blind man* have been found in Spain, which indicates that El Greco took the picture, or a preparatory study for it, to Toledo, since this canvas is carried out in a technique that is earlier than that of the first works done there. We might almost say that El Greco wished to make this version a synthesis of the best qualities of the previous two, and he did in fact achieve a greater balance in all the elements. Realising the importance of figures in the foreground as points of reference, he again placed some of the forms in this area, but instead of the dog and the sack of the first version he put a couple whose gestures betray their excitement and whose eyes are fixed on Christ at the very moment of the miraculous healing. The young man mentioned in the Parma version as a possible self-portrait is here placed behind the group on the right. The figures in the middle distance have been increased in size in an approach to greater naturalism and everything tends to emphasize the central void, harmonizing its colouring within each group. And within this tendency the clarity of the tones and the strength of the red and blue, shaded with white in order to give the luminous quality of the reflections that distinguish the Saviour's clothing, give the latter's figure an authority that provides the composition as a whole with a more successful hieratic arrangement.

In the course of the three versions the skies have been treated with increasing softness and we might say that the architecture, too, has lost some of its dramatic character. While the strength of the forms was predominant in the second version, in the third there is a tendency to seek a compromise between the intensity of the forms and the more purely narrative manner of the first version. Undoubtedly the influences of Titian and Tintoretto are present in these works, but it cannot be denied, on the other hand, that they reveal a great effort on El Greco's part, not so much to achieve full originality as to bring to perfection the formula of his Italian period. What proves the artist's mastery when he painted this third version, which was probably done in Rome —apart from the rightness of all the spatial, formal, chromatic and linear elements— is the way in which the tones are shaded to create a whole which possesses a spiritual joy that is rare in art. The harmony between the yellow and the light red is extraordinarily beautiful, as is the pink shading of the white in the architectural elements.

In the group of works considered to belong to the Roman period there are three pictures dealing with the theme of the *Annunciation,* which was to be painted by El Greco on so many occasions in his life. All three are based on a similar scheme, a scheme that owes much to Titian and is very similar to the one used in the Modena triptych. In fact the similarities of general concept, and also of technique, linking the third version we shall be studying —that in the Contini Bonacossi Collection— and the painting in the triptych provide very well-based support for the identification of the painter who signs himself Doménikos with El Greco.

The one in the Prado is a very tiny panel, painted with the meticulous precision that El Greco always bestowed on his *modelli (Fig. 24 - Cat. 18).* The fact that this painting was one of them is confirmed by a second version on canvas, of much greater size, which is its exact replica in every detail. We see a repetition of the steep perspectives and of the division of the scene by conspicuous architectural elements. The mixture of techniques, or, rather, the skilful employment of the textures according to the elements represented, may be particularly appreciated in the figure of the Virgin. Her robe, especially in the sleeve, has some strong linear strokes of highlighting; the voluminous cloak, however, which is wrapped round the greater part of her body and folded to hang over the right arm, is treated in a much more monumental fashion. The clothing of the archangel is given a linear treatment similar to that of the Virgin's robe. The heads are treated in a rather simplified way, frequent in the works of this period, especially when they are of small size, as is also the case with the *Flight into Egypt*. We may already see in this painting El Greco's interest in contrasts of materials, or, rather, in contrasts between firmly delineated forms and others only lightly sketched in (which was to be a notable characteristic of the painter's final period): compare for instance the treatment of the archangel's wings with that of the architectural elements. The quality of the luminous clouds in the upper part of the picture is very similar, both in the density and in the arbitrary form, to that of the clouds in the *Saint Francis receiving the stigmata* we have already studied.

As we have said, the second *Annunciation (Fig. 25 - Cat. 20)* is an exact replica of the little panel in the Prado and may have been painted in Spain. At present it bears a signature in Greek italics which is evidently false, but this is no reason for doubting the authenticity of the work itself, which is in the Muñoz Collection in Barcelona. The nervous qualities of the first version, which are evident even at the end of the street which provides the deep perspective, no longer exist here. There is the same strange force in the luminous clouds, but now it is softened and restrained, better controlled technically. El Greco's secret, however, after having achieved a technique comparable to that considered the most "normal" among the best painters of his time, was to be a partial re-dissolution of this technique, so that his ideas might be expressed by the pictorial vehicle rather than the iconographic one, or at least by both equally. In this version the full, ample forms are matched by modelling that is at once strong and soft and creates admirable tonal values.

The third version, which may be earlier in date than the second, but which we consider later than the first on account of its technique, was found in Italy *(Fig. 26 - Cat. 19)*. The pictorial formula is clearly influenced by Titian; from its advanced technique it may have been painted very late in the Roman period. The architectural background and the perspective effects have disappeared. The only thing that constructs space geometrically here is, as in late Spanish Gothic painting, the tiling of the floor. A great sweep of agitated curtaining on the left and a misty background are sufficient to isolate the event mysteriously from the real world. Indeed we might say that the painter —while in the other two versions he had treated the Virgin and the archangel on more or less equal terms— is here attempting to express a difference between them, presenting the archangel as an airy, half-unreal character, while the Virgin, for all her superiority, is treated as realistically as the artist can manage, whether in the rendering of the forms or in the modelling of the flesh tints, the draperies and the book and desk beside her. The clouds, which are more evanescent than in the other two versions (much more so, especially, than in the first), have come much closer to reality. The little angels seem to have been painted almost as compulsory allegorical accessories, though their forms might repay closer examination on account of the novelty of the synthesis of naturalism and distortion, above all in the lowest one. The diaphanous material that covers the body of the archangel is perhaps, apart from the technique, the most attractive feature of the picture, raising its subtle sensuousness to a higher level. We must also mention the similarity of type between the Virgin's head *(Fig. 27)* and that of the female figure emerging behind Christ in the *Christ healing the blind man* in Parma *(Fig. 21 & 22).*

There have been some objections to the attribution to El Greco of a small panel with a representation of *Christ on the Cross* in the Marañón Collection in Madrid *(Fig. 28 - Cat. 21),* but it is evident that its technique is the same as that of certain works painted in Italy, particularly the first version of the *Annunciation* and the *St. Francis receiving the stigmata.* What is surprising is the appearance, in the depths of the landscape background, of a vertical mass that coincides to some extent with El Greco's interpretation of the great tower of the Cathedral of Toledo in the landscapes he painted during his years in that city. Is this pure chance or is it possible that El Greco, after settling in Toledo, could have reproduced the technique of the works of his Italian period so faithfully?

In the inventory of the estate of El Greco's son, drawn up in Toledo in 1621, there are two paintings with the title *Blower,* more recently known, in English, as *Boy lighting a candle.* But there are two compositions by El Greco which may be described by this vague title. One represents a boy blowing to kindle the flame of a burning stick in order to light a candle-end; in the second composition the one who is blowing, for the same purpose, is a young woman placed between a laughing man and a monkey.

Of the first composition two signed versions are known: the one in the Payson Collection *(Fig. 30 - Cat. 23),* signed with Greek capitals, and the one in the Capodimonte Museum in Naples *(Fig. 29 - Cat. 22).* The latter comes from the collection of Alessandro Farnese and figures in the 1680 inventory as "by the hand of El Greco". The figure stands out against a black background and the yellowish reflections of the light affect, and indeed entirely dominate, the tone of highlights and penumbra. Accustomed as we are to El Greco's religious iconography, or to the metamorphosis wrought by his pure plastic instinct on the qualities of the materials and forms depicted, the realism and simplicity of subject-matter of this painting are surprising. It is difficult to "see" the painter in this work when our eyes are infused with his more usual images. But analysis will discover the characteristic values: the boy's right hand, the flame-reflecting quality of his clothes, the bold technique in the treatment of such details as the lips, the tip of the nose, the eyelids, etc., details that denote not only the painter's mastery but also his freedom and audacity, proclaiming the liberties he was to take with form in the future. The formal values, just because the colour is so limited in range, are very acutely specified, the work almost gaining in precision when studied in a black and white photograph, though losing its chromatic quality. The signed canvas is hardly different at all, not only in the theme and the way of approaching it, but even in technique. This indicates that we are dealing with pictures separated by a very short interval of time within the Roman period.

The idea for this composition would appear to have come from works by Jacopo Bassano. It was to prove very popular, for, apart from the two signed versions just mentioned, several old copies are known, almost all of them found in Italy. One of these, in the Uffizi Gallery in Florence, is attributed by Wethey to the painter Lattanzio Bonastri, who was El Greco's apprentice in Rome, as we have said.

The second composition, which represents a human couple and a monkey, is mentioned in the books on our painter under various titles: *Proverb, Genre scene* and *Fable (Fig. 31 - Cat. 24).* The first of these titles, which appears as early as 1878, in the sale catalogue of the Zacharie Astruc Collection, was adopted by Cossío, whose proposed interpretation of the scene is contained in a Spanish proverb that runs: "Man is fire, woman is tow; then the devil comes and starts to blow". But this interpretation has been called in question by Enriqueta Harris, followed by Wethey, as they consider the central figure of the group to be a young man rather than a woman. To tell the truth, we do not agree with this change of sex. If the title *Proverb* is unacceptable, however, there is still less reason for accepting that of *Fable,* for though it is true that there is a canvas with this name in Inventory II of El Greco's son, there is nothing to prove this identification. We might add that in the inventory drawn up in 1611 on the death of Blessed Juan de Ribera, Archbishop of Valencia, mention is made of a picture with the title: *Two male figures and a monkey which is lighting a candle by blowing on the fire.* Wethey proposes that the painting in the inventory should be identified as the one we are considering in this chapter.

We will leave it, then, with the title *Genre scene.* Of this type of composition there are three signed original versions and several old copies. The originals are housed in the V. von Watsdorf Collection in Rio de Janeiro *(Fig. 31 - Cat. 24),* in the Harewood Collection in London *(Fig. 151 - Cat. 128)* and in the Mark Oliver Collection in Jedburgh, Scotland *(Fig. 152 - Cat. 129).* There is a considerable difference in technique between the first of these —which we consider to belong to El Greco's Roman period— and the other two, which we would place as having been painted in the third phase of his career in Spain, so that we shall study them at a later stage. The canvas from the Roman period is clearly analogous in technique to some of the portraits we shall be studying shortly: a very pronounced realistic conception, big brushstrokes that make it easier to produce firm modelling, despite the fact that the luminous effects might have led to dissolution of the form, and a tendency to reflect the immediate: i.e., to dispense with any kind of idealization or allegory.

Portraits painted in Italy

The portrait of *Giulio Clovio (Fig. 32 - Cat. 25),* the Croatian illuminator who gave El Greco a helping hand on his arrival in Rome, is probably the oldest known portrait by the painter. It must, of course, have been preceded by the lost self-portrait which, according to Clovio's letter of recommendation to Alessandro Farnese, "astonished all the painters in Rome". The excellence of this portrait, moreover, shows a complete mastery of the genre. It has something of the formula of Titian, but it is really executed in a technique very different from that of the Venetian master: freer, less elaborate, avoiding scumblings and glazes. Giulio Clovio (1498-1578) is shown pointing to one of his most deservedly famous works, the book dedicated to the Blessed Virgin and finished in 1560 for Cardinal Farnese (Morgan Library, New York). The picture is signed in Greek capitals, and this portrait was undoubtedly the model for the small portrait that appears in the Roman version of *Christ cleansing the Temple (Fig. 13 - Cat. 14).* Firmly-drawn lines and

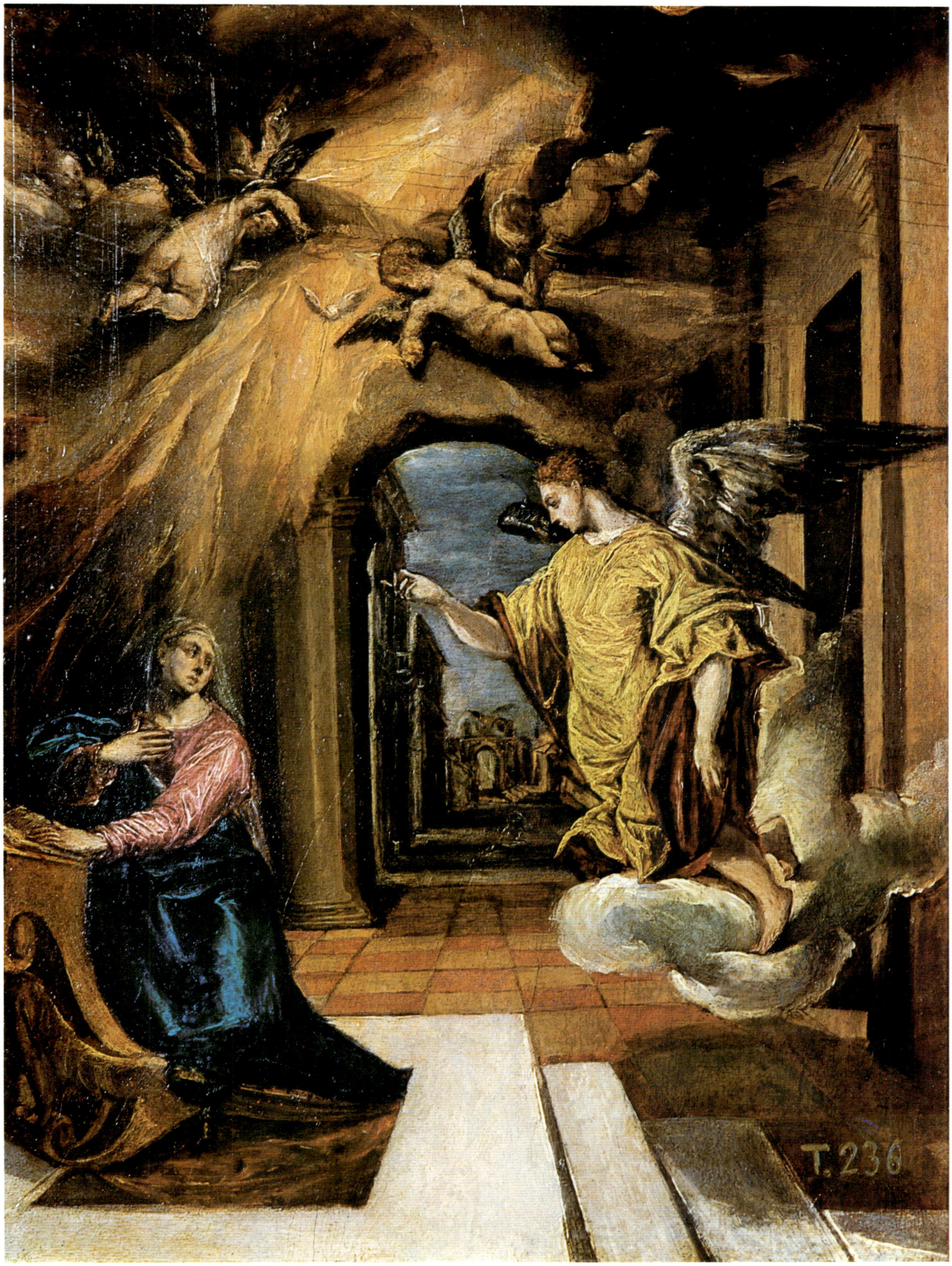

Fig. 24. The Annunciation, 1570-1575. Madrid, Prado. Cat. No. 18.

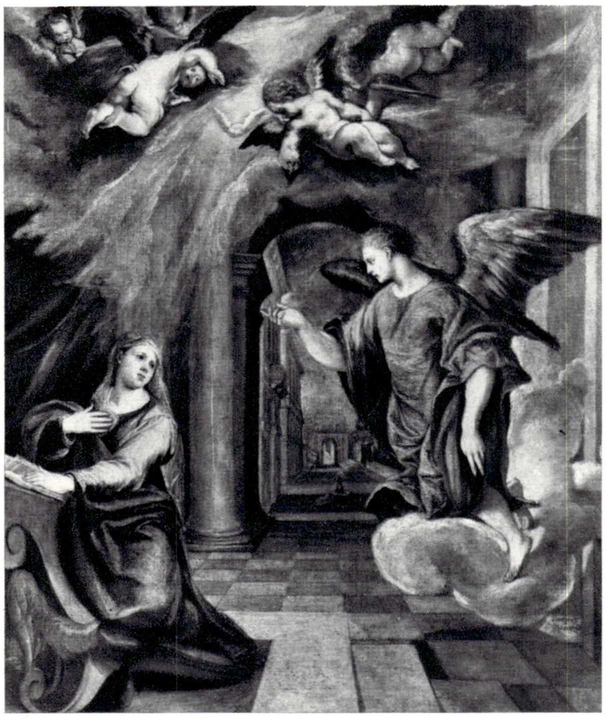

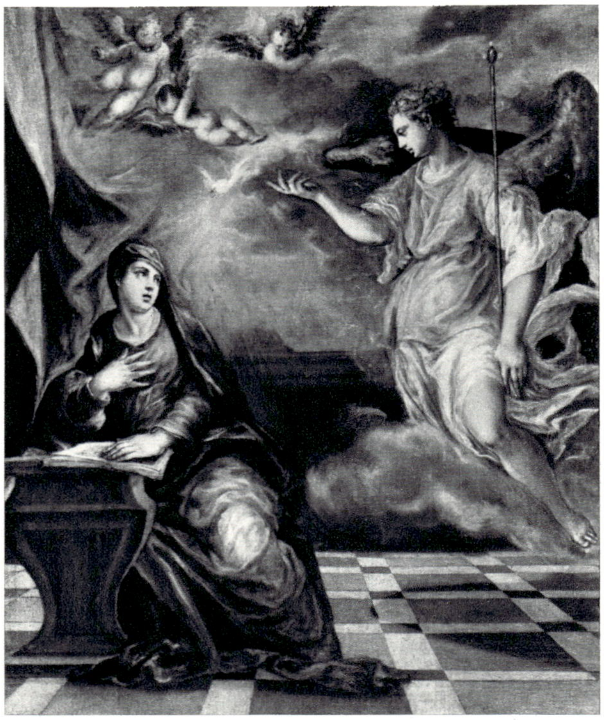

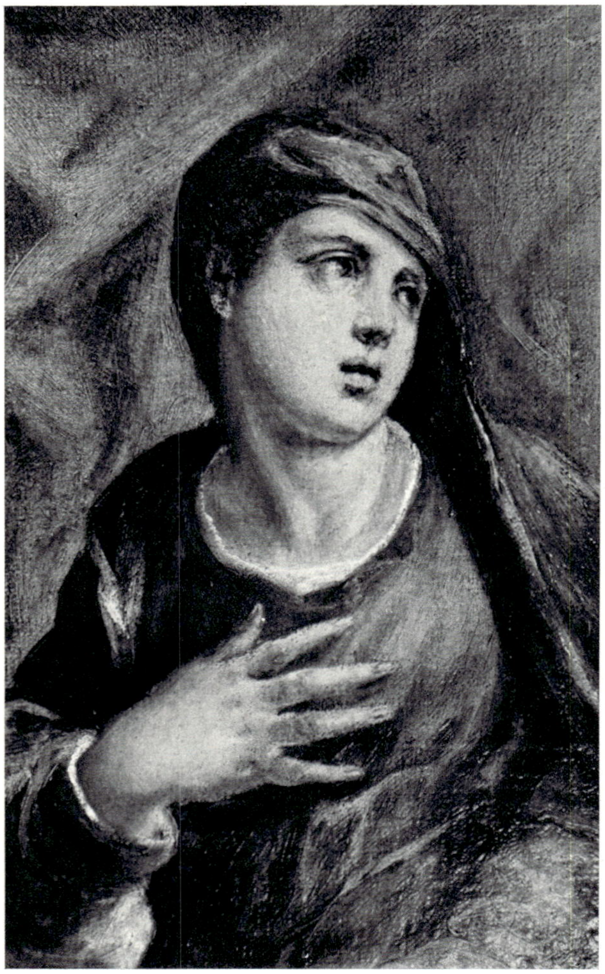

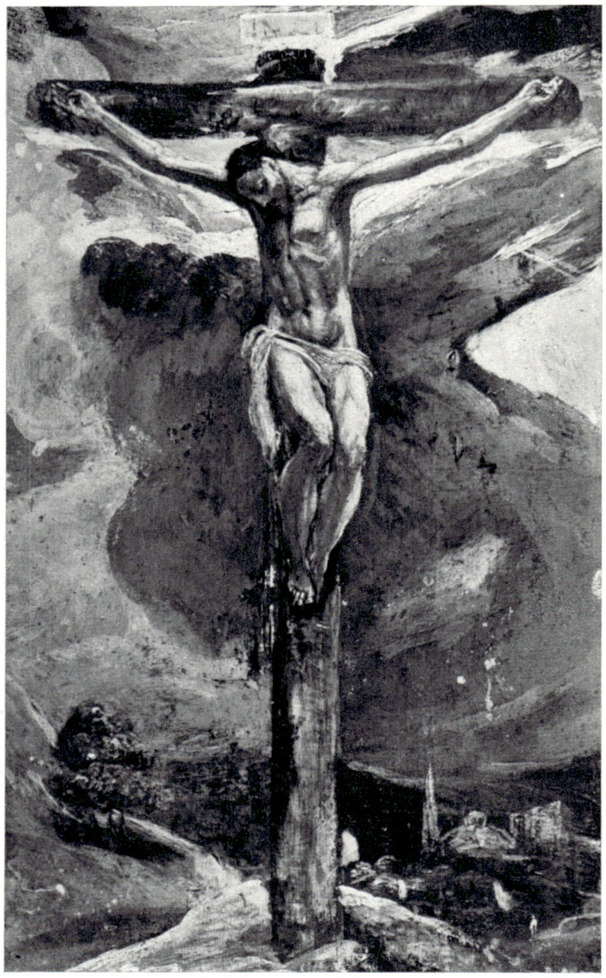

Fig. 25. The Annunciation, 1570-1575. Barcelona, Muñoz Collection. Cat. No. 20.
Figs. 26 & 27. The Annunciation, 1570-1575. Florence, Contini-Bonacossi Collection. Cat. No. 19.
Fig. 28. Christ on the cross, 1570-1575. Madrid, Marañón Collection. Cat. No. 21.

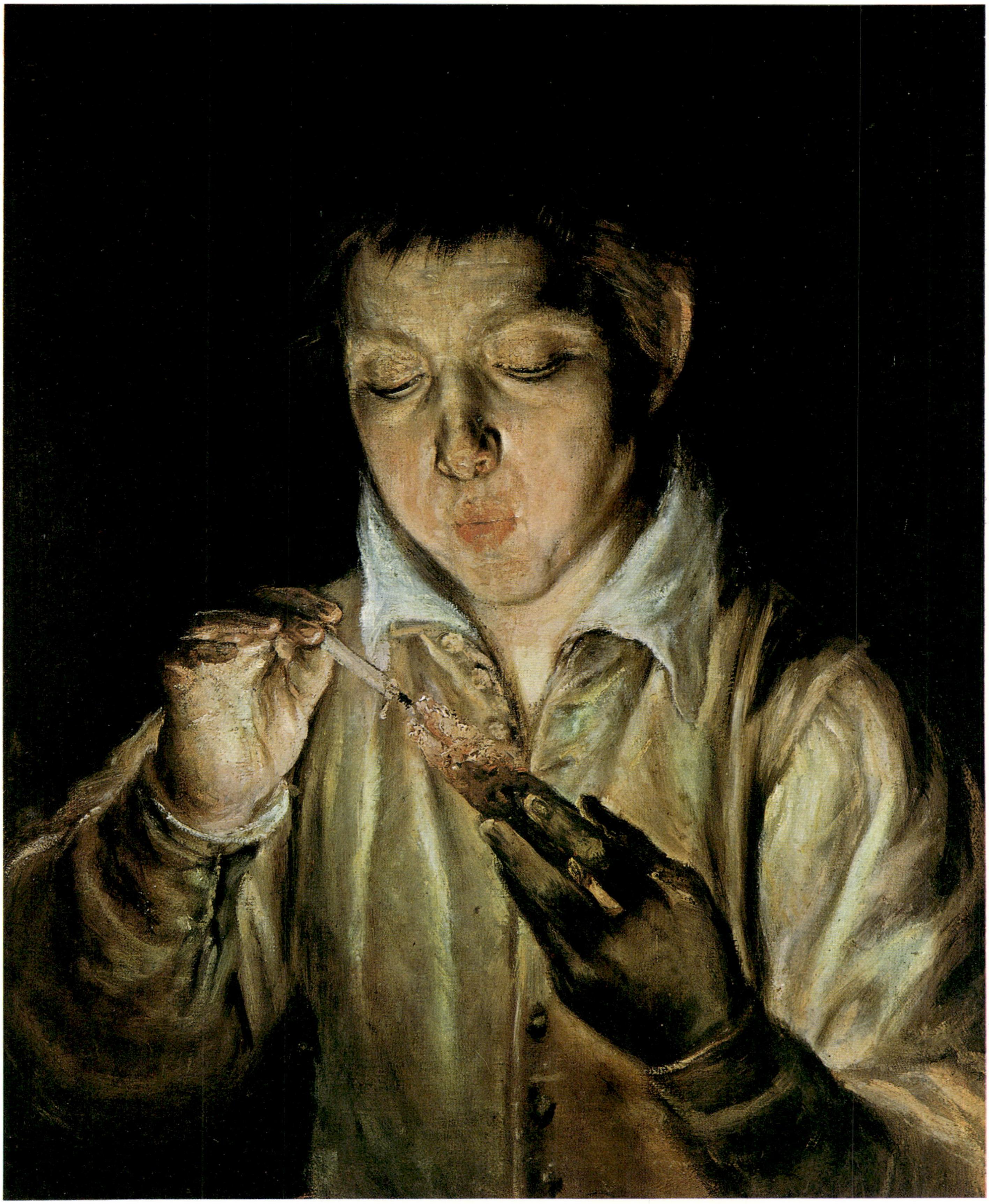

Fig. 29. Boy lighting a candle, 1570-1575. Naples, Capodimonte Museum. Cat. No. 22.

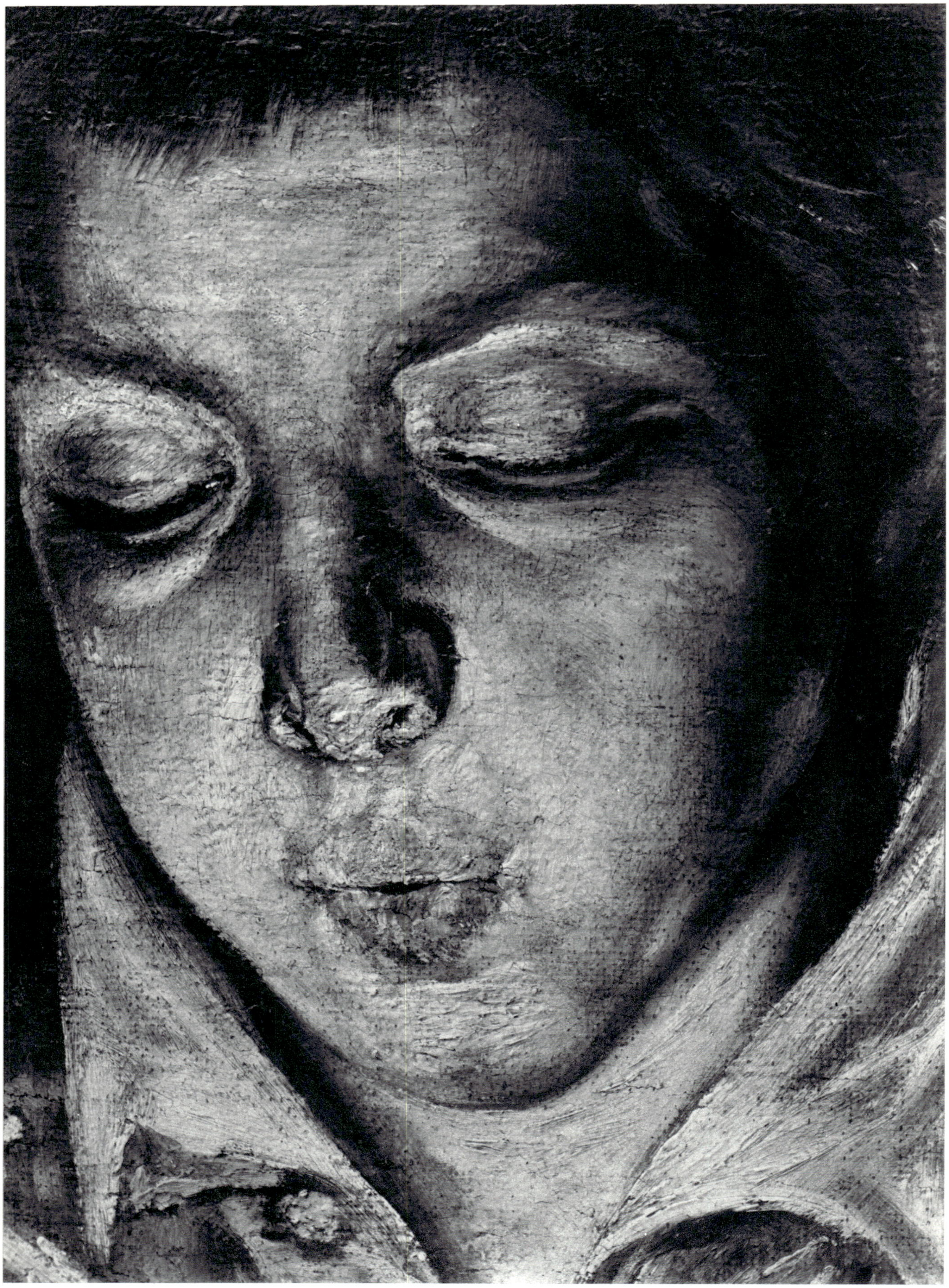

Fig. 30. Boy lighting a candle, 1570-1575. Manhasset, Payson Collection. Cat. No. 23.

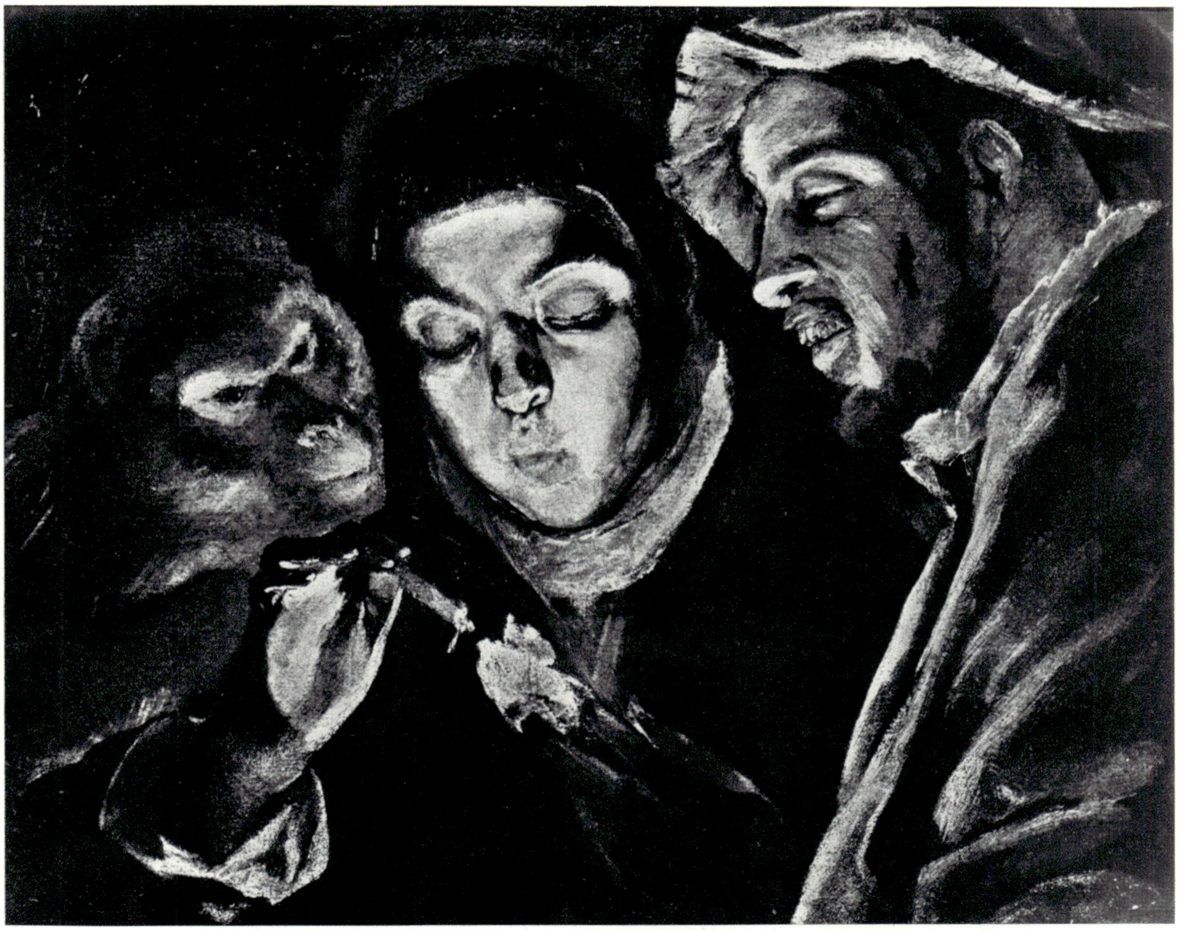

Fig. 31. Genre scene, 1570-1575. Río de Janeiro, V. von Watsdorf Collection. Cat. No. 24.

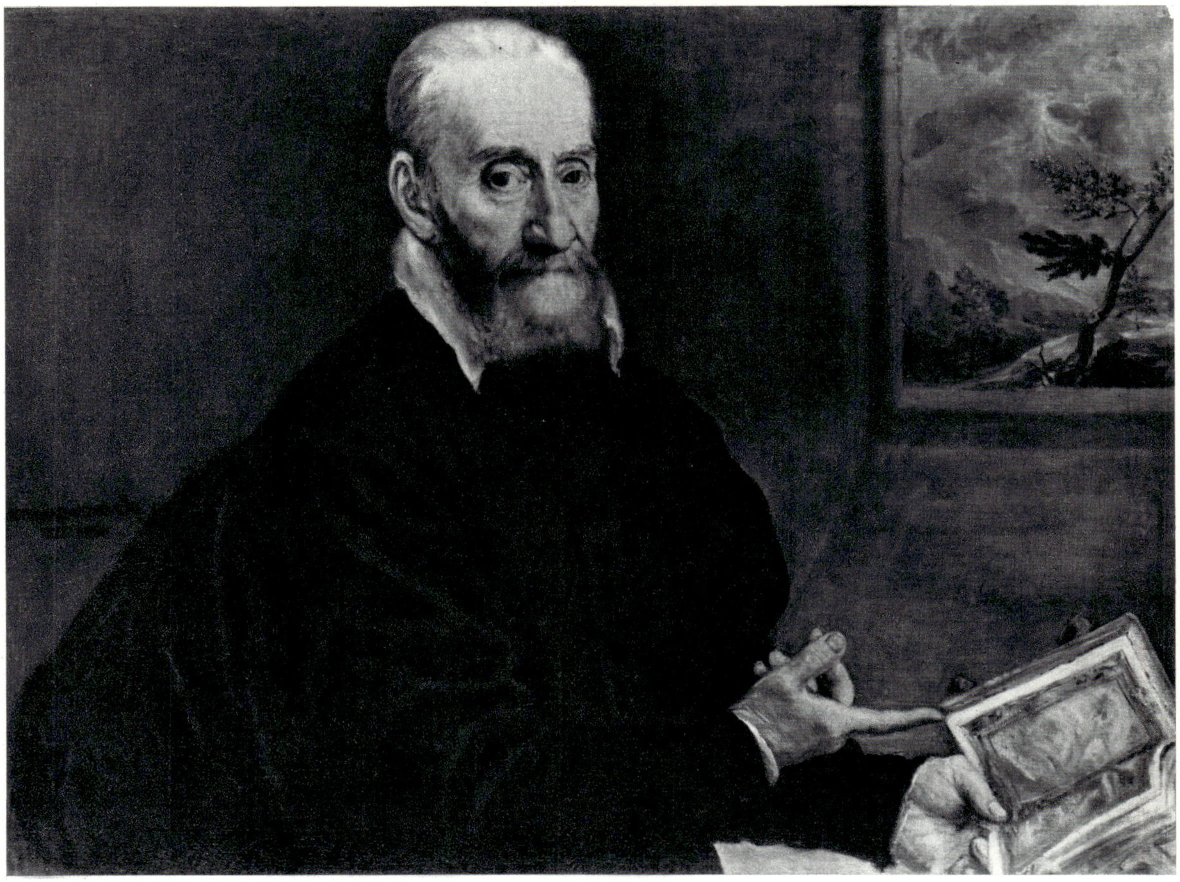

Fig. 32. Giulio Clovio, c. 1570. Naples, Capodimonte Museum. Cat. No. 25.

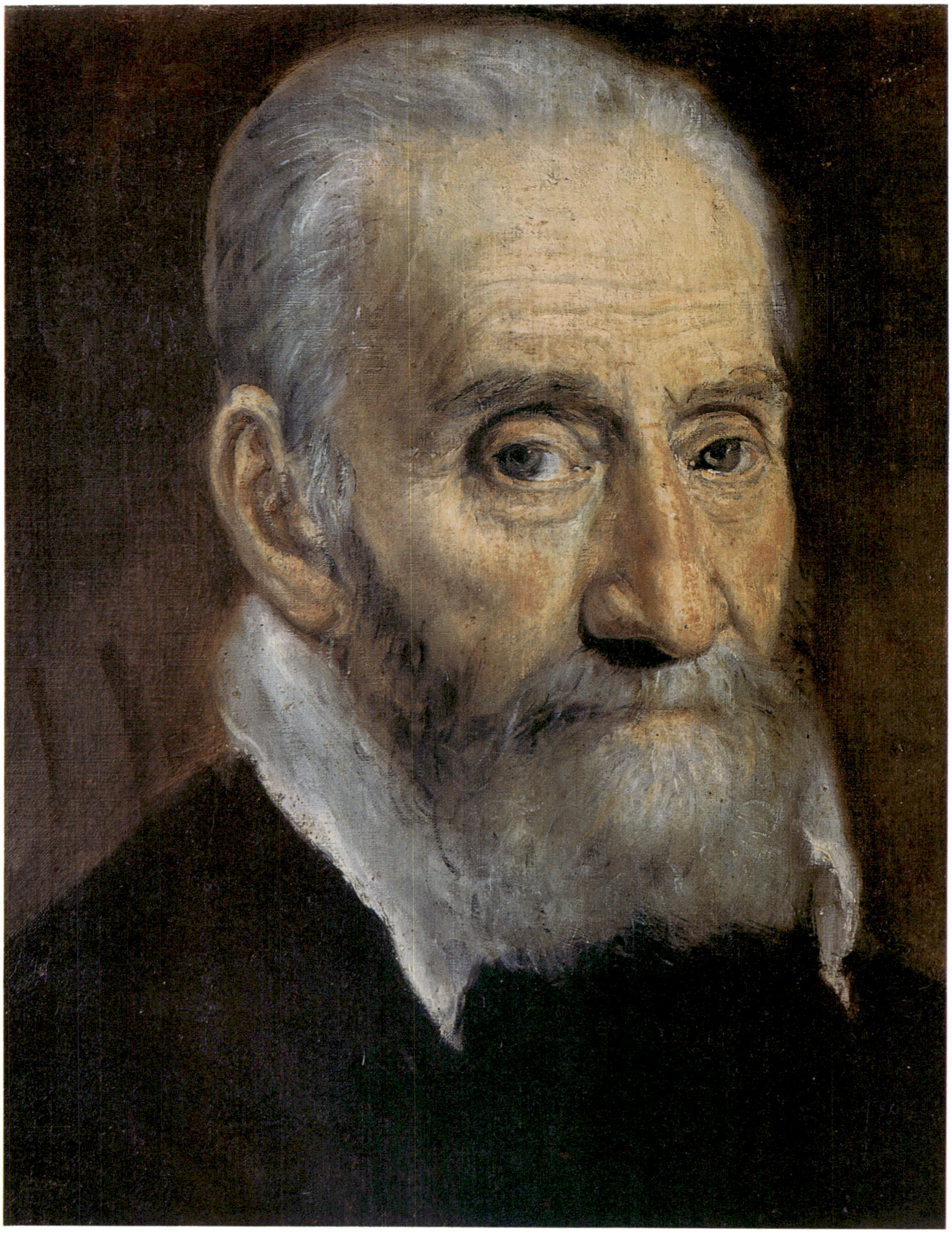

Fig. 33. Detail of figure 32.

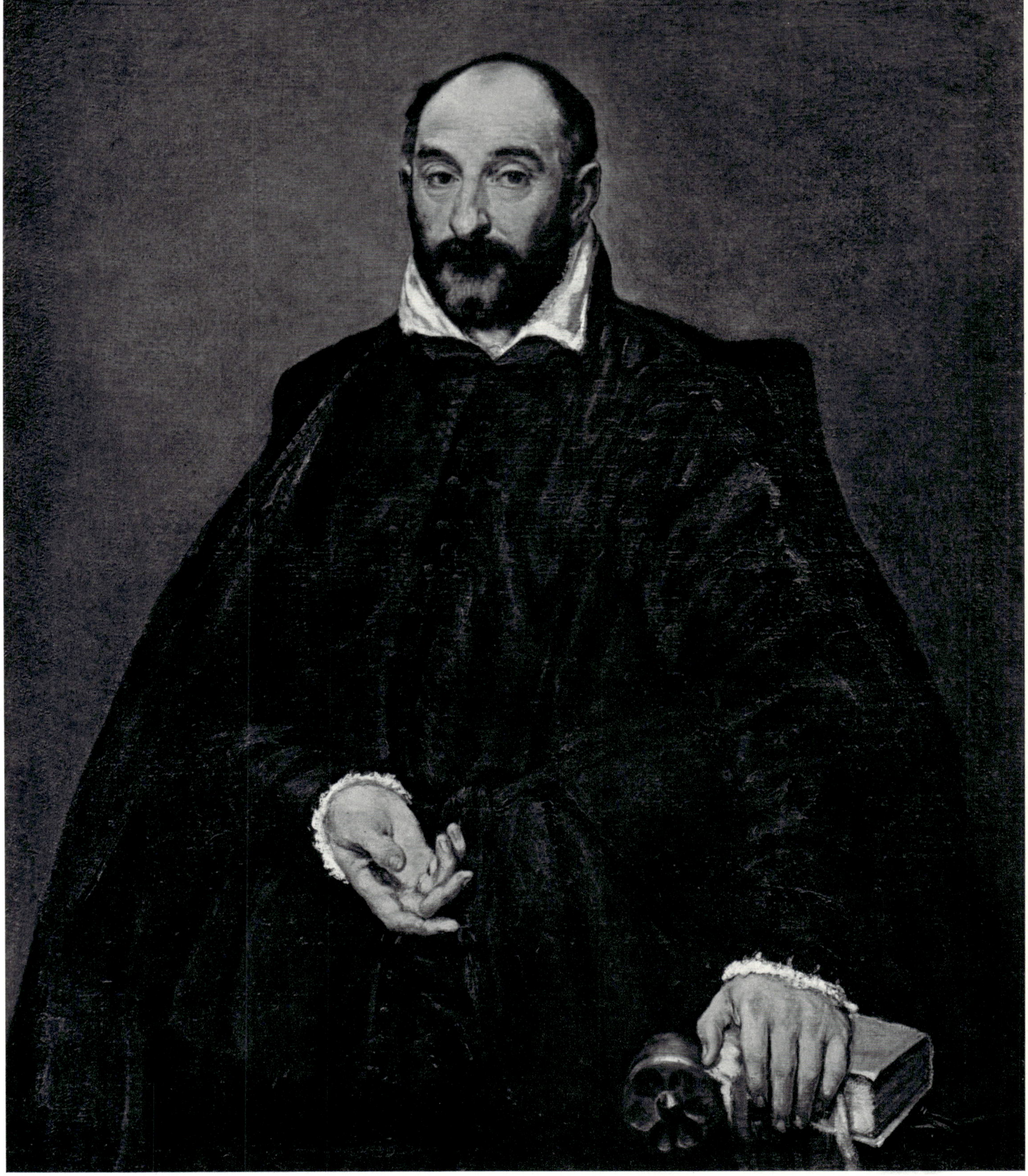

Fig. 34. Giovanni Battista Porta, 1570-1575. Copenhagen, National Gallery. Cat. No. 26.

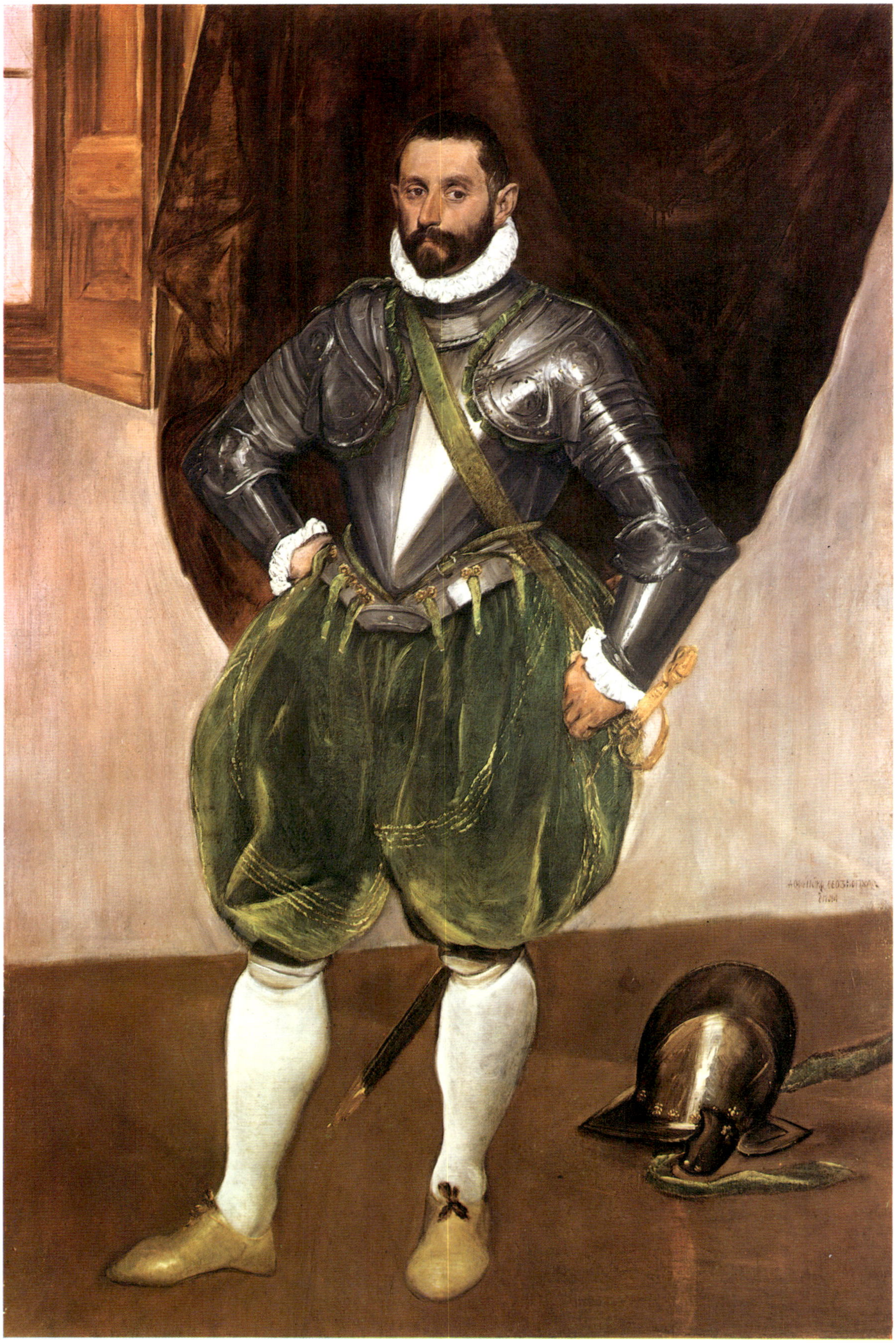

Fig. 35. Vicenzo Anastagi, c. 1575. New York, Frick Collection. Cat. No. 27.

rather large features provide an opportunity for an intense modelling that foreshadows what El Greco's typology was to be in the years to come. For El Greco, not in such a marked manner as Gothic painters but certainly to some extent, always transmitted to his models something of his own physical personality. In other words, since his spirit was something congenital with a given body and face, and since he had to see others through his spirit, the painter never portrayed these others without lending them something, at times very little, of his own being. It may, of course, be simply a question of a stylistic factor that has not yet been properly studied. It certainly can hardly be regarded as a product of his age, for at that time many other artists painted portraits and sacred images, but none of them ever created a gallery of personages even remotely resembling that bequeathed to us by El Greco. It is also possible that the Greco-Byzantine background of his early career —a factor which should never be forgotten when studying El Greco, even considering his immmense capacity for transforming, adapting and surpassing his own achievements— helped him to create those typological characteristics he always infused into the features or general aspect of his characters, though portraying them with all the honesty and visual perspicacity of a man so enormously gifted in drawing. We must repeat once more that El Greco is always the opposite of a fantastic painter. His gift for transfiguration is neither fantasy nor pure imagination, but a transformation of the real and a contemplation of the supernatural through the real; and always in an eminently painterly fashion.

We will close this study of the work done by El Greco towards the end of his Italian period with an analysis of two masterly portraits. That of *Giovanni Battista Porta,* painted in oil on canvas, may very probably be identified with the one sold at the Rubens auction, in 1641, as a self-portrait of Tintoretto *(Fig. 34 - Cat. 26).* It was recognized as El Greco's work when his signature was found on it during the restoration effected towards the end of the last century. It accepts the conventionalism that was beginning to take shape at the time: that of the full-face portrait, a little more than half-length, with the hands showing, some object that serves more or less as an attribute and a smooth background, in flat or lightly shaded tones, which is used to simulate a spatial background and to contribute to a better modelling of the volume.

This personage is quite firmly treated; we might say that there is little or no typological projection in the face. By this we mean that the painter has achieved perfect objectiveness in drawing and modelling, representing this individual according to his true character and with the utmost fidelity to his features. We feel certain, though without the slightest real grounds for thinking so, that the attitude of the right hand was not spontaneous in the model but rather suggested by the artist, both on account of the expressive value of the gesture in itself and because depicting a hand in that position is much more difficult than painting it against the body or resting on an object —as is the case with the left hand in this work, which rests on a thick book. At this time El Greco was just beginning an aspect of his work which was to be as fruitful as his religious iconography: portrait-painting. And from the start he showed that he had all the necessary talent for it. This type of portraiture enters frankly into the realms of realism, being far removed from the hieratical attitudes and the coldness that were so typical of the portrait-painters of two or three decades earlier. From this picture we can also see that, had it not been for his deeper, unrenounceable vocation, El Greco could have been an admirable portrait-painter, in the sense in which the term is used when it is applied to seventeenth-century art, which he anticipated by over a quarter of a century in these masterly portraits painted in Rome. As we shall see in the ones he painted later on in Spain, his art gradually assimilated a subtly idealizing character that modified the basic factors of the drawing and painting of real form, which in the work we are now studying triumphs completely and determines the whole direction of the picture.

In the portrait in question we see less interest in the representation of details in the clothing, though the perfect transference of tactile qualities is so marked that it becomes an important factor. This, in short, is a solid, virile, realistic portrait and somewhat harder than those of Titian by which it is evidently influenced.

Vicenzo Anastagi, a Knight of Malta from 1563, was governor of that island, took part in its defence against the Turkish attack of 1565 and died in 1586 *(Fig. 35 - Cat. 27).* This full-length portrait of him represents, particularly from the technical point of view, the culminating point in this first series of portraits painted by El Greco, a group that is characterized by its total realism, as against the more or less idealizing character that he was to infuse —though never to the detriment of the objective qualities— into the portraits of his later years. In confirmation of the period in which it was painted, we have the monumental, epigraphic signature characteristic of these works of his Italian period. Later, in Spain, El Greco replaced the signature in capitals with one in small letters.

We can tell that this painting was an important commission. Its subject is dressed in half-armour, breeches in sumptuous green velvet and white stockings. His gilt sword-hilt and the sash that crosses his steel breast-plate are indications of his high rank. The head is firm and round, with black beard and moustaches carefully clipped and trimmed. His temperament and the vicissitudes of a soldiering life are revealed in his whole *persona,* but particularly in the penetrating look. The background is a miracle of colour and tones. Instead of seeking a straightforward harmony of complementary shades, the artist has arranged curtaining in an obliquely descending line, the colour of which is an almost violet-tinted dark chestnut; but it is far from being dull, thanks to its strong contrast with the light, grey-ochre tones of the wall and the sepia of the floor. The absence of warm colour —red, orange or yellow— permits two things which basically converge: the interest of the admirably represented steel and of the face, and the dramatic quality that undoubtedly reigns to some extent over the whole picture. We should not forget, however, that this is a vague sensation rather than an explicitly displayed character, for when El Greco wished to give a work a certain feeling he was well able to do so by more forceful means. Here he is more reserved and, we repeat, realistic above all else.

Simplicity is also an important factor in this painting, both in the rather rough sobriety of the subject's attitude and at the same time in a sort of absolute indifference to everything around him. The solidity of the paint, the strength of the colour and the roundness of the form dominate the theme in which they are employed. In this work, we repeat, El Greco arrives at the style, at once realistic and deeply pictorial, of the portrait-painters of half a century later, though he himself was to turn his attention to other fields.

When did El Greco's stay in Rome come to an end? We do not know, nor have we any real clue to the date, apart from the vague reference in Mancini's text. Some of the painter's biographers have inclined to believe the hypothesis that he made a second stay in Venice, around 1575, on account of the plague which wrought havoc in the Eternal City at that time and soon spread to Venice, where its effects were even more terrible, among its victims being Titian himself. It has also been supposed by some that El Greco visited Malta, an idea suggested by the great portrait of Anastagi.

Wethey, the demolisher of so many theories that seemed to have been firmly established in the scanty "life-story" of El Greco, is in agreement with Morovic, who dismisses as apocryphal the letter by Giulio Clovio describing a visit to the painter's studio. It must be admitted that this letter is not without appeal, and so we are including it, not as documentary material but as a poetic judgment of surprising accuracy: "Yesterday I paid a visit to El Greco in order to take him out for a walk in the town. The weather was beautiful, with a delicious spring sun that seemed to fill everybody with joy. The whole town had a holiday air. But when I reached El Greco's studio I was astonished to see the curtains of all the windows so closely drawn that it was hardly possible to see anything. El Greco was sitting in an armchair, neither working nor sleeping. He refused to come out with me, for the light of day disturbed his inner light".

Wethey also reveals the mistake that was made in thinking that it was El Greco who was referred to in a satirical epigram by Giovanni B. Marino (born in 1569), entitled "Di Pittura goffa: Dal Greco". This had been advanced as evidence of the outcry raised by the intellectuals of Rome on the occasion of his extraordinary proposal regarding Michelangelo's *Last Judgment.*

II

c. 1576-1579

A HYPOTHESIS ABOUT EL GRECO'S FIRST WORKS IN SPAIN — THE *ADORATION OF THE NAME OF JESUS* — THE *ST. SEBASTIAN* OF PALENCIA — THE *CRUCIFIXION* IN THE LOUVRE — THE *KNIGHT TAKING AN OATH* AND OTHER SIGNED PAINTINGS — WORKS SIGNED "CHEÌR DOMÉNIKOU" — THE *ST. LAWRENCE* OF MONFORTE — THE ALTARPIECES FOR SANTO DOMINGO EL ANTIGUO — THE *ESPOLIO* — JERÓNIMA DE LAS CUEVAS.

The mystery surrounding El Greco's departure from Italy also extends to his arrival in Spain. It would seem logical to suppose, as do most historians, that he moved to Spain in the hope of joining the team of artists in the service of Philip II. By about that time the monastery of the Escorial had reached its final stages, in which a preponderant role would be played by the painters. Did he first settle in Madrid? It may readily be imagined that the painter, if he had decided to offer his services to the Spanish king, would first make his way to the capital of the Empire. In general the study of El Greco's work in Spain begins with the altarpieces of Santo Domingo el Antiguo (1577-1579), but there is a series of paintings —a series we consider to be intermediate between the work done in Rome and the altarpieces— which must belong to a period of transition between the Greco of Rome and the Greco of Toledo. In this series, undoubtedly carried out in Spain, the works are signed with Greek capitals, some bearing the inscription DOMÉNIKOS THEOTOKÓPOULOS EPOÍEI in a prominent position, others with the words CHEÌR DOMÉNIKOU. The *St. Sebastian* in the Cathedral of Palencia, the *Crucifixion* in the Louvre, a *St. Francis,* the *Knight taking an oath,* the sketch for the *Adoration of the Name of Jesus* and a *Sudary of St. Veronica* have the first signature. The second appears on a *St. Veronica,* a *St. Anthony* and a *St. Mary Magdalen.*

The existence of these works has induced us to put forward the hypothesis that El Greco might have arrived in Spain at least as early as 1576, a possibility regarding which there are no specific arguments for or against, but which seems logical from the technical point of view. On the other hand, a stylistic study of such paintings, which show a certain maturity and are certainly both of notable quality and numerous (since, as we shall see, they must be grouped with other, unsigned, paintings), leads us to suppose that some of them may be contemporaries of the works documented and dated between 1577 and 1579.

The "Adoration of the Name of Jesus"

The first work we shall deal with is the complex allegorical composition figuring Philip II. We think it advisable to let this admirable painting keep the title given it by Camón Aznar: *The Adoration of the Name of Jesus (Fig. 38 - Cat. 29).* Father Santos, who mentioned it for the first time in 1657 under the title of *Glory of El Greco,* interpreted its iconographical significance as "the heavens, the earth and the infernal regions adoring Jesus", a theme inspired by St. Paul's Epistle to the Philippians. Cossío gave the composition the name of *Glory of Philip II,* in order to discredit the absurd title of *Dream of Philip II* given it by Polero in his catalogue of the pictures in the Escorial, which was published in 1857 and attained widespread popularity.

Sir Anthony Blunt interpreted this work as an allegory of the Holy League, which triumphed in the battle of Lepanto in 1571, and considers that the figures we can see kneeling in the foreground are: Pope Pius V, Philip II, the Doge of Venice, Mocenigo, Marcantonio Colonna and Don Juan of Austria, admiral of the allied fleet. This last is supposed to be represented by the idealized figure on the Pope's left, resting both hands on a sword. If we recall that Don Juan of Austria died in 1578 and was buried in the Escorial a year later, we shall more easily accept the hypothesis proposed by Blunt, who considered that this painting must have been carried out as an allegory in honour of Don Juan and therefore placed in the chapel of the Pantheon of the Princes. It is there that it is described by Father Santos. The sketch, painted on a wooden panel, is still extant *(Fig. 36 - Cat. 28)*; it was at one time the property of that Gaspar Méndez de Haro (d. 1687) whom we have already mentioned, an important personage in seventeenth-century Spain. In the inventory of his collection it figures as the pair to one of the sketches for the *Espolio* at Upton Downs *(Fig. 74 - Cat. 52)* and it is, in fact, of the same dimensions. It is signed with Greek capitals, following El Greco's usual custom during his Italian period. The canvas in the Escorial, which is an almost literal enlargement of the sketch, is signed in italics.

Camón Aznar's suggestion that both works were painted by El Greco shortly before settling in Toledo is a very thought-provoking one. The technique used in both the sketch and the definitive canvas betrays clear traces of an inner struggle to achieve a new pictorial formula and seems to show the road that was to lead the artist to the masterly execution of the group in Santo Domingo el Antiguo, the *Espolio* and even the *St. Maurice,* the principal figures in which show a close relationship with the probable idealized portrait of Don Juan of Austria.

There are few differences between the definitive work and its sketch. Merely some changes of colour, an enrichment of details in the larger picture —above all in the upper part— and a more emphatic shading of the tones. The sketch pays more attention to the intermediate area, with the dynamic rhythms created by the clouds, whereas its rather emptier upper part seems to draw us dizzily into the infinite. In the final work the painter gave more human interest to this representation of the heavens, making the figures of the angels in the central area proportionally larger. To the right the clouds grow darker, in consonance with the theme of the lower area. In effect, while the multitude of the just, headed by the historical figures, appears in the foreground from the centre of the composition to the left background, the right-hand side is the area of the damned. Hell is represented by an enormous monster, with gaping maw —as in the medieval tradition— to swallow up the bodies of the sinners, and this monster floats in turn upon a kind of fiery sea. In the background arches are drawn, creating a world that represents the death of the wicked (there is even a gibbet), within a space that traces a sweeping curve towards the right background, the whole in a clear orange tone. A patch of the same colour, in the form of an elongated triangle, spreads towards the left and surrounds the multitude of the just, which, behind the foreground, is progressively wrapped in shadow, with the exception of a small group standing on an eminence to the left, where the figure of a kneeling man in a red robe stands out, making sweeping gestures with his arms.

This wonderful and eminently pictorial piece of scenography serves to frame the magnificent representation of the principal personages in the foreground, who are, from right to left: Philip II, Pope Pius V, Don Juan of Austria, Marcantonio Colonna (the figure in a blue robe with his arms crossed on his breast) and the Doge Mocenigo (who is seen with his back almost entirely turned to us, in a yellow cloak with an ermine collar). The symphony of colours is dazzling and almost makes us forget the originality of the composition as a whole to concentrate our attention on this essential area. The dominant colours are blue, white, golden yellow and vivid red, which contrast with the black clothes of Philip II, with his lean, ascetic profile. With the exception of this portrait, all the figures display an arrogance which still shows Italian influence. Hence this picture seems to be a synthesis of two ideas: that of the adoration of the Name of Jesus and that of an allegory of the victory at Lepanto. And in this there would be no contradiction, for the adoration would be an action of thanks for the triumph against the enemies of the Christian faith. After a beginning like this, at once spectacular and profound, El Greco's way was open to all kinds of speculations with space, colour and form.

The antecedents of the essential scheme of this very complex composition are to be found in the central panel of the Modena triptych *(Fig. 5),* the sixteenth-century allegorical woodcut we have already mentioned and the 1590 engraving by Andrea Andreani.

The "St. Sebastian" of Palencia

In its monumental character and comparative simplicity of form, the *St. Sebastian* in the Cathedral of Palencia *(Fig. 40 - Cat. 30)* still seems to show traces of the impact of Rome. From time immemorial this

Fig. 36. The Adoration of the Name of Je
1576-1579. London, National Gallery. Cat. No.

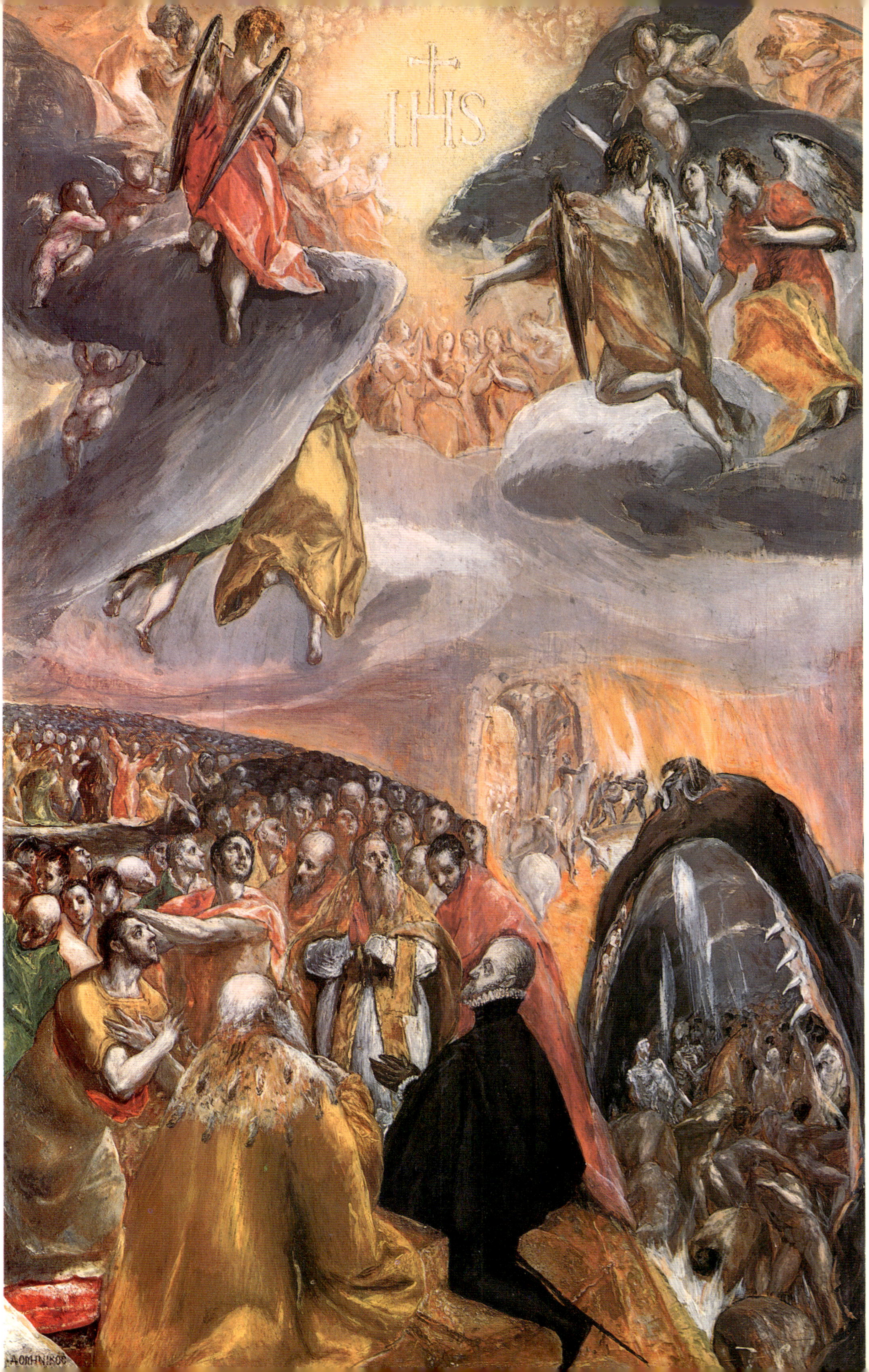
IHS

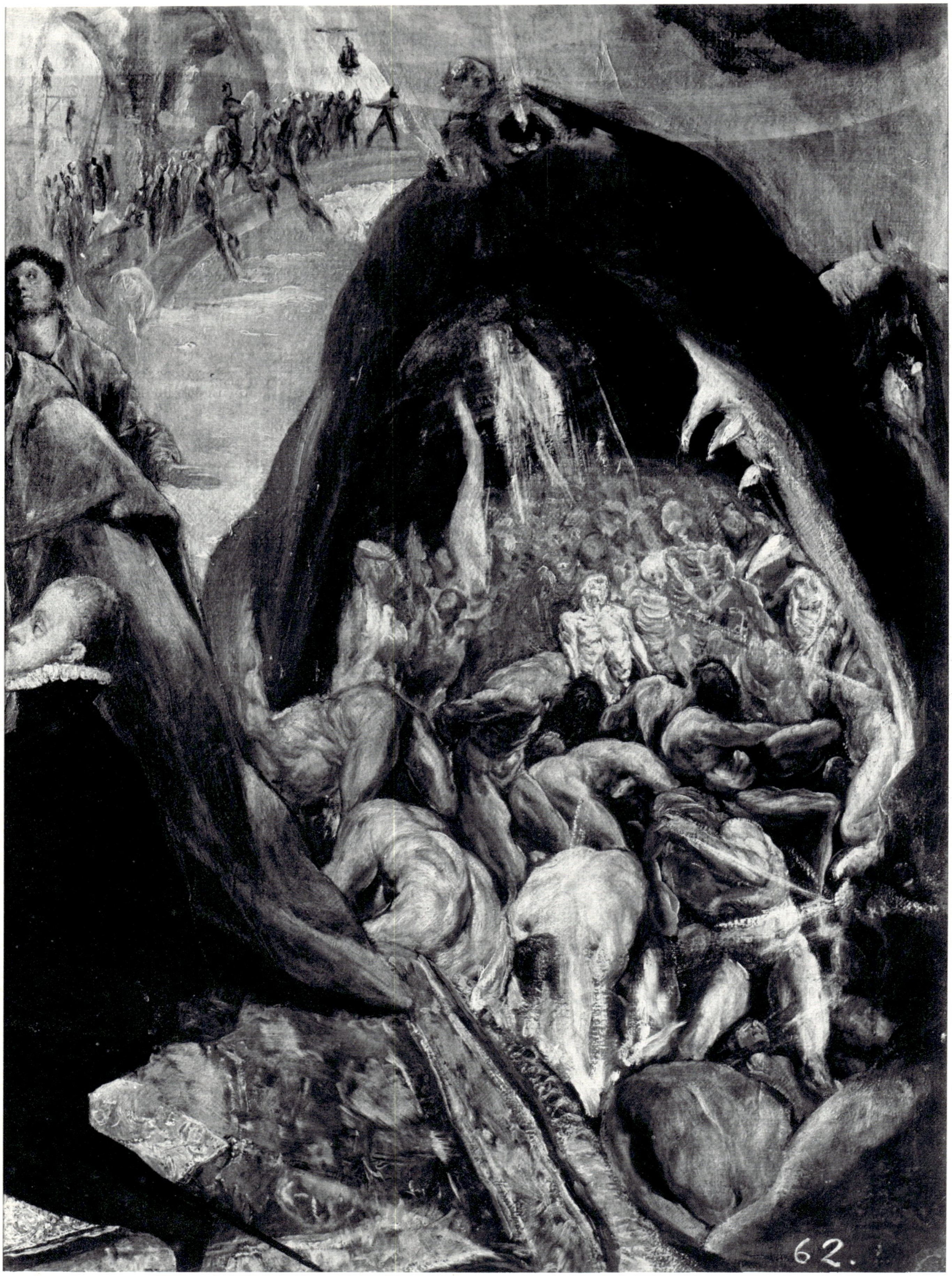

Figs. 37 & 38. The Adoration of the Name of Jesus, 1576-1579. The Escorial, Monastery. Cat. No. 29.

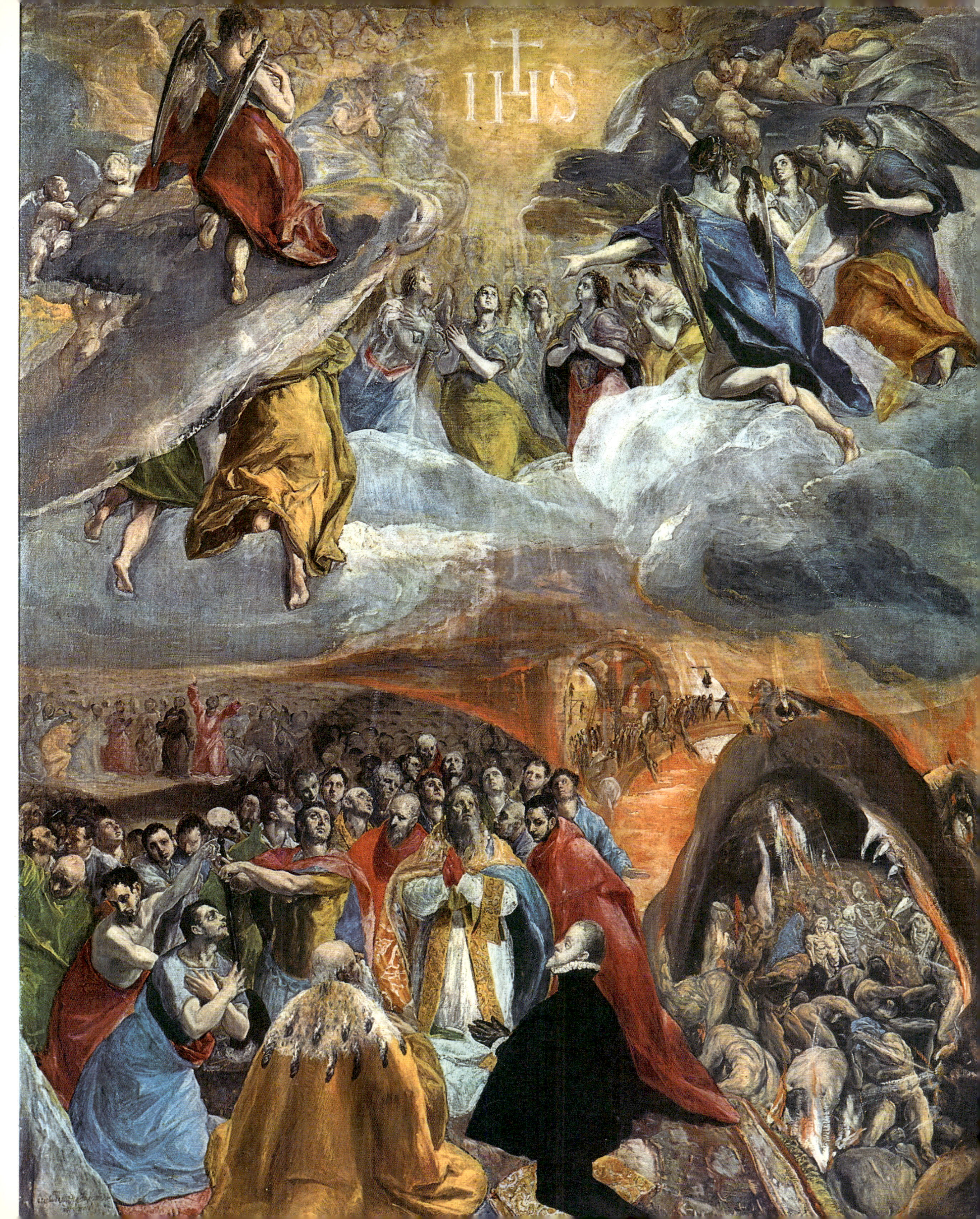
IHS

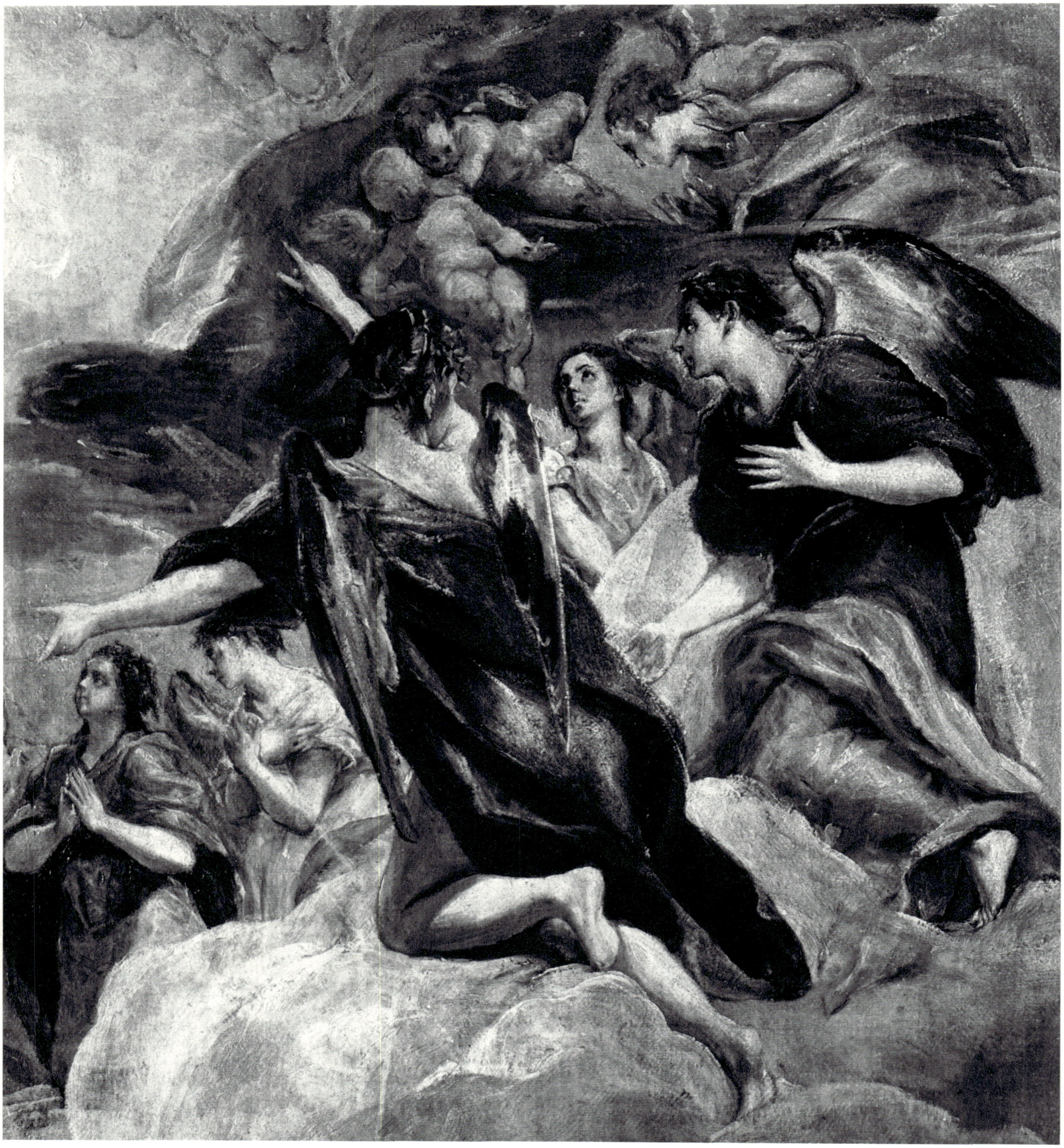

Fig. 39. Detail of figure 38.

picture hung in the buildings of the Cathedral of Palencia, but nobody seems to know how it got there. Wethey has suggested that it may have been donated or bequeathed by Diego de Castilla, the Dean of the Chapter of Toledo, who gave El Greco his great commission for Santo Domingo el Antiguo and who had also been the chaplain, and later canon and archdeacon, of the Cathedral of Palencia. It seems logical that the painter should have given him such excellent first fruits of his work in Spain, and equally logical that the Dean should have presented it to the cathedral in which he had begun his ecclesiastical career. In this admirable canvas, signed with Greek capitals, El Greco shows restraint in depicting cruelty. As against other versions, which are literally held together by arrows, he presents us with a youthful figure wounded by a single dart. The centre of the painted surface is occupied almost entirely by the figure of the martyr, against a blue sky with dense, whitish clouds which is joined to a landscape with trees that recall those to be seen in the painter's Italian works. To the right is the tree used as an execution post, which —together with the wild flowers we shall see in the foreground of the *St. Maurice (Fig. 83)*— is one of the most realistic pieces of painting in the artist's whole work. The canon of the figure is already noticeably elongated. And we can also see how soon El Greco has achieved the result of making the figure itself a sufficient theme for the work. In the portraits of the Roman period we pointed out what great possibilities El Greco might have had as a strict realist, but here we can already see the way the painter had chosen for himself. The modelling of the body in this painting is a beautiful synthesis of the form as an element modelled by light. In future he would only have to shade, vary, complicate and further deform what he had already achieved, without ever surpassing it absolutely. The *St. Sebastian* in Palencia reveals the blossoming of his genius in a theme and a style that were by now characteristic, with hardly any reminiscences of a past that El Greco had already left behind him when he first set foot in Spain. In little more than a decade he had gone from the "vermicular" technique of the icons to the imitation of the perspectives and scenographies of Tintoretto, from the figurative creation of Titian to an art that was wholly his own; an art, moreover, in which he was to stand alone for all time, with neither rivals nor followers and, for the most part, without really worthy imitators.

The "Crucifixion" in the Louvre

Another of the pictures signed with Greek capitals is the one in the Louvre representing a *Crucifixion* with two donors *(Fig. 43 - Cat. 31)*. It is almost certain that this was the work acquired by Baron Taylor in 1836 from the Queen's convent of the Hieronymite Nuns in Toledo. The three figures in the scene stand out as independent elements against a background of clouds. In them, above all in that of Christ who is represented as still alive, we see the full flowering of the concept initiated in the *St. Sebastian* of Palencia.

The clouds, as was also to be the case with his draperies, provide El Greco with a world of forms and colours in the handling of which he can develop his innate tendency to an expressionism that was to be openly unleashed in his final period. Clouds and draperies, moreover, together with flesh tints, were to be practically the only elements used by him in evolving his immense plastic eloquence. This figure of Christ is one of El Greco's great creations, being the prototype or initial model for all the figures of Christ crucified that are as milestones in his career and reflect, simultaneously with other iconographical series, his stylistic evolution and the dramatic progression of his own life. The modelling is among the purest and most perfect that he ever achieved. Strength and softness, tactile sensation and purity of line in the contours, light and shade, are all perfectly combined. We should also mention the sculptural character of the form, which was not always to be so clear and intense in El Greco, though appearing with comparative frequency.

Nothing is known of the identity of either the surpliced ecclesiastic on the left *(Fig. 44)* or the man in black. They might well be the brothers Diego and Luis de Castilla, which would be a proof that they had become El Greco's protectors in Spain while he was waiting for Philip II to make up his mind. They were to take him to Toledo with a definite commission of great importance: the altarpieces for the church of Santo Domingo el Antiguo. They were the sons of Don Felipe de Castilla, who was a direct descendant of King Peter the Cruel of Castile. The elder succeeded his father as dean of the Cathedral of Toledo and died in 1584. Don Luis, who was twenty years younger than his brother, was born in 1540 and rose to be Dean of the Cathedral of Cuenca.

From the pictorial point of view, these are two excellent portraits and we can appreciate the artist's wealth of technical resources in his way of treating every detail in the most suitable manner. In the figure of the ecclesiastic there is a wonderful contrast between the hands, with their firm, blended modelling, and the transparent surplice, which is depicted with brush-strokes in different directions and in very dense impasto, so that the separate hairs of the brush can be quite clearly seen.

The "Knight taking an oath" and other signed paintings

The *Knight taking an oath* is the title recently devised by Wethey, in the light of his research, for this famous canvas in the Prado, traditionally known as the *Gentleman with his hand on his breast,* which was inventoried in the royal collections in 1794 *(Fig. 45 - Cat. 32).* This beautiful portrait has been so maltreated that it is difficult to appreciate it in all its real excellence. The degrees of the tonal shading can be seen to be greatly altered and the image has a certain flatness which cannot have been there when El Greco painted it. In spite of this, it produces a considerable effect on the viewer, for there are some works of art —and this is one of them— which seem to be destined not so much to satisfy the capacity for enjoyment of the expert as to attract the masses, not only because of their subject-matter but also on account of that subject-matter's generic significance. It is also the mission of art, after all, to create figures, forms and even personages that will remain as witnesses to a way of life, a race, an age. In this portrait generations have seen the personification of the Spanish grandee of the Golden Age, whose hand is a sign of caste and lineage, but whose look denotes resolution and boldness. There is no need to dwell on the sober elegance of the composition: the rhythm of the flesh tints and the white against the black on which shines the finely-wrought hilt of the sword, and the more fleeting gleam of a chain against which the gentleman's fingers are pressed. With this figure and the two praying figures in the *Crucifixion* in the Louvre begins the masterly gallery of portraits that El Greco was to paint in Spain, a series in which we may trace an evolution parallel to that of his religious compositions.

The signature DOMÉNIKOS THEOTOKÓPOULOS EPOÍEI in Greek capitals appears on two more paintings. The first is the prototype of an image that was to be repeated throughout the painter's career: the *Sudary of St. Veronica (Fig. 47 - Cat. 34).* It is a face of impressive spirituality, at once sweet and vigorous, divine and human, combining the qualities of the Byzantine tradition with that profound humanism to be found in the greatest creations of the Renaissance.

The second is the representation of *St. Francis in ecstasy (Fig. 48 - Cat. 35),* a realistic figure painted with all the vigour of the technique used in the portrait of Giovanni Battista Porta. We can see how the face was analysed by the implacable drawing that followed the painter's idea exactly. The formal perfection of the hands crossed on the breast is admirable, as is the modelling of the skull. Even the effect of light is realistic, with the source in the upper left, which establishes a gentle division of the painted area, with a certain penumbra on the right and a rather subdued clarity on the other side. In the face there is a tendency to expressionism, above all in the look; we shall see later how El Greco achieved a growing intensity in this respect, giving features and looks so profound a pathos and range of feeling that this expression seems to be the sole excuse for the picture. But here we have not yet reached this stage. We might say the painter wished to "portray" the saint and did everything he could to produce an absolutely faithful likeness in forms, qualities and typology. The technique, though very pictorial, pays more attention to the drawing than is usual in El Greco, both in the internal structure of the form and in the individual touches and brush-strokes that enliven certain areas. There is an unsigned replica of this work in the Lázaro Galdeano Museum in Madrid *(Cat. 36),* which has harder qualities and tonal contrasts, so that the modelling is more intense but rather less naturalistic.

Works signed "Cheìr Doménikou"

We find the signature CHEÌR DOMÉNIKOU in Greek capitals on three paintings on canvas: a *Penitent Magdalen* once in the English College of Valladolid, a *St. Anthony of Padua* and a *St. Veronica* holding the sudary with the imprint of the face of Christ. It will be recalled that this is the signature that appears on the controversial triptych of Modena, which was studied in the first chapter of this book, and that it means "from the hand of Dominico". This signature is not found again on any of El Greco's work.

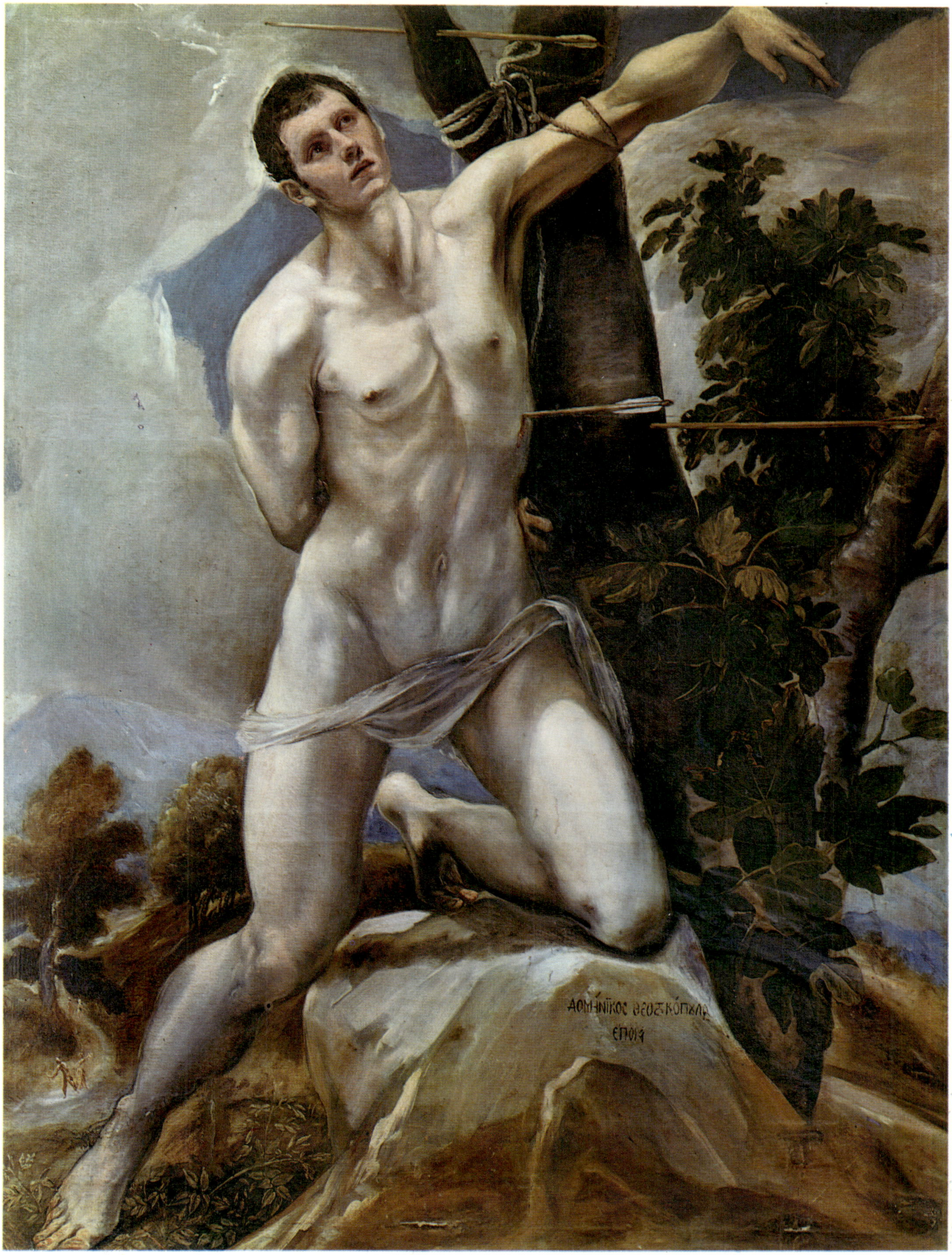

Fig. 40. St. Sebastian, 1576-1579. Palencia, Cathedral. Cat. No. 30.

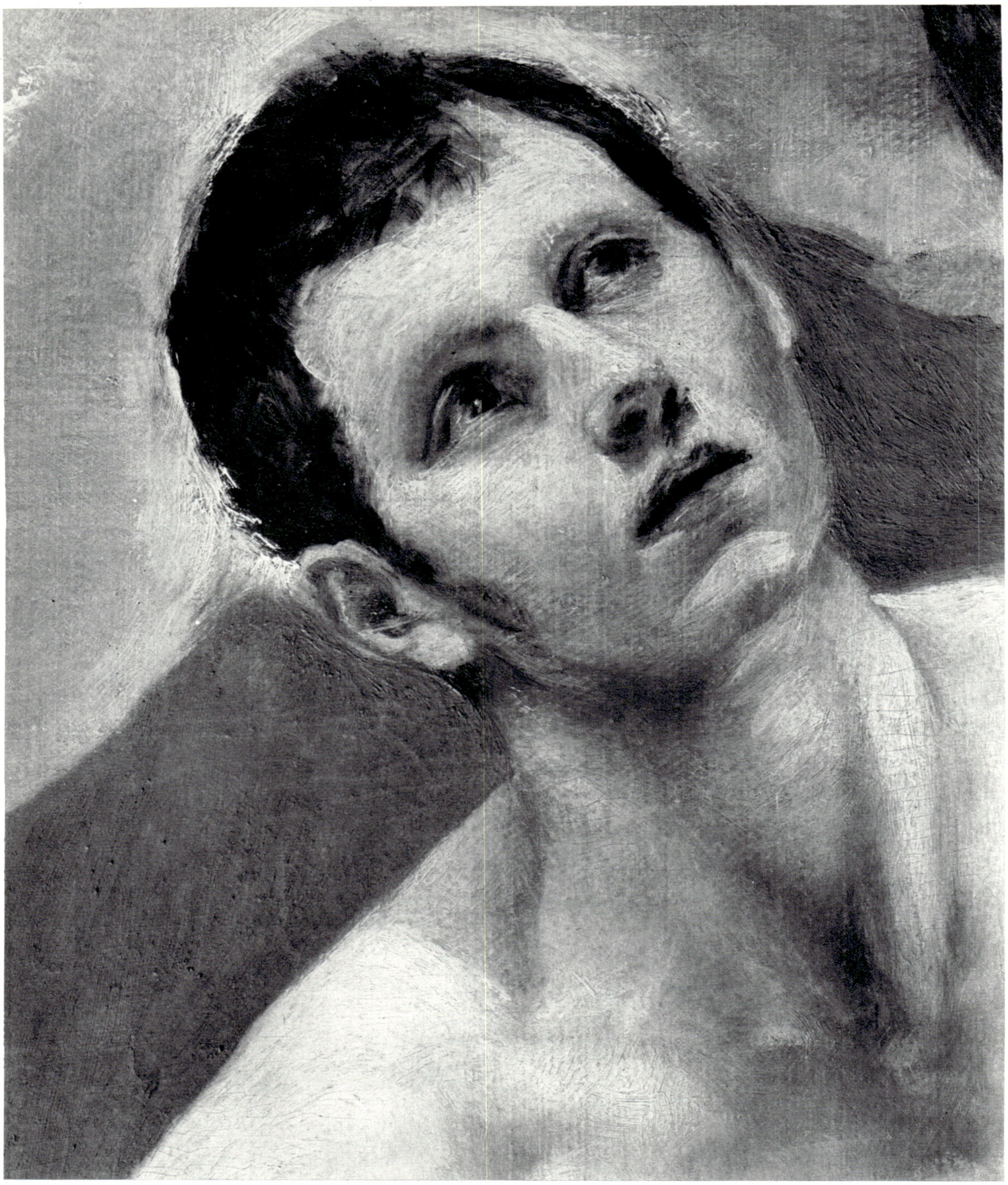

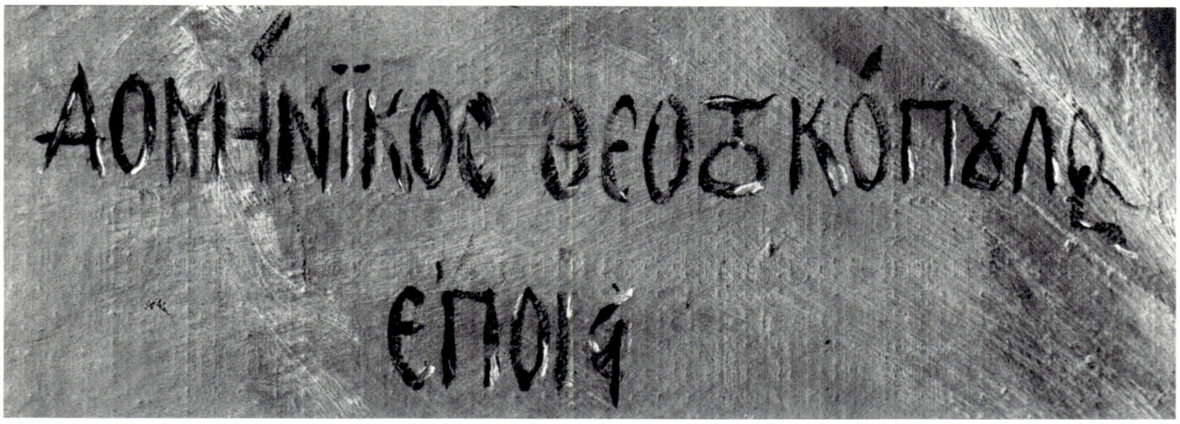

Figs. 41 & 42. Details of figure 40.

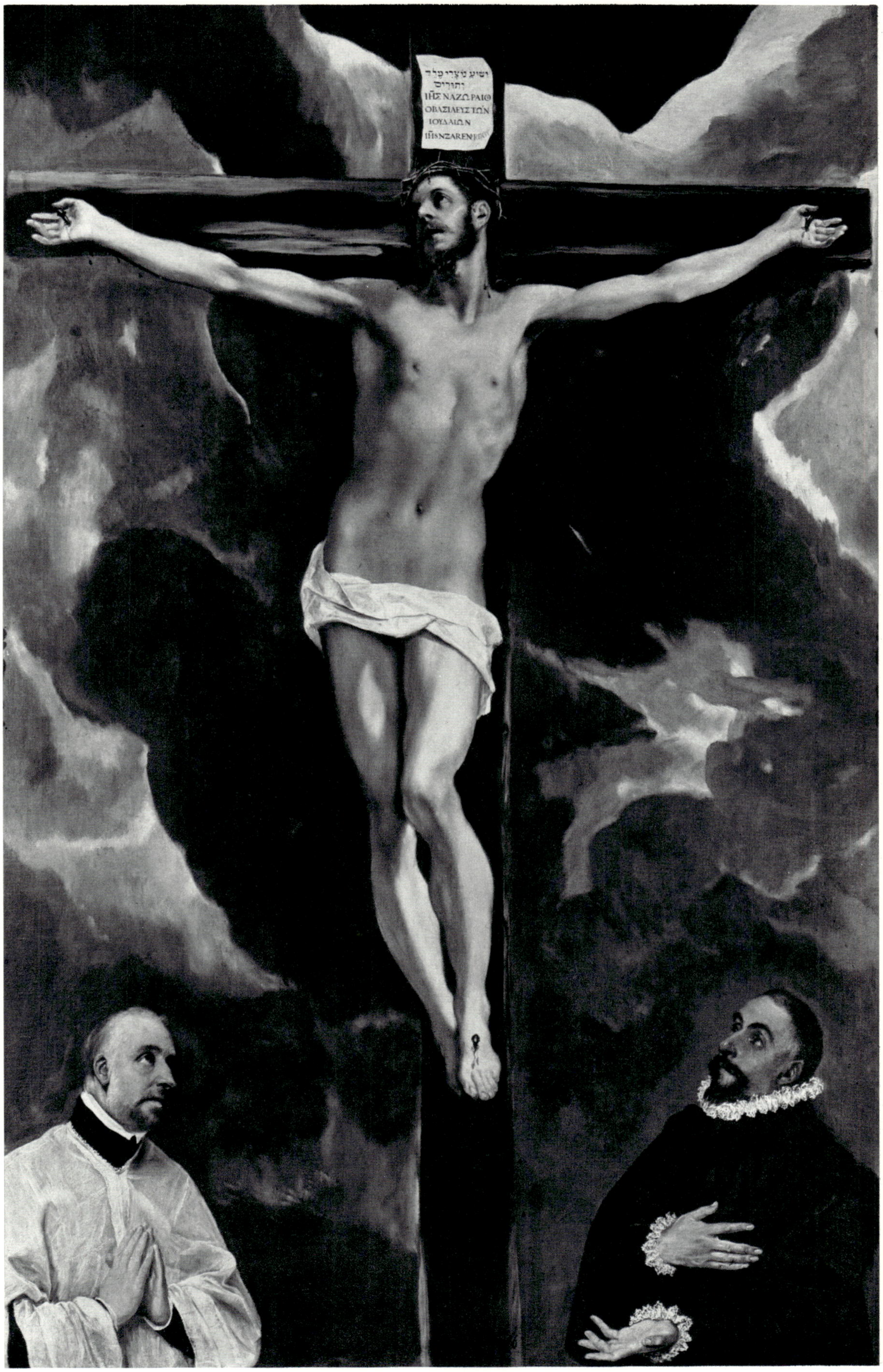

Fig. 43. Crucifixion with two donors, 1576-1579. Paris, Louvre Cat. No. 31.

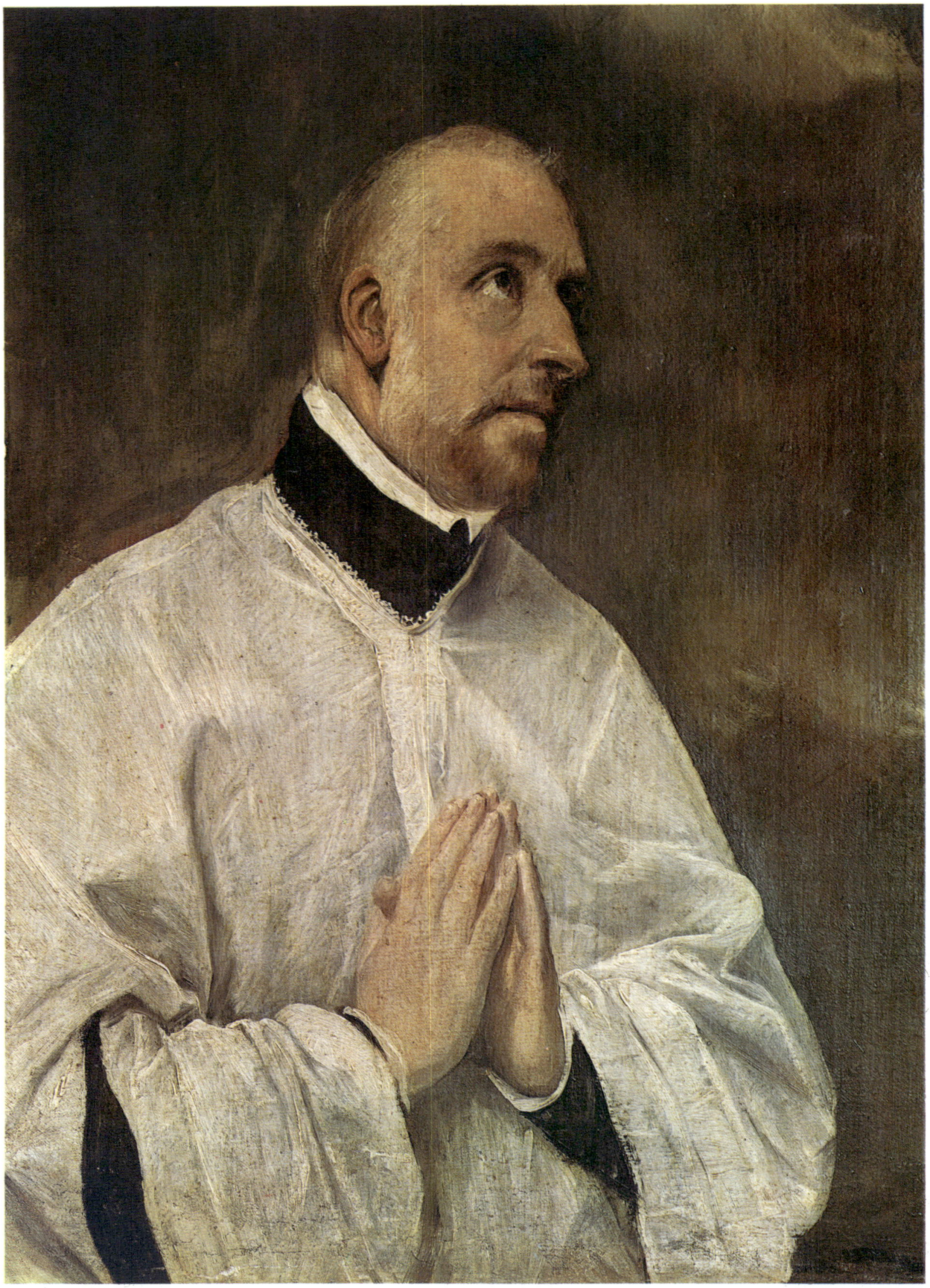

Fig. 44. Detail of figure 43.

In the *Penitent Magdalen* now in the Worcester Art Museum *(Fig. 46 - Cat. 33)* there is a deliberate effort to create beauty, with the flesh tones managed with clarity and a certain simplification, so that a blend of spirituality and sensuousness is irradiated by the saint's inner life. It is obvious that the artist's intention was to create in this work an attractive image, the viewer's interest being drawn to the saint's great eyes, an effect that is frequently repeated in El Greco's work. The figure is perfectly situated in space and the sensation of physical volume is complete. The tonal balance between the dark rock and the lights and shadows of the cloud effects shows how near in time this picture is to the *Crucifixion* in the Louvre. The elements of the setting are few but effective: the ivy straggling across the bare rock, the wonderful cloud effects and the "still-life" formed by the skull and the little glass vase.

The *St. Anthony of Padua* in the Prado *(Fig. 49 - Cat. 37),* which is almost a grisaille, is less conventional in conception than the *St. Francis in ecstasy* discussed above. The head has an extraordinary vigour, with its large and intensely modelled features. The execution of the habit is rather summary, not so much due to any neglect of the tactile qualities as because the effect has been simplified by a certain amount of geometrizing. The hand betrays the same approach, but is more delicately treated. If we make a close analysis of the execution (particularly in the head, which is the most carefully worked part), we shall see traces of El Greco's special technical tricks: scoring and rubbing, or heightening by clear, light brush-strokes on dark surfaces. It is interesting to observe what the painter achieves by such means in the suggestion of real forms and qualities — in the saint's hair, for instance, or in the eyelids and the chin.

For technical reasons, and on account of its pictorial character, we consider the *St. Veronica* to be the third of these paintings signed with the laconic CHEÌR DOMÉNIKOU. It comes from the Church of Santo Domingo el Antiguo in Toledo and is now in the collection of a colleague, María Luisa Caturla *(Fig. 51 - Cat. 39).* There is another version, almost exactly the same, which was originally in the Church of Santa Leocadia in Toledo and is now in the Santa Cruz Museum in the same city *(Fig. 50 - Cat. 38).* This composition is conceived in rather dull —almost ashen— tones. The violet border framing the sudary is modulated with yellowish reflections that match the paler tones of the hair round the Holy Face. The outline of Veronica's dark violet clothing almost melts into the black background. The fact that both of these versions of the *Veronica* come from Toledo induces us to believe that they were probably painted there. This group of works may have been done in 1577, possibly during the months that passed while the contracts for the important work in Santo Domingo el Antiguo were being negotiated and drawn up. In both versions the cloth bearing the Holy Face is an exact replica in form and colour of the one in the canvas studied in the preceding pages *(Fig. 47).* The image of Christ appearing in these three paintings seems to belong to a slightly more archaic typology than the one in the *Espolio (Fig. 69).* We should also note that the head of one of the Holy Women in the left foreground of this famous picture is an almost literal repetition of the *St. Veronica* duplicated by El Greco in the paintings we have just been studying, which goes to confirm our chronological and stylistic placing of this group of undated paintings.

The "St. Lawrence" of Monforte

Finally we come to another painting —unsigned— which is the stylistic link, so to speak, between the very coherent group we have just studied and the work done in Santo Domingo el Antiguo: *St. Lawrence's vision of the Virgin* in Monforte de Lemos (Lugo) *(Fig. 52 - Cat. 40).* Its first owner was Rodrigo de Castro, Inquisitor of the Supreme Court of Toledo in 1559, who later became Archbishop of Seville, where he died in 1600, bequeathing this canvas to the Galician monastery, together with a *St. Francis* which we shall study later on, as it is a later work *(Fig. 93).* The structure of the head and the hands of the *St. Lawrence* is reminiscent of that which can be seen in the portrait of Giovanni Battista Porta in the National Museum in Copenhagen *(Fig. 34).* As for the brocade dalmatic, with its crimsons and golden yellows, it is a premonition —and one that is very carefully worked out— of the liturgical robes of St. Stephen and St. Andrew in the *Burial of the Conde de Orgaz.* The position of the head and the intensity of the gaze approach those to be seen in the *Penitent Magdalen,* though the technique here is more abrupt and vigorous, like that of the *St. Anthony of Padua* in the Prado. The Virgin and Child —who are rather reminiscent of those in the little panel with the *Flight into Egypt (Fig. 18)*—

appear upon a cloud behind the martyr, who holds his attribute in his right hand. The pictorial concept of this work, like that of the others considered in this chapter, evidently precedes El Greco's use of elongated proportions, profound spiritualization and expressionistic distortion. In these early days of his career in Spain, El Greco had not yet wholly discovered himself, or did not yet dare to follow the dictates of his feeling. We can see, in each and every painting that he did down to the decade from 1580 to 1590, a marked desire to construct through form and to present his images with a verisimilitude acceptable to any viewer in the Spain of Philip II.

The accentuated technical eclecticism of these paintings is a sign of the ambivalent attitude peculiar to all profound and inventive artists: the retention of what they have acquired, without being afraid of repeating themselves or of replicas, and the slow but steady penetration into new worlds of form and colour. We maintain our hypothesis that these works belong to the uncertain months when he was establishing himself in Spain, though it must be admitted that some of these paintings might have been done in Toledo, alternately with the works for Santo Domingo el Antiguo and the *Espolio* or even one or two years later. The only objection that might be made to this theory is the amount of work their painting would represent, over and above El Greco's copious production between 1577 and 1579. But it is a well-known fact that most of the great geniuses of art have been indefatigable workers, especially in their years of maturity and prime of life.

The altarpieces for Santo Domingo el Antiguo

The execution of this impressive ensemble, the most important done by El Greco in all his life, was the initial reason for his settling in Toledo. In one of the documents of the lawsuit concerning the *Espolio* (1579), the spokesman for the Chapter states: "... that the work he came to do in this city, which is the altarpiece of Santo Domingo el Viejo (Antiguo), is already finished and in position . . .". It is also a testimony to the protection and affection he received from the brothers Diego and Luis de Castilla, for it was thanks to them that he was given the important commission. El Greco finally carried out three altarpieces, between August 1577 and some undetermined date in 1579. Let us now turn our attention to the history of these works.

Doña María de Silva, a Portuguese lady in the household of Charles V's wife, Queen Isabel, married Don Pedro González de Mendoza, the Emperor's Auditor General. After her husband's death she retired to the convent of Santo Domingo el Antiguo in Toledo and on her own death, in 1575, her property was left in trust for the construction of a new church to contain her tomb, Don Diego de Castilla, the Dean of the Cathedral of Toledo, being appointed as her executor. The building was constructed between 1576 and 1579, thanks to the activity and financial assistance of Don Diego, according to plans drawn up by Nicolás de Vergara and modified by Juan de Herrera, the great architect of the Escorial. At some date which is unknown, but certainly earlier than August of 1577, Don Luis de Castilla drew up an "Account of what is to be discussed with Dominico". This document shows that Luis de Castilla was the intermediary between his brother the Dean and El Greco. It should be recalled that, as we have said, the painter may have made friends with Luis de Castilla in Rome, when he was in the Palazzo Farnese. In this account we read: "The reason for giving this work to the said Dominico is because he is said to be eminent in his art and profession, and therefore choice has been made of the industriousness of his character, which no other can replace". The account also states that the work shall be executed in Toledo and that El Greco undertakes to supply the plans for the altarpieces and the models for the carved images that are to complete the iconography of the altarpiece over the high altar. He must also design the "monstrance", i.e., the ciborium. The builder and sculptor of the altarpieces was Juan Bautista Monegro.

On August 8th 1577 the Dean and El Greco agreed in writing that the latter must deliver the paintings that are to make up the ensemble within 20 months, that is to say by March of 1579. The estimate for these paintings is fixed at 1,500 ducats. In a letter written on the same date El Greco accepts the terms of this document and, graciously reducing the figure mentioned, proposes an estimate of 1,000 ducats for all his work, signing "Yo Domenico Theotokopuli afermo quanto e sopra scrito". Apparently he was not yet familiar with Spanish. On August 9th, i.e., the day after the signing of the above undertaking, he acknowledged receipt of various sums paid for the purchase of the canvases and of 51,000 *maravedis* that "I requested when I returned to Madrid", which reveals that

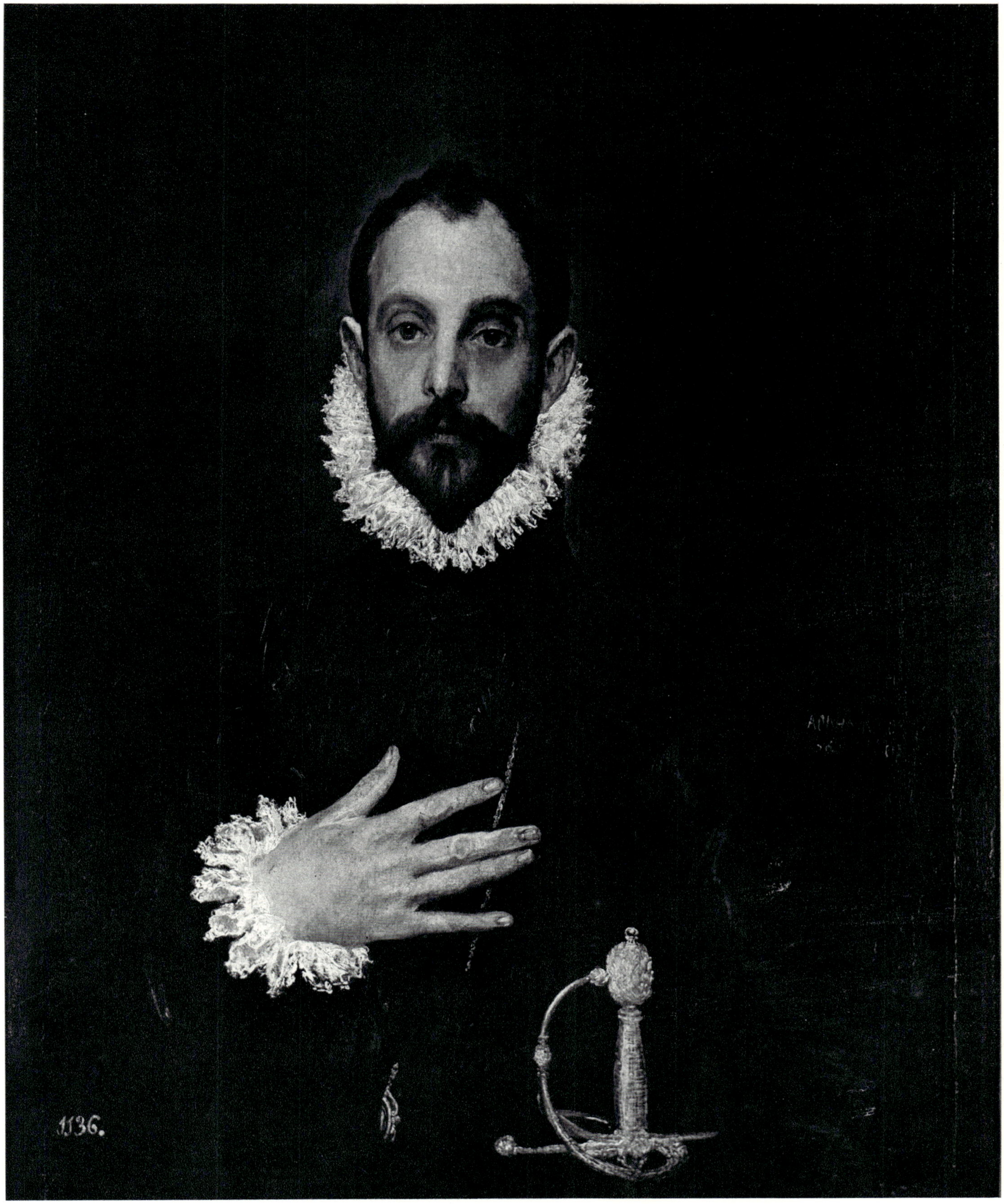

Fig. 45. Knight taking an oath, 1576-1579. Madrid, Prado. Cat. No. 32.

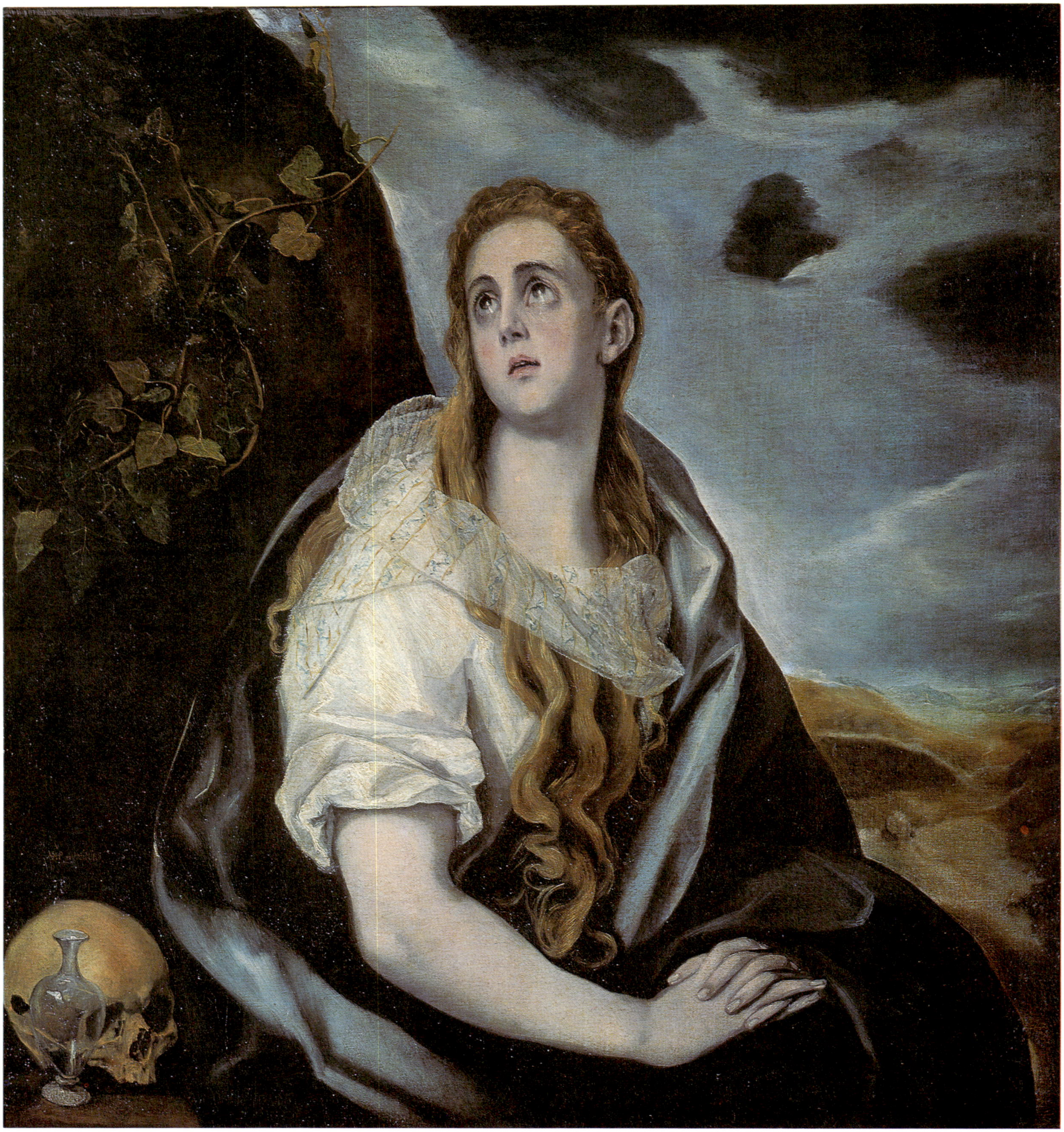

Fig. 46. The Penitent Magdalen, 1576-1579. Worcester, Art Museum. Cat. No. 33.

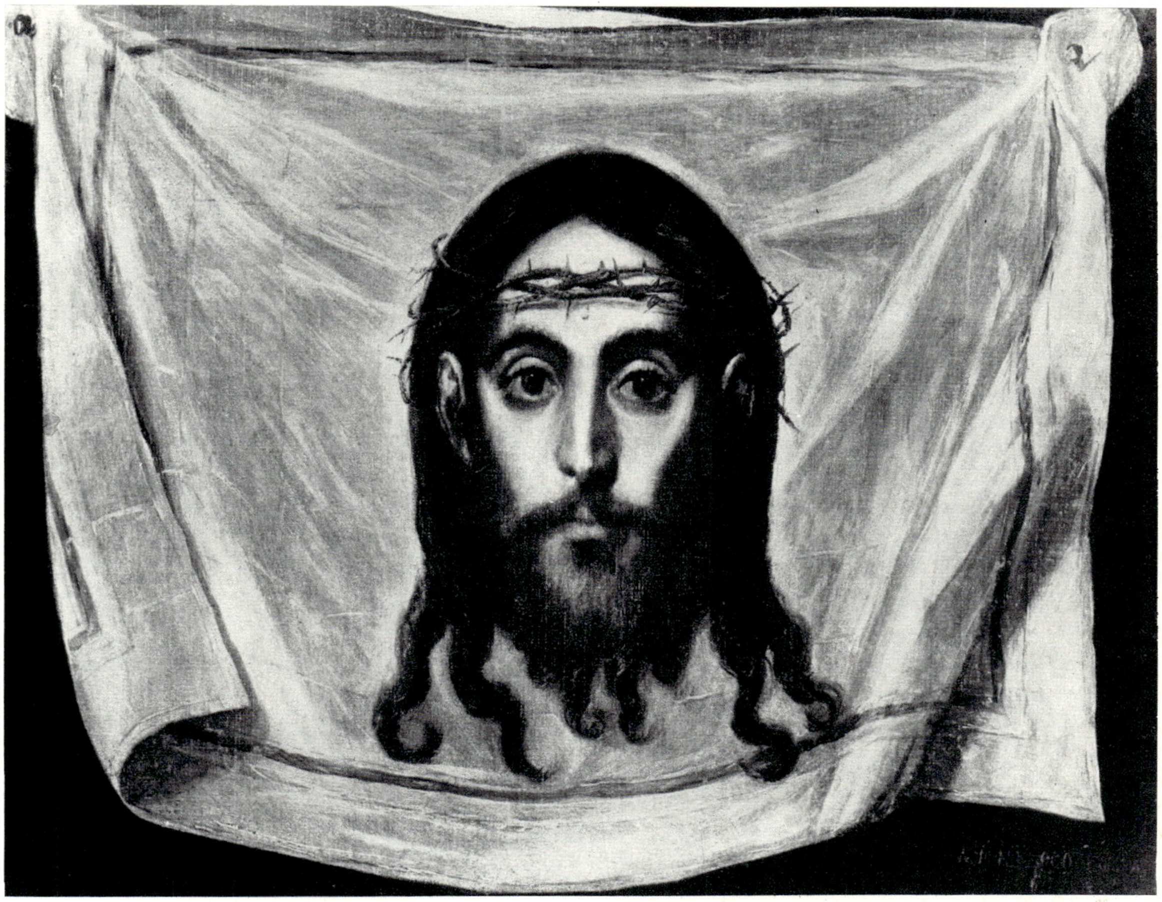

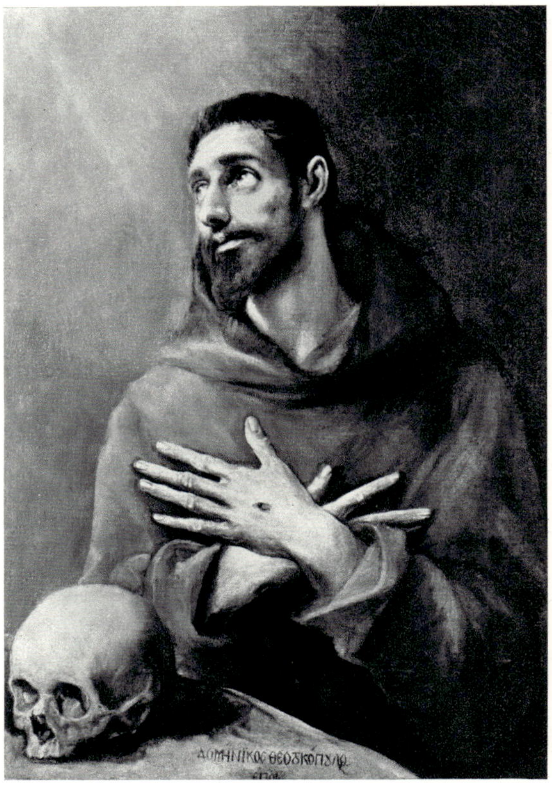

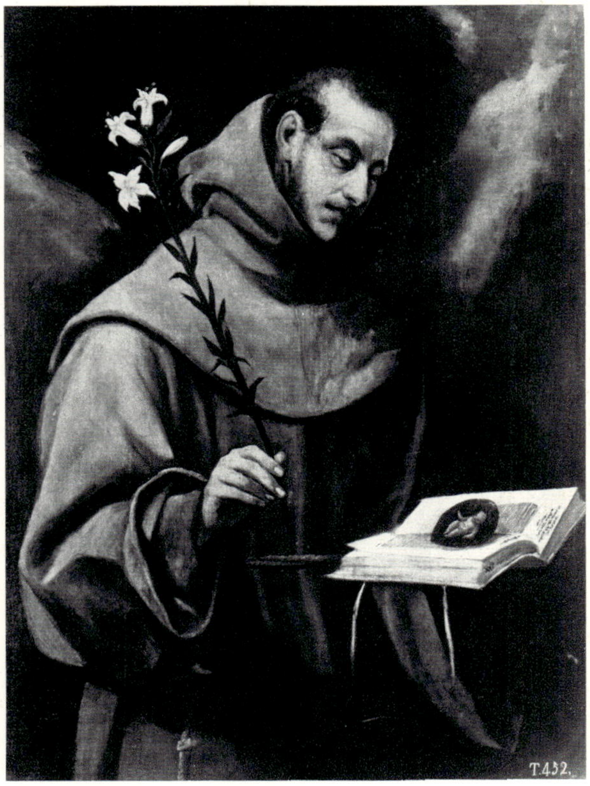

Fig. 47. The Sudary of St. Veronica, 1576-1579. New York, Basil Goulandris Collection. Cat. No. 34.
Fig. 48. St. Francis in ecstasy, 1576-1579. New York, private collection. Cat. No. 35.
Fig. 49. St. Anthony of Padua, 1576-1579. Madrid, Prado. Cat. No. 37.

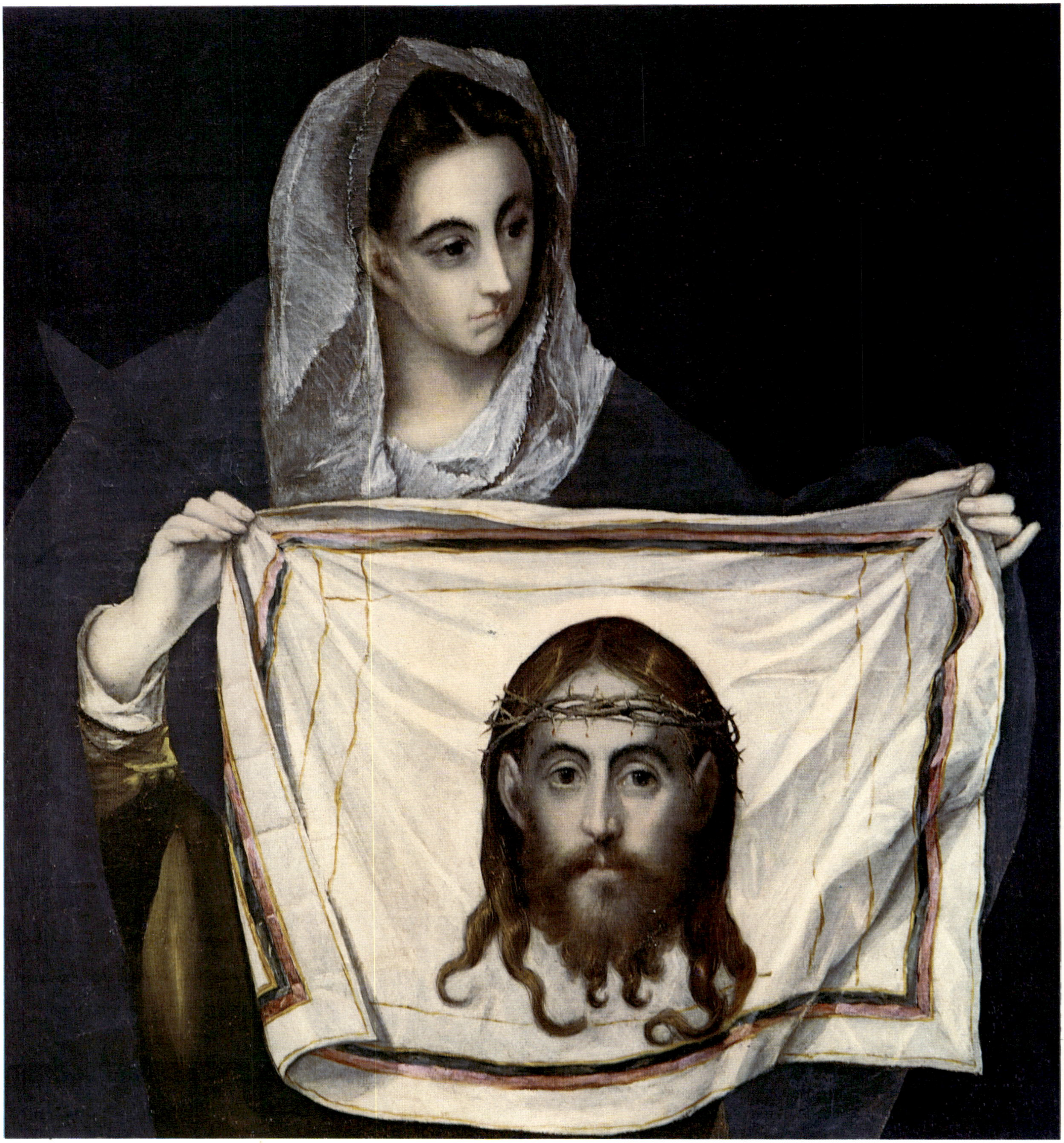

Fig. 50. St. Veronica, 1576-1579. Toledo, Santa Cruz Museum. Cat. No. 38.

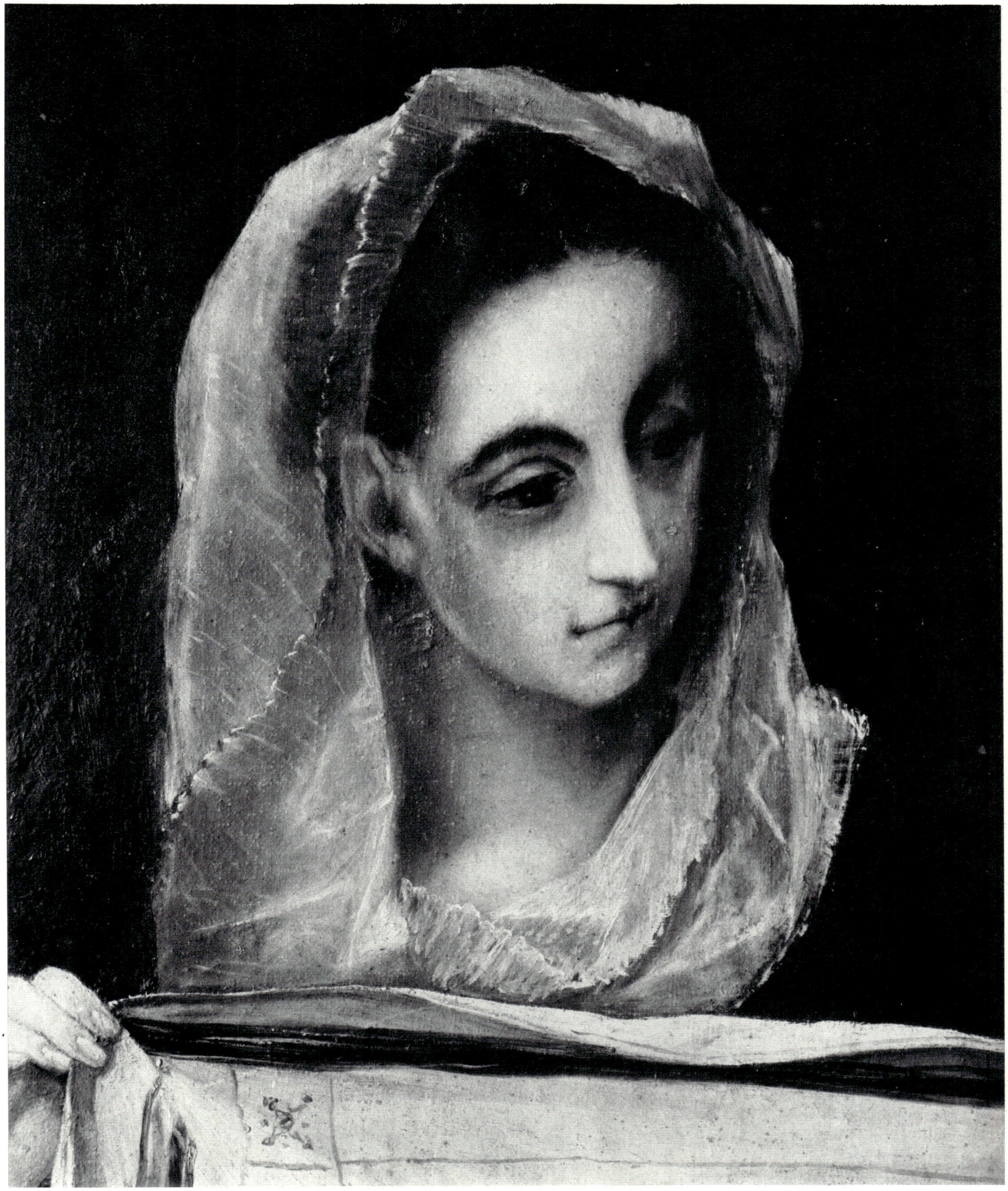

Fig. 51. St. Veronica, 1576-1579. Madrid, Caturla Collection. Cat. No. 39.

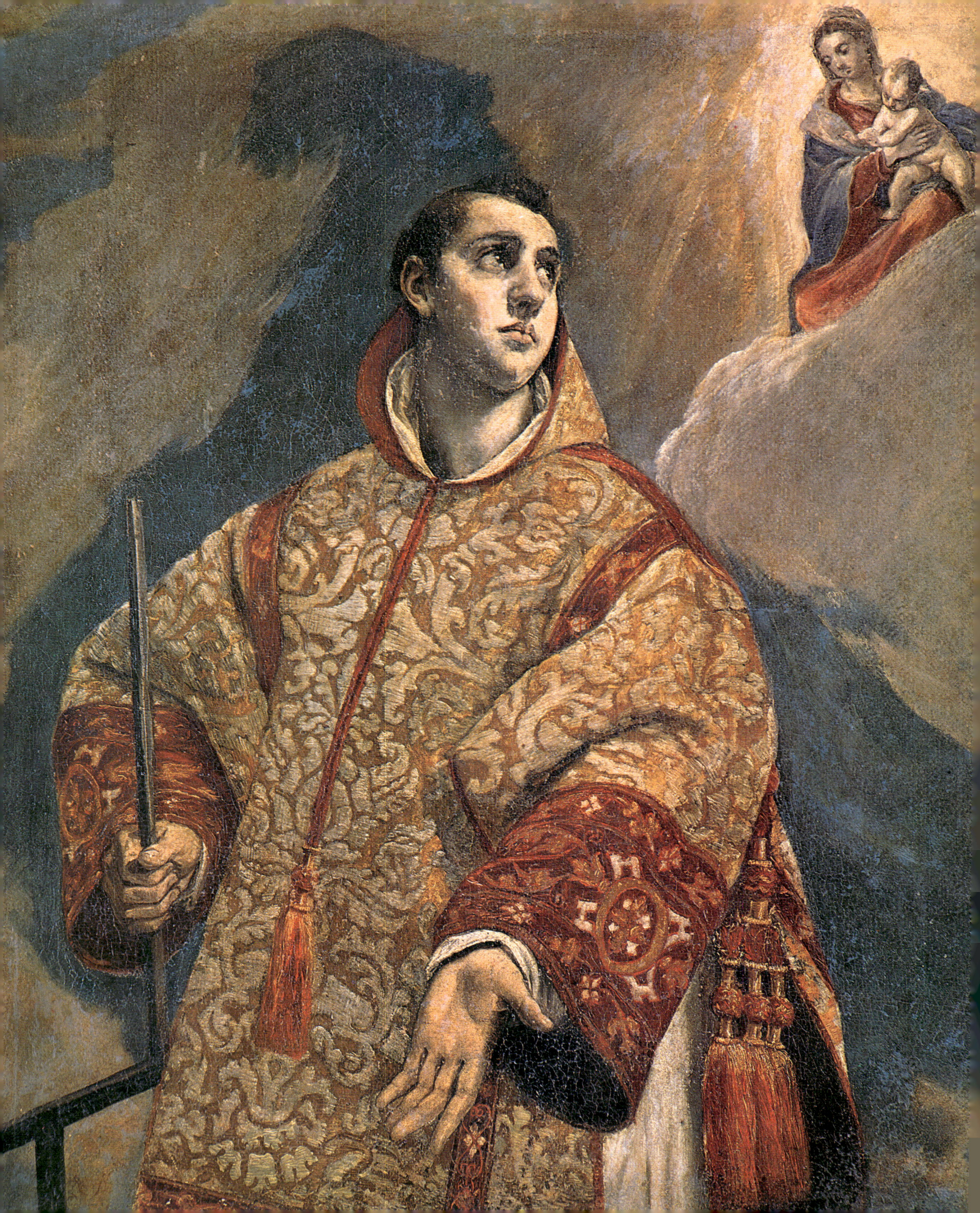

he was living in that city before he settled in Toledo. On July 27th 1578 he received the payment that completed the 1,000 ducats of the estimate. The work was probably at an advanced stage by then, though he declares that the paintings were not finished because the church itself and the carving of the altarpieces were not finished either. In the document he promises: "I shall not move from this city of Toledo until the said painting is finished by my hand". Apparently he had not yet decided to settle in Toledo permanently. Not yet abandoned, then, were his hopes of entering the circles closest to Philip II.

The pictorial ensemble of Santo Domingo el Antiguo originally consisted of nine paintings *(Fig. 53).* The first seven — the Assumption, the Trinity, the Sudary with the Holy Face and Saints Bernard, Benedict, John the Baptist and John the Evangelist— occupied the spaces assigned to them in the soberly elegant structure of the central altarpiece, which, as has been conclusively proved, was copied from Venetian models. The two side altars are mere frames for an Adoration of the shepherds and a Resurrection respectively, flanked by fluted columns with Corinthian capitals. But today this impressive ensemble has been stripped of most of its original canvases. The only ones that remain *in situ* are the two Saints John of the high altar and the Resurrection over the right-hand side altar.

El Greco made every effort to paint works that would do him the fullest justice in his new adopted country. And his achievement may be defined —and has, in fact, been so defined by critics of opposing tendencies— either as an astonishing transformation of El Greco's own creation in his previous period or as the attainment, after various experiments, of a synthesis in which all the components traditionally recognized in his art are affirmed: Byzantine idealism, Venetian colour, composition taken partly from Titian and partly from Tintoretto, the heroic style of Michelangelo modifying the latter and a manneristic elongation of the proportions. But even if this were true, El Greco's own strictly personal contribution is no less evident, a contribution that we may sum up in another series of very important principles: a deeply personal typology, with a sense of form that seems to be borrowed from nobody else; an extraordinarily personal chromatic range, a synthesis of a certain primitivism —in the accumulation of figures— and a presentiment of Baroque; the exaltation of the eloquence of gesture, which is a dominant factor in all this painter's work. At this stage in his career, moreover, he achieves the relief of a volume in space, of full corporeality, that reaches as high a level as his supposed masters in Venice.

He must have begun his work with the painting of the *Assumption,* the great canvas in the centre of the high altar, which was finished in a few months *(Fig. 54 - Cat. 41);* beside the signature, in Greek italics, he put the year: 1577. In this work we see a certain preoccupation with the composition in itself and with the relationship of the form to the structure of the volumes in space. To solve this problem he resolved to use a pyramidal composition and with this in mind gave a decided emphasis to the figure of the Virgin, reducing the importance of the angels on either side, so that the human groups in the lower part acquire greater solidity. The geometry is not confined to the scheme of the composition, for it also helped him to determine the internal form and the modelling, as may be seen particularly in the figure on the left, seen from behind with a yellow robe and a red cloak covering his body from the waist down.

We find here, moreover, an important development in the division of the painted surface —in the vertical sense— into two areas: the upper area for the celestial figures and the lower one for the humans. The viewing point, and consequently the line of the horizon, is situated between these two parts, almost in the centre of the composition. The figures are larger than life size. Perhaps as a result of this preoccupation with a more accurate and vivid typological representation, there seems to be a certain lack of connection between the groups in the lower area. Each of the apostles, who, with one exception, are not conversing though they are together, is an admirable study from life and a factor that combines with the others in this work aesthetically rather than humanly.

Nevertheless, despite the successful effort to find a satisfactory solution to the problems of space, form and colour, we can still see some of the gestures and attitudes that we have already noticed in the Italian works. Throughout his career El Greco gradually built up —with sketches and notes that he was to preserve— an ever greater repertoire of gestures, the expression of which he undoubtedly knew —or felt— very accurately, for eloquence was always one of his most constant concerns and certainly few have ever been so gifted as he in its attainment. Here we see attitudes, like that of

52. St. Lawrence's vision of the Virgin, 1576-1579.
forte de Lemos, Piarist Fathers. Cat. No. 40.

the old man with his hand on his breast in a gesture of contrition, which are the forerunners of those to be found in so many of the images of saints that he was to paint in the future. Others, like the outstretched arm of the apostle on the left, are openly declamatory, though never excessive, exaggerated or pompous.

In this composition we also see a factor that was to be comparatively frequent in El Greco: a marked tendency to *horror vacui,* to the introduction of as many figures as possible, with a minimum of environmental elements (in this case merely the sepulchre, open and empty). This tendency is accentuated still further by the parallelism, similar to that in many Gothic woodcuts, of the terminal lines of the forms, by means of which, if these lines were brought nearer, and the empty intermediate spaces suppressed, they would almost produce a compact mass. The impeccable drawing and vigorous, realistic modelling are reinforced by very free brush-work, guided by a total knowledge of the form and of the visual effects of one layer of colour over another. The material is fluid but very dense, the textures and lights being described in masterly fashion. The technique is that necessary for a rapid and powerful painting, in order to achieve a perfect balance of tone and depth, and of brilliance in the expression of every nuance. When we consider the details, especially the heads of the figures in the lower part, we see a variety of types within the overall unity of feeling and an absolute capacity for representation. The ensembles are constructed with more attention to art than to subject-matter, if such a distinction can be made. In other words, the naturalism of each element is made to serve the aesthetic idealism of each ensemble. It is difficult to know which to admire more, the sturdy and expressive volumes of some of the heads or the harmonies of the draperies. The method of treating the clothing of the Virgin was another precedent that the painter was to maintain, though distorting it, till the end of his career.

As for the angels in the upper area, they also boast a rich range of attitudes, foreshortenings and inflections. They are figures studied from life, just like the human characters, and in this upper area of the *Assumption,* too, the figurative beauty of faces and flesh tints is balanced against the geometrizing tendency of ample, swirling cloth, the folds, wrinkles and smooth surfaces of which give the painter an opportunity for rich harmonies of colour.

The crowning composition of the central altarpiece of Santo Domingo el Antiguo is the magnificent canvas of the *Trinity,* which is now in the Prado *(Fig. 57 - Cat. 42).* The majestic figure of the Eternal Father supports the body of Jesus under the dove that symbolizes the Holy Ghost. The angels at the sides help to bring the whole forward like an enormous composition in high relief. Here once again is seen in operation the principle of giving the greatest importance to the figures, resolving the tones of flesh and draperies into powerful elements of the design, in which the figures are supported only by clouds, and are either resplendent with light or are subsidiary or even merely ornamental or lyrical adjuncts, like the group of little winged angels' heads at Christ's feet. It can be seen that the picture was executed quickly, with the same technique as the *Assumption,* though perhaps a little more closely blended.

In this painting the full development of the form prevails over the vigour of the colour and the tone, and one can see how much of Michelangelo's monumental conception had been assimilated by a painter who started by peopling the architectural backgrounds of Tintoretto, after his obscure beginnings in an age-old craft. As in almost all his works of this period, and even in earlier ones, there are plenty of details foretelling what in time was to be one of his aesthetic passions — expressive distortion, not simply from a taste for torturing form but to show the inner fire of the spirit surmounting the restrictions of the given form. There is deliberate exaggeration in the foreshortening of the angel nearest the Eternal Father on the right, and also in the head of the one in the middle of the three on the opposite side. This fact is symptomatic: in all painters whose work is later to evolve towards distortion, this distortion usually appears at an early stage in secondary, marginal figures, while the principal ones are still treated in a perfectly naturalistic way, as is the case in the present painting with God the Father and God the Son.

The geometric centre of the central altarpiece in Santo Domingo el Antiguo was occupied by a *Sudary with the Holy Face (Fig. 62 - Cat. 46),* painted on an elegant medallion supported by two angels carved by Monegro, after designs by El Greco. An extraordinary strength and sweetness emanate from this face, which the artist depicts as if it were the key to his whole iconography. That is why this *Holy Face* is like a synthesis of the most utterly opposed artistic methods:

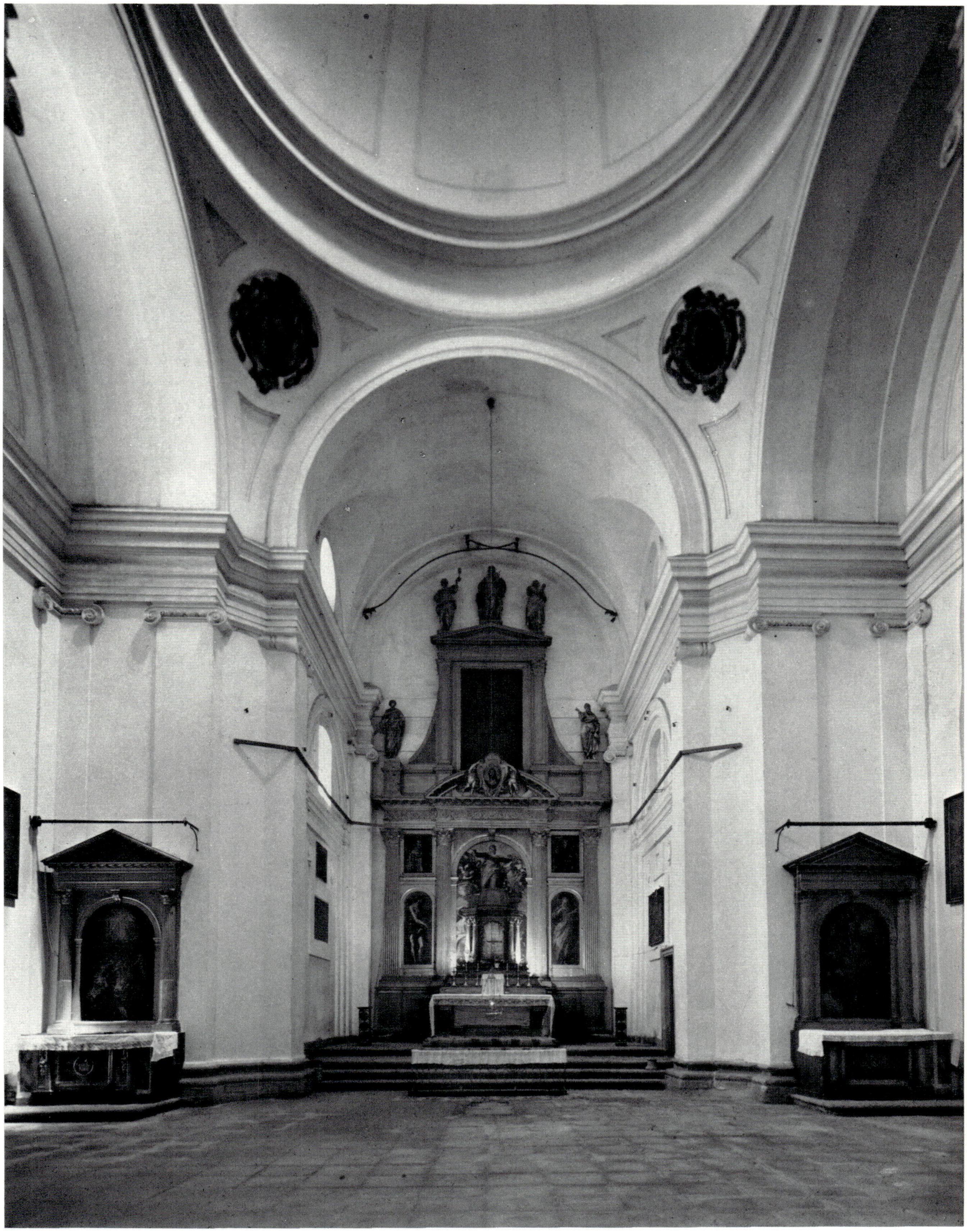

Fig. 53. Toledo, the Church of Santo Domingo el Antiguo.

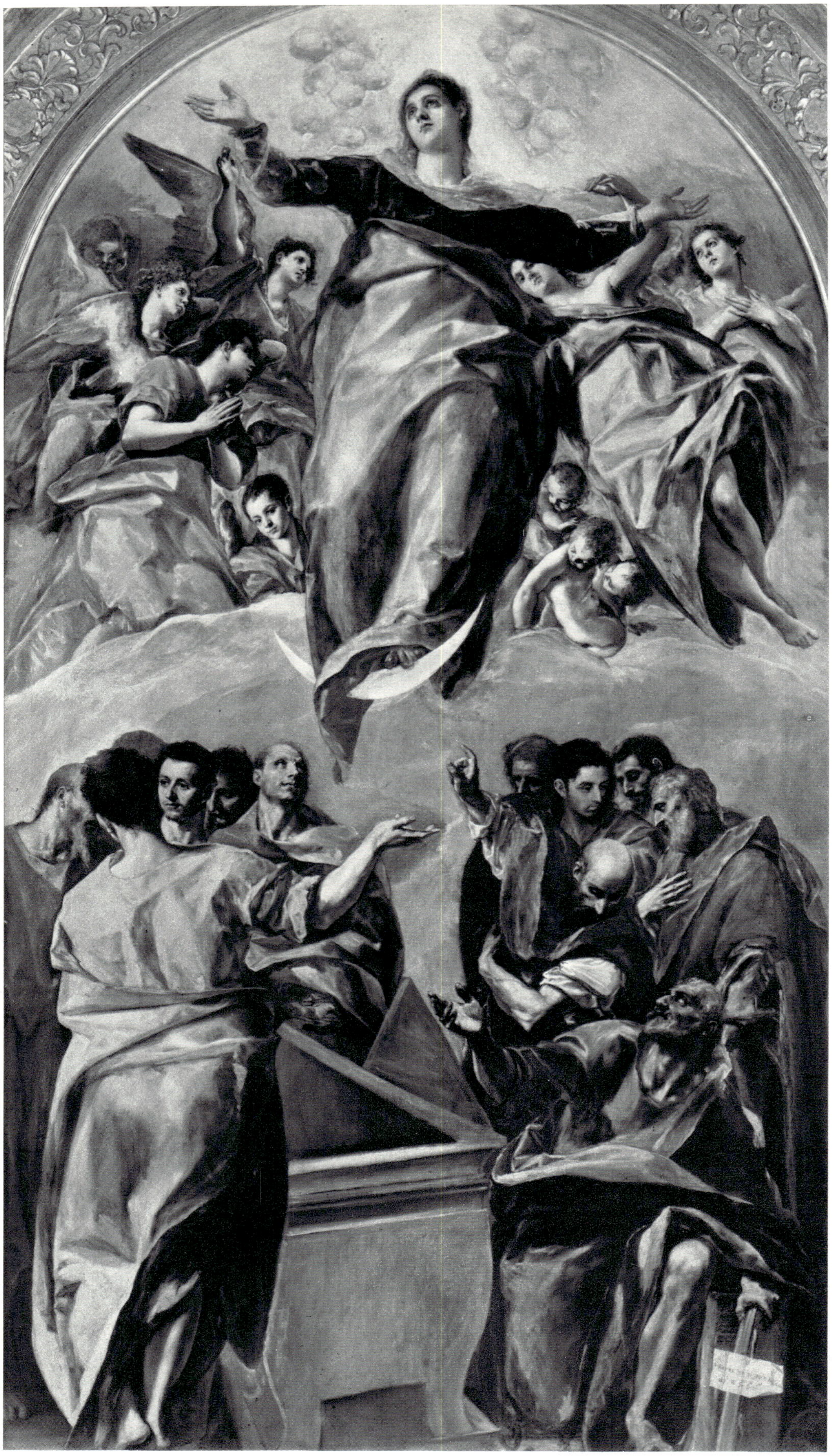

Figs. 54 & 55. The Assumption, 1577. Chicago, Art Institute. Cat. No. 41.

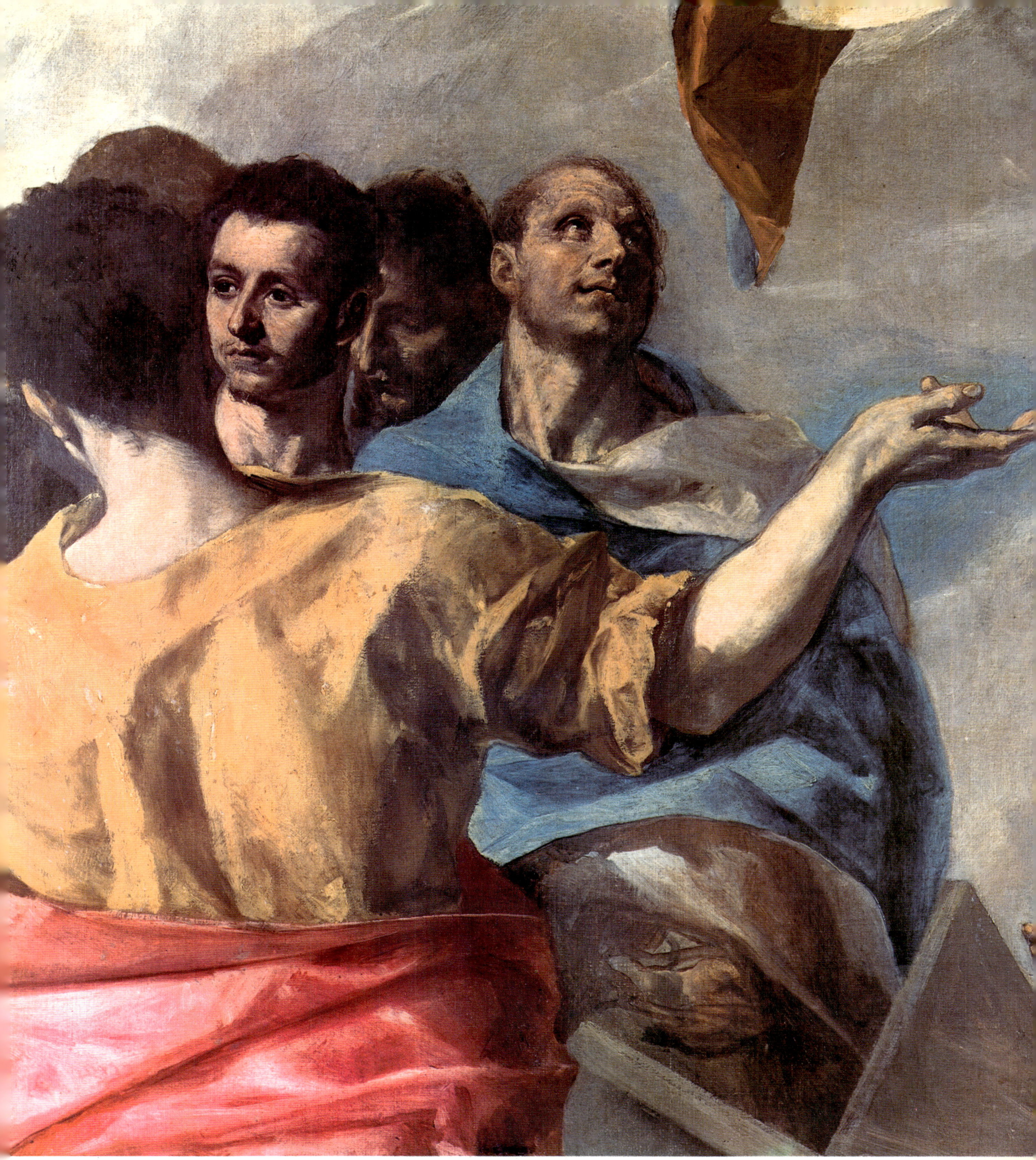

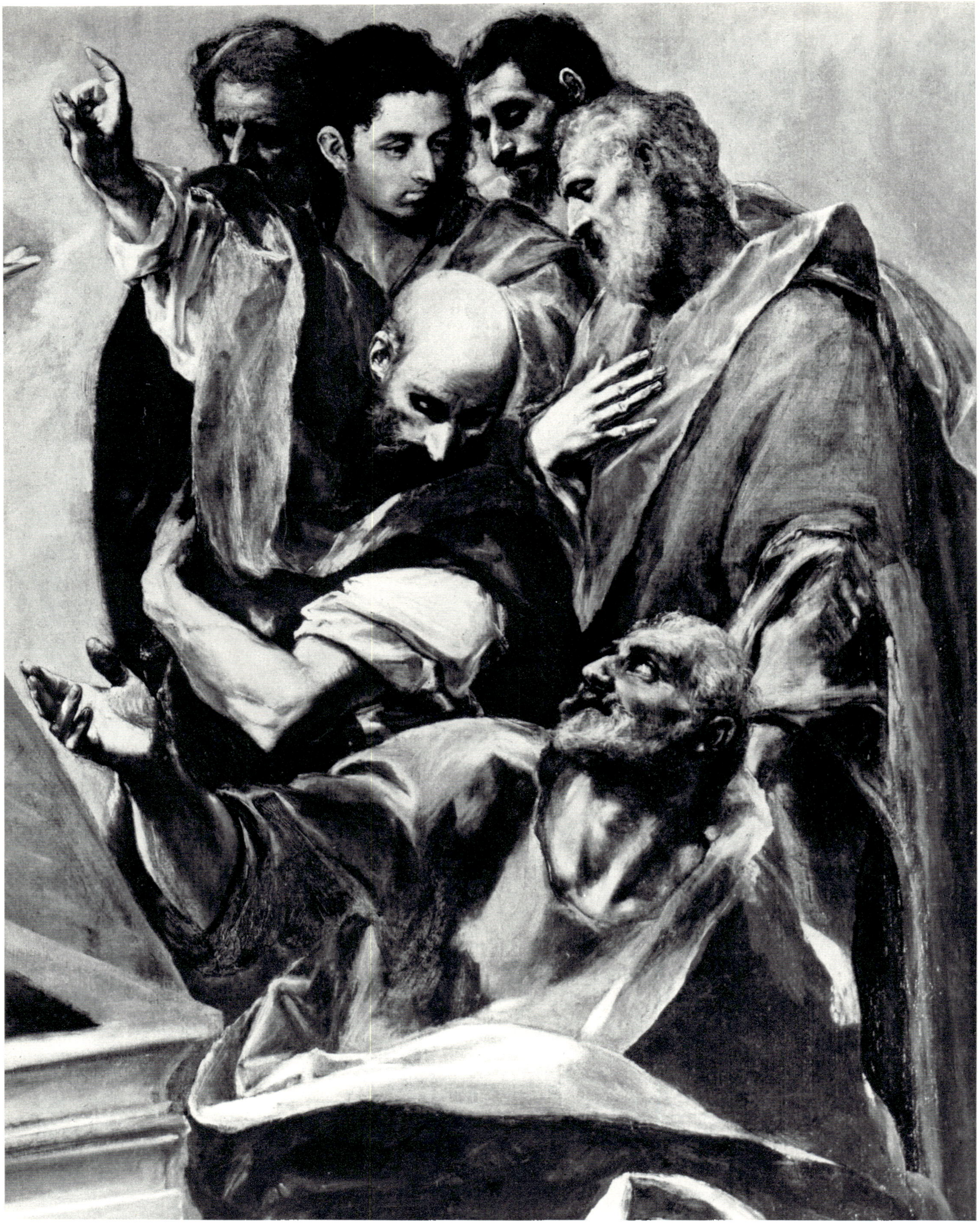

Fig. 56. Detail of figure 54.

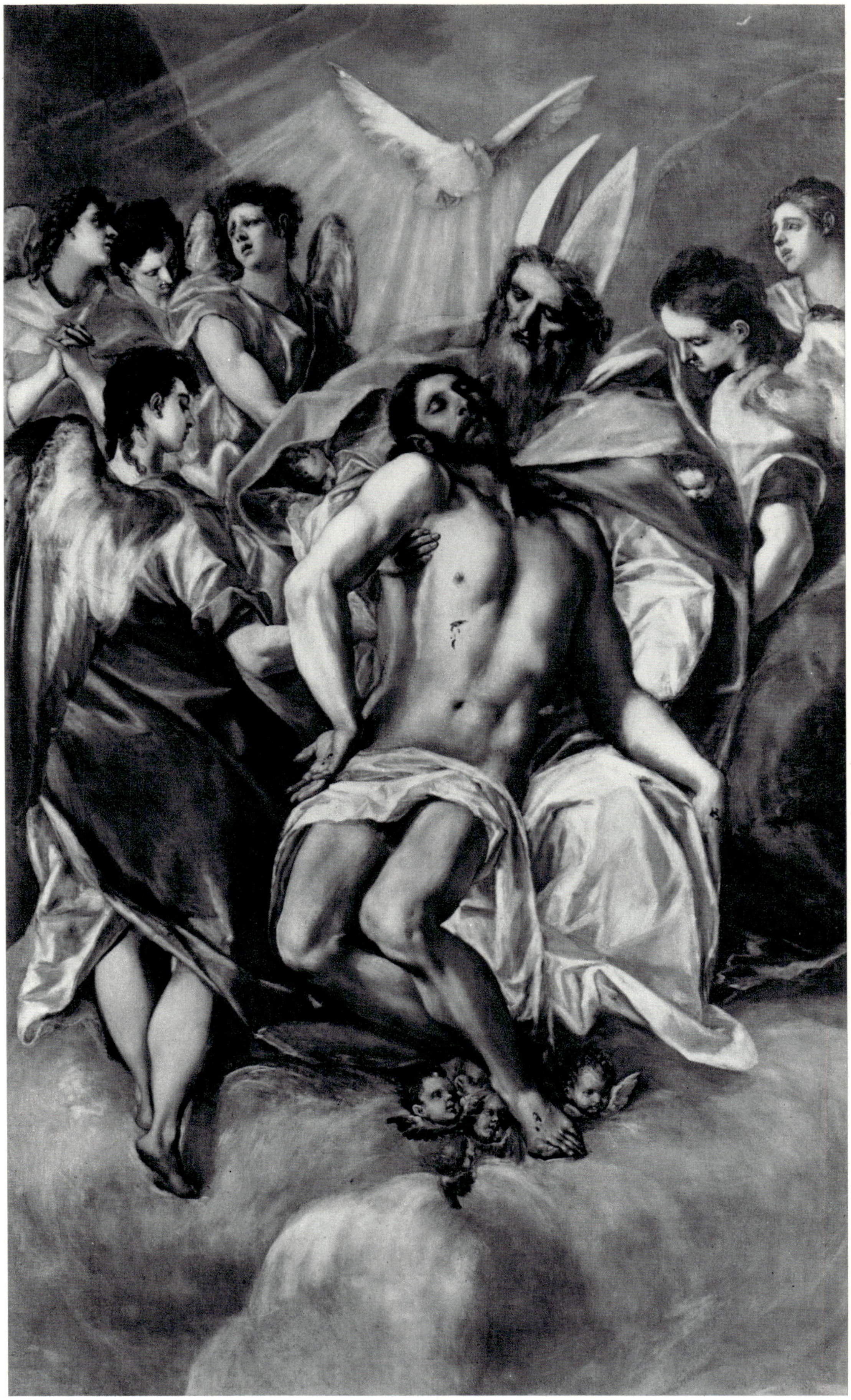

Fig. 57. The Trinity, 1577-1579. Madrid, Prado. Cat. No. 42.

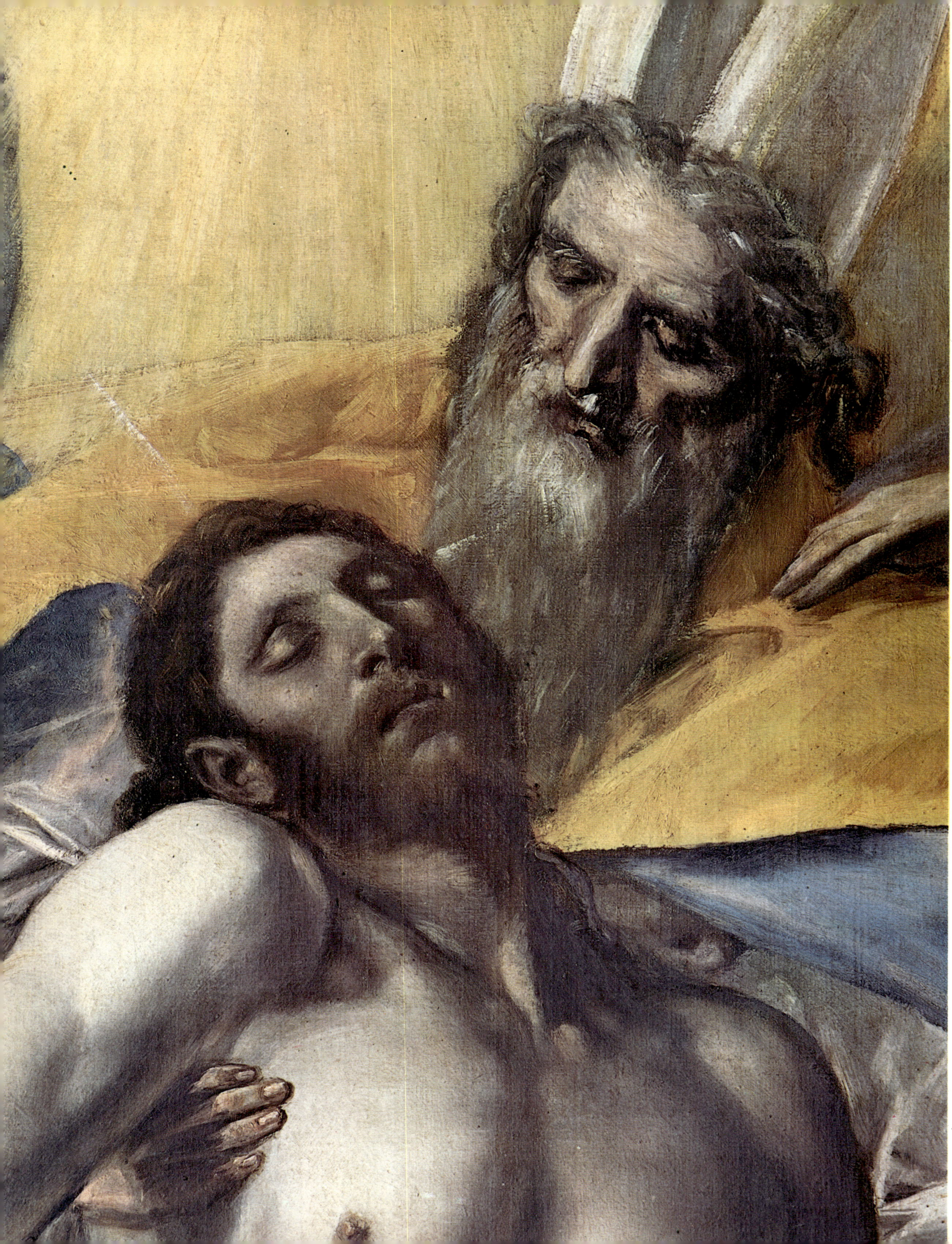

Fig. 5
Detai
figure

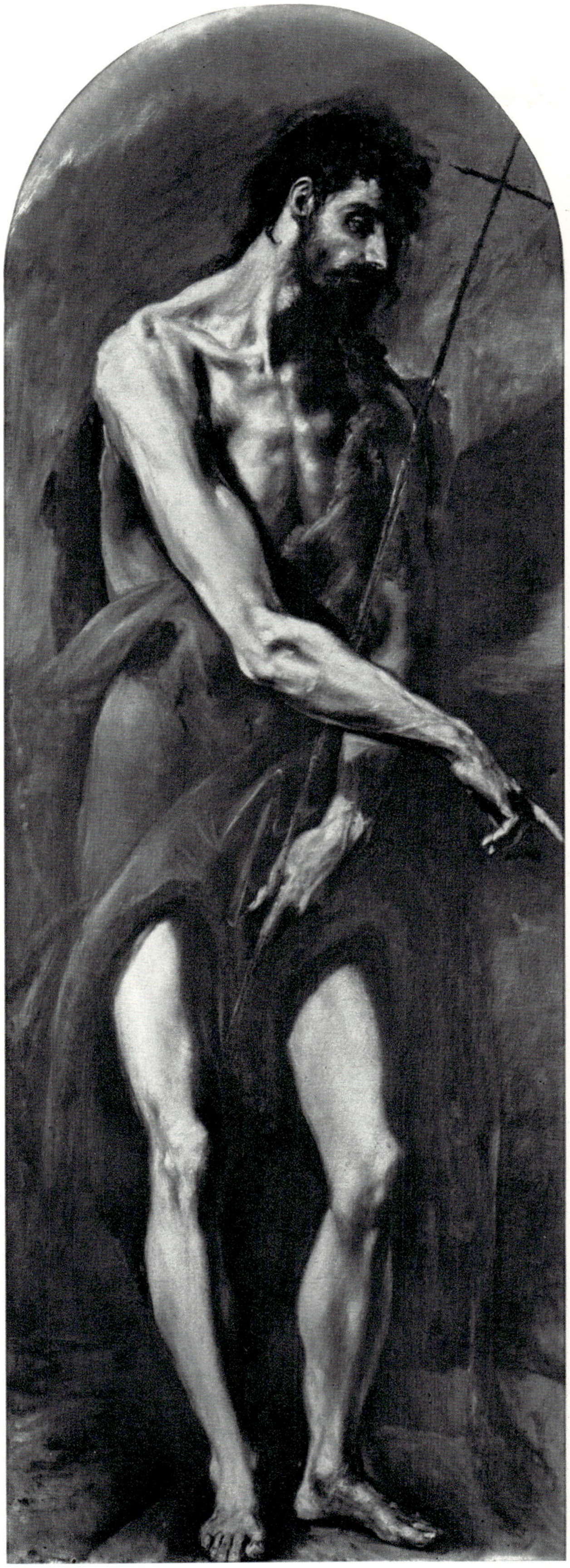

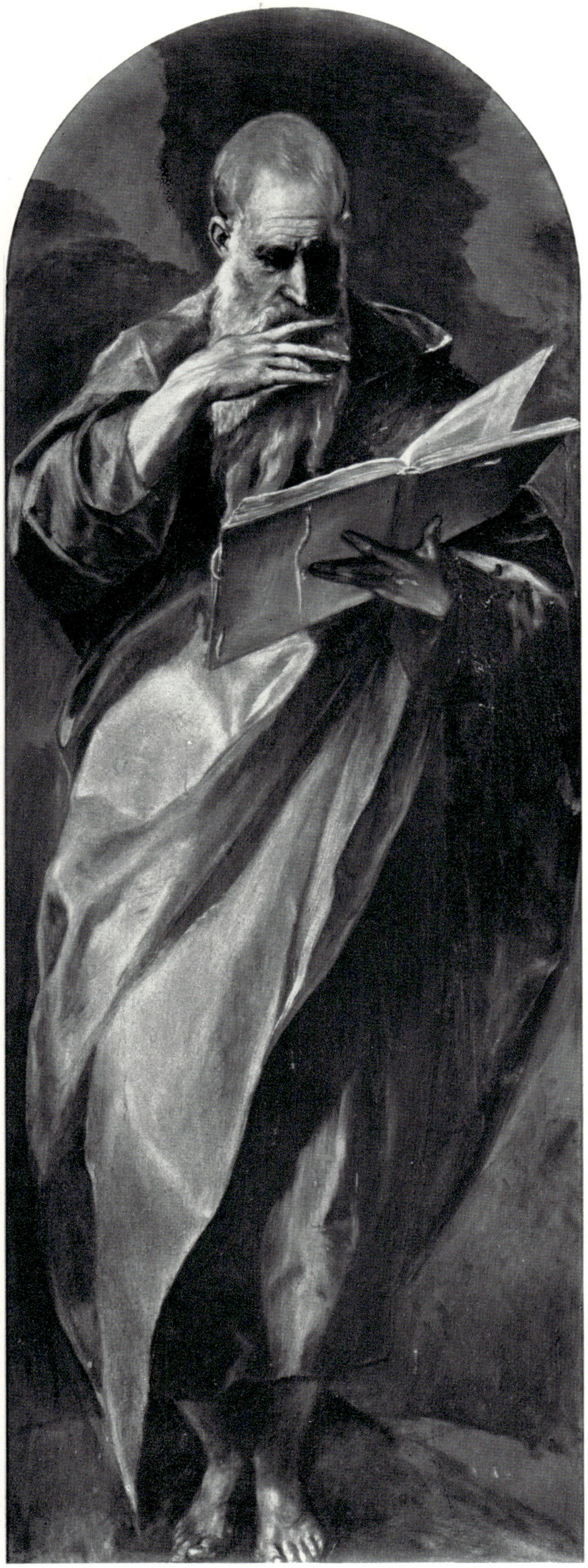

Fig. 59. St. John the Baptist, 1577-1579. Toledo, Santo Domingo el Antiguo. Cat. No. 43.
Fig. 60. St. John the Evangelist, 1577-1579. Toledo, Santo Domingo el Antiguo. Cat. No. 44.

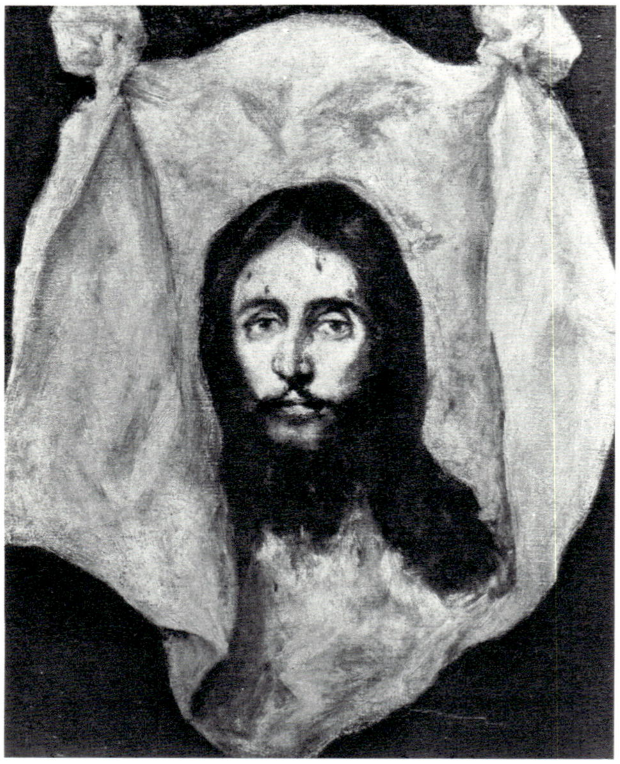

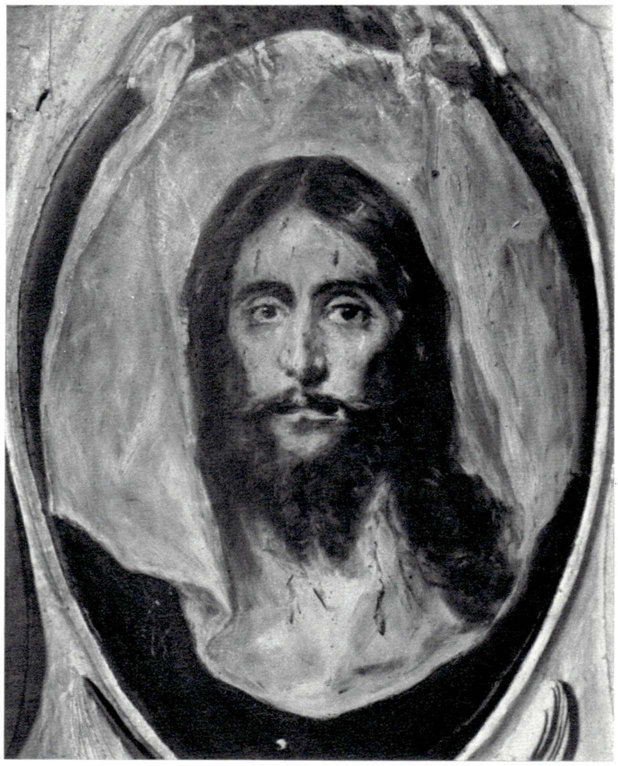

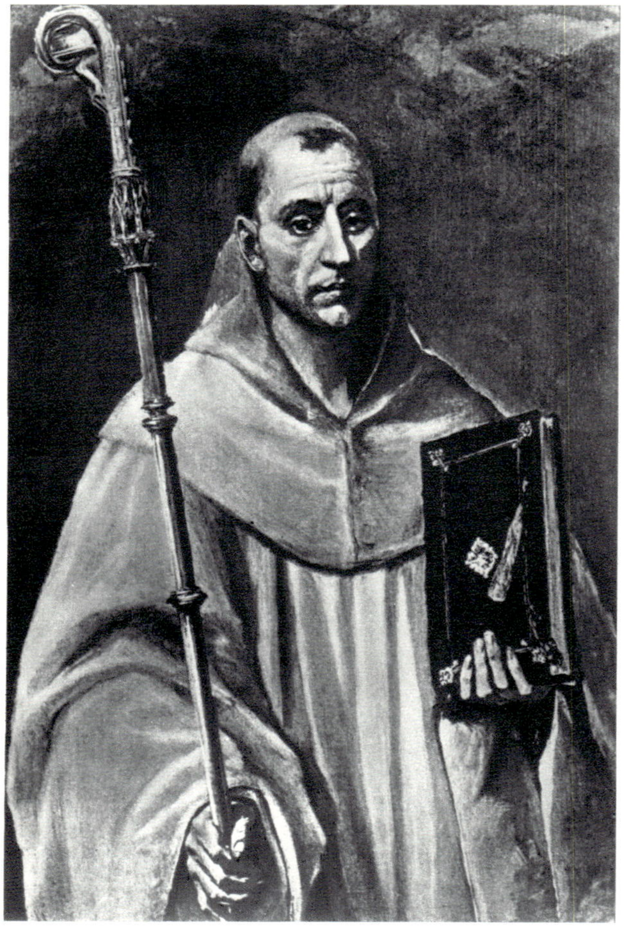

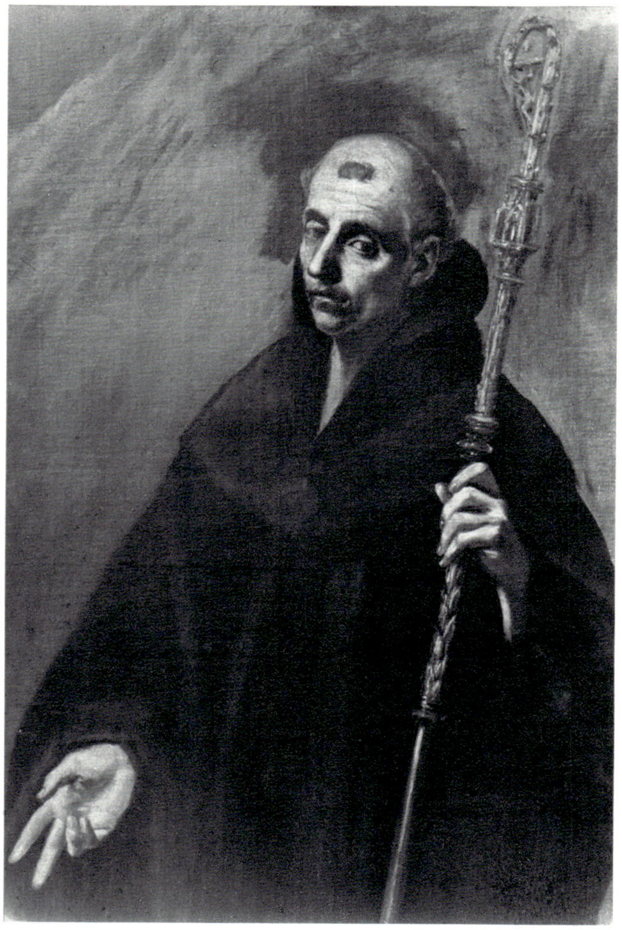

Fig. 61. Sudary with the Holy Face, 1577-1579. Madrid, Prado. Cat. No. 45.
Fig. 62. Sudary with the Holy Face, 1577-1579. Madrid, March Collection. Cat. No. 46
Fig. 63. St. Bernard, 1577-1579. Present whereabouts unknown. Cat. No. 47.
Fig. 64. St. Benedict, 1577-1579. Madrid, Prado. Cat. No. 48.

the archaism of the icon, justified by a longing to depict the supernatural in itself and to respect and maintain the features inherited from an iconography that came from the depths of history, and the sumptuous naturalism —which might be called, paradoxically enough, "sensuously spiritual"— of the beginnings of Baroque. The wonderful, impeccable drawing is entirely hidden by the painting. By this we mean that there are no linear factors, the form being modelled without any need to reveal its analytical stage. At first sight it seems to be a replica of the *Holy Face* in the sudary of St. Veronica studied above *(Fig. 47),* but in fact the differences are profound. This work is at once a display of technique and a document that attests the depth and authenticity of the painter's religious feelings. Undoubtedly, an image like this poses fewer problems than a vast composition. But this very simplicity is the cause of the great difficulty in carrying it out perfectly, for everything is concentrated in a face that does not appear either overwhelmed by human ingratitude or hurt by moral or physical sufferings. With an almost neutral expression this face looks out at the viewer, but in its look there is a question and, as it were, a mute reproach. All the features are rather large, but very beautiful and harmonious. The long hair is divided in two, as is the beard. Fine, light touches, brief and rapid brush-strokes superimposed on the dark surface, give a perfect sensation of relief. The flesh tints are given a soft modelling which is not without its contrasts and deep shadows. It is possible that a small canvas with a representation of the *Sudary with the Holy Face,* originally in the parish church of Móstoles and now in the Prado *(Fig. 61 - Cat. 45),* was the preparatory study for the image we have just been considering.

The *Assumption* in the middle of this central altarpiece was flanked by the figures of four saints: St. Bernard, St. Benedict, St. John the Evangelist and St. John the Baptist. The first two, which are like portraits, are more direct, while the representation of the two Sts. John comes nearer to the idealized manner of presenting themes taken from religious iconography. The *St. Bernard,* with his crozier in one hand and his missal in the other, is a solid, strong, realistic image *(Fig. 63 - Cat. 47).* The head harmonizes with the austere clothing and the dark background, which is not entirely a flat wash. The painter's delicacy is noticeable above all in the admirable hands. The *St. Benedict (Fig. 64 - Cat. 48),* which is similar in concept, also concentrates interest on the supremely beautiful hands. The treatment of the figure creates contrasts which have a powerful influence on the image. Both figures are modelled in heavy impasto, many brush-strokes being left unblended.

The *St. John the Baptist* is more like a relief in its conception of form *(Fig. 59 - Cat. 43).* The anatomy is revealed with great intensity and the lines of the body forcefully depicted. The light gives particular emphasis to the right shoulder and arm and to the legs; the torso and the neck are modelled with intense shadows and the head almost sinks into the penumbra. The comparatively draughtsmanlike technique used for the Evangelist is maintained and accentuated in, for instance, the lines of the veins in the thin but vigorous arms of the Forerunner. In the whole position of the body there is a supreme elegance, and it is clear that it is in discoveries like this that we witness the victory of style over naturalism, though without any destruction of the latter. The idea of form simultaneously prevails over and subserves representation — a synthesis of which Goya was to be one of the last great exponents. The effect of relief is obtained, not only by means of the position (as near as possible to frontal) of the figure's body, limbs and head, or by the way in which the figure is incorporated into its rectangular space, leaving few voids through which the background may be seen, but also by the interplay of tones, which models the figure sculpturally without giving it total volume.

St. John the Evangelist is shown full-face and at a rather advanced age *(Fig. 60 - Cat. 44).* His right hand is raised to the level of his mouth, expressing mental and spiritual concentration. In the background there are dark, cloudy contrasts which particularly dramatize the upper area of this picture with its elongated format. The cloak that covers most of the body expresses the pure plastic values of form, light, colour and movement and, at the same time, a feeling of grandeur which interprets, as it were, the expressions of face and attitude. In this ideal portrait of the Evangelist the drawing is more readily perceptible than in other works by El Greco; the right hand and the visible part of the forearm show it just as much as the admirable feet and the head, in which, thanks to its forward-bending position, there are deep shadows under the eyebrow on the right side of the face.

The *Adoration of the shepherds* from the side altar *(Fig. 65 - Cat. 49)* differs from the other compositions of Santo Domingo el Antiguo both in the lyrical, intimist character due to its theme and in the world of references El Greco sought in this work, a very different world from that on which the other paintings are based. Here the composition, form and figures are not the only important factors. Light and movement, empty space and a certain restrained taste for anecdote, all make their appearance as well. All of this, quite as much as the rustic character evoked by the shepherds, brings us back to the world of the Bassanos, who, as we know, also influenced El Greco during the years spent in Venice, even though —as in the case of Titian or Tintoretto— it is simply an external reference, a *point d'appui* used by critics, rather than a profound reality.

If we compare this composition with the *Assumption* of the central altarpiece, we shall see that, apart from the difference in formal approach, the structure of the upper area takes on a certain fantasy in its treatment of forms in that the light seems to be concentrated in the form of a great star, through whose radiance angels appear. The lower area is treated with the utmost diversification of action and rhythms. The figure we see in the foreground is St. Luke the Evangelist, whose candle sheds light on his text. In the central group the light also forms a sort of stellar irradiation in which El Greco uses, with copious variations of shadings, the experiments in lighting that derive from the *Boy lighting a candle* and the group of man, woman and monkey in his Italian period *(Figs. 29 to 31 - Cat. 22, 23 & 24).*

The face of the Virgin is solidly, almost sculpturally modelled, while that of St. Luke is based on superimpositions of light (varying from dense to evanescent) on dark, with great freedom. The shepherds are evidently intended to receive realistic treatment. A greater degree of idealization may be observed in the two figures in the right background which contrast with the further background behind them, the night sky under the moon. In them we see that dazzling treatment of the voluminous cloaks that gives the colour and form a great wealth of aesthetic qualities. Other details reveal the use of heavy impasto that leaves clots at certain points, or, on the contrary, the employment of delicate glazes. Because of the complex technique and the impetuosity of the execution, the broken brush-strokes are easily perceptible and some of the faces have been left no more than sketched in. In the naked limbs, whether arms or legs, the modelling is intense, quite evidently the same as that of the flesh tints in the *Trinity*. Needless to say, the gestures play a decisive role here, serving both to express the feeling and to mark rhythmical axes of composition, subordinate to the ones that decide the arrangement and attitude of each figure. If we look carefully at the detailing of the faces, we shall see that El Greco, like many other great artists of the past, from the beginning of the sixteenth century down to the nineteenth, uses different technical methods on one and the same picture, depending on the effect he wishes to produce or the materials represented.

The *Resurrection (Fig. 67 - Cat. 50)* was planned, and indeed executed, as a pyramidal composition, but this structure is used with a characteristic exaggeration of the vertical, i.e., of the height of the front plane of the pyramid. Nor is the effect of a third dimension disregarded, as can be seen in the intense foreshortening of the group of soldiers on the right, but it is entirely subordinated to the vertical rhythm of the picture, a rhythm that is accentuated rather than diminished by the intersecting axes created by the varied gestures of the principal characters in the action. Christ is presented as if in transfiguration, raised above the terrestrial space. St. Ildefonso appears, in an expressive attitude, as a bystander in the foreground among other main characters. On the right, with his back to us, standing in the darkness against the light that emanates from the brilliance irradiating the risen Christ, one of the guards of the tomb is looking at Jesus, but raising his left arm as if to shield his eyes from the light. The balance of this figure, as a study in the capturing of an instant of movement, is wonderful. On the left a soldier is coming towards the viewer; by leaving him in a more brightly-lit area El Greco shows us to what an extent he graduated these effects of the light as values to be taken into account in the distribution and shading of the elements of the work. Behind, rather more fully blended, we see two soldiers sleeping. The luminous cloudiness of an almost imperceptible aureole surrounds the triumphant body of Jesus, which is symmetrically flanked by two admirable pieces of drapery, the cloak on the left, which leaves his naked figure almost totally revealed, and the banner on the right, which is the sign of his victory over death. An imaginary source of light enables the painter to treat the modelling with the utmost perfection of form and texture. The gesture of the upraised arm and the look cast downwards do not make the image theatrical, for

Fig. 65. The Adoration of the shepherds, 1577-1
Santander, E. Botín Collection. Cat. No. 49.

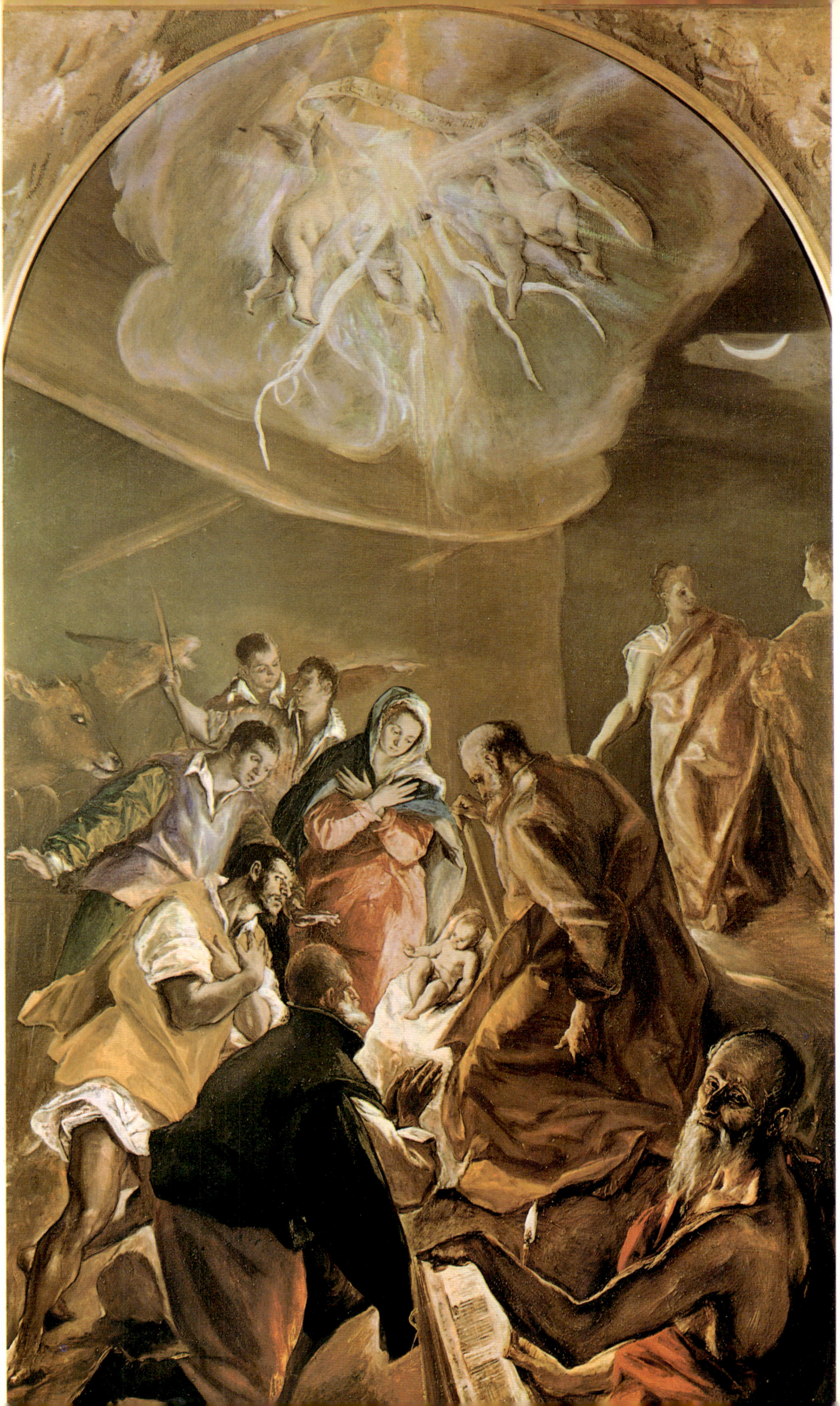

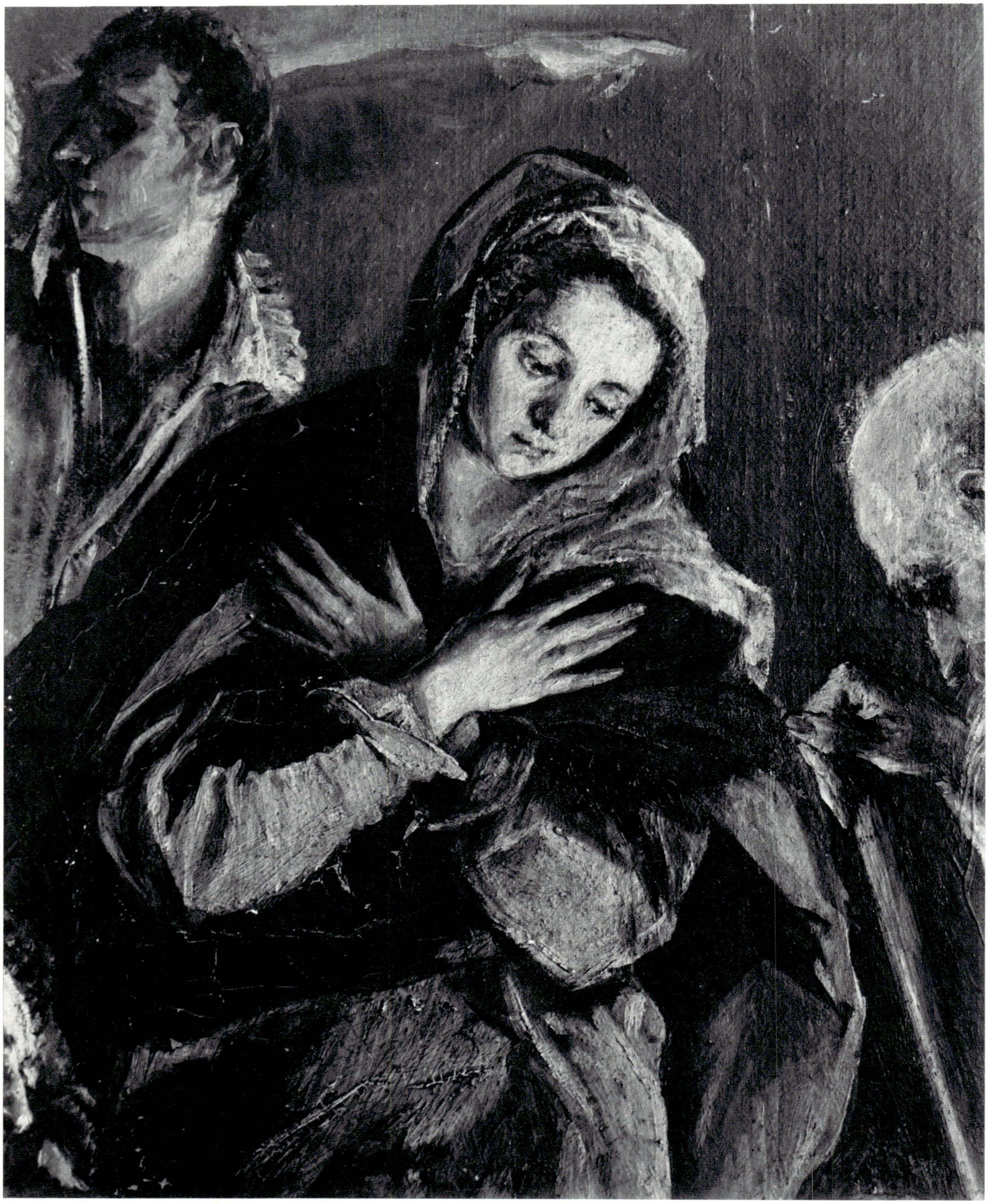

Fig. 66. Detail of figure 65.

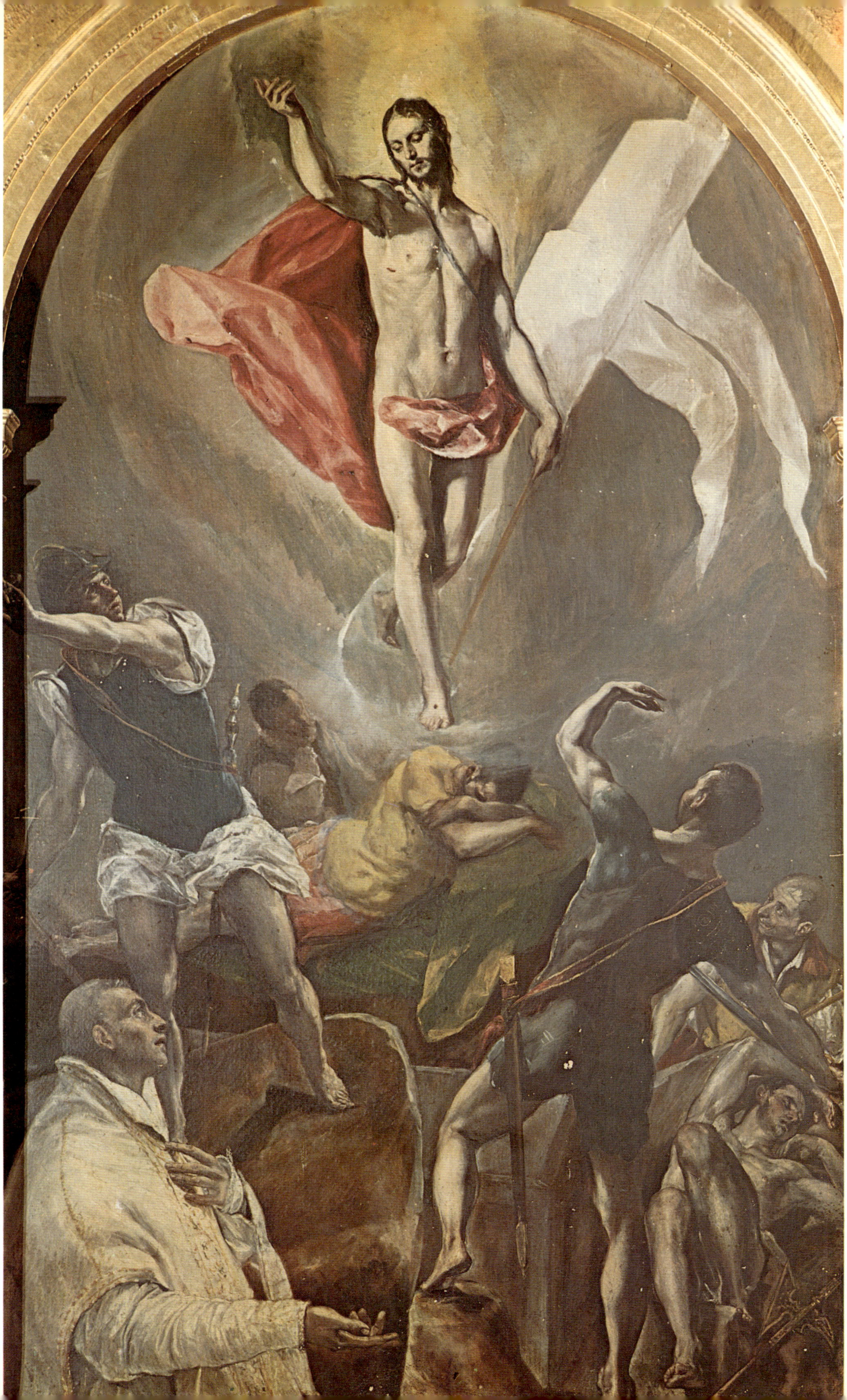

67. The Resurrection, 579. Toledo, Santo Do- el Antiguo. Cat. No. 50.

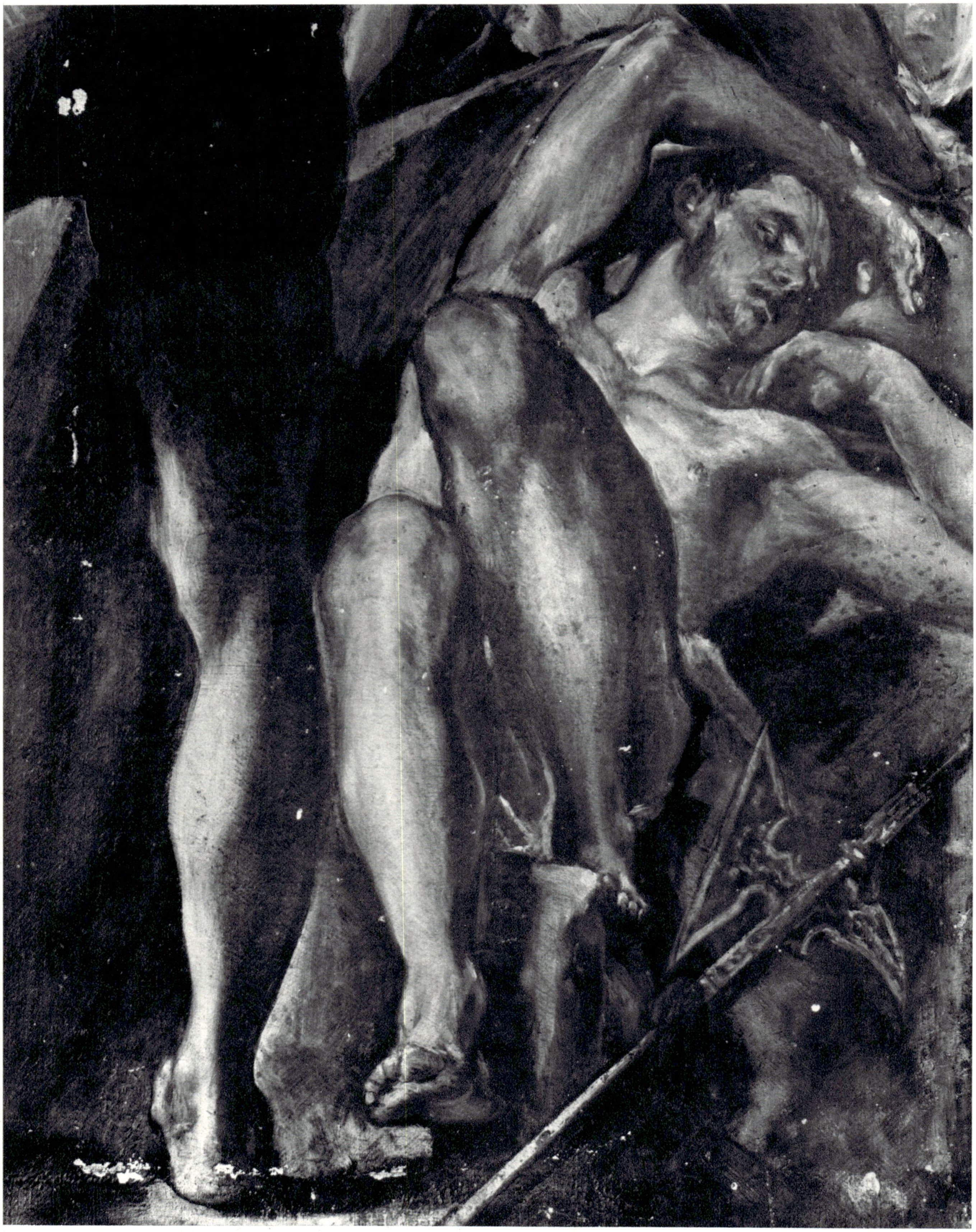

Fig. 68. Detail of figure 67.

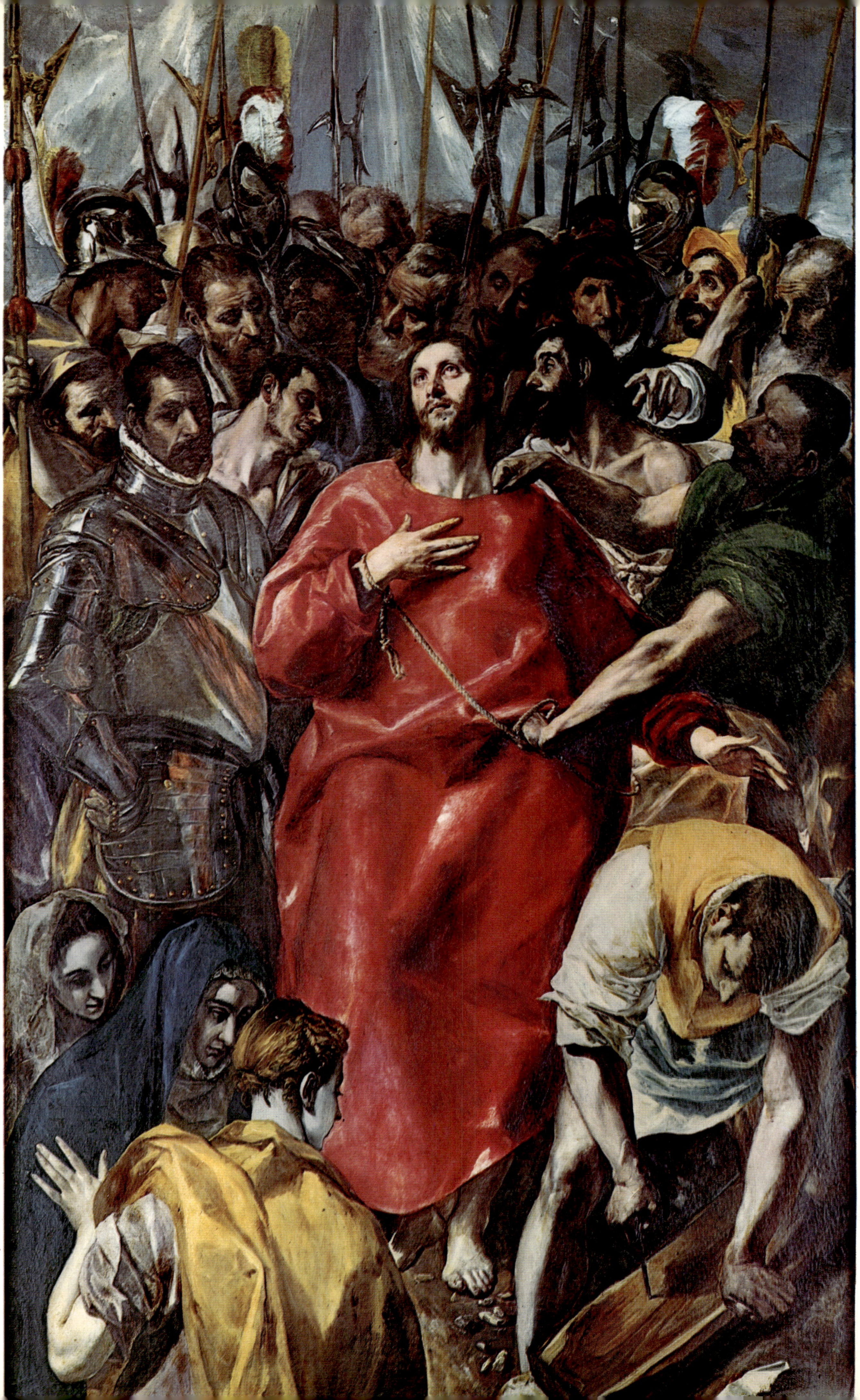

9. The Espolio (Dis-
of Christ), 1577-1579.
, Sacristy of the Cathe-
at. No. 51.

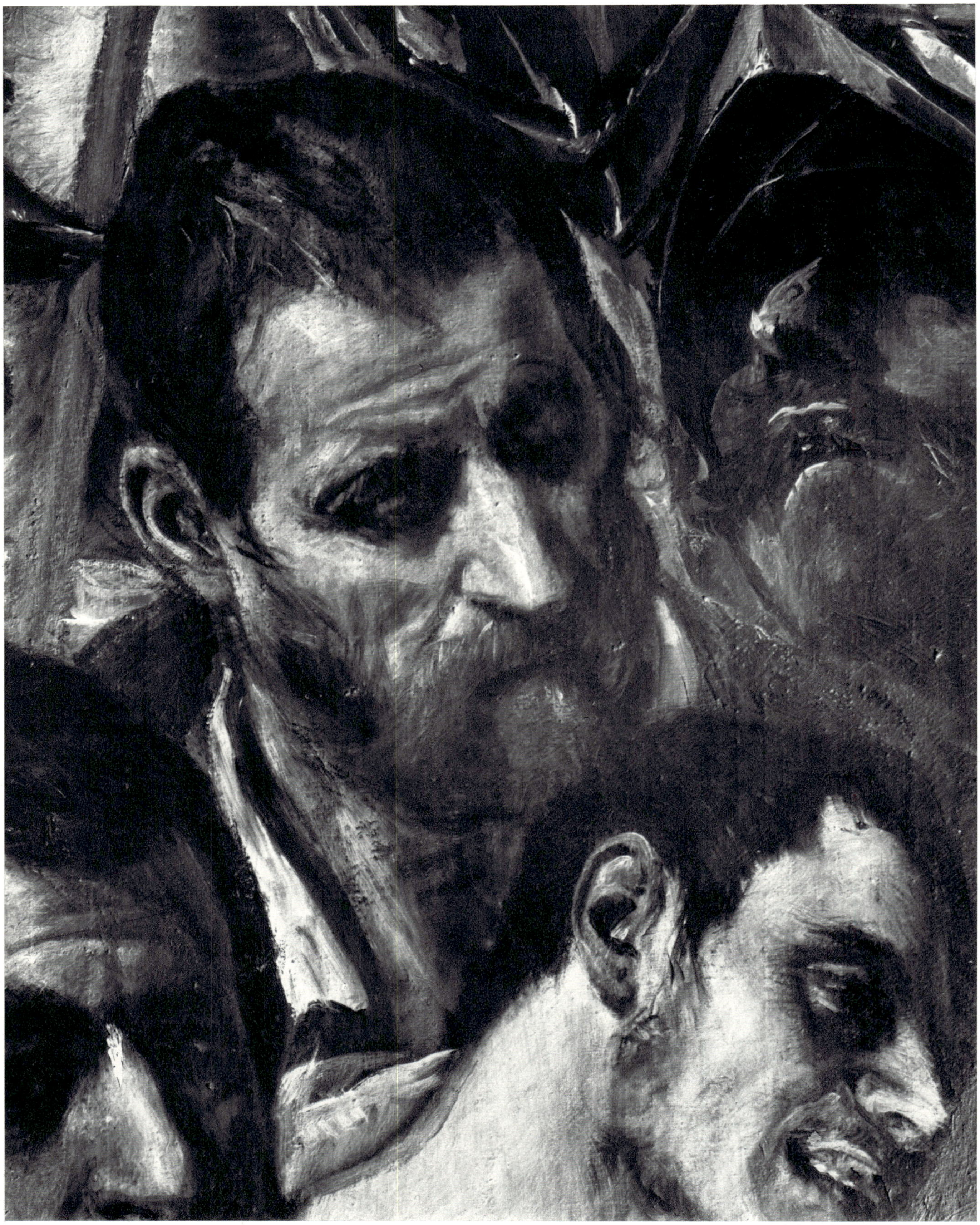

Fig. 70. Detail of figure 69.

the pictorial values prevail over those of the subject-matter at all points. There is a total absence of the theatrical, as in the *Assumption* and the *Trinity*. Form and light are used exclusively in the service of image and colour. In the modelling in this work El Greco permits himself some rather harsh effects (in secondary elements) which were later to tempt him further, like those originating in the intensity that is needed to make the bodies stand out in the penumbra on the right. In the foreground, and in a position both similar and symmetrical to that of the St. Luke in the *Adoration of the shepherds,* we find, as has already been stated, the figure of St. Ildefonso, patron saint of the Toledan Church. Cossío has suggested that this may have been a portrait of the Dean, Don Diego de Castilla. We simply mention this, without forgetting what we have said earlier regarding one of the praying figures in the *Crucifixion* in the Louvre *(Fig. 43 - Cat. 31).*

The "Espolio" (Disrobing of Christ)

The *Espolio* is one of El Greco's finest paintings and certainly a work of the greatest importance in the history of European art *(Fig. 69 - Cat. 51).* It produces an unforgettable emotional impact and is the work mainly responsible for the persistence of its painter's name and fame in the spirit of the people of Toledo down through the centuries. The composition is a work of genius, with its tightly-knit combination of plastic values and the feeling expressed through the theme and the typology of the characters. It represents Christ on Calvary, at the moment when the executioners are about to strip him of the red robe they had put on him in derision for the crowning with thorns. Considering its subject, the picture is very suitably hung: over the altar of the vestry in the Sacristy of the Cathedral of Toledo. It has no precedents in the iconography of the Middle Ages or in that of the sixteenth century. Azcárate tells us that the literary source for this canvas was most probably the book of "Meditations on the Passion", by St. Bonaventure.

The first document in connection with the execution of the *Espolio* is a receipt, signed by El Greco on July 2nd 1577, for 13,600 *maravedis* as an advance on this work. This seems to indicate that the contract, which has not been preserved, was drawn up very shortly before, perhaps on the same day. We see, therefore, that this work is the exact contemporary of the group of works for Santo Domingo el Antiguo. We may believe that it was the Dean of the Cathedral, Don Diego de Castilla, who induced the Chapter to commission the *Espolio.* At all events, the problems that arose in connection with the valuation of the picture, which were settled in such an inconsiderately cruel way by the Chapter, are at a great remove from the polite, almost ceremonious fashion in which the arrangements for the works in Santo Domingo el Antiguo were so successfully concluded. Something very serious must have happened between the Dean and the Chapter, but the documents do not reveal what it was.

In 1578 the painter was paid 37,500 *maravedis* plus 400 *reales.* The valuation of the finished work, which took place on June 15th 1579, was the occasion of very different opinions. The experts appointed by El Greco, the painter Baltasar de Castro Cintrón and the sculptor Martínez de Castañeda, declared: "that the estimate is so great that it has no price ... but that, considering the poverty of the age ... a payment may be made of nine hundred ducats of three hundred and seventy-five *maravedis* each". The appraisers appointed by the Chapter, who were the architect Nicolás de Vergara and the painter Luis Velasco, estimated the work at 227 ducats (2,500 *reales).* In his document of arbitration the silversmith Alejo de Montoya says: "having seen the said painting and [considering] that it is one of the best I have seen ... it might be assessed at so much that few or none would wish to pay it; but considering the times and what is usually paid in Castile for paintings by great artists ...", he proposes that El Greco should be paid 317 ducats (3,500 *reales).* The Chapter's appraisers attempted to justify their miserly valuation by reasons of iconography, pointing out that the heads placed above that of Christ would have to be removed, as would the three Marys, "for they were not present at this event". In the ensuing lawsuit the Chapter demanded that El Greco should either deliver the picture or pay some bail, since he had already received two hundred and fifty ducats on account and "the picture is in his hands and he is a foreigner ... and he has no reason to stay in this city, nor has he any possessions here ...". To the questions of the Chapter's lawyer El Greco replied disdainfully "that he is not obliged to give any reasons for coming to this city, and to the other questions he is asked he does not have to reply because he is not obliged to". Only when threatened with imprisonment did he capitulate and accept what they wanted to pay him, declaring besides: "I am ready to remove what they wish me to remove [from the picture] and with this the whole case ends". In fact the painting was hung without any modifications, but the painter was not finally paid the full amount until December 8th of 1581. With this sad anecdote begins the story of the artist's struggle against the miserliness of the city that was to be his new home. The conflict is all the less comprehensible when we consider the excellence of the painting that occasioned it.

The figure of Christ, in which we find again the head on the *Sudary of St. Veronica (Fig. 47)* and the gesture of the *Knight taking an oath (Fig. 45),* but treated with greater fullness and splendour, is presented as the focal point, victim of the subhuman fury of a mob that is variously characterized. The Son of God, shown as an archetype of universal male beauty in an attitude of serene triumph, here proclaims his double nature and this, undoubtedly, is one of the painter's greatest successes. He is surrounded by a crowd of evil, sinister, gesticulating characters, shouting insults and imprecations.

The only one who remains aloof from the general frenzy is the "centurion" in armour. He may represent, as Camón Aznar suggests, a personification of the indifference of Rome. But Wethey thinks that he is meant to be St. Longinus, the one who later, as he pierced Christ's side with his lance, exclaimed: "Truly this man was the son of God!" Other figures, of old men, with heads very realistically depicted, are rather more difficult to explain. In the foreground we see the three Marys. The face of the Virgin betrays weariness and pain. Just behind her we see Mary the wife of Cleophas, an exact replica of the figure of *St. Veronica,* already considered in its two versions in the preceding pages *(Figs. 50 & 51).* The rich inflexions of El Greco's drawing attain extraordinary beauty in the head and arm of Mary Magdalen. On the right we see one of the executioner's assistants boring a hole in an arm of the cross, his figure bent so intently over the wood that he gives the painter an occasion for violent —and very realistic— foreshortening.

As we have seen, the Cathedral Chapter tried to force the painter to suppress the numerous heads on a higher level than Christ's —for reasons of traditionally-observed hierarchy in religious iconography— without realizing that this was just the effect that El Greco was aiming at, in order to give a sensation of anguish and nightmare and, at the same time, the psychological contrast between the serenity of Christ and the frenzy of executioners, soldiers and other tormentors. With this effect the painter also succeeded in making the divine face rise out of its absolute immersion in the chaos of turbulent, convulsed expressions. The blues and dark tones are used to set off the white of the flesh tints, particularly in Christ's face, and the astounding red of his robe, which is, after all, the motif of the title. This robe is treated in accordance with the concept we have already mentioned, that of using it to create a form in which colour and light, modelling and folds, shall be of interest in themselves. El Greco's great concern with this treatment may be seen, indeed, in the fact that the main change made between the two preliminary studies described below and the definitive work comes from the painter's moving the figures in the foreground further left and right, so that the central space may be left freer and almost the whole of the figure of Christ may be seen, wrapped in its red robe. The textures are rendered by a combination of extremely fine scumblings and comparatively thick impasto. There is no lack of distortion, particularly noticeable in the tense attitude of the executioner, on the right of the figure of Christ, who is holding the rope and beginning to undo the robe. The jostling of all these bloodthirsty characters in their efforts to get nearer to Christ enables the painter to vary the foreshortenings and also the degree of finish imparted to each fragment. The contrast between a light area, with zigzagging brush-strokes, and a darker one with dense impasto conveys the transition from light to shade. Sometimes shadows are obtained rather by a greater weight of impasto than by any increase in tonal darkness, or even by slight superimpositions of dark tones on light, as in the veil covering the head of Mary the wife of Cleophas. The whole is unified by the tightening of all the forms in the direction of the central area and by the marked verticality that makes the great figure of Christ, at the centre of everything, dominate the composition.

The painter simultaneously infuses more light into the face of the Redeemer and makes all the surrounding heads relatively darker. From a technical point of view, the execution of this central face is no different from that of those surrounding it, but it seems better studied, even more sculptural, without losing the constant pictorial quality that prevails in all El Greco's work. The great moist eyes, the soft yet muscular throat and the short beard, which are all modelled with perceptible brush-strokes, i.e., without total blending, are unforgettable.

Fig. 71. Detail of figure

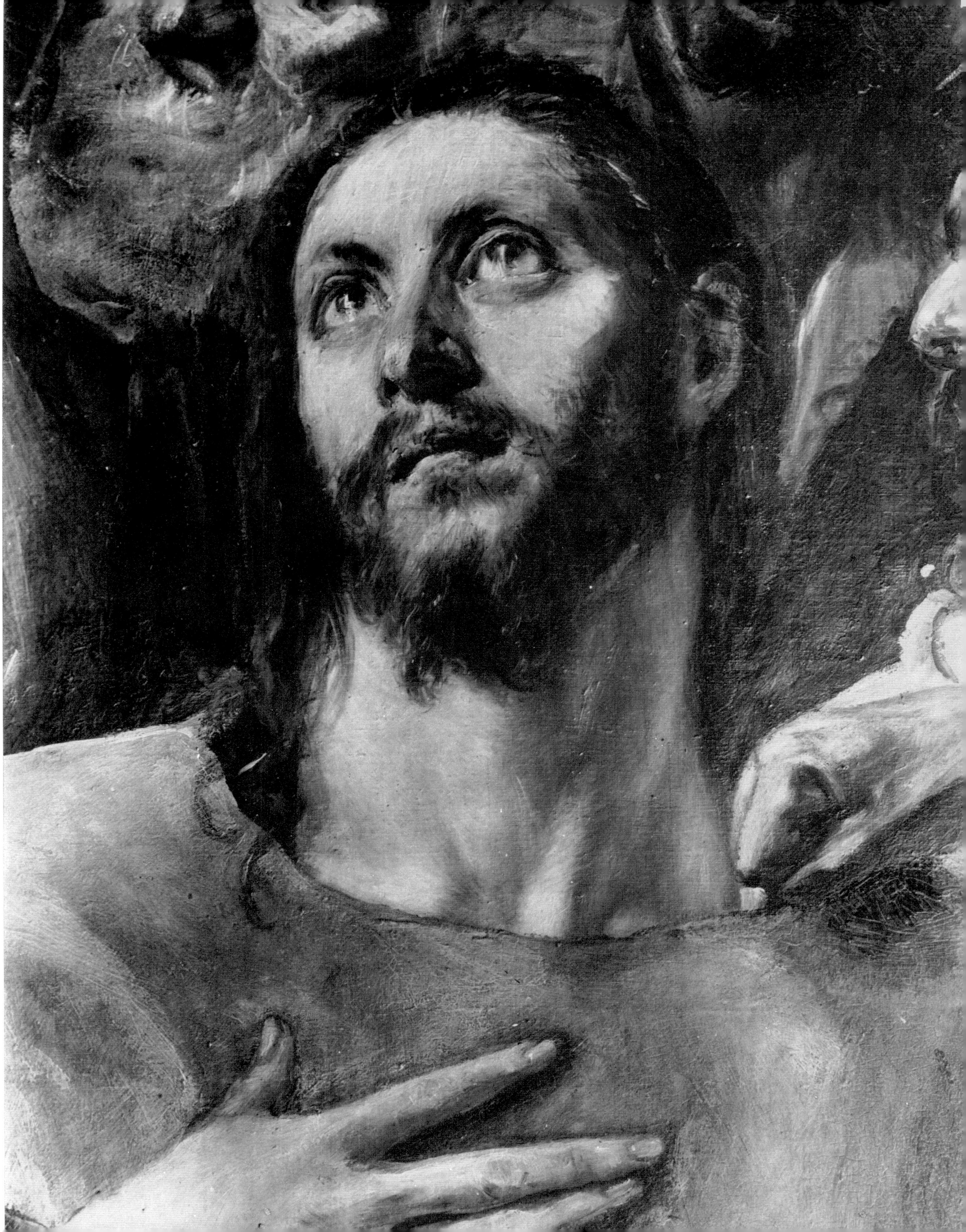

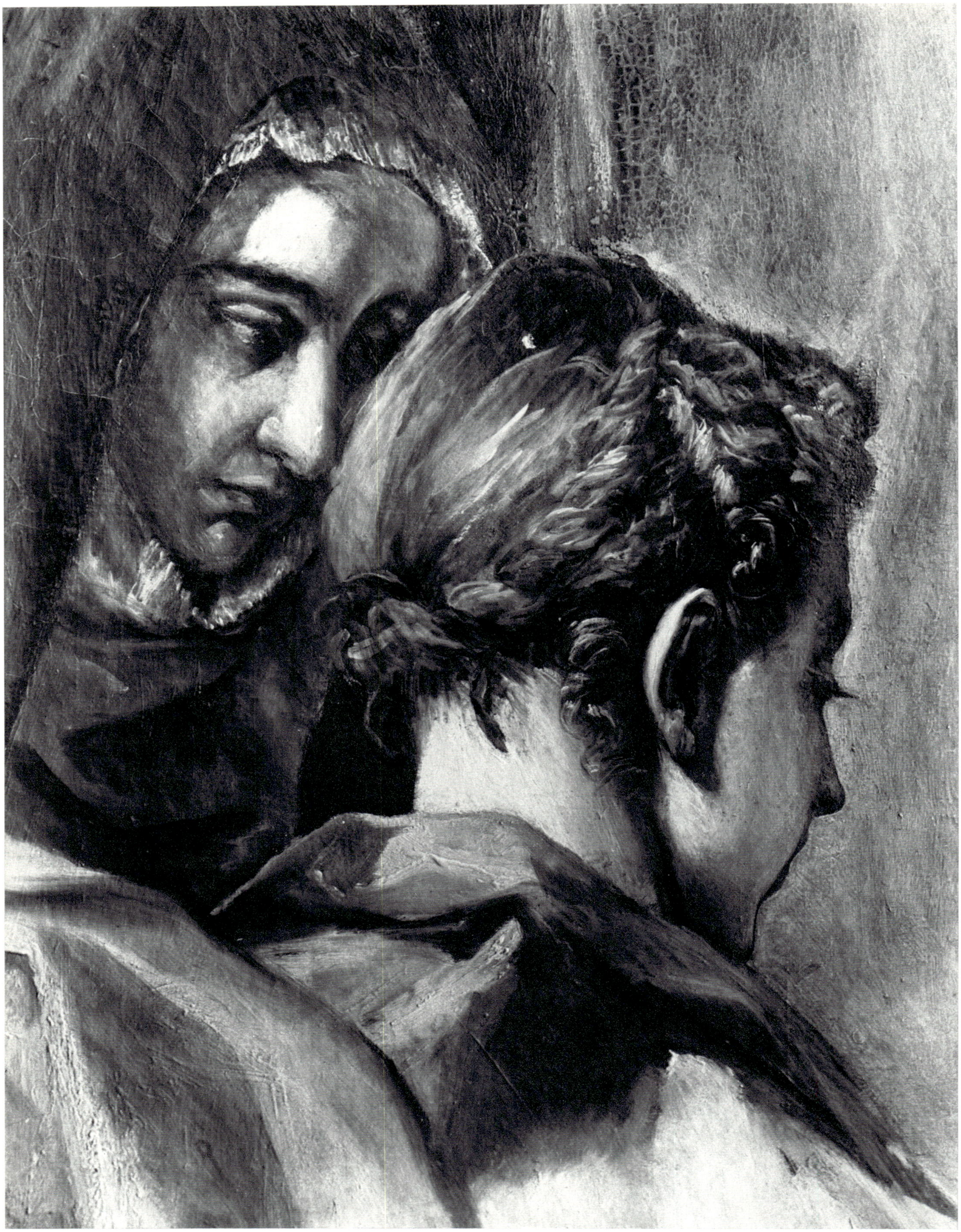

Fig. 72. Detail of figure 69.

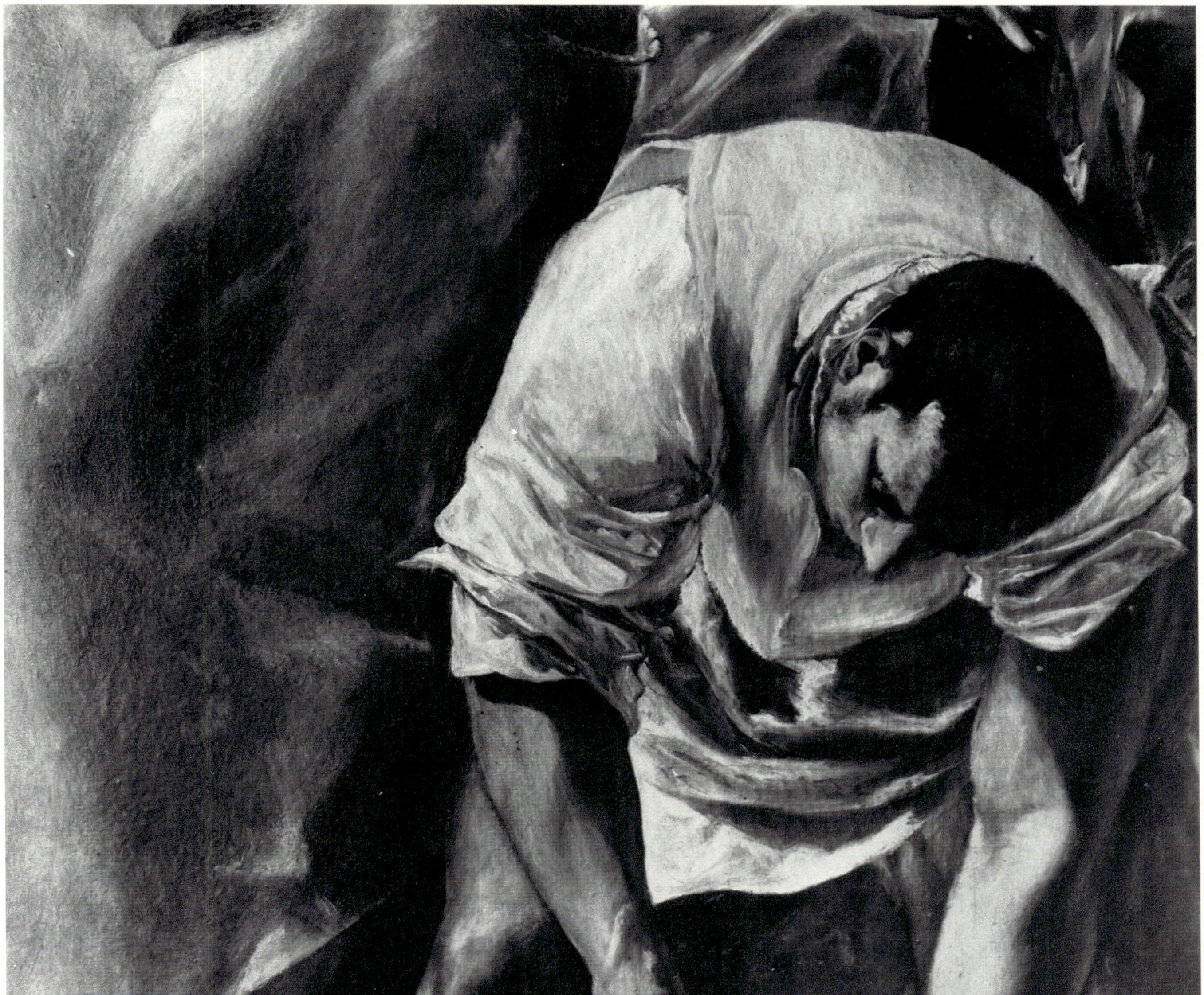

Fig. 73. Detail of figure 69.

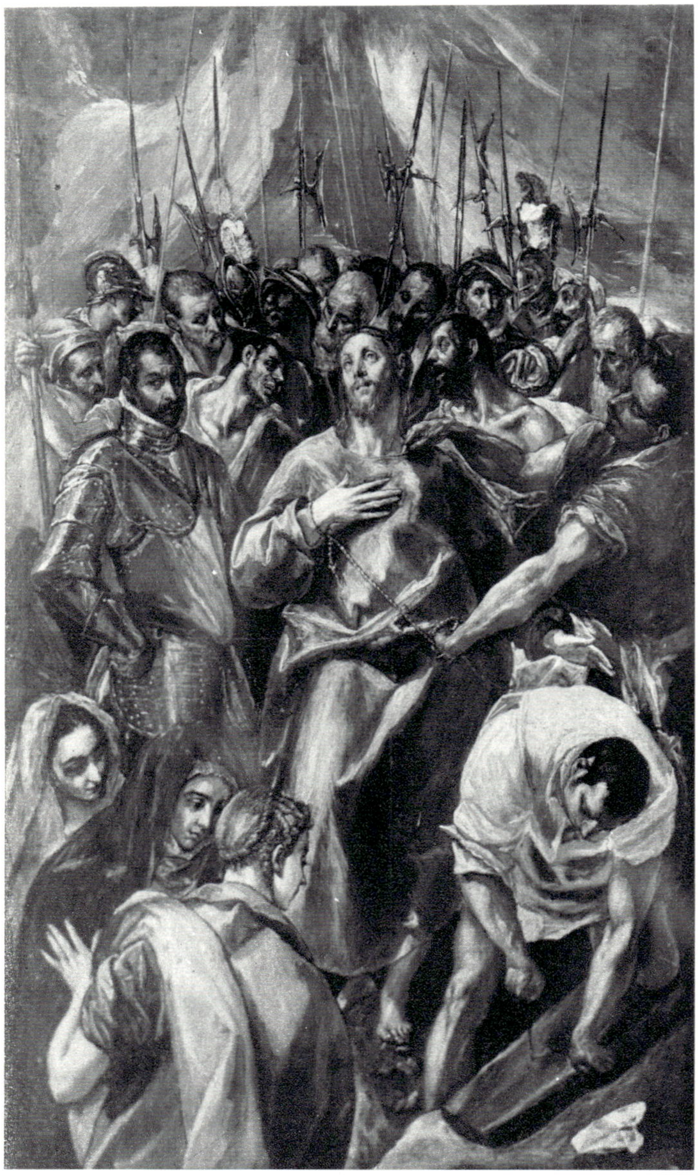

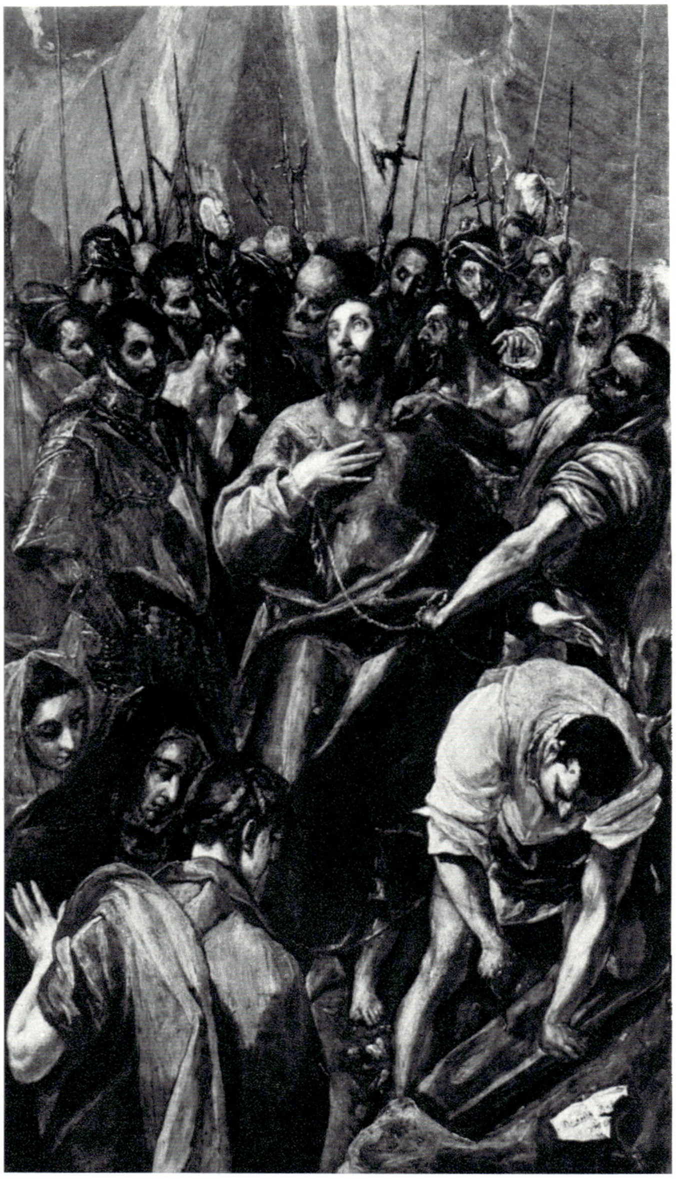

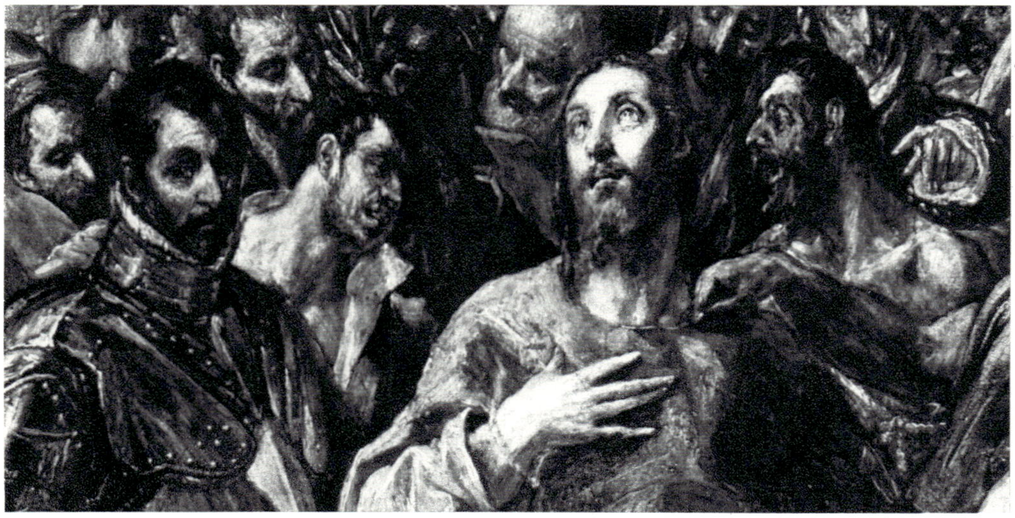

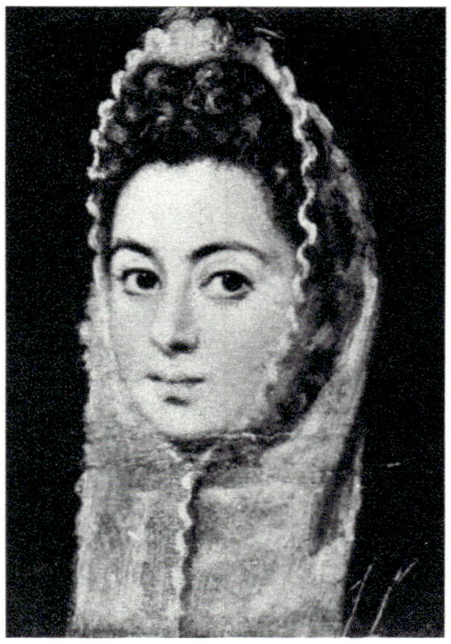

Fig. 74. The Espolio (Disrobing of Christ), c. 1577. Upton Downs, Viscount Bearsted Collection. Cat. No. 52.
Figs. 75 & 76. The Espolio (Disrobing of Christ), c. 1577. Florence, Contini-Bonacossi Collection. Cat. No. 53.
Fig. 77. Portrait of a lady (Jerónima de las Cuevas?), 1577-1579. Barcelona, Muñoz Collection. Cat. No. 55.

The *Espolio,* the crowning work in those two busy years that decided El Greco to settle in Toledo and the work, too, that was the cause of his first lawsuit, was also to be one of his favourite paintings. At least five signed versions are still extant, as well as several contemporary copies, one of them signed by his son. As we may logically suppose that there were other versions which have not survived, it would seem that El Greco's vigorous personality succeeded in making itself felt to the extent of introducing into the hermetic, suspicious world of Toledo a subject-matter which had no tradition at all, and one which had, moreover, given rise to the most virulent objections.

Among the versions signed by El Greco two almost identical little panels *(Figs. 74 & 75 - Cat. 52 & 53)* are outstanding, both executed with exquisitely meticulous technique and with all the vigour of the great canvas in the Sacristy of the Cathedral. Can these two little versions have been copies of the preliminary sketch or study? For El Greco, as we shall see, the painting of an original basic model was the usual first step in the execution of his works. The slight variations to be observed between these little twin panels and the *Espolio* in the Cathedral do not alter either the composition or the typology of the characters. The Upton Downs version is almost exactly the same size as the sketch for the famous *Adoration of the Name of Jesus* in the Escorial, which we have already studied *(Fig. 36 - Cat. 28).* The fact that the two works bear the initials D.G.H. on the back tells us that they once belonged to the collection of Gaspar Méndez de Haro. The other versions of the *Espolio* belong, in our opinion, to a later period; they will be studied, therefore, in the fourth chapter.

It might be advisable here to pause for a moment and give some consideration to the undeniable change in style to be observed between the works El Greco had done in Italy and the group painted during his first Spanish period. The first thing we notice is that the artist, both in accordance with his own impulses and as a natural reaction to his early failure at Court, which was only to be confirmed on the occasion of his superb *St. Maurice,* set his feet resolutely on the path of originality. Realizing that his art would perhaps avail him little except in essentials, he dispensed with anything that might mean the slightest compromise. We might almost say that he began again. With this in mind he geometrized his figures. His resorting to geometrization, of which there had not been the least sign during his Italian period, meant that he had to restate the form and renounce the easy manner he had acquired from his contact with the masterpieces of Titian and Tintoretto. At the same time his colour became rather colder. The ideas were more personal now and any debt to the past, however slight, was cancelled. So in the works done for Santo Domingo el Antiguo we find an almost totally integral Greco, one who has successfully risen above his first period, in which he inevitably —all the more so if we remember his humble beginnings as a "madonna-painter"— felt the impact of the great Venetians and that of Michelangelo. When we study the works of the Italian period we sometimes refer to premonitions of the essential Greco, the artist forged in Spain. But it is never more than a question of details.

In Spain El Greco "remade" himself, a process in which the grandiose compositions of Santo Domingo el Antiguo marked the first and firmest step. In them the geometrization of the form is hidden under the acute pathos that was so frequently to characterize the artist's works. It was a magnificent flowering of genius, which also left behind the realistic aspect of some of his Roman works and which, above all, went beyond those compositions in which the oblique perspectives of Tintoretto still appeared.

As from this moment, at which his work was already completely original, his creative powers were to develop in an increasingly personal way. By this we mean that the undeniable influences mentioned above — inevitable, as we have said, considering his origins and the real stature of his masters— were now thoroughly assimilated. Without losing anything of what he had learnt, he was to transform it to such an extent that the change wrought in his whole approach would hardly leave room for reminiscence. He was to incorporate the factor of realism into his mystical concept and transfigure it without either denying it or eradicating it from his work, for, despite the comments of his detractors —on the occasion of the *St. Maurice* to be studied later— El Greco was never avid for notoriety, nor can any fair-minded critic seriously accuse him of such a failing. What he did feel was an ardent impulse that drove him onward and led him into the most audacious pictorial explorations, with an absolutely original use of colour and with harmonies of form and interpretations of his subject-matter that did not always meet with his clients' approval, but which were to bring him the glory he now enjoys.

Jerónima de las Cuevas

We will close the brief period that ended in El Greco's settling in Toledo with the presentation of *Jerónima de las Cuevas (Fig. 78 - Cat. 56),* the mother of El Greco's only son, Jorge Manuel. We are assured of her existence by the painter's own statement in his last document (1614): "Jorge Manuel, my son by Jerónima de las Cuevas". This woman is one of the great mysteries in the life of El Greco. He probably made her acquaintance on his arrival in Toledo, since Jorge Manuel was born in 1578, when the painter was still working on the paintings for Santo Domingo el Antiguo and had not yet decided to settle in the city permanently. Most historians are of the opinion that there was no marriage between them, perhaps because El Greco had already been married in Italy and had a wife still living in that country. Tormo and Camón Aznar find it impossible to believe that El Greco could have lived with a Toledan woman without marrying her in the Toledo of that day and age. This problem has been very carefully studied by José Gómez-Menor, who suggests that Jerónima may have died in giving birth to Jorge Manuel, before El Greco had had time to make the wedding arrangements. According to the same historian, Cuevas is a frequent name among the middle classes in Toledo, though there is also a more important branch of the same name in Castile; one of St. Teresa of Avila's grandfathers was called Cuevas. A possible explanation of Jerónima's single state is that she may have been of Moorish ancestry. We know that a Toledan called Juan de Cuevas, probably Jerónima's brother, was married to Petronila de Madrid, who died in 1603. El Greco was present when the inventory of this lady's property was drawn up and some of the pages of this inventory are in the painter's handwriting. Among these pages we find the following entry: "Ytem, a picture of Our Lady, by Domynico".

To return to the subject of the supposed identification of the portrait of this woman, whose role in the painter's life cannot be precisely ascertained and will probably never be known, El Greco's very first biographers had no hesitation in identifying Jorge Manuel's unknown mother with the model for the portrait of a woman painted on canvas which is now in the Maxwell Collection in Glasgow *(Fig. 78 - Cat. 56).* There is not the slightest reason for believing that the beautiful woman portrayed here was Jerónima de las Cuevas. It is a splendid painting, extraordinary in execution and with a simple —though very iridescent— range of colours. The modelling of the face is outstanding in graphic precision. It may be the work of El Greco, but it is quite possible that it is not; we have included it in our catalogue, though not absolutely convinced of its authenticity. Beruete attributed this picture to Tintoretto, but the specialists in the work of the great Venetian painter did not accept this attribution. The work comes originally from Spain. It was at one time in the collection of Serafín García de la Huerta in Madrid and later passed to the Spanish Gallery in the Louvre, where it hung in 1838. It was included in the London sale of Louis Philippe's collections in 1853 and it was there that it was sold to the Maxwell family of Scotland, its present owners. We must repeat that there are absolutely no grounds for believing that the lady in the portrait is Jerónima de las Cuevas.

We also reproduce here, in the same size as the original work *(Fig. 77 - Cat. 55),* a miniature painted in oil on paper (Muñoz Collection, Barcelona). It seems to be a sixteenth-century work and the coincidence with the portrait of a woman that we have just been studying is quite evident. We present this work as a document still awaiting judgment.

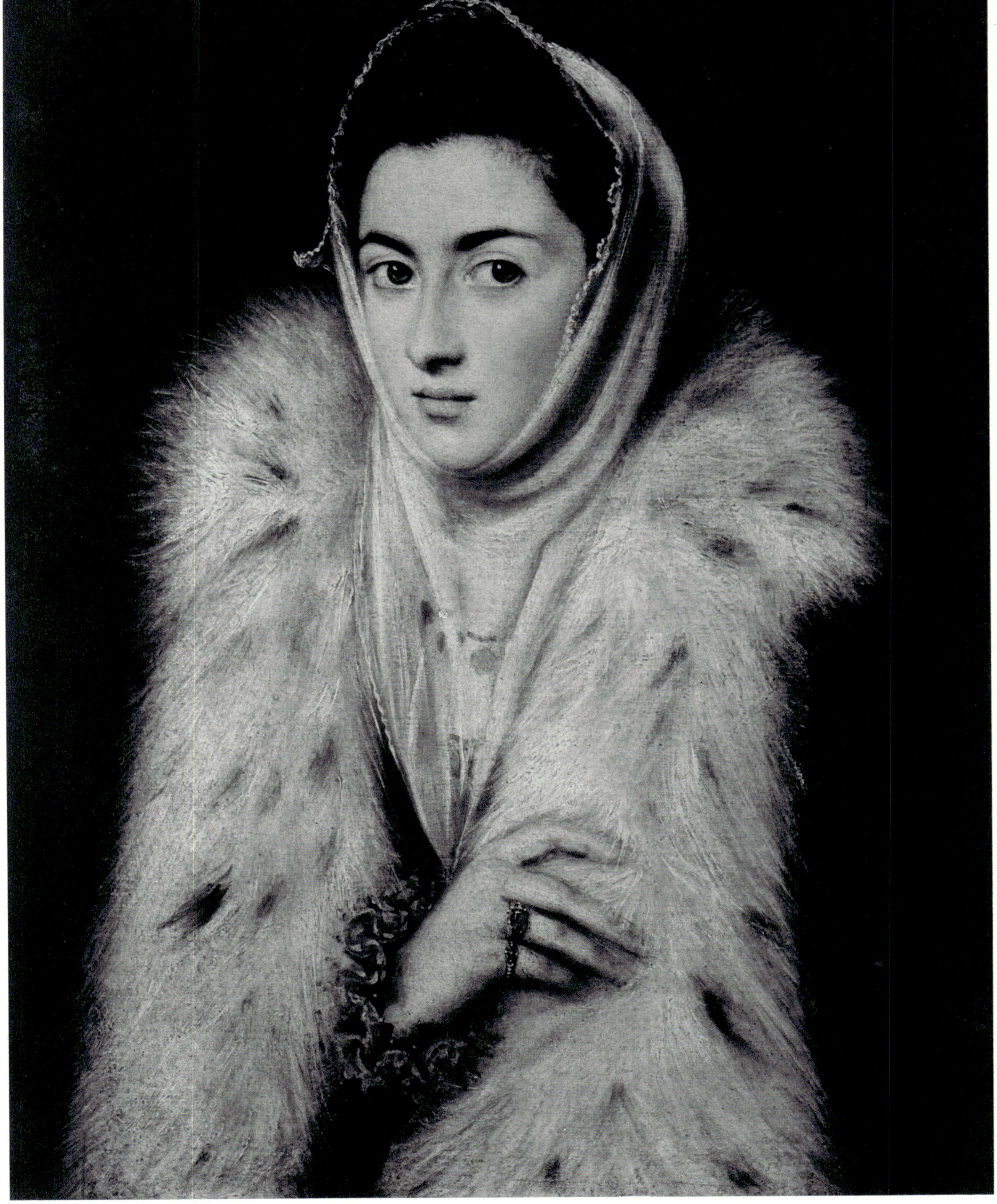

Fig. 78. Lady in a fur wrap (Jerónima de las Cuevas?), 1577-1579. Glasgow, Maxwell MacDonald Collection. Cat. No. 56.

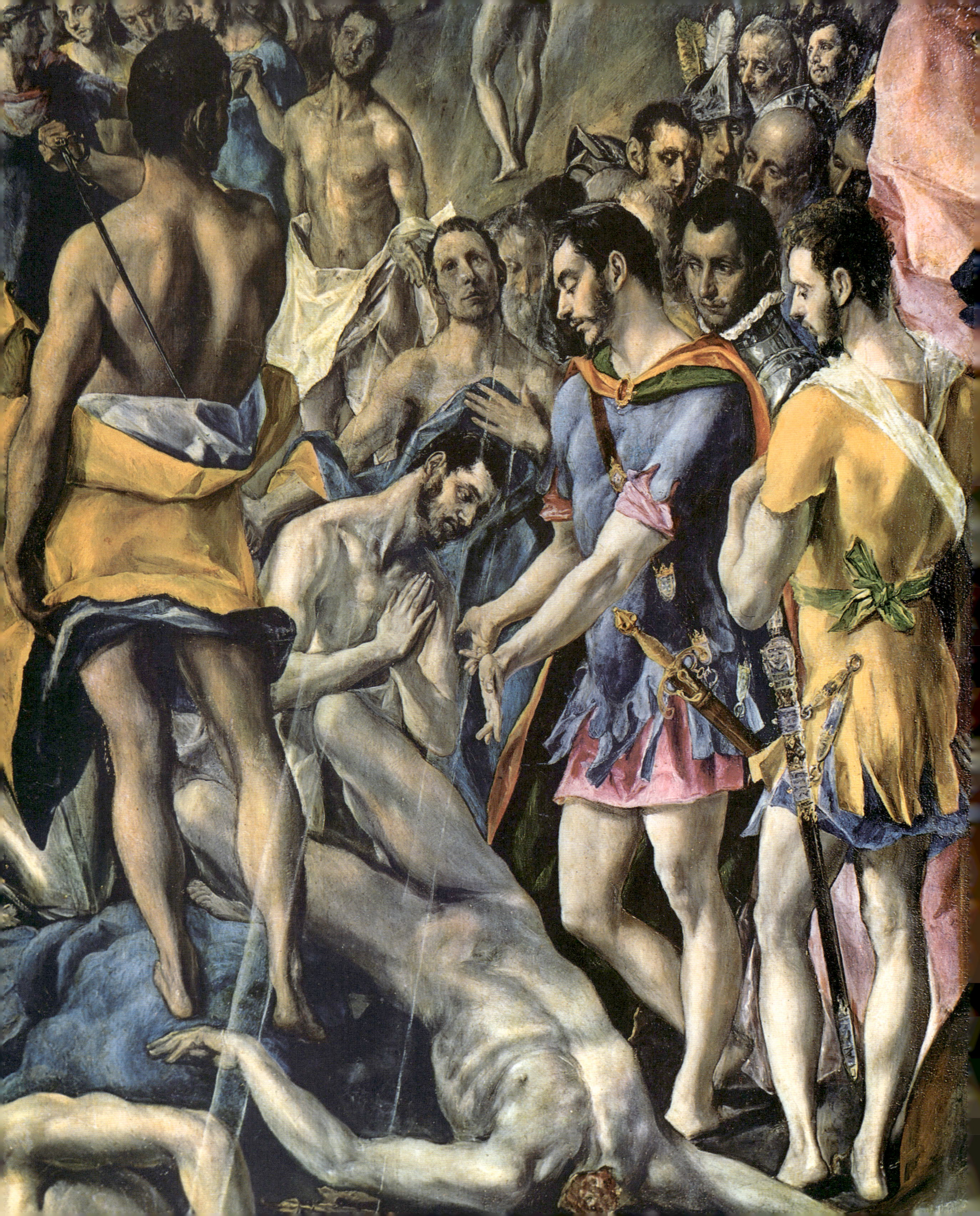

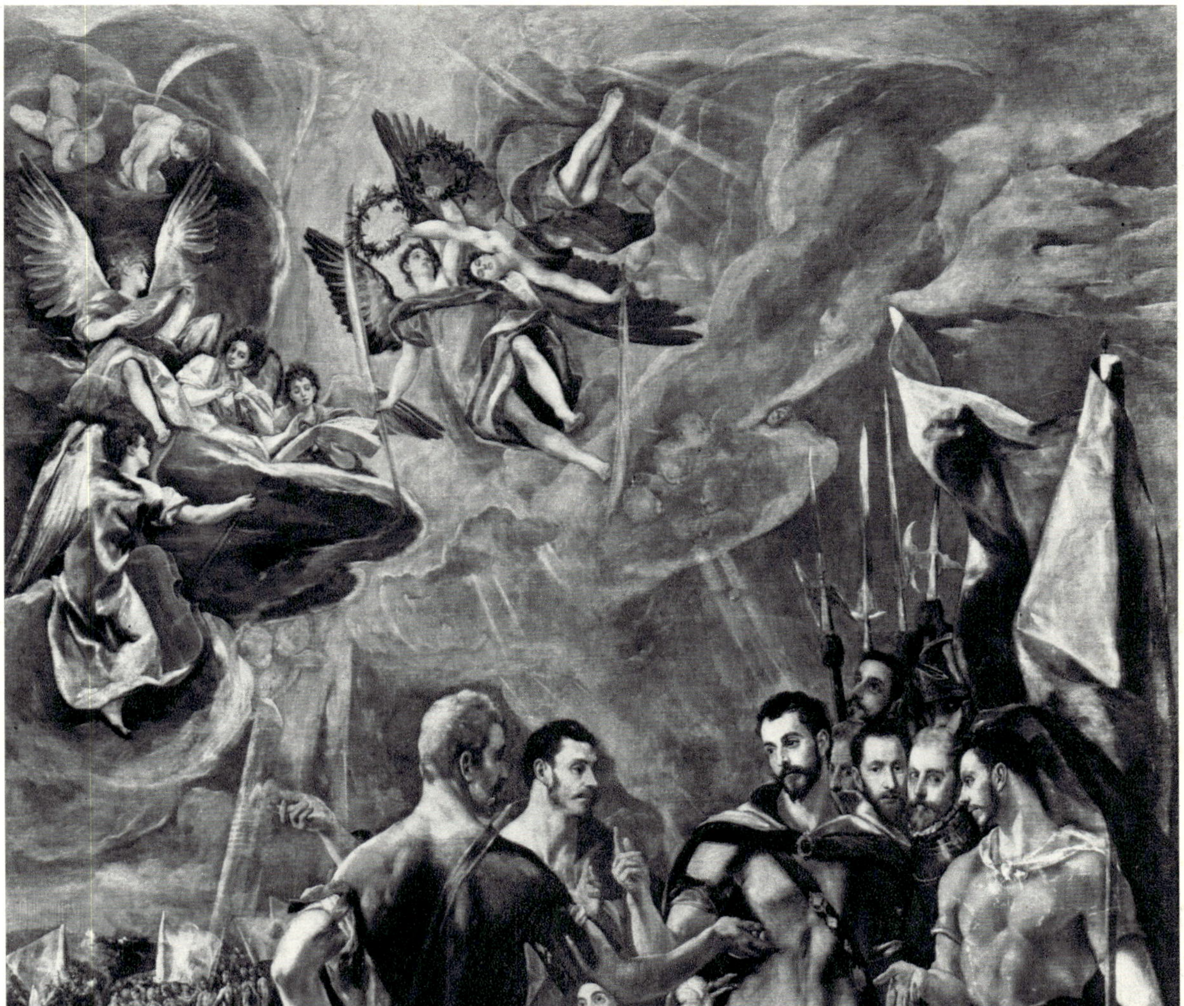

Figs. 79 & 80. The Martyrdom of St. Maurice, 1580-1582. The Escorial, Monastery. Cat. No. 57.

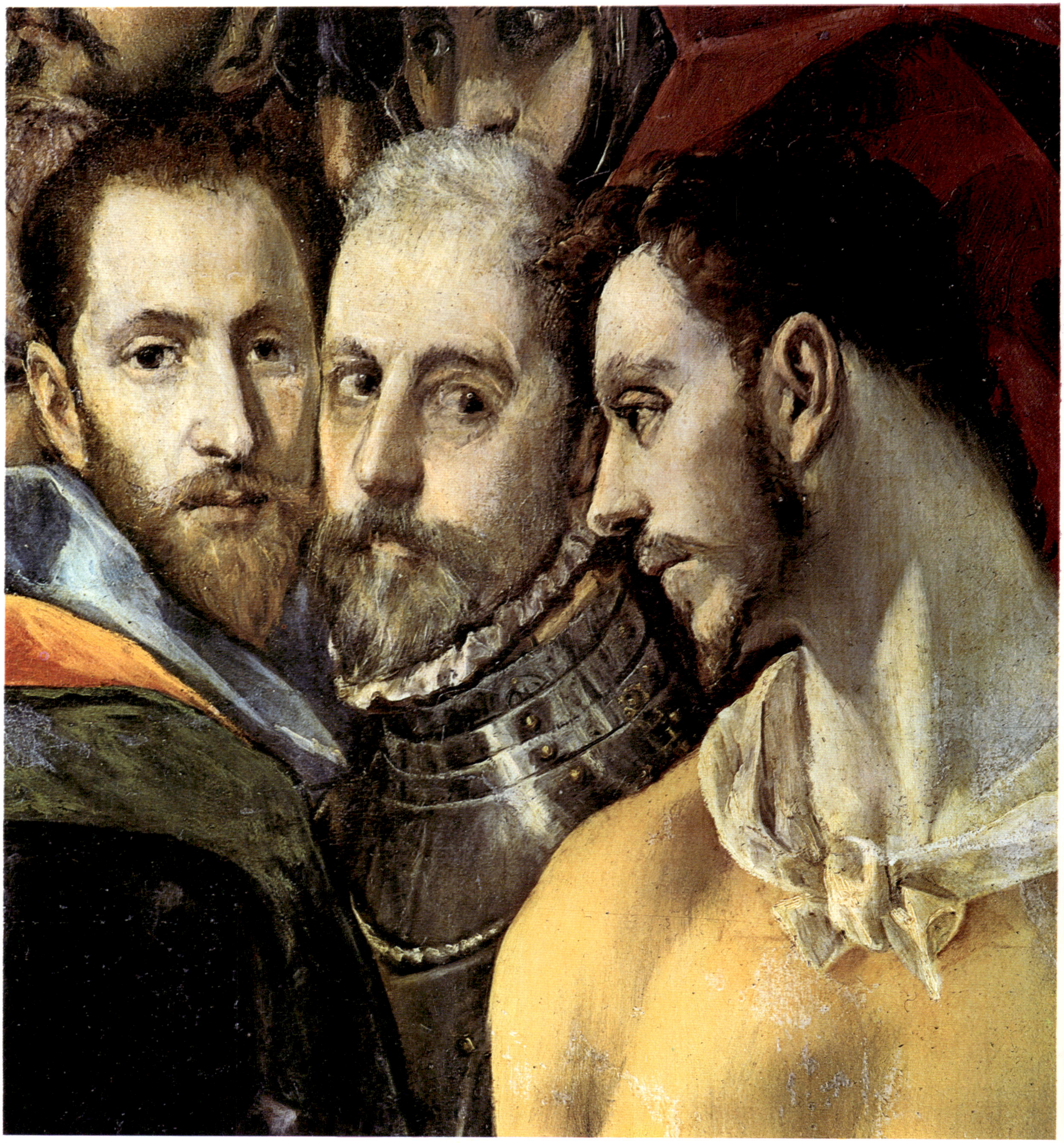

Fig. 81. Detail of figure 80.

III

1579 - 1586

THE *ST. MAURICE* IN THE ESCORIAL — TOLEDO AND THE PALACE OF THE MARQUÉS DE VILLENA — WORKS ATTRIBUTED TO THE PERIOD 1579-1586 — PORTRAITS — THE *BURIAL OF THE CONDE DE ORGAZ.*

It was probably in the autumn of 1579, after he had been in Toledo for two years and while his acrimonious controversy with the Cathedral Chapter was still going on, that El Greco received the royal order from Philip II with a commission to paint a picture representing St. Maurice and his fellow martyrs *(Fig. 79 - Cat. 57),* for the monastery of the Escorial. The exact date of this document is unknown, but it may be supposed that it was the reason for the painter's surprising refusal to continue the defence of his rights in the *Espolio* affair. We may readily believe that his good friends in Toledo would have advised him to avoid any trouble with the authorities at a moment when a road was opening before him that might lead to boundless possibilities: participation in the gigantic projects of the King. In another order, dated April 25th 1580, Philip refers to the *Martyrdom of St. Maurice* commissioned from El Greco some time before: "We have been informed that, for lack of fine colours and money, he has given up working on this project", and he therefore gives orders for an advance to be made to El Greco on account and for colours to be sent to him.

Between May 1580 and April 1583 the painter received, in four remittances, a total sum of 800 ducats. The painting, which was finished some time before September 2nd 1582, did not please the King. Since El Greco had refused to accept the results of a first appraisal of the picture, it was appraised for the second time, in the spring of 1583, by the Italian painters Romulo Cincinnati and Diego de Urbina, who were probably in part responsible for the King's adverse opinion. At any rate, the latter of these two painters was then commissioned to paint another version of the *St. Maurice* and produced a very commonplace work, which was delivered in August of 1584 and now hangs over one of the altars in the church of the Escorial. It was valued at the rather more modest figure of 550 ducats. El Greco's canvas is housed in the extraordinary gallery of paintings in the monastery of the Escorial.

In his "History of the Order of St. Jerome", published in 1605, Father Sigüenza says: "A certain Dominico Greco, who is now living and producing excellent work in Toledo, left here, in the Chapter Room of the Escorial, a picture of *St. Maurice*.... His Majesty did not like it ... not many people like it, indeed, though it is said to be very artistic and we are told that its painter is very proficient, and that many excellent things by him are to be seen".

When we stand before El Greco's masterly painting of *The Martyrdom of St. Maurice and the Theban Legion,* we cannot help wondering why the work did not appeal to Philip II. The only valid explanation, apart from the possible influence of his Italian assessors, is that Philip cannot have had any real sensitivity to painting, being only interested in its iconography. Undoubtedly he expected a clearer and more vigorous treatment of the theme, a treatment in the traditional Spanish manner. When confronted with a picture of apparent serenity, in which the executions are relegated to a rather far-off middle distance, he would naturally show his disapproval.

According to hagiographical tradition, the martyrdom of St. Maurice and his legionaries took place in Gaul towards the end of the third century, when the saint and the legion he commanded were required, on Maximian's orders, to swear allegiance to the gods of the Empire. After deliberating with his men, who were all, like himself, Christians, Maurice decided to refuse. The legion was decimated and the oath required again. Again it was refused and again one man in every ten was put to the sword. And so it went on until they had all been executed, or so we are told, though it is difficult to know how much of the story is historical and how much mere legend.

It was El Greco's intention to show the greatness of soul of St. Maurice and the officers of the Theban legion above all else. That feeling of sublime indifference to be seen in the composition was intentionally evoked in order to show the attitude with which the martyrs obeyed the dictates of their religious conscience, without any fear of their ultimate fate. And so, rather than place the emphasis on the executions, El Greco placed it on the saint himself and his higher-ranking officers, that prodigious group of figures in the right foreground whose eloquent gestures reveal what is going on in their hearts. With an execution that follows Mannerist methods to some extent, next to the large figures in this group may be seen the smaller ones in the middle distance, where the recalcitrant Christians are being decapitated. Further off a third group of soldiers approach their martyrdom. The asymmetry of the composition is counterbalanced by giving greater interest and force to the left of the picture in the upper part, which represents the heavens. And thus above the groups of minor figures we have clouds and angel musicians, while the sky on the opposite side is empty and the central space is occupied by other angels, bearing the laurel wreaths of triumph. Clearly perceptible beams of light are projected on the earth from above.

It is hardly necessary to say that here El Greco, as was his custom, represented the characters in the most varied attire, partly that of his own age and partly what he imagined to be Roman suits of armour, but giving these latter radiant tones of blue and yellow instead of the colour of leather. The figure on the right wears a sword of an Arab type, similar to that of Boabdil, while above the group of heads on the right we may see halberds and lances of burnished or gilded steel. Of the principal figures one is an adolescent —a page or squire— carrying a sixteenth-century helmet.

Atmospheric effects —of secondary interest but extremely vivid and lyrical— float between the earthly and heavenly zones. Together with the angels depicted full-length, who stand out strongly in their various attitudes and foreshortenings, we can see cherubs and winged heads, but they are so immersed in the mass of clouds that they take on its colour and are barely perceptible. The prodigious harmony of the whole is imposing. The essential chromatic range is that of complementaries: blue (with the most diverse shades, from violet to an almost white blue) and yellow, together with red, white, the earth colours, the blue of the sky and the yellowish greens of some of the various figures' robes, among them those of the angels, are the colours that compose this fundamental harmony. On the other hand, the forms of the figures and the outlines of the groups, as is frequently the case with El Greco, tend to maintain a certain parallelism, so that they would almost coincide if the intervening spaces disappeared. The dominant rhythm is supplied by the void —the diagonal line that goes from bottom left to top right— which constitutes the separation between the triangular space that contains the angels (in the upper left) and the other triangular space, in the lower right, which is filled by the main figures.

This chromatic range contributes to the extremely luminous effects which, given dynamic force by the introduction of very light shades, enliven the whole painting. This work is almost like a stained-glass window, for one might say that the light, apart from coming from above and from a source just where the viewer stands, also comes from behind the canvas. This light acquires different qualities according to the zone of the space that it touches and the characters situated in that zone. It is a typical work of El Greco's middle period, by which time his personality was completely formed and no reminiscences could disturb the absolute, original power of his painting. The group of heads on the right is the precursor of the frieze of hidalgos in the *Burial of the Conde de Orgaz*, but under a more cheerful light and with a less intense expressive force. The gestures of the central characters are almost the same, but St. Maurice's hand is pointing heavenwards, while those of the others seem to be making gestures that express their agreement with their leader's idea of the duty to be performed and the martyrdom that awaits them. Those who are unaware of the importance of gesture in El Greco's work might find these attitudes conventional, the bare feet and legs too "aesthetical". But such elements in the work as are not immediately intelligible must be understood in the context of the artist's general evolution and of the feelings he expressed throughout his career, which was so coherent in its various periods and at its high points, though it did include moments of change, like the one exemplified in the *St. Maurice.*

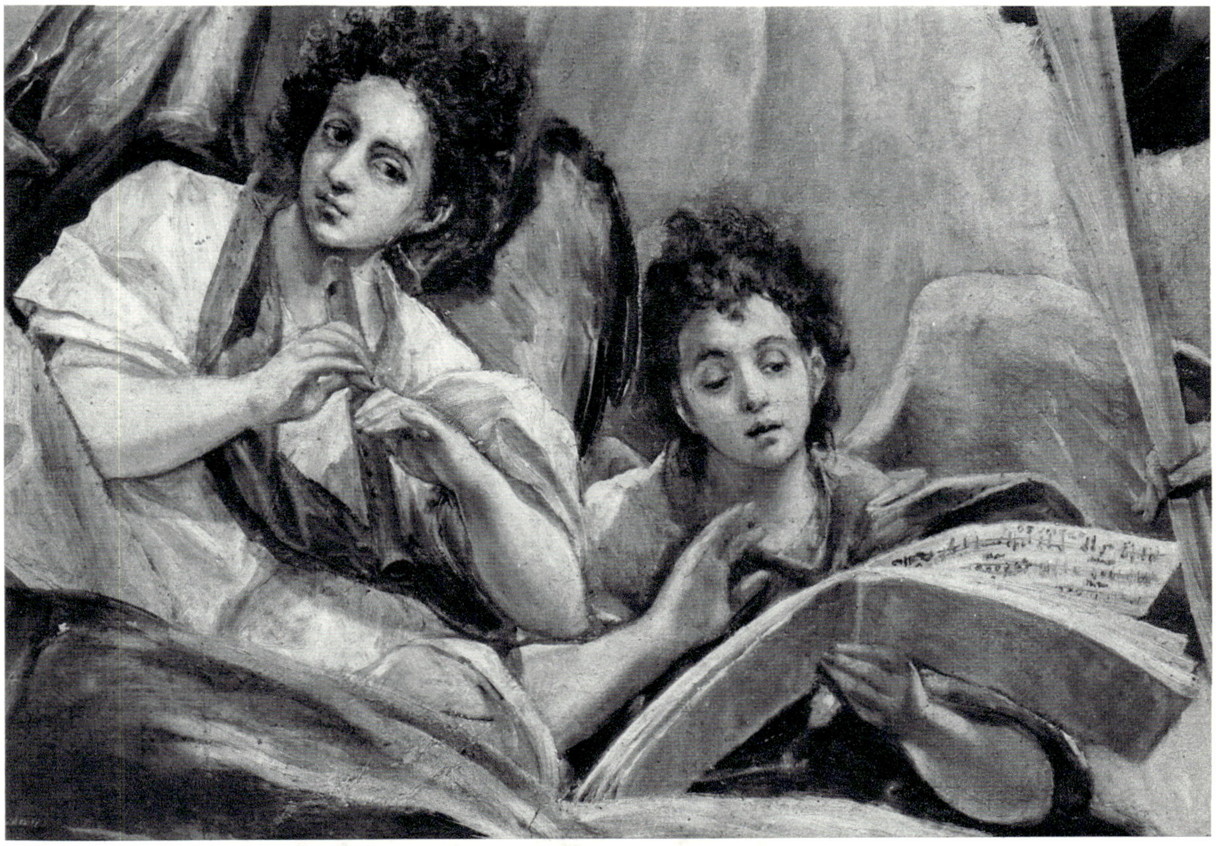

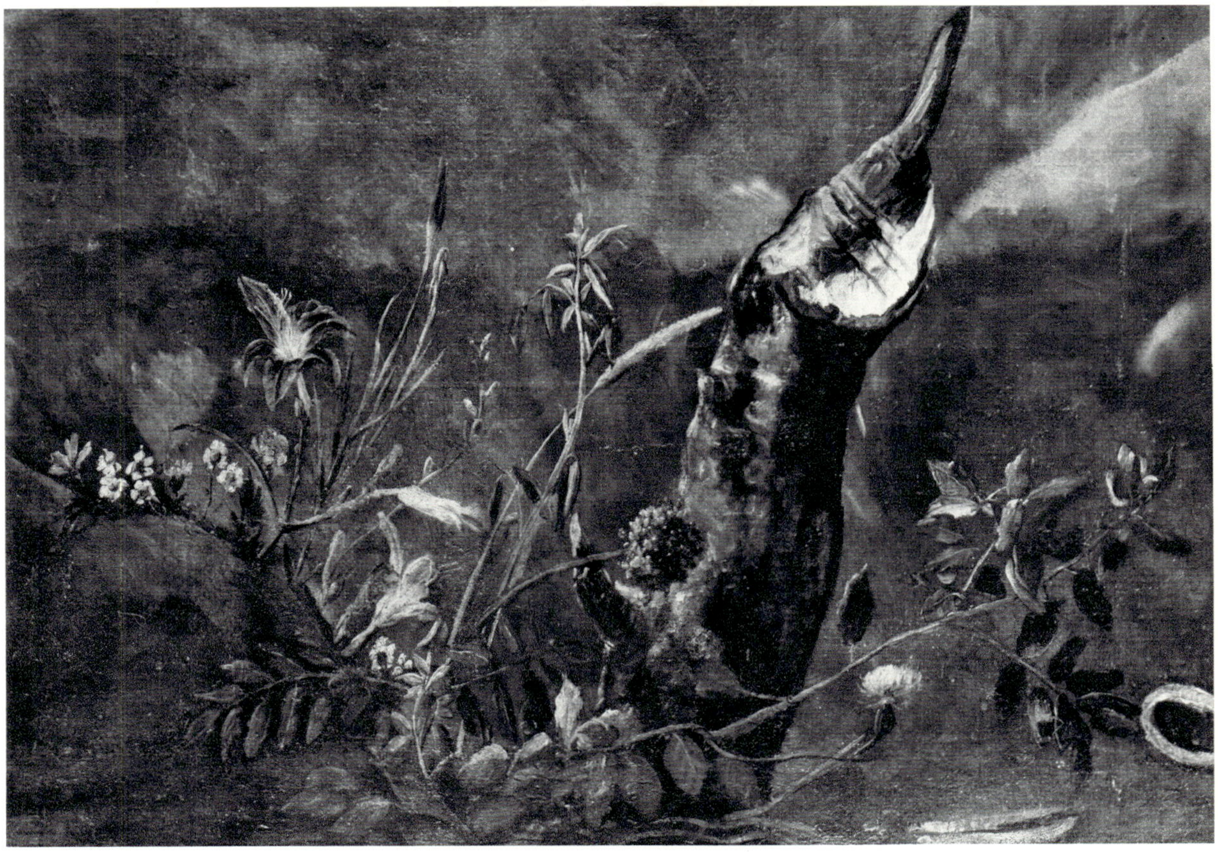

Figs. 82 & 83. Details of figure 80.

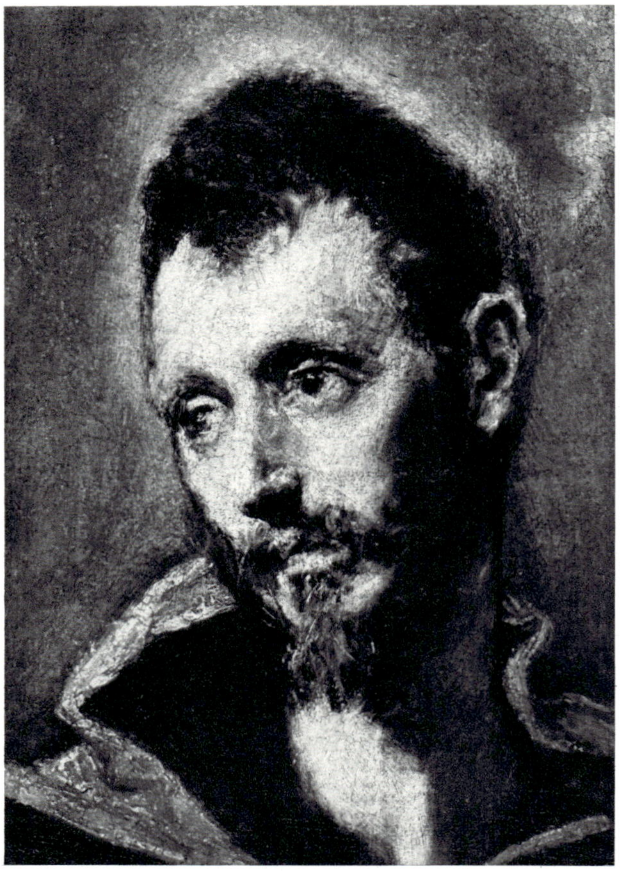

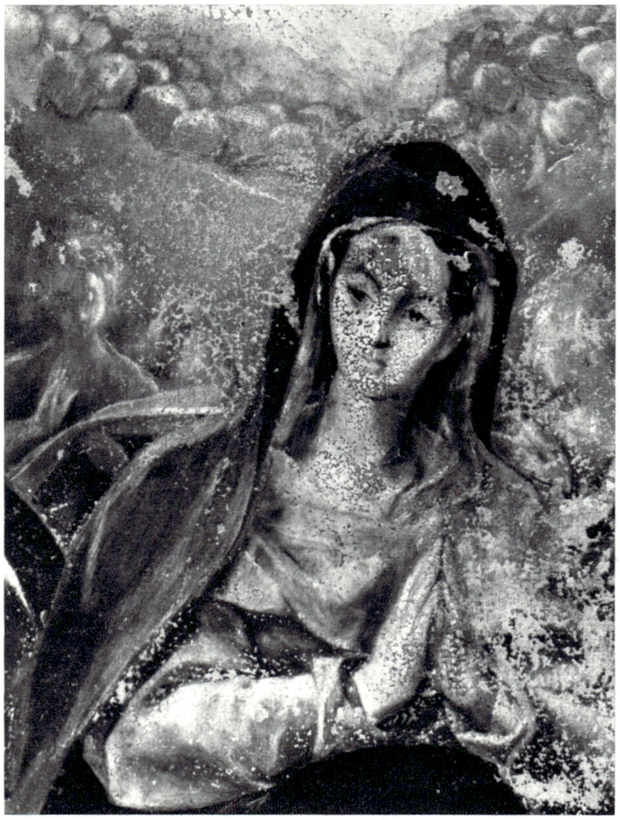

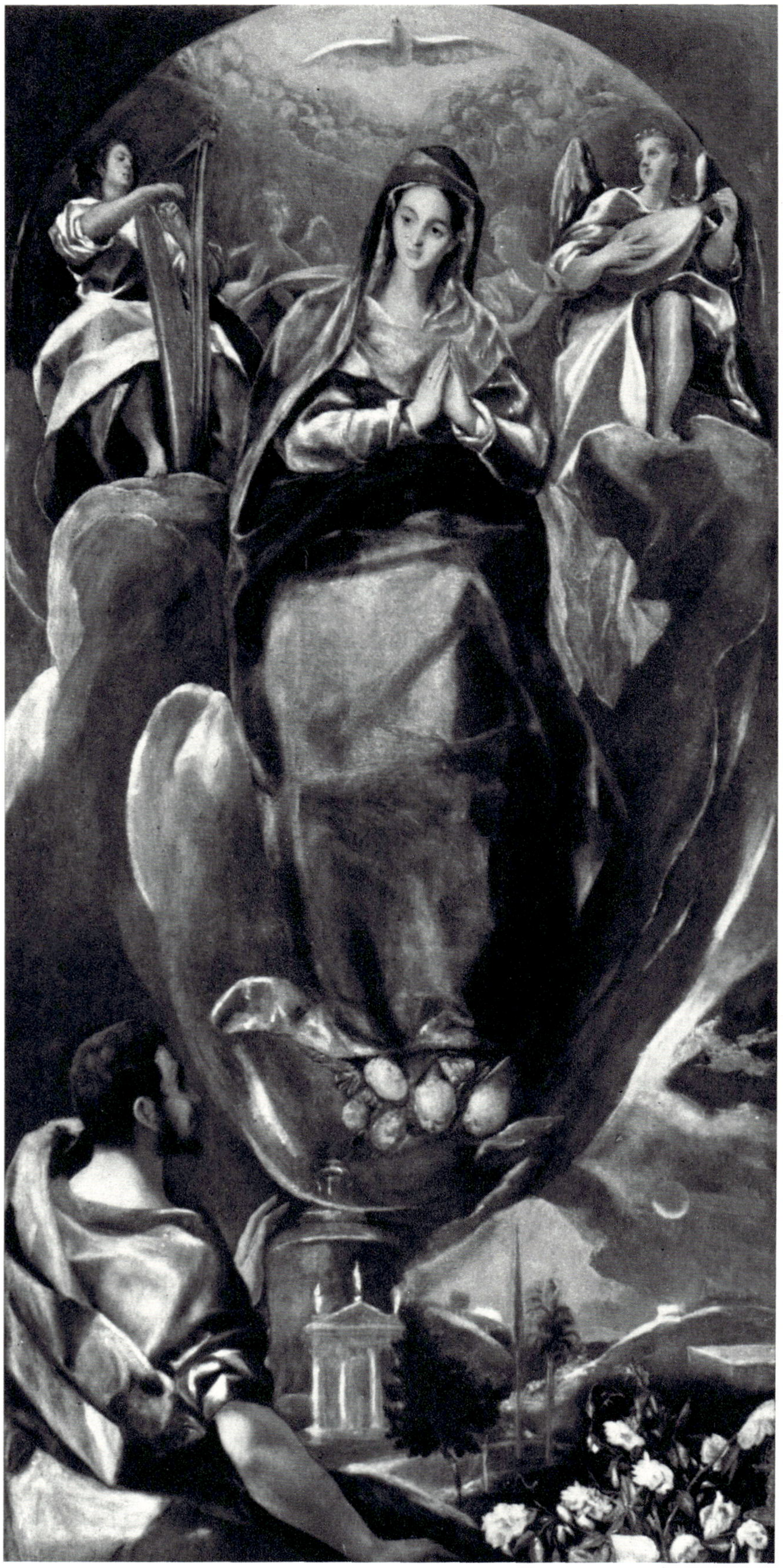

Fig. 84. Study for the head of St. Maurice, c. 1580. Montreal, W. van Horne Collection. Cat. No. 58.
Figs. 85 & 86. The Apparition of the Virgin to St. John, 1580-1586. Toledo, Santa Cruz Museum. Cat. No. 59.

In this work a new manner in El Greco's painting takes specific shape: the geometrization of the forms and softening of the modelling that had begun in the works, already studied, that represent St. Veronica and Mary Magdalen. This geometrization decides both the general scheme and the minor details and is a reaction against the more abrupt technique that characterizes the canvases of Santo Domingo el Antiguo and the *Espolio.* We can see geometrization in the figures of angels, in the clouds and in the patch of landscape with its little house that can just be seen on the horizon.

This preoccupation with geometry is very apparent, with its accentuated limitation of planes and volumes, which gives a very special air to the large figures in the foreground. In this canvas El Greco's tendency to elongate the figures becomes more noticeable, a tendency which was gradually to increase in his later development. If we compare the predominant effect of the *Espolio* with that of the *St. Maurice,* we shall see a surprising change, all the more so when we remember that there is only a year between the finishing of the first and the beginning of the second. This surely implies a deliberate intention on the painter's part, a considerable mental effort that justifies the long time it took him to complete the work intended for the Escorial. As a reaction against the exaggerated determination of line that was the result of geometrization, we now see for the first time a process that is, to some extent, the "destruction of the outline" in the larger figures. This destruction is brought about by intentional jerks of the brush and by rapid rubbing of the accumulations of colour. This rubbing, which can be quite clearly seen in the two heads in the foreground group that face the viewer, was to become one of El Greco's most characteristic features over a very long period. Another reaction against geometrization is the total realism of the flowers in the foreground at the foot of a dead tree-stump *(Fig. 83),* beside the painter's signature, which is written on a paper that a snake has picked up and is holding in its mouth.

The contrast between the plastic and chromatic concepts of the *St. Maurice* and those of the homogeneous group that includes the works for Santo Domingo el Antiguo and the *Espolio* was much stressed, as Cossío noted, by the early biographers. In an attempt to find some explanation for such a sudden change, Palomino writes: "Seeing that his works were mistaken for those of Titian, he made such extravagant efforts to change his style that he succeeded in rendering his painting contemptible and ridiculous, both in the incoherence of the drawing and in the dullness of the colour". And Madrazo tells us: "In the interval between the *Espolio* and the *St. Maurice* the artist's imagination had suffered a radical transformation, a veritable ailment of the aesthetic sense, whether as an effect of some mental hallucination or because his *amour-propre* drove him to excess in his efforts not to resemble any of the painters of his age".

The head in the Van Horne Collection in Montreal *(Fig. 84 - Cat. 58)* is an important work on account of its resemblance to that of the main figure in the *St. Maurice.* It seems likely that it was a study for the great canvas in the Escorial, perhaps his first confrontation with the subject, aimed at solving what must have been his main problem: how to give shape and life to the main character in this great chapter of the martyrology. This exquisite work was formerly the property of Antonio Vives Escudero, one of the most clear-sighted archaeologists of the turn of the century, a time when as yet El Greco's work was neither copied nor forged.

The *St. Maurice* represents a crucial moment in El Greco's life. It marks the renunciation of, or definitive failure in, the purpose which in all probability had decided him to come to Spain in the first place: that of becoming the official painter of Philip II, or at least participating in the King's great work, the Monastery of the Escorial. But as to what can have happened to him, all is pure conjecture; and even more so with regard to his reactions. The only documentary references to these years that we possess are the ones already mentioned regarding the commissioning, appraisals and payment for the *St. Maurice.*

Toledo and the palace of the Marqués de Villena

No important commission now obliged El Greco to remain in Toledo, since he was not to receive another until 1586; having worked in the city since 1577, however, he probably decided about this time to settle there for good. We do not know where he lodged, nor has his workshop been located. The ancient Spanish metropolis, possessing neither the sources of wealth that so aggrandized Seville nor the advantages enjoyed by Madrid, the new capital of the kingdom, must have been a decrepit sort of place, with its palaces and mansions abandoned by their former owners. It is difficult to imagine Toledo as a particularly monumental place, and it probably never was one. The views of the city painted by El Greco give us an image of it very similar to what it looked like only a few decades ago. In them everything seems really old, small and rather poor; a maze of narrow alleys surrounding the majestic Alcázar, the huge Cathedral, the Hospital of the Holy Cross and a few great mansions. The churches, convents and synagogues were not noticeable for their external magnificence and, though there were some other notable buildings, the beauty of Toledo was to be found above all in its secluded corners, its mysteriousness and its topographical situation, which had made it necessary to construct two truly monumental bridges. Its real wealth, in El Greco's time as much as in ours, was in the great number of works of art which withstood, perhaps better than in any other city in the world, the advances of civilization with its attendant transformations.

A document dated September 10th 1585 throws some light on El Greco's material circumstances at this time. It is the contract of a lease to the painter by Juan Antonio de Cetina of a suite of rooms in the "Houses of the Marqués de Villena", an old palace now pulled down which, according to San Román, occupied part of the modern street called the "Paseo del Tránsito", just beside what is now known as "El Greco's House", in what used to be the Jewish quarter of Toledo and near the point at which the city begins to slope down to the Tagus. The "Houses", apparently, were a cluster of buildings of some elegance, the remains of what had been one of the finest residences in the city, with elements of Mudejar architecture set among courtyards, gardens and tiny orchards. It was built towards the end of the fifteenth century by Enrique de Aragón, Marqués de Villena, who made use of parts of the mansion of Samuel Leví, treasurer to Pedro I (Pedro the Cruel) of Castile (d. 1369). Tradition had it that the palace possessed secret passages leading down to the banks of the Tagus, where the rich Jew was supposed to have hidden his treasures. From Amador de los Rios, who studied the ruins of the buildings, still visible at the end of the nineteenth century, we learn that it had been one of the finest buildings in Toledo, similar in type to the recently restored mansion of the Conde de Fuensalida.

Towards the end of the sixteenth century the "Houses" were leased by sets of rooms rather arbitrarily divided. According to the contract, El Greco took "three apartments, one of them being the great hall, with the main kitchen, and another at the entrance between the first and second courtyards, with a basement adjoining the well in the said courtyard, and also a great hall called the 'hall of the sideboards', together with a room on the way down the staircase to the cellars". For all this El Greco paid 596 *reales* a year, a much higher rent than was paid by the other tenants in the mansion, which probably means that he occupied the principal rooms. The chaotic description of his rooms shows us what a labyrinthine rabbit-warren this palace converted into apartments must have been.

During these years another character appears in El Greco's life: Francisco Preboste, a painter by trade. We know that he was an Italian, born in 1554, and he makes constant appearances in documents concerning the painter, as a servant often empowered to sign contracts. His personality as an artist and possible collaboration in the copious production of El Greco's workshop cannot be established with any certainty, but we are convinced that the material assistance of Preboste was of decisive importance. After 1607 there is no further mention of him.

Works attributed to the period between 1579 and 1586

We will now turn our attention to a group of works on religious subjects which, for various reasons, may be dated in the period between the *St. Maurice* and the *Burial of the Conde de Orgaz*. In this short space of time, unencumbered by works expressly commissioned, El Greco returned to the system he had followed in Italy: the painting of devotional pictures intended for possible clients. We know, from the inventory of the pictures the artist left to his son, that El Greco had kept some of the works executed in Italy. He probably used them as models for certain subjects and as "samples" to show to his first clients in Toledo. As a matter of fact, he organized his work just as he had done in his youth, according to the traditions of the Greek "*Madonnieri*" of Venice. Without in any way compromising the extraordinary artistic level he had attained, he gradually created an iconographical repertoire that he developed down through the years, following a course ranging from the brilliant to the hallucinatory, a course which we shall follow step by step. He must have been given confidence to work in this way by finding himself in a

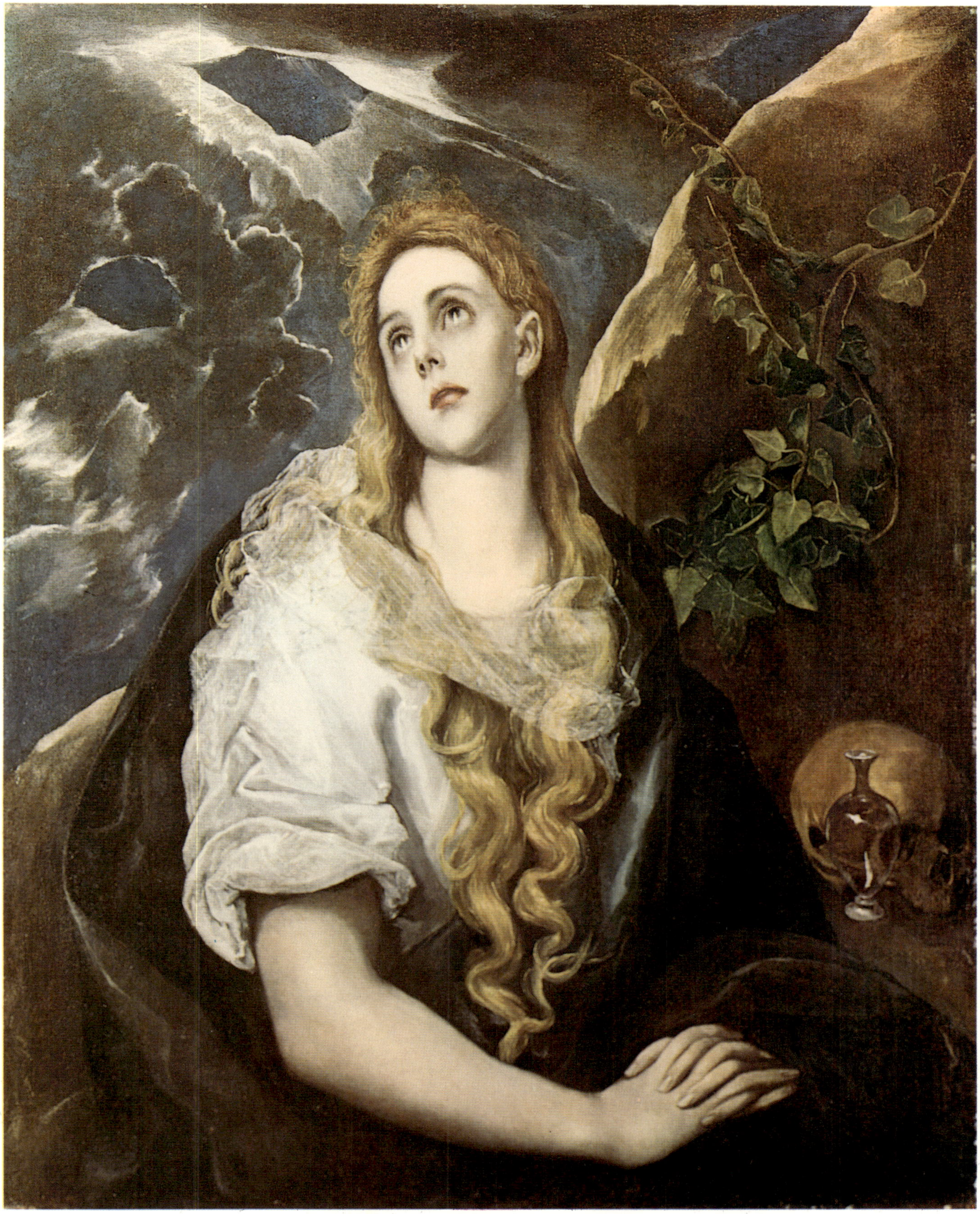

Fig. 87. The Penitent Magdalen, 1579-1586. Kansas City, W. Rockhill Nelson Gallery of Art. Cat. No. 60.

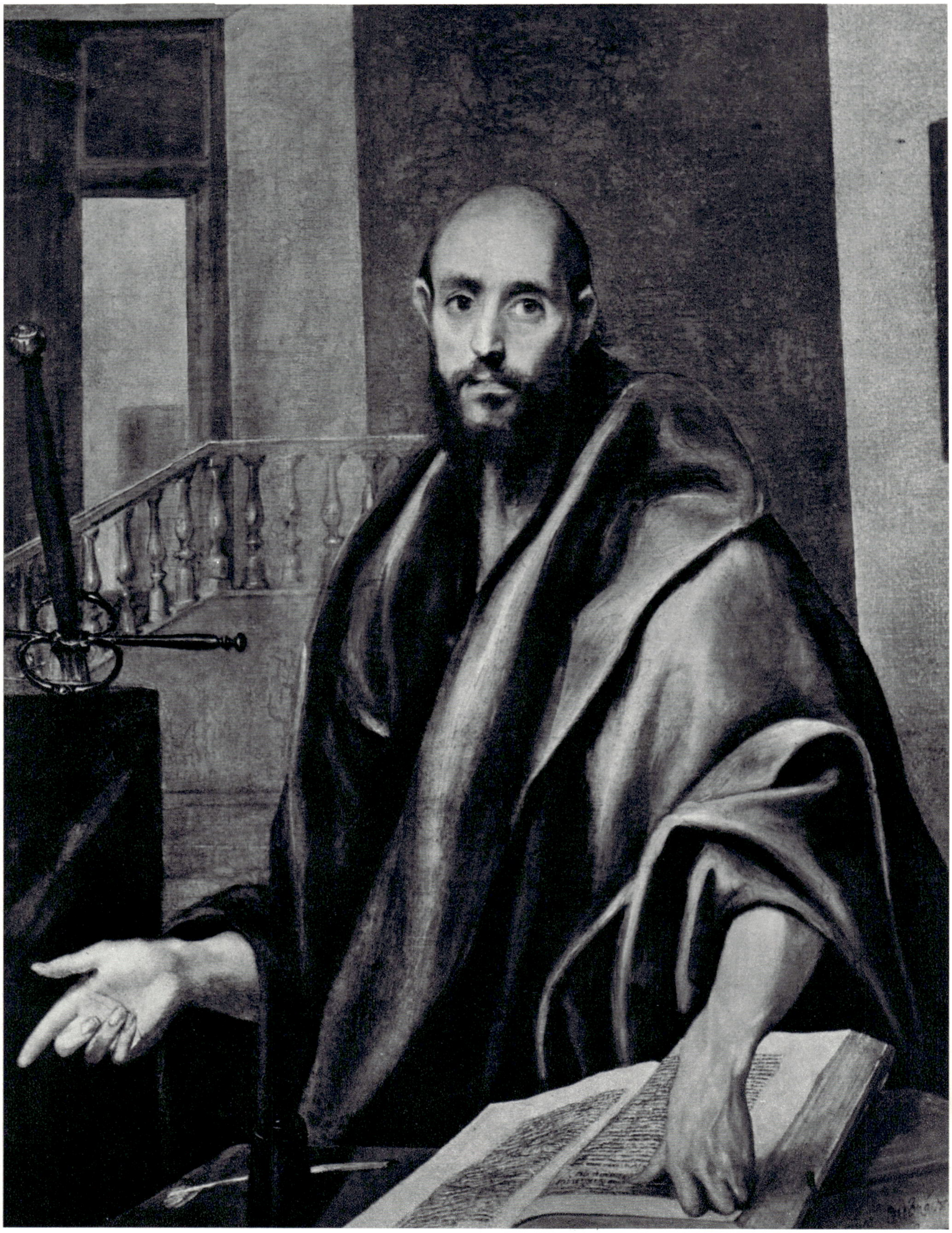

Fig. 88. St. Paul, 1579-1586. Madrid, Marquesa de Narros Collection. Cat. No. 61.

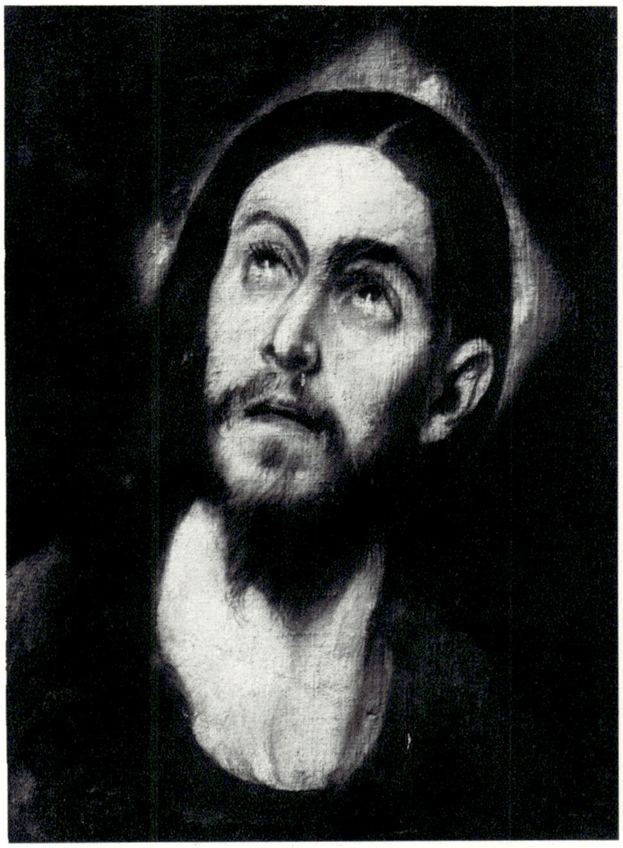

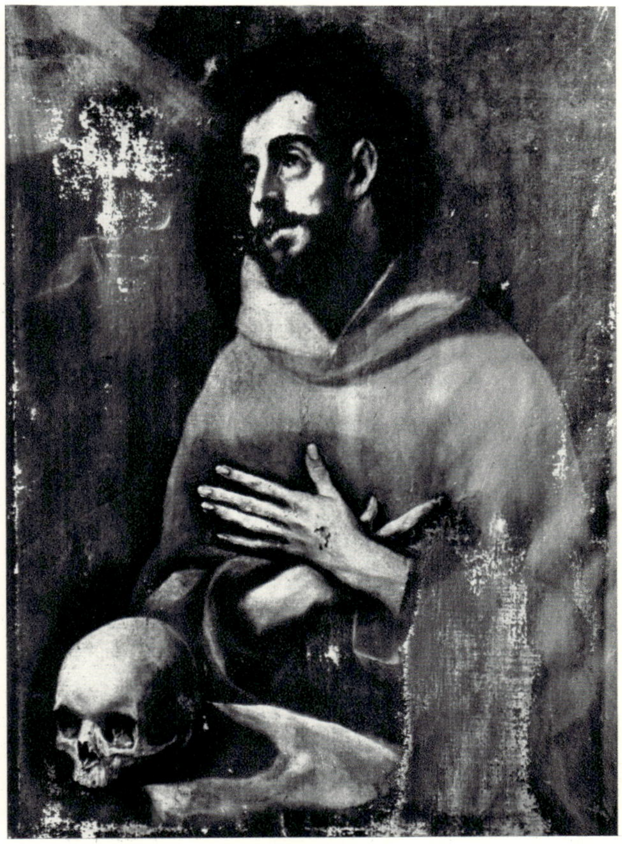

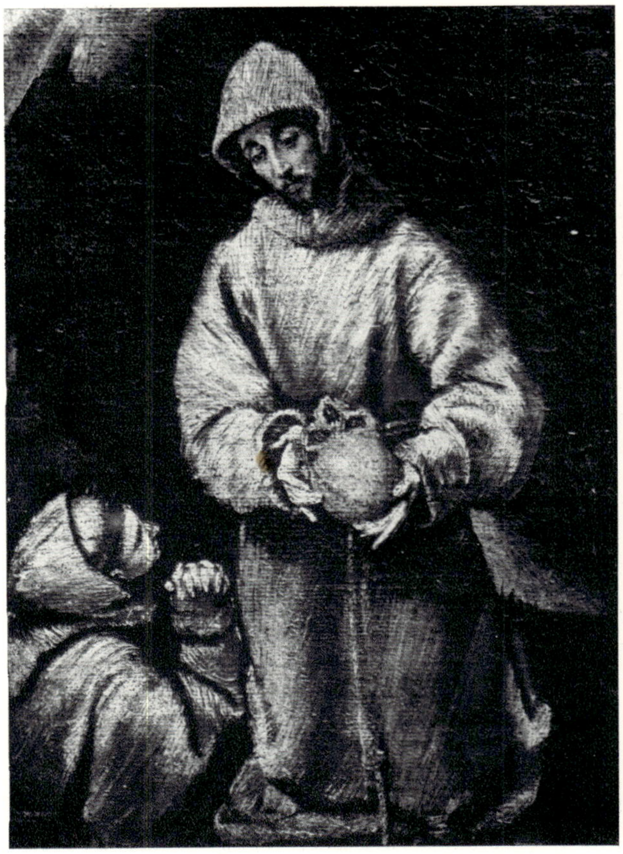

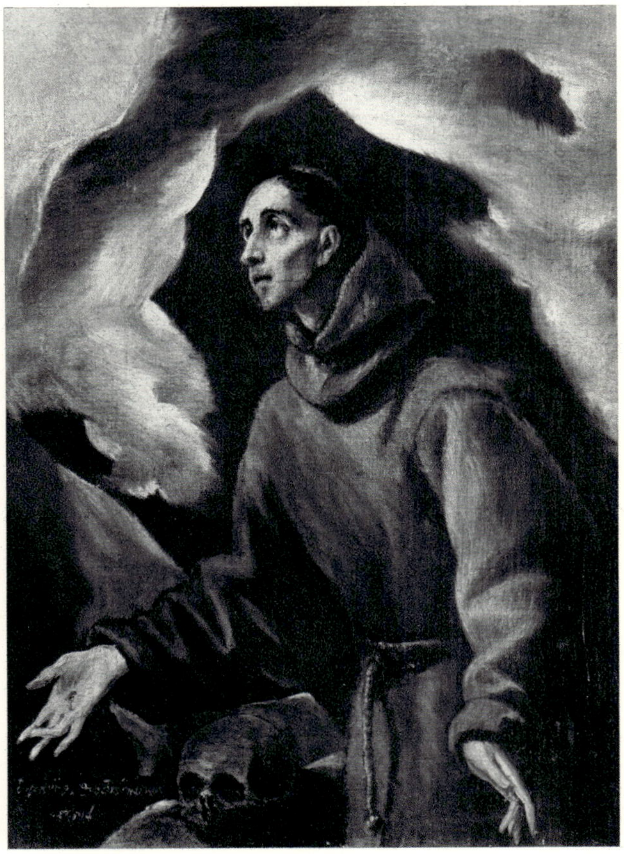

Fig. 89. Head of Christ, 1579-1586. San Antonio, McNay Art Institute. Cat. No. 62.
Fig. 90. St. Francis in ecstasy, 1579-1586. Present whereabouts unknown. Cat. No. 63.
Fig. 91. St. Francis and the lay brother, 1579-1586. Present whereabouts unknown. Cat. No. 64.
Fig. 92. St. Francis receiving the stigmata, 1579-1586. Present whereabouts unknown. Cat. No. 66.

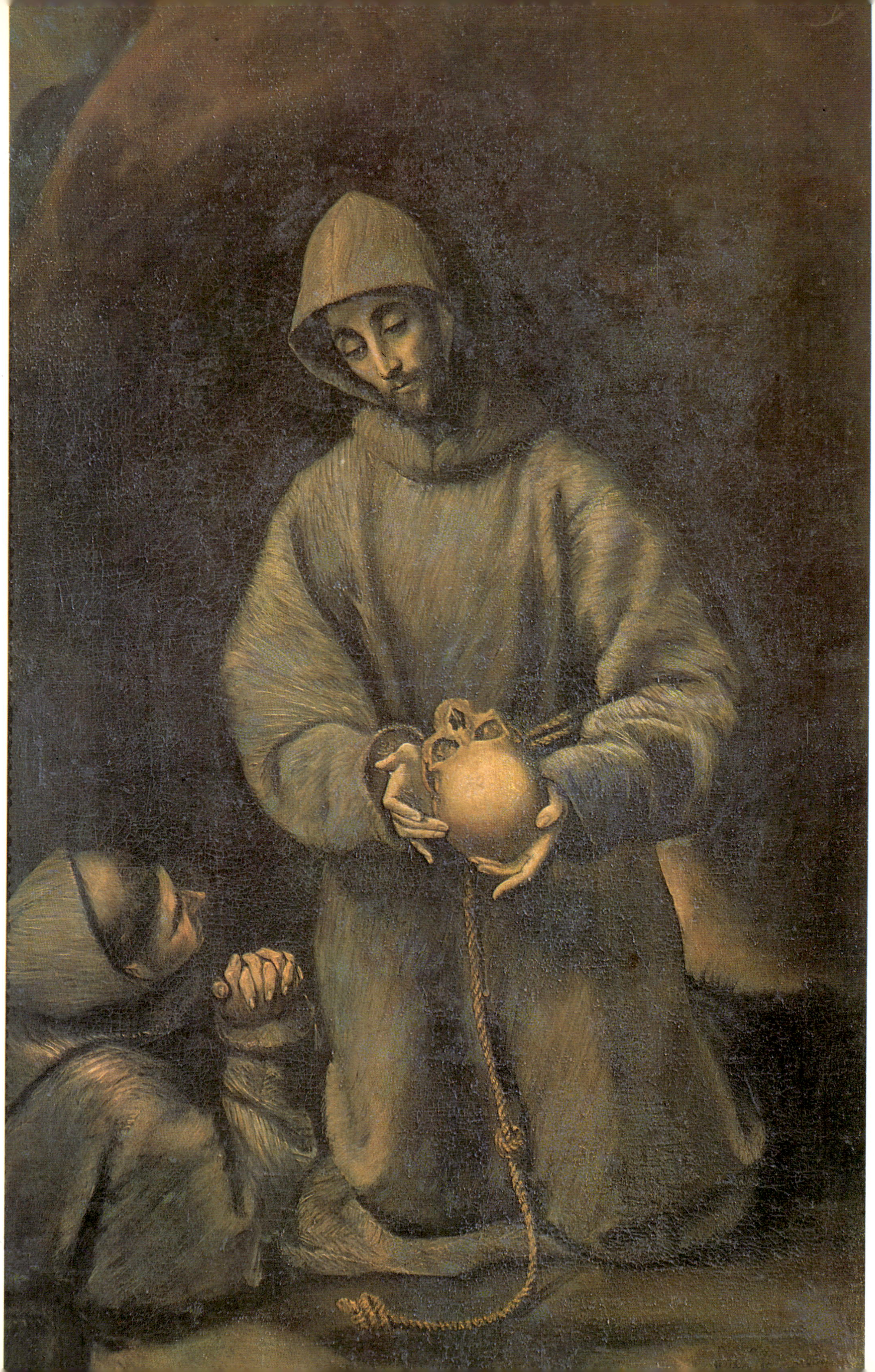

country which, unlike the sensuous Italy of the Renaissance, had not yet opened its doors to mythological themes or to nudes, a country in which medieval traditions still prevailed, though transformed in art by the technical advances of the sixteenth century. He knew that he could count on a clientele for a profoundly religious art, for which his particular gifts suited him perfectly.

The most important work we can attribute to this period is the *Apparition of the Virgin to St. John* which originally hung in the church of San Román in Toledo *(Figs. 85 & 86 - Cat. 59)*. This canvas has come down to us in a lamentable state of preservation, but though excessive restoration has appreciably altered its overall aspect the work is still a very notable one. Its concept and technique are very close to those of the *St. Maurice.* The Virgin is the essential factor in the composition, and to heighten this effect El Greco followed his new tendency of using elongated proportions, which improves rather than disturbs the image. The figure is presented on a sort of throne of opaque clouds, in imitation of the Byzantine ovals. The head is flanked by two angel musicians treated with idealized naturalism, together with others that melt into the clouds, like the cherubim surrounding the Holy Ghost. This vision of St. John, who is shown, half-length, in the foreground, takes place in an idyllic landscape with extraordinarily beautiful chromatic effects: the sun and the moon, a temple, a fountain and a masterly bouquet of roses in the foreground are all allusions to the Virgin Mary.

The *Penitent Magdalen* in the Kansas Museum *(Fig. 87 - Cat. 60)*, which is very similar to the canvas with the same subject from Valladolid that we have already studied *(Fig. 46)*, seems to have been painted in the period we are now considering. In this new version the painter takes the work from a closer point of view. He changes the position of the ivy tendrils, the skull and the little glass jar, but not that of the saint herself, maintaining the rhythm that goes from her brow to the clasped hands on her lap. The moulding of the form seems softer and slightly more sensuous, an effect which is heightened by the long tresses of hair, which are wavier and fairer in this version. Nor is the pictorial formula the result of such intense geometrization as in the *St. Maurice.* After the latter painting, in fact, El Greco partially returned to a more blended and spontaneous modelling. If there is still any geometrization, it is hidden under the "skin" of the pictorial finish and is mainly in connection with the structure of the drawing.

The *St. Paul* in the collection of the Marquesa de Narros *(Fig. 88 - Cat. 61)* achieves almost the same clarity of form as the *St. Maurice,* but its colouring is grave and muted. The saint, who is shown standing in a room, is gesturing eloquently, with one of those gestures to which the painter resorted in his attempts to escape from the limitations of painting— an essentially mute art —and make his work speak. Besides a two-handed sword, which is the saint's attribute, we can see a pen and an inkpot, an evident reference to the extraordinary activity of the author of the Epistles. At the back of the room we see a staircase and an opening in the wall. The interplay of spaces determined by the architecture is very skilful, its neutral tones being used as a foil to the admirable figure of the saint, the typology of which is undoubtedly that of a portrait. It is neither an impersonal face nor an idealization of a vision of the painter (or of the transformation of a model); rather would one say that St. Paul himself is posing for El Greco. This face looks out at the viewer directly, with a look that expresses interest rather than passion but which also tells us something about the saint's energy. The flowing cloak of thick but supple cloth, with its strange curves, has a quality of almost abstract form, of the kind that can sometimes be seen in Gothic draperies. We shall see later on how El Greco gradually endowed such materials with ever greater interest, as a means of creating coloured forms which would possess sufficient aesthetic power but which, needless to say, are always confined in his art to the strict function of serving the figures to which they belong, just as the figures in turn give us the sensation that they are never placed in his pictures for no reason at all, but as an act of service to man.

Another work in the group we are now considering is a *Head of Christ* painted as a picture for family devotion *(Fig. 89 - Cat. 62),* which is a simplified version of the head of Christ in the *Espolio.* We should observe the similarity of modelling, expression and character —despite the obvious differences inherent in the subject matter— between this picture and the second version of St. Mary Magdalen which we have just studied.

It is our belief that three pictures of St. Francis of Assisi may also be assigned to this period. The first, which was formerly in the parish church of Santa Olalla, in the province of Toledo *(Fig. 90 - Cat. 63),*

93. St. Francis and the lay brother, 1579-1586.
forte de Lemos, Piarist Fathers. Cat. No. 65.

is a geometrized copy of a similar canvas already studied *(Fig. 48)*. The composition and feeling are the same; all that is changed is the technique, for in this second version ample use is made of the process of dispersing the pictorial material by rubbing. It also strives after technical effect in another way: the accentuated darkening of certain parts of the background, which gives an outline of pure black to elements that already stand out quite boldly on their own account. This outlining in black was gradually to become a formula El Greco used profusely in the treatment of later works.

Of the second representaion of St. Francis there is what we believe to have been the sketch, once in the Pidal Collection in Madrid *(Fig. 91 - Cat. 64)*, as well as a finished version on a larger scale, which is in Monforte de Lemos, in the province of Lugo *(Fig. 93 - Cat. 65)*. These are two masterly works, between which hardly any difference can be seen. In the final version the spatial effect is perhaps broader and more intense, and there is a narrow empty area in the foreground. Both works represent St. Francis full-face and kneeling, with a skull in his hands and with Brother Leo praying at his feet on the left. We believe that these two paintings were the prototypes for the largest series of paintings of St. Francis produced by El Greco. Counting replicas by the painter's own hand, paintings from his workshop and contemporary copies, this representation is repeated in over fifty canvases. The *St. Francis* in Monforte, like the *St. Lawrence* previously studied *(Fig. 52)*, was bequeathed by Don Rodrigo de Castro, Archbishop of Seville, in the year 1600. Between this new representation and the one in Santa Olalla there is a considerable change of concept from the iconographical viewpoint. The Santa Olalla painting represents the saint more directly; we might almost say that the painter is seeking an immediate relationship with his subject, whom he treats in the spirit of a portrait. In the Monforte painting and the sketch for it, however, the representation is rather more what we expect from a devotional picture. There is a greater sense of spiritual distance, the distance that separates the common run of mortals from this man whose love of God was so great that it caused the wounds of Christ to appear on his body. The difference between the sketch and the painting in Monforte de Lemos is in the effects of the relationship between form and execution, which inevitably derive from the format. In the sketch the brushwork is quite large and noticeable in proportion to the figures and there is no lack of the rubbing effects that give the habit a worn texture. In the larger work this texture, though still present, is much less intense. The modelling of the flesh tints, moreover, is softer and more blended, while the tonal contrasts, though perhaps less abrupt, seem greater. The contrast between the qualities represented is greater than in the sketch, for in the latter the quality of the actual paint itself is more important. This difference in effects between sketches or small pictures and medium to large paintings should always be borne in mind. The drawing, too, not as mere substructure but rather as a clear definition of the form, is more perceptible in larger, definitive works. This will be clearly seen in the present case if we compare, for instance, the treatments of the area of the hands holding the skull which is the object of the saint's meditation.

The *St. Francis receiving the stigmata* in the collection of the Marqués de Pidal in Madrid *(Fig. 94 - Cat. 67)* seems to be the prototype for another extensive series. The saint is represented rather more than half-length and in three-quarter profile to the left, bending slightly forward in an attitude of offering. An admirably painted misty sky forms the background and in the upper left there is a small crucifix from which rays of light emanate, marking the course followed by the wounds of Christ which are to appear on the saint's body. The modelling of the latter's figure is soft enough, but we still find the simplification and geometrization that derive from the *St. Maurice*. Since it was a simple model, and one that could be quickly carried out, it was well suited to the new principles adopted by El Greco in setting up professionally in Spain. As we shall see, it was not long before he was required to execute replicas and variations of the same model, which shows how right his instinct was in his choice of subjects and in his way of depicting them. The fact of having different versions of the same saint readily available, as it were, obviously enabled him to give greater satisfaction to his potential clientele, though it would be quite wrong to consider El Greco's new course as having been wholly dictated by commercial motives; just as wrong, in fact, as imagining that he could wholly ignore such realistic motivations in his position as a foreigner very recently established in Spain, without either personal fortune or any kind of official backing. Part of El Greco's greatness, in fact, as has been the case with some other artists in his

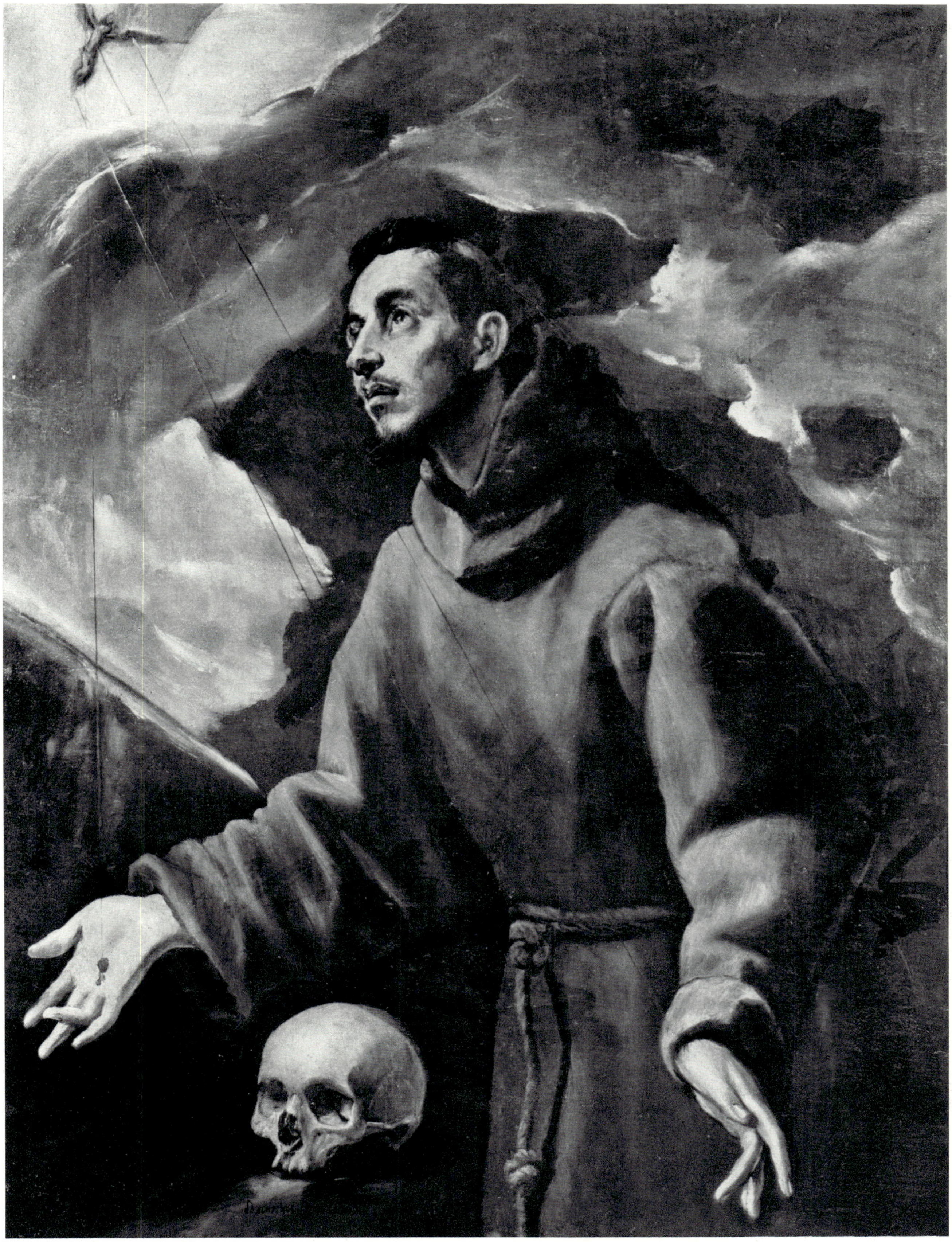

Fig. 94. St. Francis receiving the stigmata, 1579-1586. Madrid, Marqués de Pidal Collection. Cat. No. 67.

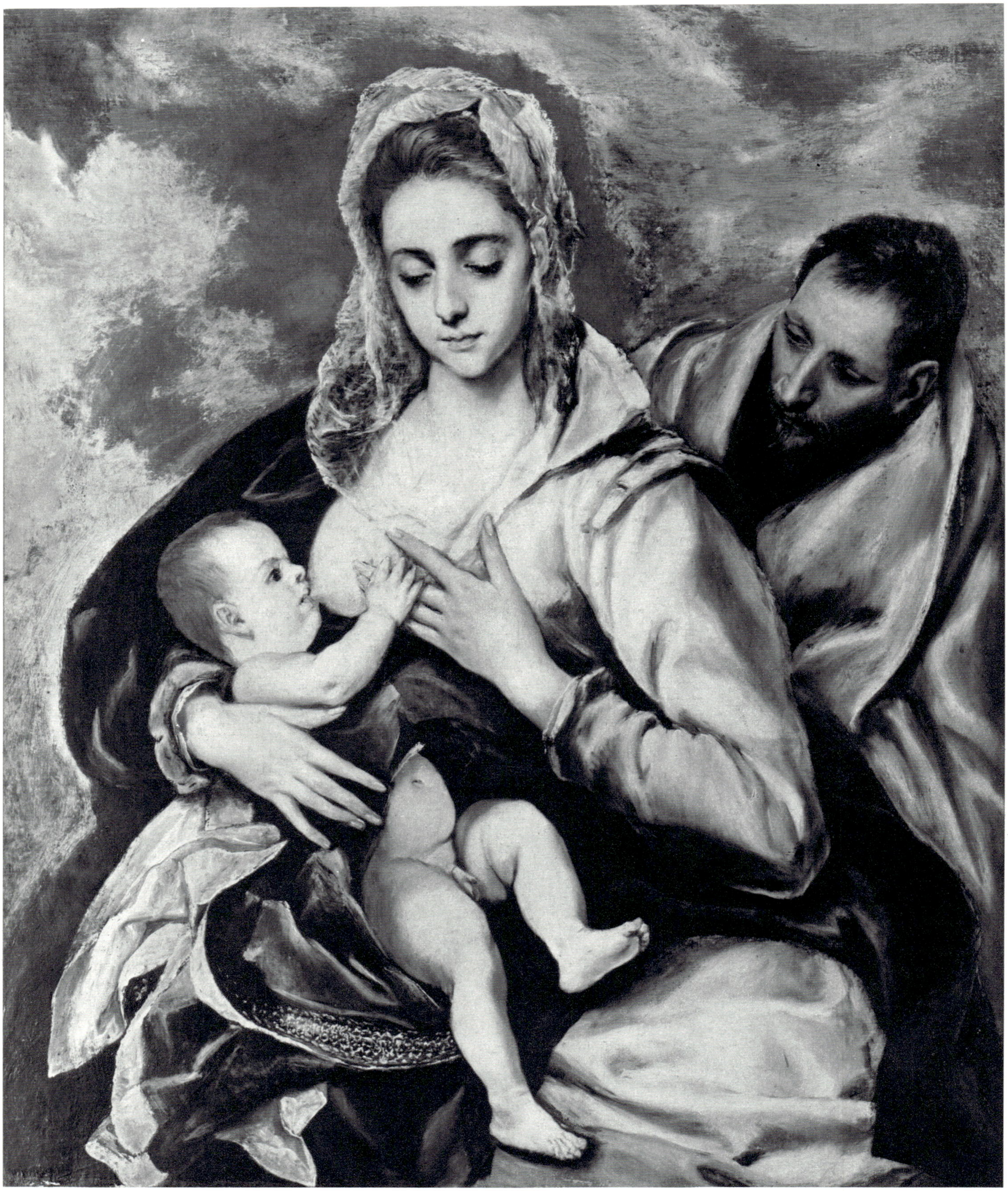

Fig. 95. The Holy Family, 1579-1586. New York, Hispanic Society. Cat. No. 69.

situation, was his ability to reconcile the demands of everyday life and the maintenance of his family with his inner vocation and the inclination that led him to express mystic sentiments through the medium of painted images. It is quite possible that the smaller canvas *(Fig. 92 - 66)* was a sketch for the preceding picture.

During this same period he painted the first known version of another religious subject: the *Holy Family* owned by the Hispanic Society *(Fig. 95 - Cat. 69).* The execution of this picture takes us one step nearer to that of the *Burial of the Conde de Orgaz,* painted in 1586, which it must have preceded by a very short space of time. The Virgin here is extremely beautiful. The reader may well seek, as have all the historians, resemblances between this very human nursing Virgin and the supposed portrait of Jerónima de las Cuevas; both figures certainly belong to the same type of deep, serene beauty, one that is modest under all its grace and splendour. The chromatic range of this painting is one of the artist's great successes within his tendency to clarity and simplification. It moves away from the coldness of the *St. Maurice,* but without becoming absolutely warm in feeling, and maintains a balance that seems to have been struck quite naturally and without the slightest effort. We should not forget the background of blue sky and clouds when we are considering the chromatic harmonies, for this background plays a most important role in the unification, not only of the colours but also of the tones and even of the formal rhythms.

With the *St. Peter in tears* in the Bowes Museum *(Fig. 96 - Cat. 70)* we find ourselves at some remove from the direct, portrait-like treatment of the *St. Paul* already studied. This picture may be the first in the series of images of the first apostle that El Greco painted throughout his career. In position, angle of vision and even setting, it calls to mind the *Penitent Magdalen* in the two versions studied above. We can even see the rock and the ivy, though in a rather more diffuse pictorial conception. Following the Mannerist technique of arranging small figures to contrast with larger ones —in perspective— El Greco includes here, in the left background, one of the three Marys walking away from the Saviour's tomb which is guarded by an angel. We might say that these images of pure mist, so closely bound up with the evanescent landscape, are the connecting link between the phosphorescent angels in the *Apparition of the Virgin to St. John* that we have studied above and the multitude that goes to make up the *Burial of the Conde de Orgaz.* But we should observe once more how El Greco tended to renew his images using what he had done before as a starting-point, though always adding new elements. Though the way of depicting the face, the eyes and the joined hands and arms in this picture is very similar to that used in the two versions of *Mary Magdalen* —with the obvious exceptions deriving from such a marked difference between the two characters, however similar the mystical feeling— the background of sky and clouds is treated in a new way: blending it into the scene of little figures to be seen on the left. The supernatural light emanating from this area combines perfectly with the agitated movement of the cloud effects and provides a background at once lyrical and dramatic. In the treatment of the thick stuff of the robe, however, this St. Peter is to some extent similar to the *St. Paul* in the collection of the Marquesa de Narros *(Fig. 88),* though here the form encloses the body more tightly, modelling it instead of establishing upon it a system of forms that would be valid in themselves. Another successful feature of this picture is the contrast between the tones. It is remarkable how the painter makes the dark robe stand out against the clear tones of the background, and the clear flesh tints against the dark colour of the sky. The ivy is used as the attribute of a life of penitence, but the skull in the picture of Mary Magdalen (an allegory of death) has been replaced by the empty tomb (evidence of the Resurrection of the Lord, whom St. Peter had denied). The emotional quality of this picture comes from our almost unconscious perception of all these elements, but above all from the fact that the saint's face tells us everything by itself. It is curious to observe, from the typological —or, rather, psychological— point of view, that Mary Magdalen's expression is more serene and trustful than that of the apostle, which we might almost describe as anguished. El Greco knew how to show all this with precision and eloquence. Although our analyses may pay more attention to execution and plastic values than to iconography with all its implications (including the one we have already mentioned), we cannot doubt that in a truly great painter all these qualities are found together. This is especially true in the case of an artist who was very far from subscribing to the concept of "art for art's sake" —who was, on the contrary, a fervent adherent of the ideal of service in the cause of a divided religion and a shaken faith.

Portraits

Let us now turn our attention to four male portraits which, to judge by their technique, complete the work done during the period we are now studying. In formal concept they are related to the praying figures of the *Crucifixion* in the Louvre, and to the *Knight taking an oath* especially, marking the transition from these two works to the great concentration of human figures that forms the frieze of the lower part of the *Burial of the Conde de Orgaz*. The subjects of these portraits are: *Rodrigo de la Fuente,* a Toledan doctor who died in 1589 *(Fig. 100 - Cat. 74)*; an anonymous *Gentleman of the house of Leiva*, whose portrait comes from the Cathedral of Valladolid *(Fig. 97 - Cat. 71)*; *St. Aloysius Gonzaga*, whose portrait this is supposed to be and very probably is *(Fig. 98 - Cat. 72)*, painted before the young man had yet attained the glory due to his spiritual merit, for we know that Aloysius Gonzaga was in Toledo in 1583 as page to Philip II's son, Prince Diego; and, finally, the impressive *Head of an old man* in the Metropolitan Museum, which for so many years was considered to be a self-portrait of El Greco *(Fig. 99 - Cat. 73)*. Considered together, these are paintings done in a minor key, modelled by chiaroscuro as in a grisaille and using effects which have tempted all the great colourists in history, most probably with the intention of resting and renewing their vision of colour. It would be rash to indulge in suppositions regarding the spirit of these portraits, the identification of which is clouded by the shadow of doubt. Sixteenth-century Spain, however, had a character of its own, a character it owed to the men of the age, and thus the factor of "collective psychology" cannot be denied. In the *Burial of the Conde de Orgaz* we shall see that, despite the differences of expression, attitude, age and feeling to be found among the gentlemen present at the burial of the Conde, there is a great character of unity. This unity is already to be seen in these four portraits conceived independently.

The *Gentleman of the house of Leiva* is a young man of about thirty or thirty-five, dressed in black, which provides a beautiful contrast with the white lace cuffs and ruff of his suit. Typologically it is admirable to see how, in these sixteenth-century fashions, the suits and the restrained adornments harmonize with the faces. Before the later periods in which sumptuous clothes were fashioned in the brightest of colours, these Renaissance gentlemen dressed for ceremonial occasions in a silky or velvety black which was an incomparable foil for the fineness of their flesh tints and their aristocratic features. The technique used is a comparatively complex one, a different treatment being employed for each type of texture. The way in which the lace is painted is really beautiful, the white paint being crushed, as it were, against the canvas and thus made to open out; El Greco was to use the same technique in the figures of the gentlemen at the *Burial*. We should also observe, however, the rich interplay of transparencies in the black suit, the reflections of the light and the density of the wholly dark areas. The flesh tints, by way of contrast, are treated with an extremely soft, blended modelling which is really very draughtsmanlike.

The supposed portrait of St. Aloysius, who is seen from closer at hand, before an open book and with his right hand raised, is reminiscent, in the strong painting of the face, of some of the portraits of El Greco's Roman period. The boy seems imbued with intense will-power and resolution, and under his apparent lack of expression one would say that he was consumed by an inner fire. The black of the suit in this portrait is absolutely solid, with slight superimpositions of light grey to indicate the lines of projection and light.

We also have the picture which was formerly considered to be El Greco's self-portrait. It is rather similar to the *St. Paul* we have mentioned above, the difference being that it represents a man who is at least twenty years older. The big nose, which even from the front can be seen to be rather hooked, and the half-inquisitive, half-evasive expression of the eyes seem to imply that the character is probably of Jewish origin. That it is not a self-portrait of El Greco may be deduced from the date attributed to the work (when the painter would have been about forty, while the man in this picture seems to be over sixty). It is one of the most carefully worked portraits in the group we are now dealing with. The fur of the collar provides the painter with a further contrast of textures, but he still concentrates the interest on the head. Particularly worthy of notice are the way of painting the temples (with slight brushstrokes of white on darker tones), the subtle shading of the forehead, the mobility of the eyes and the slight asymmetry of the whole face.

In the portrait of Dr. Rodrigo de la Fuente we see, as well as the qualities already mentioned, the

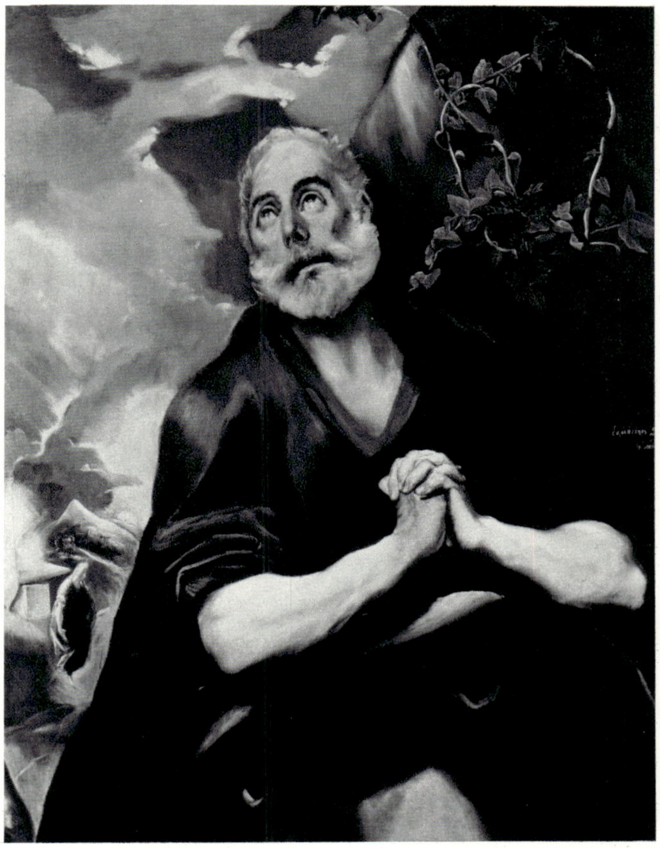

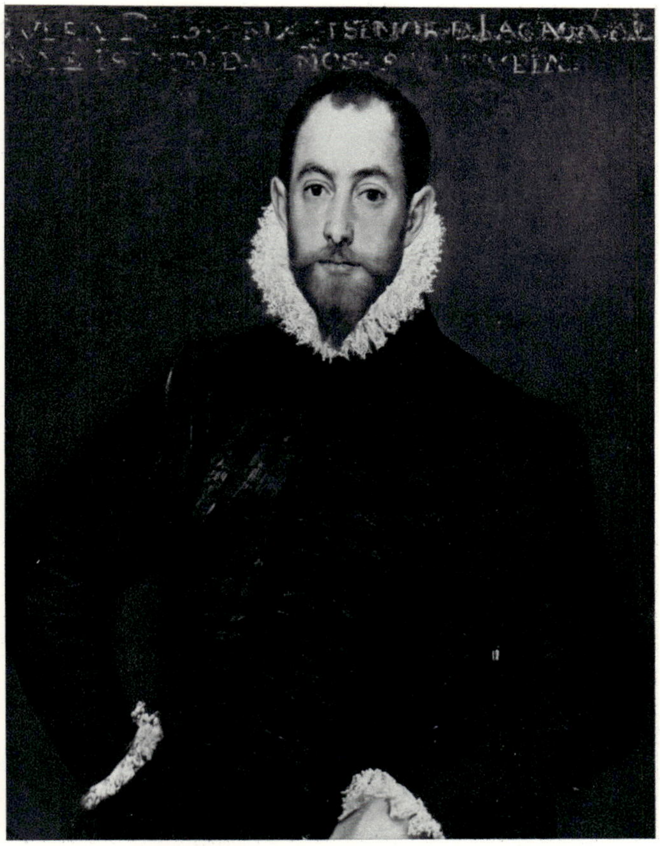

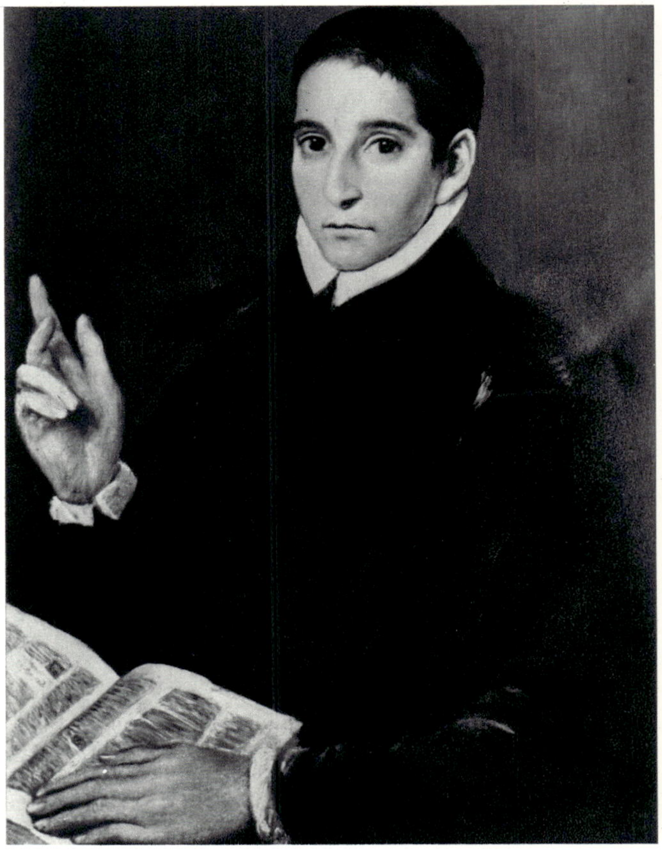

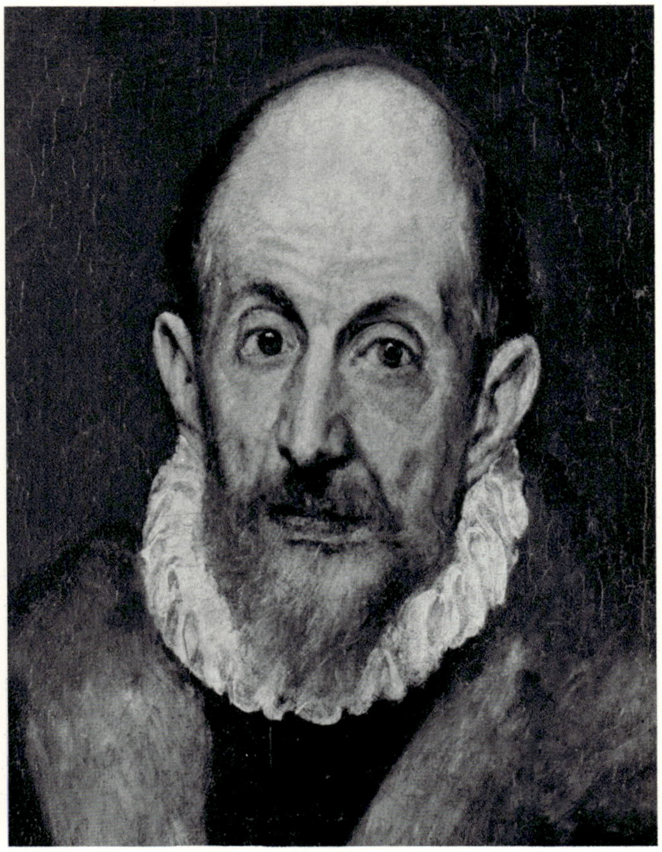

Fig. 96. St. Peter in tears, 1579-1586. Barnard Castle, Bowes Museum. Cat. No. 70.
Fig. 97. A Gentleman of the house of Leiva, 1579-1586. Montreal, Museum of Fine Arts. Cat. No. 71.
Fig. 98. St. Aloysius Gonzaga (?), 1579-1586. Santa Barbara, Converse Collection. Cat. No. 72.
Fig. 99. Head of an old man, 1579-1586. New York, Metropolitan Museum. Cat. No. 73.

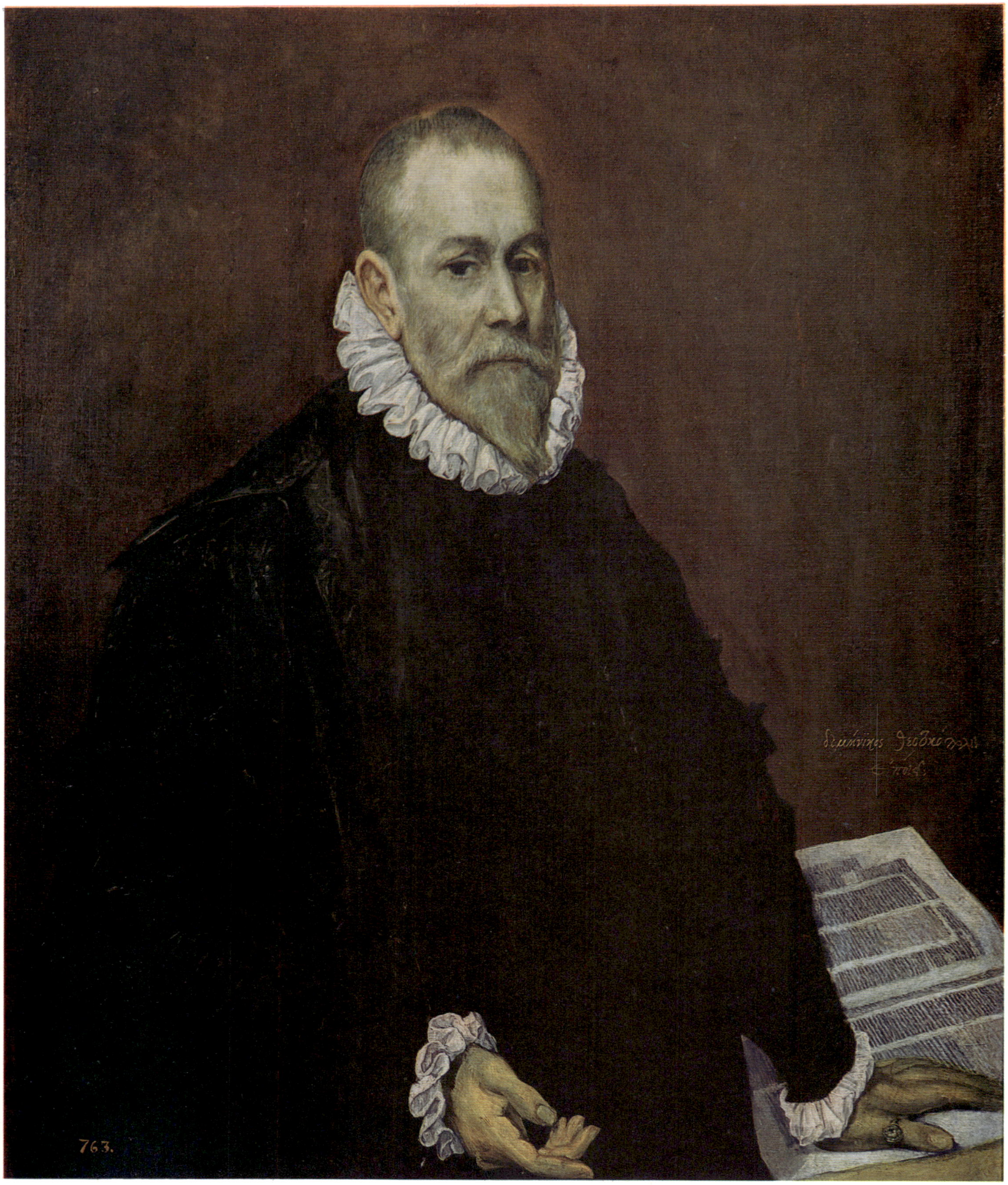

Fig. 100. Rodrigo de la Fuente, 1579-1586. Madrid, Prado. Cat. No. 74.

painter's desire to represent the character proper to a man of science. As in the *St. Paul* and the supposed portrait of St. Aloysius, we also find here an open book on which the subject rests his hand, but this fact enables us to perceive differences rather than analogies among the three works. This gesture, in the *St. Paul,* speaks of the transcendental importance of the book in question, in which the saint's hand seems to be indicating some particular passage. In the *St. Aloysius* the relationship is more indifferent, though the sense of invocation of the text is not lost. In the portrait of Dr. de la Fuente, however, the subject rests his hand rather more authoritatively on the book, as if to say that in him we could find as much science as in any text book or even more. On the other hand, it is a portrait of undeniable power, though at the same time full of humanity within its sense of austerity and severity. The ruff, for all its arbitrariness, can do nothing to modify this effect, which derives from the very solidity of the subject and from the face, which is expressive without any attempt to be so, but which has evidently been moulded by years of study and experience. Admirable, too, is the drawing of the right hand, which advances into the foreground right on the central axis of the painting, under the figure's grey beard. The clothing is treated in a rather diffuse way, without blending into the dark green background; we can see that its mission is to support the noble bearing of the intense, dignified head.

The "Burial of the Conde de Orgaz"

This third chapter in the life of El Greco comes to a close with his most famous work, the *Burial of the Conde de Orgaz,* which still hangs in its original place in the church of Santo Tomé in Toledo *(Fig. 101 - Cat. 75).* Let us first consider the history of this painting. Don Gonzalo Ruiz de Toledo, Chancellor of Castile, tutor to the Infanta Beatriz and lord of the town of Orgaz, caused the church of Santo Tomé to be rebuilt at his expense. On his death in 1323 he was buried in one of its chapels. The funerary inscription, carved on the stone in Latin and Castilian, tells us of the miracle of his burial: "When the priests were preparing to bury him, to the wonderment of everybody St. Stephen and St. Augustine came down from Heaven and placed his body here with their own hands!". The apparition of the two saints was considered a sign of their gratitude to the charitable gentleman for having obtained a lodging for the monks of the Order of St. Augustine and a new church dedicated to St. Stephen. The inscription goes on to say: "in his will he left to the parish priest and minister of this church, as also to the poor of the parish, 2 sheep, 16 chickens, 2 full wineskins, 2 wagonloads of firewood and 800 of the coins we call *maravedis,* which they were to receive annually from the townsfolk of Orgaz". With the passing of time, however, it would seem that the authorities of the town of Orgaz, which is in the province of Toledo, refused to make their annual contribution to the parish of Santo Tomé. So the parish priest, Andrés Núñez de Madrid, sued them and won his case in 1570, and it was to commemorate this that Archbishop Quiroga authorized the painting of the picture in 1580. The contract with El Greco was signed on March 18th of 1586 and the painter fulfilled his promise to finish the work by Christmas of the same year, which means that he carried out such a complex painting as the one we are about to study, measuring 4.8 × 3.6 metres, in nine months.

Luis de Velasco and Hernando de Nuciva appraised the work at 1,200 ducats, but at the request of the parish council of Santo Tomé, who considered this price excessive, the work was appraised again, this time by Hernando de Avila and Blas del Prado. They, however, judged the excellence of the painting so highly that they raised the appraisal figure to 1,600 ducats. Finally, after lengthy negotiations, both sides agreed to accept the first appraisal on July 20th 1588. The painter had to put up with being paid partly with a silver monstrance and partly in money, which passed directly into the hands of one Medina, "linen merchant", and of other creditors of El Greco's. But the long negotiations did not prevent the painter from presenting the parish priest of Santo Tomé with a canvas portraying Andrés Núñez himself praying before a crucifix; this work, according to the Conde de Cedillo, was bequeathed by Andrés Núñez to the parish church of Navalperal in 1601.

Ever since it was painted this magnificent work has been the high point of any visit to Toledo, though of the church built at the expense of the charitable lord of Orgaz, who did not live to enjoy the title of count bestowed on his successors, only the elegant Mudejar tower remains. If El Greco had long before this reached maturity in style and technique and achieved a synthesis of the component factors of his art

—as we have seen— it is nevertheless in the *Burial of the Conde de Orgaz* that this synthesis acquires its full spiritual significance and attains to its most absolute and convincing development.

If we compare this composition with others by El Greco divided into two areas (one celestial and the other earthly), we shall see that the space given to the former is here considerably enlarged. Still firmly resolved to avoid localized and detailed settings, he used the lower part of the canvas as no more than a space for expounding the central theme of the picture: the miraculous burial. It should be noted that in this case there is a certain integration of the two spaces, due to the fact that two heavenly characters have become leading figures in an event on earth. For the throng of gentlemen the burial of their friend is not just another ceremony but an occasion for considering once more the idea of their own mortality. The celestial part of the painting, therefore, does not only express the painter's vision, but is the image evoked by each of the characters. Clouds treated in that special, unusually solid technique that we have seen in the *St. Francis receiving the stigmata,* painted in Italy some fifteen years before, are shaded with opalescent tones, peopled inside and out with angels and used to construct a mass upon which rises the edifice of those beings who live in glory. Contrasts of tones and shadings, ranging from well-defined colours to indefinable nuances, fill the whole of that dynamic area which seems to be swept by a whirlwind round a central space expressing the direct contact between Christ, on high, and the temporal world below. Flanking the entrance to the celestial regions we see the Virgin and St. John receiving the Conde's soul, which, carried by an angel, attains to glory in the shape of a child, as translucent as a mist.

In the centre of the lower half a youthful St. Stephen and a white-bearded St. Augustine hold the Conde's body wearing its partially gilded steel armour. The clothing of the two saints enables El Greco to introduce paintings within the painting, like the little scene that shows the martyrdom of St. Stephen or the vertical border with its frieze of saints. Gold, yellowish white and red are the predominant colours in this central group, apart from the metallic tones of the Conde's armour, which reflect the figure of St. Stephen, the hand of the knight of Santiago in the middle of those attending the burial and other subtle images that recall, under an abrupt and miraculously precise technique, the naturalistic discoveries of the Flemish painters of the fifteenth century.

The main effect of this work derives, in principle, from the whole theme of the painting as an idea that impresses itself on the mind of the viewer, whether he be a passionate connoisseur of art or simply a sensitive layman. The factor second in importance is the prodigious and complex balance between static effects and suggestions of movement. The central group really appears to be moving. The frieze of gentlemen, on the other hand, even the awed attitude of the priest on the right, are static. In the upper part of the canvas the restrained attitude of the Virgin contrasts with the eloquent posture of St. John, just as the spiral movement of the cloud in the upper left, revealing the seated figures of David, Moses and Noah and, above them, St. Peter, is counterbalanced by the compact group on the right. Among the venerable saints the painter has seated two well-known figures: Philip II, who was still on the throne when this picture was painted, and Cardinal Tavera, who was dead by then.

It is quite clear that in this work El Greco did not intend to produce one sole effect, but rather a predominant impact that was to be accompanied by a whole series of secondary effects, skilfully apportioned according to their relative importance in the whole. The realism of the vision is progressively diminished from the lower to the upper part; it is never lost in vagueness, however, but rather consists of a logical graduation of the dematerialization, from the Conde's armour to the idealized figure of the Redeemer, who, though placed so close to His Mother and the Precursor, nevertheless seems to be situated in his own space, at once near and far.

El Greco's skill in depicting gesture is given fresh opportunities here, though in general the work is surprising in its restraint and severity. The most dynamic elements in the whole composition are, undoubtedly, the angel carrying the dead man's soul, the other little angel on the right, the almost naked figure of St. John (the anatomy of which is perfect despite its elongation), the gesture of the same saint's arm and the position of his left leg. If the central group has an effect of latent dynamism, this is due, first of all, to the tremendous sensation of life with which the figures are imbued and, secondly, to the way in which the weight of the dead man makes itself felt, as we can see in the posture of the two saints stooping over the Conde as they hold him up. There are other expressive

Fig. 101. The Burial of the Conde de Orgaz, 1
Toledo, Santo Tomé. Cat. No. 75.

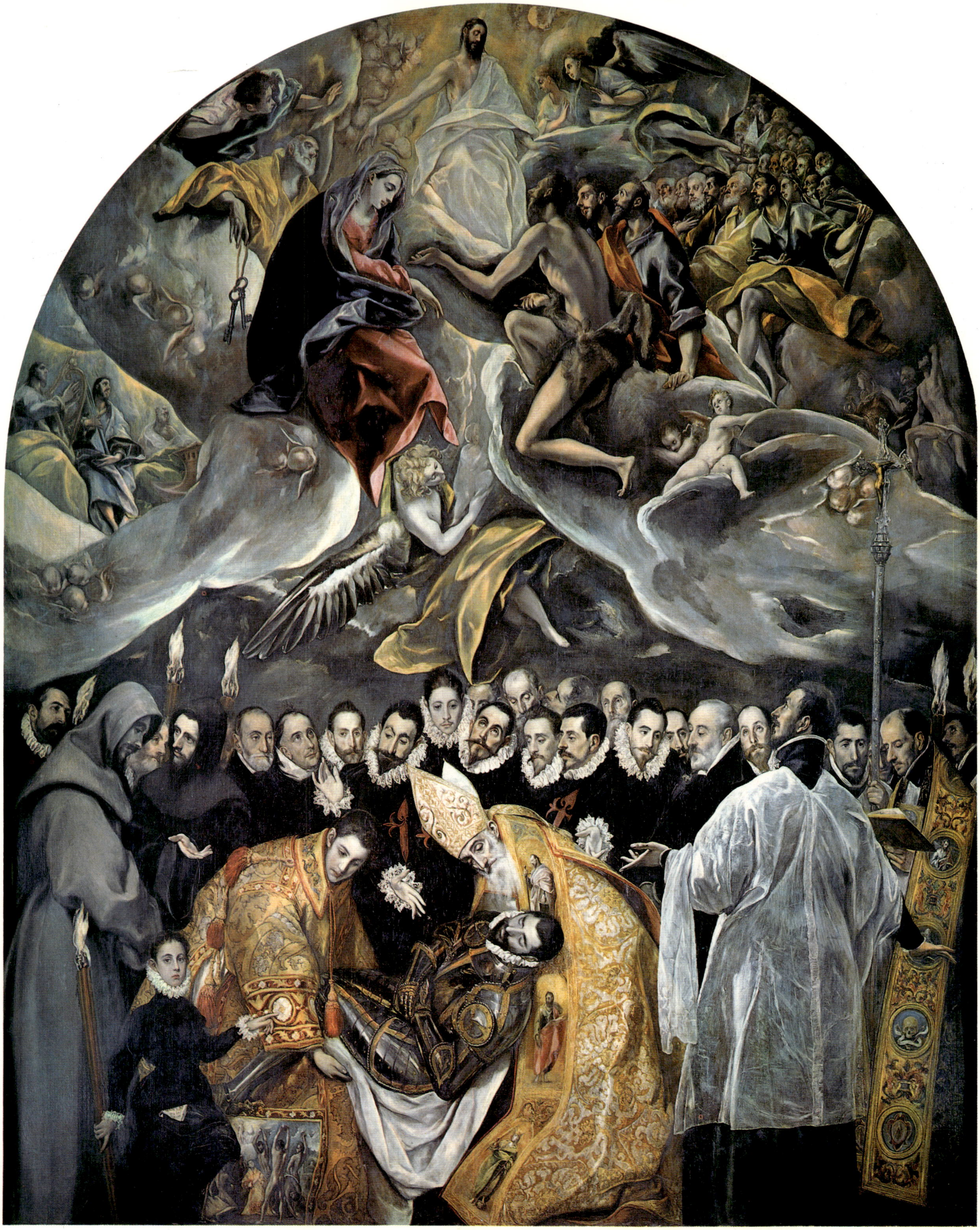

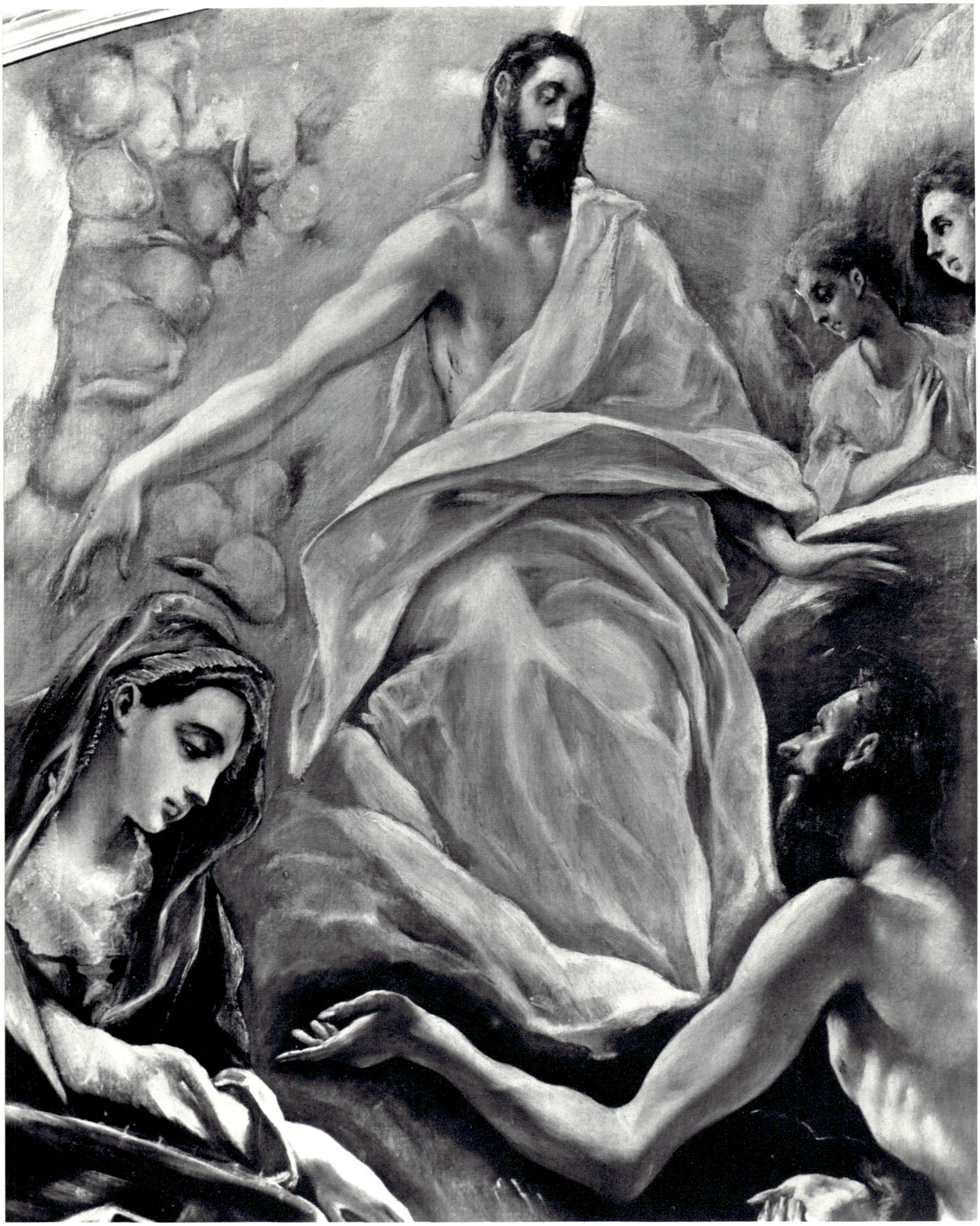

Fig. 102. Detail of figure 101.

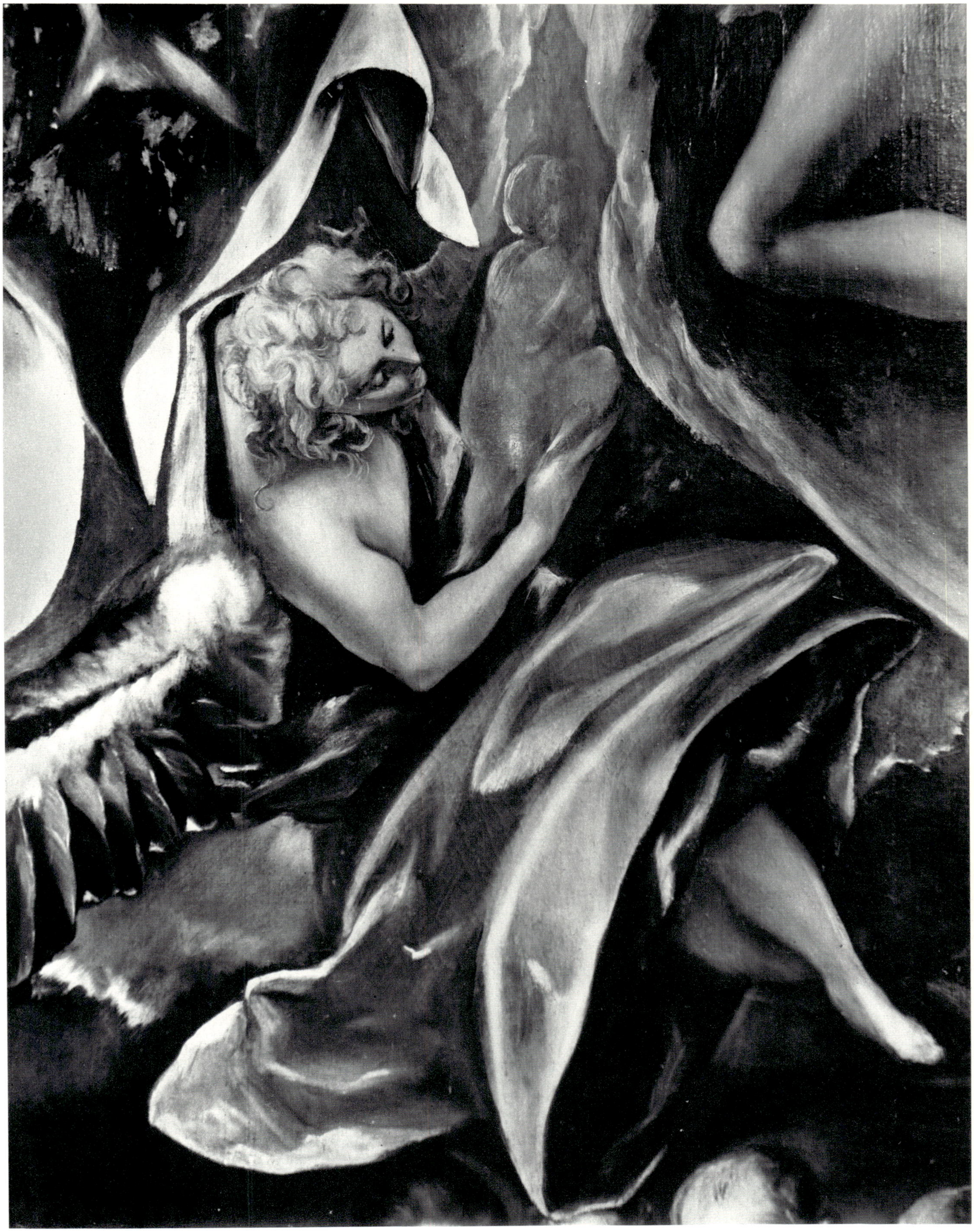

Fig. 103. Detail of figure 101.

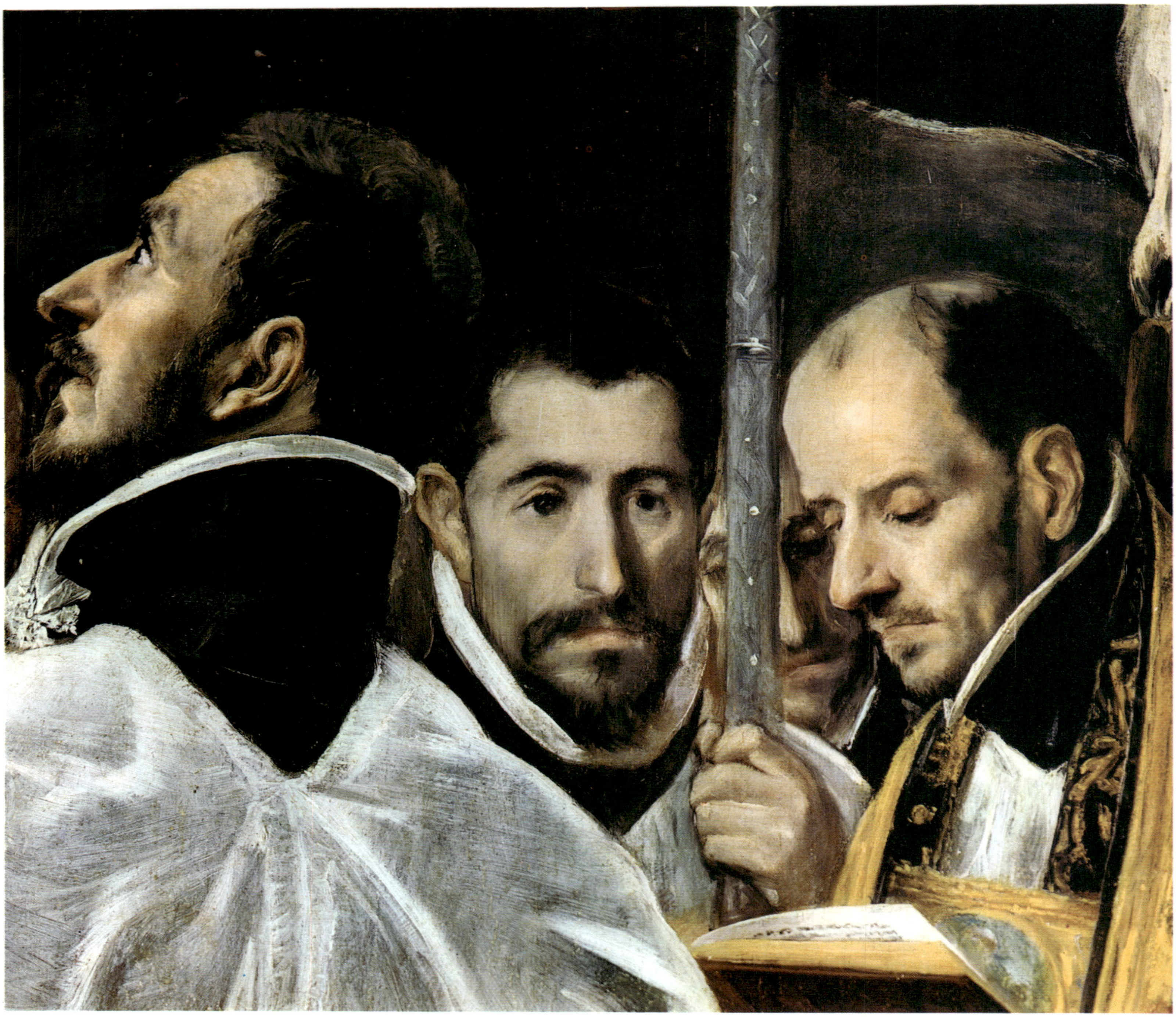

Figs. 104 & 105. Details of figure 101.

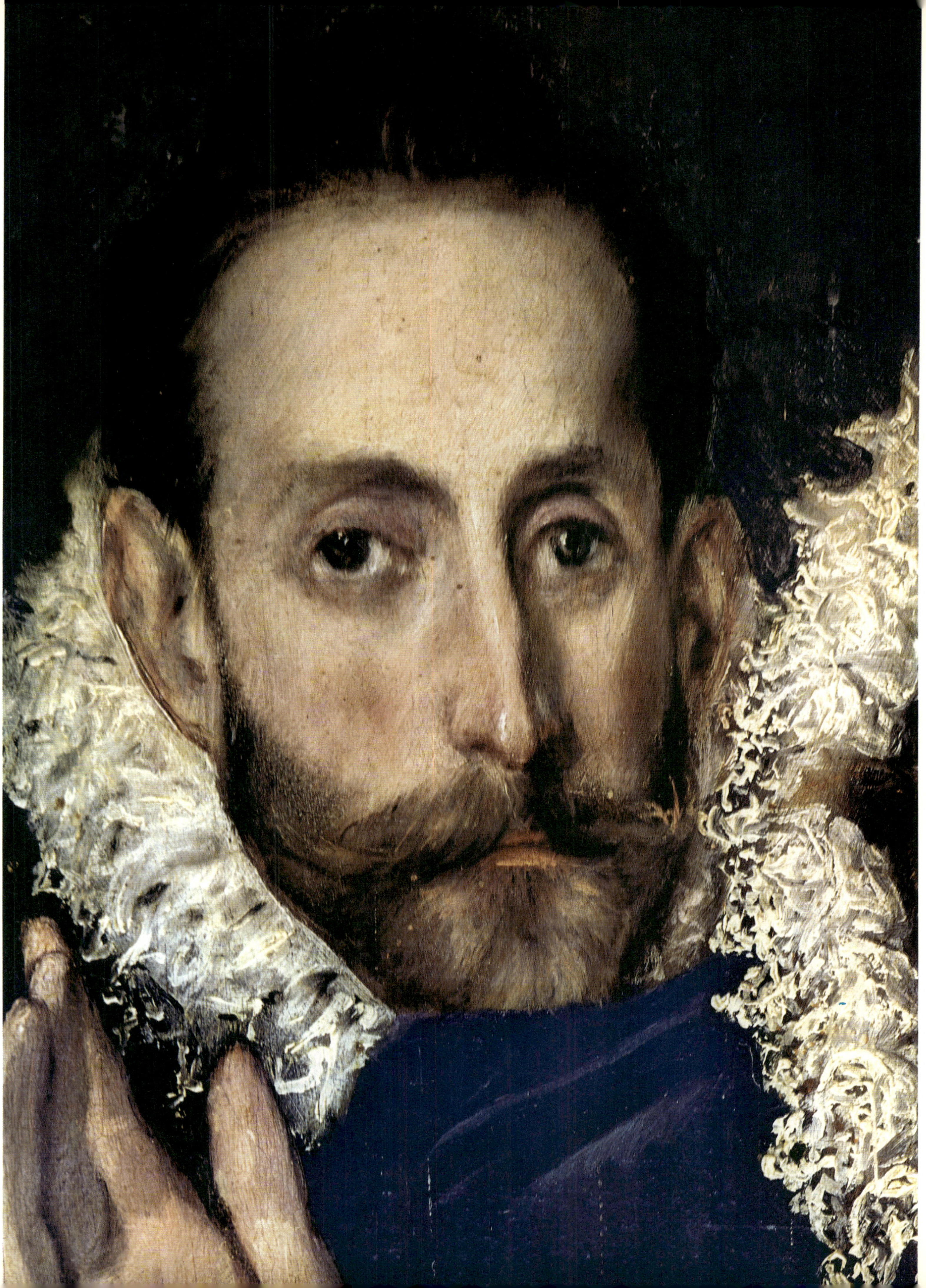

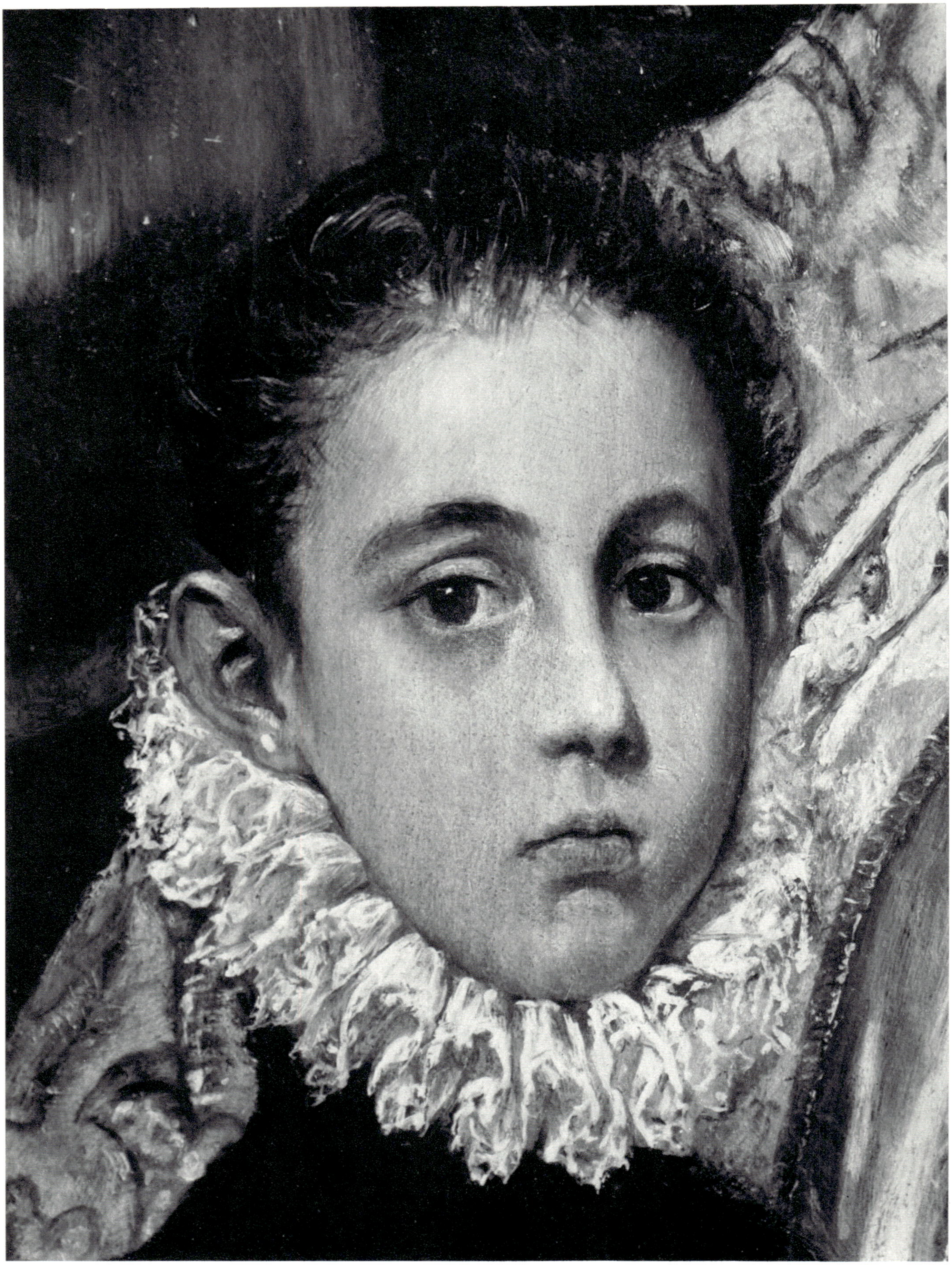

Fig. 106. Detail of figure 101.

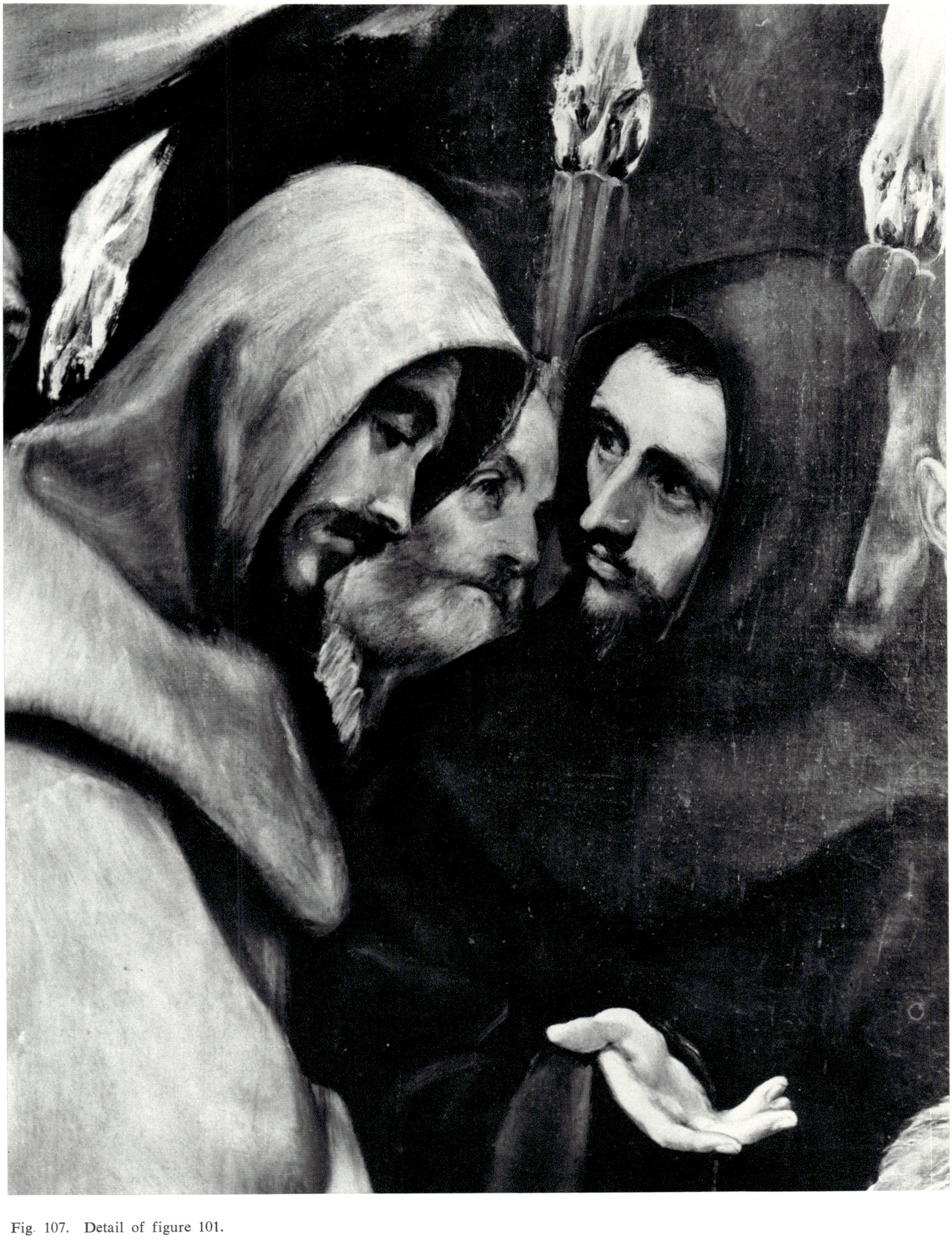

Fig. 107. Detail of figure 101.

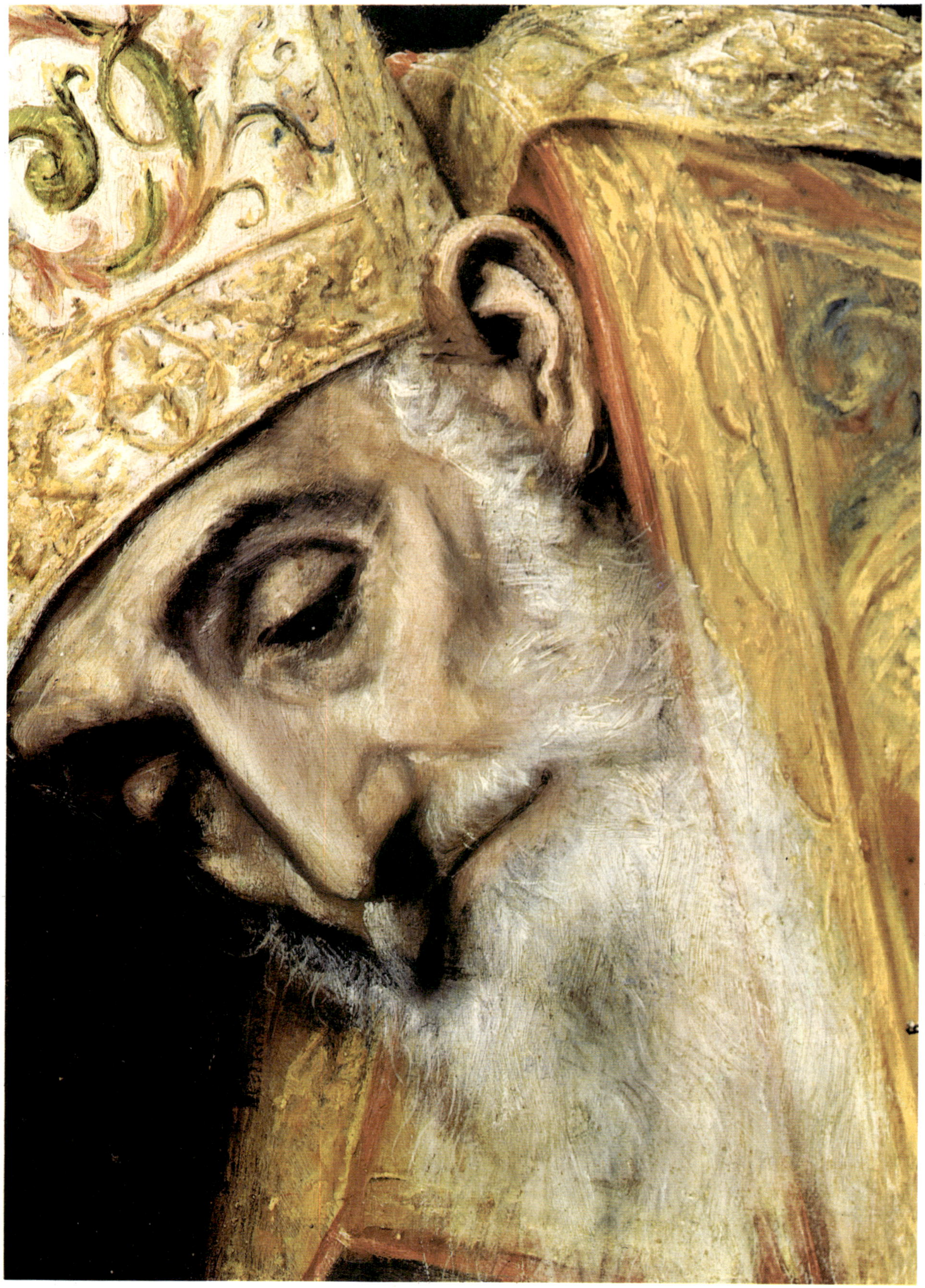

Fig. 108. Detail of figure 101.

attitudes to be found in the hands, so wonderfully painted with the white contrast of their lace cuffs against the black of the suits and the red crosses of Santiago, and in the faces. The gentlemen and priests here echo the work done in that phase of realism we have seen during El Greco's Roman period; he was by then already in control of his technique, but now —all problems solved— he was in absolute possession of a superhuman facility, a facility the viewer will recognize from the moment he first glances at the picture, without need of further analysis. Every head is a masterpiece, every hand a proof of incomparable draughtsmanship. Moreover, the varied expressions (resignation, acceptance of the divine will, hope, curiosity, unspoken opinions of the virtues of the dead man, etc.) all show the painter's wealth of psychic perception, his gift for understanding and representing human beings, which was as great as his ability to show the diverse degrees of participation in Glory, and his genius for depicting the divine beings themselves by idealizing traditional types.

The exceptional chromatic quality of the composition comes from what we might call its "sumptuous pathos", evidenced in the predominance of black and dark tones, which serve as a background to set off whites and pale greys, greenish or golden yellows and various shades of red, together with a sparingly employed secondary range that includes violets, blues, greens and opalescent lights —all this quite apart from the magnificent flesh tints. If we analyse the details, we shall see the painter's tremendous sureness, the technique that alternates soft modelling with sharp accents and creates the most astounding contrasts of texture. The ruffs and other pieces of lace are painted in pure white with a rather thick impasto. The hands, first lightly traced in white, are then modelled with very soft pink shades. The eyes, those eyes to which El Greco succeeded in imparting a liquid gleam, are essential elements throughout the composition; even when we cannot see them under drooping lids, the strength of the drawing makes us feel their gaze with all its human intensity. The different stuffs give El Greco occasion to display his technical mastery, from the transparent surplice of the priest on the right, which harmonizes with the white robe of Christ at the top of the composition, to the heavy gold and velvet brocades of the dalmatics worn by St. Stephen and St. Augustine. The head of the dead Conde is another fragment of extraordinary power, above all in its contrast to the thoughtful figures of the surrounding company, animated by the life of the feelings rather than by that of the body.

The child in black holding a torch that we see in the foreground pointing to the miracle is Jorge Manuel Theotokópoulos, El Greco's son *(Fig. 106)*. The painter gives us a clue to the identification of this portrait by inscribing the date of his son's birth (in 1578) on the handkerchief peeping out of his pocket. The vivid beauty of this little portrait stands out even in the masterly series of portraits that constitutes the soul of this painting.

This picture, which, together with the *Espolio,* preserved El Greco's fame at all times, has given rise to infinite, and usually passionate, encomia down through the centuries. The first of these appears in the "Description of the Imperial City of Toledo", written by F. de Pisa in 1612, which tells us: "it is one of the best pictures in Spain; foreigners come to see it and are filled with admiration, while the people of the city never tire of admiring it, constantly discovering new things in it". It is believed that all the figures attending the miraculous burial are portraits of people of El Greco's day. Many attempts at identification have been made, but the whole question is really very uncertain. It seems sure that Antonio de Covarrubias —the famous humanist and friend of El Greco's— is portrayed in the white-bearded cleric shown in profile in front of the priest standing with his back to us in the foreground.

The gentleman in the centre may be the Duque de Benavente, whose portrait by El Greco is in the Museum of Bayonne. The cleric holding the cross is supposed to be a portrait of Rodríguez de la Fuente, son of the man painted by El Greco *(Fig. 100)* and related to Mother Jerónima de la Fuente, whose portrait by Velázquez is in the Prado. It is also thought that the priest with the white surplice is Andrés Núñez, the parish priest of Santo Tomé, who brought the suit against the authorities of the town of Orgaz and commissioned this painting to honour the memory of the dead man who is its protagonist. We are told the painter included himself among the bystanders, but of that we will speak at the end of this book, when we discuss all the supposed self-portraits of El Greco.

IV

1587 - 1597

THE ALTARPIECE OF TALAVERA LA VIEJA — NEW COMPOSITIONS — THE NIARCHOS *PIETÀ* — FRANCISCAN ICONOGRAPHY — OTHER WORKS — PORTRAITS — REAPPEARANCE OF AN ITALIAN MODEL.

We continue our study of El Greco's work into a period of his life which may be supposed to have been stationary in every aspect. The only dated work is the altarpiece of Talavera la Vieja, which was painted in 1591. He and his assistants continued to paint devotional pictures, but that does not exclude the constant invention of new compositions. What information we have regarding his life is certainly scanty enough. On July 1st 1588, El Greco and Francisco Preboste empowered two persons residing in Seville to receive payment for a picture of St. Peter and one of St. Francis, sent to Don Diego de Velasco. This first sign of expansion beyond Toledan circles would seem to prove the existence of a contract of association between the artist and his servant or assistant. On December 27th 1589, El Greco undertook to pay the rent of the palace of the Marqués de Villena, where —as we have seen already— he had been living and working since the end of 1585. Apparently this undertaking was not kept, for towards the end of the same year El Greco found himself obliged to move to a rather humbler and more economical lodging, which is where we shall find him for some years thereafter; this shows that the sale of pictures to private patrons had proved less profitable than he had imagined at the outset.

The works we are about to study will help us to perceive the existence of three "levels" in El Greco: the major compositions, like the *St. Maurice* and the *Burial of the Conde de Orgaz*; fairly complex and carefully-coloured paintings on religious themes; and devotional images which, though by no means executed in merely routine fashion, yet do not attain the profound brilliance that we always find in the paintings of the first two groups. These three groups, of course, do not include portraits. A painter who could not count on a fairly steady stream of important commissions, who —when he was given any— was often paid little and late and found himself embroiled in lawsuits, who led a difficult life in a declining city that had lost its former greatness, naturally had to go back to the medieval conception of pictorial production. He painted for his very livelihood and did a much larger number of works than he should have done, which forced him to employ procedures that would make his task easier. The first of these consisted in re-adapting elements from his earlier compositions, of which he kept the preparatory studies; the second was to accept the collaboration of his assistants, however few they might be —at times, perhaps, only the faithful and mysterious Preboste.

As we have said, the only documented work in the period we are studying is the altarpiece of the Virgin of the Rosary in the parish church of Talavera la Vieja, in the province of Cáceres, which was preserved in almost complete form until 1936. Mélida, in his "Catalogue of the Monuments of Cáceres", gives a detailed account of the original contract, which is kept in the Register Archives of Toledo, and a vague description of the work itself: a central image carved in wood, gilded and polychromed, and five oil paintings depicting the Annunciation, the Presentation in the Temple, the Coronation of the Virgin, St. Peter and St. Andrew, the description stating that the first two are not the work of El Greco. Paul Guinard published the only photographs still extant of the altarpiece *in situ,* which show the whole structure, though not very clearly, and the rather fine wooden image. When the church was destroyed in 1936, the altarpiece was dismembered and, after long wanderings, the three canvases painted by El Greco became part of the collection of the Santa Cruz Museum in Toledo.

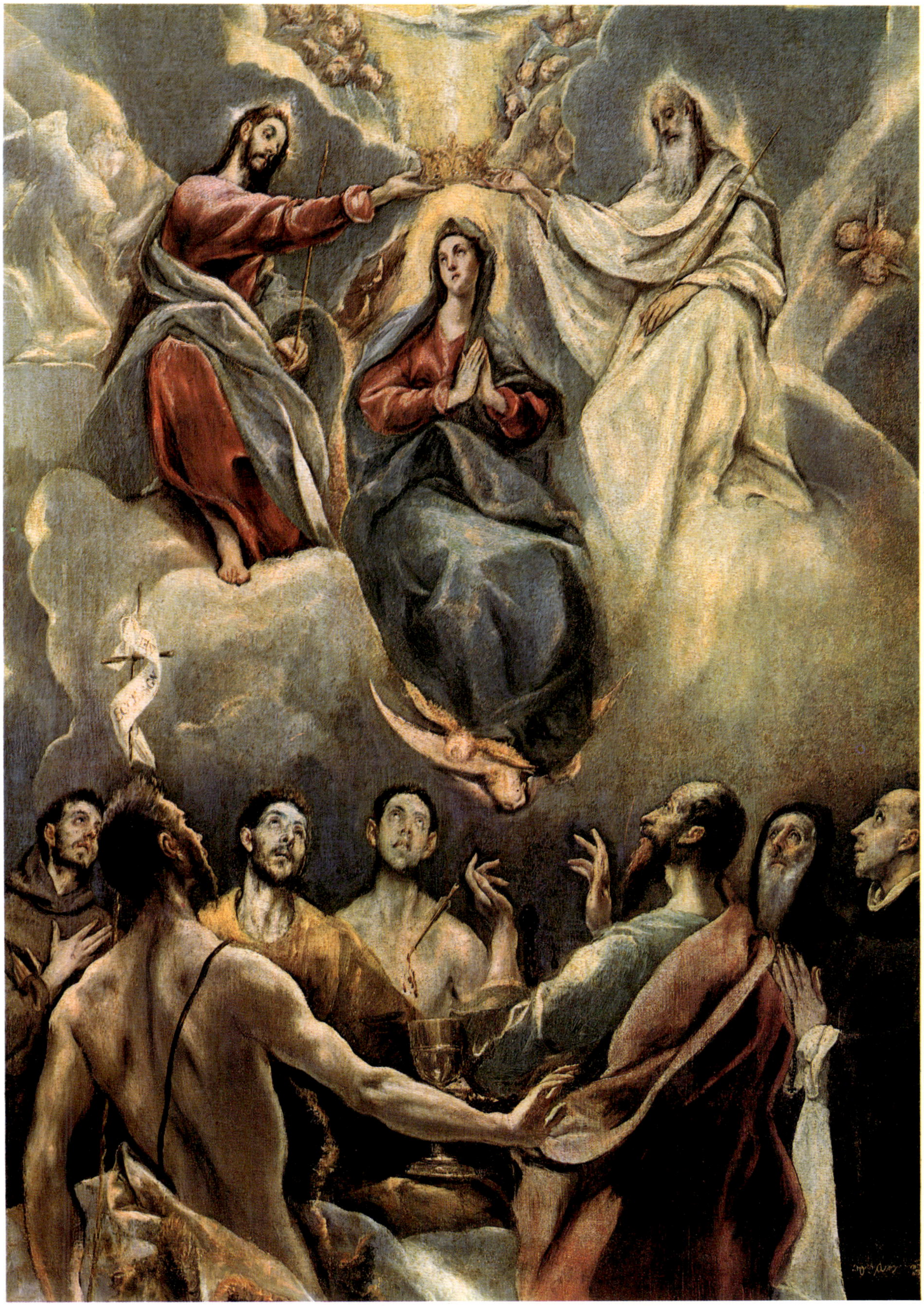

Fig. 109. The Coronation of the Virgin, 1591-1592. Toledo, Santa Cruz Museum. Cat. No. 76.

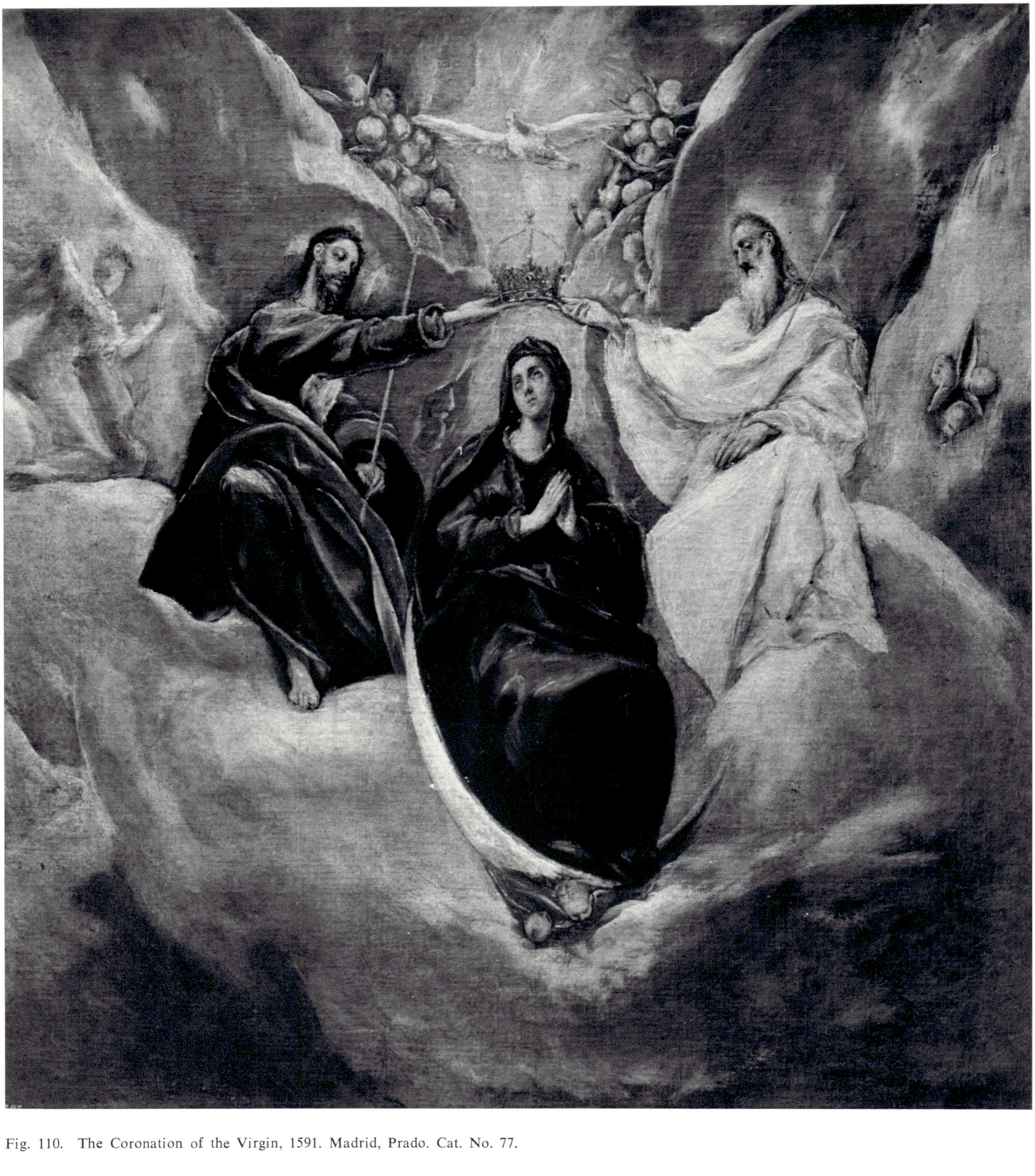

Fig. 110. The Coronation of the Virgin, 1591. Madrid, Prado. Cat. No. 77.

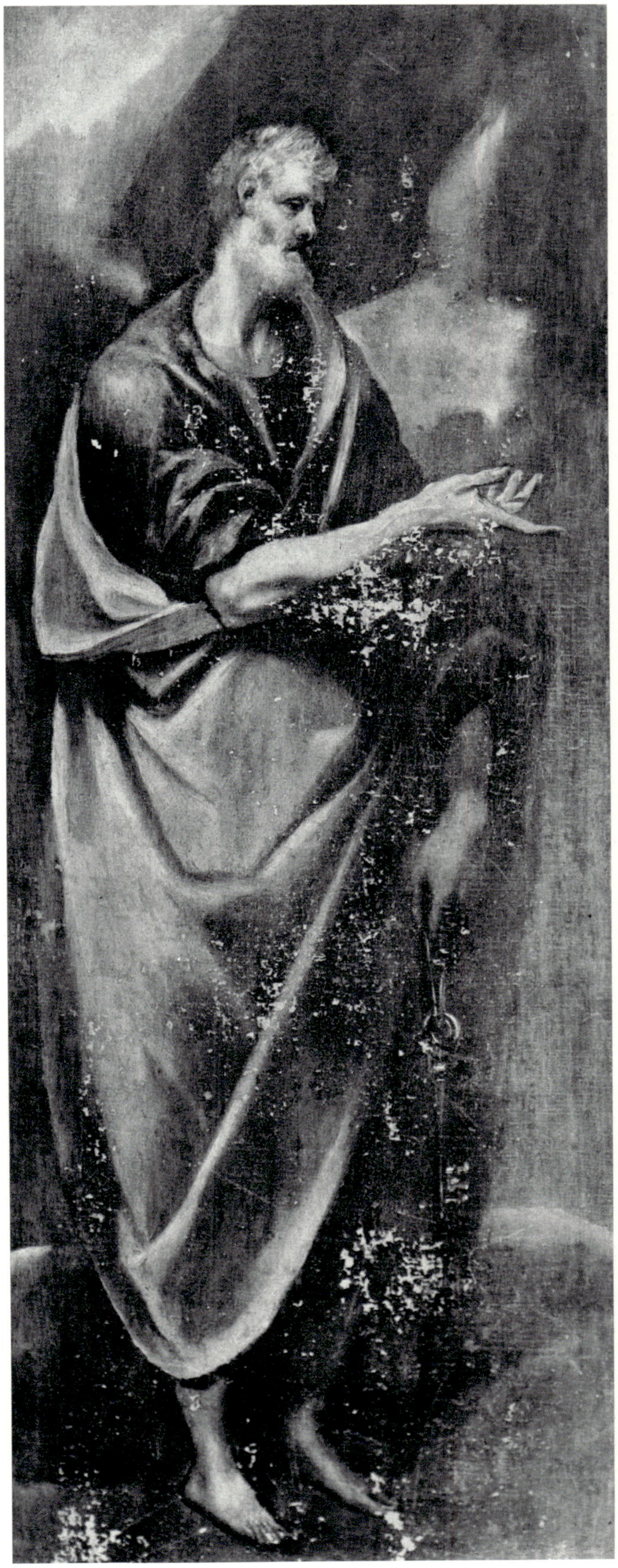

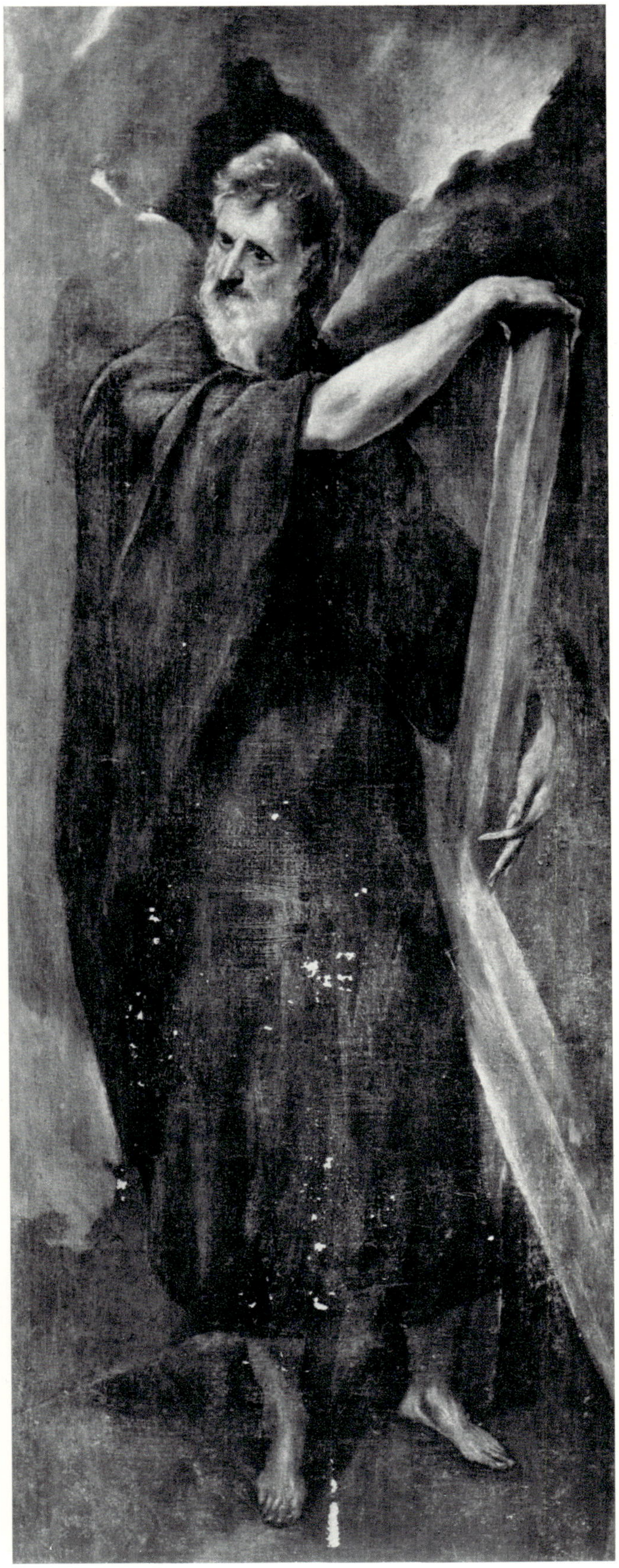

Fig. 111. St. Peter, 1591-1592. Toledo, Santa Cruz Museum. Cat. No. 79.
Fig. 112. St. Andrew, 1591-1592. Toledo, Santa Cruz Museum. Cat. No. 78.

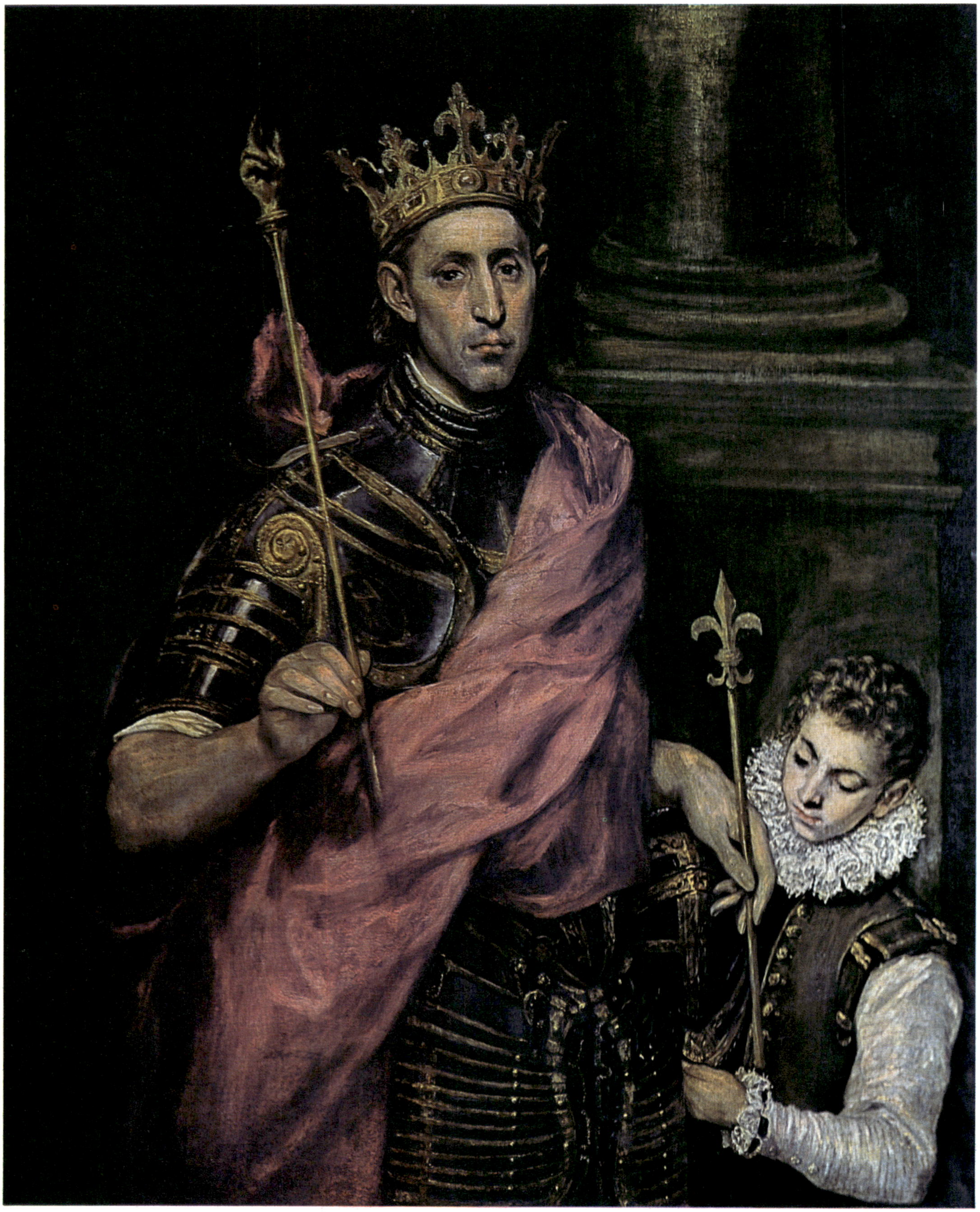

Fig. 113. St. Louis of France, 1587-1597. Paris, Louvre. Cat. No. 80.

The aforesaid contract, between El Greco and the representatives of the Confraternity of the Rosary in Talavera, among whom was the parish priest, Hernando Márquez, brother of a famous Toledan goldsmith who was a friend of the painter's, was drawn up on February 14th of 1591. The date fixed for delivery of the work was July 25th of the same year, but the parish books of Talavera register the payment of 300 ducats, the price established in the contract, at a late date in 1592.

The three paintings of the altarpiece of Talavera la Vieja are of great interest if we wish to know how El Greco painted when he was about fifty years old, five years after the execution of the *Burial of the Conde de Orgaz*. In the Prado we find what was, very probably, a partial study for the painting of the *Coronation of the Virgin (Fig. 109 - Cat. 76 & Fig. 110 - Cat. 77)*. As we shall see, this sketch or model was used in other compositions of later date. El Greco's process of spiritualization, though this may sound like a cliché, can be seen quite clearly by comparing the figure of the Eternal Father in this composition with that in the *Trinity* of Santo Domingo el Antiguo *(Figs. 57 & 58)*. In the latter work God, though of great majesty and beauty, was still treated with a certain realism which brought Him close to human beings, but here the Creator is a distant, majestic figure, imbued with profound peace and highly idealized, though without thereby becoming impersonal or dissolved. The painter's lively humanity is never absent; it can be seen in this figure and in all the others of this composition, marking a step towards greater freedom, towards the image for its own sake.

The painter shows great daring in making the chromatic balance of the work frankly asymmetric, without the least hint at compensation. Both Christ and the Virgin wear robes of an almost purple red and blue cloaks, which provide intense notes of colour. On the right we see God the Father in robe and cloak of the purest white and seated on clouds that are much lighter in colour than those on the opposite side. On the opposite side, too, the rhythms are much livelier. In the definitive work the composition is completed with a circle of saints, painted rather longer than half-length, surrounding the chalice of St. John. This group is almost entirely symmetrical, and where there is a slight asymmetry it is to give even greater weight to the left-hand side, which has four figures as against the three on the right. This asymmetry is counterbalanced by the intense luminosity irradiated by the white of the Eternal Father, which shows the important role that El Greco gave to light in composition and, at the same time, his absolute self-confidence and his refusal to accept any kind of conventionalism. The pictorial concept is derived from the *St. Maurice,* but the mystical sense is appreciably accentuated and the form is more in accordance with this feeling; its flexibility is extraordinarily well-fitted to the iconographical idea. The concept of form for form's sake, which could be seen in some compositions of earlier years, such as those of Santo Domingo el Antiguo, and even the idea of a certain formalism, as in the *St. Maurice,* have here been abandoned. One could almost think that the artist painted this work without any need either to work it out or to construct it, so great is the effect of incomparable facility. Gesture is still an important factor in the composition, above all in the human figures.

The two figures of *St. Peter* and *St. Andrew* belong to the conception of isolated figures already established by the painter in the images of this type in Santo Domingo el Antiguo *(Figs. 111 & 112 - Cats. 79 & 78)*. The proportions are elongated and almost the whole of the canvas is filled by the figure, which is given a highly plastic treatment, almost as if it were a sculpture or a relief. But this is only as regards form. All the other elements —colour, feeling, gesture, expressions, misty backgrounds, flowing draperies— are dazzlingly pictorial. Despite the evident simplification of the figures, every detail has sufficient intensity and vigour. The head of St. Andrew, turned to the left with peculiar power, is so strongly expressive that there are hardly any precedents for it in El Greco's previous work. These two canvases have now been restored; the photographs published here were taken before this restoration and show that nothing essential had been damaged. In the details it can be seen that the simplification is not so great as might appear on viewing the works in their entirety, which is due to the elongation, the monumental quality and the tonal and chromatic intensity of the enveloping draperies. There is not the slightest distortion in the position of arms, legs or feet, and the elongation —and consequent slenderness— is consonant with his idea of proportion. The use of shading is as masterly as the more complex technique of the heads, with superimpositions, transparencies, scrapings and little, light brushstrokes on the beards and hair, which suggest the different materials with great exactness.

New compositions

We will now discuss a group of paintings attributed to the period between 1587 and 1597. This chronological attribution is based on what stylistic analysis reveals, in connection with the "milestones" of the painter's development as determined by the dated works. Most of them are new models in El Greco's extraordinary typological sequence and will be repeated in other signed versions or used as prototypes for the products of his workshop.

In the first place we have the admirable *St. Louis of France,* of which the only version extant is the one in the Louvre *(Fig. 113 - Cat. 80).* The simple range of colours —the dark background, the shining black armour with its gilding, the gold of the king's crown and sceptres, the red of the cloak thrown over his shoulder, the white and sepia of the page and the varied shading of the flesh tints— does not prevent the painter from showing his great skill as a colourist. He reaffirms his indifference to harmonies of complementary colours, preferring to arrange the different parts of the form by gradations in the intensity of colour and tone. This picture of the saintly King of France is painted as if it were a portrait, being neither a devotional work nor an idealized representation. As far as the typology is concerned, El Greco cannot have been acquainted with any of the old miniatures or other representations of the king, for he literally invents his character, giving him a much more Spanish than French appearance. He evidently considered that the attributes of royal power and the vaguely mystical expression of his St. Louis were enough to give the image probability in the sense of what it was intended to represent. The contrasts of textures are brilliantly managed, so that this is one of the painter's most realistic works. The tonal modelling is masterly and the sensation of immediate presence produced by the figure is almost obsessive. In order to avoid an archaizing effect of immobility, the two sceptres carried by the king are situated at different heights, though the hands are at almost the same level. The cloak, brilliantly executed, is the nearest approach to El Greco the visionary, with its *sfumato* qualities and the sudden reflections of the material, the diaphanous quality being accentuated in order to give greater intensity to the hardness of the metal armour. The page is an enchanting little figure and also serves to heighten the idea of the main figure's strength and power. It might even be a new portrait of Jorge Manuel.

El Greco painted St. Peter and St. Paul together on several occasions. His taste for eloquence and his attitude as an artist of the counter-reformation inclined him to unite these two saints, who are truly the keystones of the whole edifice of historical Christianity. A whole typology of New Testament characters was developed down through the Middle Ages, from the end of the Early Christian period, and this El Greco took up and adapted to his own temperament and gift of expression. It is our belief that the impressive canvas in the Art Museum of Catalonia, in Barcelona, is his first known version of this theme *(Fig. 114 - Cat. 81).* He presents the two saints as closely united friends, putting their heads at the same height and joining their hands. Although they are represented with mantles "in the antique mode", without any further archaelogical exactness, St. Paul's sword —both in this and in other versions— is a two-handed one of the painter's own age. El Greco chose his living models very well, modifying them to make them conform to the "idea" he had of each saint, both in deference to his own feelings and in more or less specific obedience to traditional typology. In the heads, which are full of gravity and profound strength, the painting sticks closely to the drawing, with some slight distortion which is due rather to the painter's desire to indicate the spiritual sense of the characters than to that intrinsic passion for distortion which was later to gain possession of his style to such an extent, above all in the foreshortenings of complex compositions. The technique here is less realistic and structural than in the *St. Louis* studied above, but shows no greater tendency to abandon the straightforward and realistic in favour of the visionary. The background of sky most skilfully establishes a different shade for each character, without thereby disturbing the unity. Thus the figure of St. Peter stands out against a patch of blue, while that of St. Paul contrasts with whitish greys and more evanescent tones. The brilliant tones of the cloaks in this work are of greater interest than the form created with majestic, enveloping rhythms.

At about the same time El Greco created the justly celebrated *Holy Family with St. Anne* from the Tavera Hospital in Toledo *(Fig. 115 - Cat. 82).* In it he used the same scheme as in the canvas in the Hispanic Society already studied *(Fig. 95).* On account of the beauty and profound humanity of Our Lady, many

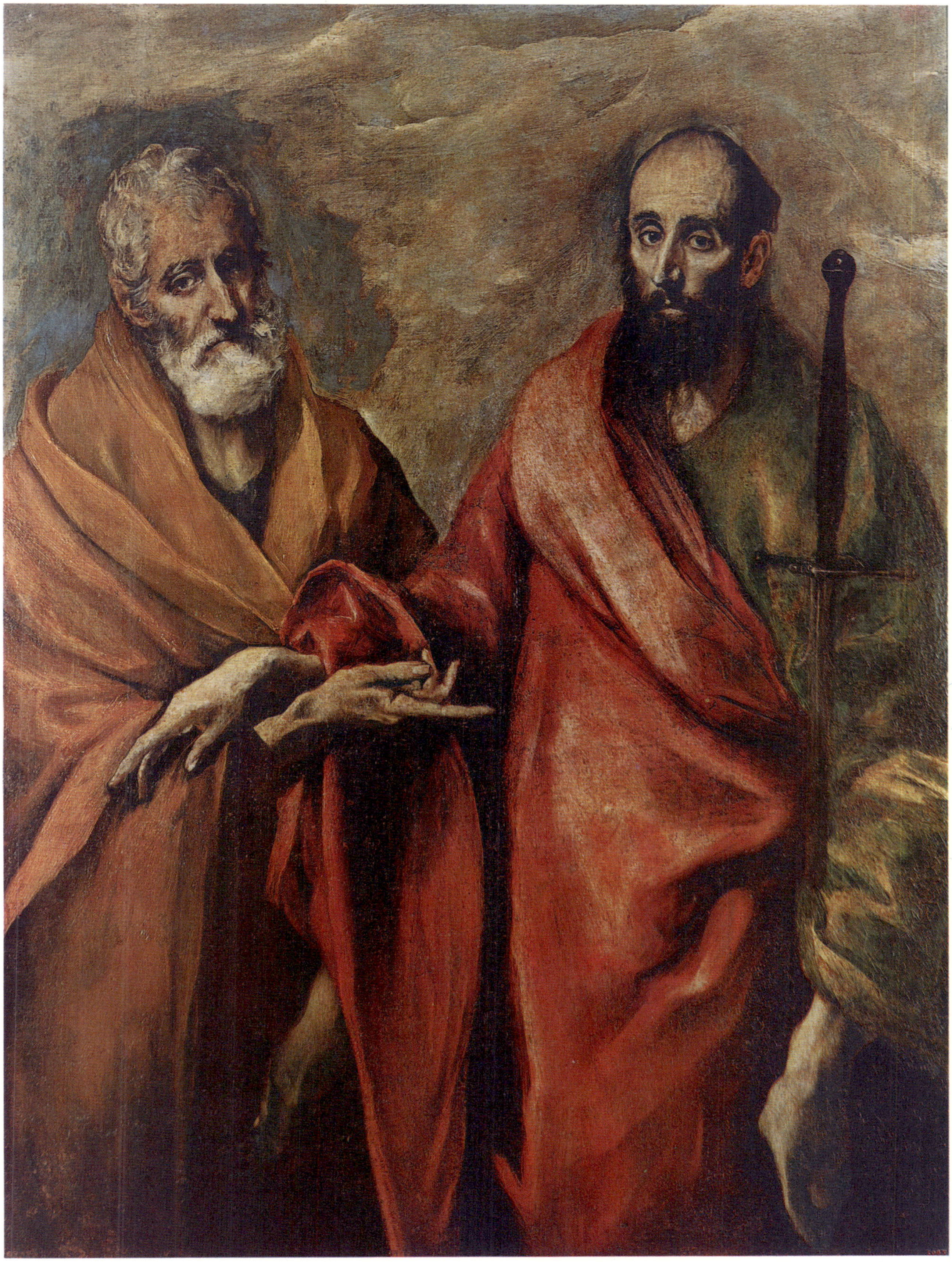

Fig. 114. St. Peter and St. Paul, 1587-1597. Barcelona, Art Museum of Catalonia. Cat. No. 81.

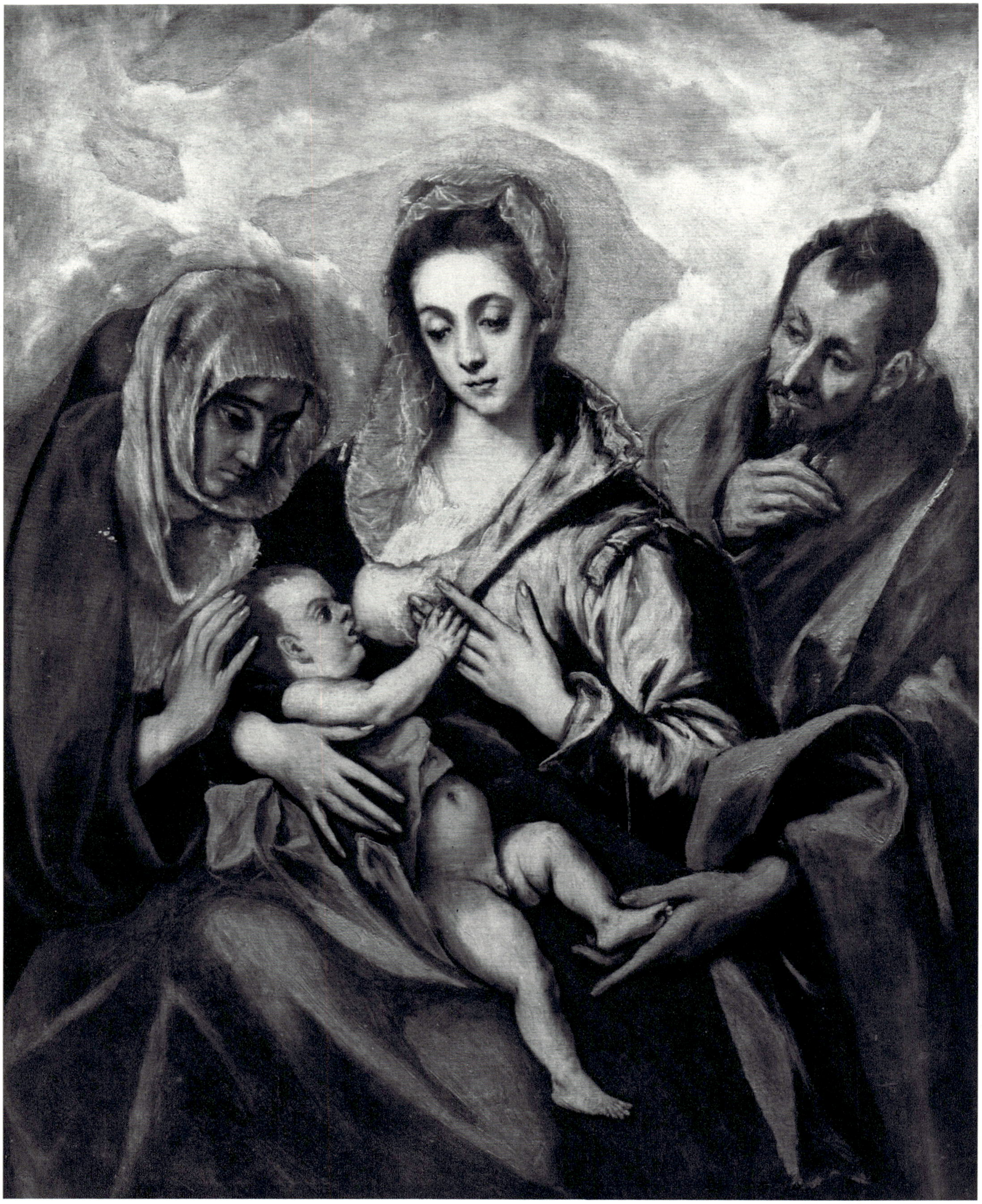

Figs. 115 & 116. The Holy Family with St. Anne, 1587-1597. Toledo, Hospital de San Juan Bautista de Afuera. Cat. No. 82.

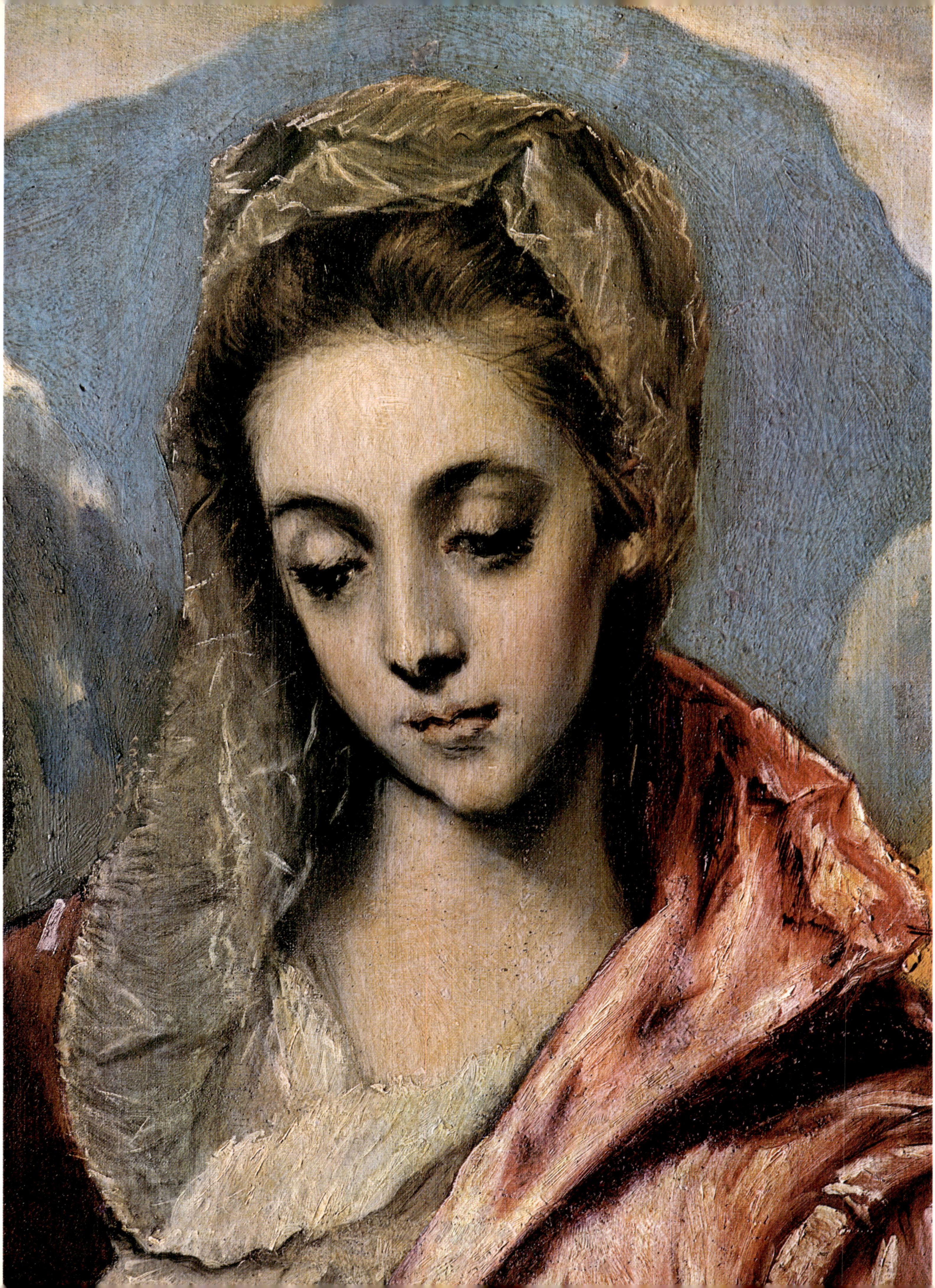

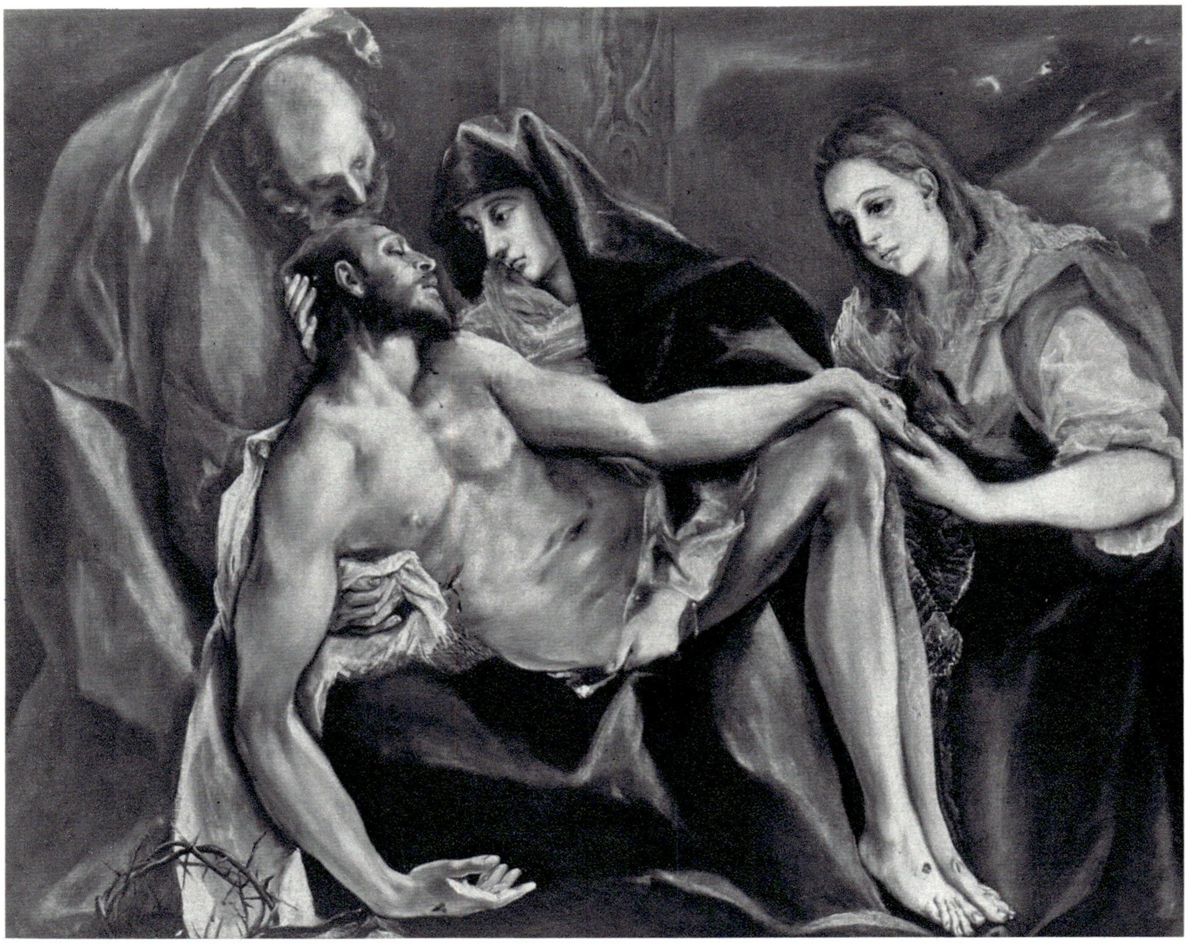

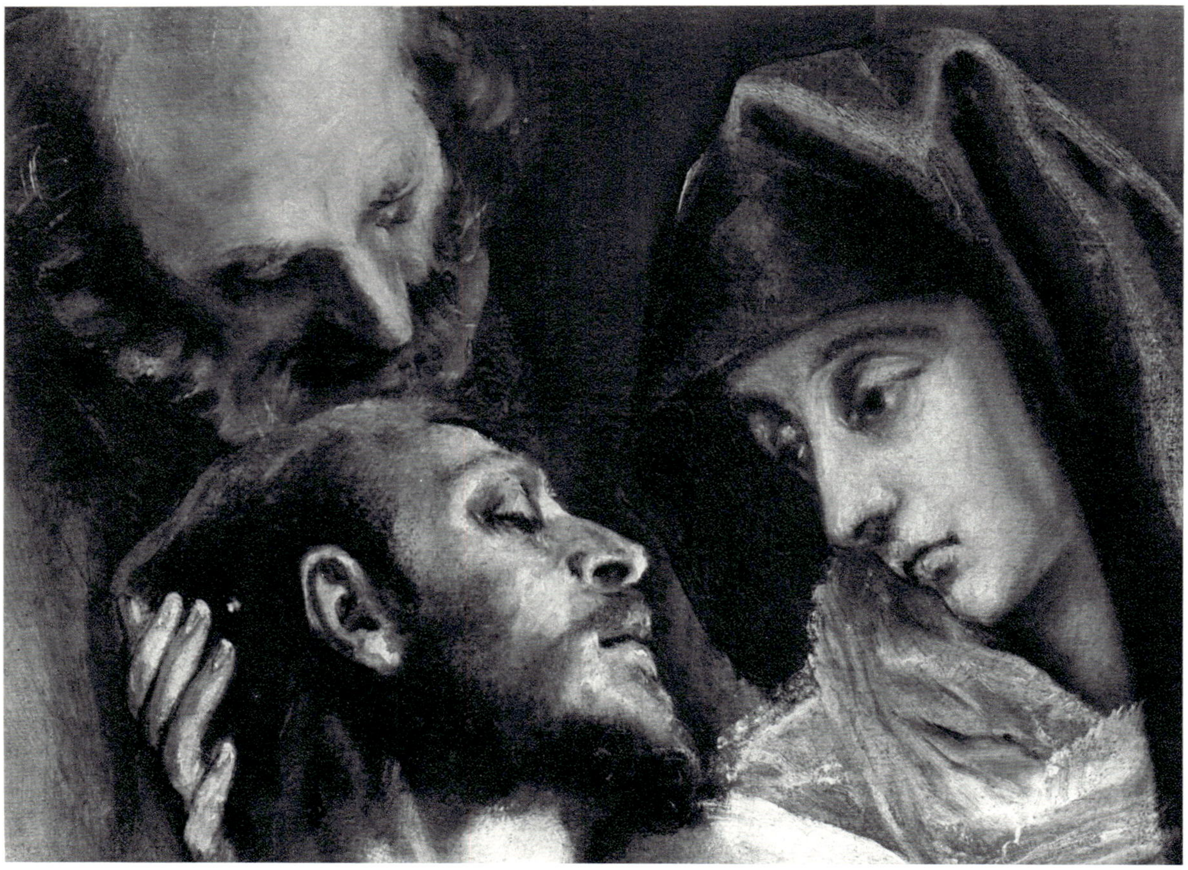

Figs. 117 & 118. Pietà, 1587-1597. Paris, Niarchos Collection. Cat. No. 83.

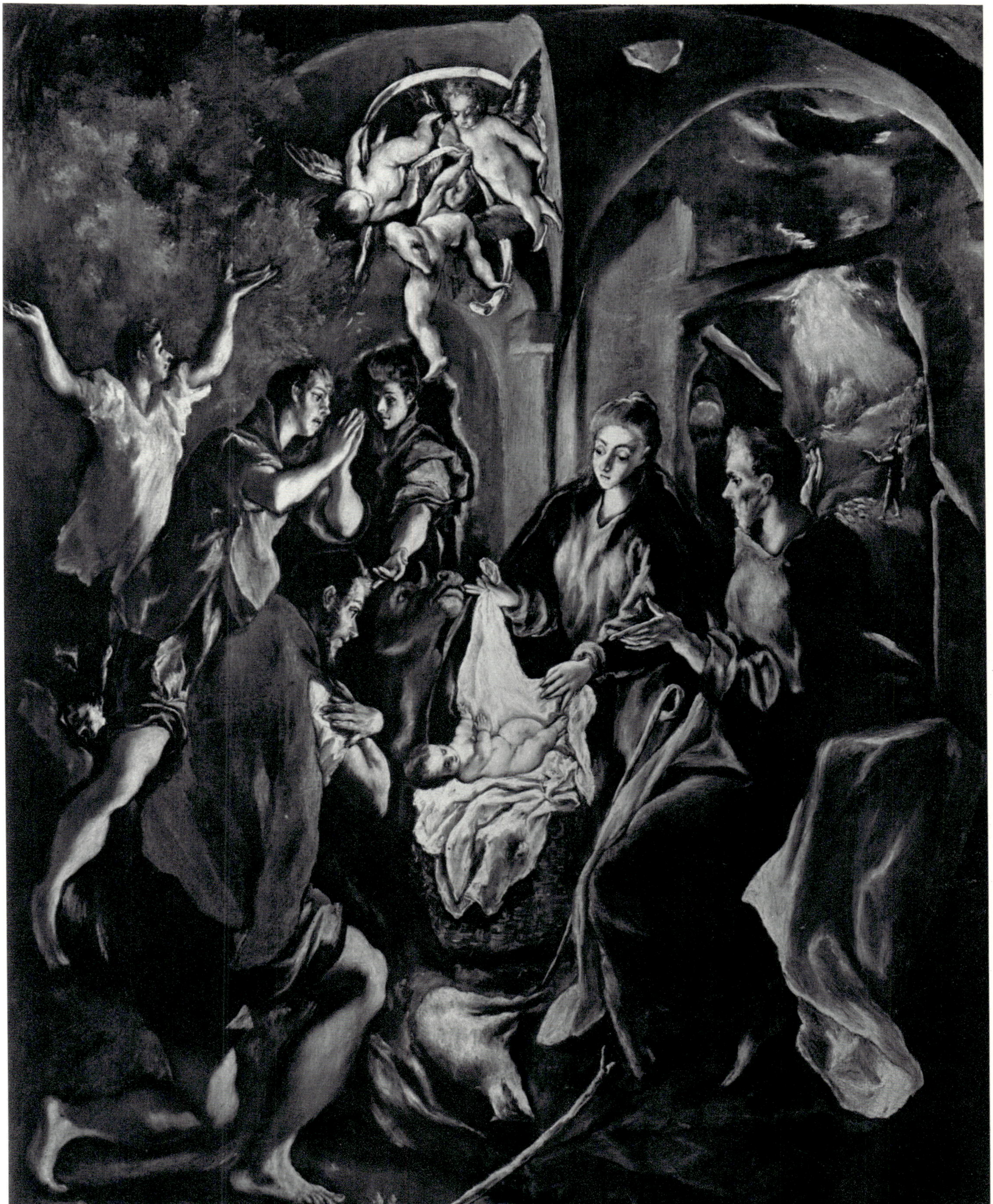

Fig. 119. The Adoration of the shepherds, 1587-1597. Valencia, Colegio del Patriarca. Cat. No. 84.

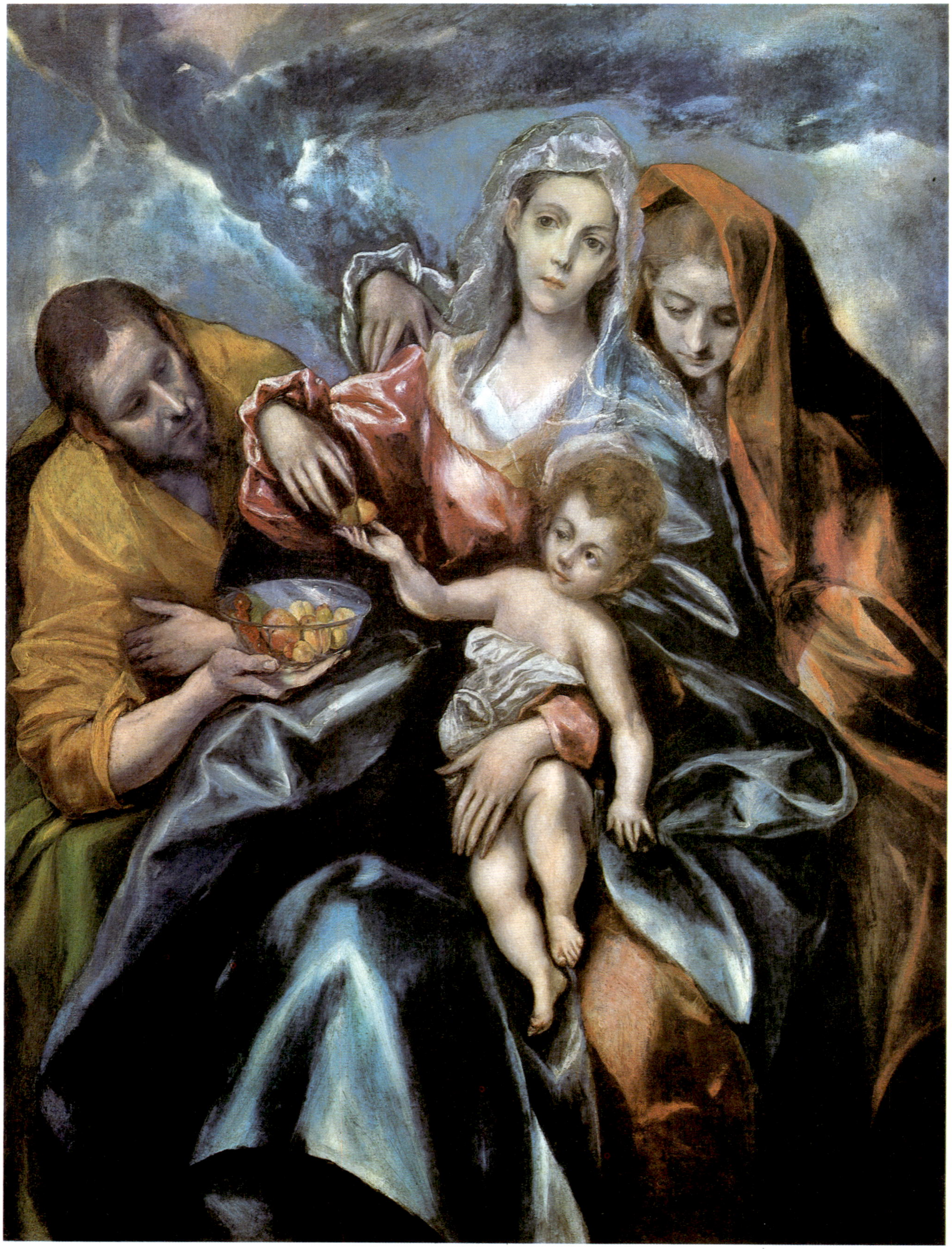

Fig. 120. The Holy Family with the Magdalen, 1587-1597. Cleveland, Museum of Art. Cat. No. 85.

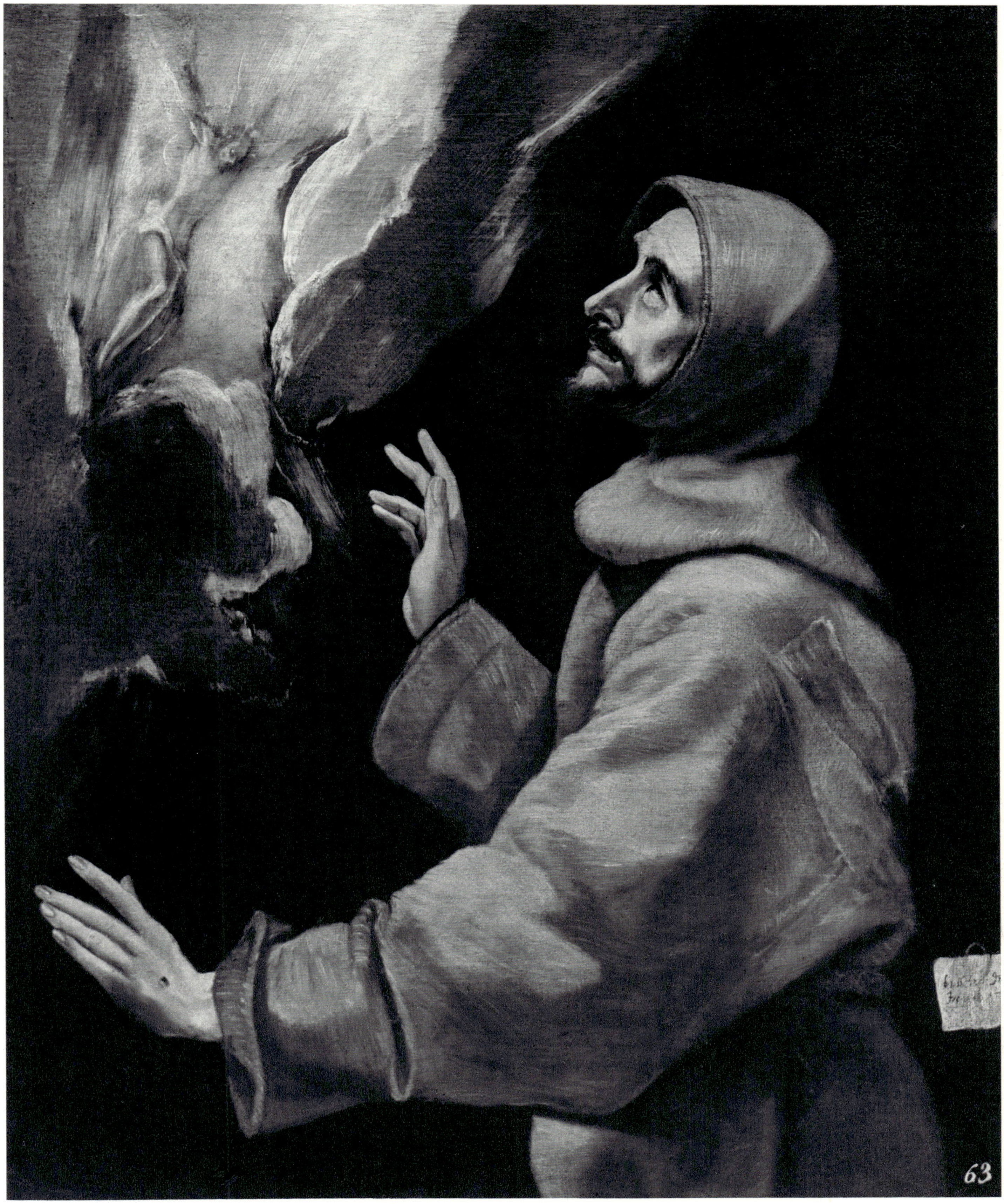

Fig. 121. St. Francis receiving the stigmata, 1587-1597. The Escorial, Monastery. Cat. No. 86.

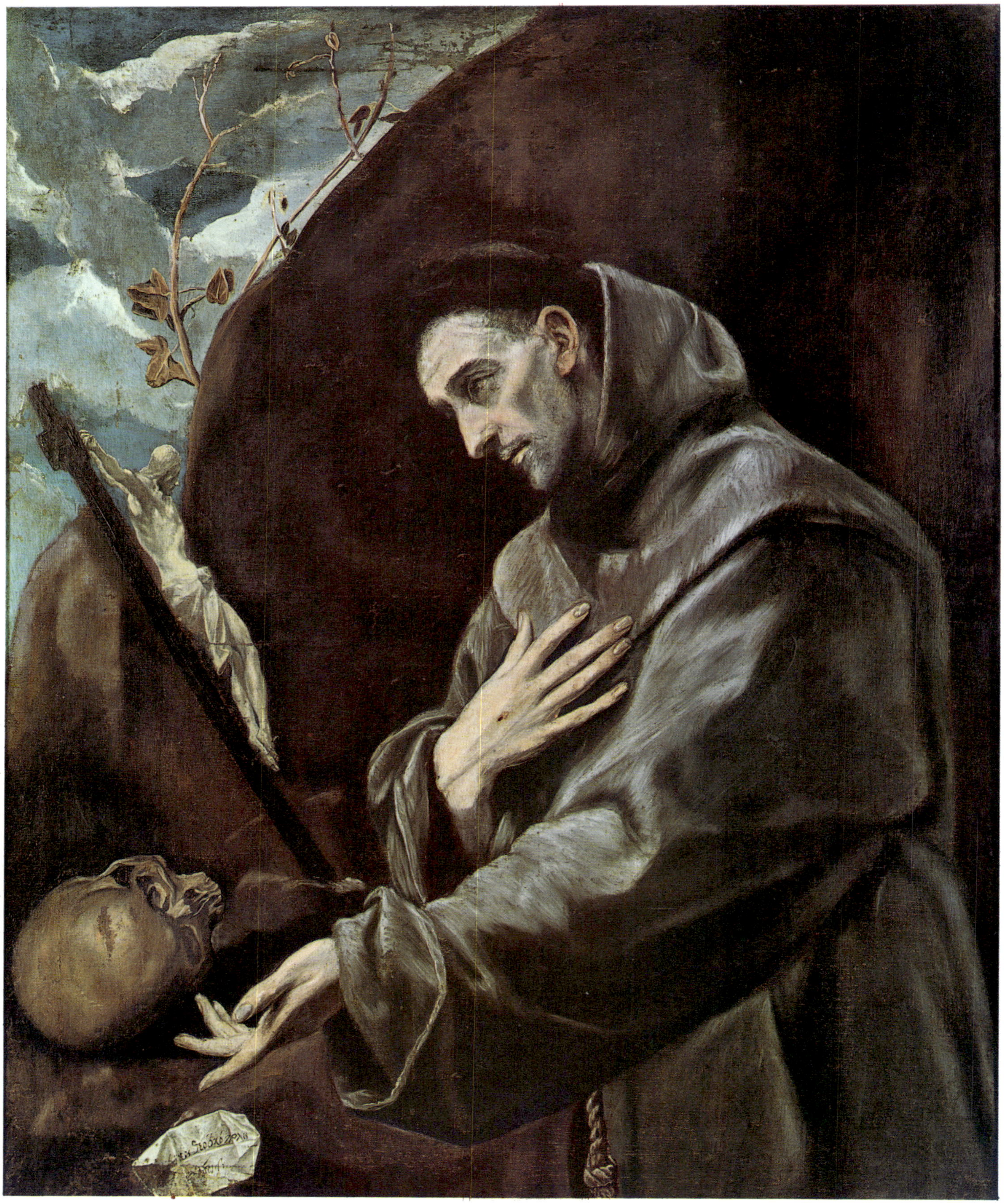

Fig. 122. St. Francis in meditation, 1587-1597. Barcelona, Torelló Collection. Cat. No. 89.

attempts have been made to identify this figure with that of Jerónima de las Cuevas, the Cretan painter's only known love. It is the image of a typically Spanish woman, but in its most ideal and spiritualized form, which conforms at bottom to the painter's normal rule with all his models. Her beauty is the true centre of the composition: all the other elements seem to revolve around that roseate head, with its chestnut hair half-covered by a transparent veil of pinkish ochre. There is no other aureole than that skilfully formed by a gap between the clouds, through which we can discern a background of blue sky. It is interesting to observe —as a probably conscious effect and one that shows El Greco's fidelity to archaic formulas within his advanced style— the bilateral symmetry produced by the two smaller openings in the clouds, which also let us see the blue sky in the background and are placed over the heads of St. Anne and St. Joseph respectively. The clouds grow denser towards the centre and form a kind of great arc over Mary, which contributes to the profound effect of symmetry that this picture has on the viewer, even though the symmetry is then animated by the marvellously depicted interplay of life and by the movement of the draperies, centering on the vivid pink of the Virgin's clothing. The precision of tone is very delicate and, as in many of El Greco's pictures, the intertwining of hands creates a rhythm of feeling and plasticity that enlivens the whole.

The Niarchos "Pietà"

We consider that the highest point of the period following the painting of the *Burial of the Conde de Orgaz* is reached in the magnificent *Pietà* in the Niarchos Collection *(Fig. 117 - Cat. 83),* in which some of the details might be interpreted as reminiscences of Tintoretto, though without thereby losing any of the splendid originality and force of the whole. The most surprising feature is the way in which the image is conceived. In order to create a *Pietà* of more vigorous effect than any he had done hitherto, El Greco here places himself, so to speak, in the very interior of the action, giving the figures an impressive sense of nearness. Four figures fill the whole space, leaving small gaps in the upper part through which can be seen the wood of the cross and the sky. It is in Mary Magdalen —and also, perhaps, in the figure on the left— that the Tintoretto aspect is most evident, though some relationship may also be admitted in the monumental quality of the body of Christ, thrust so far into the foreground. But this is a reminiscence, not the reflection of a concept or even any deep similarity in results or in style. This picture admits no background, no perspective effect, no sensuousness, affirming in all its implacable truth the drama of the Passion of Christ. It is one of the greatest works in El Greco's whole career. Few pictures exist in which all the elements are so perfectly and so necessarily united. The body of Christ is the dominant factor, not only because the theme demands it, but also because the painter succeeded in arranging this form so that it becomes both the centre of attention and an element that binds all the other factors of the composition together. The vertical rhythm of the fallen right arm leads our eyes to the crown of thorns, the symbol of the Passion. The head, lovingly held up by the Virgin's right hand, forms the essential nucleus of the whole. The bearded male figure (Joseph of Arimathea) bends over the Redeemer, his bald head standing out against the ample cloak that closes the composition on the left. Christ's left arm, stretched over the bloodless body, marks an evident horizontal axis, while the nail-pierced hand that rests on the knee is held by Mary Magdalen in her own hands. Here we find once more that beautiful feminine character, whose features we already know from the versions of the *Penitent Magdalen* painted before the present work. Even the clothing is very similar, as are the loosely flowing golden tresses, the transparent veil and the bared forearms. The deep folds of the Virgin's cloak form a background to the body of the dead Christ. The fact that the painter has worked from a viewpoint so close to the figures not only increases their monumental quality and the dramatic character of the scene, but also deepens the vital intensity of the colour, the form and quality, and the pictorial effects required to reflect each of the materials depicted. In almost every area of this composition the eye cannot fail to notice and appreciate the beauty of the actual paint itself, as something to a certain extent independent of the reality it is recording on the canvas. This is the case with the firm, unctuous, whitish paint of Christ's left shoulder and arm, with the flesh tints and the cloak of the Virgin and with the details of Mary Magdalen's clothing, especially with her exquisitely painted veil, treated with that freedom of execution that is the privilege of genius. It cannot be denied that El Greco, logically enough, made greater efforts when he was creating a composition that he had not painted previously. Hence the importance of all his prototypes, though we must admit there may be something of speculation —of pure supposition— in these opinions of ours, for a lot of El Greco's work has been lost and is unknown to us today, so that what we believe to be prototypes may sometimes be nothing of the sort.

Next to be considered is the *Adoration of the shepherds* bequeathed to the College of Corpus Christi in Valencia by its founder, the Blessed Juan de Ribera, and included in an inventory drawn up in the year 1611 *(Fig. 119 - Cat. 84)*. This composition is arranged by means of broken rhythms which give rise to a series of flame-like movements in different parts of the scene, which is unified rather by the movement than by the static structures. The distortions here are no longer merely optical, as in previous periods; now they are beginning to constitute a sort of expressionism which will be further evidenced in later works by El Greco. But they also form a way of conceiving the faces, in very strongly-marked ovals, with appreciable volume and simple but effective modelling; these ovals are sometimes subjected to lateral twisting, but this never deprives them of their beauty or reaches the verge of caricature, though they are not devoid of a certain Mannerism.

For El Greco draperies and gestures are always positive elements in the rhythmic expression, which is what really constructs the picture, apart from the colour. Thus certain details of linear unification are of interest in the picture now before us. We should observe, for instance, how the broken line of the wall in the background, just behind the corner of the swaddling-cloth that is being held up, is almost parallel to the line of the back, shoulder, neck and head of a shepherd, so that his outline may stand out better against the dark night that can be divined behind the line of the wall. The fact that this canvas was reproduced in an engraving published by Diego de Astor and dated 1606, which we shall study later, does not imply that the painting is of that year.

The *Holy Family with the Magdalen* now in the Cleveland Museum of Art comes from the Convento de Esquivias in Torrejón de Velasco (Toledo) *(Fig. 120 - Cat. 85)*. It is a very effective painting in spite of its bad state of preservation, which was not much improved by the restorations to which it was subjected when in various collections. In a vivid harmony of colour we see the three members of the Holy Family, in their traditional attire, with Mary Magdalen, who is wrapped in a brilliant cloak that even covers part of her fair hair. This composition permits El Greco to create one of the youngest and most beautiful Virgins in his whole career, in which Marian iconography occupies such a prominent place. The contrast established between her and Mary Magdalen, all the more noticeable because their two faces are so close, could not be a more felicitous exaltation of the Virgin, for the saint, whose face is shown bending downwards and in foreshortening, really presents a psychological type which we can guess to be complex and tormented and which, for that very reason, sets off the radiant serenity of the Virgin. St. Joseph also appears in semi-foreshortening and somewhat slanted, so his dominant rhythm follows the very evident oblique axis imposed by the right hand of the Virgin and that of the Child. The ample folds in the lower area and on the right, together with the beautiful cloud effects, envelop and heighten this admirable ensemble of elegance and feeling. As we shall see in the following chapter, some elements in this composition are the immediate forerunners of those in the canvas over one of the side altars in the Chapel of San José in Toledo.

Franciscan iconography

The beauty and deep religious feeling that emanate from El Greco's paintings of St. Francis justify the words of Pacheco in his *Art of Painting*: "It is certain that if Antonio Mohedano had followed these indications, in my opinion he would be the best painter of St. Francis known at this time. But we will leave this glory to Domingo Greco, for he kept more closely to what history tells us. Yet he dressed him roughly in coarse cloth, like a hermit, which was not his real habit...." It may be supposed that this objection to the quality of the clothing with which the scrupulous Pacheco modifies his spontaneous praise of El Greco's Franciscan paintings was the more or less general opinion at that time. We should not forget that iconographical precision was considered inviolable in those days, given their feelings regarding realism. Nor should it be forgotten, however, that this accuracy affected clothing to a lesser degree. We have

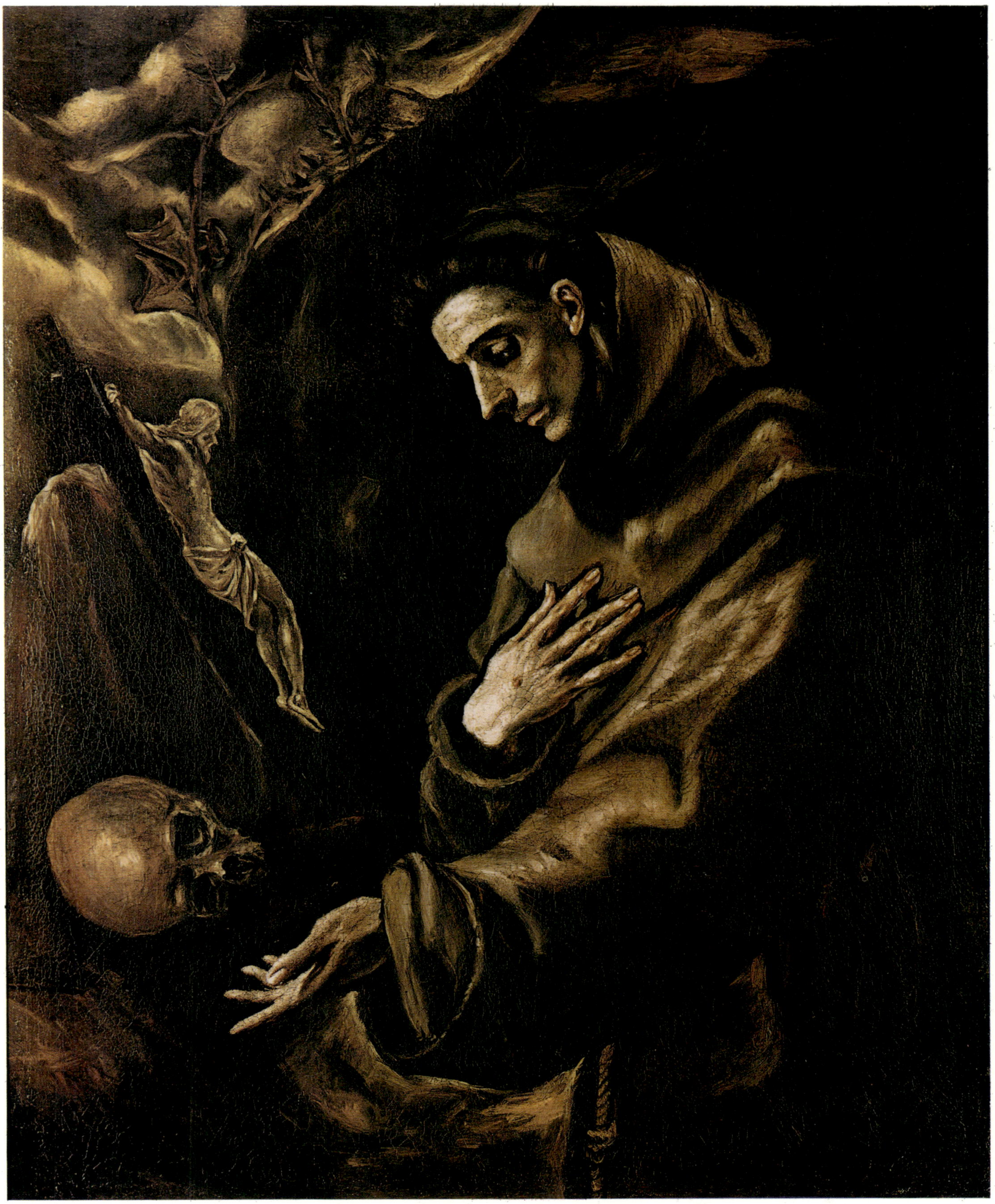

Fig. 123. St. Francis in meditation, 1587-1597. Valencia, Montesinos Collection. Cat. No. 90.

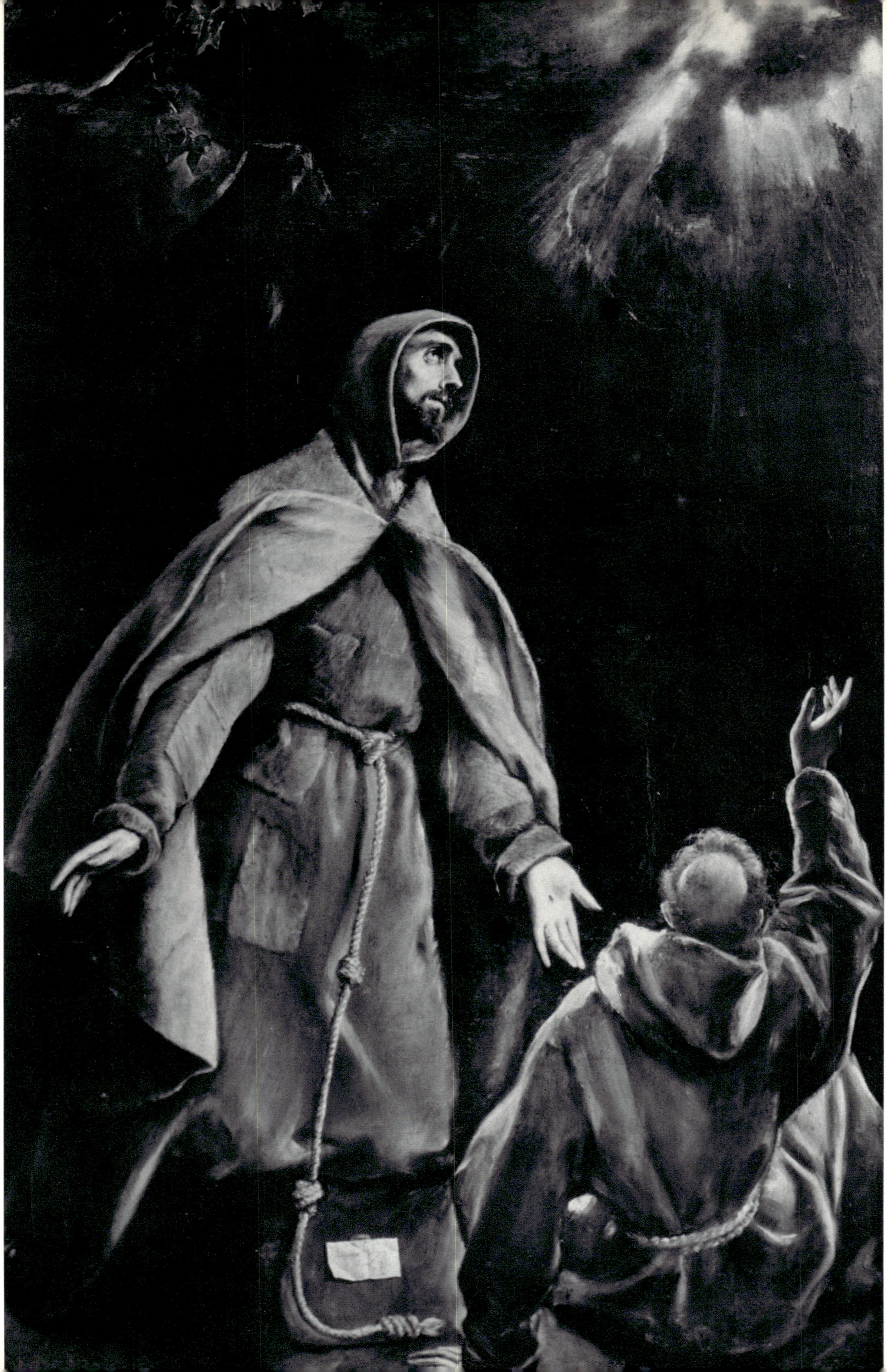

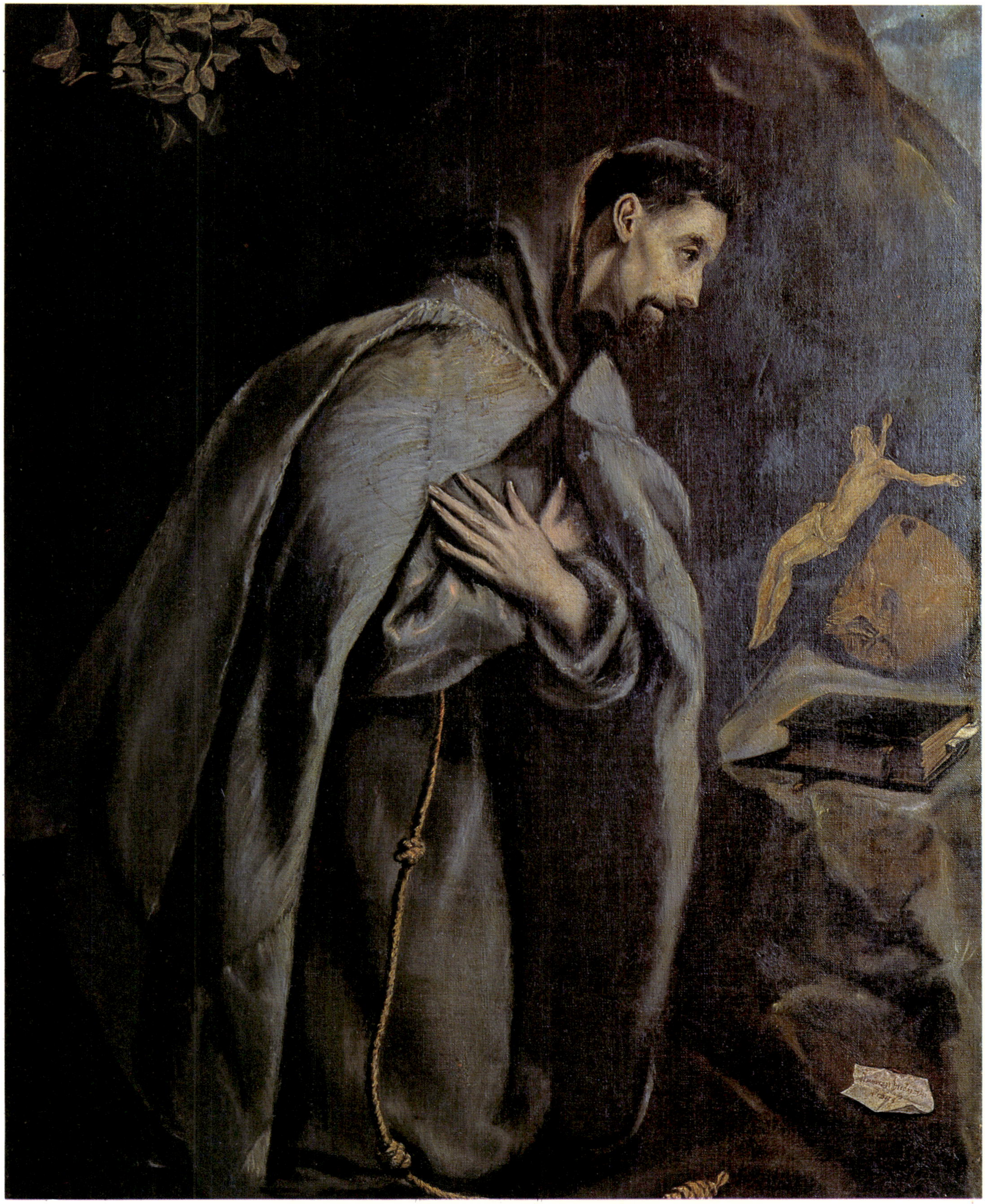

Fig. 124. St. Francis receiving the stigmata, 1587-1597. Cadiz, Hospital de Nuestra Señora del Carmen. Cat. No. 92.
Fig. 125. St. Francis kneeling in meditation, 1587-1597. Bilbao, Museum of Fine Arts. Cat. No. 94.

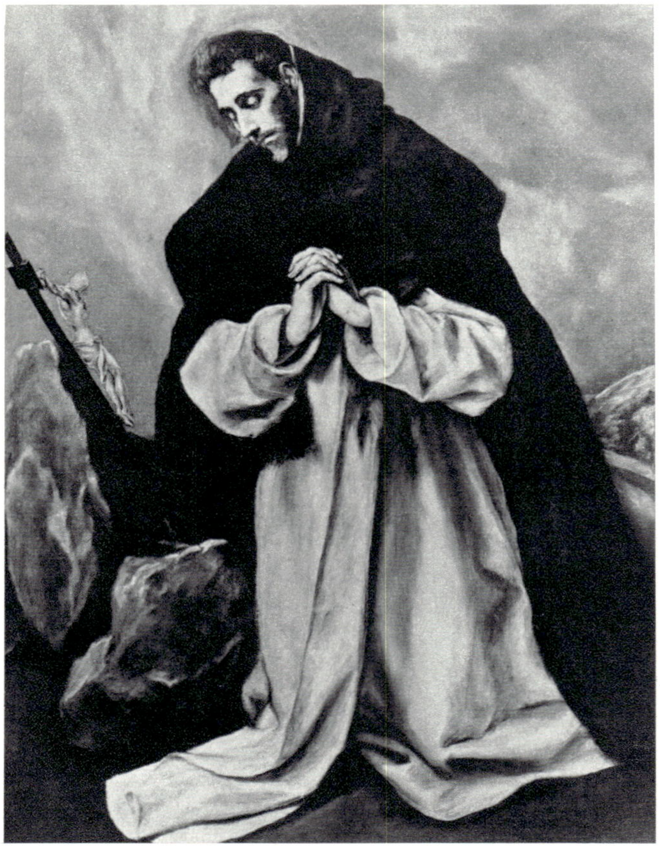

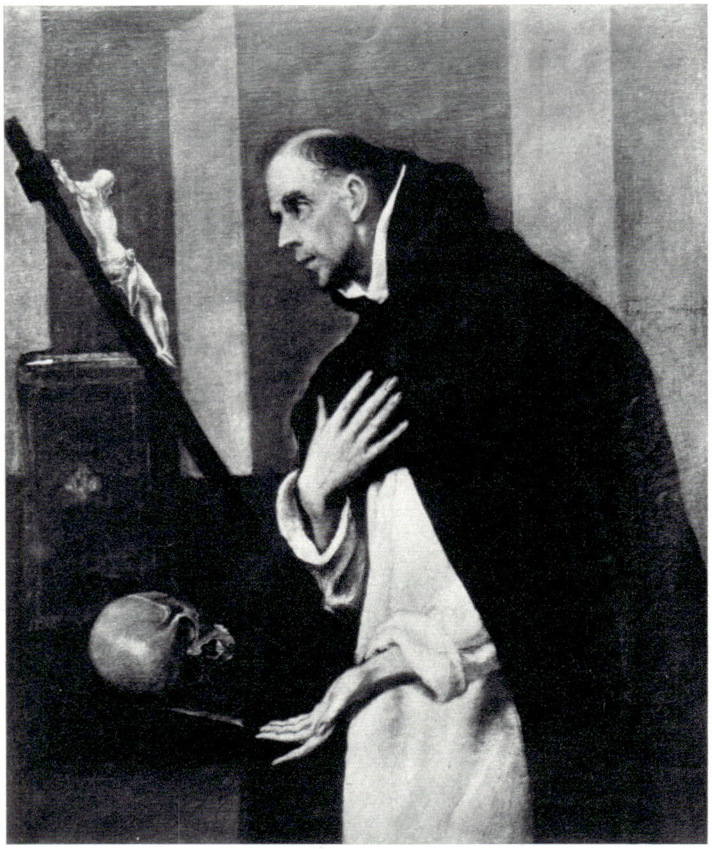

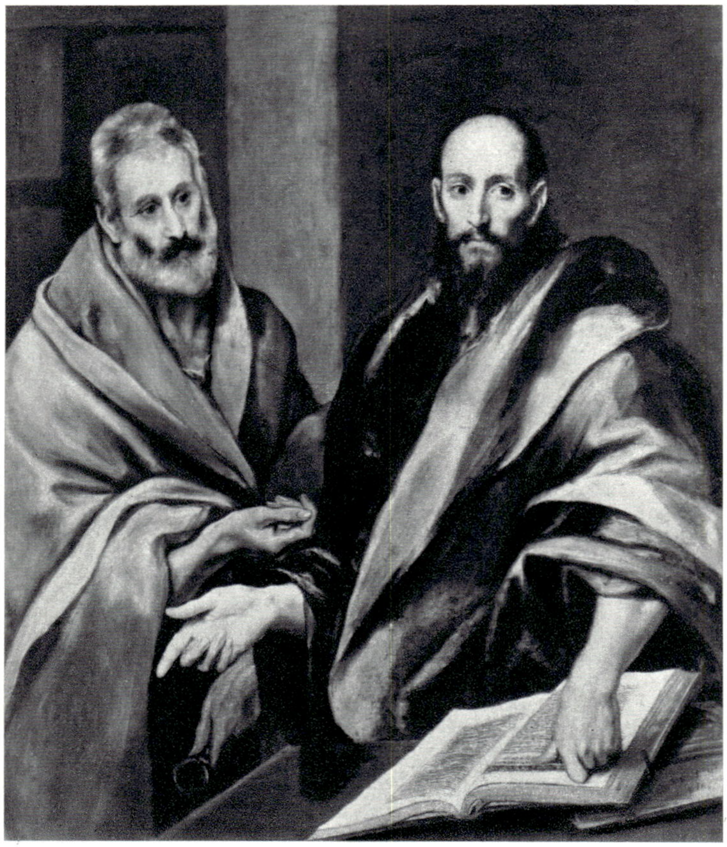

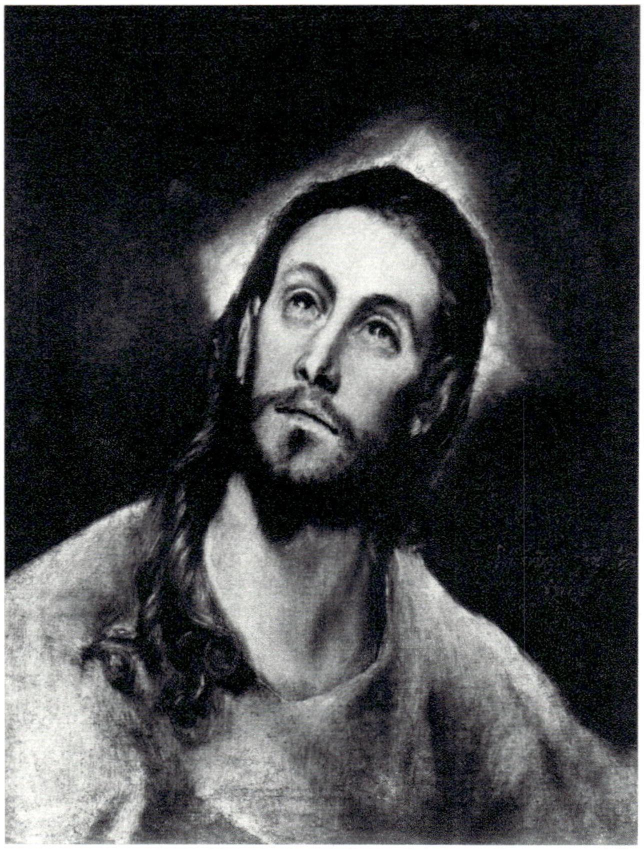

Fig. 126. St. Dominic in prayer, 1587-1597. Madrid, Urquijo Collection. Cat. No. 95.
Fig. 127. St. Dominic in prayer in his cell, 1587-1597. Newport, J. Nicholas Brown Collection. Cat. No. 96.
Fig. 128. St. Peter and St. Paul, 1587-1597. Leningrad, Hermitage. Cat. No. 97.
Fig. 129. Head of Christ, 1587-1597. Prague, Museum. Cat. No. 98.

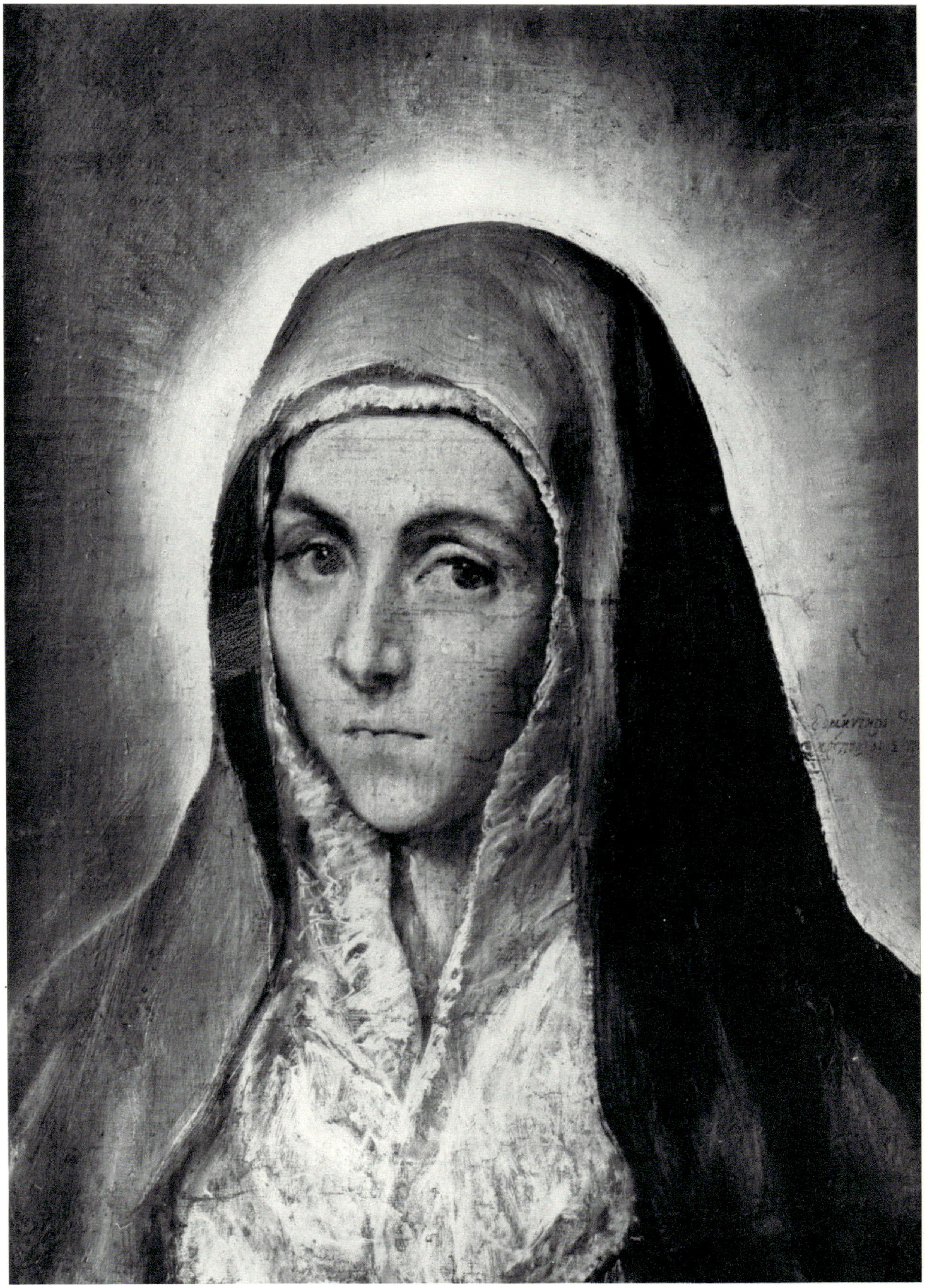

Fig. 130. Mater Dolorosa, 1587-1597. Strasbourg, Museum. Cat. No. 99.

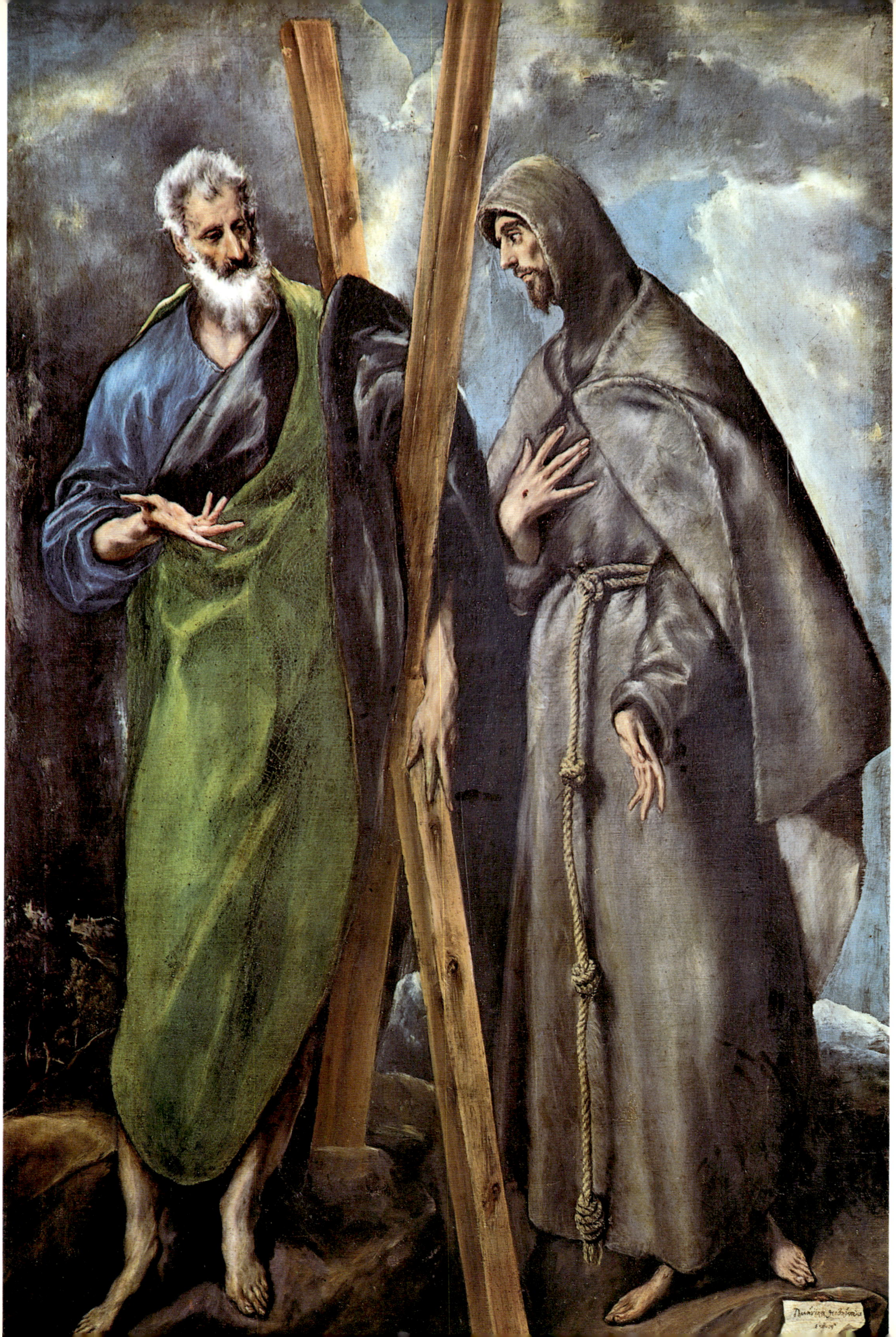

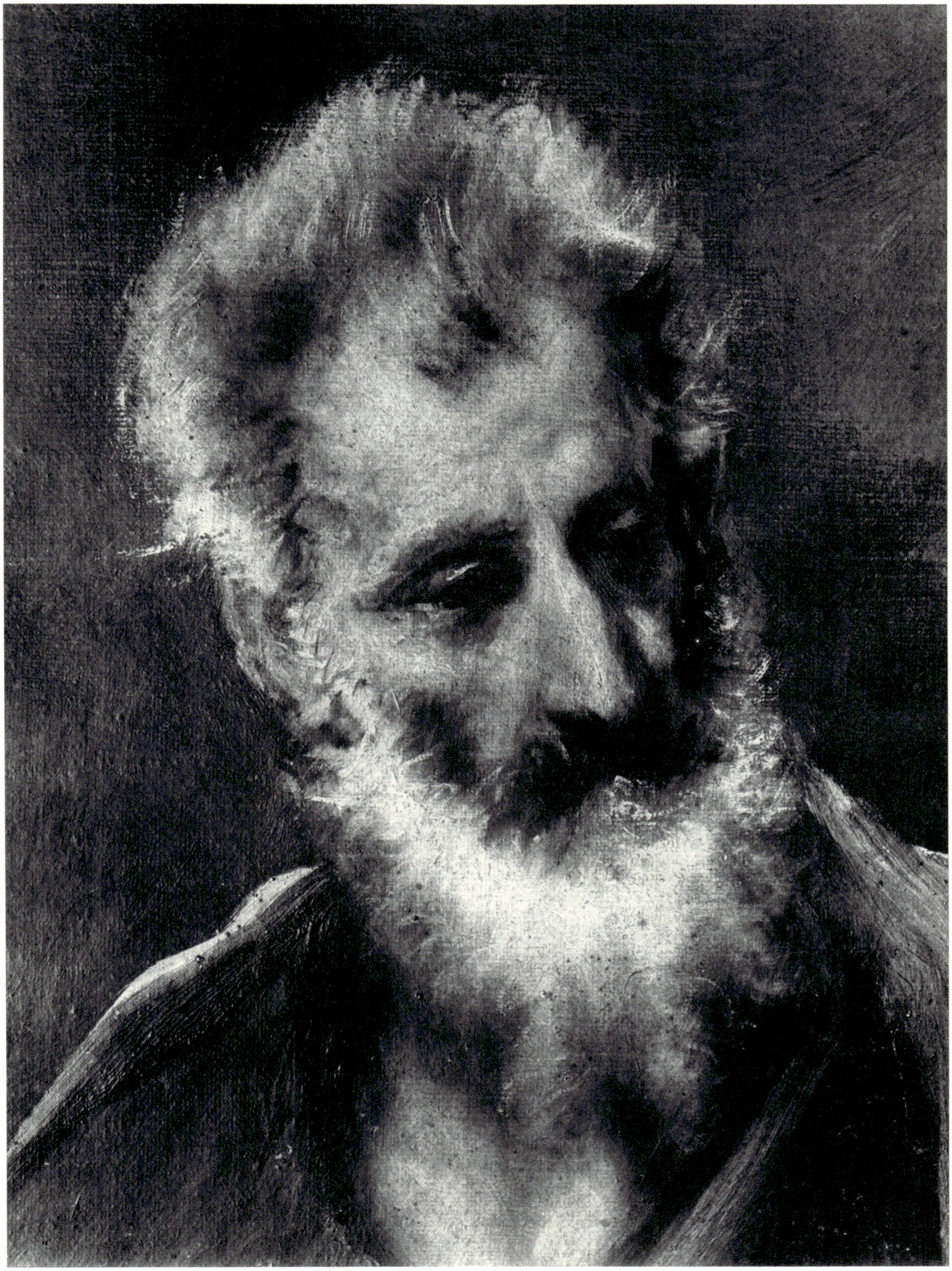

Figs. 131 & 132. St. Andrew and St. Francis, 1587-1597. Madrid, Prado. Cat. No. 100.

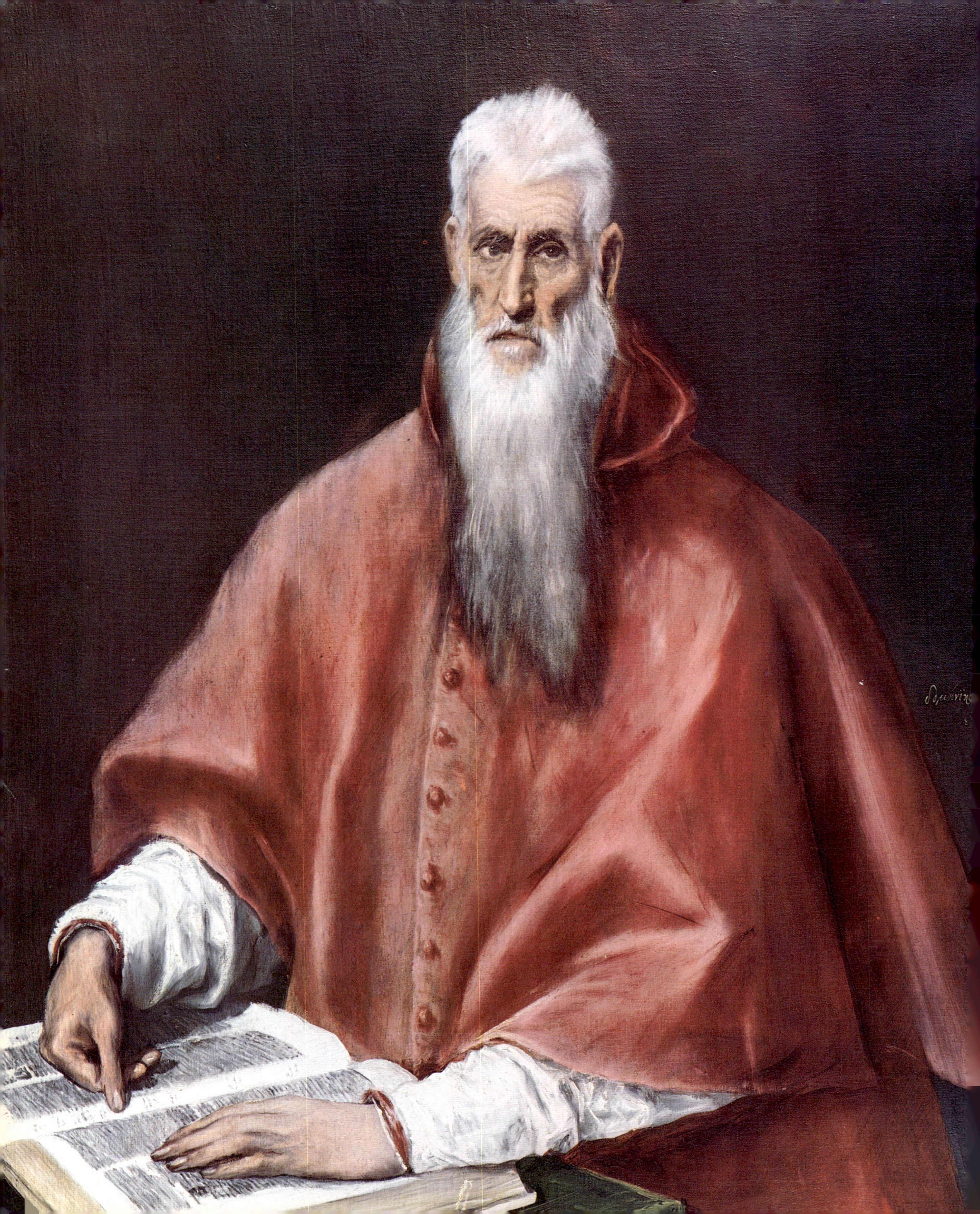

already seen how El Greco represented the warriors of antiquity with armour of the sixteenth century.

A very fine canvas in the Escorial represents *St. Francis receiving the stigmata*; with an expression of awe, the saint contemplates the apparition of the crucified Christ between radiant clouds *(Fig. 121 - Cat. 86)*. We may observe the painter's overriding desire to establish clear contrasts between all the elements and areas of the form, as may be seen above all in the wonderful habit, so directly and forcefully modelled. Here we have one of the tricks that El Greco was to develop conscientiously in other similar representations, giving the cloth inflections that transform it into pure expression without affecting the realism of texture and form. The tonal contrast, which is so vigorous in this work, was to be attenuated in the following ones, the artist probably having noticed that a soft expression and treatment suited St. Francis better than this dramatic contrast of light and dark, barely mitigated by the apparition of Christ.

At this point in his career El Greco developed a definite preoccupation with light and made use, in fact, of themes that were somehow related, if not repeated with some degree of precision, to experiment with natural light as a factor of variation and change. Let us consider a new type for the image of *St. Francis in meditation*, of which three signed versions are known to us. They can be differentiated by the effect of the light, certain qualities of texture and the physical appearance of the saint. The version that hangs in the Joselyn Museum in Nebraska *(Cat. 88)* depicts him almost in the full light of day, the one in the Torelló Collection in Barcelona *(Fig. 122 - Cat. 89)* shows him at twilight, while in the third, which is in the Montesinos Collection in Valencia *(Fig. 123 - Cat. 90)*, the light comes from the moon. All three versions have the same emotion, the same serene, restrained eloquence, which is shown in the gesture. They show the painter's extraordinary capacity for capturing the spirit of his ideal personages, a gift which, it is evident, was necessarily based on his skill in transmitting his own emotionalism to the models represented.

Within El Greco's work as a whole, in pictures that are less vividly coloured, in those that are sadder in tone and even in expression, as is the case with these pictures of St. Francis, we can also make wonderful discoveries. To compare these three pictures —to be able to see all three side by side— would be an immense aesthetic pleasure, for then we might see how the painter managed to vary one and the same composition and theme by skilful gradations. The idea of gradually changing, from one version to the next, both the light and the physiognomy of the saint, but without altering his features in any essential, is a really astounding one. It is very possible that these variations, apart from their aesthetic value, were a device hit upon by El Greco to enable him to reiterate his images without entirely repeating himself. To prove this a direct study of the replicas is essential, for what may seem exact replicas in black-and-white photographs are, in fact, canvases endowed with fresh originality created by changes of tone, lighting and execution.

The course followed by El Greco is plain to be seen in the extraordinary *St. Francis receiving the stigmata* in the Women's Hospital of Cadiz *(Fig. 124 - Cat. 92)*. It appeals to our emotions through its vehemence and through the intimate relationship between space and figures, light and gestures, as expression. The realism of the scene, the effect of the light and the nearness of the painter's viewpoint all foreshadow the work of Caravaggio, as does the vivid tonal contrast. But the Cretan painter lacks the Italian's naturalistic obsession and the trenchant oppositions of light and shade that became Caravaggio's principal stylistic formula.

Astonishing indeed is the quality of realism achieved in the textures, which also appears in all the details of the picture, particularly in the habits of the monks and the knotted cords round their waists. The explosion of light in the sky, in the upper right-hand corner, is sufficiently dazzling to serve as a sign of the truth of the miracle. It is easy to understand how this type of art appealed to the ordinary people (a question which it would be interesting to analyse more fully) in late sixteenth-century Spain. Quite evidently, El Greco was one of the painters who did most for the popularity of St. Francis in Spain. The series of pictures of this saint either signed by him or done in his workshop, if we are to take into account all the versions and variants he created which we shall study, is really impressive and constitutes a true act of homage, the highest point of which is reached in this work in Cadiz.

El Greco also repeated in a fair number of canvases another type of the saint of Assisi, a model which must have been a novelty during the period we are now studying. It represents the saint praying in a cave, kneeling before a crucifix that is resting on

133. St. Jerome as a cardinal, 1587-1597.
York, Frick Collection. Cat. No. 101.

a skull. As in the previous case, the repetitions are all very similar, nor is it an easy task to decide where the painter's own hand leaves off and an assistant's brush takes up the job. We publish here as a signed version, and one that belongs to the period now under consideration, despite the fact that there are other signed versions of equal quality, the one which comes from Cuerva, near Toledo, and now hangs in the Bilbao Museum of Fine Arts *(Fig. 125 - Cat. 94).* There can be no doubt, as we have said before, that when El Greco created a composition, even one based on a theme and person already dealt with, he felt more inspired than when he came back to the same composition to repeat it. Or perhaps an additional reason —for we cannot forget the psychological attitude of the viewer, even when he is an historian— is that the impact produced by the hitherto unknown is deeper. However that may be, this new image of St. Francis, in profile against a background of shadows and with the wonderful still-life made up of breviary, crucifix and skull, seems to reveal a new side to the Franciscan mystique of El Greco. If we examine the details, we shall observe his use of the technique of rubbing, in order to give quality to those details and, above all, to produce that impression of movement that animates the character and gives him life, a representation very different from the purest and most perfect "coloured drawing". Pictorial to an extreme, El Greco was a forerunner in procedures that were to be habitual in Goya and in some details he went even further, or, rather, he outdistanced him in different ways (visionary and idealistic ways rather than expressionistic). The face of this St. Francis is impressive enough in its basic drawing, but still more so in its execution, which is a most skilful amalgam of discipline and freedom in tackling the problem of depicting the form. The great quality of this painting is to be seen even in the slightest details.

Other works

There is just as much emotional quality in a kneeling image of *St. Dominic in prayer* in the Urquijo Collection in Madrid *(Fig. 126 - Cat. 95),* which presents the saint full-length from a low and very close viewpoint, as a result of which the figure is monumentalized and projected, as it were, against the sky. But this effect does not render the character heroic, thanks to his intensely withdrawn and humble expression. The saint is represented as aloof from all temporal circumstances and entirely given up to his religious vocation. A broad sky covered with clouds enables the painter to use the richest of shadings to frame the intense tonal contrast of the Dominican habit.

The *St. Dominic in prayer in his cell* in Newport (Rhode Island) *(Fig. 127 - Cat. 96)* is a literal adaptation of the praying figure of St. Francis in the versions studied above, but the typology is different and so is the expression. While the representations of St. Francis were conceived as expressions of his dedication, here the arching of the saint's eyebrows, the slight trembling of the lips, which seem to be half-open, and even the hinted movement of the left hand are all rather signs of questioning.

In the Hermitage in Leningrad there is another version of the *St. Peter and St. Paul,* which, though engraved by Diego de Astor in 1606, we believe to belong to the period we are now studying *(Fig. 128 - Cat. 97).* Here the two saints are shown in an interior. In the background we can see a tall vertical rectangle, rather vague as an architectural element, but sufficient to separate the two figures in space. One might almost say, indeed, that these are two figures taken from two different previous typologies and now brought together by the artist. Unlike the Barcelona painting, therefore, each figure in this work in the Hermitage seems to be isolated in his own world, lost in inner thought. The St. Peter, on the left, recalls in his typology the version we have already mentioned of St. Peter in penitence, though here the head is taken from another angle of vision. The St. Paul comes from another version of this saint by himself, which has also been previously studied. Typologically, these two characters are less similar to those hallowed by traditional iconography, though not different in essentials. It is their temperaments that separate them: St. Peter is presented as a dreamy, spiritual character, St. Paul as a resolute man of action. They are two men preoccupied by a task which seems —and in fact was— too much for mere human strength. It is important to remark on these typological and iconographical details, for they show that El Greco's preoccupations were both technical and psychological. It is on account of the latter, evidently, together with the magic of his luminous colour and contorted forms, that he has reached the hearts of the masses who have hardly any interest in pictorial matters, if they have any at all.

Another religious picture may be included in this group and period: a *Head of Christ*, gazing heavenwards on a background that is dark, though separated from the head by a brilliant aureole of light *(Fig. 129 - Cat. 98)*. This picture, in the Prague Museum, illustrates the technical complexities that went to make up the simplicity of El Greco: the rubbing of the robe on the right, the thick, pale impasto on the forehead, especially to the left, and a whole broad mass emphasizing the outline of the forehead just at the beginning of the hair. Liquid luminosity in the eyes, which is obtained by touches of white applied partly on the black of the iris and the pupil and partly on the less vivid white of the cornea. Abrupt and thick impasto on the bridge of the nose, between the eyes. A dark line of great depth marking the middle of the mouth, at the joining of the lips. White spots and specks, unevenly applied, on the sparse hair at the beginning of the beard; and even apparently motiveless flecks of white on the black hair to the left, at the height of the cheek. The whole, though very different from the pointillism and "optical blending" of some nineteenth-century artists, is nevertheless identical at bottom. The idea is to enliven the whole and the impression received by the viewer through technical procedures far removed from the academic. In the seventeenth century Rembrandt was to be another consistent cultivator of such "tricks", which enabled him to create soft backgrounds, like a sort of fluid atmosphere, against which he projected his figures. But neither the Dutchman of the Baroque period nor the Hispanicized Greek of the late sixteenth century was to stray far from the normal path of representation, for they used these methods only to intensify the sensation of life in their figures.

Here we may place the admirable *Mater Dolorosa* in the Strasbourg Museum *(Fig. 130 - Cat. 99)*, which is notable for its simplicity and its penetrating expressiveness. The head is covered by a blue mantle, over a white veil of gauzier texture which is fastened at the level of the throat. All the interest is centered on the face and, in it, on the penetrating look. It is an understanding gaze, imbued with meditation, which confirms the fact that the figurative painting of the great periods was never a simple affair of aesthetic qualities (though these, too, it possessed in the highest degree), but also an art of human and divine themes, one that admitted the iconographical principles on which it was based and also feelings. Here again El Greco shows his skill in using the radiance behind his sacred figures as a kind of halo or aureole, in order to give the volume a roundness that is intensified by this contrast.

The picture depicting *St. Andrew and St. Francis* in the Prado *(Fig. 131 - Cat. 100)* was given to the Convent of the Incarnation in Madrid in 1676 by the daughter of the Duke of Abrantes. Here we have two figures in elongated proportions, depicted full-length against a landscape background with a very low horizon which is barely hinted at on each side of the two figures. St. Andrew's green cloak is folded over his X-shaped cross, the black of its lining being placed in bold contrast to the cobalt blue of his robe. The shaded grey of St. Francis's habit, with tones enlivened by touches of colour, is bound up with the leaden grey of the clouds and the blue of the sky to form a strange chromatic harmony with the predominant colours in the figure of St. Andrew. Here we may see yet again how the painter absolutely dispenses with harmonies of complementary colours and seeks his unity in the effects of rhythm, the colour being treated as a factor rather of exaltation and differentiation than of connection. This is the only version of this work, though from it were to come various interpretations and derivations, especially in the case of St. Francis. It is undoubtedly one of El Greco's finest iconographic creations. In it we find a certain element of disintegration and evanescence, in which the shadows, the forms (hinted at rather than really represented) and the lights are all based on an underlying drawing of great precision, but one whose lines can only be noticed in certain areas of the picture —in the admirable hands and feet of the figures, for instance. The general expression of the work takes us into a region of very marked religious feeling, of greater intensity than in earlier periods.

The *St. Jerome as a cardinal* in the Frick Collection *(Fig. 133 - Cat. 101)* is another of El Greco's most impressive creations. It comes from the Cathedral of Valladolid and there are various signed versions and others from the painter's workshop. An exact replica of the painting in the Frick Collection was formerly in the collection of the Marqués del Arco and now hangs in the Lehman Collection, also in New York. This figure is depicted with all the spirit and living force of a portrait. By this we mean that El Greco used a model whom he represented with objective realism, but whom he transferred, by a mysterious stroke of genius, to a higher plane, at the same time giving him that depth which transforms a person into the paradigm of a race and an age. What with the Byzantinism evoked by the elongation and the sense of idealism that imbues the realism, this is the most exact of all representations of a figure who must have been of essential importance in Spain from the Middle Ages: the high-ranking churchman. Men whose study, meditation and ascetism remade, as it were, their whole personality and, creating a specific human type, made it the highest representative of what a certain moment and place in history valued above all else. Let us ignore, for the moment, the more profound sense of the image —the considerations aroused by typology alone— and observe its extraordinary chromatic harmony. It foreshadows the harmonies in grey and crimson of Velázquez, but in another register and with greater intensity, for here the grey is a white modelled with greys, a purer white in the sleeves showing under the crimson and greyer in the figure's long beard and hair. The execution is complex, above all as far as the hair is concerned, and is based both on the fine brushstrokes that draw lines as if in relief created by light and on the scoring, with a paintless brush, of a light, basically evanescent mass, thus suggesting the indefinite multiplicity of the hair. The flesh tints have an intensity that is rarely achieved. The hands, resting on an open codex, are equally expressive, very fine but at the same time as hard and implacable as the gaze. This picture is the psychological forerunner of the portrait of *Cardinal Niño de Guevara*, which we shall be studying later on.

Another work that appears to have been painted during the period we are now studying, and one which El Greco was to repeat with great frequency, is the one that represents *Christ carrying the cross (Fig. 134 - Cat. 106)*. The figure of the Saviour with the great cross fills almost the whole of the canvas and only the misty sky provides the necessary chromatic and spatial foil. The noticeably static character of the image is surprising. The painter has presented Christ as though he were stopping for a moment on the terrible march to Calvary. The eyes are raised heavenwards —those great, luminous, liquid eyes that we have mentioned several times already— and the representation is entirely faithful to the traditional typology, which El Greco knew so well how to transform, adapt to his manner and therefore personalize, in both senses of the term: i.e., both with reference to the person of Christ and to that of the creator of his image, in this case El Greco himself. The extremely beautiful hands resting on the cross are almost as important as the face. El Greco was a prodigious painter of hands, both in the beauty of form that he gave them, with its precise inflection of straight lines and curves in the definition of each finger, and in the perfect suggestion of the volume and the different tensions —muscles, bones, the outer integument of skin— to be found in them. The voluminous cloak, emblem of royalty and mockery, and the crown of thorns, which does not need the exaggerations of Grünewald to be awe-inspiring, are the only accessories, together with the heavy cross, that appear with and around the flesh tints of Christ and his sublime expression. The expression is one of emotion and sacrifice rather than triumphant serenity. This version, which shows Christ advancing almost diagonally from left to right of the picture, with the head on the axis of the body, was, as has already been pointed out, one of the painter's favourites. We know of three signed contemporary versions, in the Art Museum of Catalonia, in the Lehman Collection in New York and in the National Museum in Buenos Aires, but there are other notable replicas executed with considerable participation on the part of the master himself. As we shall see, this *modello* was used in other versions painted during a later period.

It seems likely that the original version of the theme of *Christ carrying the cross* is the picture in the Brooklyn Museum in New York *(Fig. 135 - Cat. 111)*. Astonishing indeed is the head of this Christ, in which we can see, not only all the qualities of expression, but also the supreme freedom of El Greco's pictorial concept. The head is painted in not very marked but extremely difficult foreshortening without distortion of the form, which shows the painter's total mastery in drawing. Whenever he used distortion it was intentional and was only an exaggeration of the necessary alteration imposed on the form by a given posture or angle of vision. The drawing in this work is subordinate to the pictorial execution. In other words, the line is of less importance and the blended modelling disintegrates at certain points, though without losing any of its force and precision of representation, in order to give greater emotion to a detail, in this case a pictorial rather than a mystical emotion, though the latter is also abundant in this work. The best example of this partial disintegration of the modelling is to be found in the area of the right eye, with the

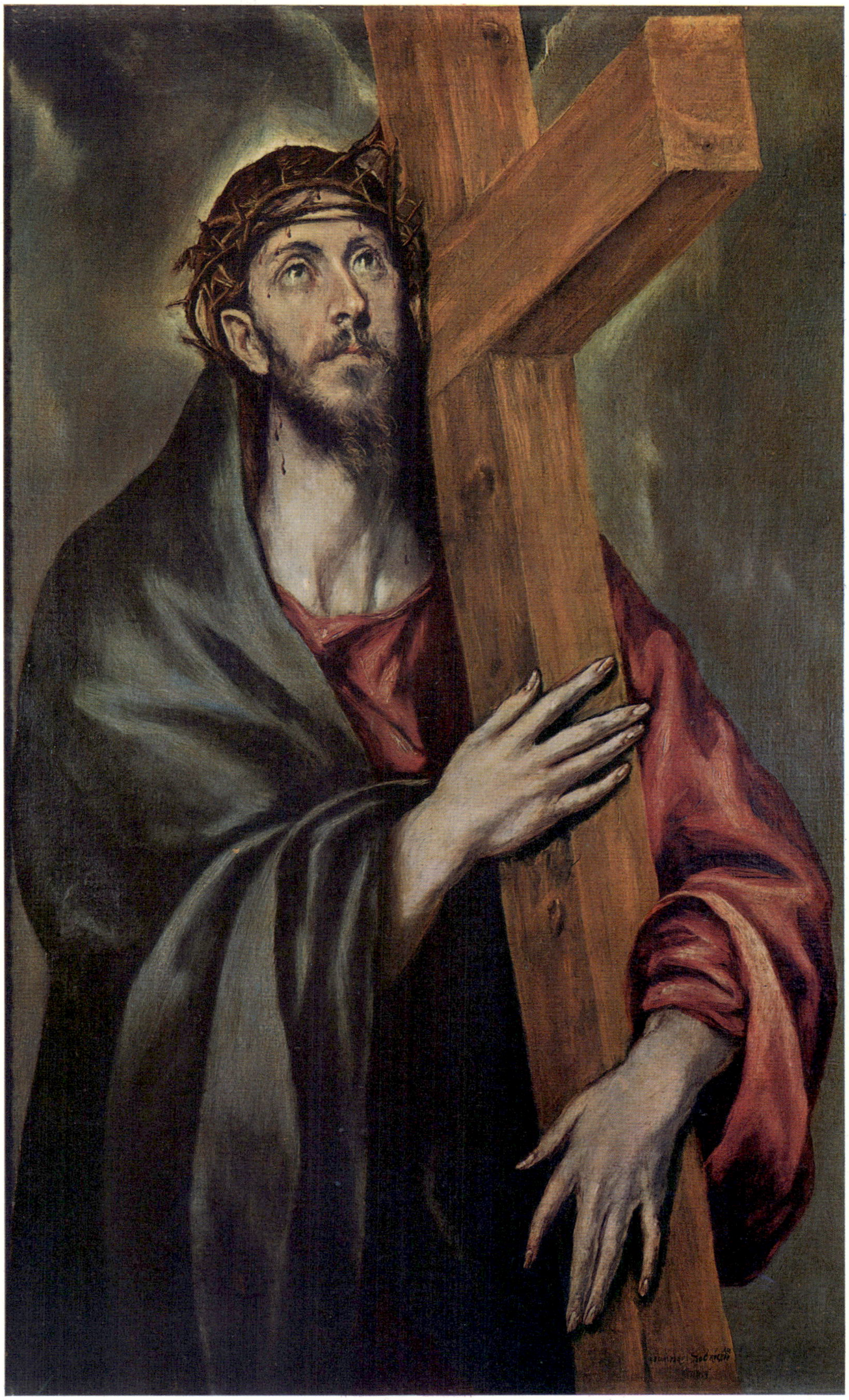

Fig. 134. Christ carrying the cross, 1587-1597. Barcelona, Art Museum of Catalonia. Cat. No. 106.

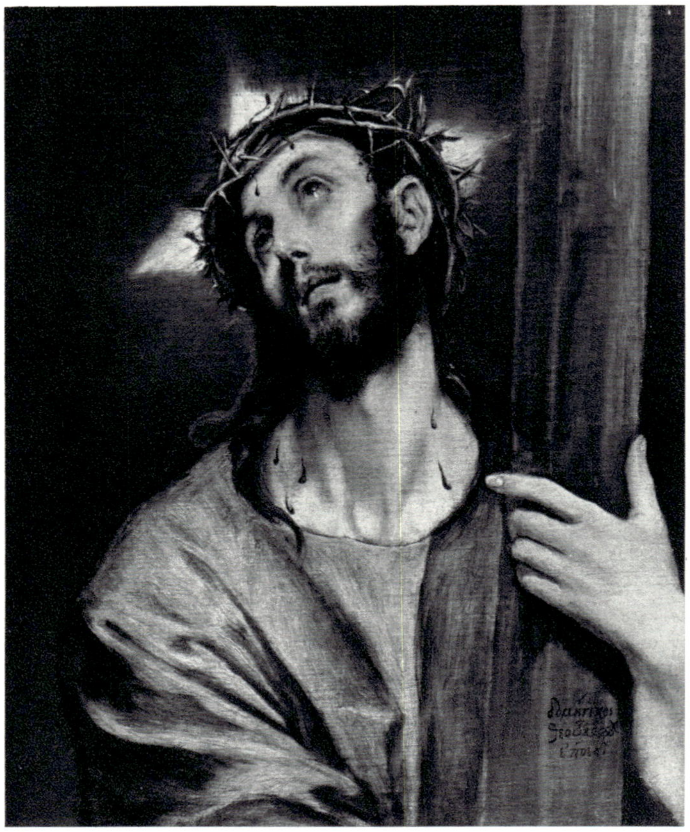

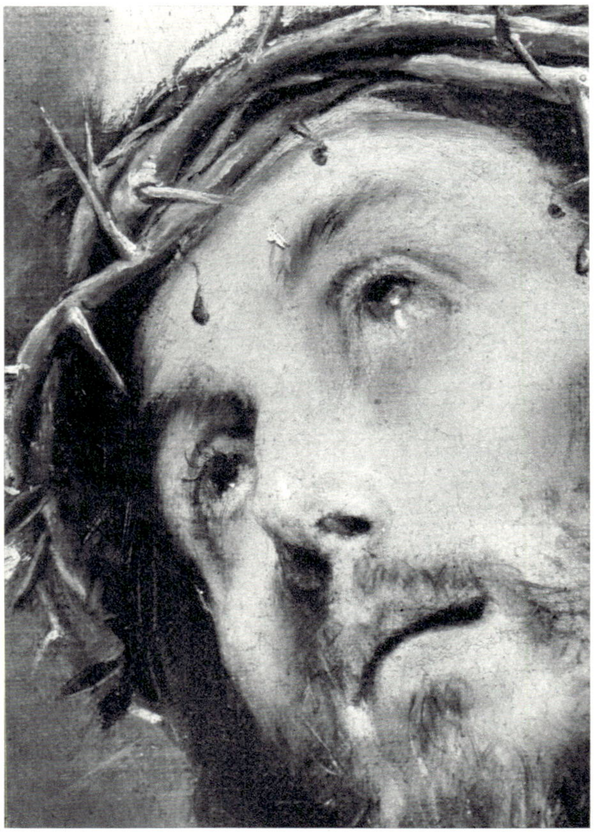

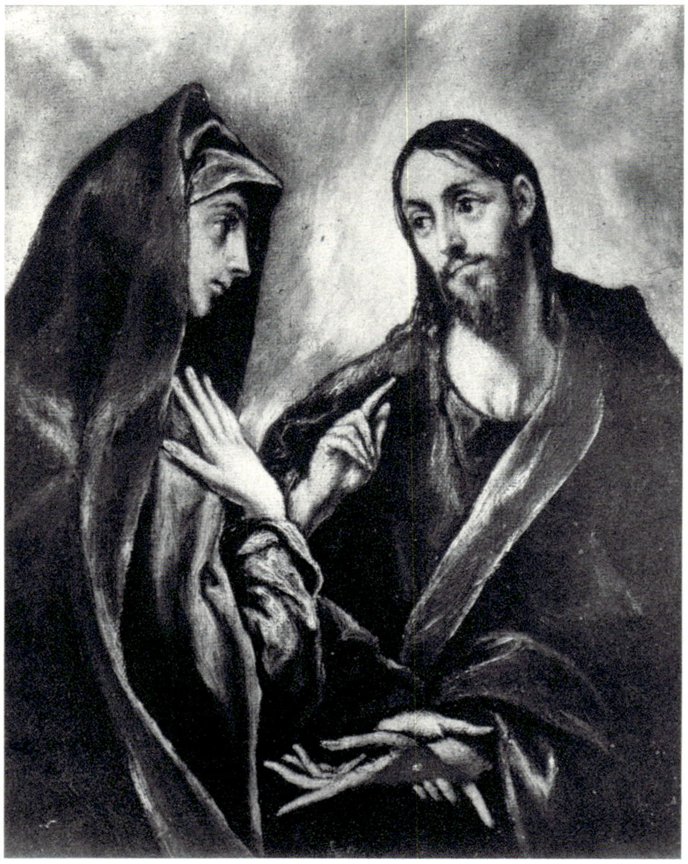

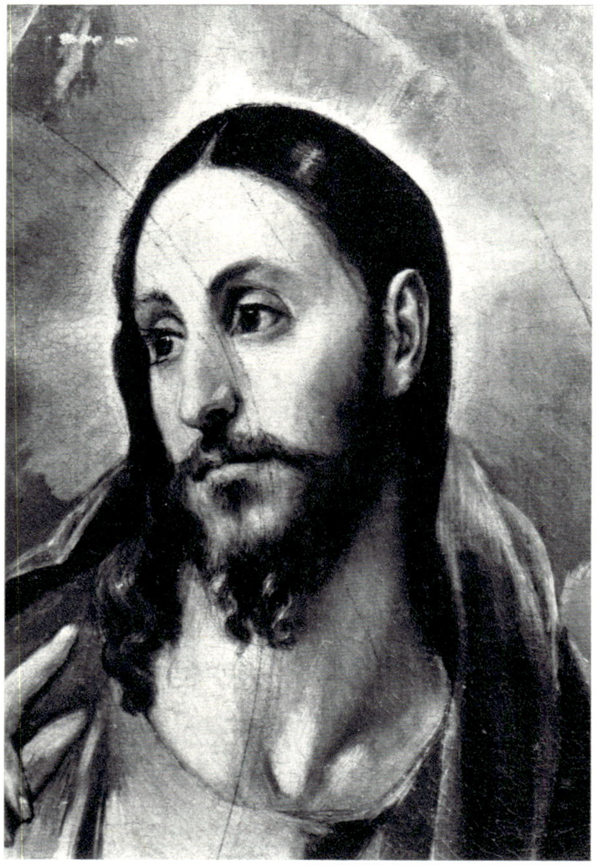

Figs. 135 & 136. Christ carrying the cross, 1587-1597. New York, Brooklyn Museum. Cat. No. 111.
Fig. 137. Christ saying farewell to his mother, 1587-1597. Sinaia, Royal Palace. Cat. No. 113.
Fig. 138. Christ saying farewell to his mother (detail), 1587-1597. Toledo, Santa Cruz Museum. Cat. No. 115.

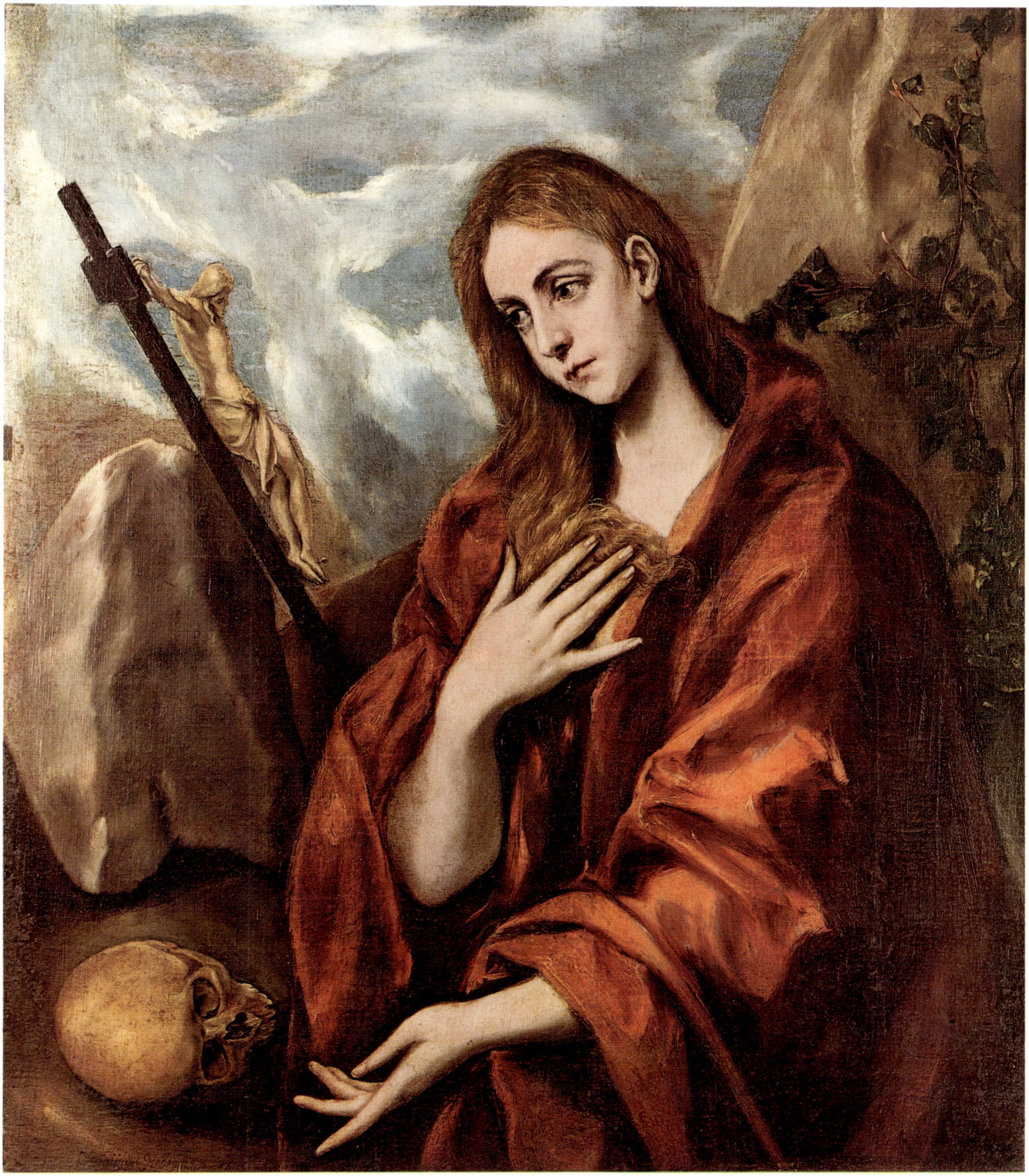

Fig. 139. The Penitent Magdalen, 1587-1597. Sitges, Cau Ferrat Museum. Cat. No. 116.

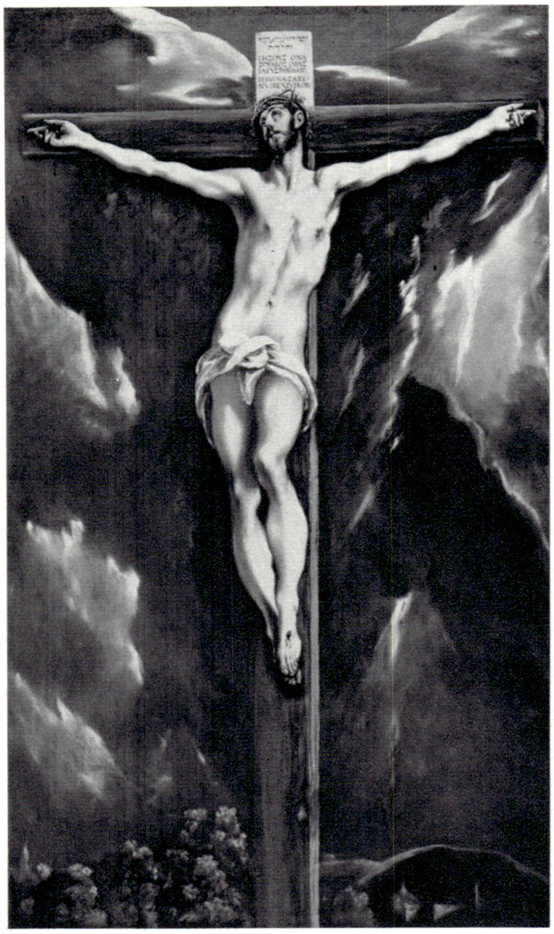

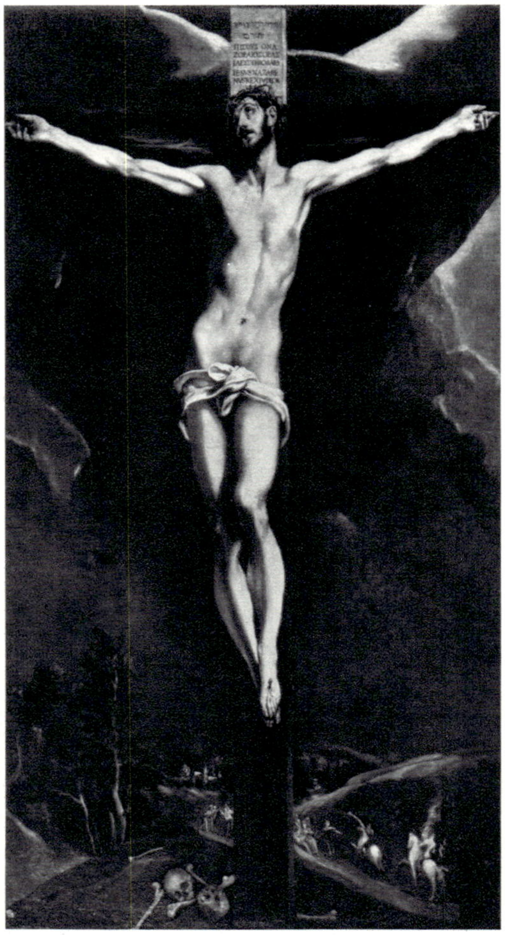

Fig. 140. Christ on the cross, 1587-1597. Cleveland, Museum of Art. Cat. No. 117.

Fig. 141. Christ on the cross, 1587-1597. Seville, Marqués de Motilla Collection. Cat. No. 118.

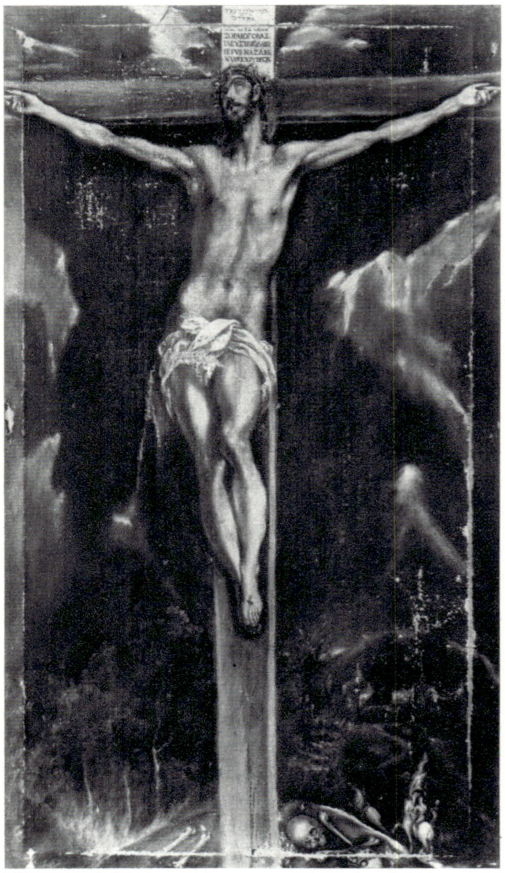

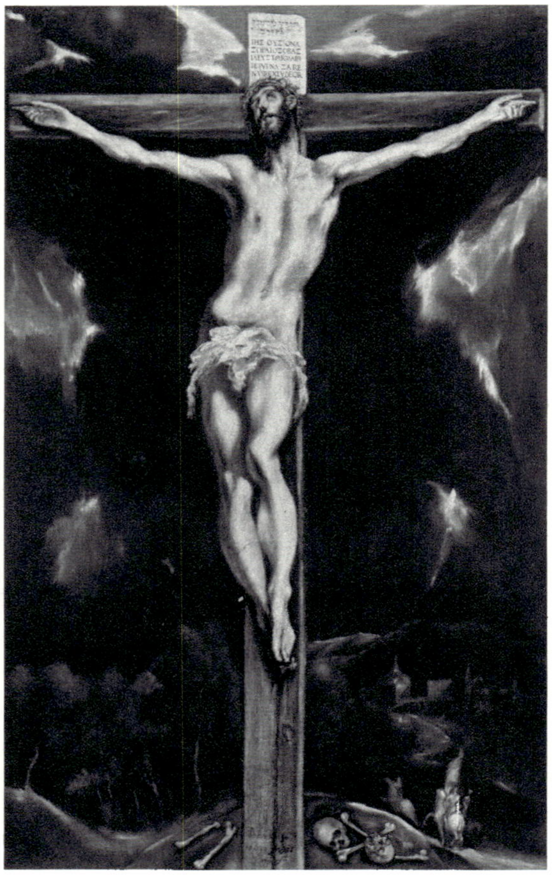

Fig. 142. Christ on the cross, 1587-1597. Toledo, Santa Cruz Museum. Cat. No. 119.

Fig. 143. Christ on the cross, 1587-1597. New York, Wildenstein Galleries. Cat. No. 120.

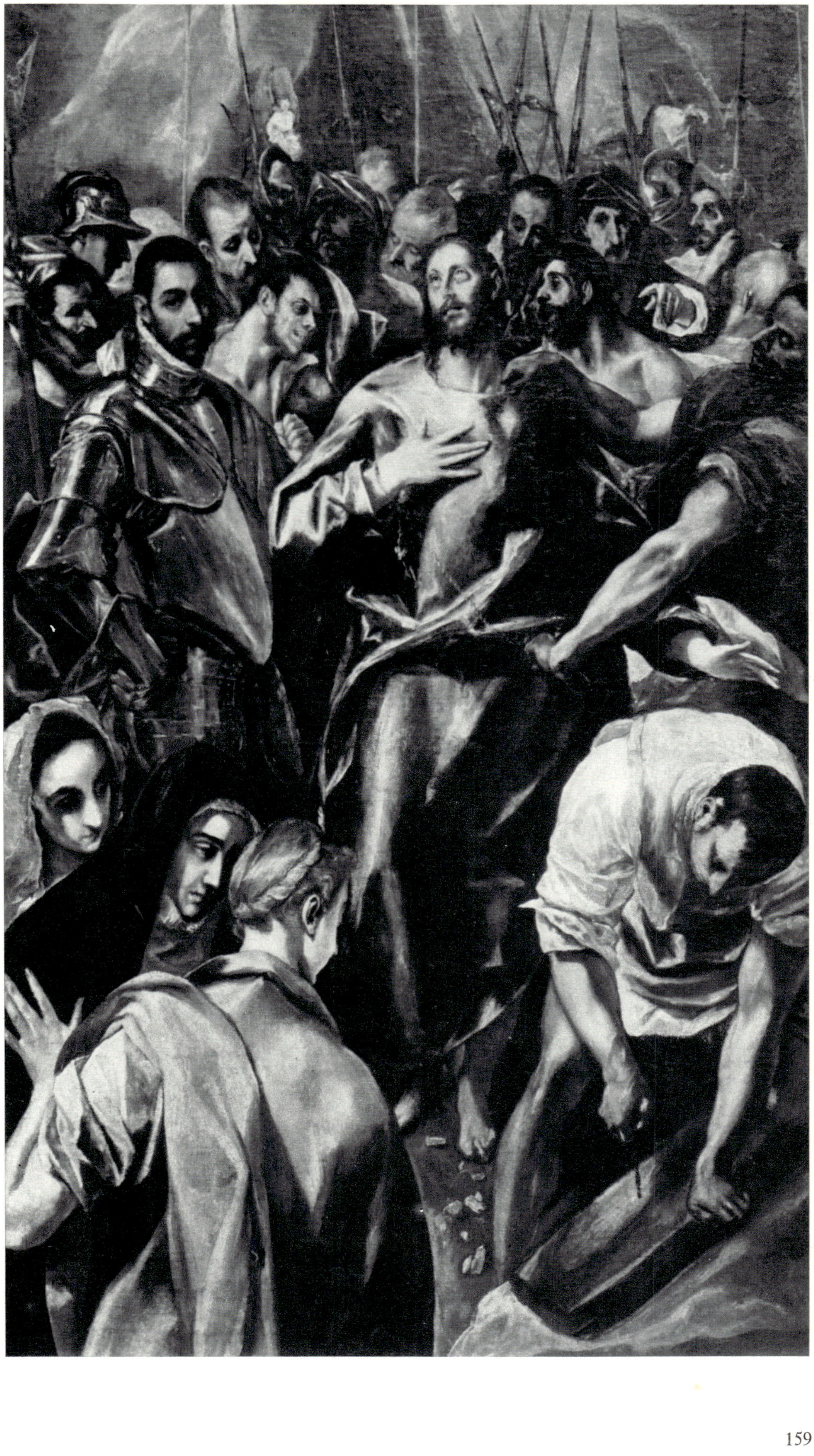

Fig. 144. The Espolio (Disrobing of Christ), 1587-1597. Munich, Alte Pinakothek. Cat. No. 121.

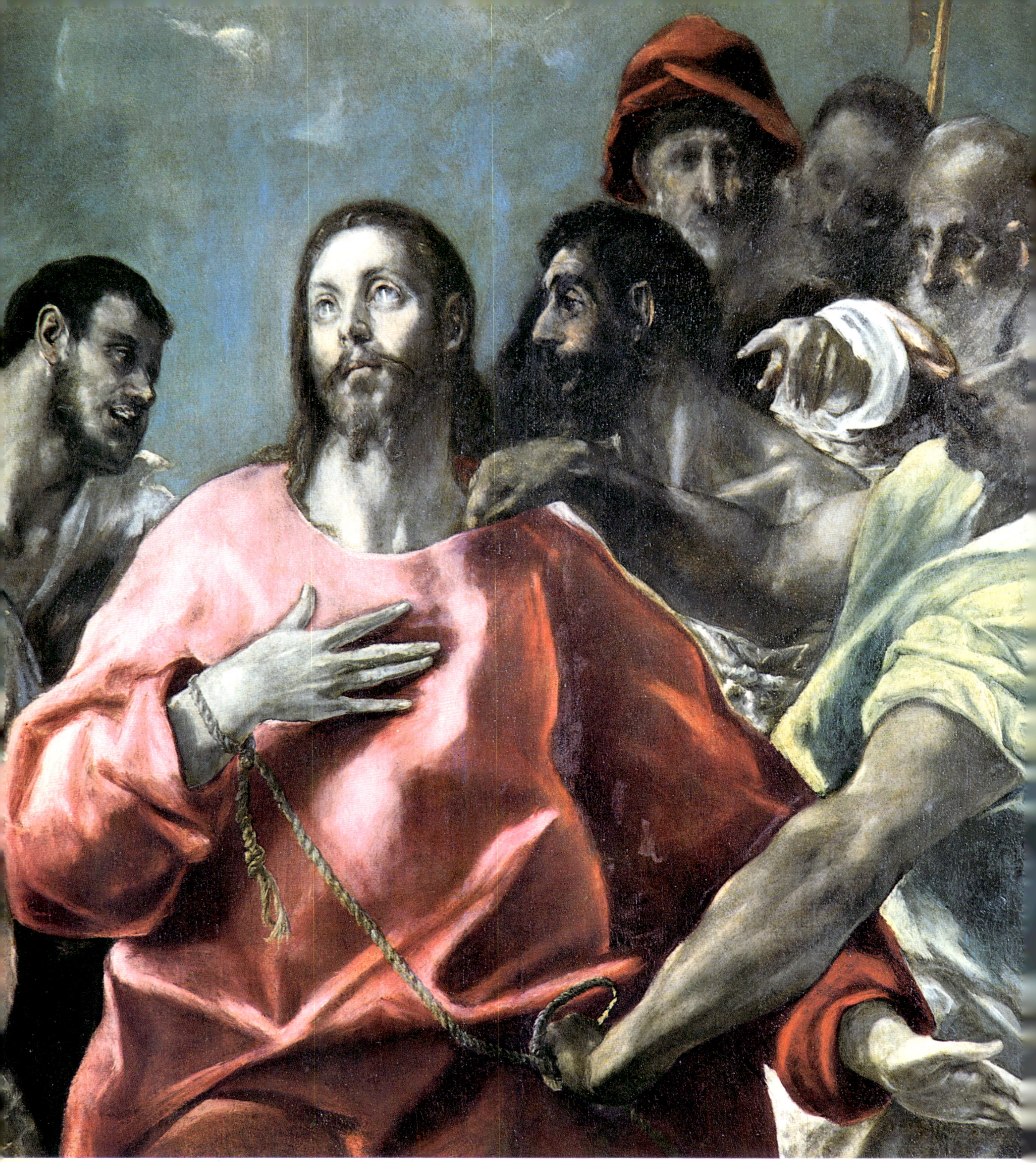

Fig. 145. The Espolio. (Disrobing of Christ) (detail), 1587-1597. Private collection. Cat. No. 122.

lower eyelid, the arch of the eyebrow and the cheekbone all suggested and traced by a drawing that is underlying rather than explicit and linear.

Among the compositions created during the period we are considering, let us now look at the *Christ saying farewell to his mother* in the Royal Palace of Sinaia (Rumania) *(Fig. 137 - Cat. 113)*. We believe this small canvas to be a preliminary sketch or study of this theme, which appears in its definitive version, with life-size figures, in the impressive painting in the Danielson Collection *(Cat. 114)*. The first version betrays that "short" relationship between form and brushstroke that is to be found in all pictures of smaller format.

It was executed, however, with extreme refinement and succeeds in its endeavour to give the tonal values their absolute quality, above all in the figure of the Virgin, which is one of the most successful in El Greco's whole career, not only on account of the admirable profile and the beautiful hand resting on her breast, but also in the grace and originality of the form assumed by the folds of the cloak enveloping her head. Of all El Greco's works, this is one of those that best solve the real relationship between two figures, for frequently, as we have said before, when there are two or more figures in his works they are linked together by an action, but without participation clearly expressed by the feeling. It cannot be denied, notwithstanding all his foreshadowing of Baroque, that this is an archaizing trait in El Greco, just as much as his preference for very elongated forms. But in this *Farewell*, without going so far as to "tell a story", the expression is enough to make us understand what each of the sacred personages is feeling. The light, which is more radiant in the area surrounding the head of Christ, above all in the central area, does not here allude directly —as in other images— to any supernatural splendour, but it does not thereby fail to possess this meaning. El Greco, since he could not paint like the primitives on backgrounds of gold, chose cloud effects and luminous skies as their most suitable equivalent and the only one admitted in a period of history which had already known the inclusion of detailed, story-telling landscapes (Flemish art and its consequences) in pictures on religious themes. We should not fail to observe this important regressive simplification, which El Greco practised quite intentionally.

On the other hand, since he was always deeply interested in plastic values, the harmony of gestures and suggested feelings was as important for El Greco as the colour, the form or the arabesque of the line. This *Farewell* corroborates all of this in exemplary fashion. At the same time one can see in this painting the tension of spiritual life, that tension that was later to lead the painter to exaggerate form in itself, distorting it and giving greater vibrancy to the colours, almost breaking the literal representation in his endeavour to achieve a type of image which is something unique in the whole history of painting, for such precedents as may be invoked are of no importance in comparison with the radical change to which El Greco subjected the elements he gradually picked up during his formative period or inherited from some ancestral source that gained strength in his early years as a "*Madonniero*". The originality of El Greco is so evident that it hardly needs to be mentioned, but it is also so dominant and so unerringly channelled within the beauty and iconography that it serves that we cannot simply pass over it. The definitive version of this sketch comes from the church of San Pablo in Toledo. According to Wethey, it was probably presented to the church by Cardinal Niño de Guevara.

In another version of the same theme, which hangs in the Santa Cruz Museum in Toledo *(Fig. 138 - Cat. 115)*, the original work was only the upper part of the canvas. One can see a line joining it to the lower part, in which the hands and draperies, though skilfully painted, are the work of an imitator, who also modified the image of the Virgin. It is, therefore, a characteristic work by El Greco and an assistant. The form, in El Greco as in all great artists, is very carefully thought out and overflows with an inner life that justifies and explains it. When we are faced, however, with the creation of a copyist, no matter how skilful, we can see that the form has been reproduced from the outside in and lacks that force and spontaneity in which even the imperfections (or unfinished details) are signs of life and inner fullness. The head of Christ is certainly by the hand of El Greco. The background of cloud effects and light is interesting and belongs entirely to the concept of this period, so that it is evident that the painting was executed at this time.

We continue our study of this period with works which seem to belong to the same group, as much on account of their theme or style as in technique. The chronology of these works is, of course, that of the order in which they are studied, though this need not be taken to mean any more than a coherent working hypothesis. What we do consider unquestionable is that all of these paintings belong to the period between 1587 and 1597, since their characteristics situate them between the great dated works done before and after these two years.

The canvas depicting the *Penitent Magdalen,* which is the third version of an image that was to be repeatedly painted throughout El Greco's career *(Fig. 139 - Cat. 116),* was bought in Paris in 1894 by the Catalan painter Santiago Rusiñol and borne in triumph to his "Cau Ferrat" in Sitges in a civic procession of intellectuals and artists. This event, which marked the rediscovery of El Greco, was commemorated by the erection of the first monument to the great Cretan. In this image the scheme and the essential elements are derived from the *St. Francis in meditation* which we have discussed in its three versions. The saint has exchanged the worldly raiment of the previous versions for a loose, voluminous robe of orange-tinted red which is treated as a formal element of interest for its own sake, being modelled not so much by superimposition of light tones on red in the luminous areas as by the insertion of black in the depths of the folds and drapery. The fair hair gives way to reddish chestnut locks, while the visionary expression is succeeded by one of serene, meditative sweetness. It is evident that the whole is also influenced by the painter's experience while dealing with the theme of St. Francis. The harmony of the red with the light blue of the sky and the flesh tints is essential to the composition. The ivy that is the attribute of penitent saints is also present, on the right.

As is logical, the theme of *Christ on the cross* could not fail to be included in the iconographical series created by El Greco for popular devotion. For this purpose all he had to do was to adapt the wonderful image of the great canvas in the Louvre which we have already discussed. In the numerous paintings representing the crucified Christ that may be ascribed to the painter or his circle, the scheme of this first model is repeated in general lines, but there is an evident stylistic development in both the execution and the form. Most of these paintings are not signed and so belong to the workshop category; they cannot therefore be properly discussed here, given the purpose of the present work. Two Crucifixions on canvas, both large enough but rather smaller than life-size, are undoubtedly by the painter's own hand, as can be seen from a stylistic analysis, which places them, moreover, in the period we are now studying. One of them hangs in the Cleveland Museum *(Fig. 140 - Cat. 117)*; it is incomplete in its lower part, of which all that remains is part of the landscape with a cupola, probably a reminder of that of the Escorial. The effects of chromatic and tonal contrast in the clouds are vivid and dynamic. The figure of Christ is long, idealized and modelled under a light that is very intense but lacking in great contrasts. The fluctuation of the form and the tendency to outline the volumes prepare us for what was to be the painter's later period, a sign of the absolutely original expressionism of El Greco. The magnificent head is similar to that of the Christ carrying the cross which we studied earlier, both in typology and technique, which indisputably indicates the short space of time that elapsed between the two works. El Greco could always reproduce a composition —the most external factor of a painting— at a distance of several years, but he does not usually reiterate the technical effects, the typology or the expression; he could not do so, in fact, because these are factors that are most closely bound up with an artist's development, whether in his purely pictorial conception or in his psychology as it reacts to the normal events of life. The Crucifixion in the collection of the Marqués de Motilla in Seville *(Fig. 141 - Cat. 118)* is the second of these versions. It has an interesting landscape which includes a distant view of the monastery of the Escorial —a nostalgic memory for El Greco— with people walking and riding along a road. The body of the Saviour, which in this version also stands out against a cloudy sky, is still more emaciated and tense than that in the previous painting, with more noticeable modelling in which shadows are more intensely indicated. We also present here, as signed variations on the theme of *Christ on the cross*, two canvases of considerably smaller size *(Fig. 142 - Cat. 119* and *Fig. 143 - Cat. 120).*

In our study of this period we now come to two versions of the *Espolio* which are characterized by a certain disintegration in the technique. It is difficult to explain why so many versions of a rather exceptional iconographic theme were painted. It is possible that, since the original work hung in the Cathedral of Toledo, El Greco may have been asked to paint a replica and may then have become interested in the theme again and thought it feasible to produce various identical, or almost identical, works so as to increase his repertoire of pictures intended for possible patrons,

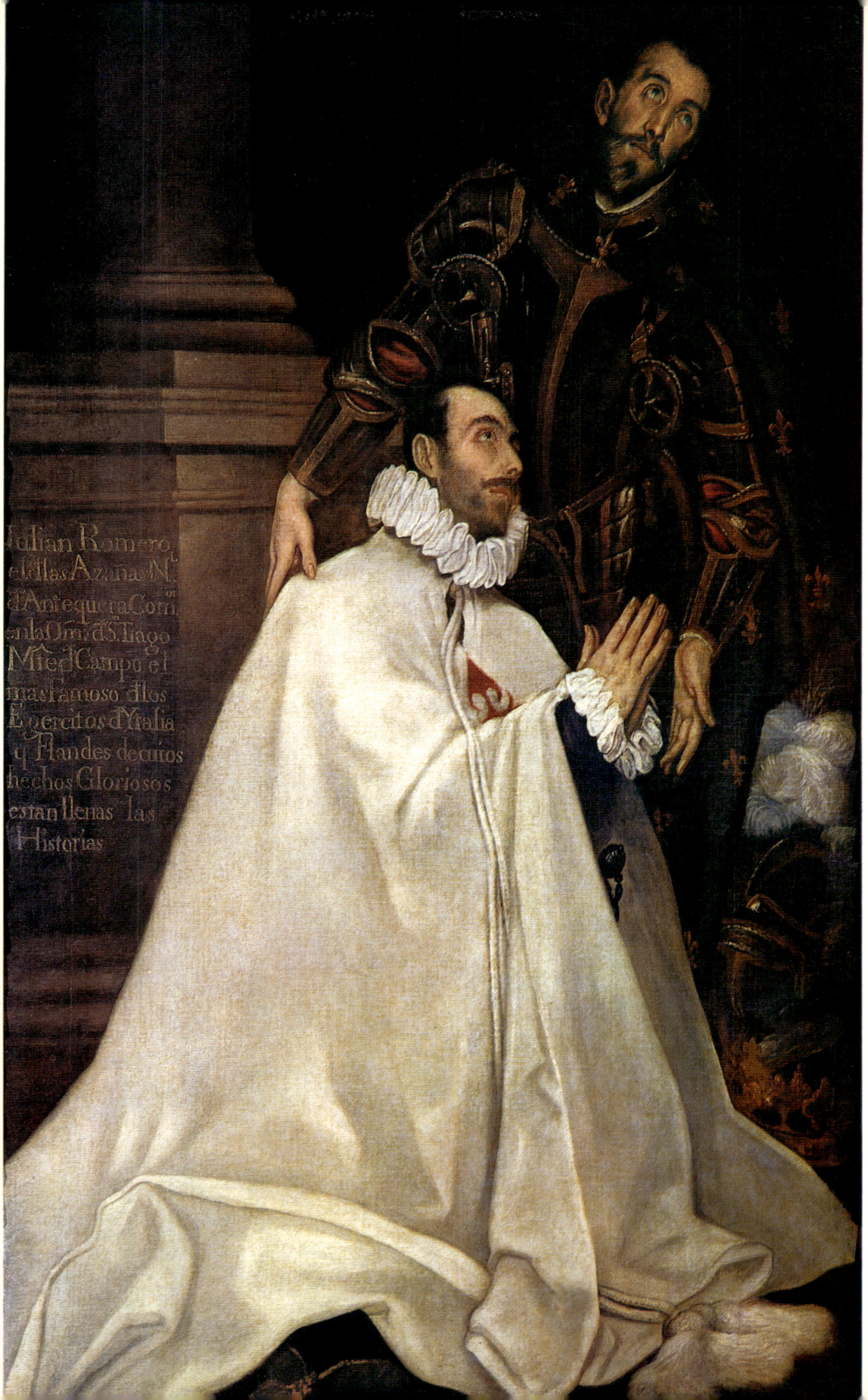

146. Julián Romero
s Azañas and St. Ju-
1587-1597. Madrid,
. Cat. No. 123.

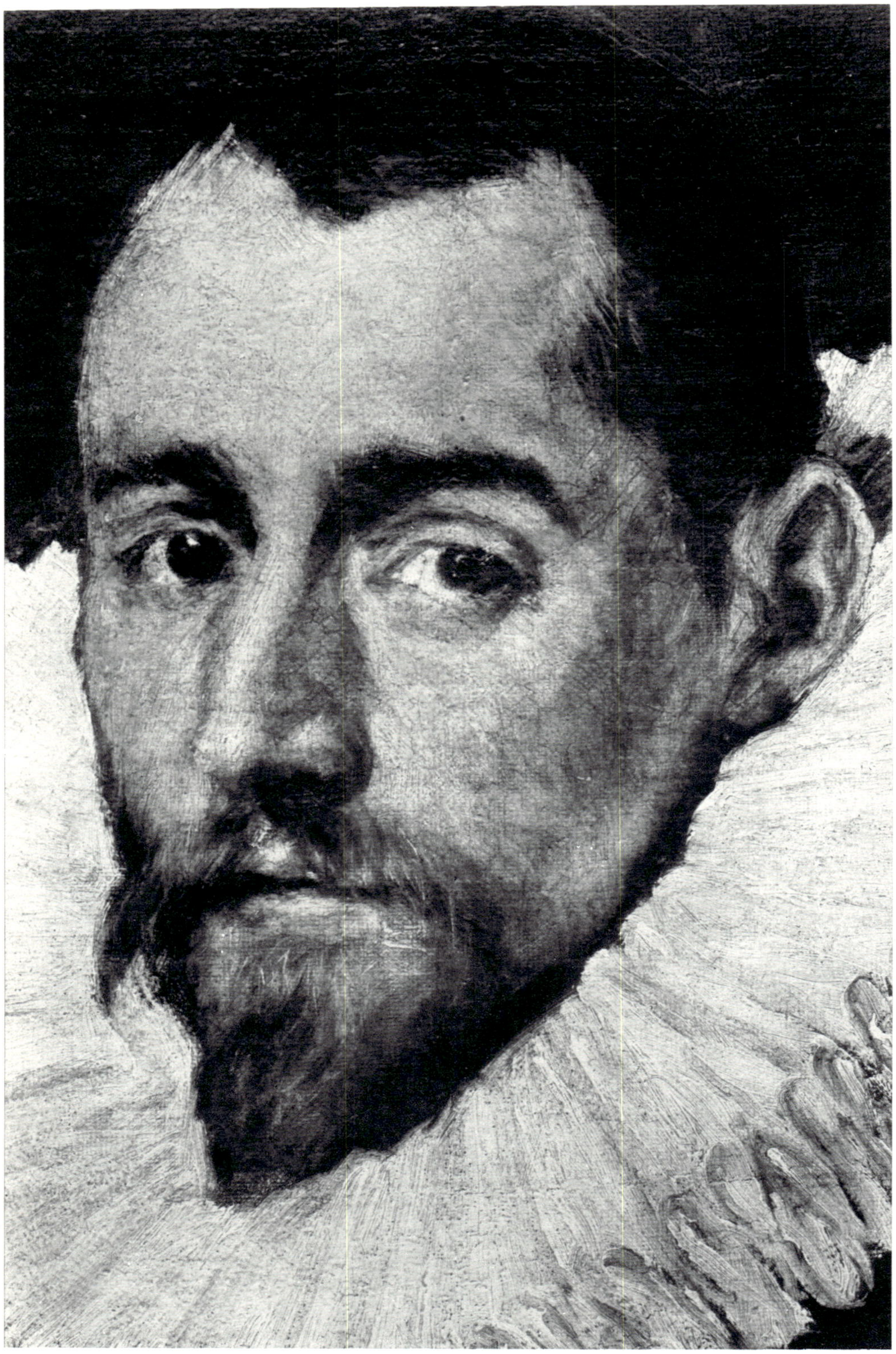

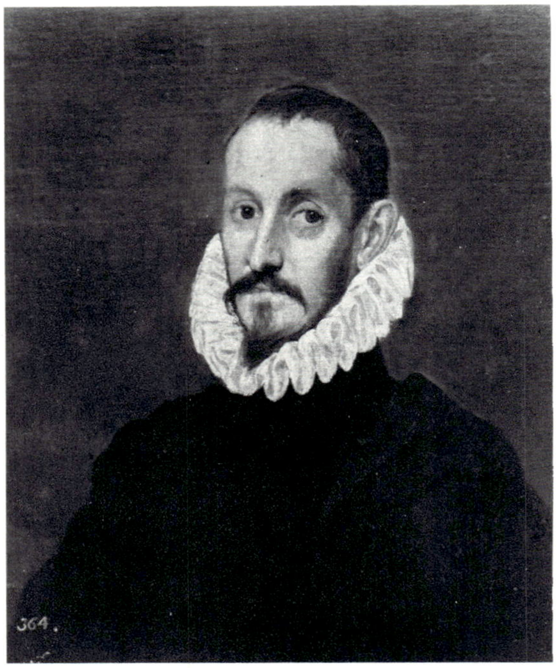

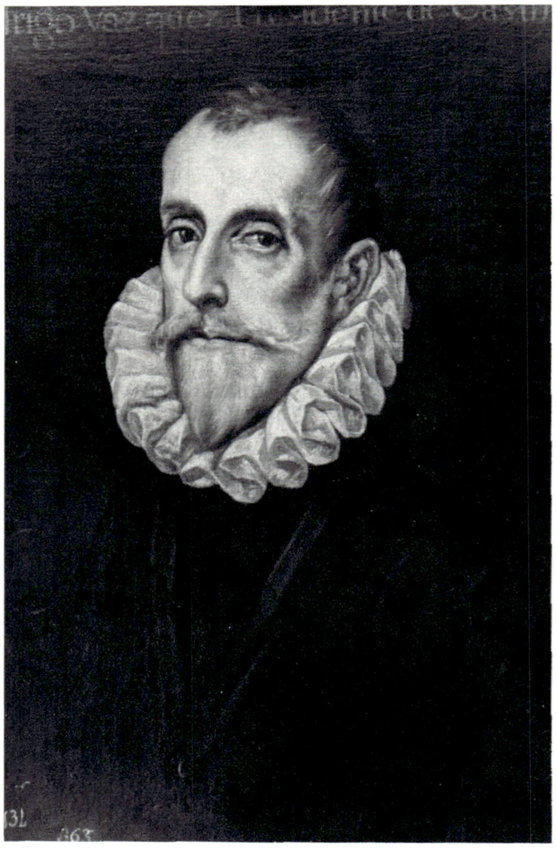

Fig. 147. Portrait of a young gentleman, 1587-1597. Madrid, Prado. Cat. No. 124.
Fig. 148. Portrait of an unknown gentleman, 1587-1597. Madrid, Prado. Cat. No. 125.
Fig. 149. Rodrigo Vázquez, 1587-1597. Madrid, Prado. Cat. No. 126.

i.e., of works not previously commissioned. Of the two versions we present here (they are not the only ones, but the others, one of which is signed by Jorge Manuel, are products of the workshop), the more outstanding is the one we will study first. It is a partial replica in a format wider than it is high, in which the main figures of the central area are reproduced half-length *(Fig. 145 - Cat 122)*. In the nineteenth century this painting hung in the palace of the Marqués de la Cenia in Majorca, where it was "restored" by Vicente López with generous repaintings which covered the whole of the cloud effects and a great part of the figures. A recent cleaning has revealed the very beautiful original painting, which is most certainly an authentic Greco, in technique, execution and outstanding quality. It contrasts with the painting in the Cathedral of Toledo in its technique and in the spatial variations. The dramatic crowding of figures around the Saviour is reduced, while the background of sky becomes more important. The expression is softened and the dramatic quality, though still there, loses some of its tension. The atmosphere, which is more mystical, is suggested by an evanescent technique, rich in strange contrasts of light and shade. The figure of the Saviour is as admirable as in the first version, as may indeed be said of all the other figures in this work, which is really a great painting.

The other version of the *Espolio,* which is an almost literal reproduction of the painting in the Cathedral of Toledo, shows certain details in the execution which lead us to consider it a product of the workshop, though with considerable participation by El Greco himself *(Fig. 144 - Cat. 121)*. The most obvious change from the Toledo painting is the head of an old man, with his back to the viewer, who appears behind the executioner beginning to strip Christ of his robe. This head is introduced almost surreptitiously and there seems to be absolutely no need for it from any realistic point of view. We may also observe geometrizations of the form, rather as if El Greco's original solutions had been "academicized". The foregoing comments do not presuppose any absolute, or even very intense, transformations, but they do indicate facts or modifications sufficiently significant to be taken into account in a deeper analysis. An *Espolio* from the church of Santa Leocadia in Toledo, which now hangs in the Santa Cruz Museum, is very similar to the preceding work. Although the essential purpose of this book is to present the absolutely authentic works of El Greco, we think this painting worth mentioning, since it belongs to that indecisive area that surrounds the authenticated work. For various reasons artists have often had to organize their production in some more flexible way than direct painting by one and the same man in every case, and it is this that provides art historians with their most inextricable problems, though with time these problems are gradually being cleared up.

Portraits

We will now pay some attention to a group of portraits which must be included in the same period. The first of these is that of *Julián Romero* in the Prado *(Fig. 146 - Cat. 123)*, the composition and typology of which constitute a remarkable variation on the painter's usual iconography. The personage is identified by a lengthy inscription which, judging by the historical errors it contains, must be of later date than the painting itself. Julián Romero, Commander of the Order of Santiago, had died in battle near Cremona in 1577, after having fought in the armies of Spain in Flanders, Italy and France. He is the hero of a work by Lope de Vega. Probably, as was supposed by Tormo, this was a votive picture. The knight is shown kneeling, praying beside St. Julian and covered by the great white cape of his Order. His patron saint is wearing armour similar to that of the Conde de Orgaz. The drawing in general, the form and the expression are admirable, but the technique is rather disconcerting in its unusual smoothness, though it possesses a skilful flexibility that denotes the work of the great master. The marked tendency to eloquence in the two figures is also entirely characteristic of El Greco.

It is probable that the period we are now studying also saw the execution of four male portraits which have been listed in the inventories of the Royal Patrimony of Spain since the seventeenth century. It is certainly difficult to date them on technical grounds, since the development of El Greco's pictorial concept is not so readily perceptible in the portraits as in other compositions. The first of them *(Fig. 147 - Cat. 124)* is the bust of a young gentleman in a full ruff, executed with firm brushwork and keen sensibility — one of the most attractive characters in the whole hallucinatory gallery of portraits by El Greco.

Another portrait, simpler in technique, is fairly similar to the first in the way in which the sitter is presented *(Fig. 148 - Cat. 125).* It is less intense than the preceding work, but presents the sitter as a man of vigorous personality and with nothing about him, generically speaking, that makes him much different from the rest of the noblemen and hidalgos portrayed by El Greco. The technique does have some peculiar features: the outline was rubbed to give it a more evanescent character and the ruff is treated with a light and flexible, but more effective, technique, giving a certain sensuousness to the white that contrasts with the flesh tints and the black of the suit.

The portrait of *Rodrigo Vázquez,* also in the Prado *(Fig. 149 - Cat. 126),* depicts the sitter in accordance with much the same scheme as the preceding painting. But the technique is very different, opaque and rather hard, which led Wethey to relegate this work to the ranks of the copies. At all events, it cannot be less than a contemporary copy, executed in El Greco's workshop by a hand gifted with extraordinary powers of imitation. It is, therefore, a key element in studying the extremely vexing problem of the great painter's assistants. This portrait is much more draughtsmanlike and precise, but less daring and advanced in technique, than the two that immediately precede it. The bust of a man dressed in black and wearing a ruff *(Fig. 150 - Cat. 127)* is one of the most beautiful works of the period now under consideration. The sitter belongs entirely to the typology that El Greco immortalized in the frieze of gentlemen in the *Burial of the Conde de Orgaz.*

Reappearance of an Italian model

This period almost certainly includes two paintings that repeat the *Genre scene* with three figures, that mysterious canvas painted by El Greco during his Roman period *(Fig. 31 - Cat. 24).* One of them, signed in Greek italics and now in the Harewood Collection in London *(Fig. 151 - Cat. 128),* confirms the attribution of these three paintings, which are almost identical yet clearly differentiated by technique and pictorial concept. That is why we have situated the two versions now presented in these years of artistic ripeness and, apparently, economic misery. The version that seems to be the later one *(Figs. 152 & 153 - Cat. 129),* which is in the Oliver Collection in Jedburgh (Scotland), reveals full acquaintance with the painter's recent discoveries. Diffuse lighting and flashes in the dark satisfy his taste for disintegration, which we have already indicated to be characteristic of this phase and which affects even the profiles of the figure-outlines. Seen in detail, this work shows extraordinary quality and is of fundamental importance in the appreciation of El Greco's technical development. Observe, first of all, the fresh triumph of skill in capturing a moment in everyday life. Puffed cheeks, a pouting mouth about to blow on an ember and the profile of a smiling companion. The spontaneity of the scene is also astonishing and the execution is exactly what the subject demands, with each element placed so as to suggest the movements just made and what is going to happen the next moment, quite perfectly. The tonal contrasts model the form and at the same time characterize the expression of the whole. In the version in the Harewood Collection, which is identical as far as composition is concerned, there are some differences of execution in representing the light effects, as can be seen in the hands, especially in the left hand of the woman blowing.

Once more we are led to speculate on the evolution of El Greco's art —that evolution that never took place— and to wonder what would have happened if, instead of devoting himself to the world of religious themes, he had interested himself in capturing the real life all around him and in strict naturalism. We cannot doubt that he would have anticipated many of the achievements of seventeenth-century Spanish art.

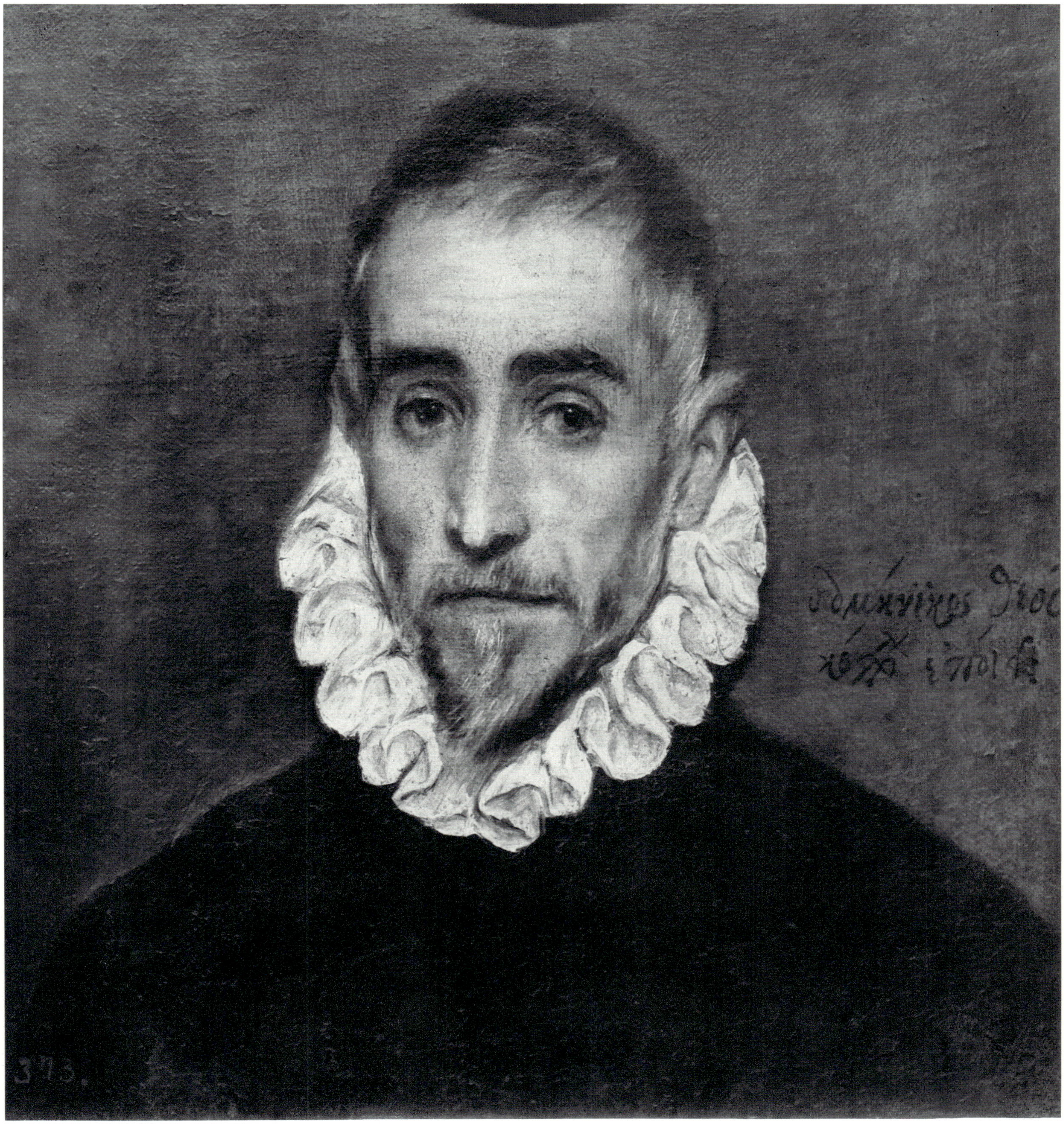

Fig. 150. Portrait of an elderly gentleman, 1587-1597. Madrid, Prado. Cat. No. 127.

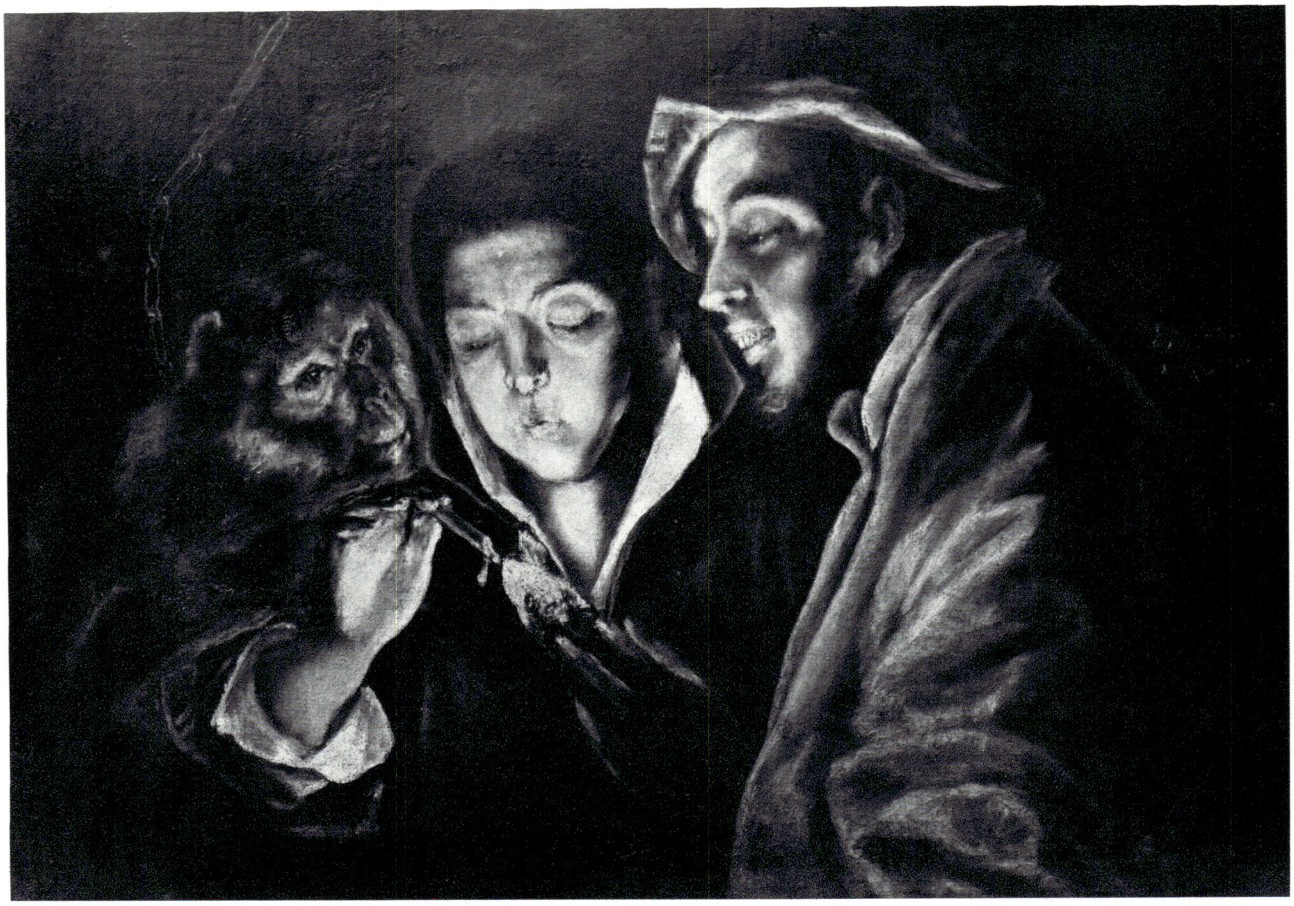

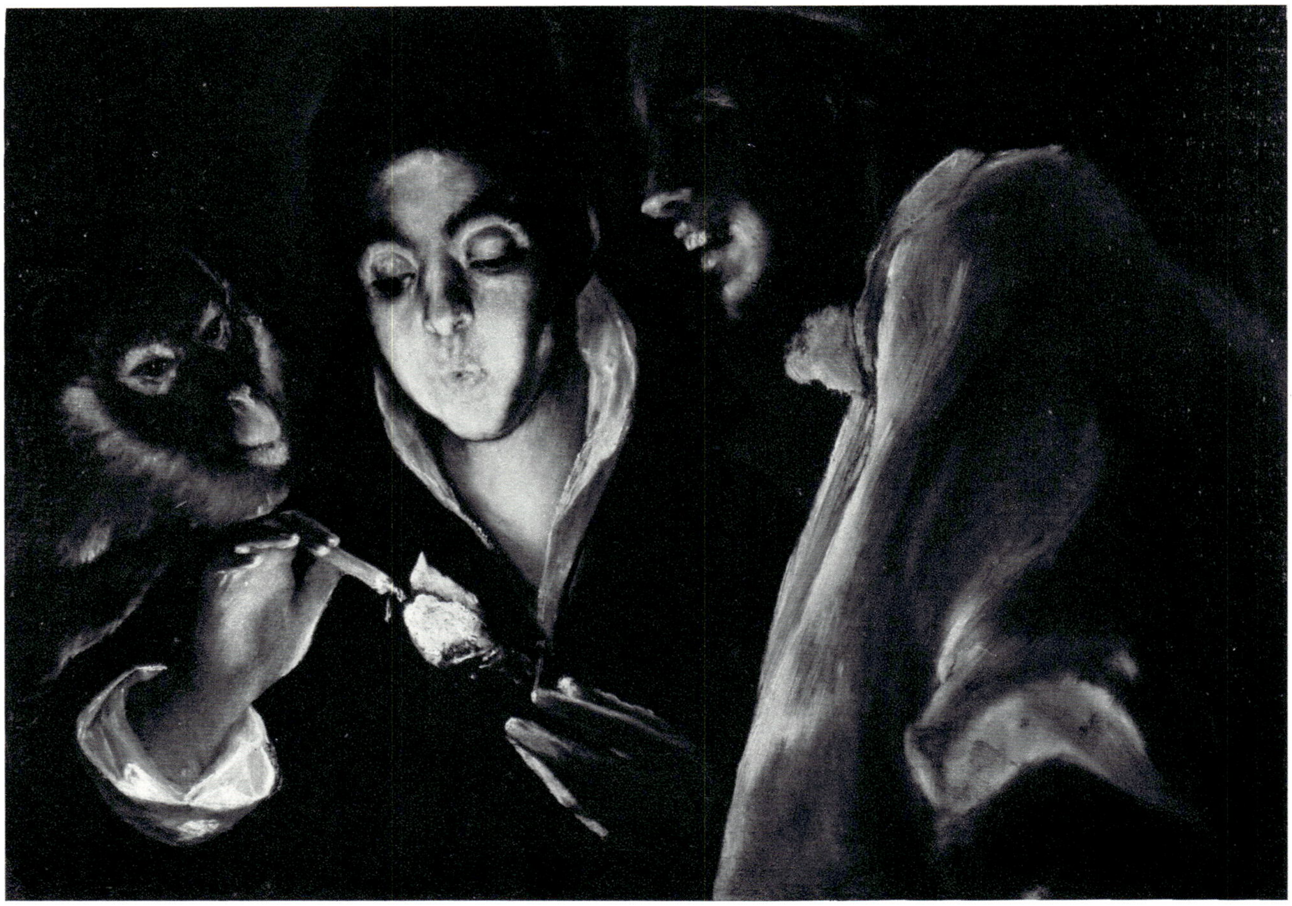

Fig. 151. Genre scene, 1587-1597. London, Lord Harewood Collection. Cat. No. 128.
Fig. 152. Genre scene, 1587-1597. Jedburgh, Mark Oliver Collection. Cat. No. 129.

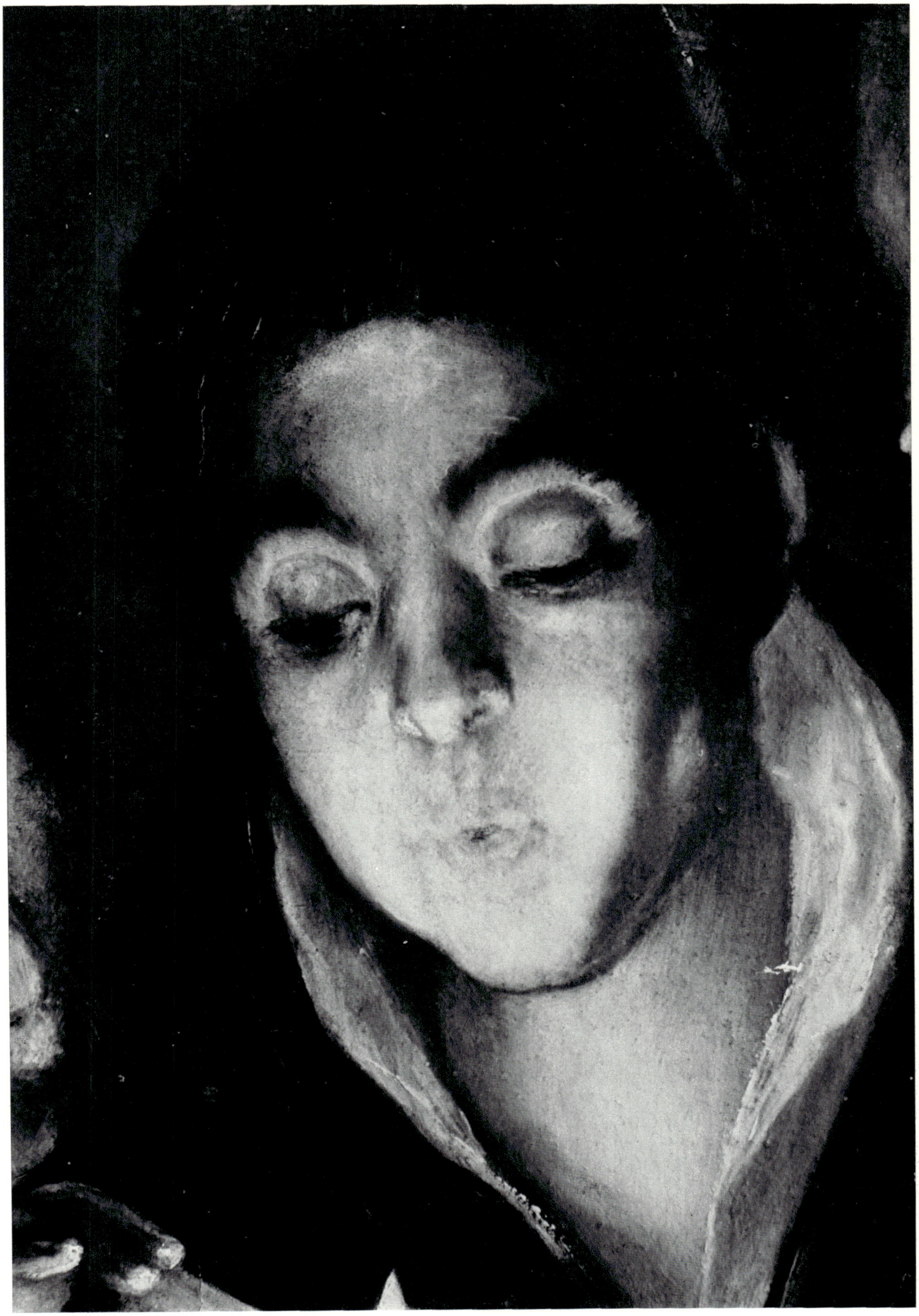

Fig. 153. Detail of figure 152.

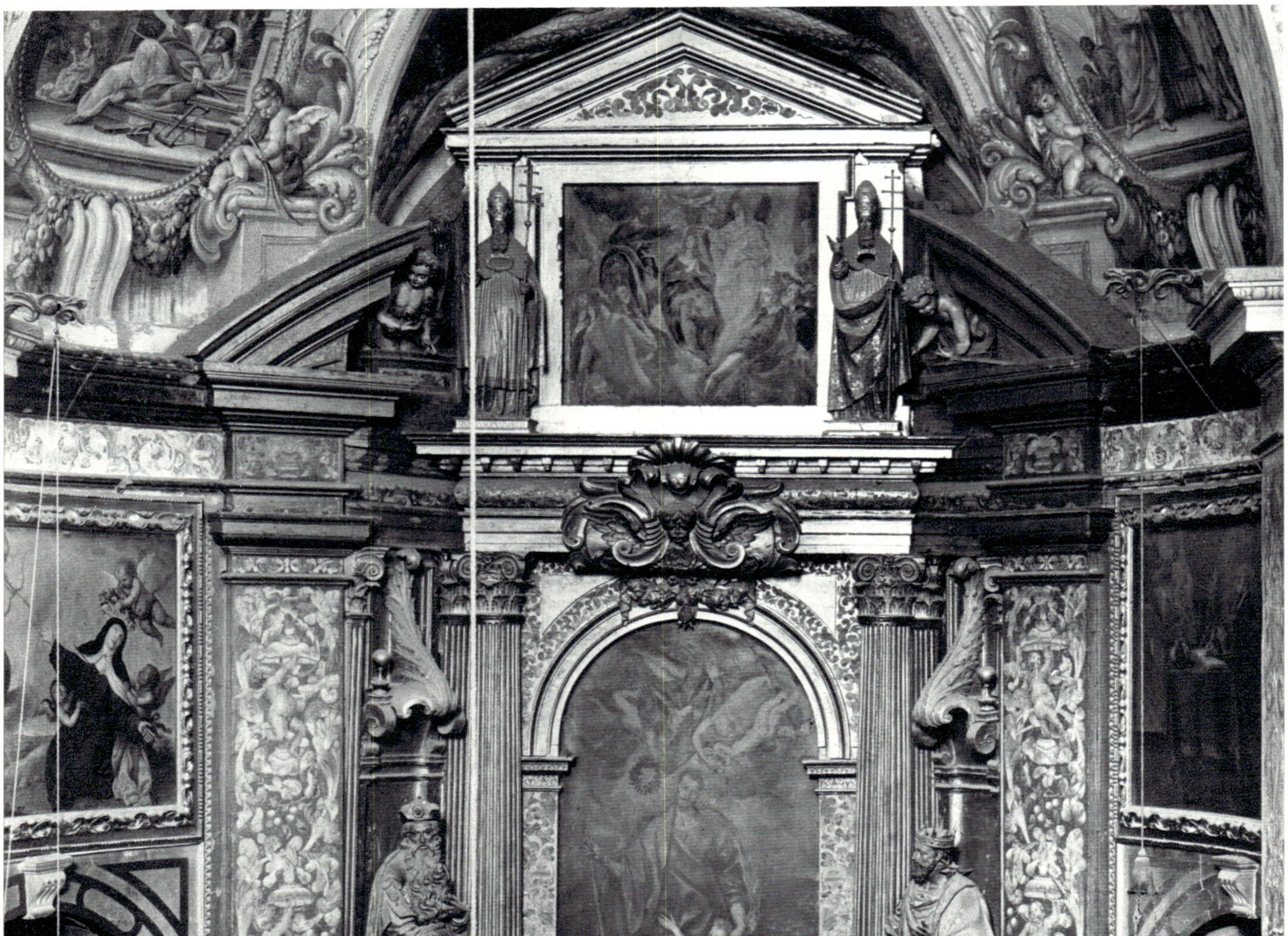

Fig. 154. Toledo, the Church of San José.

V

1597 - 1603

THE ALTARPIECES FOR SAN JOSÉ, TOLEDO — THE ALTARPIECES FOR THE COLEGIO DE DOÑA MARÍA DE ARAGÓN, MADRID — THE *VIEW OF TOLEDO* — WORKS ATTRIBUTED TO THE PERIOD 1597-1603 — PORTRAITS.

This new period is marked by the production of two important works: the altarpieces for the chapel of San José in Toledo and the one for the Colegio de Doña María de Aragón in Madrid. Leaving aside for the moment all the data and documents referring to these two ensembles, the specific information we have regarding El Greco's life and work in the six years we are about to study is the following.

On April 16th of 1597 a contract was drawn up for the construction of an altarpiece for the high altar of the monastery church of Guadalupe. A period of eight years was fixed for the execution of this work, which was certainly an important commission, and the sum agreed upon for the estimate of the total costs was 16,000 ducats. The document also says that, in the event of Dominico's death, the work is to be continued by his son, Jorge Manuel, and Francisco Preboste. This contract was never carried out, for the altarpiece of Guadalupe was constructed by the sculptor Giraldo de Merlo a few years after El Greco's death.

On May 24th of 1597 El Greco and Francisco Preboste jointly empowered one Agustín Ansaldo, a Genoese citizen residing in the city of Seville, "to ask, demand and receive payment from Pedro de Mesa, a Sevillian embroiderer"; according to the document, "images of painting, canvases and other things" had been sent to this man for him to sell. Ansaldo is authorized to discover what has happened to these works and to receive payment for such of them as have been sold. This document is of the greatest interest, for it shows that El Greco was trying to build up a deposit of works for sale in Seville. This confirms what we have said about the organization of his workshop for the production of religious paintings, and also, possibly, of themes of sumptuary or decorative interest, all of them intended for chance purchasers. The business mentioned in the above document would not have been an isolated case. In confirmation of this we have a reference to El Greco in a book entitled "Apólogos Dialogables", published by Francisco Manuel de Melo fifty years after the painter's death: "Compelled by necessity and following the advice of his friends, Theotokópuli went to Seville when the fleet was about to sail for the Indies, and on this occasion he succeeded in selling so many paintings that he made his fortune".

It may be believed that at this time El Greco had quite a sizeable workshop. His ability to accept commissions as important as the ones referred to in the above-mentioned documents is an unquestionable proof of this. Jorge Manuel, who in 1598 was 20 years old, was probably working in this workshop of his father's as supervisor of the works, for his ability as a painter was extremely limited. This probably induced his father to turn the establishment into a centre for producing, in their entirety, the great carved structures that constituted the altarpieces then in fashion, together with their subsequent gilding and, of course, the paintings that were fitted into them. To tell the truth, however, we have no specific references to this organization. At the time we are speaking of, it would seem logical that, besides his son and the faithful Preboste, El Greco should have various salaried assistants and workmen. To establish a precise distinction between the work done exclusively by El Greco himself and that in which any of the painters who passed through his workshop over the years participated has become a problem of capital importance, on account of the vast number of pictures that exists over and above those paintings which are indisputably his alone, paintings perfectly attested by the corresponding contracts, in which he was required to carry out the works "by his own hand".

Some years before, as we have already said, El Greco had been forced to leave his spacious lodgings in the palace of the Marqués de Villena. A document dated December 12th 1600 reveals that the painter was then living in a house owned by Juan Suárez de Toledo; the document in question is a receipt for 2,535 *reales* in settlement of rents due. In various payments made between February and July of 1601, El Greco also settled a debt of 83,214 *maravedis* that he owed to the heirs of Juana López. All of this provides clear evidence of financial difficulties.

Although the data we have regarding the preliminary negotiations for the construction of the great altarpiece of the Colegio de Doña María de Aragón are of earlier date than the contracts for the altars of San José in Toledo, we will begin by studying the latter, for to judge by the concept of the paintings they were probably done before the other work.

The altarpieces for San José, Toledo

The church of San José, built with funds bequeathed by Martín Ramírez (d. 1569), was consecrated in 1594. The execution of its three altarpieces, which stand in their original place, was agreed upon on November 9th 1597 with the signing of a contract between another Martín Ramírez, nephew of the original benefactor, and El Greco. The painter undertook to carry out the whole of the work: the architectural structure, the complementary carvings and the painted canvases *(Fig. 154)*. In the document are set forth the themes for the two canvases of the altarpiece of the high altar: the image of St. Joseph in the centre and the "Coronation of Our Lady with two virgins at the sides" in the upper panel. On the day the contract was signed the artist was paid 1,600 *reales*; on receiving the commission, at some unknown date, he had already received 7,000 *reales*. He was also to be paid 1,400 *reales* at the end of January 1598, plus a further 1,500 when the altarpieces were in position, which was to be on Our Lady's Day in August of 1598 (August 15th). In an agreement dated November 13th 1599, the executor of the will paid the total sum of 2,827 ducats (31,328 *reales)*, this considerable delay being due to the fact that he considered the valuation placed on the work by experts, whose names are unknown to us, to be excessive.

The *Coronation of the Virgin*, the composition in the upper panel of the centre altarpiece *(Fig. 155 - Cat. 130)*, is based on the sketch we have already studied for the altarpiece of Talavera la Vieja *(Fig. 110)*. But the more oblong form of this new version of the theme obliged the painter to bring the saints in the lower part nearer to the Coronation group —almost, in fact, to superimpose them on it. Among them we find two new figures in El Greco's hagiography: the apostle St. James and a St. John the Evangelist with his head turned towards the viewer. We believe that this image is a portrait of Jorge Manuel; it is enough to compare it with the portrait of El Greco's son, palette in hand, which is studied in the following chapter *(Fig. 196)*. The main canvas of the same altarpiece represents St. Joseph as a wayfarer, lovingly protecting the Child Jesus *(Fig. 159 - Cat. 133)*, both of them depicted wandering barefoot through the world. The "world" in this instance is a panoramic view of Toledo and one that is an almost literal reproduction of the elements of the famous picture in the Metropolitan Museum of New York *(Fig. 172)*. Was it painted, perhaps, as a preliminary for the latter picture? The idea of painting a landscape without any particular purpose might perfectly well have occurred to El Greco, bearing in mind the principles of absolute freedom on which he based his approach to artistic creation. However that may be, there is an unmistakable relationship between the celebrated landscape and the background to this picture of St. Joseph. To counterbalance the profoundly human feeling with which the two main figures are treated, three angels with a crown and flowers come down from the sky and fill the upper part of the picture. As on other occasions, their positions are all very different and the interplay of their rhythms gives dynamism and a three-dimensional sense to this very beautiful area. They are placed just above St. Joseph's head, as if forming a halo. Deep blue skies and clouds fill the sides, especially to the right, with those marvellous effects of ragged clouds that the painter created with such mastery, mixing or opposing greys, whites and blues for his tonal effects. The flowers, alone or in bunches, are soft or vivid notes of colour that help to give a very lyrical feeling to this elegant picture, a basic work in the iconography of St. Joseph. Joseph's figure, like

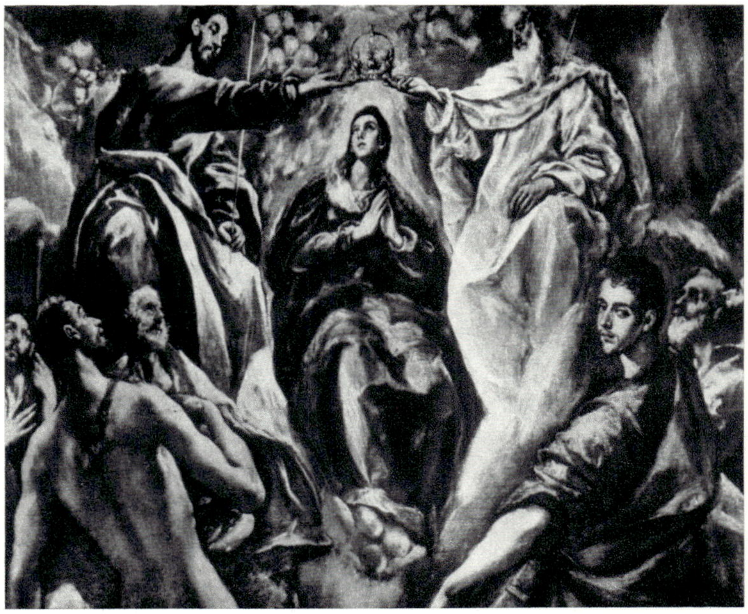

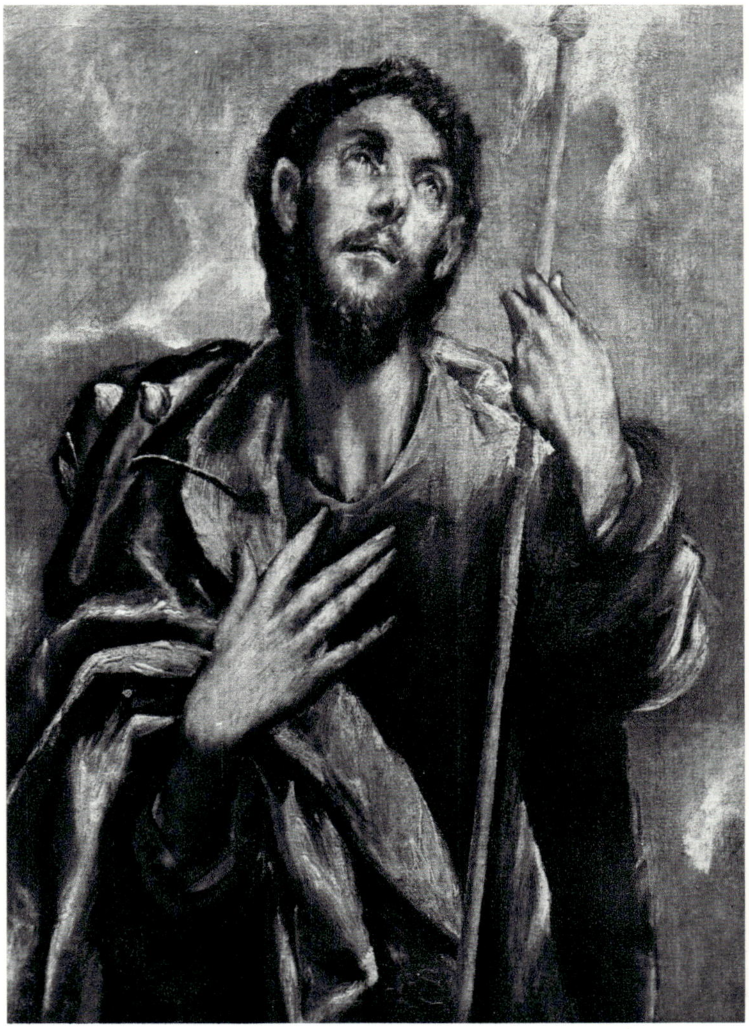

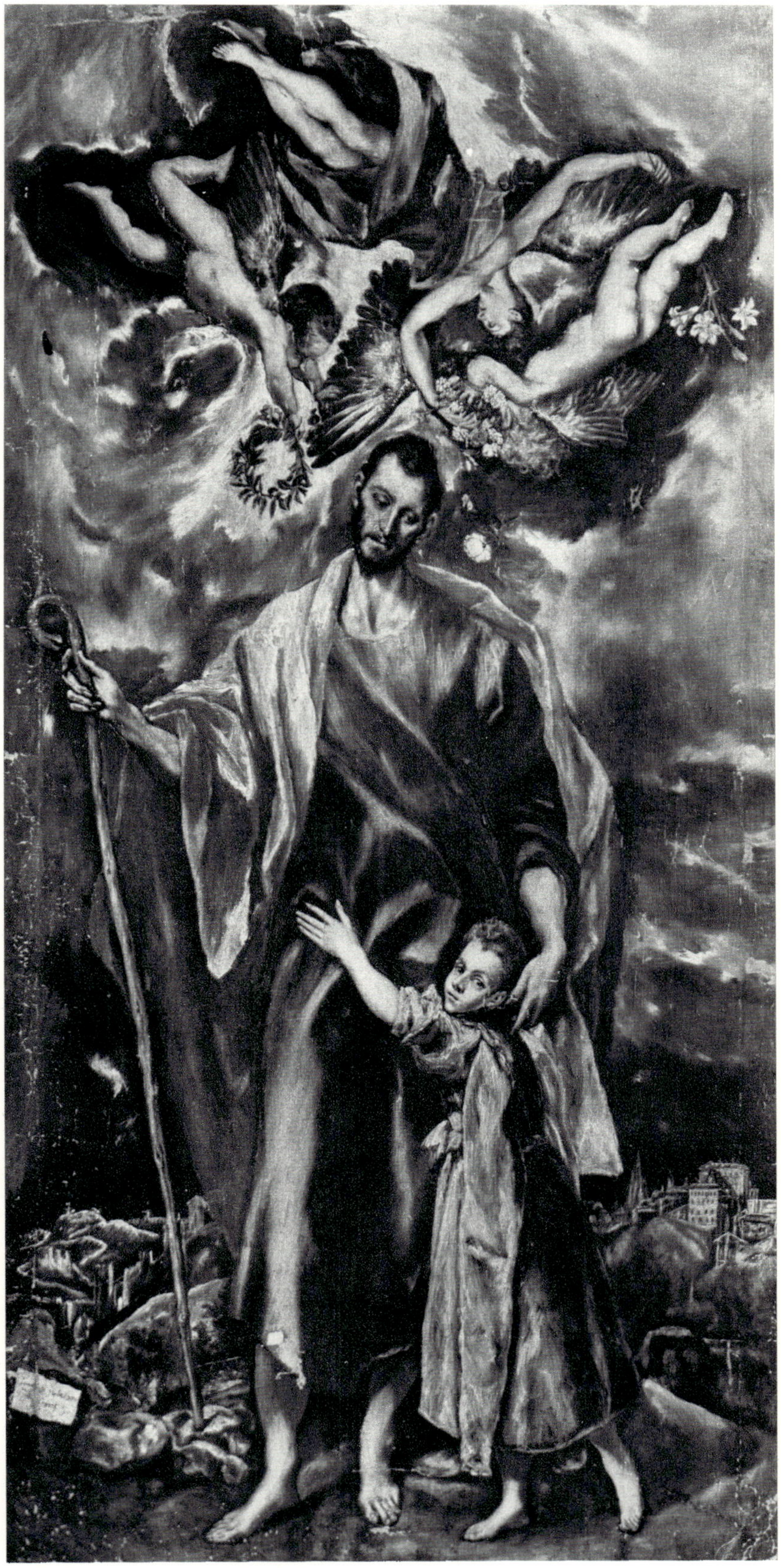

Fig. 155. The Coronation of the Virgin, 1597-1599. Toledo, Church of San José. Cat. No. 130.
Fig. 156. St. James the Great as a pilgrim, 1597-1599. New York, Hispanic Society. Cat. No. 131.
Fig. 157. St. Joseph and the Infant Christ, 1597-1599. Toledo, Santa Cruz Museum. Cat. No. 132.

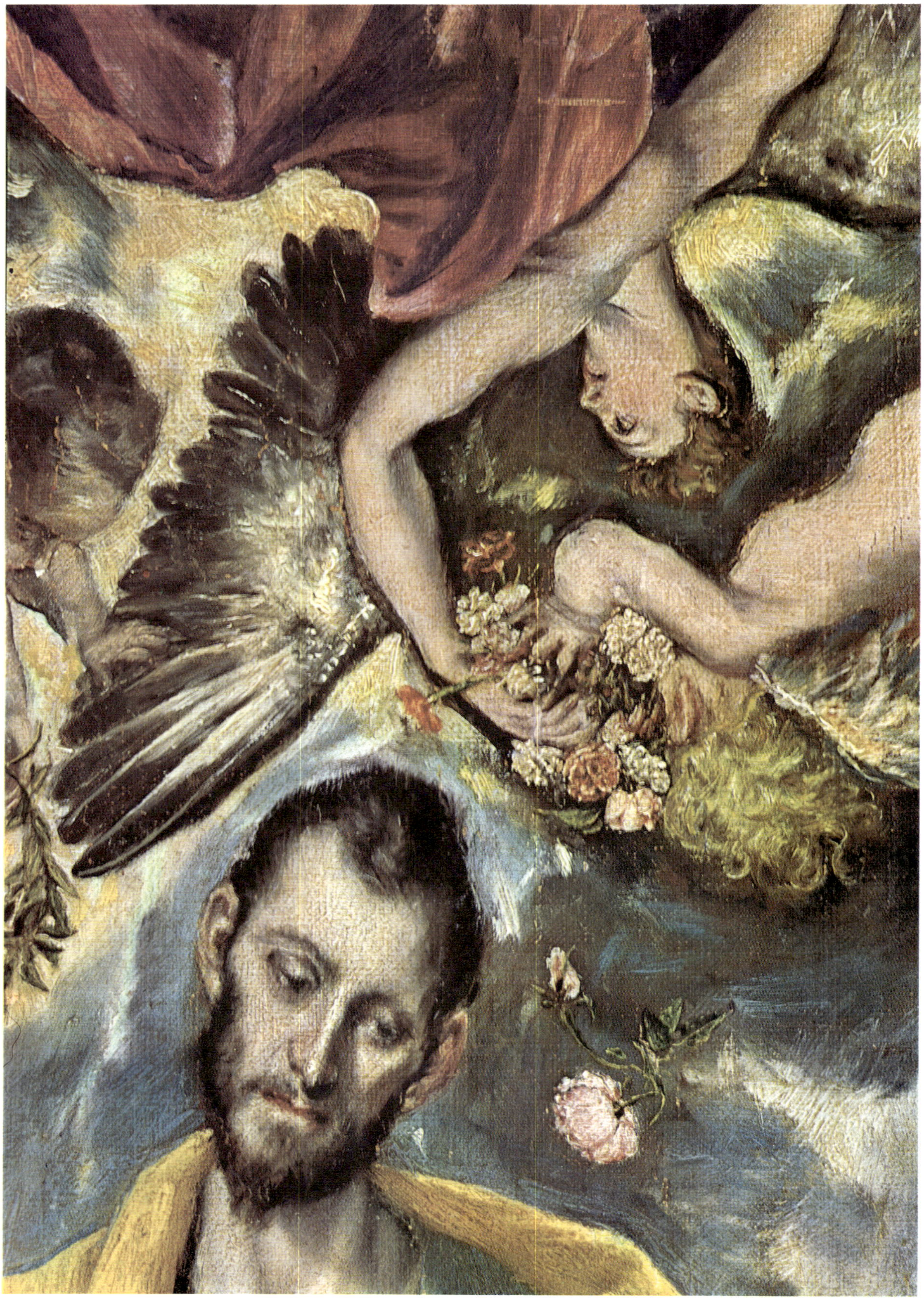

Fig. 158. Detail of figure 157.

others of biblical characters or saints, is expressed through the refined and almost melancholy head and in the sweeping draperies of his robe and mantle, elements which El Greco usually considered as important as the facial expressions from the pictorial point of view. The same occurs, though less intensely, with the little figure of the Child Jesus. The incomparable fineness of the drawing is evident in each and every detail of this work. The rhythmic interplay of the draperies, with their diagonal axes and sumptuous surfaces, gives the figures a comparatively abstract character, though without thereby dehumanizing them. Here we have, undoubtedly, El Greco's most profound secret: the one which, as we have said several times before, springs from his spirit, derives from his Byzantine origins or comes from both sources intimately and inextricably blended. El Greco knew, better than anybody else has ever known, how to show man's double nature, earthly and spiritual, and he personified this dual character with particular intensity in his saints. In this St. Joseph we have one of the best examples of this, for it was painted at a time when the artist, having overcome all his technical problems and all his preoccupation with representation in itself, succeeded in endowing reality with sufficient suppleness to express that mystery of the divine, or the spiritual, that is so deeply rooted in man. His displays of angels, cloud effects or flowers are simply an accompaniment —the least he could or would permit himself— of that profound and constant manifestation of religious feeling in man to which his whole work bears witness.

The whole is a faithful copy of the extraordinary sketch that hangs in the Santa Cruz Museum in Toledo *(Figs. 157 & 158 - Cat. 132)*, a work which, far from being painted in "sketch style", is very carefully finished, each detail being given the greatest possible perfection and clarity. The meticulous and lyrical, rather than fiery, execution may be seen particularly in the most delicate areas of the picture: around the head of St. Joseph, with the descending angels bearing crowns, and in the view of Toledo in the landscape background on the lower right.

The ensemble of San José in Toledo is completed by two side altarpieces, of very simple structure, with only one painting in each. The original canvases, replaced by copies some years ago, now hang in the National Gallery in Washington. The side altarpiece on the left *(Figs. 160 & 161 - Cat. 134)* is dedicated to the *Virgin and Child with St. Martina and St. Agnes.* It is a picture of rigorous symmetry. The simplicity of the composition, only enriched by lighting effects and the little winged heads of angels almost blending into the clouds, is made up for by two factors: the very carefully thought out delicacy of the measured gestures and the extraordinary refinement of the technique, which seems to surpass the unsurpassable, by which we mean the other compositions of the altarpiece and the sketch already studied. The tonal values possess a sweetness and strength that one would think it impossible to bring together. The hierarchical grading of the characters is shown in the degree of individualization given to their faces: the admirable Child Jesus, the extraordinary image of the Virgin, the faces and hands of the saints and, finally, the more impersonal figures of the angels.

The clouds and lights form a sort of white tapestry that, thanks to the intensity of form and colour, very strongly sets off the excellent modelling of the Virgin's figure, with flowing draperies that express almost as much as the faces or hands. Unlike what happens in other pictures, the distortion here is not so evident in the upper part of the picture as in the lower; one might suppose that El Greco is endeavouring to give the Virgin and the angels objectively serene forms. The Child is depicted with greater boldness in the form. But it is in the two saints that he concentrates all his lyrical impulse, which is translated into distortions of vivid yet delicate expressiveness. The modelling causes the forms to fluctuate in a succession of soft, undulating widenings and narrowings, which gives them a certain tension —but not too dynamic or pathetic— as well as an interest of their own. The variety and richness of treatments convey each quality perfectly. The stuffs of the cloaks, the silky softness of the robes, the clarity of the flesh tints and the diaphanous quality of the veil covering the head of the saint on the right are among the most successful pieces of painting ever done by El Greco.

In this work, apart from the representation of textures, El Greco seems to be delighting more in the purely professional aspect of his work, in his ability to cover the canvas with perfect forms which assimilate the distortion as just another element required for their own quality. And this is because the distortion, as we have said, is not the result of instinctive impulses but derives rather from optical motivations —which it exaggerates but does not oppose— and, above all, from a mystical necessity, which would bring us back —as we have also said— to the elongated images of Byzantium, if we seek its most likely beginnings, for from his earliest years the painter had intuitively felt that the representation of divine beings or those near the celestial regions should be different from any realistic vision of common mortals, and this is undoubtedly a Byzantine concept.

The picture in the altarpiece on the right represents St. Martin in the act of slashing his cloak with his sword in order to give half of it to the beggar, a theme frequently found in the Middle Ages *(Fig. 162 - Cat. 135)*. Like the Conde de Orgaz, the patron saint of chivalry is dressed in steel armour gilded and bronzed, but with more gilding and, above all, illuminated by a radiant light. His white horse is projected upwards and fills a great part of the painted surface. The setting consists of clouds against a blue sky and a landscape which partially reproduces the famous landscape of Toledo already mentioned. The beggar, almost entirely naked, has a body with rhythmic modelling that seems to make it grow, as we have seen with other figures by El Greco. The form follows a series of undulations marked by the fluctuating tone, and this gives it a flame-like character. The management of the space is perhaps the most successful feature in this picture of restrained expressiveness. The gestures, though eloquent, are sober. The right hand of the beggar seems to allude to his nakedness, while the saint's look and his slightly inclined head seem to express the fulfilment of a promise rather than any sentimental compassion. The horse is in harmony with the ensemble in drawing and quality; but, while the two men have undergone El Greco's process of "spiritualization by elongation", the horse is represented in his normal proportions.

The colour, too, is of great importance in this picture and El Greco takes all kinds of liberties with it, like a man who finds himself in his real element. Instead of producing harmonies of complementary colours, he creates them by repetition, as we may see in the effect produced by the green cloak in conjunction with the green of the landscape background in the lower part of the picture. These twin canvases are signed, that of the Virgin with small initials in Greek italics. This is the first appearance of this form of signature, which we shall find in various works of smaller format, especially in the *Apostle Series* studied in the final chapter.

The Colegio de Doña María de Aragón, Madrid

A work of great importance in this period (and, indeed, in El Greco's life as a whole), the only one he painted to be hung in the capital of Spain, is the altarpiece for the high altar of the church of the Incarnation in the Colegio de Doña María de Aragón. In 1581 Philip II granted the land for the building of this "Chapter of Nuns of the Order of St. Augustine", which was called after the lady who paid for the construction: Doña María de Aragón, a lady-in-waiting to the Queen, Doña Ana de Austria. The contract for this altarpiece, which has not been preserved, was signed in December of 1596 and El Greco undertook to have it ready and in position by Christmas of 1599. In a power of attorney granted by El Greco to Francisco Preboste on the twentieth of the same month, we are told that he was to be paid 500 ducats "then", another 500 when he sent the designs, another 2,000 ducats at the end of each year as long as the work lasted, and "the rest of what the said altarpiece might amount to" fifteen days after its valuation.

As usual there were delays in the execution, and it was not until July 12th 1600 that definite arrangements were made for transporting the altarpiece from Toledo to Madrid, the cost of this transport being 1,800 *reales*. When it was finally in place, it was appraised by Juan de la Cruz, on behalf of Doña María's executors, and Bartolomé Carducho, on behalf of the painter. And the really high figure of 63,500 *reales* (5,920 ducats) was accepted by both parties. This, it is true, included carving, polychromy and the painting of the canvases. The payments, however, were not made with the punctuality set forth in the contract, for El Greco had to seek a distraint on the income from the inheritance of Doña María de Aragón, part of which was in the town of Illescas in the province of Toledo. As late as June 2nd 1601 we find El Greco empowering Preboste to receive payment of 125,000 *maravedis* in connection with this work. There are no specific references either to the structure or to the iconographical themes depicted in the altarpiece. From vague references previous to its dismemberment we know that the *Annunciation* in the Balaguer Museum of Villanueva y Geltrú *(Fig. 164 - Cat. 138)* was the central composition. The Catalogue of the Museo de la Trinidad, moreover, tells us that the *Baptism of Christ* now in the Prado *(Fig. 168 - Cat. 140)* was once part of the same altarpiece. From the similarity of

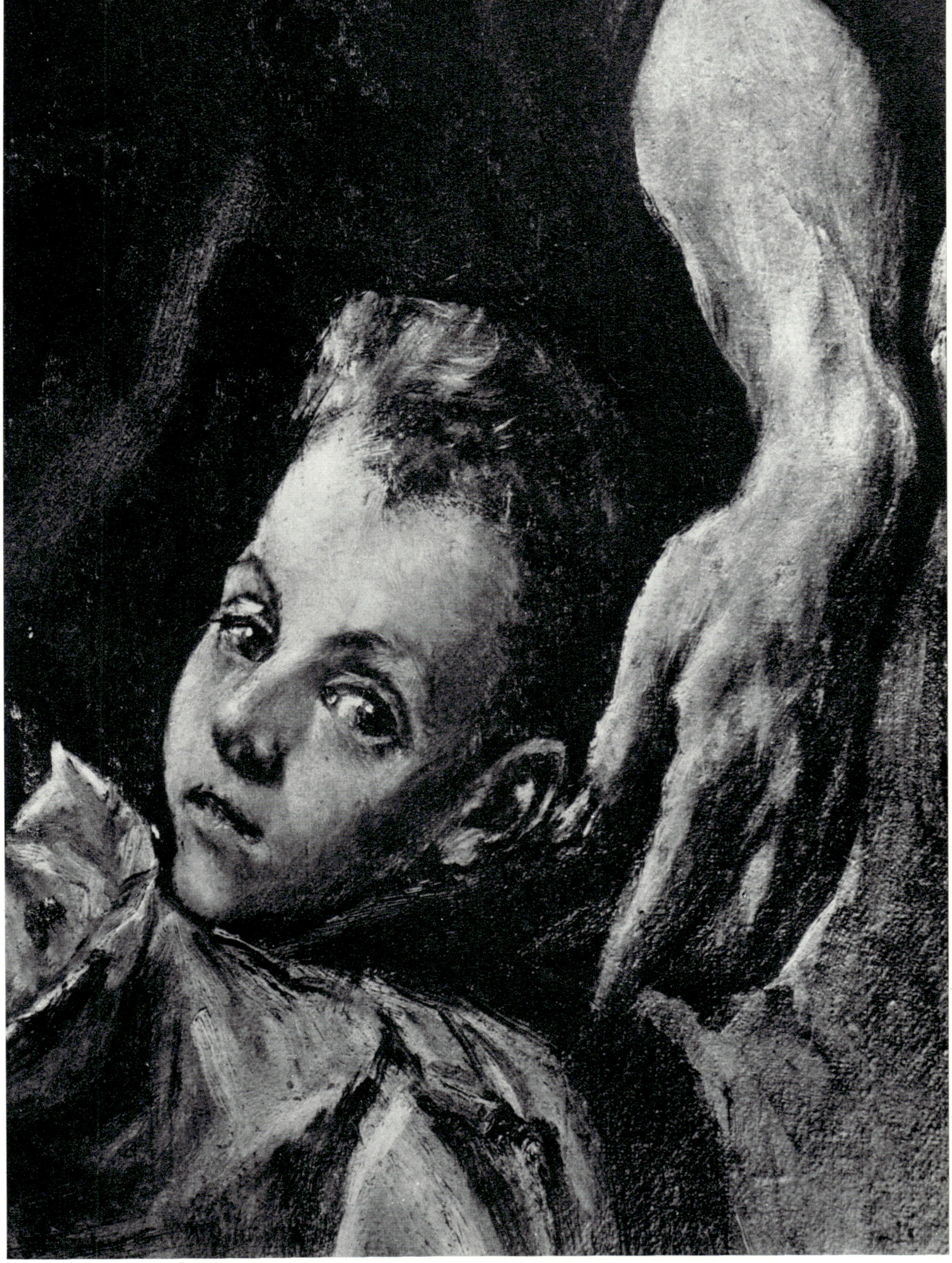

Fig. 159. St. Joseph and the Infant Christ (detail), 1597-1599. Toledo, Church of San José. Cat. No. 133.

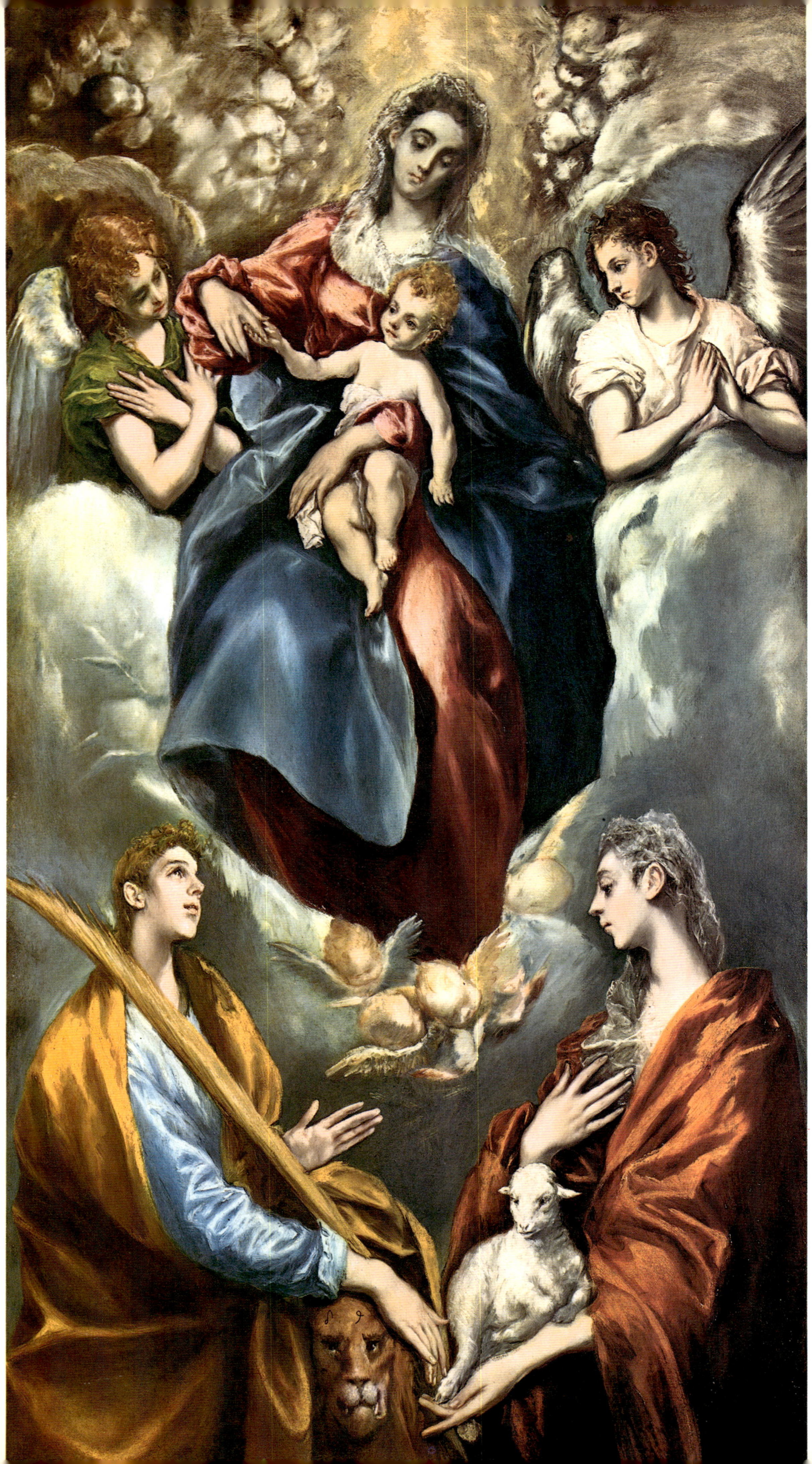

Fig. 160. Virgin and Child with St. Martina and St. Agnes, 1597-1599. Washington, National Gallery. Cat. No. 134.

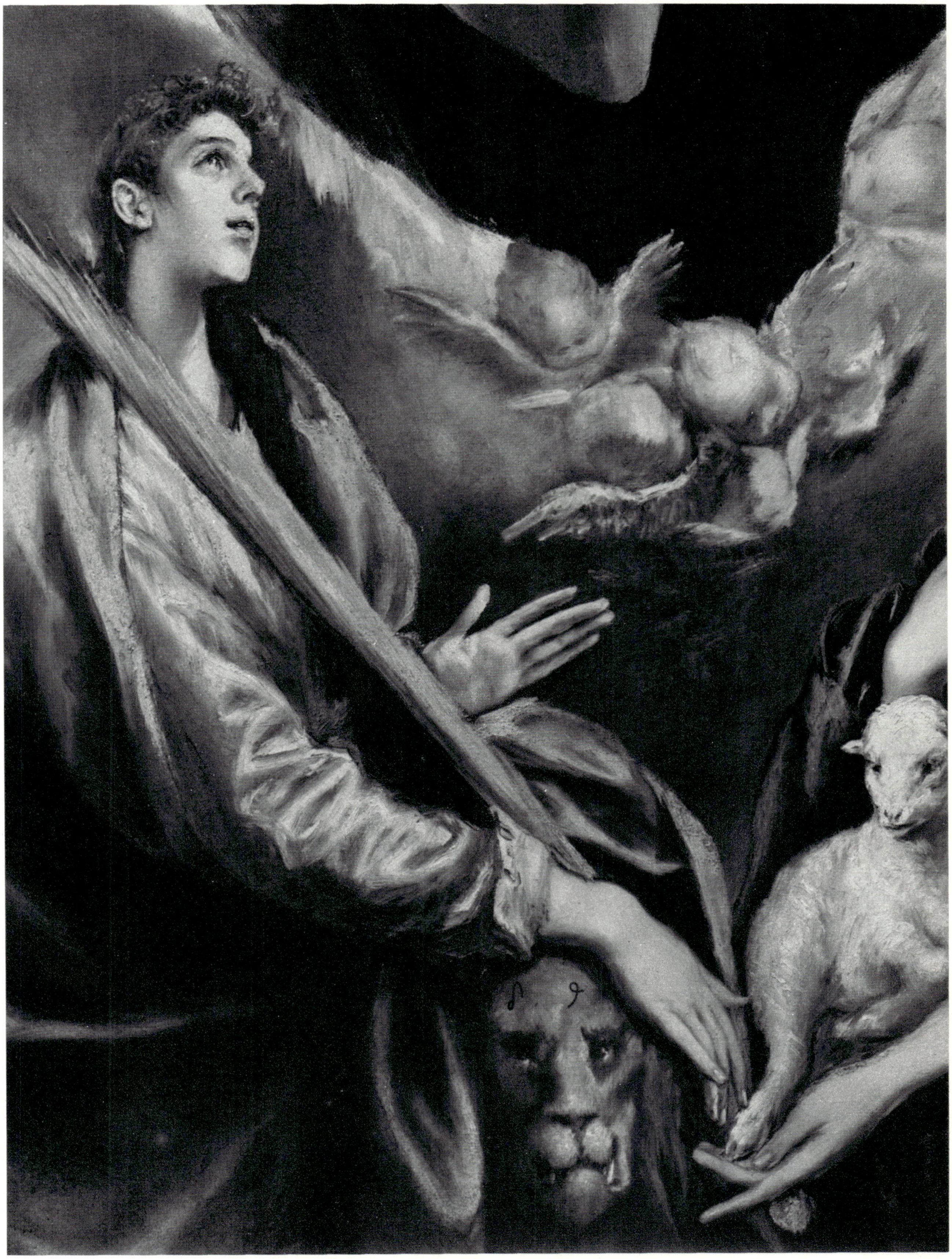

Fig. 161. Detail of figure 160.

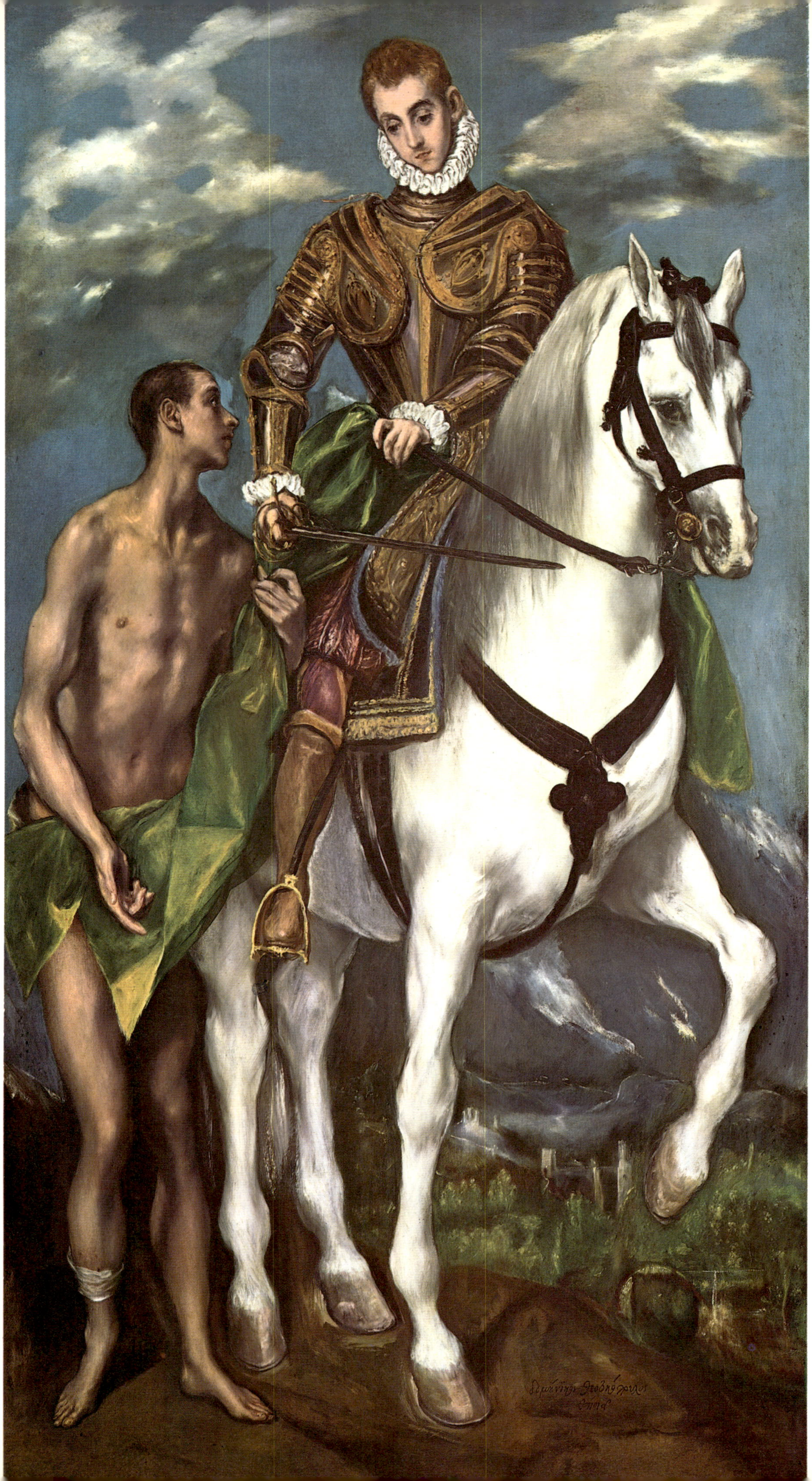

Fig. 162. St. Martin and the begga
1597-1599. Washington, National Ga
lery. Cat. No. 135.

dimensions and suitability of subject matter, it may be deduced that the *Adoration of the shepherds* in Bucharest *(Fig. 171 - Cat. 142)* was the composition that balanced the preceding one on the other side of the ensemble. Of the sculptures which, we are told, completed the altarpiece, nothing is known.

Of the three pictures of the altarpiece painted for this Madrid convent the preparatory studies are still preserved and hang in the Thyssen-Bornemisza Collection and in the Galleria Nazionale in Rome *(Figs. 163 & 165 - Cat. 136, Fig. 167 - Cat. 139* and *Fig. 170 - Cat. 141).* They are, like all El Greco's sketches, works that combine great delicacy with extraordinary vigour. Everything is already determined in them and the definitive versions are simply replicas on a considerably larger scale, though executed with such mastery and passion that each element is created afresh, with a new magic but without any perceptible alteration in the form. It is only on analysing them that we discover profound transformations, due both to the difference in format, which gives rise to different relationships of size between a given form and its brushwork, and to the fact that El Greco never copied himself exactly as far as procedures were concerned, though he did stay faithful to the colour, the scheme of the composition and the drawing, both in general and in each separate detail.

This *Annunciation*, unlike practically all the other paintings he did on the theme, emphasizes what we might call the painter's "symphonic" concept *(Figs. 164 & 166 - Cat. 138).* El Greco knows that when the Archangel Gabriel transmits the message from on high to Mary something very profound occurs in the celestial regions and it is this that he seeks, successfully, to represent. For this purpose he divides the composition, as is frequent with him, into two areas: the lower one, in which the events of this earth take place, and the upper one, which is a vision of heaven, in this case only represented by angel-musicians. We have already spoken of the great formal interest of the "intermediate area", which serves as a separation, and at the same time as a link, between heaven and earth. It is like a sort of downpour of light that joins the two areas. It would be naïve to suppose that El Greco's interpretation of the *Annunciation* consists only of the theme itself; i.e., of the representation of a group of angels playing musical instruments in heaven, to celebrate what is taking place on earth. This motif gives the painter a pretext for refusing to repeat the usual composition, with earth (or floor), figures and spatial setting —closed or open, but cut short at the upper limit of the picture. The division of the surface into two distinct areas enables him to invent a new type of composition, which gives rise to new rhythms and internal dynamism —in upward flight (which was, as we know, an obsession of his)— and at the same time to vary and increase the interplay of formal, tonal and chromatic harmonies.

In the *Annunciation* we are now studying, this fact can be seen with a force and clarity rarely equalled in their revelation of the degree to which the subject became a pretext for the composition. If we attempt to make an imaginary division of the composition along the line of the archangel's wing, on the right, the whole picture disintegrates. For we might almost say that the main interest does not lie in the figures but in the ascending movement of light that goes from the figure of the Virgin to the central area of the upper part, passing through the intense white of the dove of the Holy Ghost. The little heads of angels are inserted, as usual, in the mass of clouds that the painter uses to create this "channel" of communication between the heavenly and earthly parts of the picture. But this movement is partly offset by the oblique axis in vigorous ascent that is formed, from left to right, by the open book on the lectern, the outline of the Virgin's head, the head of the archangel and the tip of his left wing. This powerful line, moreover, is paralleled below by the different levels at which the painter has placed the feet of the Virgin —hidden by her pinkish red robe— and those of the archangel. This relationship heightens the one between the two figures and the very beautiful —and not complementary— contrast between the vivid green of the archangel's robe and the blue and crimson of the robe and mantle worn by the Virgin. The yellow, greenish, whitish and greyish tones of the background successfully unite the whole and produce the same neutral base in the upper area, where marvellous figures of angels form two groups: a larger one in the centre and on the left, another one on the right. The elongated, zigzag form of the angel in the centre, with his leg projecting downwards covered by an orange-tinged crimson robe, is also used to establish a rhythmic communication with the whole figure of the announcing archangel.

To analyse the subtleties and harmonies of this work would be an endless task. Its sketch, as we said, differs from it only in execution. with its brushwork seeming larger on account of the smaller format of the work, while the technique is more spontaneous and at the same time more "dissolved" and less noticeably drawn. In the definitive work, however, El Greco also leaves the forms rather vague, on account of his technique of rubbing the paint and thus partly effacing its limits. But in the field of expressive sentiment he remains extremely faithful to his first version, as may be verified by comparing details of the Virgin's head in the sketch with the same details in the larger work. The outline of the face varies slightly, the execution is not exactly the same, but the turn of the lips and the look convey exactly the same meaning in both cases. This capacity for the exact repetition of a feeling and for variation in the execution would be sufficient evidence —even if we had not much more besides— to prove the pictorial genius of El Greco. Even in the replica of this sketch, which is in the Bilbao Museum *(Cat. 137)*, the expression is identical, though somewhat "wearier" or less tense.

In this work we can see that El Greco, like Rembrandt and Velázquez, knew perfectly well that the secret of painting is the perfect integration of everything that forms part of it: a brushstroke is as important as a colour, a form or the apparently arbitrary way of giving life to a foreshortening as important as the whole ensemble of composition and theme. The reason is that it is only in analysis that it is all —artificially— separated, whereas in its creation it all sprang up in one and the same act.

The *Baptism of Christ*, another painting from the altarpiece for the Colegio de Doña María de Aragón *(Figs. 168 & 169 - Cat. 140)*, is hardly to be distinguished from the sketch as far as the scheme of composition and subject matter is concerned. Apart from the difference we have constantly pointed out in the execution (smoother qualities and more cleanly drawn forms in the larger work), in this case El Greco's modifications were minimal: he raised the level of the rock on which the Baptist is standing, in order to give greater justification to the stature of this figure, which is gigantic in comparison with that of Christ. Besides —and this is very important— his features are more realistic in the sketch, but as the painter wished to give a sensation of distance in the upper part of the composition, he softened and simplified the forms in such a way that they seem more idealized. We also find here the optical effect already mentioned in connection with other works: in the upper part of the surface the space appears to drop backwards or to be situated on a deeper or more distant plane. In the lower part the painter contrived a device of great pictorial effect, making the five angels in this area (one of them seen full-length between Christ and St. John) hold up the flowing mantle of the Saviour, between Him and the middle distance. In this way the very beautiful body of Christ, modelled with a technique of flowing, curved forms, stands against the ample, outspread cloth, and of four of the angels all we can see is their hands and heads. The simplification of form in combination with distortion produced by accentuated foreshortening is already to be found here and it gives an effect that could be described as expressionistic. Qualifications apart, we have here one of the most daring and beautiful pieces of painting in the whole history of art.

The simplification and distortion, however, are still more accentuated in the upper area. The Eternal Father is rather the image of an idea than of a being. How far we are here from the humanization of God the Father in the Trinity of Santo Domingo el Antiguo! Besides, El Greco finds another way of idealizing and transfiguring these representations of heaven: giving more life to the qualities of the void (or background of light and flaming cloud effects), while greatly reducing the specific character of the textures of the personages appearing in it. In this way he diminishes the contrast, or difference, between figures and background and creates —without falling into confusion or formlessness— a new world of beauties and expressions never known before. The whole is justified by the dizzy rhythm of upward flight that this composition constitutes. The lower area, with its sinuous, flame-like rhythms, is already formed in such a way as to lead the eye upwards, a fresh stimulus being provided by all the active elements in the intermediate area: the luminous dove of the Holy Ghost, angels who seem to be literally flying upwards, various groups of little angels in positions that are as diverse and as opposed to the law of gravity as possible —and, above all, the stream of light flowing upward and finally blending into the white robe of God the Father. From the point of view of tone, the lower part seems to have been treated almost as a relief, thanks to the intimate linking of the figures and the exactitude of the rhythms. But above, from the group of angels' heads to the top of the oval of light that surrounds the Almighty, a symphony of luminosity and colour

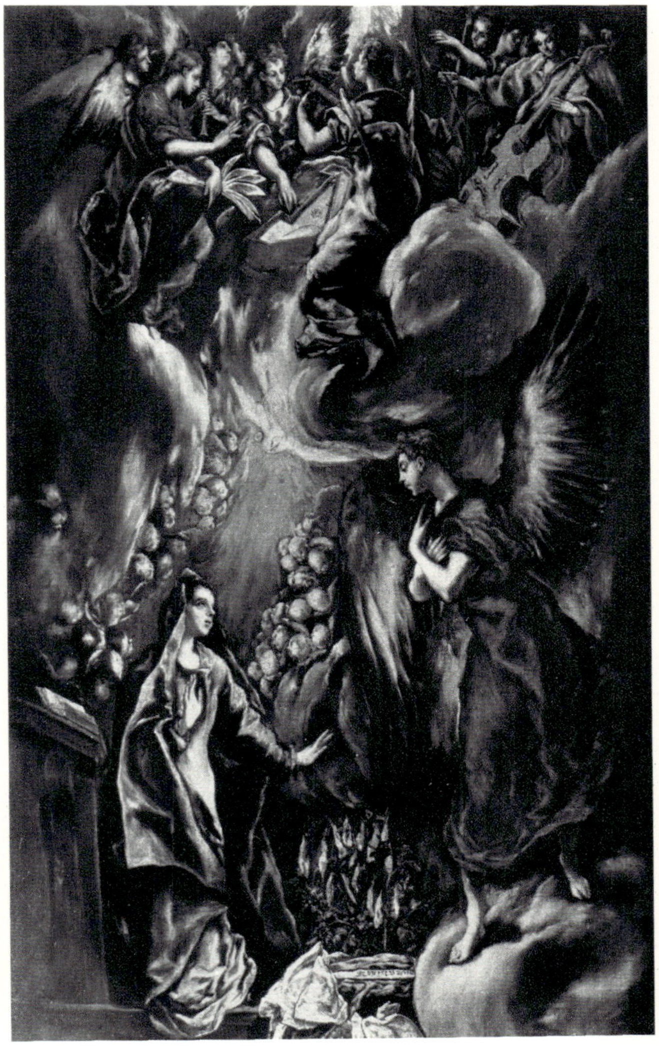

Fig. 163. The Annunciation, 1597-1600. Lugano, Thyssen-Bornemisza Collection. Cat. No. 136.

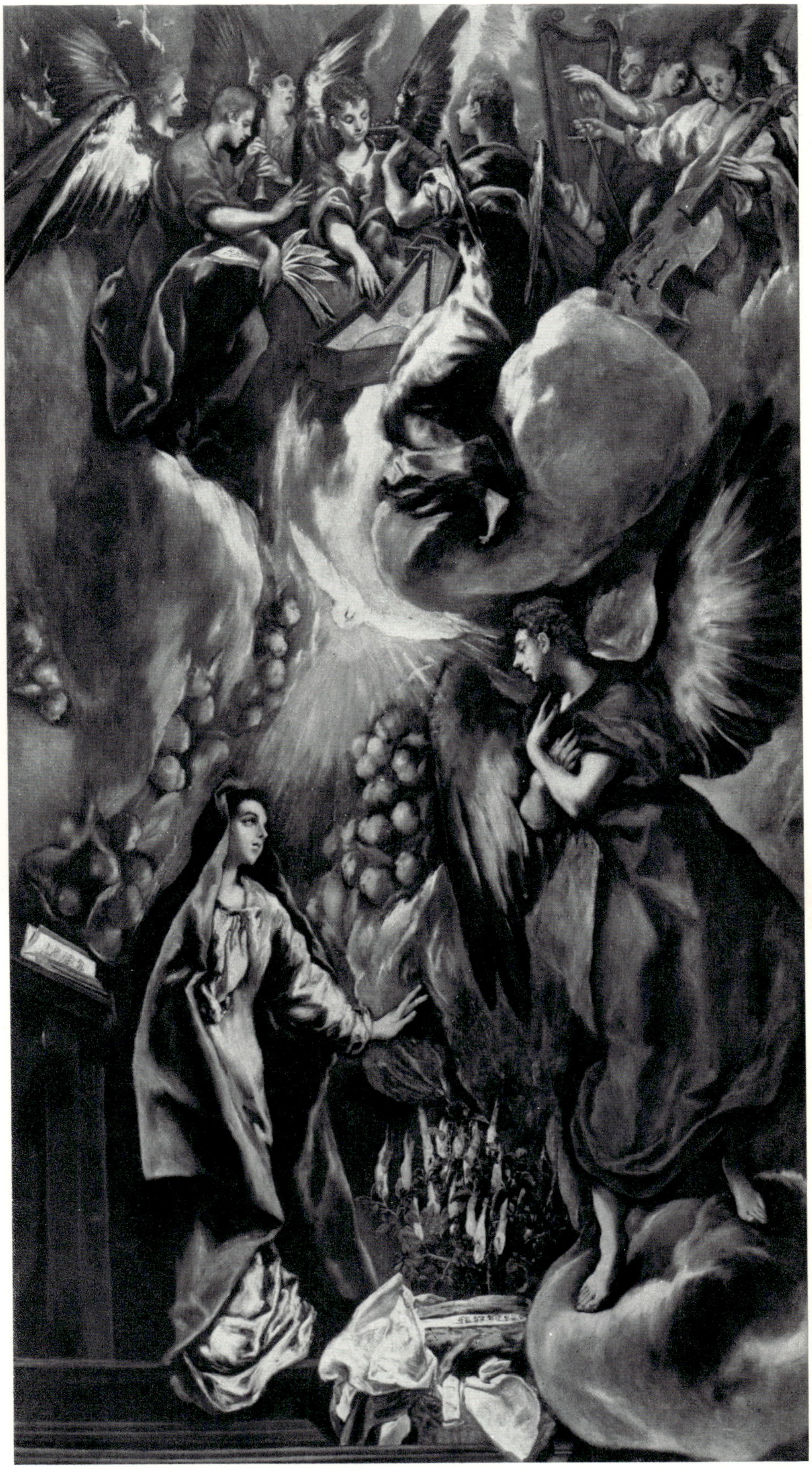

Fig. 164. The Annunciation, 1597-1600. Villanueva y Geltrú, Balaguer Museum. Cat. No. 138.

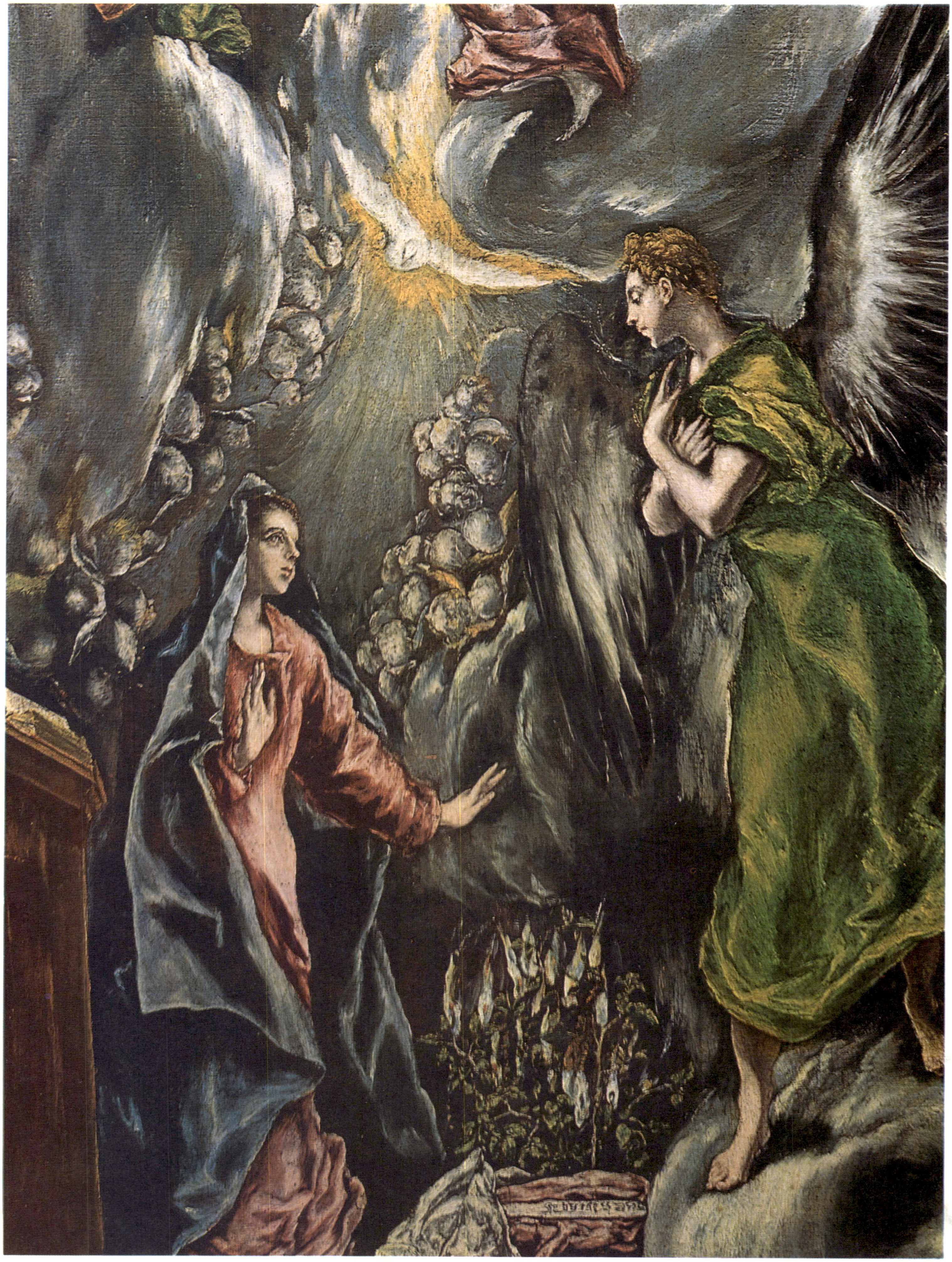

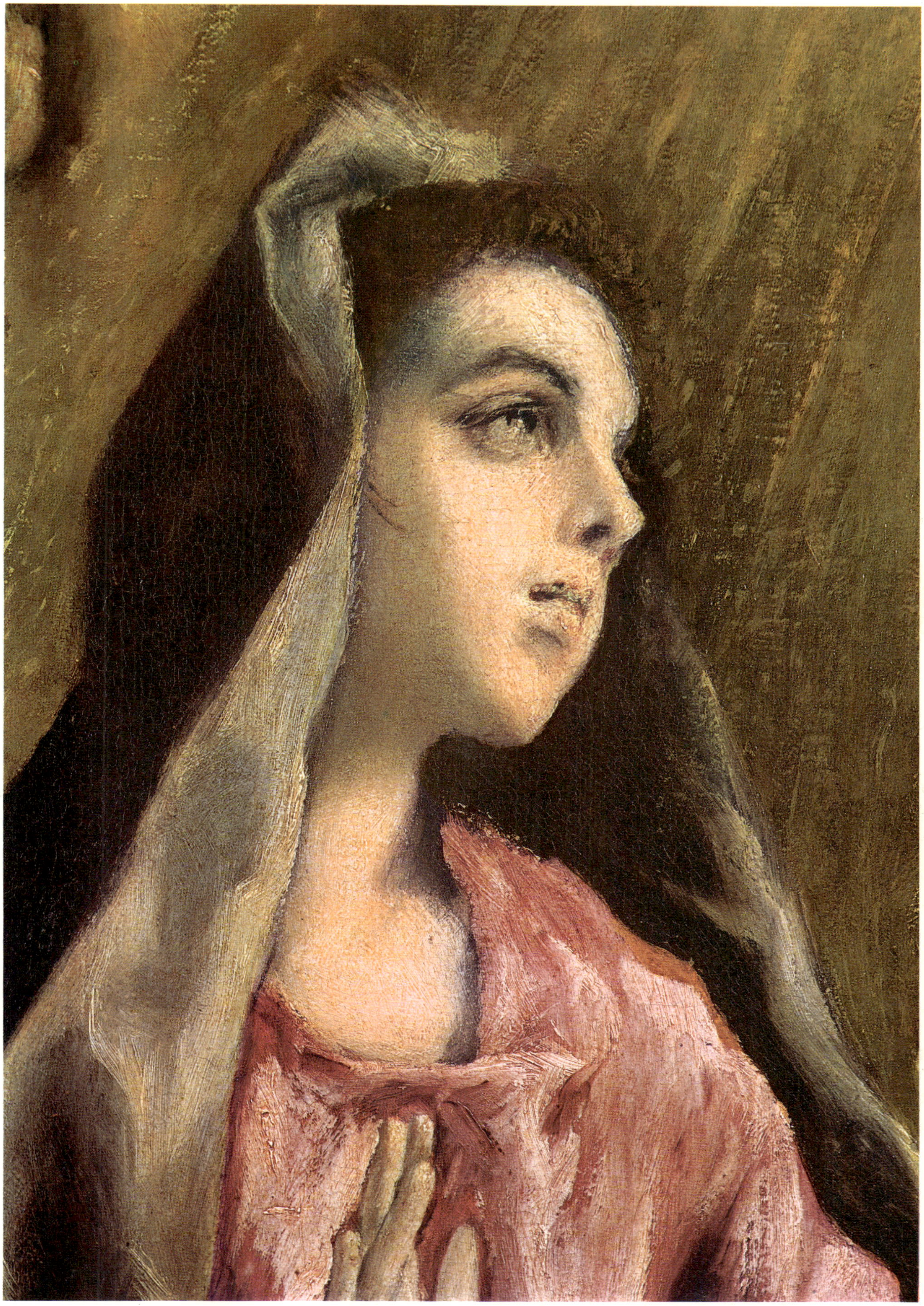

Fig. 165. Detail of figure 163.
Fig. 166. Detail of figure 164.

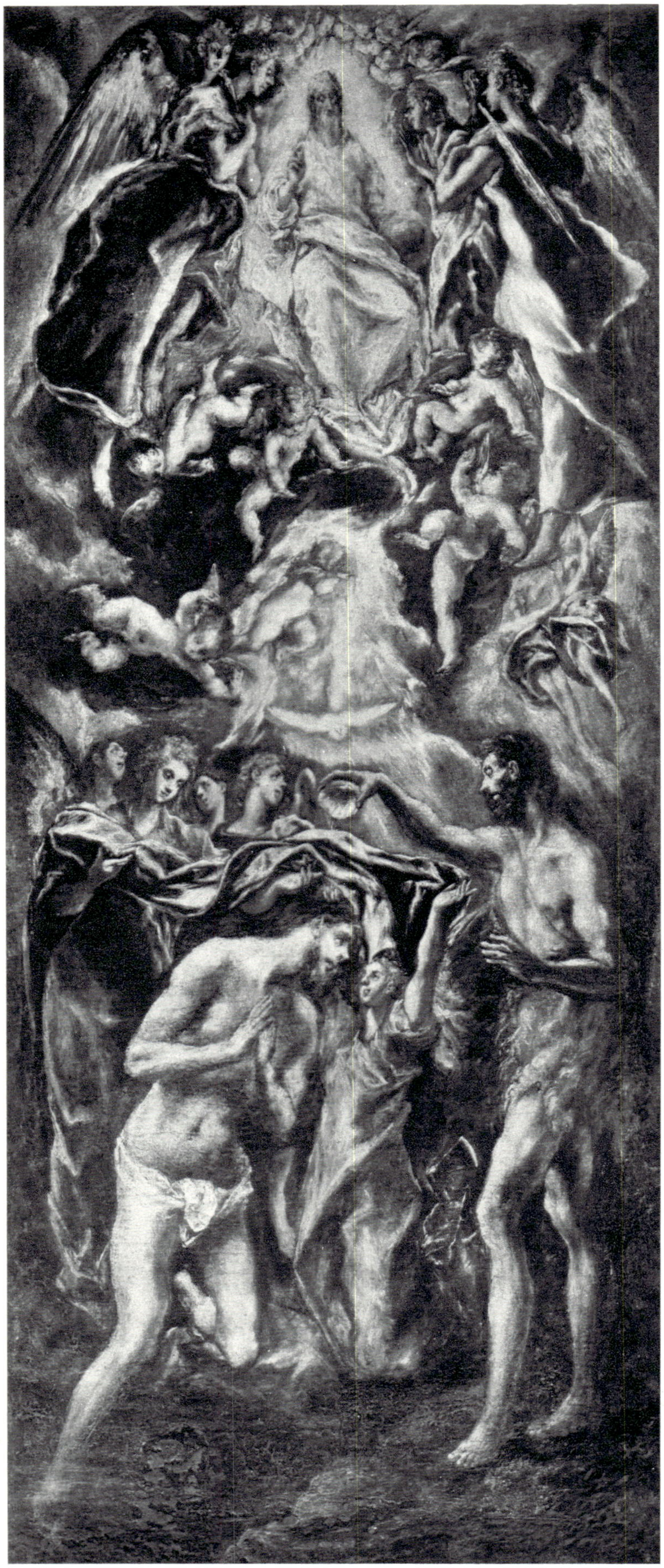

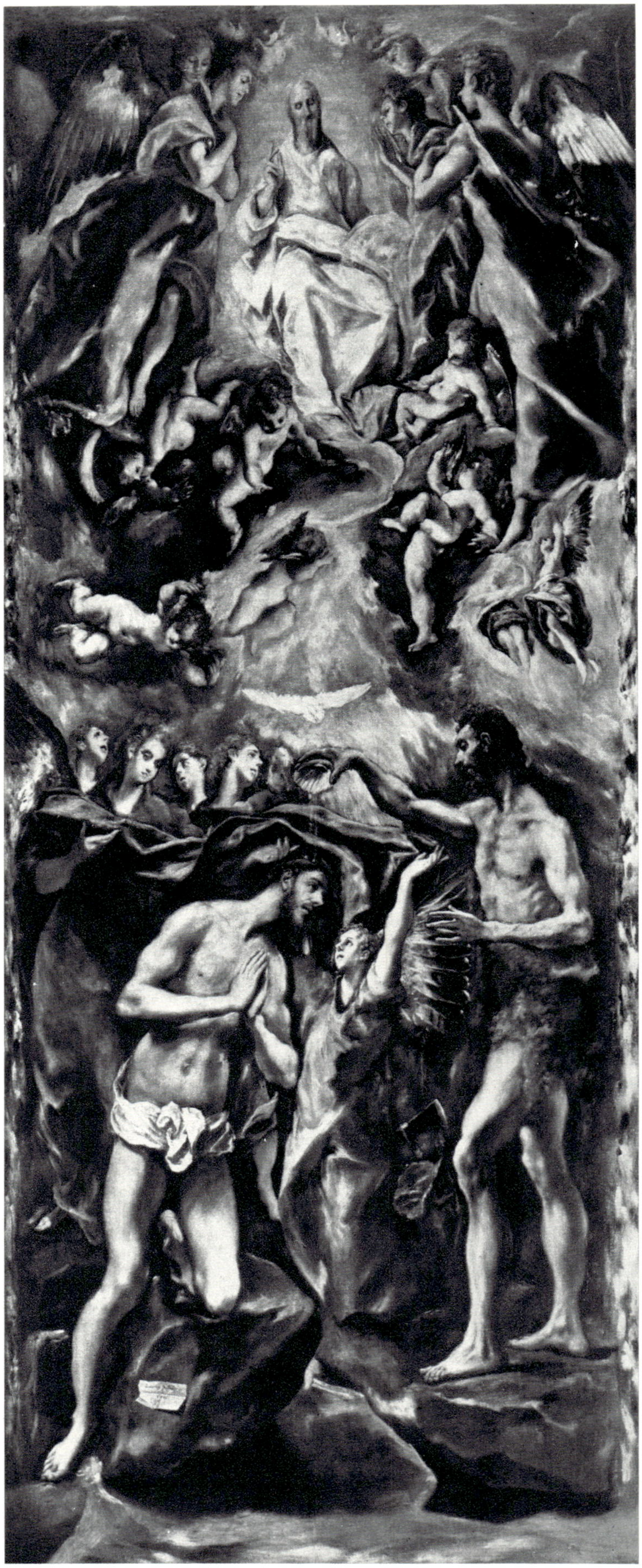

Fig. 167. The Baptism of Christ, 1597-1600. Rome, Galleria Nazionale. Cat. No. 139.
Fig. 168. The Baptism of Christ, 1597-1600. Madrid, Prado. Cat. No. 140.

develops, driving the whole upwards. In the sketch this ascending movement may seem less intense on account of the greater force of the brushwork, which, as we have said, lessens the differences of intensity among the various elements. The foreshortenings, however, are exactly the same and the distortions almost identical, except as regards the treatment and the execution properly speaking.

In the *Adoration of the shepherds* that hangs in the National Museum of Romania *(Fig. 171 - Cat. 142)*, we may at first seem to find elements (light effects, secondary figures, etc.) that might be considered typical of the work of Bassano. But this is only due to the fact that El Greco, in the reiteration of these traditional themes of religious iconography, always used previous works of his own as a starting-point and so, in this advancing movement, even though he created new metamorphoses, he still retained elements from his earlier periods, in typology, gestures, expression of feelings and effects of the setting. In this version, however, we may observe a more appreciable ascending movement between the upper and lower areas, the heavenly regions being separated from the earthly by architectural elements, the vaults of the building in which the sacred characters are situated. There is a double dynamic suggestion in this composition: upward and circular. This second movement seems to be centered on the vigorous, though fragmented, axis of the intermediate area, represented by the pillar supporting the vault. But, thanks to those effects of displacement towards the viewer and towards the background which are quite common in El Greco, in the lower half the centre is placed considerably further forward than the architecture: it is the figure of the Child Jesus, bathed in intense light. The movement of the angels on high with scrolls follows the same rhythm. Pink, crimson, white and pink or rather yellowish luminosities are contrasted with dense blues. If we examine the details, we shall see that the form is treated with the boldest of brushwork, with details half-disintegrating, but turning out to be "reconstituted" when we consider the ensemble as a whole.

In these three works executed for the Colegio de Doña María de Aragón we find confirmation of what we said regarding the paintings done after 1590. El Greco totally rejects both the judgments and valuations of the social world around him and all his own preoccupation with "formalism". After his previous period of great "classical" achievement, from the altarpiece of Santo Domingo el Antiguo to the *Burial of the Conde de Orgaz*, knowing himself to be in full mastery of all factors of his art, at this high point he loses interest, or, rather, he no longer needs to interest himself, in what might be called restraint, correctness or formal exactitude. Having created a technique, a conception and a world of his own, he uses them as his sole starting-point in a development that will increasingly accentuate the most audacious distortions, an art in which there will also be frequent accentuation of the *horror vacui* that prevails in these compositions of 1597-1599, together with the upward flight and the elongation of proportions. To the repertory of gestures which, as we have said, is an important factor in the evolution of El Greco's work, yet another is now added: that of the two raised arms of the angel in the centre foreground, a gesture which was later to lose the practical function it fulfils in this work and become an expression of pathos, as in the Apocalyptic vision painted in his last years.

Differentiated by a certain nuance of feeling, derived from the theme, these three compositions are closely related as regards their scheme, form, colour and rhythmic movement. They are among the best works of the painter, who, after his great previous achievements, now knows exactly what means he possesses and how far they will permit him to go, despite all his material failures and the unworthy treatment he is at times subjected to, treatment which will bring him, in the now fast approaching last years of his life, almost to the verge of indigence.

As has already been said, a study of the paintings in San José in Toledo logically establishes a chronological connection with two original works by El Greco of unknown date: an image of *St. James the Great* in the Hispanic Society, New York *(Fig. 156 - Cat. 131)*, and the famous *View of Toledo* in the Metropolitan Museum of the same city *(Fig. 172 - Cat. 143)*. The first of these two canvases was probably painted before the *Coronation of the Virgin* which is in the top panel of the altarpiece in the church of San José *(Fig. 155)*, since exactly the same image figures among the saints depicted in that composition. It is quite possible, however, that this image of the patron saint of Spain is of later date than the picture in San José, as it was by no means El Greco's invariable practice to include such images among the lesser details of his compositions.

The "View of Toledo"

The *View of Toledo* was a basic element in El Greco's work for the establishment of landscape backgrounds, like that in the great *St. Joseph* and its sketch and the one in the representation of *St. Martin.* This would imply that the extraordinary landscape itself was painted before 1597. In documents referring to El Greco there are sporadic references to painted "countrysides". In the inventory of the estate of Salazar de Mendoza, drawn up after his death in 1629, we find "a countryside of Toledo, towards the Alcántara bridge", without mentioning any painter's name. This might well be, as San Román supposed, the canvas we are now studying, for Mendoza had been the administrator of the Hospital de Afuera, the great foundation of Cardinal Tavera, and, as we shall see in Chapter VIII, played a very important role in the last years of El Greco's life. On the other hand, the inventories drawn up by Jorge Manuel after his father's death include canvases: "a Toledo" and "two countrysides of Toledo".

The *View of Toledo* in the Metropolitan, or another very similar picture, was also used as a model for the backgrounds of other compositions, which were undoubtedly painted after 1600 and which we shall be studying in the following chapters. Before using Toledo as a landscape background, El Greco sometimes put the Escorial to this use, as we have seen. The present landscape —one of the first in the history of Spanish painting since the Middle Ages— is seen under a stormy sky which projects livid lights upon the earth. Thus it is hardly surprising that, together with touches of ochre, the picture is totally dominated by three shades: green, a grey that is somewhere between bluish and white —in the buildings— and a greyish blue in the stormy cloud effects. One of the most successful features of the composition is the displacement to the right of the central mass of the "acropolis" of Toledo, with the huge bulk of the Alcázar brooding over it; to the left are the Alcántara bridge and the castle of San Servando. A road that starts out from the lower left rises abruptly to the tower guarding the Alcántara bridge, is continued in the rhythms of the bridge itself and then gently climbs the crest of a ridge situated at about the same height. This is one of El Greco's greatest paintings, however much it might be faulted for the disproportion in the tiny figures —certainly much too small— that can be seen in the river in the middle distance. The ones walking along the road leading to the bridge are on a more suitable scale. But this is mere hair-splitting when we consider the astonishing expression that emanates from the picture as a whole. Never has a city been "portrayed" with such genius, captured in all its mysterious sum of deep forces, which seem to rise to the surface under the livid light imposed by the atmospheric conditions. The build-up of rhythms and the perfect coordination of masses of earth covered with vegetation and skies covered with clouds (of almost the same amplitude), with the grey buildings of the ancient Spanish capital in the middle as a link between the two, create a unique whole. The execution is meticulous and brilliant in every element, with a succession of very finely-nuanced contrasts between areas of light and shade, which gradually model the grounds, from the foreground, with treetops, spreading undergrowth and the dark channel of the river, to the sharp point of the cathedral tower. El Greco intentionally darkened the lower area of the sky, in order to increase the contrast between the grey buildings and the atmospheric elements. Thus he created a work in which the pictorial force is equalled only by its own psychic intensity.

Works attributed to the period 1597-1603

We will now turn our attention to a considerable series of undated works which, for reasons of style and execution, should in our opinion be placed in this period of transition from the sixteenth to the seventeenth century. There are compositions with various figures, images of saints and portraits: variety of subject matter, but unity of style. In some cases the new images are copies of previous designs, revived and simplified at the same time. But in most of these works the great Cretan's inexhaustible creative talent surprises us with new ideas.

Among the first of these is the wonderful *Annunciation* in the Museum of Toledo (Ohio) *(Fig. 174 - Cat. 144),* which derives from the little *modello* brought by El Greco from Italy and now in the Prado *(Fig. 24).* There has evidently been a great transformation in the process of simplification that began with the Contini-Bonacossi version *(Figs. 26 & 27).* The only elements of the setting are the workbasket

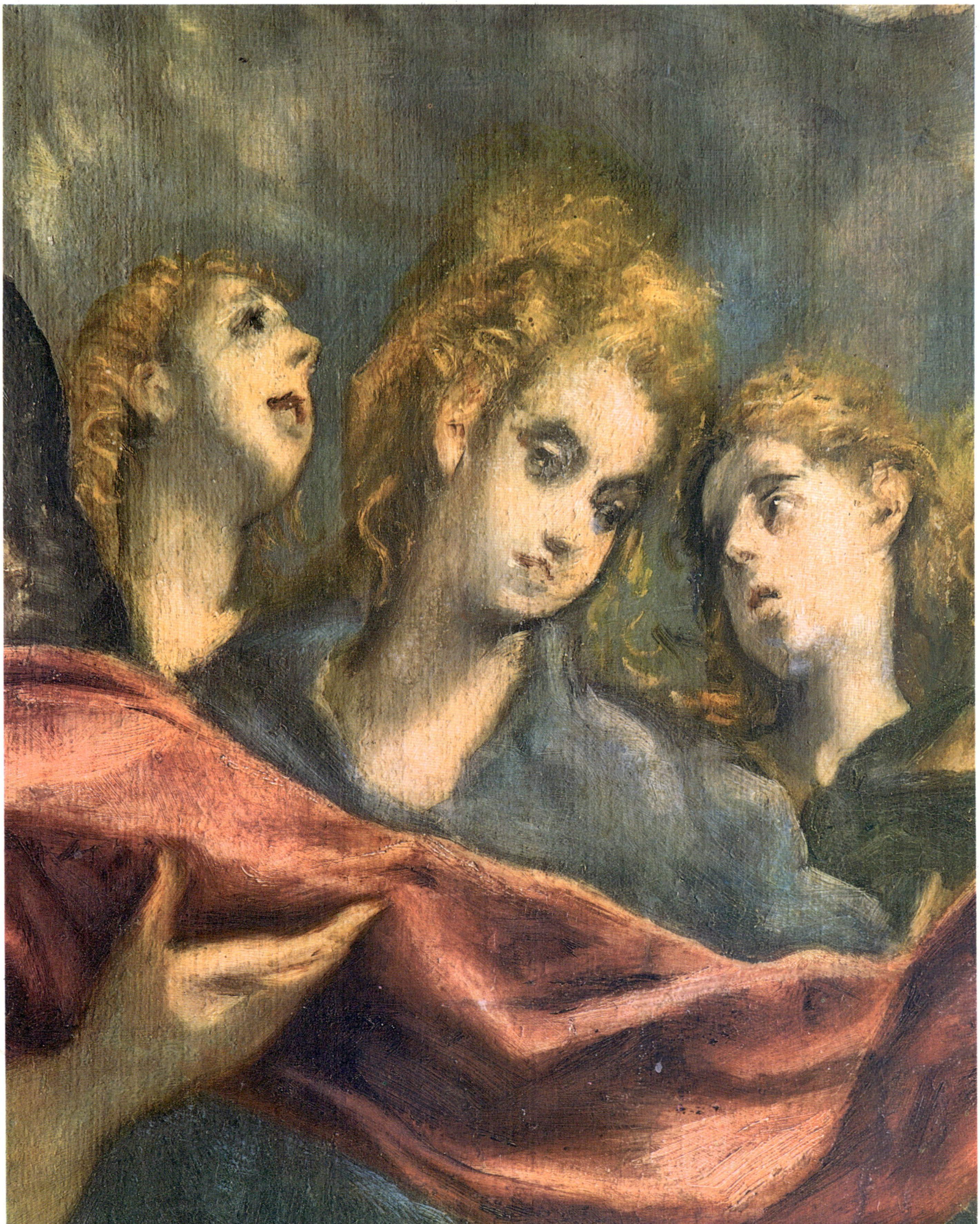

Fig. 169. Detail of figure 168.

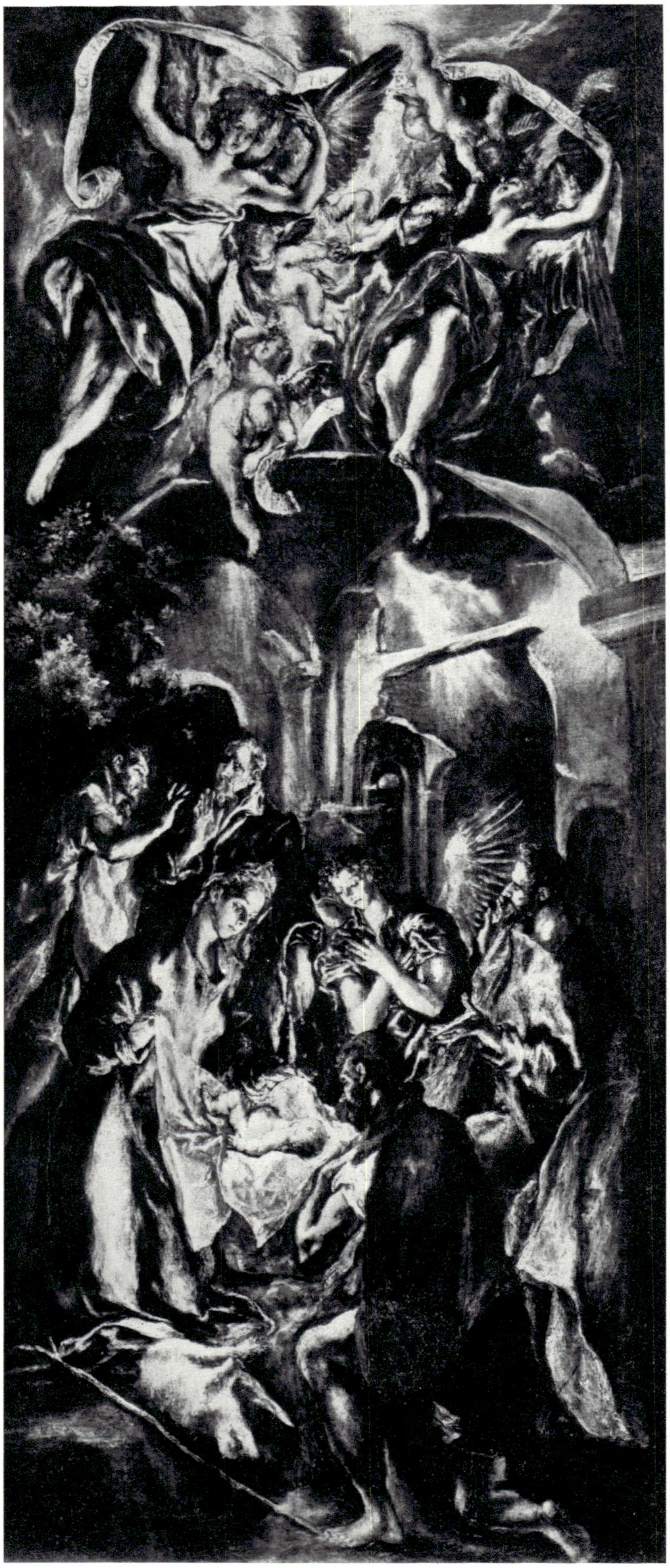

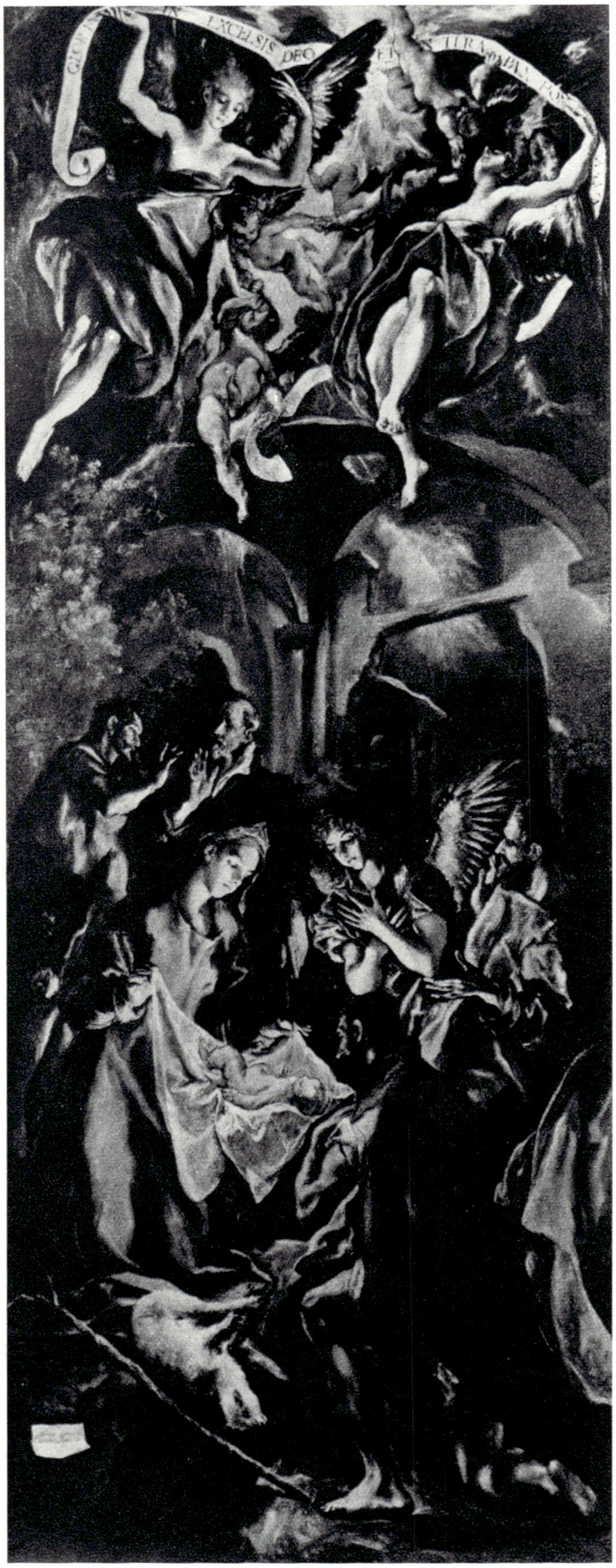

Fig. 170. The Adoration of the shepherds, 1597-1600. Rome, Galleria Nazionale. Cat. No. 141.
Fig. 171. The Adoration of the shepherds, 1597-1600. Bucharest, National Museum of Romania. Cat. No. 142.

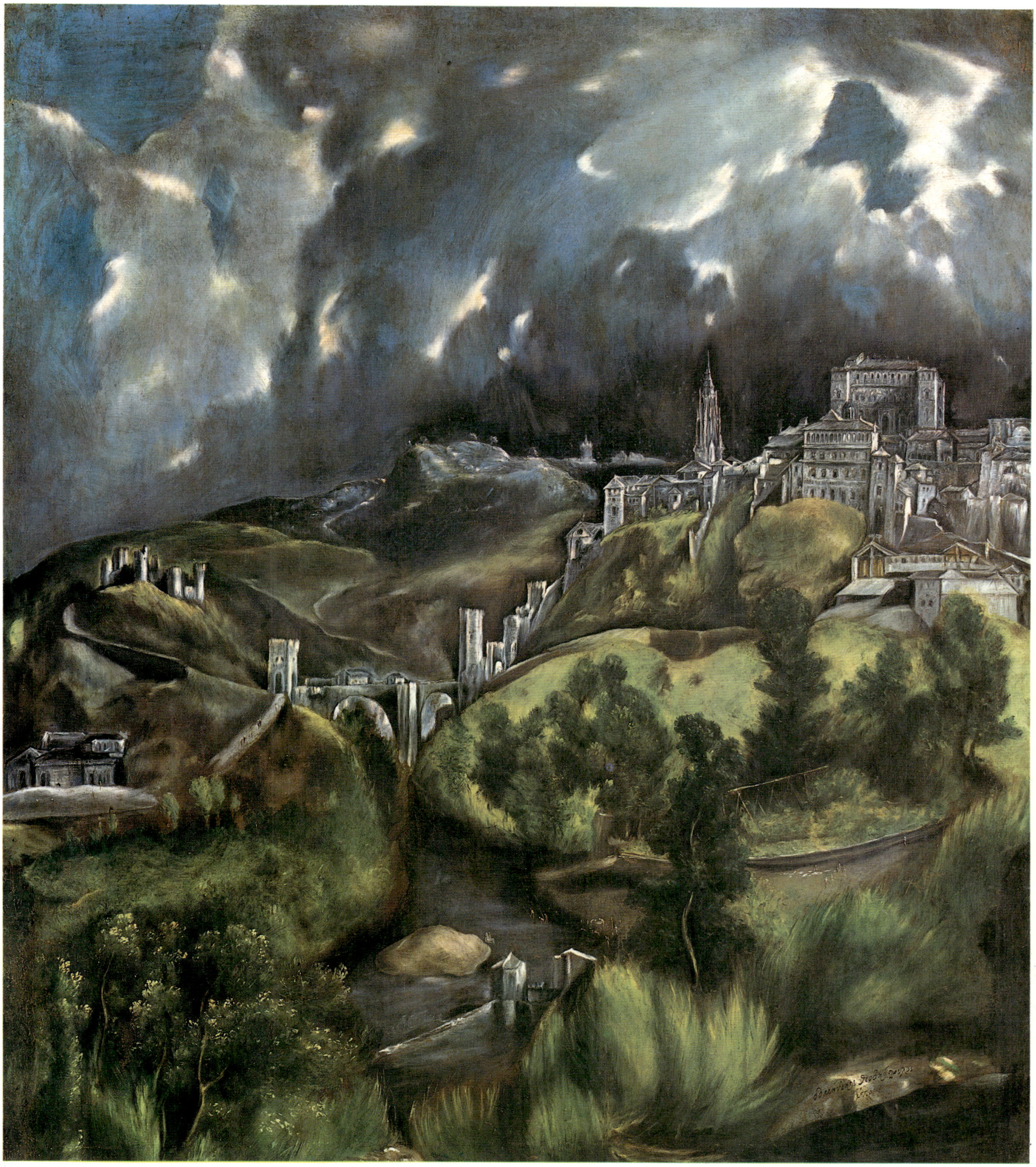

Fig. 172. View of Toledo, before 1597. New York, Metropolitan Museum. Cat. No. 143.

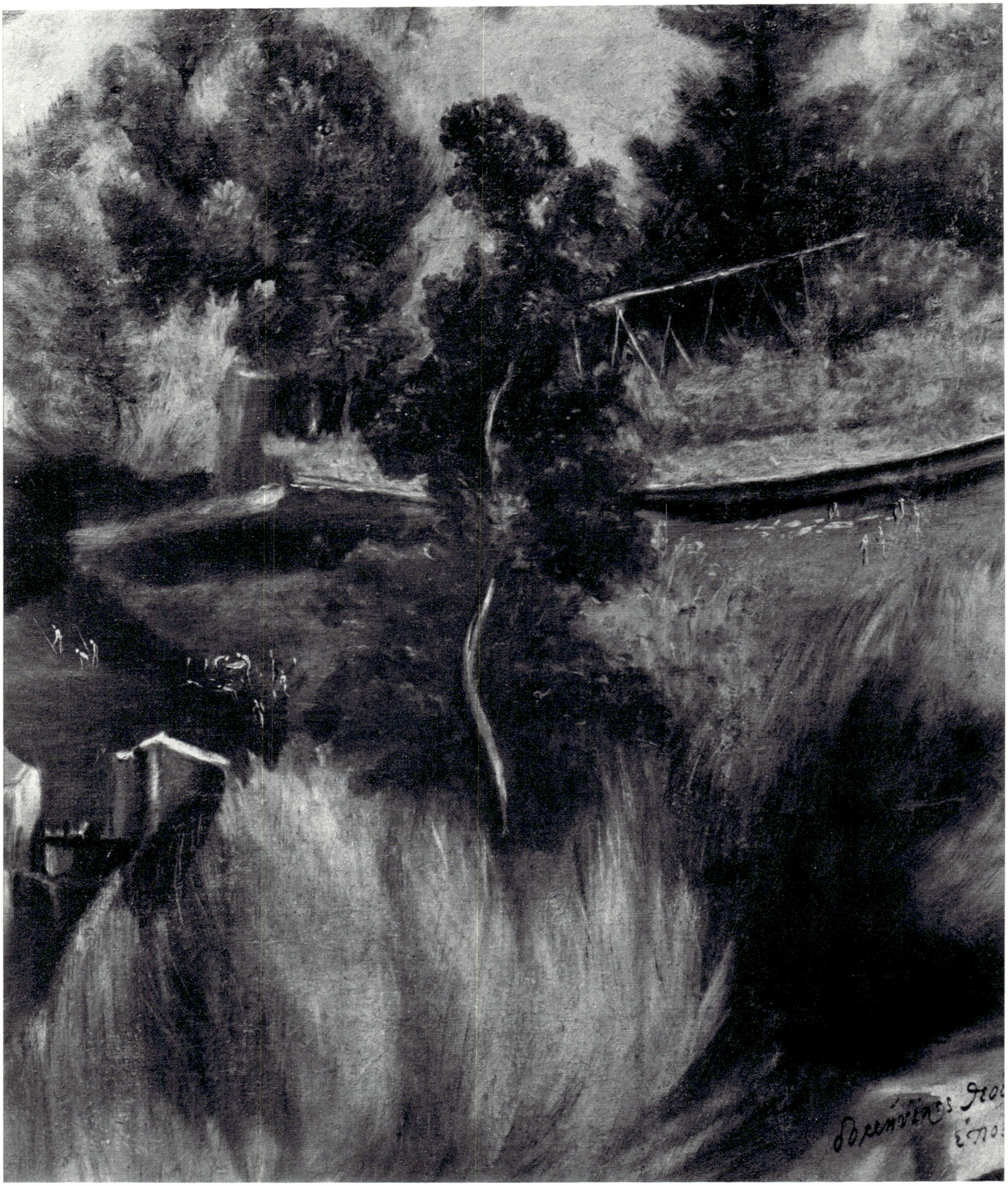

Fig. 173. Detail of figure 172.

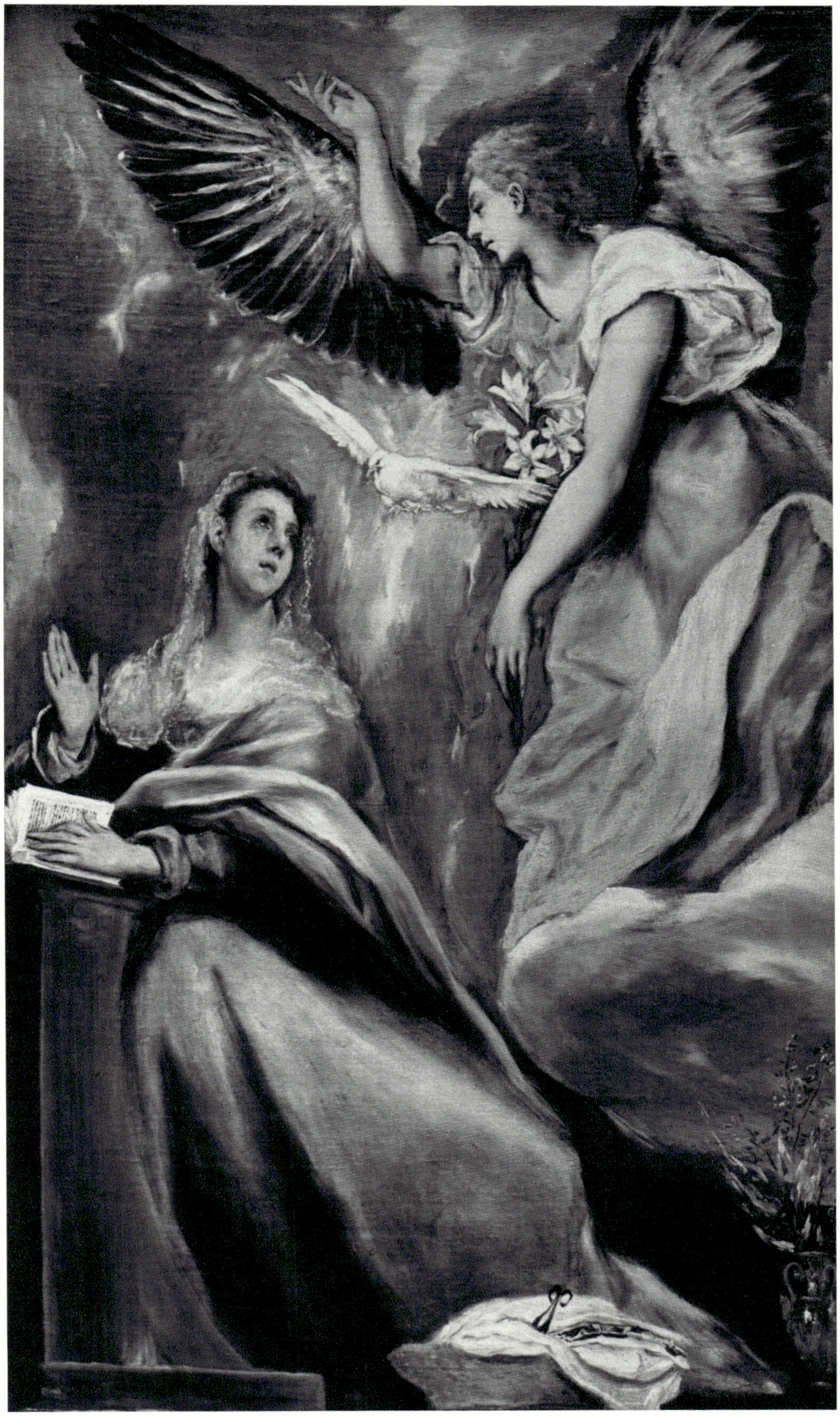

Fig. 174. The Annunciation, 1597-1603. Toledo (Ohio), Museum. Cat. No. 144.

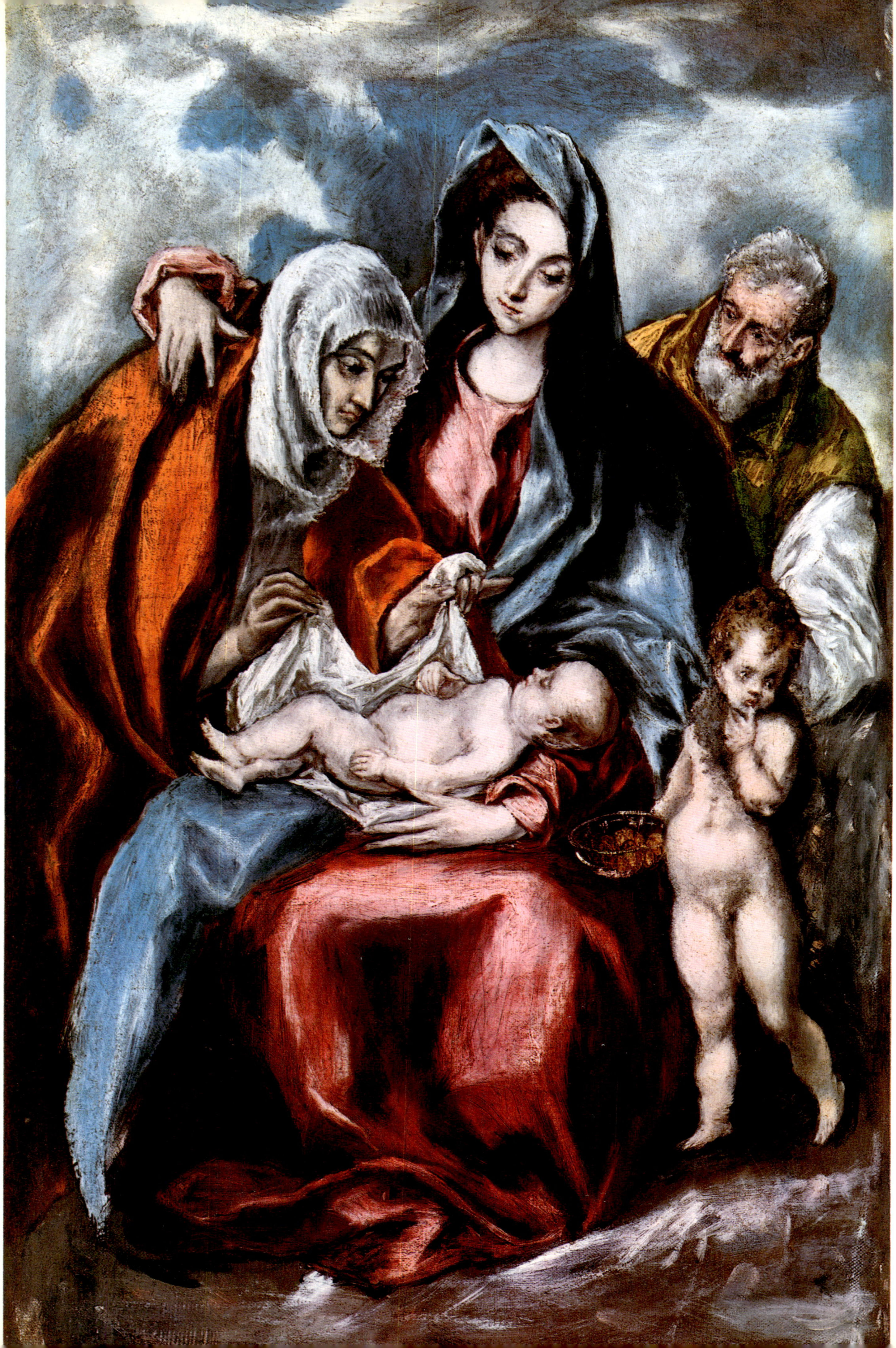

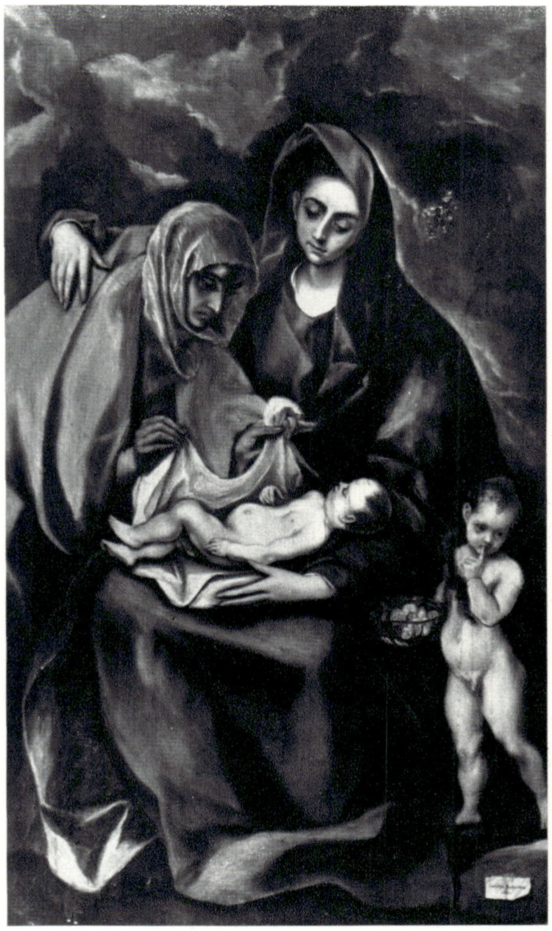

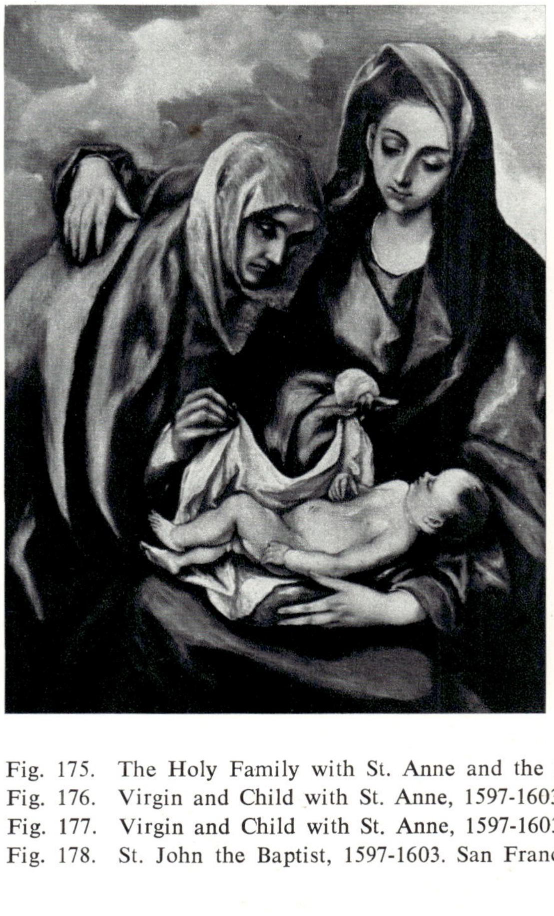

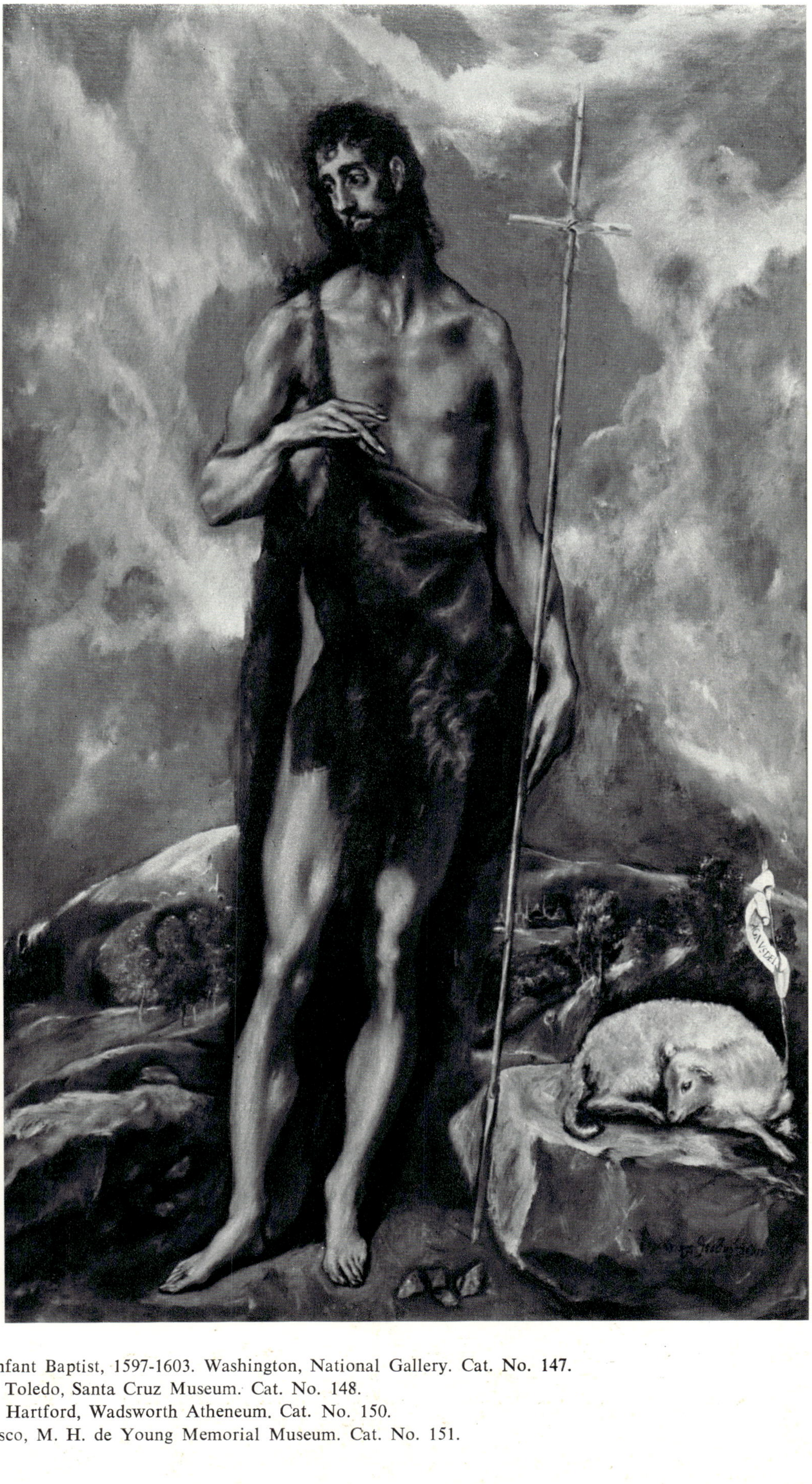

Fig. 175. The Holy Family with St. Anne and the Infant Baptist, 1597-1603. Washington, National Gallery. Cat. No. **147.**
Fig. 176. Virgin and Child with St. Anne, 1597-1603. Toledo, Santa Cruz Museum. Cat. No. 148.
Fig. 177. Virgin and Child with St. Anne, 1597-1603. Hartford, Wadsworth Atheneum. Cat. No. 150.
Fig. 178. St. John the Baptist, 1597-1603. San Francisco, M. H. de Young Memorial Museum. Cat. No. 151.

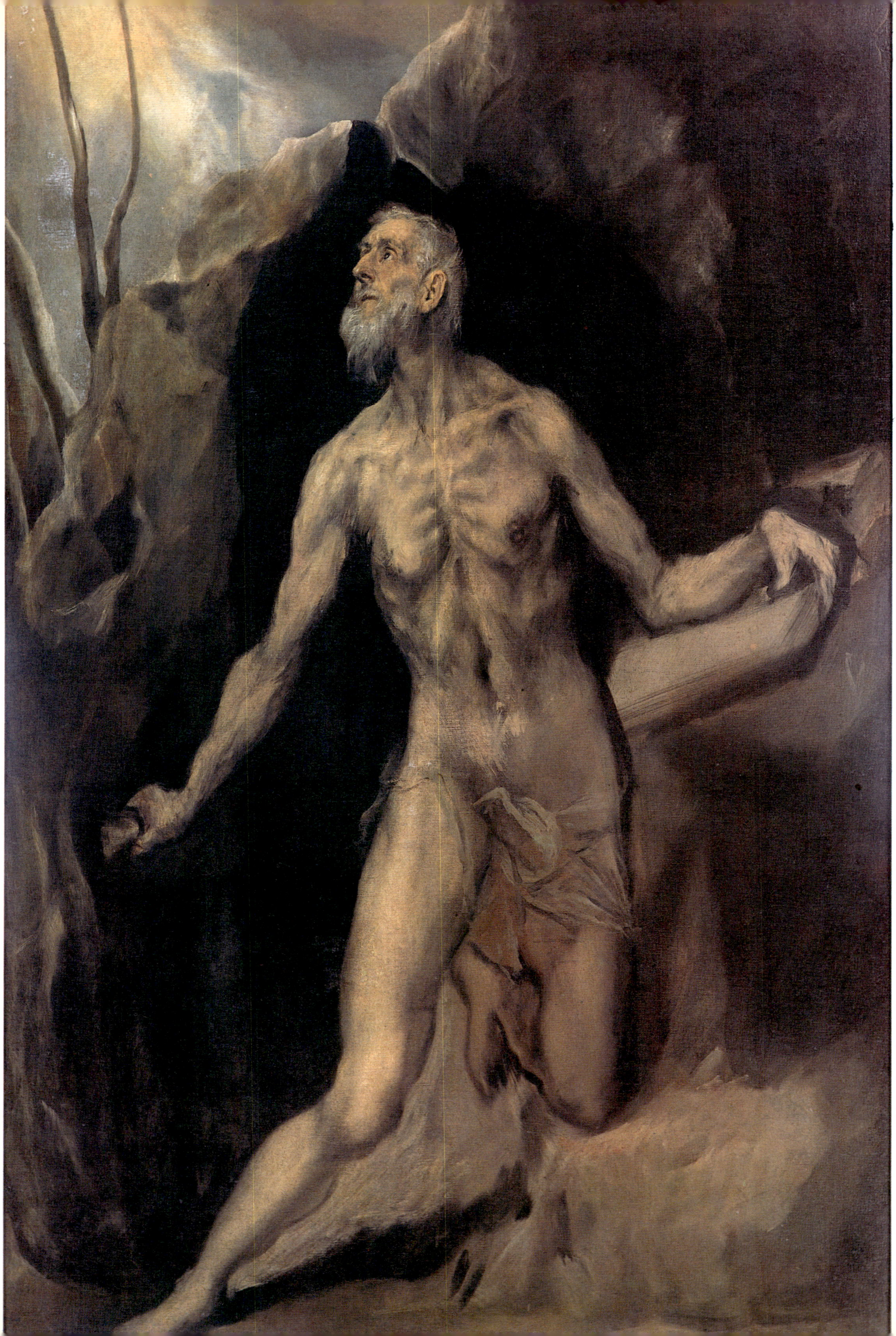

on the floor in the foreground and the little vase of wild flowers —a simple yet beautiful still life that foreshadows the strange and sometimes anguished simplicity that characterizes the impressive sequence of Spanish paintings in this *genre.* The slightly dimmed yellow of the archangel's robe harmonizes with the bluish greys and greyish whites in his great wings and in the background. The form is marvellous and the effects achieved by contrasting qualities almost give the sensation of a relief, particularly in the figure of Gabriel, with his face in profile and his left arm magnificently modelled. There are various replicas of this prototype, some of them probably painted in the following period.

The *Holy Family with St. Anne and the infant Baptist* is a composition created during the period we are now studying, to judge by the pictorial concept of a small-scale version, the quality of which seems to point to its being the original model, in the National Gallery, Washington *(Fig. 175 - Cat. 147).* As is always the case, the original work of a typological series possesses all the vigour of the fresh idea, the spontaneity of the impulse and enthusiasm that go with the first creation. Though repetition may not necessarily cause weariness, replicas are paintings without problems —being born with their problems solved, so to speak— and so the articulation of their elements cannot possess the force and freshness of the prototypes, as we have said before. In this version in Washington every element has great life and richness, though the distortion of the Virgin's face, thanks to the foreshortening occasioned by its inclined attitude, may be more intense than in other known versions of the same model. The Santa Cruz Museum in Toledo has what we believe to be a contemporary replica on a larger scale, in which the image of St. Joseph was —inexplicably— removed by the painter himself, since the sketch of his head shows through the modelling of the clouds that cover it *(Fig. 176 - Cat. 148).* In the Wadsworth Atheneum in Hartford (Connecticut) there is another signed version which is still further simplified: the Virgin and St. Anne are represented only half-length, without St. Joseph and without the infant Baptist *(Fig. 177 - Cat. 150).* In the Prado there is yet another replica of the complete work, in which St. Joseph is shown with a black beard *(Cat. 149).* The whole interplay of draperies is extraordinary in all these versions, though this hardly needs to be mentioned, since it is one of the most characteristic virtues of El Greco's painting, a painting usually devoid of setting and relying completely on flesh tints, draperies, sky and cloud effects and the eloquence of the gestures.

The standing figure of *St. John the Baptist* in the De Young Memorial Museum of San Francisco *(Fig. 178 - Cat. 151)* originally hung in the convent of the Discalced Carmelites in Malagón (Ciudad Real). It undoubtedly belongs to the period now under consideration and is the earliest example of another series of images repeated by El Greco and his assistants. It is like the paradigm of the human concept El Greco used at the height of his career. This St. John is a perfect image of the ascetic applying his virility and the whole temper of his soul to his struggle against the passions. The landscape, which includes the well-known view of the Escorial, acquires resplendent qualities in the distance, thanks to the lighting effect of the sky, which consists —as on so many other occasions— of a struggle between half-torn clouds and empty spaces through which we can see the blue of the sky. We should observe the cleverly composed landscape, with its gentle gradation of shades towards the hill in the background, its alternating lights and shadows, clumps of trees and areas in penumbra, the whole very realistic yet transfigured at the same time by a unique vision. The openly heroicized proportion places the head at an anomalous height, but it is so well balanced by the ascending rhythms of all the parts of the body and by the interplay of fluctuating forms that it only accentuates the mystical sense of the character. In the Museum of Valencia there is another, less brilliant, signed version of the same design, which may have been done a short time later *(Cat. 152).*

An almost totally naked *St. Jerome* in the National Gallery in Washington *(Fig. 179 - Cat. 153)* also belongs to the group of works we are now studying. The anatomy of the man, who is no longer young, is a matter of nerves rather than muscles and the typology is wonderfully served by the representation, thanks to perfect drawing and vigorous —but not heavy— modelling, with loosely-worked impasto which permits skilful interpenetrations of light and shade. The saint is shown as a penitent, in a cave that is open at the top and to the left, with some vegetation and intense lights contrasting with the dark background. The pose has a certain dynamic quality and the saint is shown turning to the left, his eyes gazing heavenwards through the opening of his solitary and voluntary

179. St. Jerome in penitence, 1597-1603.
…ington, National Gallery. Cat. No. 153.

prison. This is possibly an unfinished work, but, equally, the painter may have intentionally left it in its present state.

During this period we find a considerable number of canvases intended for potential patrons and for churches and religious communities. In them *modelli* from previous periods are repeated, though naturally modified and often improved as the painter developed. An example of this worth quoting is that of the repetition of the *St. Francis and the lay brother,* a design of which there are over twenty known replicas. The composition is a copy of the work in Monforte de Lemos that we have already studied *(Fig. 93),* a picture done during the first years in Toledo. Although El Greco was an extremely rapid executant we cannot doubt that his assistants did a lot of the work on these. Their classification as replicas (i.e., duplicates totally executed by El Greco himself), workshop versions with more or less intervention by the master and copies, with the painting of which he had absolutely nothing to do, is an arduous problem for the analysing historian. In some cases we can only reach a satisfactory conclusion when we study the works after they have been cleaned of all the dirt and old restorations which so often turn them into veritable enigmas. As this is almost never possible, the enigmas persist. We have therefore selected the three versions which seem to be of the highest quality: the one in the Max Bollag Collection in Zurich *(Cat. 155),* the one in the Ottawa Museum, which is from the parish church of Nambroca, in the province of Toledo *(Fig. 180 - Cat. 154),* and the one in the Barnes Foundation in America, which was formerly in the Colegio de Doncellas Nobles in Toledo *(Cat. 156),* all three very similar in image and technique.

We must insist on the fact, already mentioned, that El Greco succeeded in inculcating in his assistants a spirit of technical discipline which entailed some degree of mimicry, and this mimicry sometimes achieves such high quality that it gives rise to serious problems of attribution in many cases, even for the professional with suitable means of comparison at his disposal. In the three canvases in question the similarity is so great that it is obvious that the painter had simply decided to repeat exactly the same design without any variations. The spatial conception, the situation of the main figure, the expression on the face, the typology and the very restricted range of colours are all nearly identical, as is the drawing.

The painting in the Max Bollag Collection has a less open background space and this may contribute to its greater darkness, though the poor state of preservation of the work is also partially responsible for this. The canvas in Ottawa, on the contrary, which is the best preserved of the three, is the one with the largest opening in the background, which gives it greater lightness in the colour range. The figure of the saint is rather thinner than in the other versions, which it resembles, however, even in the creasing of the habits. In all three versions El Greco has depicted thick, ill-fashioned habits of coarse cloth, to which he sometimes gives qualities that are almost like fur. He represents St. Francis as he very possibly was in reality: a meditative, lyrical temperament on which his asceticism and life as a monk left deep marks, forming his character, expression, aspect and gestures. Simply from having so often painted this theme in different versions, El Greco became what we might call a specialist in images of St. Francis and was undoubtedly the most eminent of his day, as was said.

To judge merely by the execution, we must also assign to the beginning of the seventeenth century another group of canvases representing the saint of Assisi, canvases which repeat one of the versions of the previous period, though with appreciable variations. As unquestionably authentic works we may mention the one in the Araoz Collection *(Fig. 181 - Cat. 158),* which is from the convent of the Capuchin nuns in Toledo, and the one in the Blanco Soler Collection *(Cat. 159),* both in Madrid. Here the saint is shown in an eloquent attitude, his right hand laid on his breast and his left hand stretched out across the foreground, behind which one can see the skull with the crucifix resting on it. The open area on the left of the rocky background, through which we may see the overcast sky, is larger than in the previous compositions, and this helps to enliven the colour range. The tactile quality is looser and harsher than in the two groups mentioned above and that fur-like quality we have spoken of before is more accentuated here. The features of the face are more strongly marked, undoubtedly with the idea of giving greater intensity of communication. The tonal interplay is richer in nuances, but the quality of the works in this sub-group is no higher than that of the version we mentioned above as a new approach to the theme.

The Franciscan typology of El Greco is completed in this period by another image of the saint in

Fig. 180. St. Francis and the lay brother, 1597-
Ottawa, National Gallery of Canada. Cat. No. 15

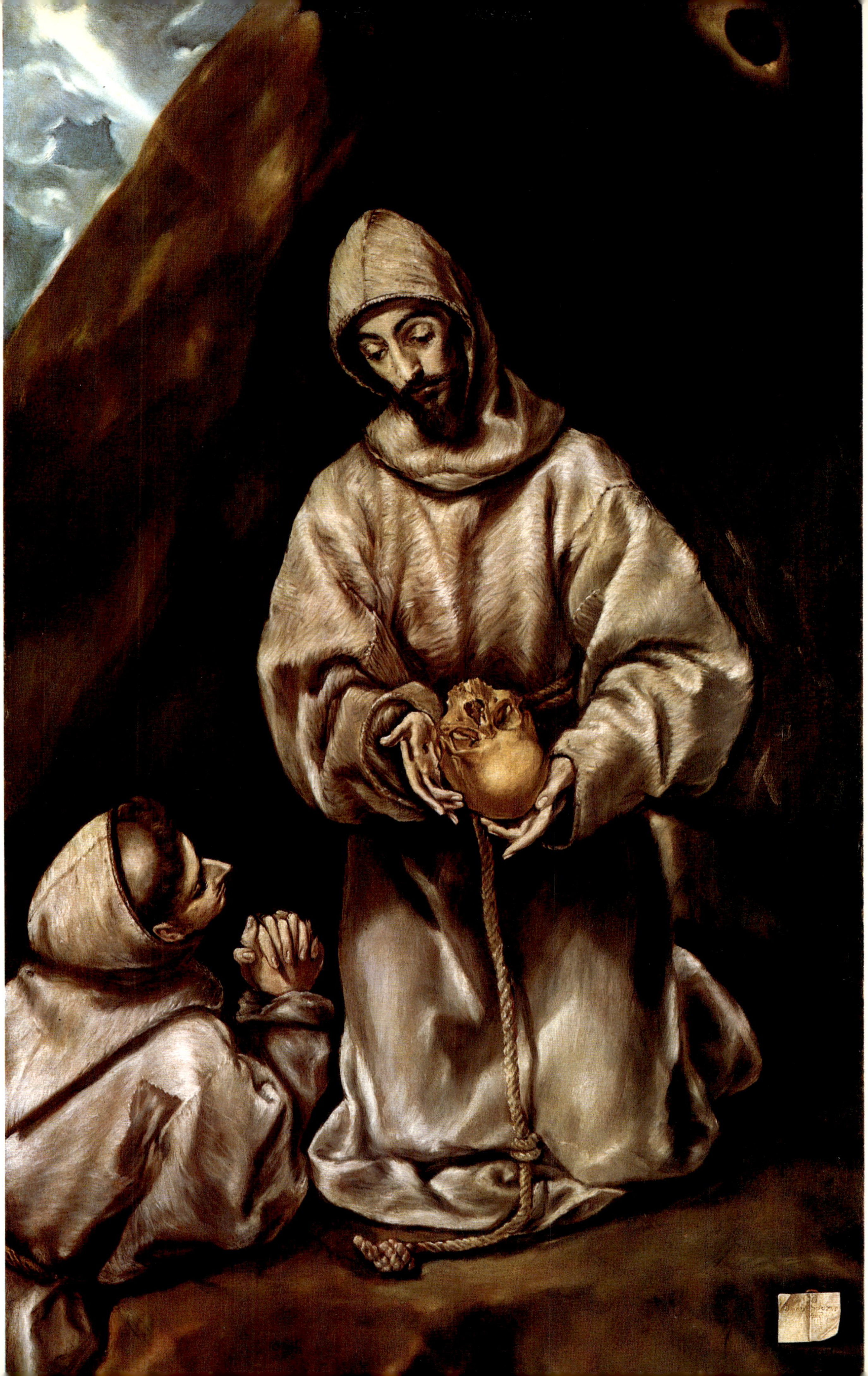

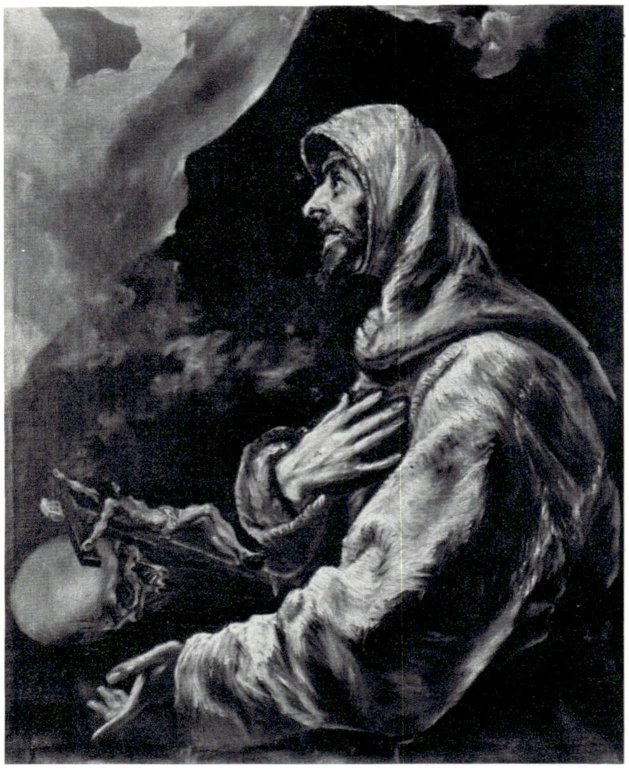

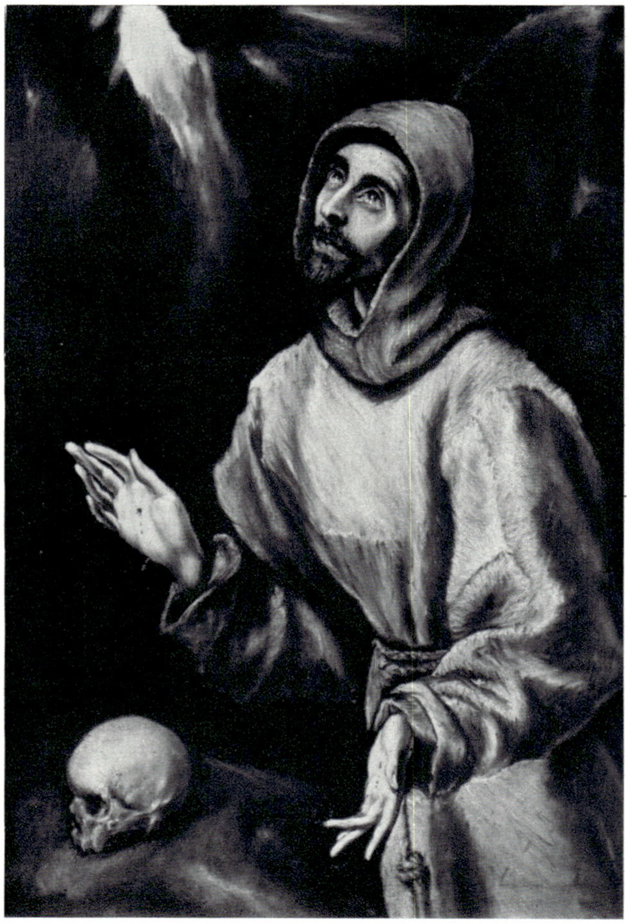

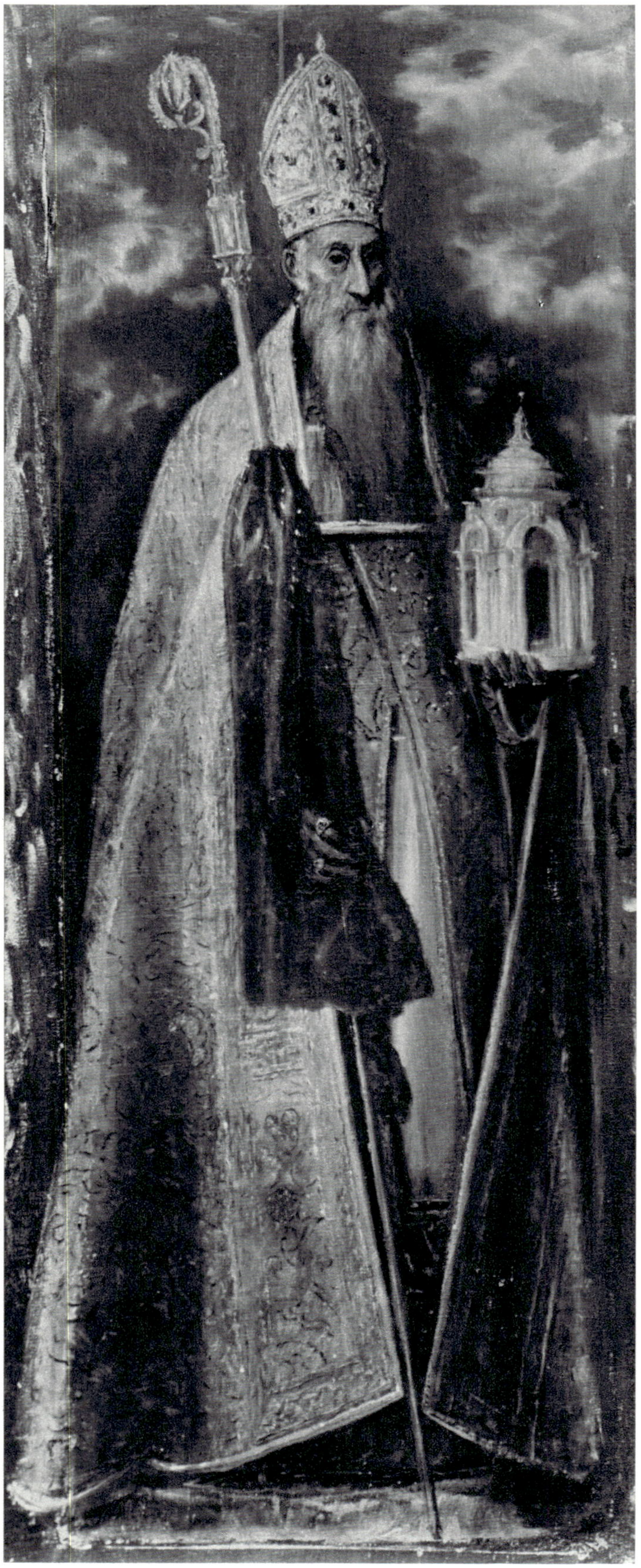

Fig. 181. St. Francis in ecstasy, 1597-1603. Madrid, Araoz Collection. Cat. No. 158.
Fig. 182. St. Francis in ecstasy, 1597-1603. Pau, Musée des Beaux-Arts. Cat. No. 160.
Fig. 183. St. Augustine, 1597-1603. Toledo, Santa Cruz Museum. Cat. No. 165.

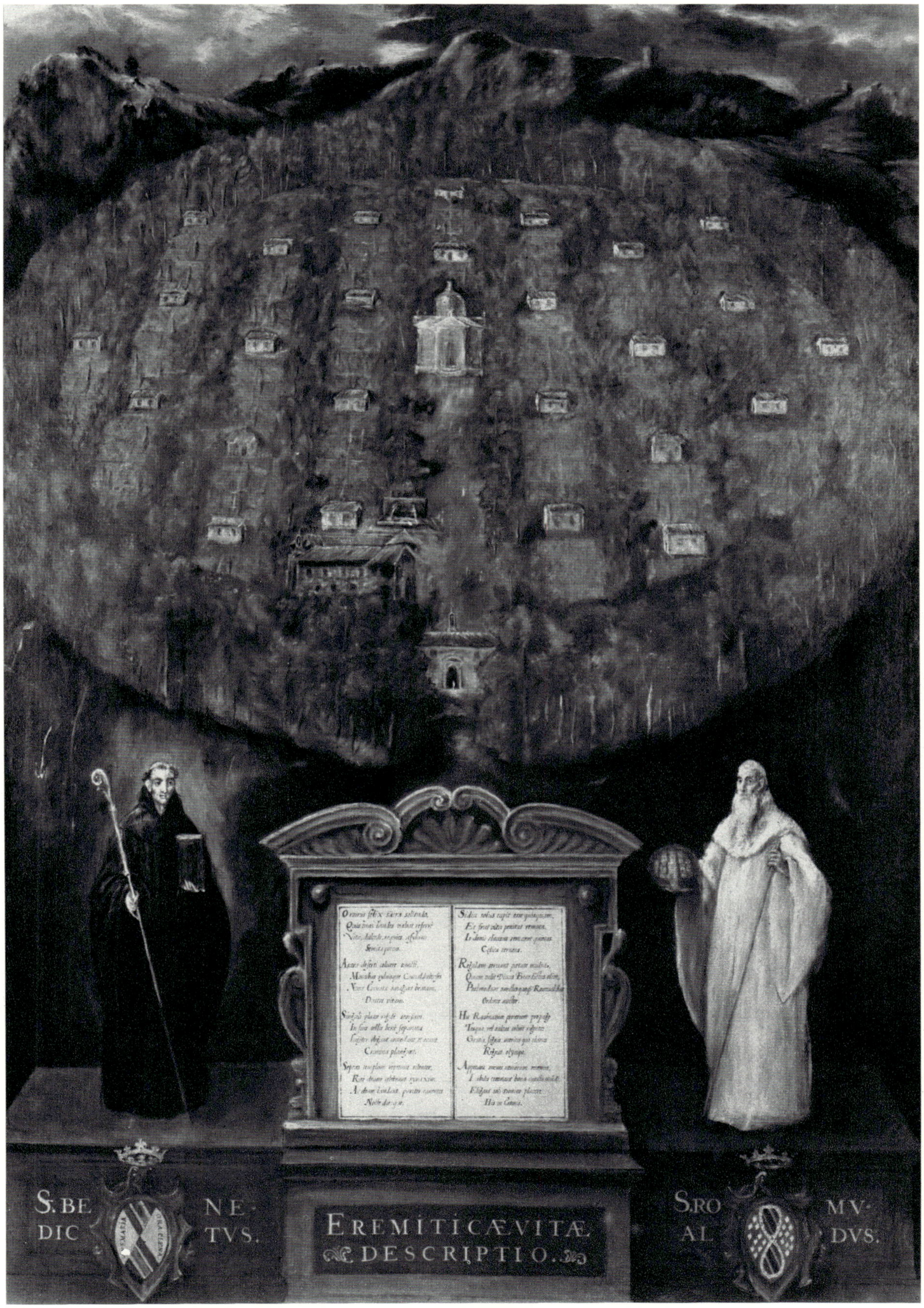

Fig. 184. Allegory of the Camaldolite Order, 1597-1603. Madrid, Instituto de Valencia de Don Juan. Cat. No. 166.

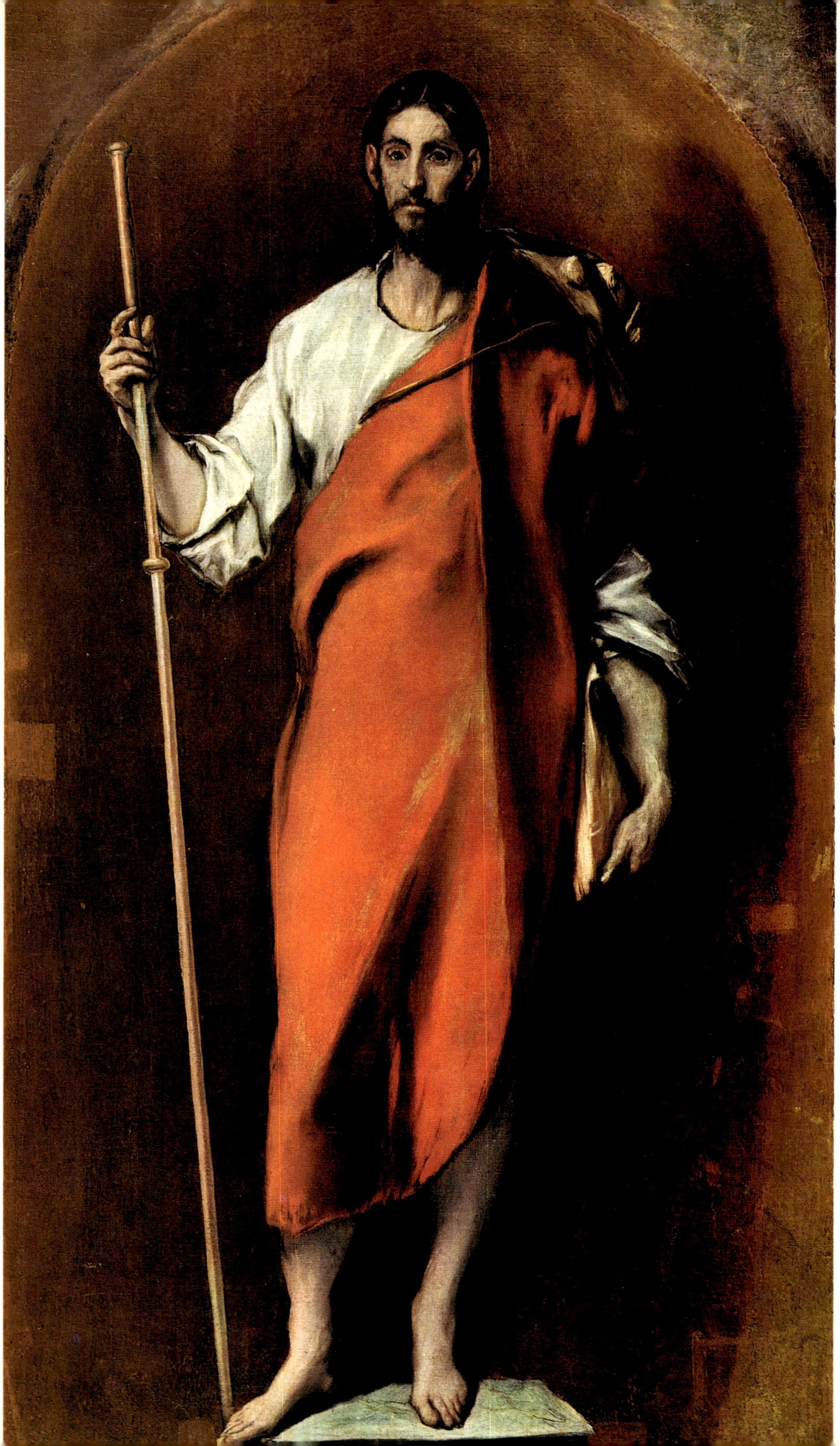

Fig. 185. St. James the Great as a pilgrim, 1597-1603. Toledo, Santa Cruz Museum. Cat. No. 168.

ecstasy, a version created for adaptation to smaller canvases *(Fig. 182 - Cat. 160)*. Here we have a visionary St. Francis, whose gaze is not directed at the cross (which does not appear) or at the skull (which is beside him), but upwards, to heaven. El Greco probably reduced the format in order to create a type intended for less wealthy patrons. All these series of images must have been very successful and the painter could probably count on regular sales; otherwise we can hardly explain such a constant insistence on this theme. There are also various authentic replicas of this last work, as well as a multitude of workshop copies which can be differentiated principally by their execution. The most beautiful of the replicas by the master himself is in the Museum of Pau. The popularity and persistence of this design among seventeenth-century painters is evidenced by the literal copy signed by Blas Muñoz in 1683, which is in the Museum of Toledo. Here we see the saint as a voluntary victim of his own adoration of Christ crucified, the only object of his desires, so that he lives apart from his fellow-men but in the eternal company of the Lord. We can readily understand the success of this theme in the Spain of that time, which witnessed the fullest flowering of mysticism. It was not so long after the deaths of St. Teresa (1582) and of St. John of the Cross (1591), and the spirit of their writings and those of the other mystics was probably still very much in the air.

El Greco never painted a replica of any of his original works without endowing it with variant elements —more or less perceptible, more or less "secret"— which make it impossible to attribute it to any of his assistants. This is evident once more in the two little *Allegories of the Camaldolite Order*, which are very far from being identical, despite their similarity *(Fig. 184 - Cat. 166)*. In presenting to the public the version that hangs in the Instituto de Valencia de Don Juan, Madrid, Sánchez Cantón gave it a date some time in or about 1597, because it was in that year that Fray Juan de Castañiza sought Philip II's permission to establish this monastic order in Spain. It is a surprising composition, for it has the structure of an engraving, the landscape being placed in the upper part, with a perspective that is only admitted in emblematic representations. In the lower part of the canvas we see Saint Benedict and St. Romuald, with their attributes, wearing black and white habits respectively and standing on either side of a kind of architectural structure inscribed with texts and set upon a plinth which also bears inscriptions. This painting is probably rather later than the date given by Sánchez Cantón, for though the landscape in its upper half links up with the *View of Toledo* already described, the treatment of the figures of the two saints is more advanced, more typical of El Greco's work in the seventeenth century.

It is very interesting to observe that, though El Greco here painted, as has been said, a landscape of a field with individual cells arranged at regular distances round a church (which lends a certain "primitive" feeling to this landscape), in his technique he displayed a fine naturalism in textures and lights and this, as we have mentioned, brings the work closer to the celebrated view of Toledo. In the top part of the picture, above all, beyond the circle of the field that belongs to the community, we see mountains with reflections of lights and very intense and theatrical shadows that enliven the whole of this part of the work. They do not form a contrast to the rest —which had to be conceived in a conventional way, given the subject matter— because of the small area they occupy in the total painted surface. The contrast of this community of hermits is heightened by the architectural structure below it, the great texts of which, under the rather Baroque pediment, are what mainly produce the noticeable effect of an engraving or even of a frontispiece. But the images of the two saints at the sides are impressively pictorial. The two figures are markedly elongated and are treated in a technique that is at once complex and simple, intense and extremely subtle, using the rubbing process very successfully to give the line —of the hands and fingers, for instance— expressive values of great intensity, though very much confined to such details.

The replica preserved in the Colegio del Corpus Christi in Valencia *(Cat. 167)*, which may possibly have belonged to the Blessed Juan de Ribera, shows, as has already been remarked, certain variations. The most notable of these has to do with the lower part of the work. The pediment with its complicated curves is here placed inside a larger, triangular pediment, while the curves on either side of this structure in the version in the Instituto de Valencia de Don Juan are restrained in the replica by severe verticals. The form of the hermit community is the same as in the other version, but the execution is subtly different, as is the case in the upper part of the picture, with the mountains under the cloudy sky. The figures of the saints are more dramatic and their features more precisely stated in the Corpus Christi version, being stronger and, perhaps, a little stiffer. This is particularly the case with the figure of St. Benedict.

We now come to the altarpiece from the church of San Nicolás in Toledo, with a sculptural figure of St. Barbara in the central niche and three painted panels representing St. Augustine, St. Francis of Assisi and St. James the Great, all shown full-length. The *St. Augustine* who is shown in his bishop's robes, carrying his crozier in his right hand and the model of a shrine in his left *(Fig. 183 - Cat. 165)*, shows a strong resemblance, in height and in the features of the face, to the St. Jerome described above. He also wears a long, white beard; but the expression lacks the questioning intensity of the other figure; if El Greco used the same model —as is probable— he succeeded in modifying and re-interpreting him, which is a proof of his mastery in this question of "superimposing" on an image (in itself impersonal, or even ordinary) a character that is undeniably projected by the spirit of the artist. The *St. Francis*, arranged in symmetry with St. Augustine, is a reproduction with very slight variations of the image of the *Poverello* in the Prado picture, in which the saint is accompanied by St. Andrew *(Fig. 131)*. The *St. James the Great*, which is the crowning composition and the most important of these three images *(Fig. 185 - Cat. 168)*, shows the saint wearing a white robe and an ample red mantle modelled with ochre yellow. The outlines are powerfully silhouetted in black. The effect of the red and black —a not infrequent harmony in El Greco's work— on the gold background is really extraordinary, as is that of the painting of the noble face of the saint, a young man with a short black beard, whose visage, though not his expression, is not without a certain Christ-like air.

The theme of the *Agony in the Garden* was treated by El Greco in two compositions, one oblong and the other vertical. Three versions of the first are still extant, but only one of these, the one in the Museum of Toledo (Ohio), is entirely by the master's hand *(Fig. 186 - Cat. 169)*. It undoubtedly belongs to the end of the period we are now studying. The vertical composition, of which there is a whole series of replicas, was painted in the following period and we shall therefore deal with it in a later chapter, in accordance with the chronological order we are following. In the first canvas El Greco makes use of all his powers of invention. In the first place, he uses the spatial variety of which he already showed signs in the *Adoration of the Name of Jesus (Fig. 38)*, though without so much development of secondary themes. In the second place he employs geometrical forms that are not exactly regular in order to create areas in which he places, as if in compartments of their own, the essential elements of the composition. He also uses the similarity of outlines to accentuate the value of a form, the main example of this being in the figure of the kneeling Christ looking to the left. The rock behind the figure looks like its shadow, suddenly become huge, raised up and turned to stone. The sleeping disciples, on the other hand, are placed in a kind of hollow on the left of the composition, while the angel above them, who is given a character both lyrical and monumental, brings Christ the chalice that symbolizes the Passion. The folds of Christ's robe, which rest upon the mantle spread on the ground, form a sort of wonderful pedestal for the magnificent face of the Redeemer, which follows the typology of the *Espolio*. On the right, behind the great rock already mentioned, we see a landscape winding away into the background, with low hills, illuminated as in the *St. John the Baptist* previously studied, under an ominous sky. The little figures in this landscape are those of the soldiers, led by Judas, who are coming to arrest Christ.

Despite the lively and extraordinarily original interplay of forms that we have described, the main interest of this painting, as in so many others by El Greco, is the colour. It is used to give original beauty and harmony to every element in particular and to all of them in general, but also to increase the dynamic power of these elements by tending to bring them closer together. This capturing of movement —which is a way of representing time, the immediate time of the event depicted— is one of the great resources of the art of all ages, but especially of Baroque. The gesture indicates the action. And though it is not necessary for the viewer to complete it mentally, it acts on his mind and contributes enormously to the effect of life produced by this work. We should also notice the delicacy of the foliage and flowers dappling the foreground, the rock behind and the bush on Christ's left. The function of all these elements, apart from their beauty, is to heighten the earthly character of the scene, which might well be overwhelmed by the visionary power of the composition as a whole. We may —indeed, we should— observe at this point that, even apart from his great works like the *Burial of the Conde de Orgaz* and their importance in his *oeuvre*, El Greco never ceased to advance.

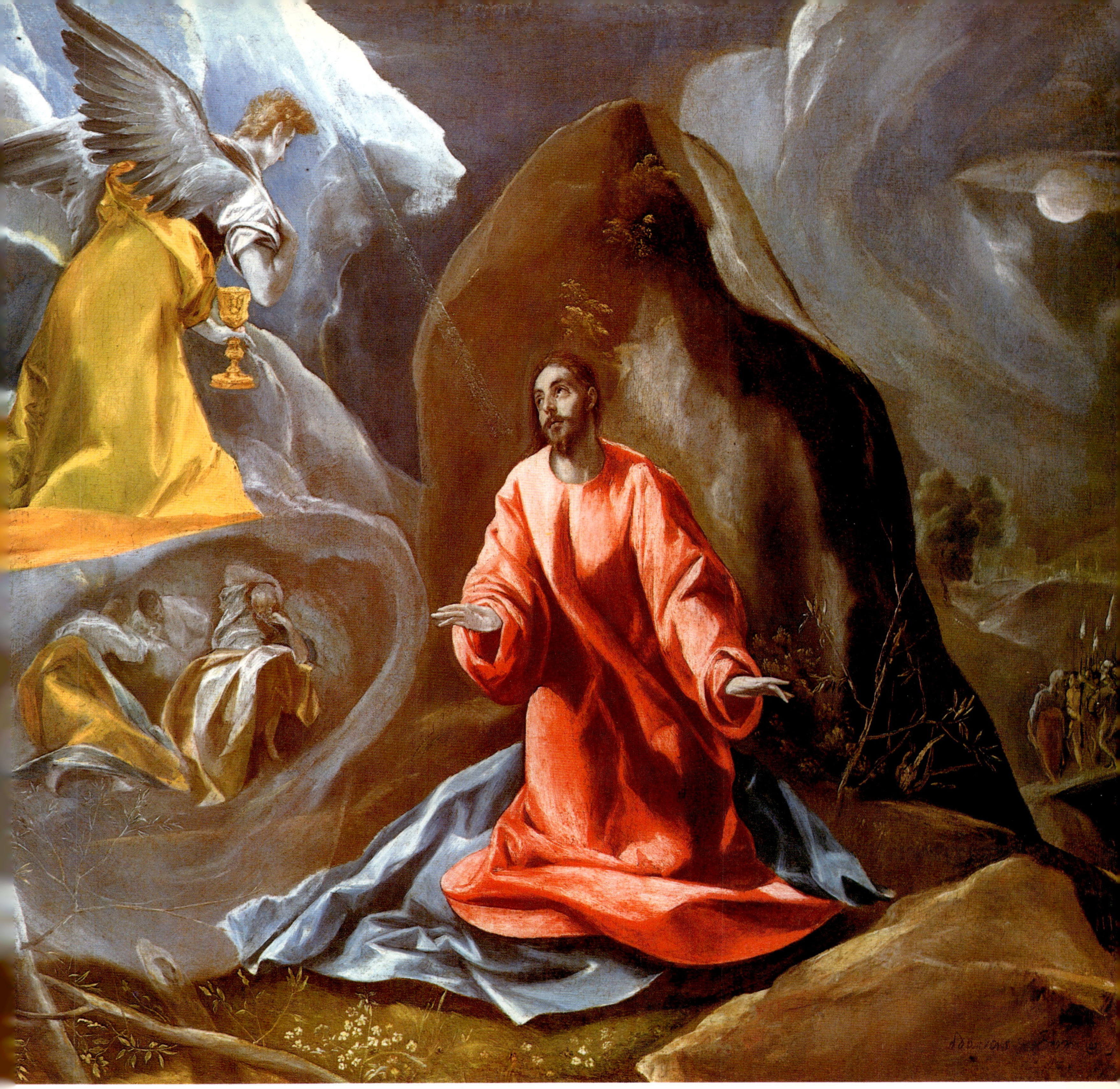

Fig. 186. The Agony in the garden, 1597-1603. Toledo (Ohio), Museum. Cat. No. 169.

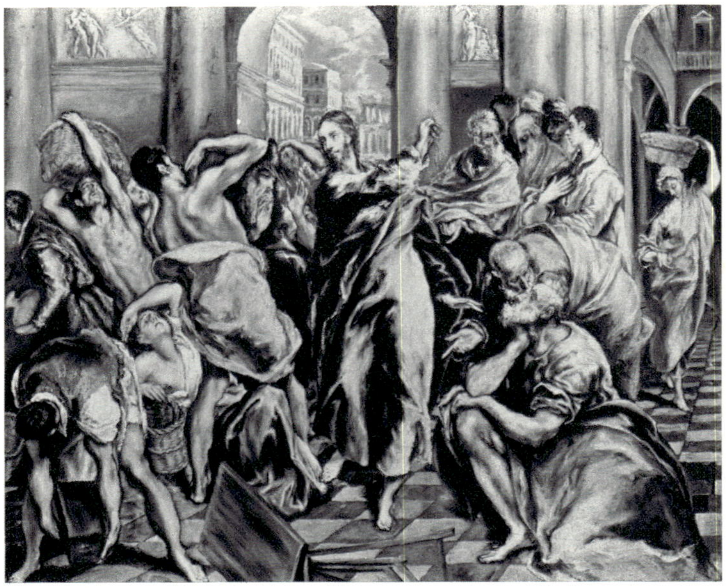

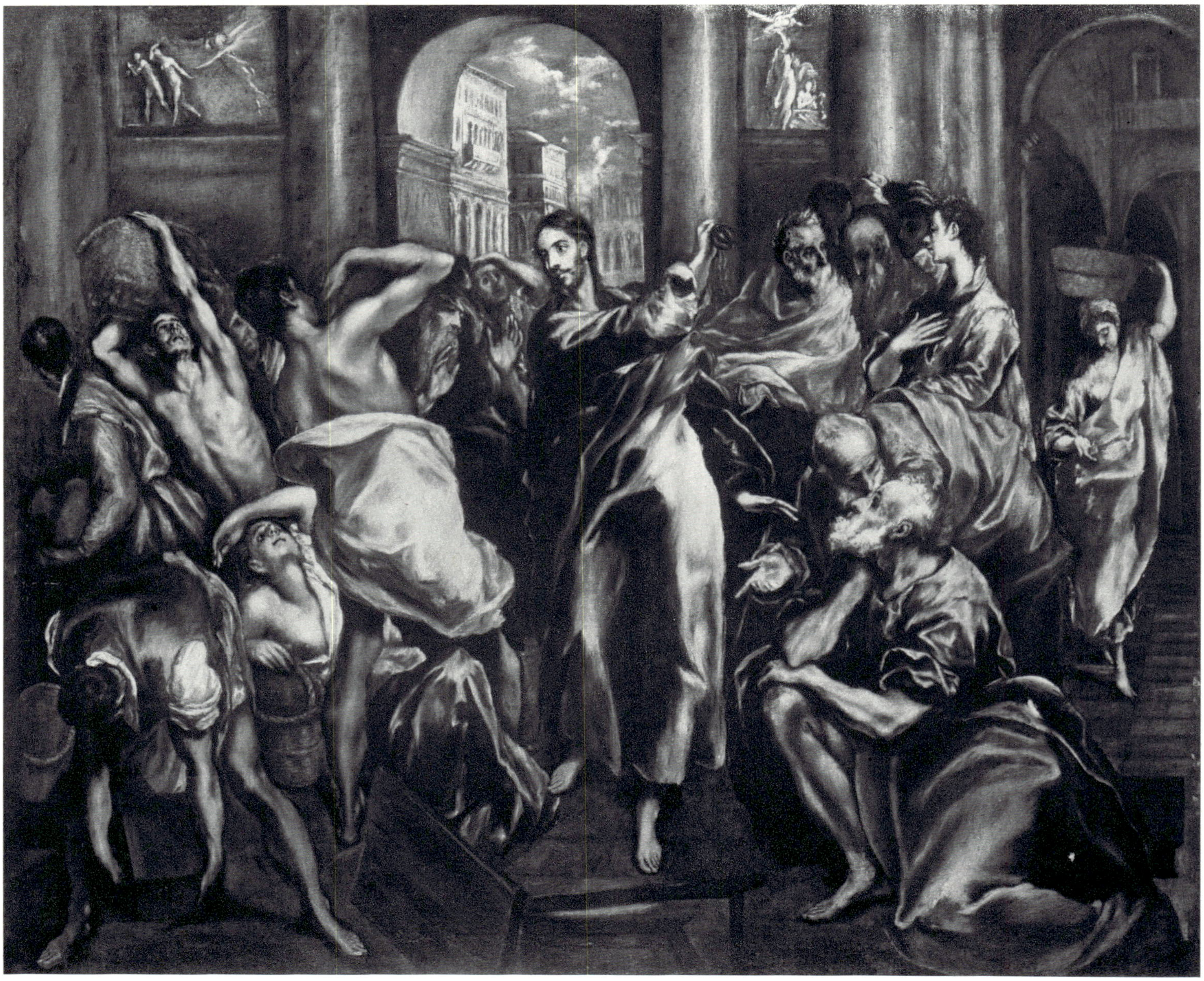

Fig. 187. Christ cleansing the Temple, 1597-1603. New York, Frick Collection. Cat. No. 170.
Fig. 188. Christ cleansing the Temple, 1597-1603. San Sebastián, Várez Collection. Cat. No. 171.

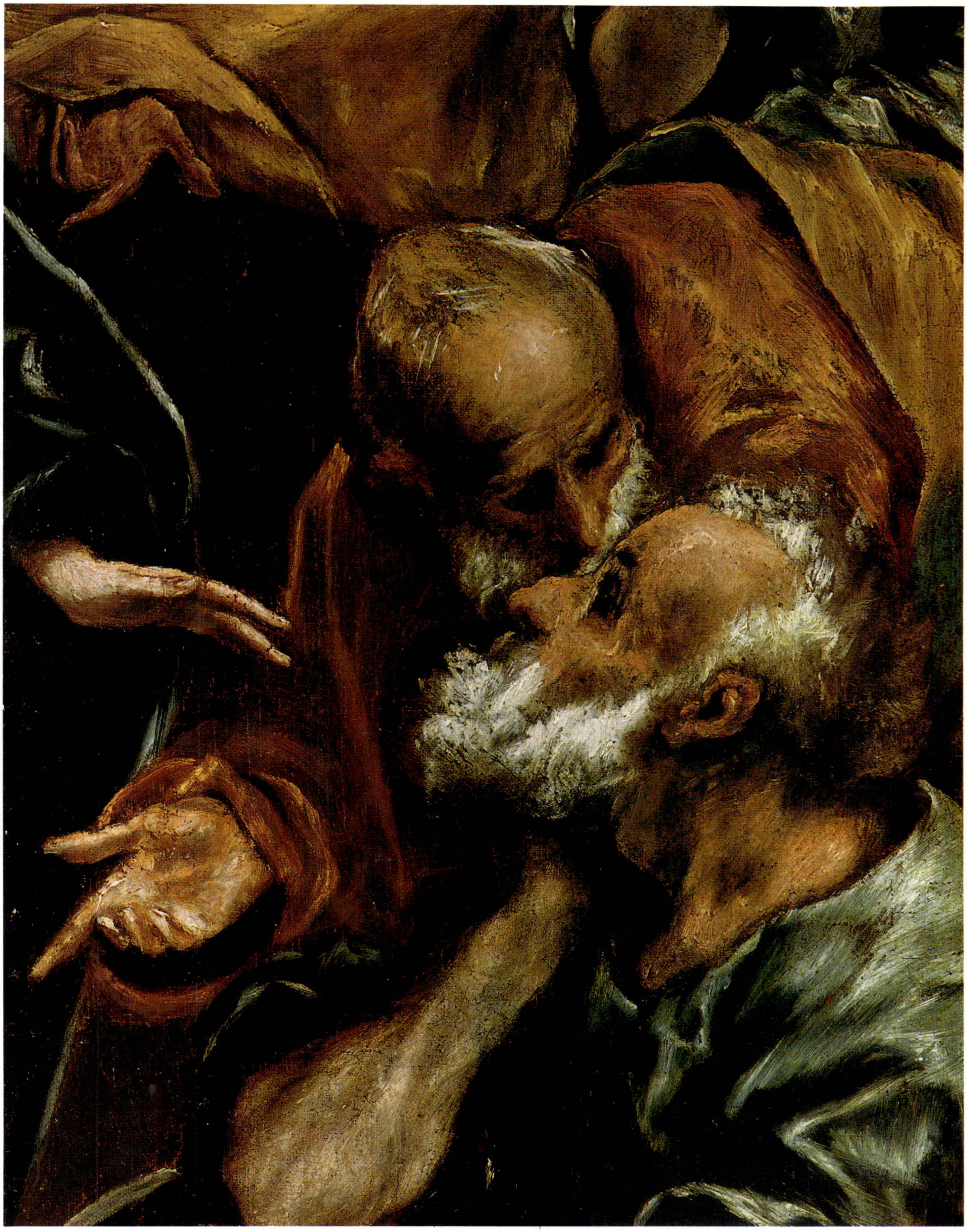
Fig. 189. Detail of figure 188.

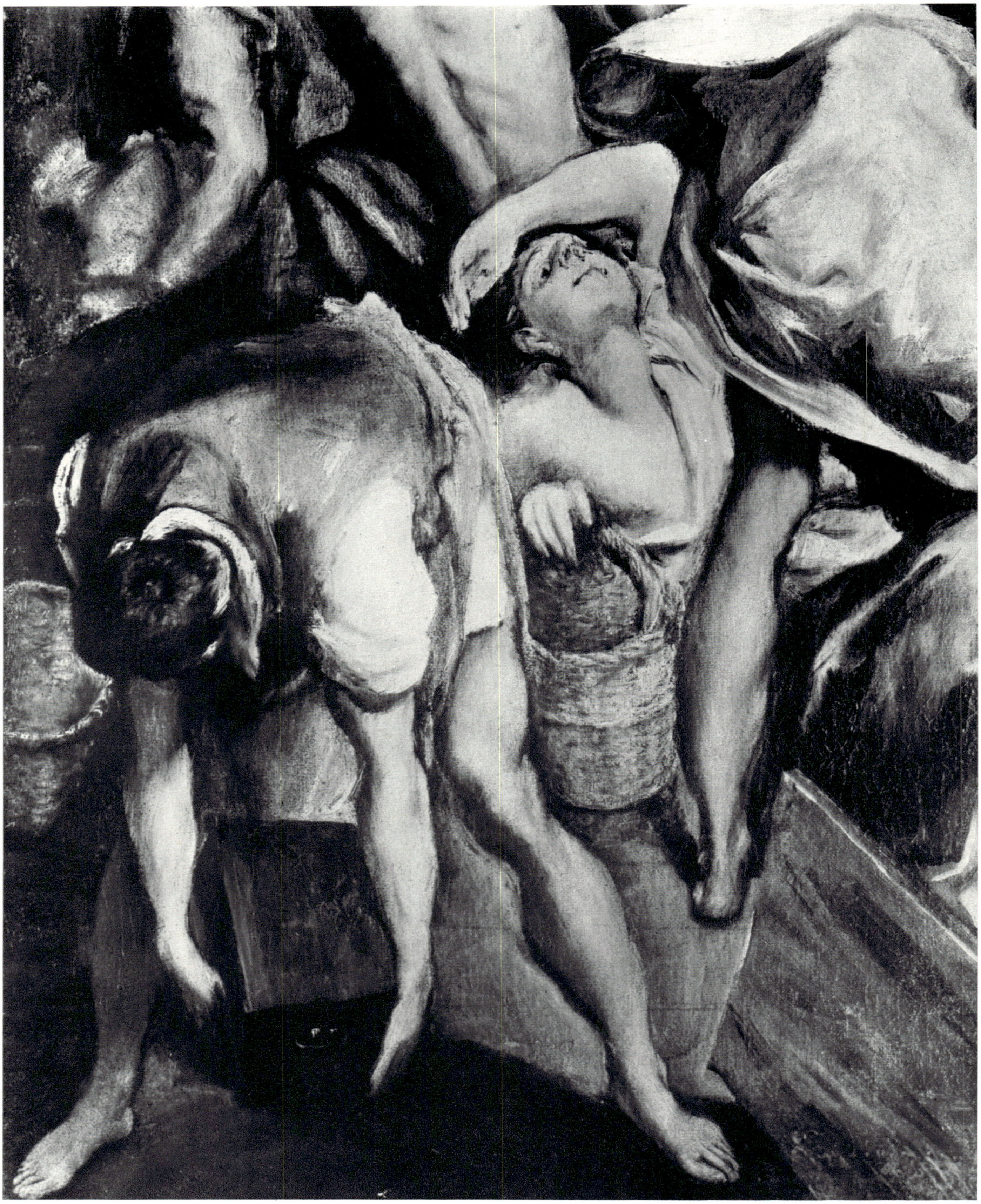

Fig. 190. Christ cleansing the Temple (detail), 1597-1603. London, National Gallery. Cat. No. 172.

Fig. 191. Cardinal Fernando N
de Guevara, c. 1600. New Y
Metropolitan Museum. Cat. No.

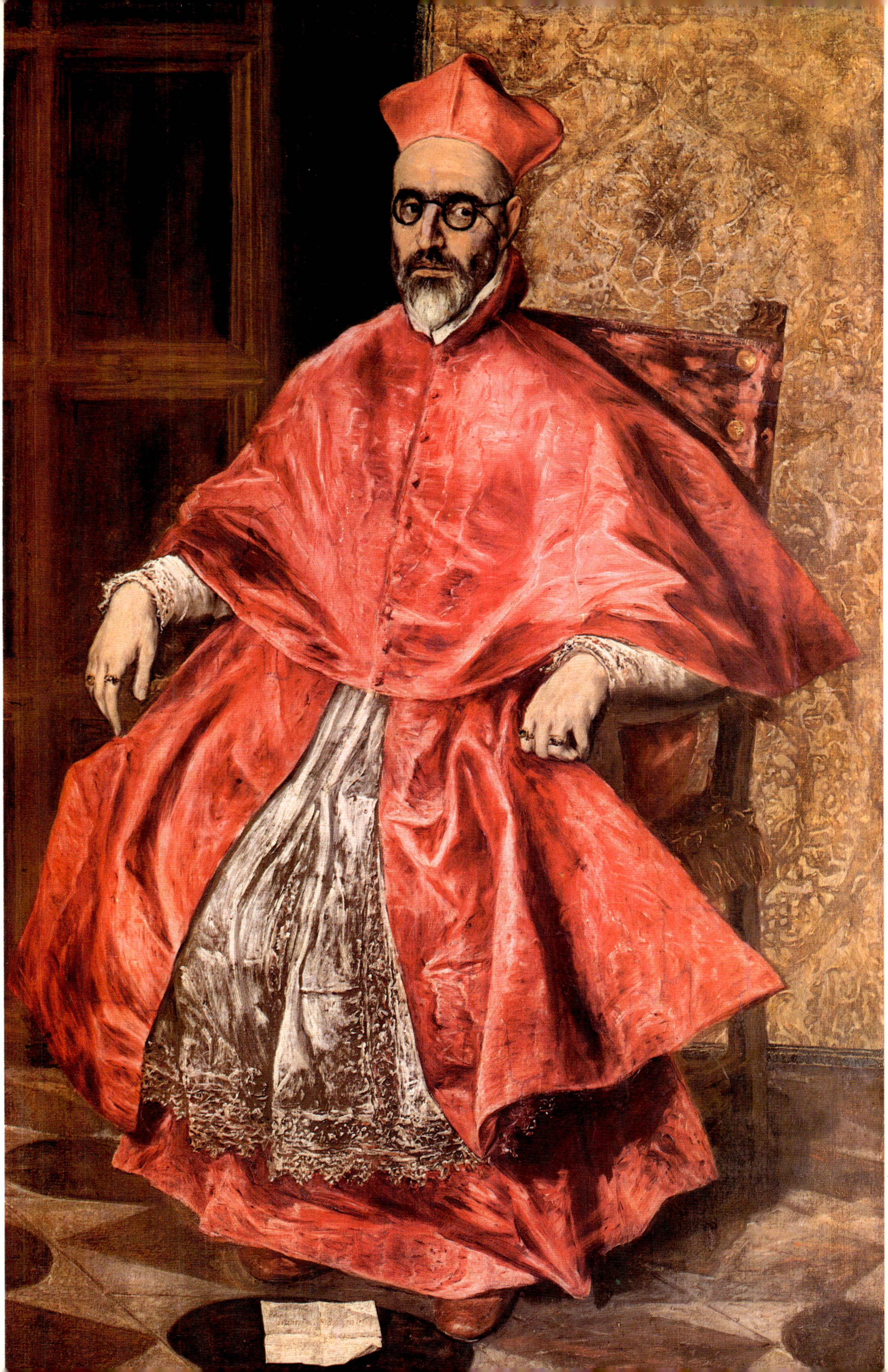

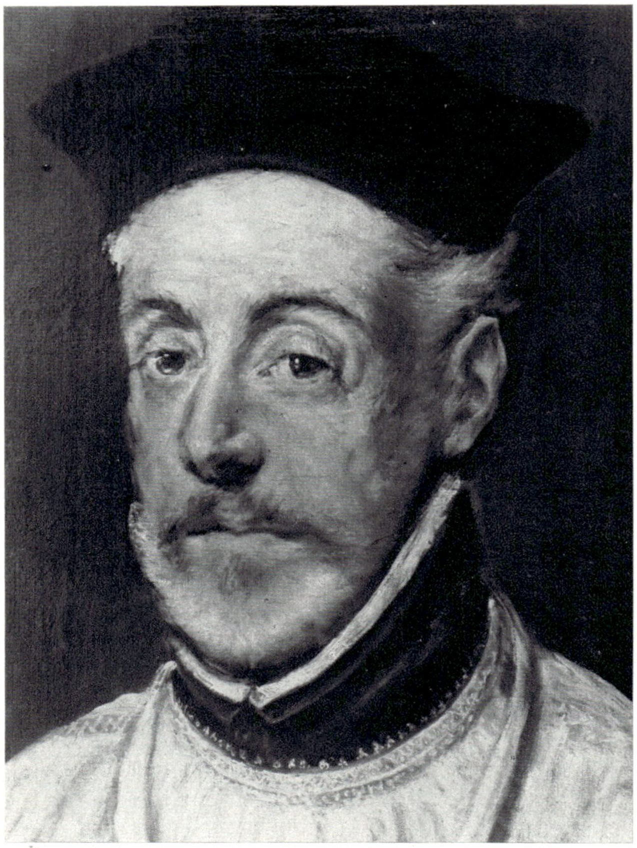
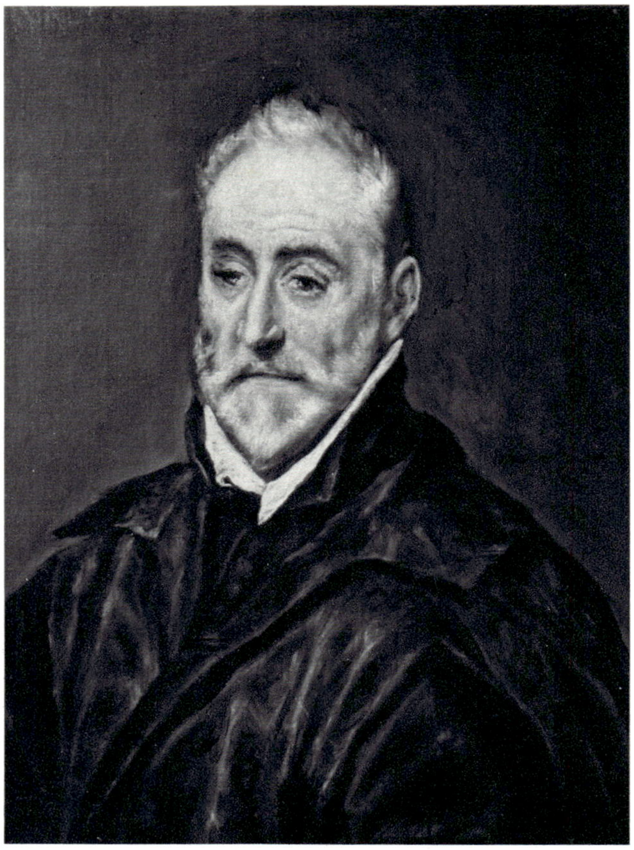
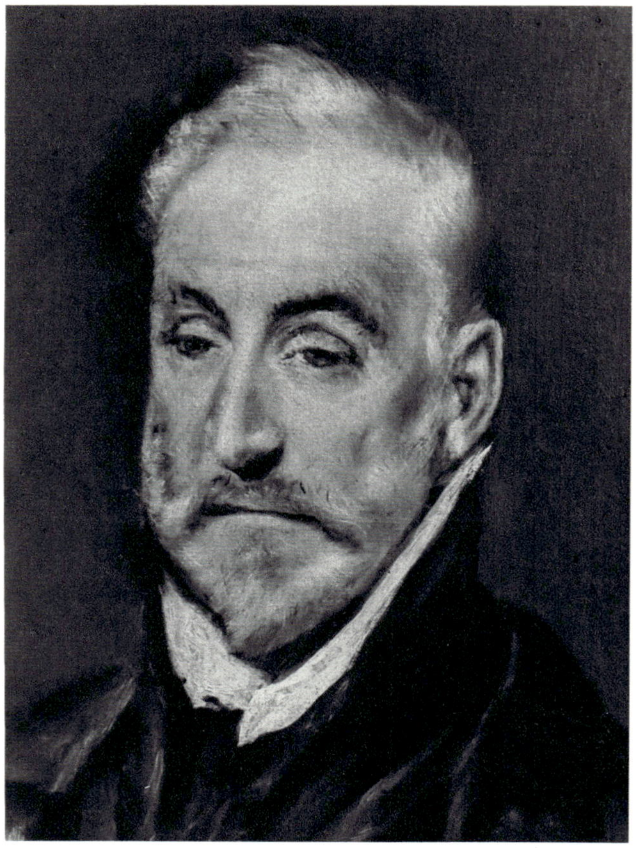
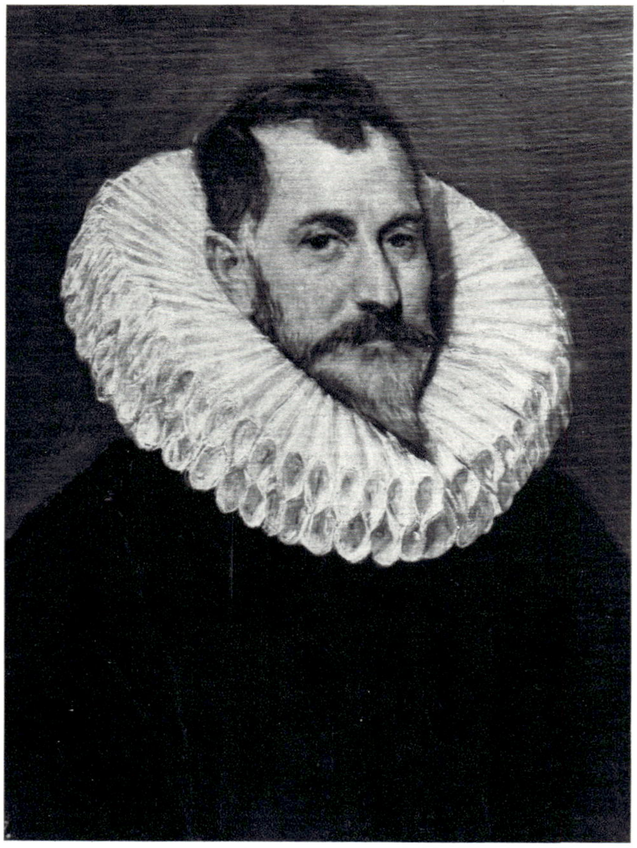

Fig. 192. Diego de Covarrubias, 1597-1603. Toledo, Greco Museum. Cat. No. 174.
Fig. 193. Antonio de Covarrubias, 1597-1603. Toledo, House of El Greco. Cat. No. 175.
Fig. 194. Antonio de Covarrubias, 1597-1603. Paris, Louvre. Cat. No. 176.
Fig. 195. Portrait of an unknown gentleman, 1597-1603. Madrid, Prado. Cat. No. 177.

Among the works we believe to have been painted around the beginning of the seventeenth century there is a new version of what Camón Aznar called the "Tridentine" theme of the *Cleansing of the Temple*; an original version, though derived from the two that El Greco painted in Italy. Every element of the theme here re-created reflects the long way El Greco had come in the development of his own personality. It seems more than probable that the first form of this third version is the little canvas in the Frick Collection *(Fig. 187 - Cat. 170).* If we compare it with the Roman version *(Fig. 14),* its predecessor by some thirty years, we shall see more considerable changes than those between the Roman version and the one executed in Venice. Consistent in his growing indifference to the details of the setting, El Greco here, though not quite eliminating the architectural features of the two earlier versions, does reduce them greatly. The figure of Christ with the scourge becomes the central axis of the composition. The group of merchants on the left has been simplified; the two men stripped to the waist remain, as does the rather Niobe-like girl between them; the Titianesque seated woman has been replaced by a boy bending to lift a box. The group of apostles remains faithful, in essentials, to the scheme of the first version. A woman with a basket on her head appears on the right as a new character. On the other hand, El Greco completed the allegorical sense of this biblical passage with the addition of two sculptural reliefs: the expulsion of Adam and Eve from Paradise and the Sacrifice of Abraham, prefigurations of the Cleansing and of the Redemption respectively. The pictorial concept, always so personal in El Greco, continues its ascending rhythms in this work with the peculiar fashion of representing the volumes, the luminous colours and the vivid interpretation of flame-like rhythms. The whole achieves unity by a kind of higher force.

El Greco transferred this design to a larger format, following his usual organized system for the repetition of his subjects, and executed two almost identical replicas: one of them now in the Várez Collection in San Sebastián *(Figs. 188 & 189 - Cat. 171)* and the other in the National Gallery in London *(Fig. 190 - Cat. 172).* The *Cleansing* in the Várez Collection, despite the relinings and restorations undergone over the years, still possesses part of the edges beyond the limits of the composition. As in other canvases now hanging in the Prado and the Museum of Toledo, El Greco used these empty areas to test his tones and to clear his brush of any excess pigment that might impair the precision of his brushwork. These irregular strokes, which are now —quite rightly— left visible, are an essential factor in any profound study of El Greco's technique; a way of discovering the formulas of the great Cretan painter, which have been the subject of so much argument.

We may say, in passing, that those critics who have declared that the disappearance of local colour and the conscious or instinctive application of simultaneous contrast began with Delacroix are quite wrong; in the canvases of El Greco we may already see, as has been said, "pointillist yearnings", and local colour is modified by them. Similarly, El Greco does not paint shadows by darkening the local colour (by adding black), but paints coloured shadows —another discovery of Delacroix, according to many critics. In his general treatment of colour El Greco, as we have already said several times, dispenses with complementary colours and seeks rather a general harmony that includes rhythm, colour and form and is based, moreover, on the predominance of a central shade and form. In the present case it is the crimson modelled with white of Christ's robe, surrounded by greens, blues, yellows, orange or earth colours, together with the shading of the flesh tints, fair or dark, and the marmoreal tone of the architectural frame, the arch of which reveals very little of the sky.

Portraits

El Greco continued to paint portraits. This was probably work done quite on the side, unconnected with the general activities of his workshop, which was organized for the production of religious compositions. One of his finest portraits is that of *Cardinal Niño de Guevara* (1541-1609), who received his cardinal's hat in 1596; in 1600 he was appointed Inquisitor General and, in 1601, Archbishop of Seville *(Fig. 191 - Cat 173).* This superb portrait, which first hung, apparently, in the church of San Pablo in Toledo, was probably painted around 1600. It represents a man of tough appearance, with a look at once frank and perverse. The idea of the Church militant evidently found a warmer welcome in his heart than that of the Church suffering of the ancient martyrs. The extraordinary power of this psychological hardness is startling. The perceptible brushwork and also the accumulated tonal contrasts add to this sensation of vigour. The treatment of the cloths, both in the reflections of the silky red stuff with the black and white that model it and in the alb, the lace of which is painted with free brushstrokes and also with scorings made with the brush-handle, constitutes an unbelievable identification with the material represented; this alone would suffice to make this painting one of the high points of El Greco's career. The mass of red and the golden background form a perfect accompaniment to the vital intensity of the Inquisitor himself and are used both to compose the chromatic form and harmony and also to denote the spirit by which the work abides. Apart from the excellence of the technique, it is the fact of depicting both the personal and generic features of the model that makes this work one of the greatest portraits ever painted. As in the case of other outstanding portraits, we find here the convergence of an artist of genius, perfect technique and a fortunate moment, but we also have a model who must be considered a prototype of the country, the age and the civilization that he represents.

Among the other personages painted by El Greco we may mention the two sons, both priests, of the famous Toledo architect Alonso de Covarrubias. Diego, the elder brother, died in 1577 *(Fig. 192 - Cat. 174).* Antonio, the celebrated humanist, who died in 1602, has already been mentioned as one of the identifiable bystanders in the *Burial of the Conde de Orgaz*. This portrait of him is now in the Louvre and was probably painted shortly before his death *(Fig. 194 - Cat. 176).* There is a replica of it in the House of El Greco in Toledo *(Fig. 193 - Cat. 175).* As a pair to this replica the House of El Greco also has the only version still extant by the master himself of the portrait of Diego de Covarrubias. El Greco never met this brother and he painted his portrait from another one, by an unknown painter, dated in 1574. These two portraits are probably the ones mentioned in the inventory of the estate of Pedro Salazar de Mendoza, which was drawn up in 1629.

They are much simpler and much less ambitious works than the portrait of the cardinal studied above. They are painted bust length, but done with remarkable energy. That of Antonio, which El Greco painted from life, evidently possesses more qualities, and there are observable differences between the two versions (the one in the Louvre and the one in the House of El Greco). In the latter the look is less frank, the eyelids seem to droop rather more and the modelling is slightly more blended. At all events, El Greco liked to paint with stiff-bristled brushes which left their mark. This factor —to some extent a linear one— is not very precise, but it does contribute to the freedom of the execution. The chiaroscuro is perfect. The sitter's personality comes over strongly. The portrait of the elder brother, Diego, shows us a character apparently less strong-willed and more acquiescent.

Judging by the technique, the period now under review may also include the *Portrait of an unknown gentleman* with a ruff, painted in accordance with the formula systematized by the painter —half-length figure, black suit, broad, dense white ruff, dark background *(Fig. 195 - Cat. 177).* It is done in a kind of deliberately free technique, using a network of extremely fine brushstrokes superimposed on a solid modelling, which constructs the form and brings out all the structures with their corresponding tensions. Observe, for instance, the contrast in quality between the end of the nose and the smooth hardness of the forehead, or the different flexibility of the hair in the moustache and that on the top of the head; the sitter's regard is frank and challenging, but not aggressive. This work appears in an inventory drawn up in 1794 on the country estate of the Duke of El Arco, which by then was one of the royal possessions.

VI

1603 - 1607

JORGE MANUEL THEOTOCÓPULI — THE RETURN TO THE PALACE OF THE MARQUÉS DE VILLENA — PEDRO ORRENTE AND LUIS TRISTÁN — THE DISAPPEARANCE OF PREBOSTE — THE ALTARPIECE OF ST. BERNARDINO — THE ALTARPIECES FOR THE HOSPITAL DE LA CARIDAD, ILLESCAS — WORKS ATTRIBUTED TO THE PERIOD 1603-1607 — PORTRAITS.

We now come to a period in El Greco's life which was short but busy. In 1601 the painter had reached the age of sixty and the activities of his workshop were constantly expanding, with the engagement of new assistants and the now full-time employment of his son, Jorge Manuel, born in 1578.

From 1602 onwards El Greco was to find himself involved with some frequency in problems that arose on the arrival in Toledo of certain fellow-countrymen of his. They would come to Spain, after long, heartbreaking voyages, in order to obtain funds for ransoming other Greeks captured by the Turks. Among such pilgrims, attracted by the memory of the battle of Lepanto, there were a Moldavian prince and several bishops. In the documents concerning these Greeks in Toledo we find references to Manoussos (Emmanuel) Theotokópoulos, El Greco's brother, who has already been mentioned at the beginning of this book. It was probably about this time that he came, old and poor, to leave his bones in the Castilian city under the protection of his brother.

The dated works of this period are the small altarpiece of St. Bernardino, which was finished in 1603, and the ensemble of altarpieces, paintings and sculptures in the sanctuary of the church in the Hospital de la Caridad in the town of Illescas (Toledo).

As will be seen in the following pages, the Illescas affair was a lamentable business, giving rise to an interminable lawsuit which was waged with great bad faith and what we can only call bloody-mindedness by the Board of Works of the Hospital. El Greco's guarantor on this occasion was his great friend in Toledo, Dr. Gregorio Angulo. And from this unfortunate case arose a fresh suit brought by the *alcabalero,* or sales-tax collector, of Illescas to claim from El Greco the *alcabala* (sales-tax) on the work executed. This second suit may have been brought at the instigation of the diabolical members of the Board of Works of the Hospital, in an endeavour to sink the painter's morale under a flood of summonses and citations. But El Greco kept his head and with great fortitude defended before the judges the principle that the work of artists, since it redounds to the honour and benefit of the nation, should not be subject to any tax. He won his case and the verdict, accepted thenceforth as a principle of jurisprudence, saved artists from having to pay the *alcabala* on their work in the future. The event is recorded with enthusiasm by Palominos in his *Dialogues of Painting.*

Jorge Manuel Theotocópuli, as he signed his name all his life, was 25 years old in 1603. It must have been about then that he married Alfonsa de los Morales, since their first son, Gabriel, was christened in March of 1604. Jorge Manuel, who had to resign himself to the incontrovertible evidence that he had no talent for painting, probably urged his father to turn the workshop into a centre for the production of more ambitious projects. Unfortunately, as will be seen, he had no luck and, to judge by the works still preserved, constructed under his supervision in his father's workshop, he was never any more than a mediocre draughtsman and a rather careless organizer. The altars of Illescas, in comparison with those built at that time in other Spanish workshops, are coarse and inelegant, and the same can be said of what is left of another, and still more ambitious, enterprise of his: the altarpieces for the Hospital de Tavera in Toledo, which are studied in the next chapter. El Greco himself cannot be held responsible for such mediocre works. In our opinion it would be a grave mistake to attribute to the great artist the design and supervision of the stunted forms that frame his marvellous paintings in Illescas, or the still worse one that survive in the altarpiece of the high altar in the Toledo hospital. The good San Román, that fervent defender of El Greco, preceded us in the endeavour to persuade critics and historians to refrain from calling Doménikos Theotokópoulos an architect.

The portrait of a young painter which hangs in the Museum of Seville *(Fig. 196 - Cat. 179)* has been identified as that of Jorge Manuel, since the features do, in fact, coincide with those of one of the figures under the mantle of *Our Lady of Charity* in the composition that crowns the main altarpiece in the Hospital of Illescas *(Fig. 199)*. In the documents that refer to the lamentable lawsuit between the painter and the Board of Works of the Hospital this identification is explicitly declared. This portrait is one of the liveliest ever painted by El Greco, who, as we have seen, frequently tended to give his sitters an idealized or spectral air. But here the enormous ruff, in the style of Philip III, keeps the young man's head very straight and erect; the clothing is black and the background in a dark, flat tone. Many of El Greco's portraits, it should be noticed, are noticeable for the vigour of their drawing and the propensity to realism. If, when considered together, they seem to suffer from a certain conventionalism, this is not pictorial, but rather the result of the affinity conferred upon them by the fact that they are of the same time and country, of a civilization which, though the predecessor of our own, is distant and difficult to recognize for us, and this fact unifies to some extent the features of people who are really quite different.

The return to the palace of the Marqués de Villena

The Illescas contract and the increase in minor commissions and chance sales that can certainly be seen in the great number of canvases attributable to this period on technical grounds very probably gave rise to ideas of expansion. Since the workshop-cum-dwelling occupied by El Greco and his family since 1590 was probably insufficient, it was decided to return to the spacious apartments in the palace of the Marqués de Villena, where, as we know, El Greco had lived some years earlier. The move seems to have taken place about the middle of April 1604, for in the new contract, signed on August 5th that year, arrangements are made for the payment of 1,929 *reales* for the coming year, plus 429 *reales* for the three months and thirteen days that had elapsed since the move. Francisco Preboste signed as a witness to this document.

El Greco's assistants

With the increasing participation of Jorge Manuel, which is certainly reflected in the growing number of commissions, El Greco's workshop needed more assistants. We know little enough of the great painter's assistants at the various stages of his working life and everything leads us to believe that our information regarding them is hardly likely to increase in the future. Apart from Jorge Manuel, whose personality as a painter is comparatively well-known, and Francisco Preboste, who is still a mystery as far as his work is concerned, there are two fairly celebrated names at this time in connection with the workshop of "Dominico the Greek": Pedro Orrente and Luis Tristán. Of the former (c. 1570-1645), who was a friend of Jorge Manuel and godfather to one of his children, we know that he arrived in Toledo at the beginning of the century and was employed in El Greco's workshop. But it has not been possible, even as a working hypothesis, to determine the extent to which he participated in the work produced. On the other hand, his copious later work, which was done in Valencia and Murcia, does not reveal the slightest trace of the style of his master in Toledo. Luis Tristán (c. 1586-1624), on the contrary, who worked with El Greco from 1603 to 1607, continued to be influenced by him till his premature death. As we shall see later on in the present chapter, his sojourn in the painter's workshop left a deep mark.

Throughout the period we are now studying, Preboste, whom we have mentioned so often, still acted as El Greco's right-hand man in all kinds of jobs. El Greco gave him powers of attorney and employed him, year after year, as the most suitable person for signing contracts, demanding payments and acting for the artist in appraisals and legal business. On April 29th 1607 he was granted the fullest powers he had

Fig. 196. Jorge Manuel Theotocópuli, c.
Seville, Provincial Museum. Cat. No. 179.

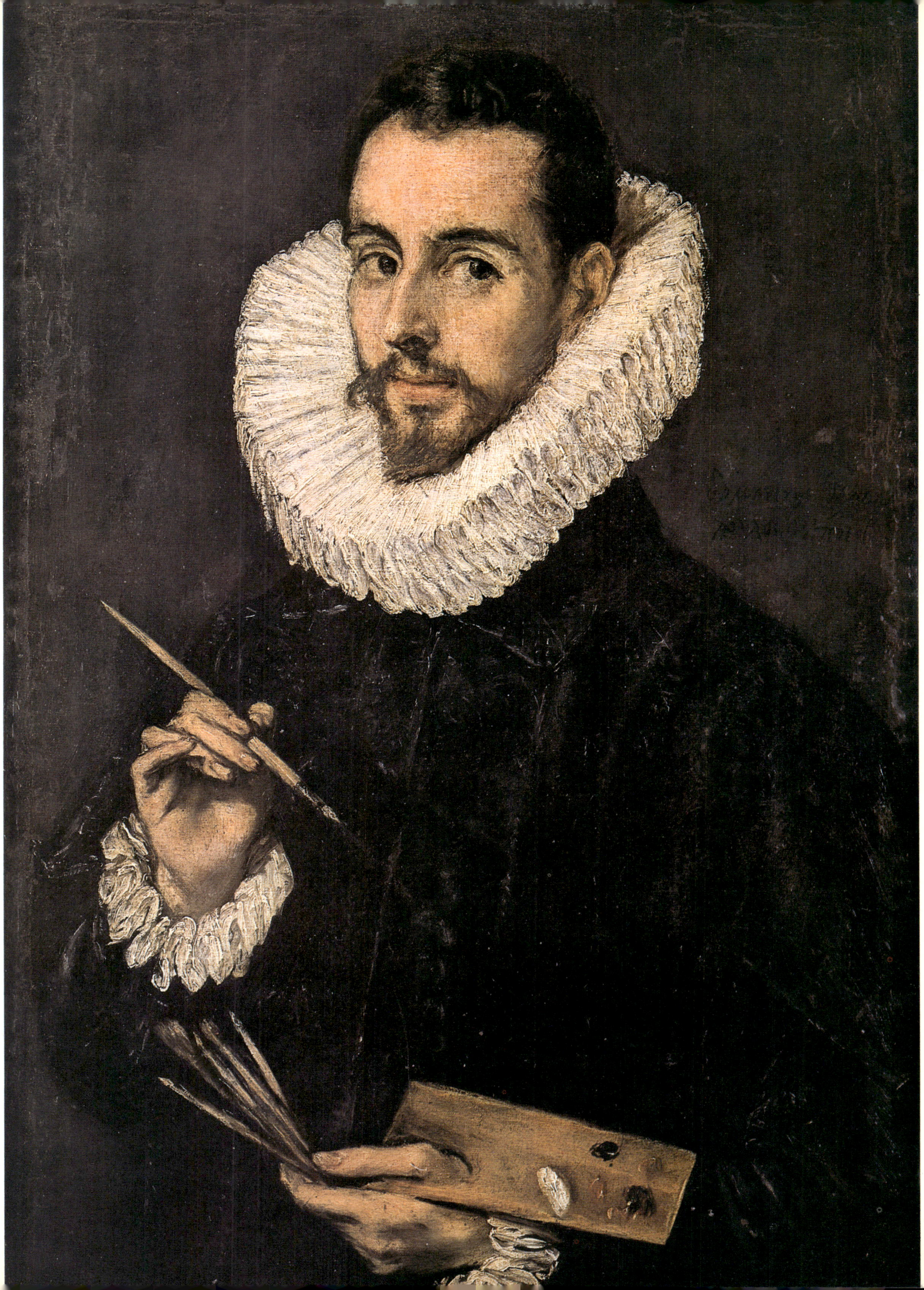

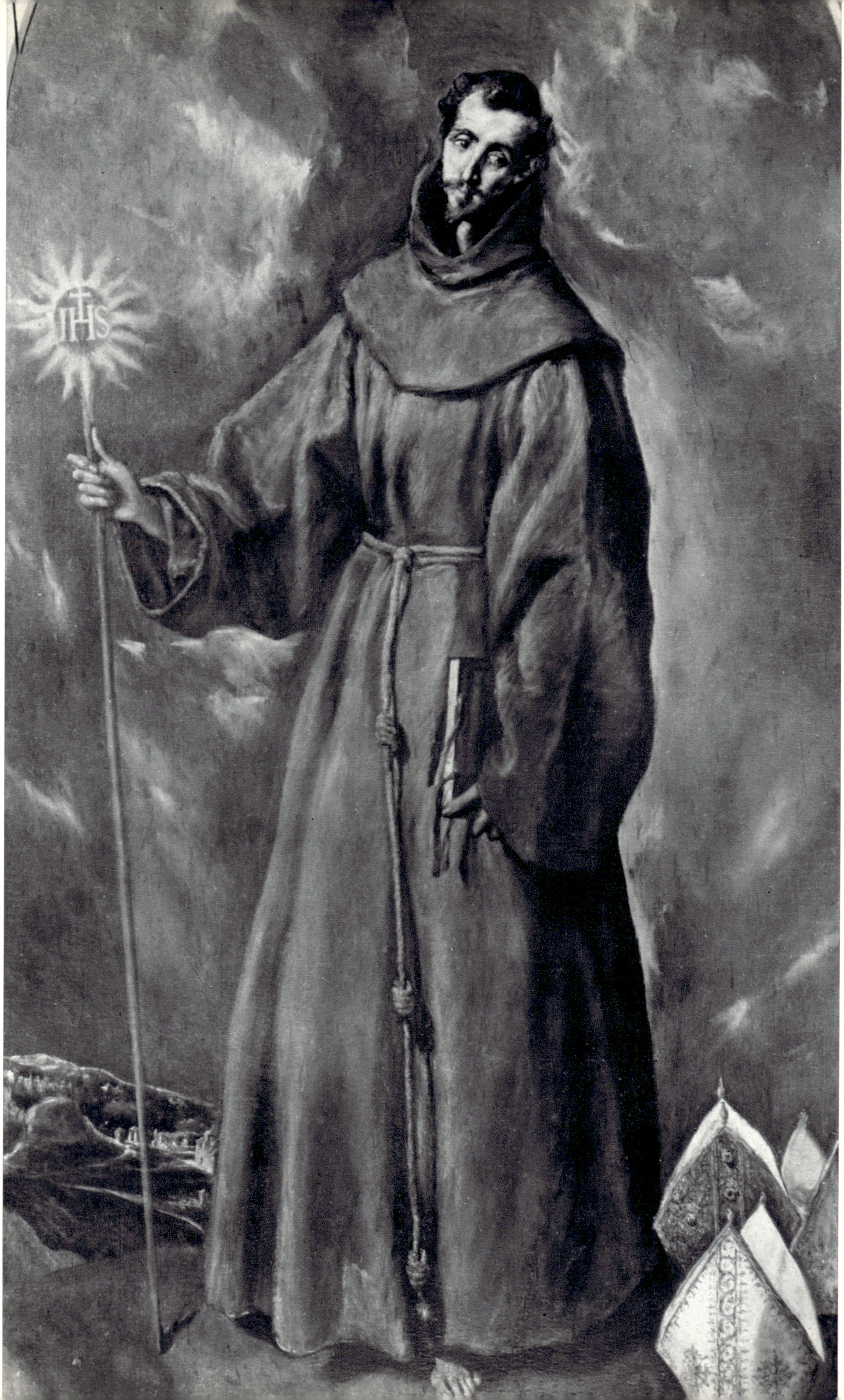

Fig. 197. St. Bernardin
c. 1603. Toledo, Gre
Museum. Cat. No. 180.

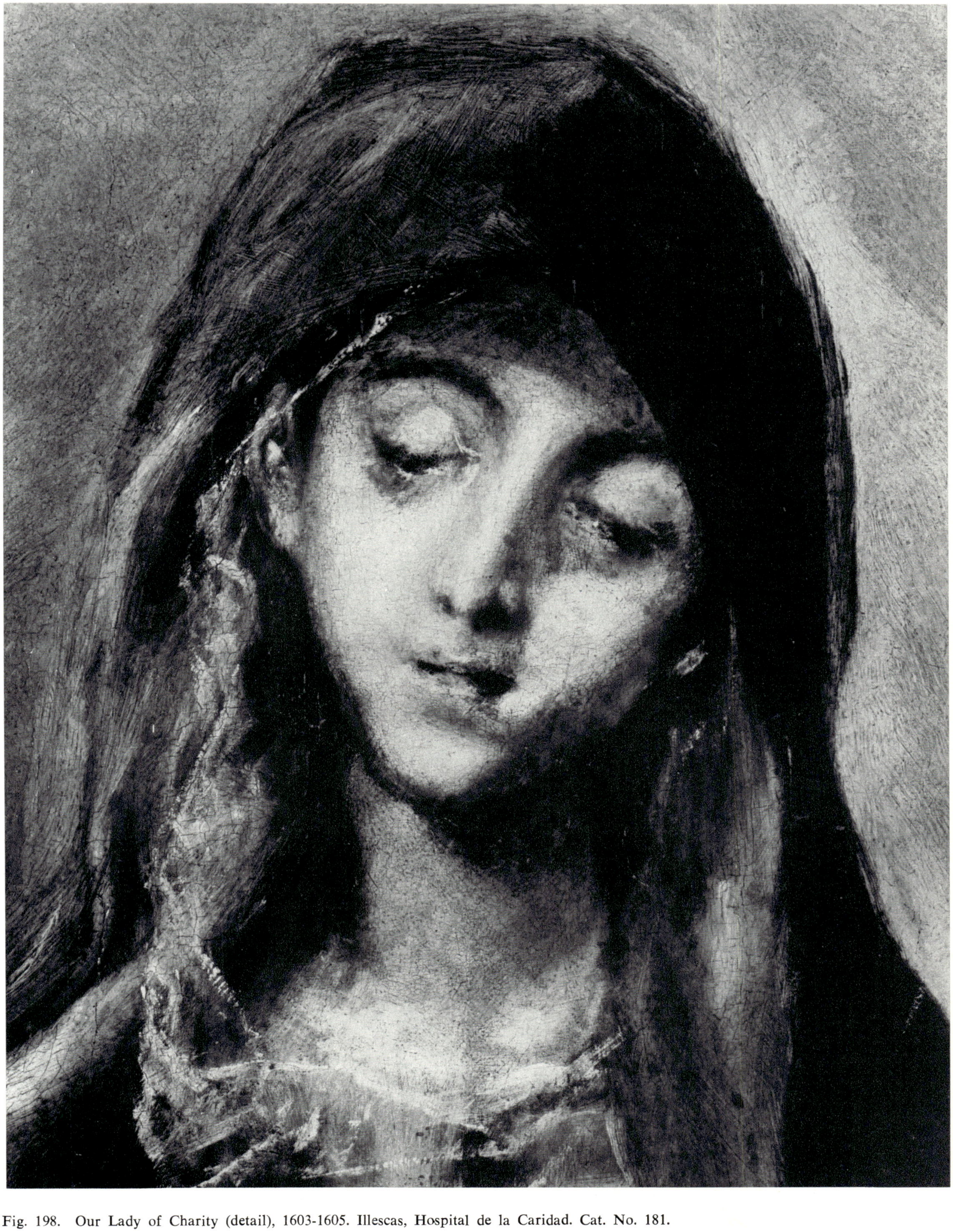

Fig. 198. Our Lady of Charity (detail), 1603-1605. Illescas, Hospital de la Caridad. Cat. No. 181.

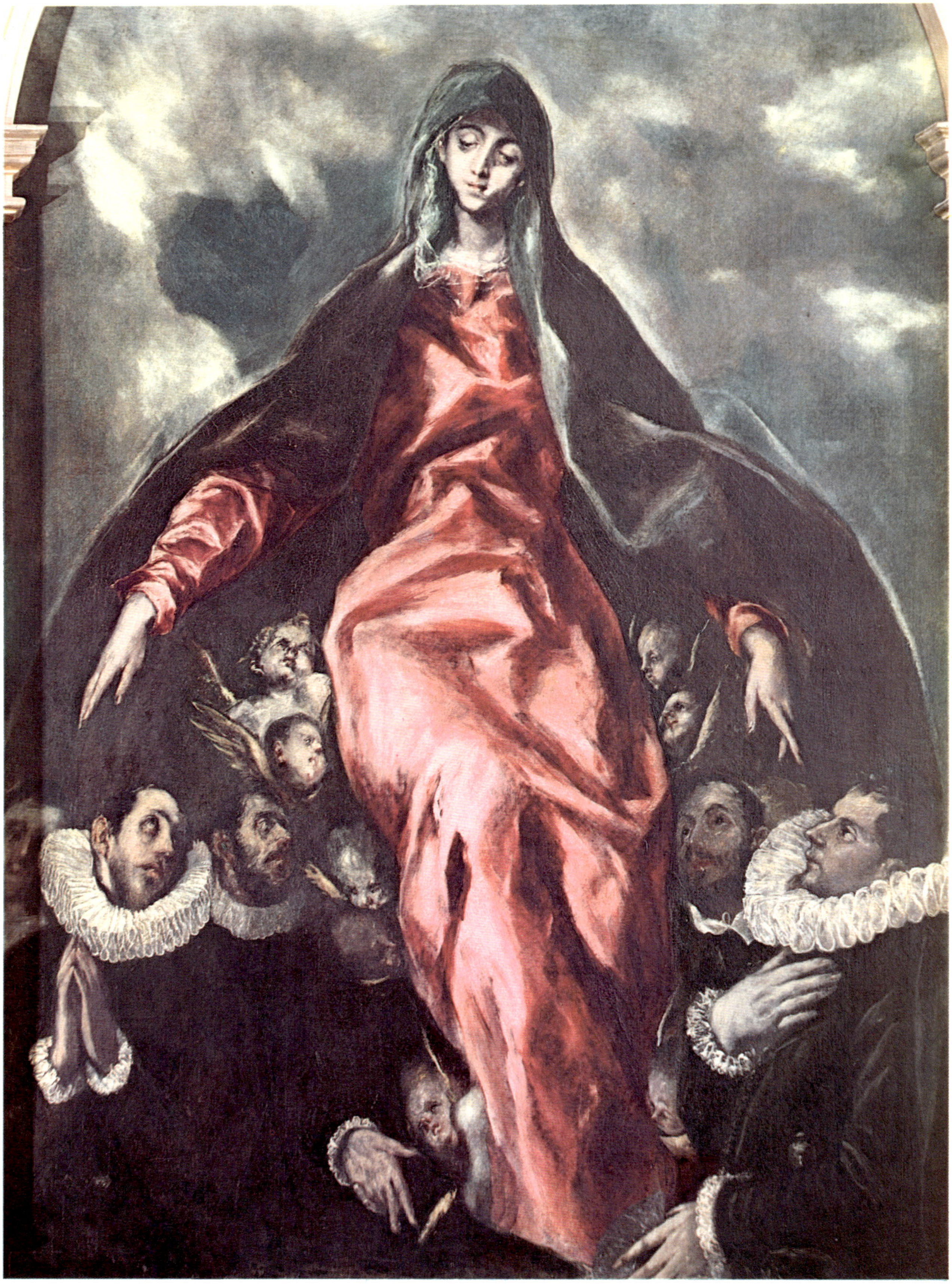

Fig. 199. Our Lady of Charity, 1603-1605. Illescas, Hospital de la Caridad. Cat. No. 181.

ever received, exactly the same powers that El Greco later granted to Jorge Manuel, of which we shall speak later. But after this document the faithful servant disappears without leaving a trace even in the register of deaths of Santo Tomé, which was his parish church. Did he die away from Toledo on one of his frequent missions? Or did he return to his native Italy after so many years spent at the side of the great painter with whom his fate was linked? We take leave of him with a certain regret, though whatever work he did as a painter is lost for ever in that enormous number of canvases that we have put on one side in this book as being workshop productions, but which still figure in so many other books, not to mention collections and galleries, as authentic Grecos.

The altarpiece of St. Bernardino

We begin our survey of the paintings belonging to this period with the impressive image of *St. Bernardino*, the central canvas in the chapel of the convent that formerly existed in Toledo under the protection of this Sienese saint *(Fig. 197 - Cat. 180)*. The contract for this work has not survived, but a receipt to the account of Jorge Manuel, dated February 3rd 1603, informs us that the price agreed upon for the altarpiece was 3,000 *reales*. The work was finished within the year, as we learn from a document signed by El Greco empowering Francisco Pantoja y Ayala "to receive payment from the Chapter of St. Bernardino... of six hundred *reales* owed to me by the said Chapter as part of a larger amount... for the altarpiece I executed for the chapel of the said Chapter". The final payment for the work was made on September 10th 1604.

In Inventory II of Jorge Manuel's estate, No. 128 is listed as a *St. Bernardino* of one *vara* and a third (111.5 cm.) in height by three-quarters of a *vara* (62.7 cm.) in width, which must be the study for the work now hung in the House of El Greco. With the closing of the convent towards the middle of the last century, the architectural part of the altarpiece, which is a simple frame of Ionic columns, was transferred to the convent of Santa Isabel de los Reyes in the same city. The typology of the character is very marked. The figure is extremely elongated and seems still more so on account of the ascetic face and the small hands and visible foot. Of great interest is the spatial conception of this work. On the one hand there is an oblique descending axis, marked by the fact that the line ideally joining the two hands ends on the right with the symbolic —and pictorially very beautiful— group of mitres in the lower foreground. Secondly, the heavy clouds seem to trace a rotating rhythm round the saint's head and this sensation of movement is accentuated by the incredible sharpness of his gaze. In the left background a strip of Toledan landscape gives greater intensity to the image, since it establishes a contrast between the ideal —the head lost among the clouds and the radiant circle— and the reality of this earth. As in all his works, El Greco here uses the clothing to create forms and colours that are expressive in themselves, independently of the theme. The brushwork used in every detail is the one most suitable for conveying the texture of what it depicts. As usual, he uses a different technique for every element, flesh tints, cloths, cloud effects, earth, etc., but creates such an interpenetration of them all that the result is admirable in its unity. El Greco was possibly the painter who, before Rembrandt, made the best use of a variety of techniques within a unity of conception and expression.

The altarpieces of the Hospital de la Caridad, Illescas

The church of the Hospital de la Caridad in the town of Illescas was built to the plans, and under the supervision, of Nicolás de Vergara between 1592 and 1600. El Greco signed the contract for the work on the high altar on June 18th of 1603, undertaking to finish it by August 31st of the following year, August 31st being the feast of the miraculous image of the Virgin which was to occupy the central niche of the altarpiece. This contract has not been preserved, but we still have the deed of confirmation of the commission, which is signed by Domingo Griego and Jorge Manuel, "painters", as the contractors. The loss of the contract itself, unfortunately, has left many points still obscure. The undertaking was an ambitious one, for it included the construction, gilding and polychroming of five wooden altars, the decoration of the vault and walls of the chapel of the high altar, the painting of various canvases and the carving of sculptures.

In the first appraisal of the finished ensemble, which was carried out on August 4th 1605 by order of the Hospital, the work was valued at 2,430 ducats. El Greco refused to accept this appraisal and the Diocesan Council appointed new appraisers, who one month later arrived at an overall valuation of 4,437 ducats. A further appraisal ordered by the Council placed the value of the work even higher, the sum determined being 4,835.52 ducats. Since the Hospital refused to pay, the Council ordered an attachment on their goods, but this had no effect. After another year of legal proceedings and mutual recriminations, the Hospital requested a new appraisal, which fixed the price at 2,093 ducats, i.e., less than the sum El Greco had refused to accept two years earlier. But the unfortunate painter accepted the appraisal this time, weary of so much litigation and of spending on it a considerable proportion of his miserable remuneration for the work carried out. The four pictures on the high altar —Our Lady of Charity, the Coronation, the Nativity and the Annunciation— were given, by this accepted appraisal, a value of 213 ducats, i.e., 87 ducats less than what he had been paid three years before for the painting of St. Bernardino. The prolonged Illescas lawsuit does not mention the *St. Ildefonso* that still hangs over the altar at the left-hand enclave of the central aisle, but to judge by its style it was probably painted at this time. Nor is any mention made of the canvas representing the *Marriage of the Virgin* which, according to Fray Gaspar de Jesús, occupied the altar matching this one on the right in 1709. The admirable painting in the National Museum of Romania *(Fig. 255 - Cat. 229)* may be a copy of this one.

In the paintings for the Hospital de la Caridad El Greco takes a noticeable step forward in his subjective tendency. Without accepting the attitude of those who began the painter's financial and moral decline, we must endeavour to understand the shock it must have been for people without any aesthetic training —mere seekers of subject matter for devotion —to be confronted with these works, in which, though we cannot say the iconography is only a pretext, it does seem evident that it is used as a springboard for leaping to areas of thought and art to which not all —very few, indeed— could follow the painter, especially in his own age and in the atmosphere of a Spanish city which, despite its brilliant tradition, was already immersed in irremediable provincialism.

In effect, the representation of *Our Lady of Charity* crowning the altarpiece of the high altar *(Figs. 198 & 199 - Cat. 181)*, in which the Virgin emerges like the Byzantine Theotokos over a void and shelters a group of figures under her mantle, could not be understood in the same way as the traditional images of Byzantium, produced within a culture which was uniform, hieratic and made for maintaining such iconographical types. And so, being the work of one single person (albeit a great artist, a genius) rather than of an iconographical tradition, this image naturally produced feelings of alarm. To the subjective tendency of the elongated proportions, partial dissolution of the forms, colouring of dazzling lights, etc., we must add here a new monumental quality of the form in itself (one that already appeared in the works for Santo Domingo el Antiguo, but which is now transformed in an expressionistic way and loses part of its formal quality), a monumental quality which one would say had been imposed by a psychological compulsion of the painter rather than by demands of any objective character, which is the reverse of the previous case.

But how can we describe this image, which should have been soothing but in fact proves tremendous? The Virgin, contrasted with the flaming sky, is principally defined by the form taken by her crimson robe with white lights, which contrasts with the dark blue mantle. The abnormal smallness of the head, which is the seat of the sentiment and action of that charity which is supposed to be the theme of the picture accentuates the dramatic effect of the figure and even more so, as we were saying, of the reddish "form in itself", which is crossed by the violent zigzag created by the folds and wrinkles of the cloth. On the other hand, the very beautiful face is not without a certain ambiguity, a distant, suffering expression, though the gesture of protection is unequivocal and easily dominates the composition, with the symmetry of the two arms descending in a gentle curve to protect those sheltering under her mantle.

On the right, finely drawn in profile and with all the character of a portrait, we see the figure of El Greco's son, Jorge Manuel, the young man whose head emerges from a voluminous ruff. On the left there is a gentleman seen in full face, with his head tilted to one side and his hands joined, and just behind him, a little further to the left, there appears the blurred face of another character. This last figure enables us to make some comments on the technique. It is very possible that El Greco left it unfinished, that is to say (using the term so often employed in contemporary references to his work), "sketched in". It is an indistinct figure, swept by the vigorous passage of a brush without paint, the stiff bristles of which left their traces marked in the colour. These brushstrokes do not follow the structure of the sketch, for their purpose was to blend rather than to efface, leaving the bright sections more evident with amazing skill.

This operation must have been carried out when the colours were just on the point of drying; at the moment when the dark tones, painted with thinner paint, were beginning to set. The painter also took into account the uneven drying of the different colours, evidently calculated beforehand. Once the whole was dry, he gave the work its final form with spontaneous brushstrokes, without any later retouching, or at least with the retouching deliberately disguised, seeking an apparent spontaneity in the slightest stroke of the brush. In some cases we have the impression that the artist must have used a metal comb with very fine teeth, instead of a brush, for these "rubbings" or "sweepings". Sometimes, after finishing the final touches, he passed the brush over the surface again, without colour, to eliminate excessive thicknesses of paint which might alter the aspect of the real structure of the impasto by an optical effect. As we have pointed out before, the works of El Greco betray the use of different processes, not always visible at first glance, but which on closer examination reveal the vast range of resources the painter had at his disposal to enable him to achieve, in every area of the picture, in every element or detail, exactly the effect he wanted.

The inventories drawn up by Jorge Manuel after his father's death mention a picture of *Our Lady of Charity* measuring three-quarters of a *vara* by two-thirds (0.63 × 0.55 m.), which was probably the sketch for the canvas just studied.

In the *Annunciation*, a circular canvas painted to embellish the vault of the high altar chapel in the church of Illescas *(Fig. 200 - Cat. 182)*, the dove is at the centre of the source of light that pours down on the Virgin, whose figure, with the usual crimson robe, is very daringly treated. The artist wished to paint both the movement and the expression of wonderment. In the figure, therefore, especially in the bust and the right hand, there is a kind of evanescence that seems to come from movement. The figure of the archangel, which is totally in profile, would seem to be treated as a relief were it not for the intensity of the luminous green of his robe, enriched by yellow reflections that respond to the greyish-blue mantle of the Virgin. The whole is treated without lines, with brushstrokes of thick colour running in different directions and tending to blend. Subtle touches give a sensation of volume or an effect of distance in the third dimension, but, seen in detail, the whole upper part of the Virgin's figure is blurred, as it were, and at the same time possessed of an unusual intensity that is mainly the result of the close and very real connection between the look and the gestures of the head and the hand raised under the rays of golden light. The background is painted in a similar tone to the *prie-dieu*, with a tendency to simplify and reduce as much as possible the naturalistic effect of a specific setting in time and space. More and more as time went on, El Greco was not so much depicting the events related in the Gospels as what might be called their timeless image.

In this canvas we may observe a juxtaposition of the levels and a sort of subtle swaying movement checked by the exact position of the vase of flowers, which is used, therefore, not only allegorically but also as a factor in the composition that provides the scene with a more static quality. The head of the archangel, whose arms are crossed on his breast, is in accordance with a normal typology in this character, so often painted by El Greco; but the execution is most unusual, as may be seen in the extremely varied forms and lengths of the brushstrokes, especially behind the nape and the head. Quite perceptibly in the hands, but also in the projecting left wing, the painter used the rubbing technique and also the process of applying a light brushstroke or a few points of apparently arbitrary colour, to enliven particular areas of an element.

In dealing with El Greco we should never forget his constant endeavour to achieve an intimate combination of the flaming idealism of his visions and the factor of realism. He never lets his imagination run away with him in his works, nor does the technique ever cease to be effectively subordinated to the image in all its details, each of which receives the treatment most perfectly suited to it. In the composition now before us, for instance, this may be seen in the way in which he renders the texture of the vase, with a heavy impasto that contrasts with the airy lightness of the flowers and the precise texture of the cloths.

In the *Nativity*, which is the second canvas in the Illescas vault *(Figs. 201 & 202 - Cat. 183)*, he dispenses with complementary tones. The intense —almost dazzling— white accent of the swaddling-cloth on which the Infant Jesus is laid produces an extraordinary impression which affects all the shades and forms with its reflections. The boldness of the spatial arrangement has a suitable complement in the way in which the enormous head, which looks more like that of a bull than of an ox, is placed in the foreground. This head, violently twisted upwards and to the right, forms a great mass which is, as it were, the dominant weight of the composition, being placed almost in its centre.

The technique of infusing light in the colour reaches its absolute limit in this picture. It is not so much a question of a luminosity peculiar to certain tones —a technique on which a large proportion of nineteenth-century art was to be based— but rather that the cloths, and also in this case the little figure of the recumbent Jesus, seem to give off a true light, as if they were realistic sources of illumination.

In the *Coronation of the Virgin*, the third theme in the Illescas vault *(Figs. 203 to 205 - Cat. 185)* and one so often treated by El Greco, the characteristics we have noted in the case of *Our Lady of Charity* are accentuated. The angels, skilfully placed in the most diverse postures of weightlessness, the clusters of winged heads and the luminous rays are only employed to create the most suitable background for setting off, with superhuman force, the three main figures. We should observe the symmetrical rhythm —two ascending diagonal axes from the centre to the edges— formed by the robes of Christ and God the Father at the height of the knees. The projection of these axes leads to the most luminous point of the Virgin's blue mantle. This detail proves once more the great care El Greco took with his compositions from the point of view of their latent geometry. That is why he was able —on so firm a basis, reinforced by his infallible drawing within such distortions as might be present— to embark on the most daring ventures; i.e., on the practice of art as he felt and conceived it to be, even though this might possibly prejudice his career and the appreciation of his work by patrons and clients, with the results of which we have already spoken.

We could analyse every or any element in this work with the certainty of finding, if not a radical innovation (within his own system), at least a step forward in the evolution of his aesthetic and procedural bases: the treatment of the Virgin's robe, for instance, or the wonderful foreshortening of the face, with that softest of blended modelling in the cheeks and some abrupt strokes between the eyes and the eyebrows. This work is a constant flow of different densities, with reflections ranging from white to dark blue and a discreet use of crimsons and golden yellow. Equally surprising is the finish of the whole lower half of the picture, with the white stream of light on the left, the intense greenish blue of the central part, on which float the winged heads that are so wonderfully expressed and captured, and the yellowish green of the right, also invaded by a stream of white light that seems to continue the sheen of the Eternal Father's robe. The harmony of colour and tones is obtained in such a way that the flesh tints hardly stand out as such against it. This would have meant an excessive humanization of the theme for the painter's sentiments at this stage in his development. The crimson and white of the robes, the pink and light blue reflections of the white robe of God the Father and the material of the clouds were all intended to make the flesh tints offer, if not the appearance of blending into them, at least as little contrast as possible. In the Epstein Collection in Chicago there is the sketch of this *Coronation of the Virgin*, the last version of a theme constantly returned to by El Greco *(Fig. 204 - Cat. 184)*, a theme, moreover, from which he always succeeded in producing both supernatural beauty and also a feeling that we might almost describe as mystical, without this being meant as an opinion of the painter's character.

The *St. Ildefonso* that hangs over one of the side altars in Illescas *(Fig. 206 - Cat. 186)* would suffice, as it belongs to an ensemble immersed in idealizing expressionism, to show that El Greco was perfectly capable of returning, when he wished to or his theme demanded it, to less venturesome ways, more in accordance with what might be defined as a neutral vision or one unaltered by any sentiment. It is not that the painter's creation in this case differs in quality or technique. The only thing he does, while maintaining his usual technique (and anything else would be unimaginable), is to restrain his propensity to great, expressive distortions, unusual illuminations and unbridled eloquence in the gestures and in the image as a whole. This explains the consistent naturalism of his portraits and the difficulties that arise in attempting to arrange them in chronological order based on stylistic comparison with his sacred compositions, perfectly well dated and more imaginative. There are two main points to notice in this work. The first is the congenial, human character the painter succeeded in giving to his subject, whose goodness and spiritual delicacy can be guessed

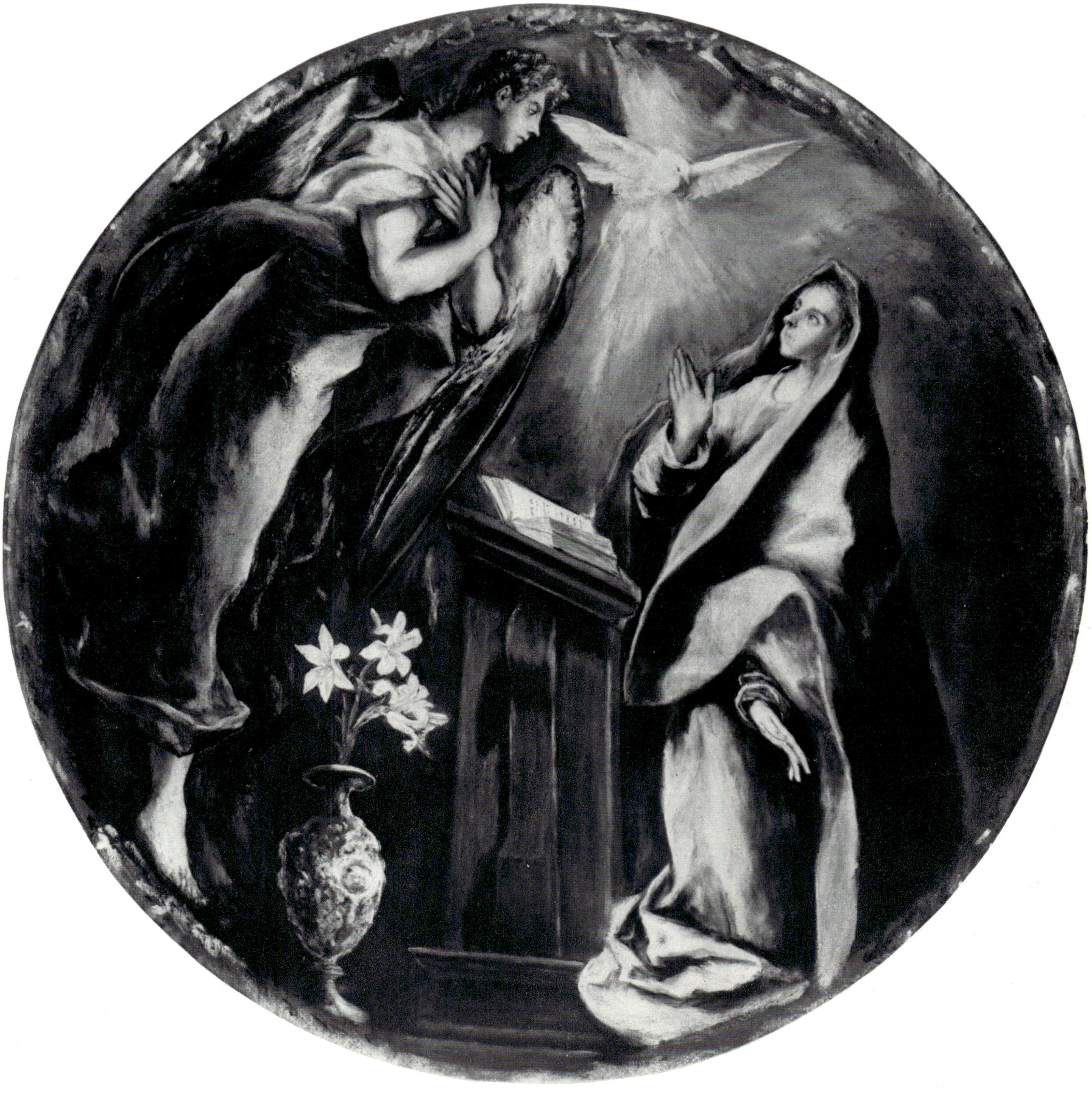

Fig. 200. The Annunciation, 1603-1605. Illescas, Hospital de la Caridad. Cat. No. **182**.

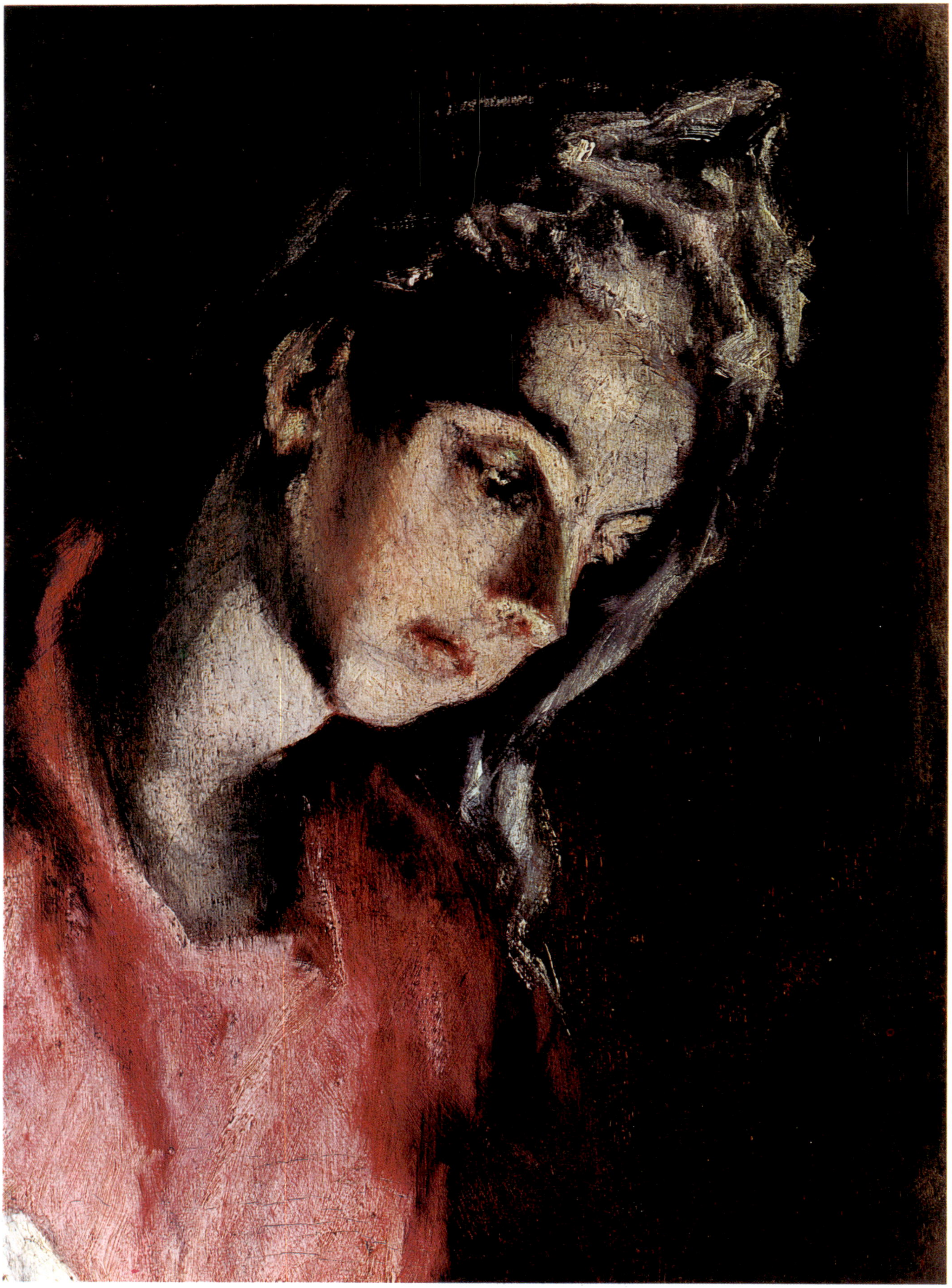

Fig. 201. Detail of figure 202.

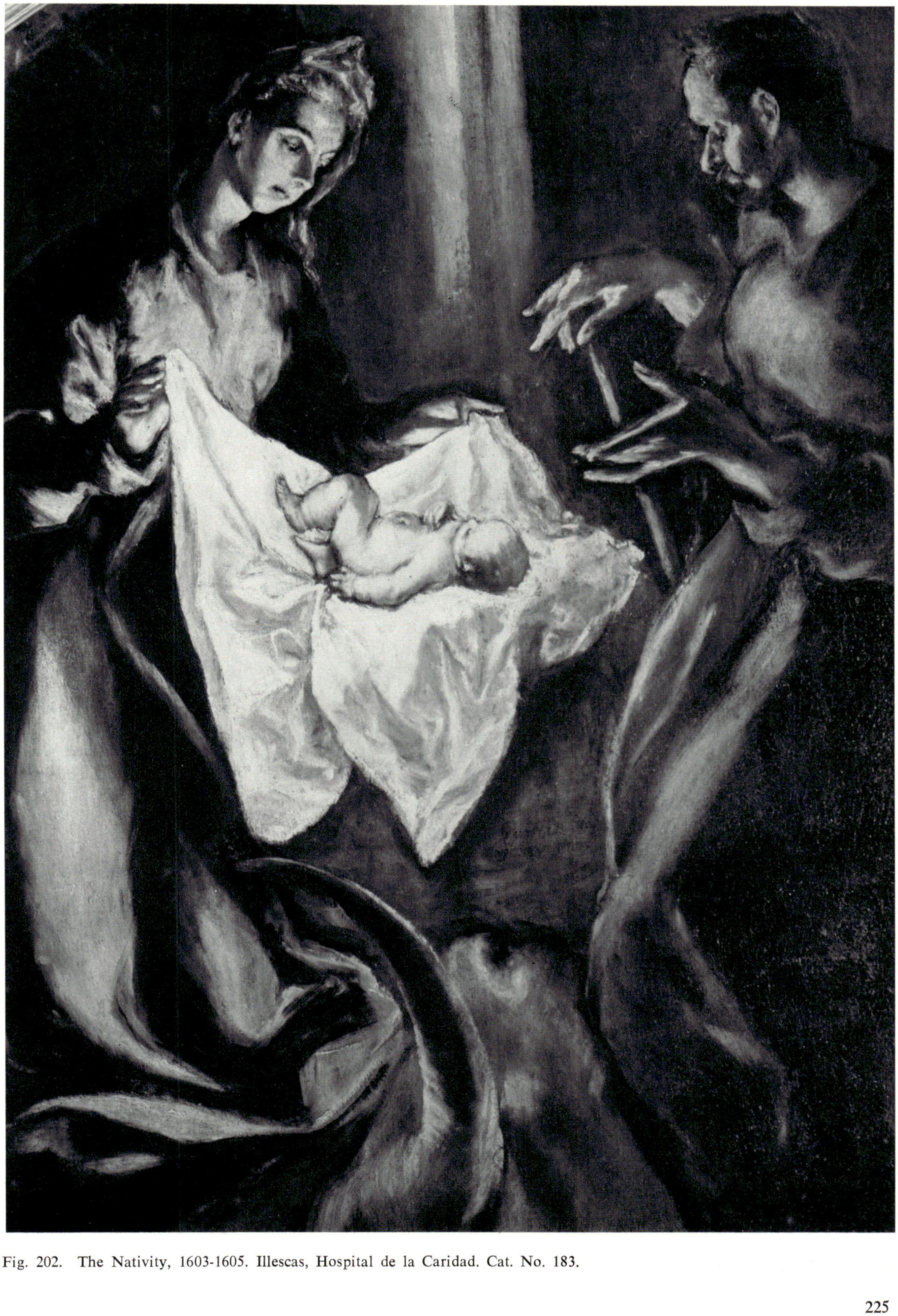

Fig. 202. The Nativity, 1603-1605. Illescas, Hospital de la Caridad. Cat. No. 183.

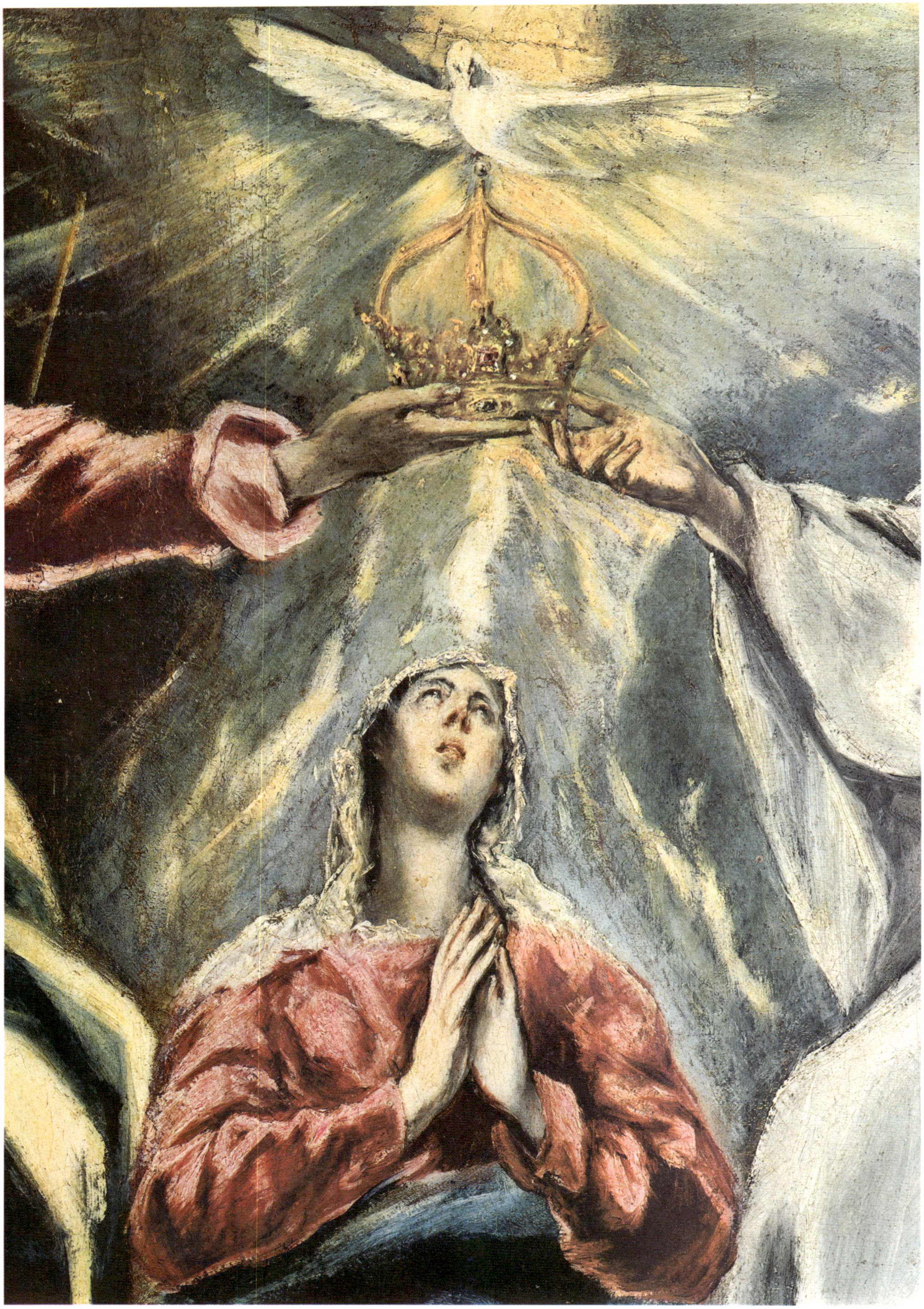

Fig. 203. Detail of figure 205.

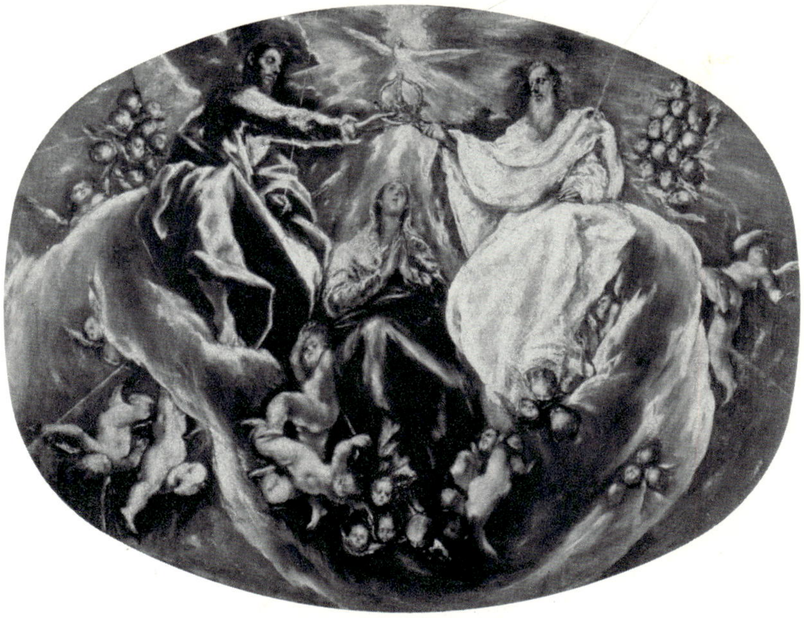

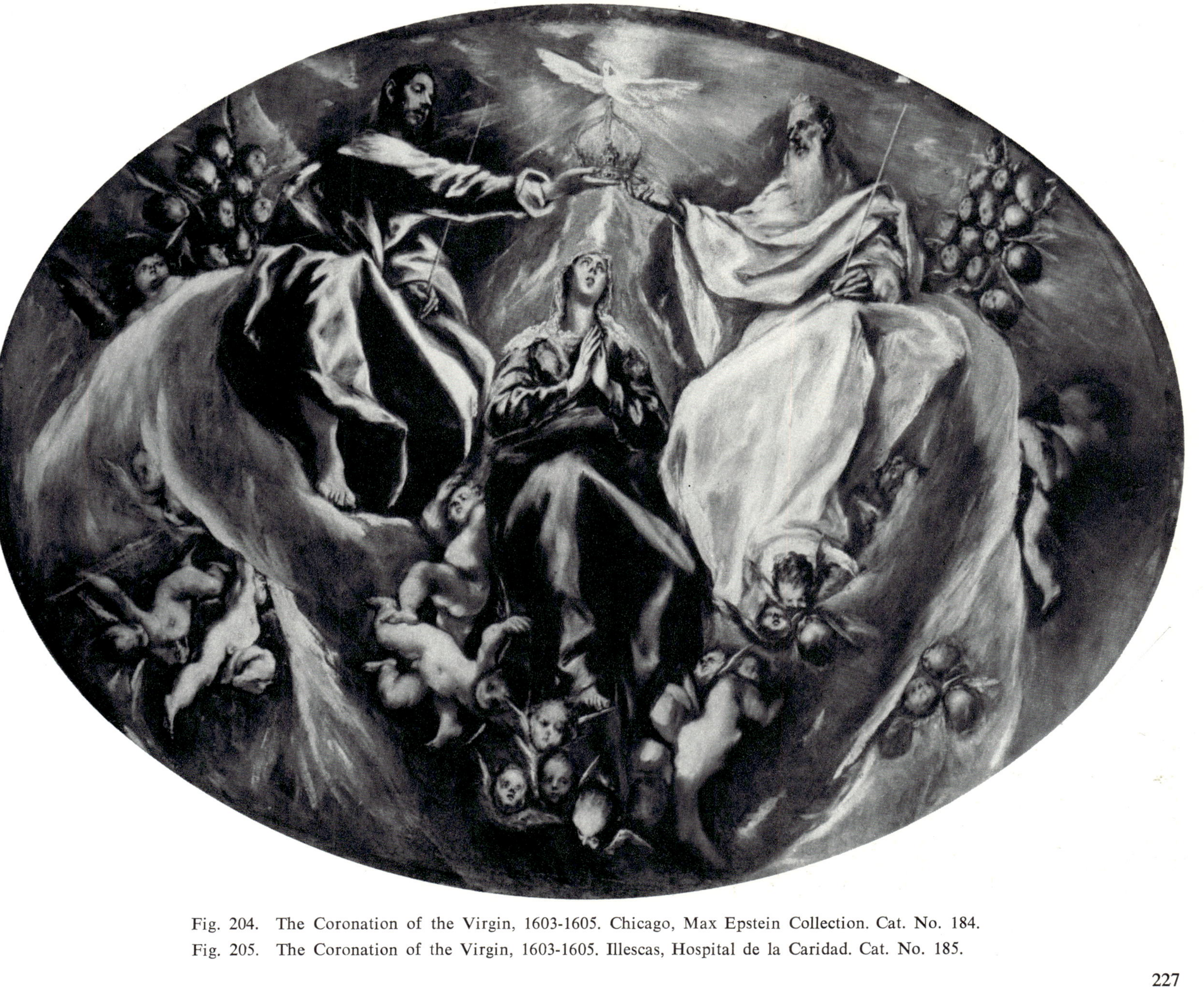

Fig. 204. The Coronation of the Virgin, 1603-1605. Chicago, Max Epstein Collection. Cat. No. 184.
Fig. 205. The Coronation of the Virgin, 1603-1605. Illescas, Hospital de la Caridad. Cat. No. 185.

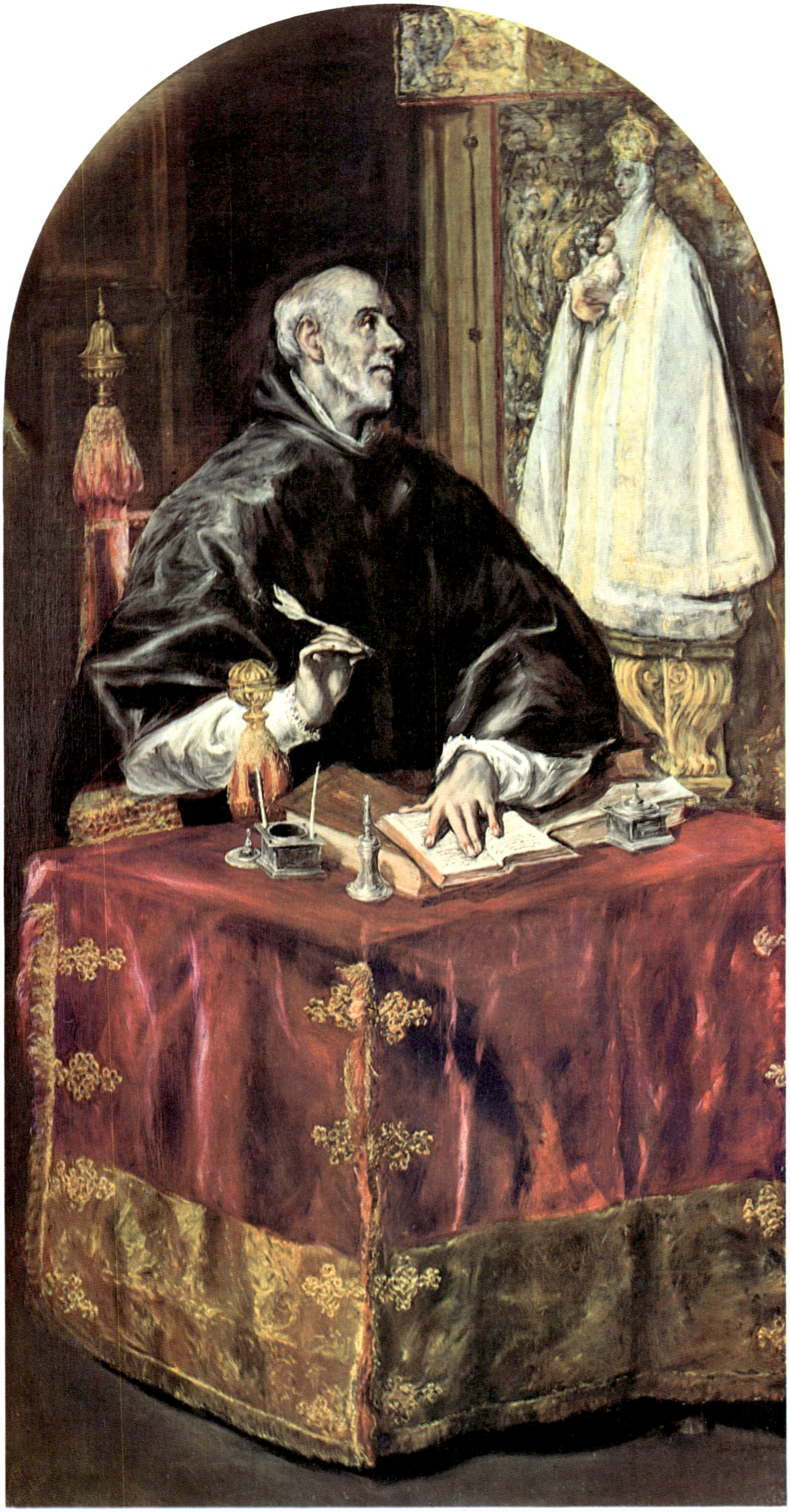

Fig. 206. St. Ildefon
1603-1605. Illescas, Hos
tal de la Caridad. C
No. 186.

at in his face and in his hands. the right hand holding a pen, the left, with the fingers separated, resting on an open book. The second is the intensity with which the different stuffs are represented: both the rich velvet that covers the table and hangs down to the floor and the black and white clothing of the saint. The black has touches of pink, white and blue in the lines of light that mark the projection of folds and creases, while the white of the sleeves receives, in inverse fashion, dark shades of colour, but not black. The whole power and gentleness of El Greco's technique stands out splendidly in this image and its setting. The white handling of the Virgin's robe and mantle harmonizes wonderfully with the black of the saint's habit, both being sustained by the harmony of reds and golds. Here El Greco did not attempt any experiments, unless we count as such his treatment of the black and white as complementaries, at the same time giving the black enough shading and luminosity to harmonize with the crimson, while the gold and the white rest on the warm ochre tones in the background of the room.

This picture, then, in its realistic restraint and even strictness as much as in its execution, synthesizes two of the paths followed by El Greco: that of his portraits —for this image is evidently painted in the spirit of a portrait— and that of the iconographical ensemble to which it belongs.

Works attributed to the period 1603-1607

We will now study that considerable group of works which, to judge by their pictorial concept, were painted during the same period as the works done for Illescas. Some of them are replicas of earlier models, their only variations being those to be expected from the profound transformation undergone by El Greco's concept of painting in the opening years of the seventeenth century. In others the modifications also affect the scheme of the elements and attitudes of the characters that go to make up the composition, so that it must be supposed that in these cases, as we have seen in the case of the Illescas *Coronation*, the painter created new designs.

At all events his creative spirit, enriched by each passing year, continued to produce absolutely original compositions. A good example of this is the *Crucifixion* in the Prado that originally hung in San Ildefonso, the Jesuit church of Toledo *(Fig. 207 - Cat. 187)*, which represents Mary Magdalen and the angels collecting the blood of the crucified Christ. The colour is very interesting in this work. Against a dark background, its most vivid tones seem to be altered by iridescent lights. Green and red in St. John, blue and crimson in the Virgin, very light green with yellow in the two figures at the foot of the Cross, red in the angel on the left and yellow in the one on the right, the whole given unity by —and centering on— the livid flesh tints in the figure of Christ. The folds of the mantles create harmonies of form and colour around the great tonal contrast of the centre. One may observe a kind of revolving movement, only barely hinted at, in the rhythms of the figures, apart from the marked ascending impulse, particularly strong in St. John the Evangelist, whose body seems to stretch upwards so as to bring his head closer to Christ. The representation of the cloths is incredibly free, the pictorial material being shown quite openly in its own textures, without using any outlines to enclose the form and with untidy brushstrokes that are at once soft and brutal. The modelling of the anatomy of Christ is more intense than in El Greco's earlier *Crucifixions*. Despite the earthly and angelical company that surrounds Him at the moment of His death, the "hole" created by the painter around the body of the Redeemer, by skilful use of the dark background, leaves the central figure of the scene in a kind of essential solitude.

We will now turn our attention to one of El Greco's finest works, the great *Adoration of the shepherds* which not so long ago was transferred from Santo Domingo el Antiguo to the Prado, after a most perilous passage even before it had left the church in Toledo *(Figs. 208 & 209 - Cat. 188)*. In 1618 Luis Tristán declared that he had seen the master painting this picture —it will be recalled that Tristán worked for El Greco from 1603 to 1607. On the other hand, it has been asserted that this *Adoration of the shepherds* was the central composition of the altarpiece that El Greco placed in a chapel of the church of Santo Domingo, the crypt of which was granted to the artist as a family tomb in 1612. In it he was to be buried, in April of 1614. But Jorge Manuel, after a lawsuit with the community of Santo Domingo, bought another burial vault in the church of San Torcuato in 1619 and to this, it would seem, he transferred his father's remains. The altarpiece was left in Santo Domingo, but El Greco's *Adoration* was replaced in it a few years later by an *Annunciation* painted by Carducho which is still there, our painter's incomparable canvas being relegated to the most preposterous places.

If we are to go by stylistic analysis, it is difficult to accept the dating in 1612 for this *Adoration*. We prefer to think that it was painted at the same time as the Illescas ensemble and intended for some other altarpiece, for which no contract has been preserved and which was never finished. This would concur with the above-mentioned declaration of Tristán. It seems very probable that another, but much smaller, *Adoration*, formerly in the collection of the Marqués del Arco and now in the Metropolitan Museum in New York *(Figs. 210 & 211 - Cat. 189)*, was the preparatory design. The compositions are almost identical, though the scene seems to have been painted from a rather closer viewpoint in the smaller work, so that the space is less important and the figures take up more of it. But the position of each of the figures, and even their expressions, were left quite unchanged in the larger version. We will make a detailed study only of this latter, since it is unnecessary to deal with both works on account of this great similarity. The composition follows two principles to be found in other, similar works by El Greco: the division into two areas, heavenly and earthly, and the arrangement of the figures, as if round an invisible vertical axis, producing a sensation of rotary movement —accentuated by the gestures— that almost leads to vertigo. As in other such scenes, Jesus and his white swaddling-clothes are the source of light for the whole composition. The light is projected upwards, with its luminosities and vivid reflections. The architectural elements are reduced to a minimum and their function much less important than in earlier compositions of the same kind. Some clouds appear on the left, like flying reflections of light, below the legs of the angel whose figure dominates the upper left of the picture.

In this picture we may see, at their very height, the distortions of the painter's last period. The figure of the shepherd on the right, whose legs are vividly illuminated, would suffice to show how El Greco succeeded in synthesizing naturalistic truth and visionary distortion. The proportions of this figure, and of its opposite on the left, are very elongated, as are also those of the angel on the right. Robes and mantles are treated less as articles of clothing than as accents of colour and light, valid on that account. Finally, even in the execution a marked tendency to dissolution can be seen. If we look closely, we shall see the most unexpected mixtures of colours, even in the flesh tints, while the linear factor seems to be broken up by brutal brushstrokes, clots of paint and rubbings, all of which tends to evoke at once the effect of light on the form, movement and the life that animates the interior of the form. The face of the Virgin is the most serene, that of St. Joseph the most affected by El Greco's expressionism here. Black is used to outline forms and to give greater contrast to the quality and to the clear shade of the tone. There is a certain geometrization of strokes, as may be seen in the transparent white veil of the Virgin, which is treated in rapid zigzags over her left arm and shoulder. We may even observe a hierarchy of values, in which form and colour are subordinated to light, space and movement, this last being a spiritual expression rather than a physical reality.

To this same phase belong a *Resurrection* and a *Pentecost*, two canvases of equal size and both with the upper part finishing in a semicircle *(Figs. 212, 213 & 214 - Cat. 190 & 191)*. Some historians held that they formed part of the altarpiece for the Colegio de Doña María de Aragón, but this hypothesis has been discredited. Now in the Prado, they were both transferred there from the Museo de la Trinidad, which seems to suggest that they originally hung somewhere in Madrid. It is possible that the *Resurrection* is the one Palomino mentions as hanging in the shrine behind the altar of Nuestra Señora de Atocha in Madrid. It is probable that they both belonged to the same altarpiece, but one of which nothing is known, and, for reasons to be adduced later, it seems probable that the second from the right in the line of figures in the upper part of the *Pentecost* is a self-portrait.

A comparison of this *Resurrection* with the one in Santo Domingo el Antiguo *(Fig. 67)*, painted some thirty years earlier, when the painter was still painting under a certain Italian influence, shows us the profound evolution of El Greco's work. That first version of the theme is rather analytical and careful in execution, its naturalistic form being slightly geometrized in its planes. In the composition the artist endeavoured to create a certain illusion of a third dimension, and in any case he formed a true represented space. The figures in the foreground are there to mark the space and to ensure, by contrast, that sensation of depth which is otherwise partially denied by the appreciably advancing character of the figure of Christ and its

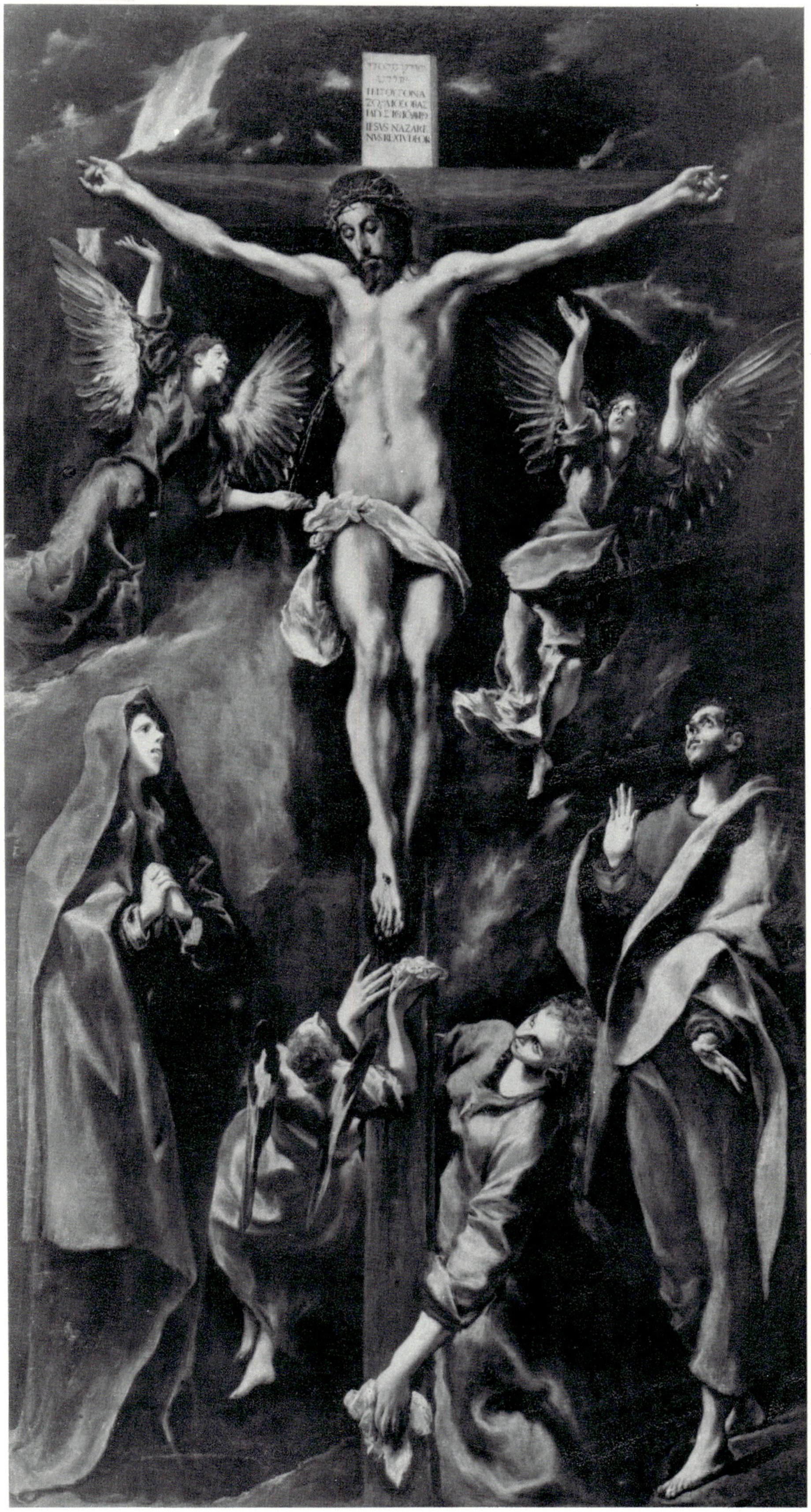

Fig. 207. The Crucifixion, 1603-1607. Madrid, Prado. Cat. No. 187.

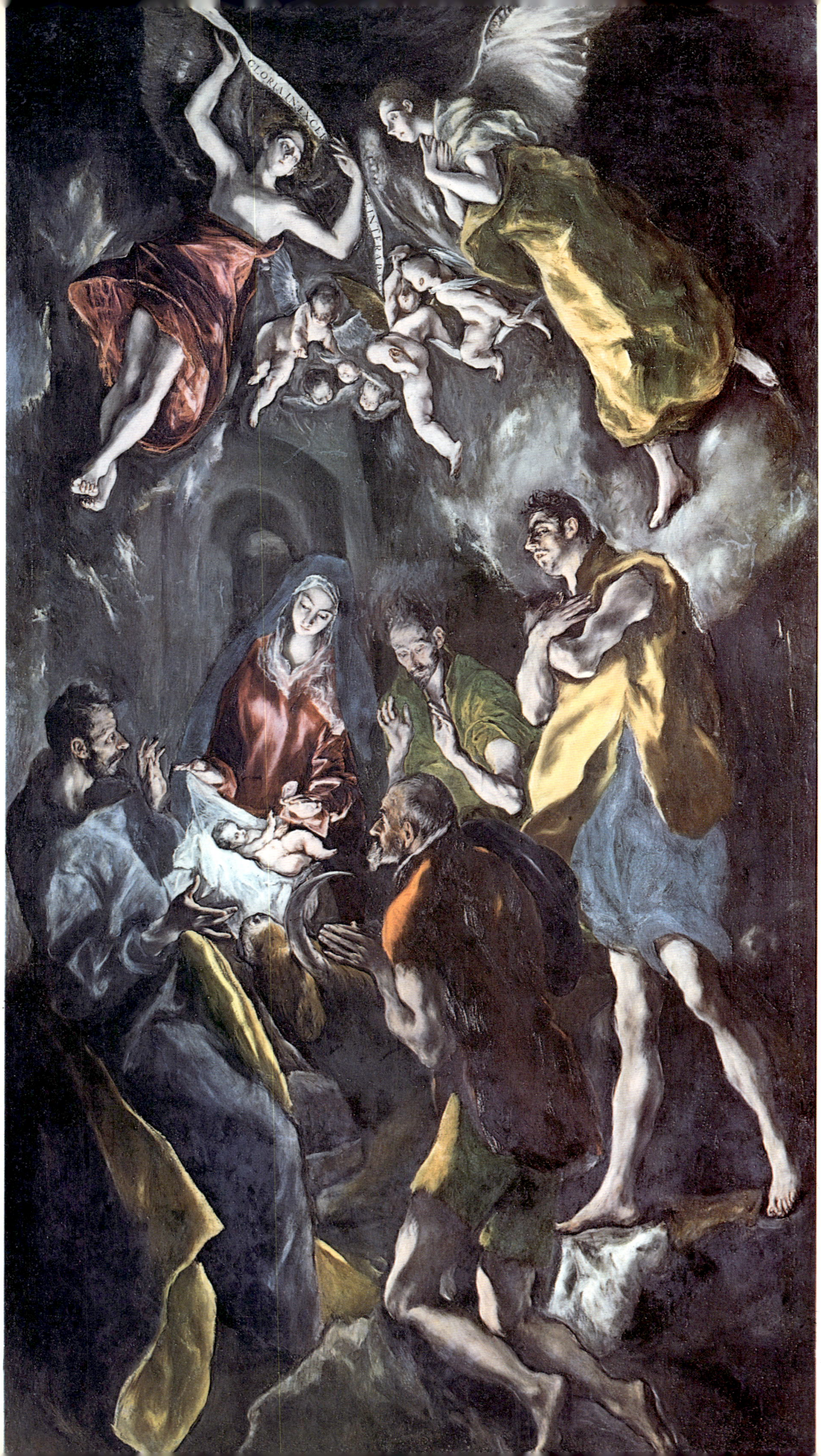

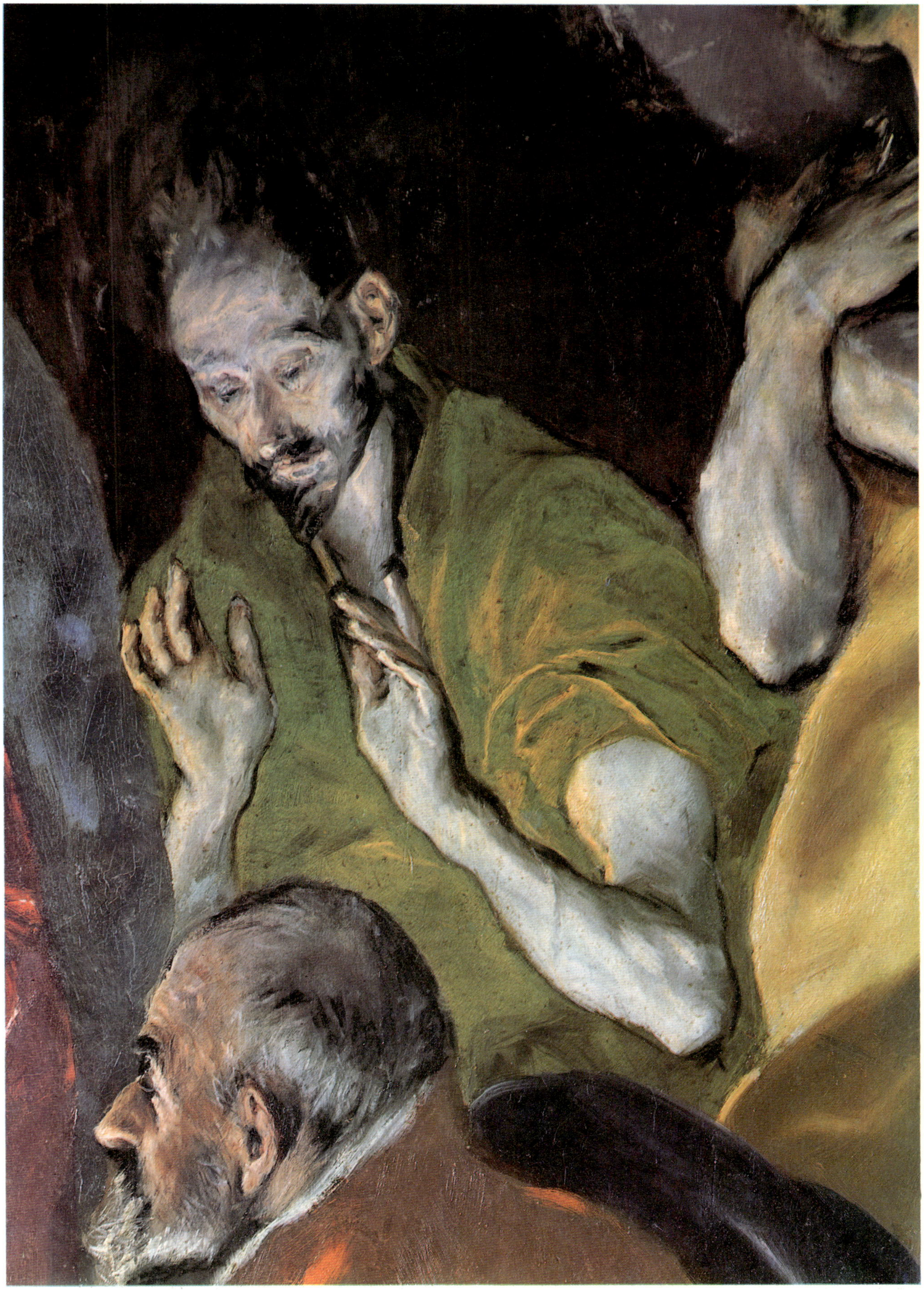

Figs. 208 & 209. The Adoration of the shepherds, 1603-1607. Madrid, Prado. Cat. No. 188.

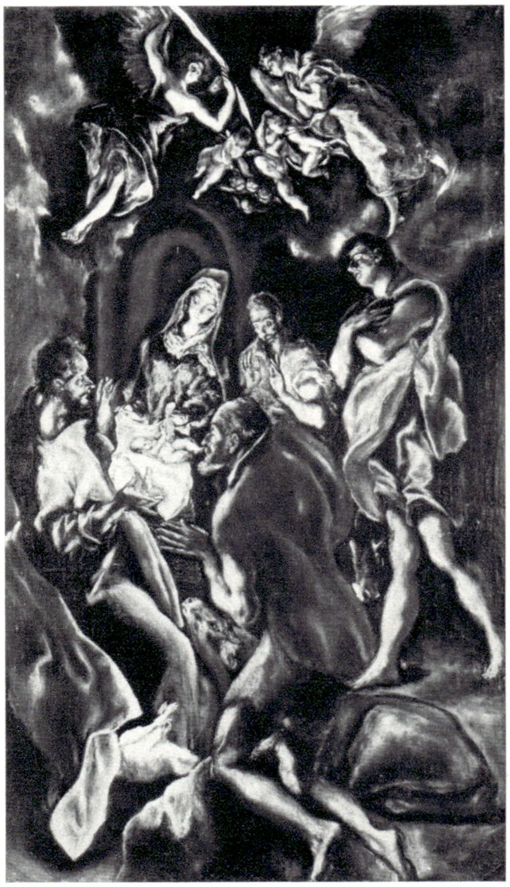

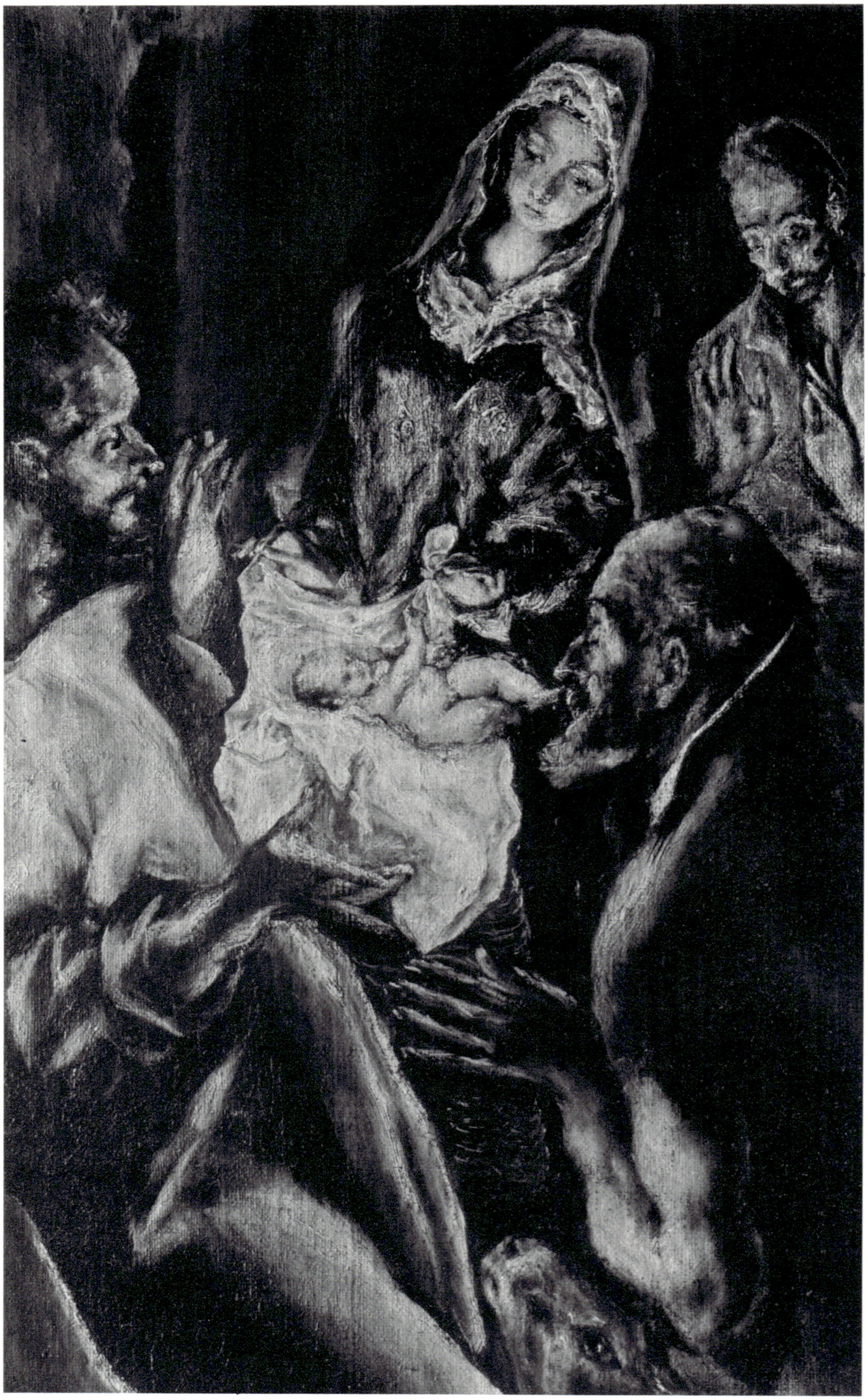

Figs. 210 & 211. The Adoration of the shepherds, 1603-1607. New York, Metropolitan Museum. Cat. No. 189.

warm, brilliant colours against the cold tones of the foreground figures. But in this later work the space exists only as an emanation of the same force that projects the figure of Christ upwards. The naturalistic basis is no longer submitted to any analytical geometrization, but to the pre-Baroque stylization of the painter's last period, combined with the half-dissolved execution —which is nevertheless firm and perfectly capable of modelling the form. The colours have grown more intense, the range warmer, deeper and more dramatic. The secondary characters are less individualized and constitute a kind of infernal company that has been routed. Here we have the most daring and exaggerated foreshortenings, most noticeably in the two figures on the left with heads bent back, and a greater degree of distortion than that to be seen in the figures in the last version of the *Cleansing of the Temple*. The flesh tints are subjected to expressive tensions; their movement, which follows winding, flame-like lines, does not contradict the anatomy, but rather El Greco makes use of the fluctuations of the natural form, accentuating and giving them meaning in order to create the climate of the composition.

Going one step further with our comparison between the *Resurrection* painted during the artist's first years in Spain and this one from his last period, we might say that the first was an attempt to depict an historical —though supernatural— moment, giving the image the precision of earthly truth, while the later work presents a spiritual concept, the eternal triumph of the Godhead over death and evil. It is very possible, of course, that El Greco did not concern himself with the problems of the philosophy of his art, but that does not alter the fact that his development enabled him to advance, not only in execution and in the creative freedom of genius, but also in ideological depth. In passing from the concrete to the dynamic, El Greco was not only acting logically in accordance with the artistic evolution of his time, but anticipating all the possibilities of that expressionism which, in this final period of his that began with the works of Illescas, asserted itself ever more vigorously.

The *Pentecost* is composed with a tendency to fill the whole space. As in other compositions with a fair number of figures, El Greco here uses a circular rhythm, though the frieze of heads in the upper part is given a flatter character, to provide the work with greater serenity. The gestures of the figures in the foreground are arranged so as to reveal as many faces as possible, as well as the greatest possible variety in representations of the human figure. On the other hand, the almost hysterical movement of the disciple in the right foreground is used to establish an axis of movement that enlivens the whole design, having its counterpart in the raised arm of the apostle who appears higher up on the left. There is a similar correspondence between the gestures of the figure in the left foreground and of the apostle on the upper right. This forms two crossing diagonal axes, which meet almost at the feet of the Virgin.

The heads are all very interesting; some of them belong to the typology of the *St. Peter* in the Escorial, which is studied below, and the execution is also the same. Particularly interesting is the representation of the Virgin, which, despite the freedom of treatment and the slight but intense distortion of the eyes, is extremely beautiful. As for the execution, there are evident inequalities to be found between different fragments of the work, but we should not forget that this painting is rather darkened and perhaps somewhat damaged by an old restoration. This helps to alter the subtly balanced values and explains why there should have been some talk of parts of the work being done by another hand than El Greco's. As regards the degree of distortion, this is undoubtedly no greater than that mentioned in speaking of the *Resurrection*; since, in fact, it does not even go so far as certain effects to be observed in the latter work, we see no reason, as we have said, why we should not suppose the *Pentecost* to have been painted at much the same time.

In this period, too, we must place two large images of *St. Peter* and *St. Ildefonso,* which were painted as a pair and now hang in the Escorial *(Figs. 215, 216 & 217 - Cat. 192 & 193)*. They are mentioned in the 1698 edition of the description of the monastery written by Father De los Santos. As they do not figure in the previous edition of this book, published in 1657, it has hitherto been supposed that they arrived in the Escorial some time between 1657 and 1698 and that they came from the altarpiece of the high altar of the church of San Vicente in Toledo, which until recently had exact copies of these pictures (now in the Santa Cruz Museum, Toledo). It was thought that these copies must have been painted to replace the two signed pictures in the Escorial. But the analysis of the San Vicente paintings shows they are replicas carried out in El Greco's own workshop.

The canvases in the Escorial, therefore, must be the *St. Peter* and the *St. Ildefonso* mentioned in Inventory II of those drawn up by El Greco's son. They were probably sold by the latter or his heirs and later presented in some way or other to the great monastery. The same inventory mentions two smaller canvases of the same subjects, which were probably preparatory studies; their present whereabouts is unknown.

To judge by their technique, we might say that with these two works of genius the painter's last period begins, after the crucial and critical point marked by the Illescas paintings. The elongation and distortion are predominant, and we can see a more Baroque character than in works of earlier periods, as well as a freedom of execution which did not exist previously. The painter's tendency to turn clothing into a form that is valid for its own sake, apart from its representative function, is also heightened. Pictorialism asserts itself throughout, and the perfect drawing is literally overwhelmed by the immense force of the colour and the textural quality. The dominant colours in the *St. Peter* are the yellow of the enormous cloak and the greyish tones of the cloud effects. But the tonal values are particularly noticeable in the interior of the form, with the accentuation of the lightness of the areas in projection and the darkness of those left in shadow. This creates a series of forms that harmonize with those of the sky, with its contrasts of clear and opaque. The technique is that of El Greco's most spontaneous tendency, which became more accentuated with time and consists of softness combined with vigour, in a misty *sfumato* that does not go so far as to upset the quality of the material in question, but does give it a second sense. In his folds and flowing draperies, in other words, El Greco achieves the same results as the artists of the final period of Gothic, but with a completely different vision and technique. The light undoes the concrete quality of the line to a great extent and it is only the artist's immense capacity for representing volumes and suggesting the internal mass of the body under the cloth that prevents these phantasmagorical figures of his from collapsing. Let us observe once more, however, the way in which the painter's apparent impetuosity, that of a Romantic before his time, is corrected by his technical expertise. He destroys the line, especially in the interior of the form, but he takes care to accentuate the outline sharply where necessary, as can be seen, in this portentous *St. Peter*, in the left shoulder and the upper part of the arm of the figure, which he illuminates and edges with very light brushwork to contrast it with the dark background, while he does just the opposite in the lower part of the cloak, at knee level. The combined qualities of inventiveness, improvisation and dissolution are splendidly displayed in the spectacular head.

Though within the same concept and technique, the figure of *St. Ildefonso* seems somewhat more restrained, undoubtedly due to the fact that clothing demanded greater precision of representation. But this impression is largely an apparent one, as can be seen, on detailed examination, from the way of executing the upper part of the crozier, the gold brocade and the sky. In contrast to the almost defiant head of St. Peter, that of St. Ildefonso inclines forward in meditation, though no less endowed with character.

The pictorial concept that obtains in the two great canvases in the Escorial is continued without much technical variation in a series of religious paintings of rather less ambitious typology, probably works produced by El Greco as a "side line" to his commissioned works — more or less potboilers, in fact, to help him maintain his workshop, his house and his team of assistants. The *St. Sebastian* in Bucharest, now cut into an oval which we hardly think was its original form, is an image that lacks the sensuousness with which this theme was represented by some of the Renaissance painters *(Fig 218 - Cat. 194).*

In this picture El Greco, despite the personal character of his concept and technique, achieves a kind of "objectiveness" superior to that of the Italian painters. On the other hand, there is no architectural background or scenography of any kind, but only, as is the almost absolute rule in his paintings, a background of cloudy sky and the indispensable stump of a tree to which the martyr was tied to be transfixed with arrows. But the element of landscape regains considerable importance in the *Penitent Magdalen* in the Valdés Collection in Bilbao *(Fig. 219 - Cat. 195).* The hand of the master himself is quite evident in this beautiful canvas, a new version of a frequent theme in El Greco's iconography, but certain details betray the intervention of his assistants.

St. Dominic in prayer in the Cathedral of Toledo *(Fig. 220 - Cat. 196)* is an advanced replica, chronologically and in execution, of a design we have studied in Chapter IV *(Fig. 126).* We have also included in our catalogue two very beautifully executed replicas, which hang in the Contini-Bonacossi Collection

Fig. 212. The Resurrection, 1603-1607. Madrid, Prado. Cat. No. 190.

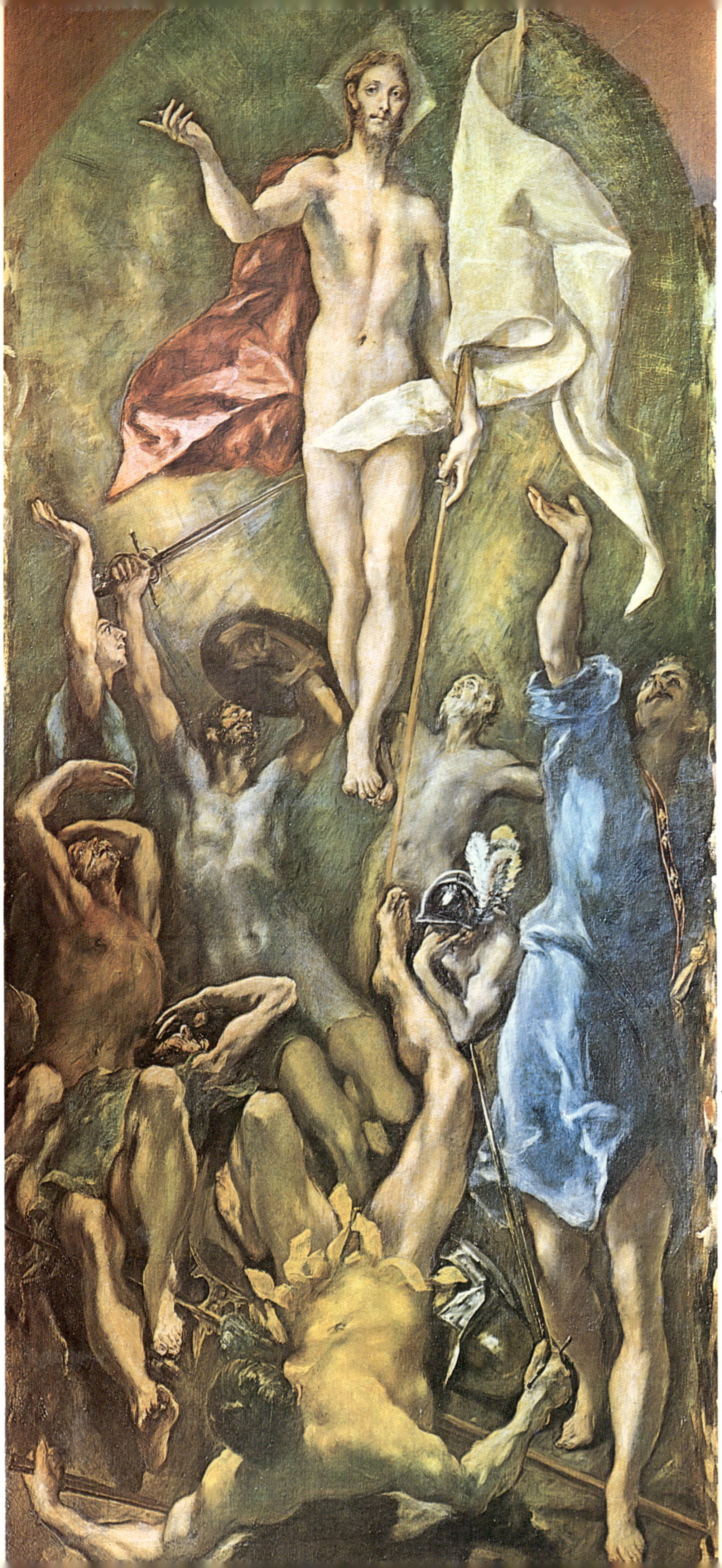

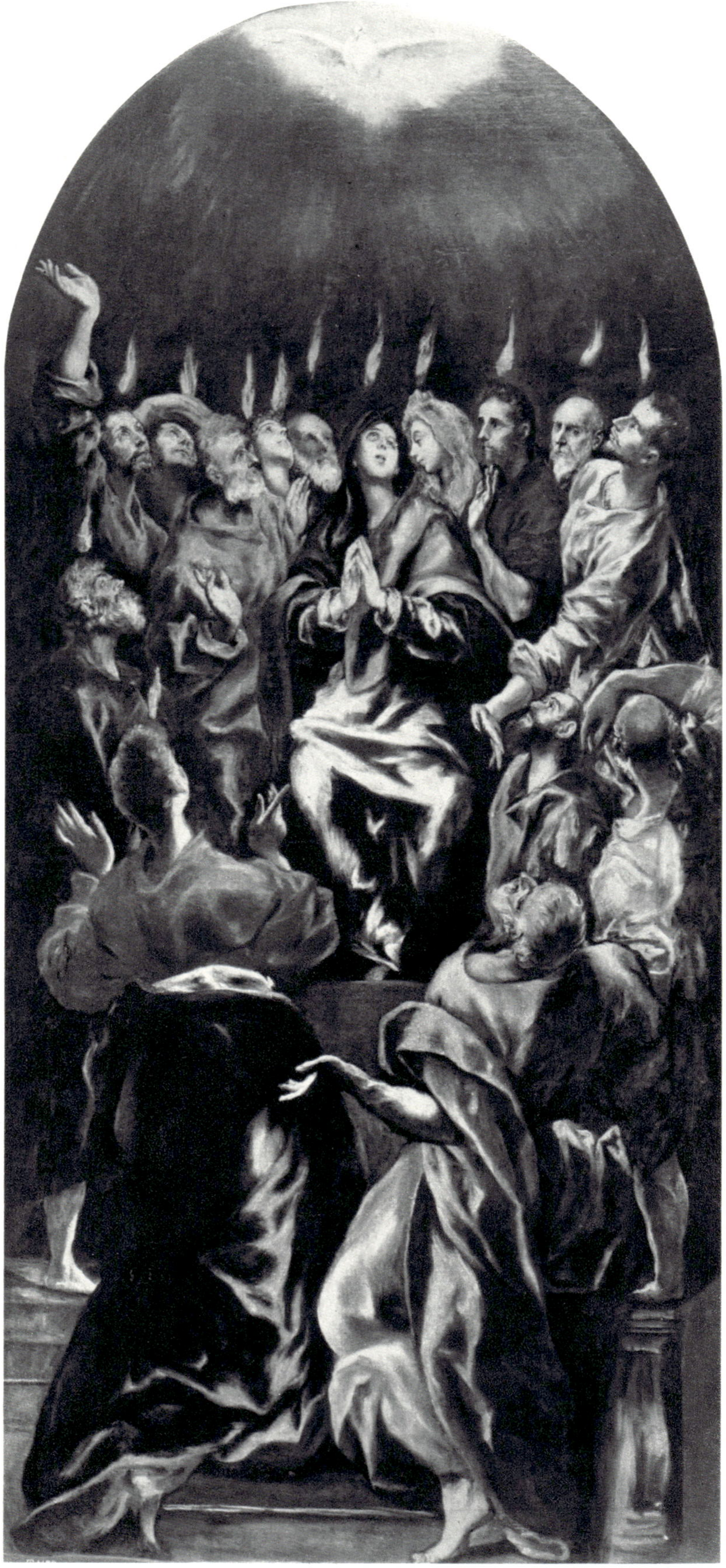

Fig. 213. Pentecost, 1603-1607. Madrid, Prado. Cat. No. 191.

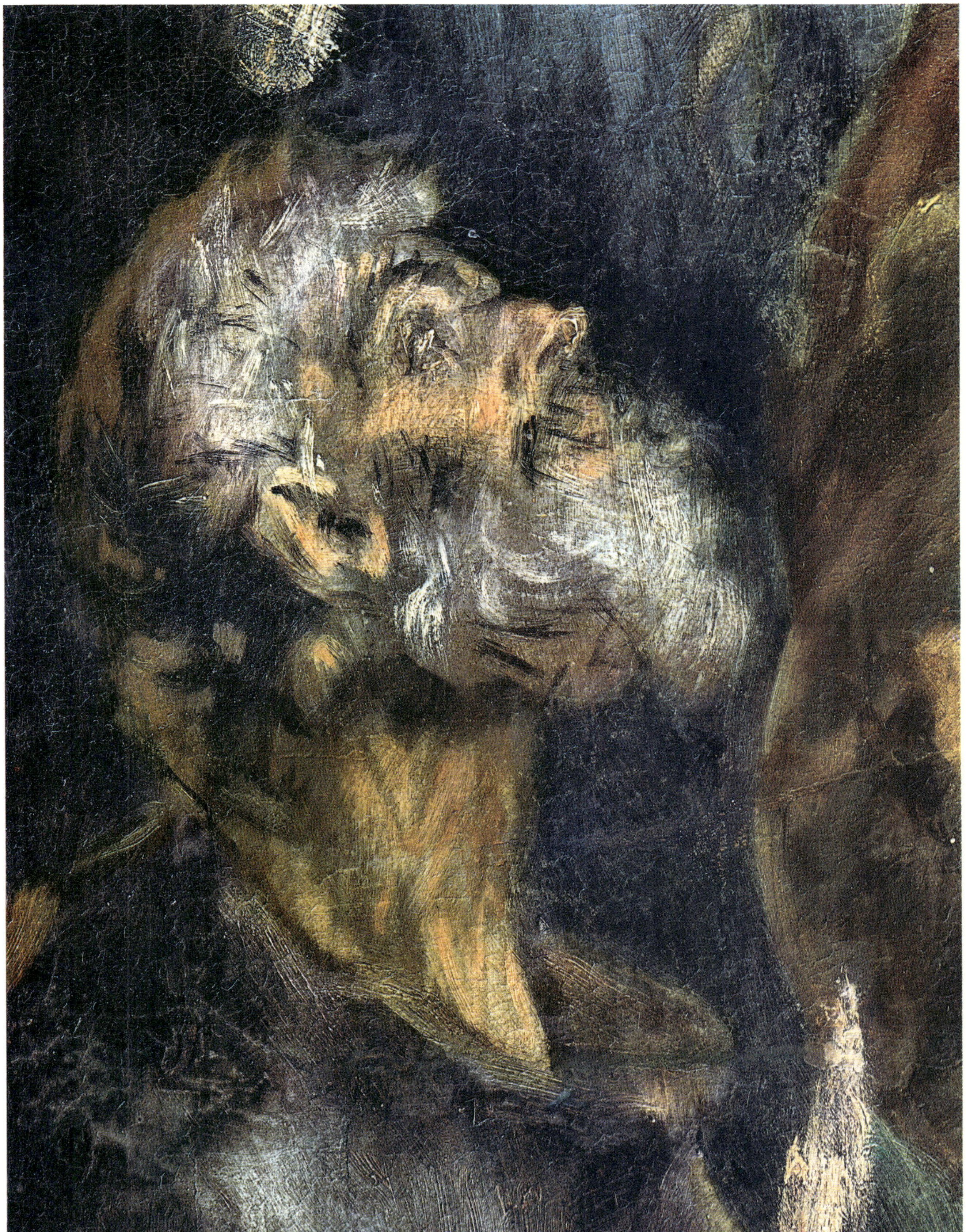

Fig. 214. Detail of figure 213.

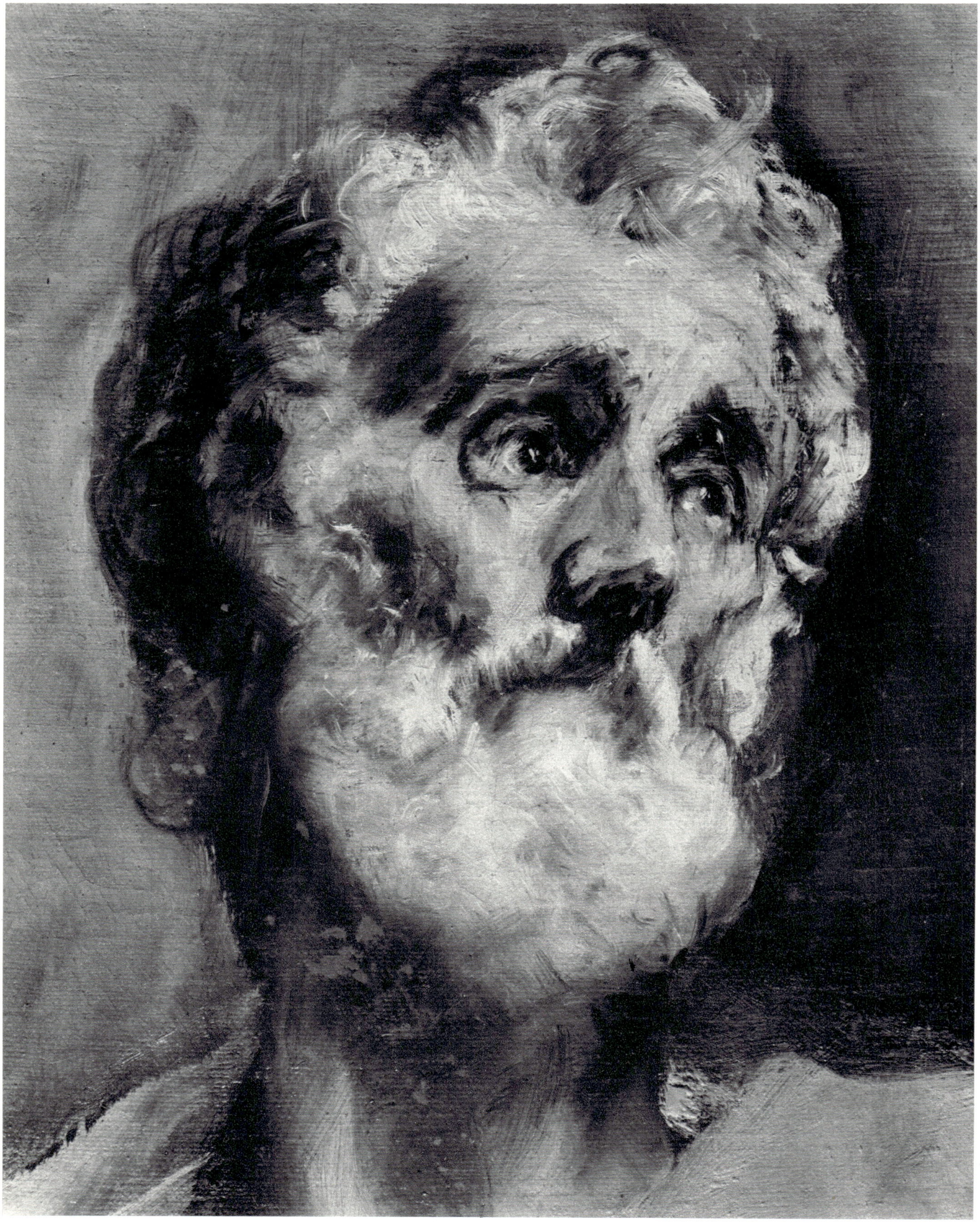

Fig. 215. Detail of figure 216.

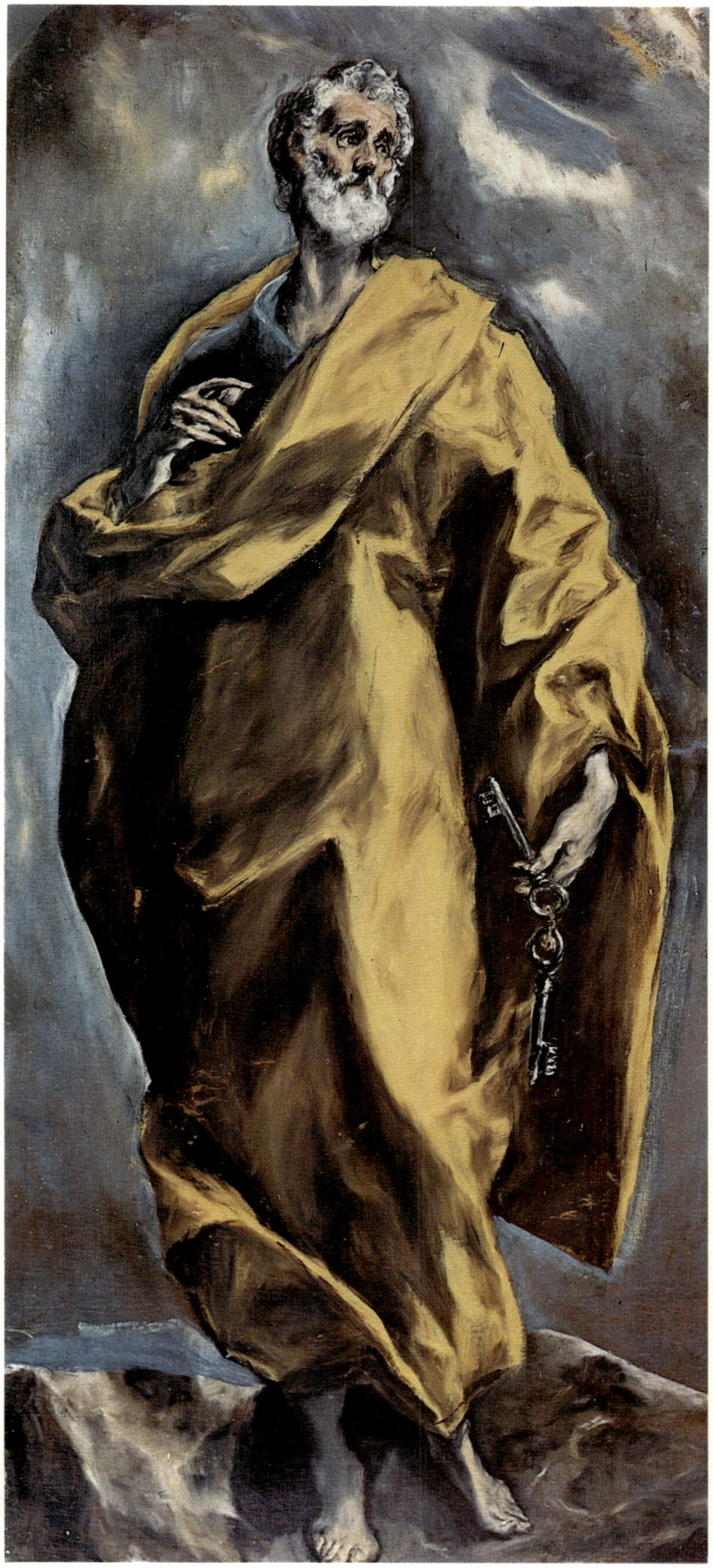

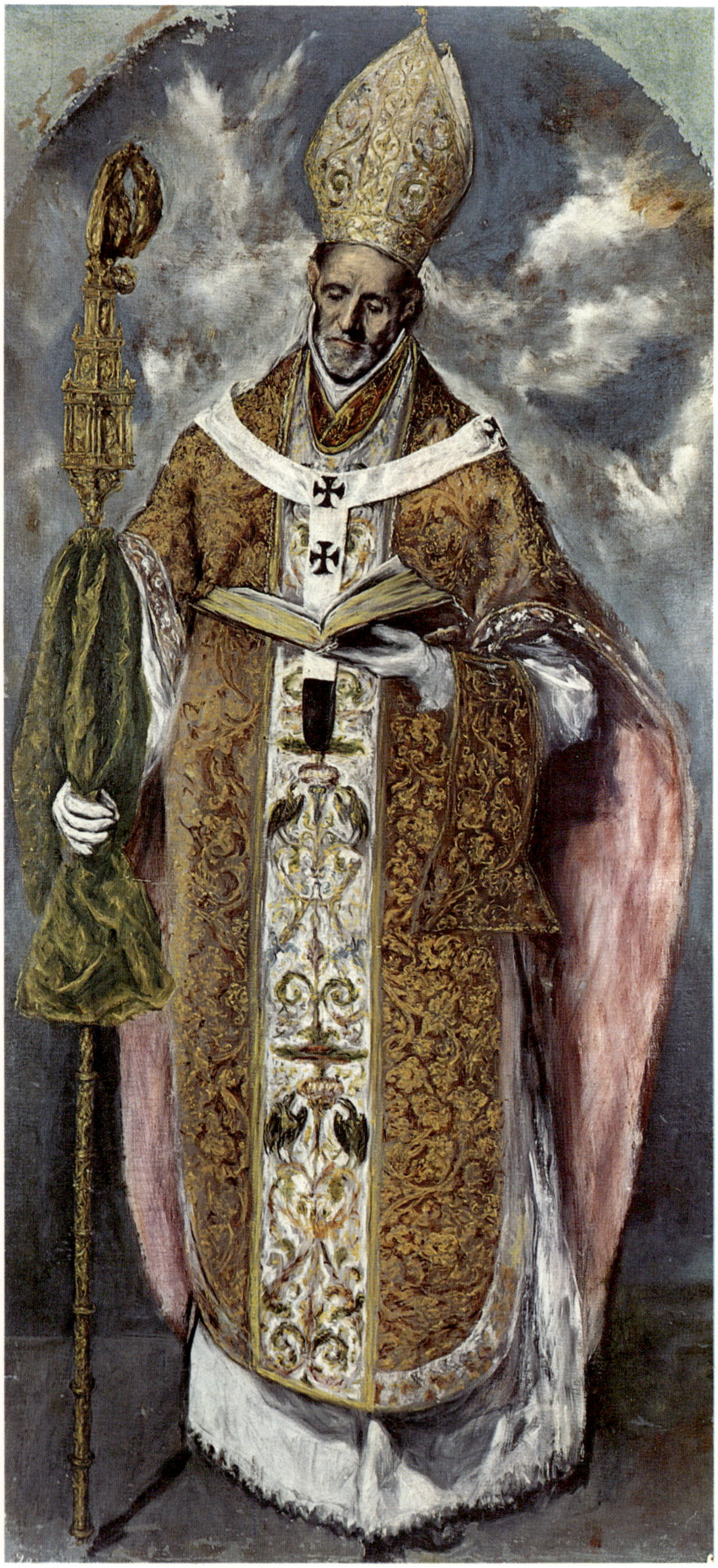

Fig. 216. St. Peter, 1603-1607. The Escorial, Monastery. Cat. No. 192.
Fig. 217. St. Ildefonso, 1603-1607. The Escorial, Monastery. Cat. No. 193.

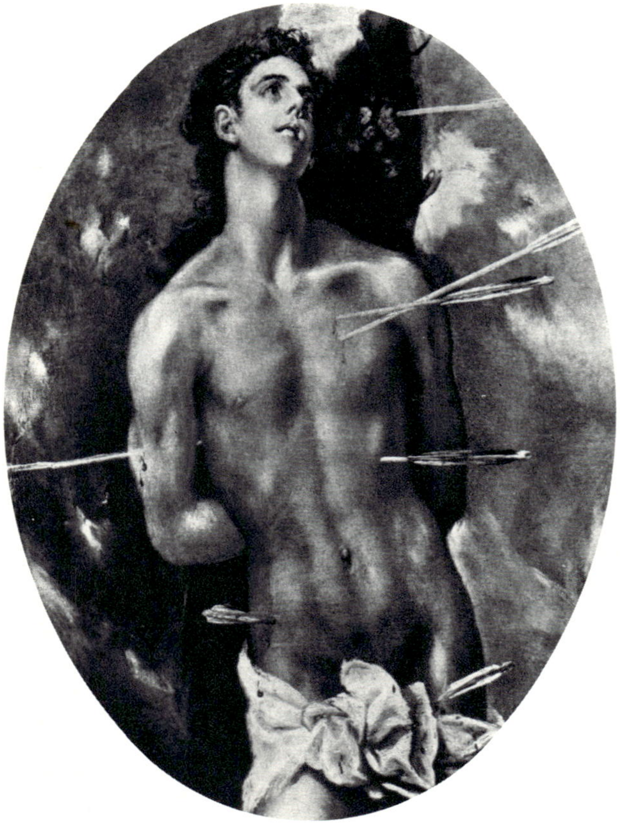
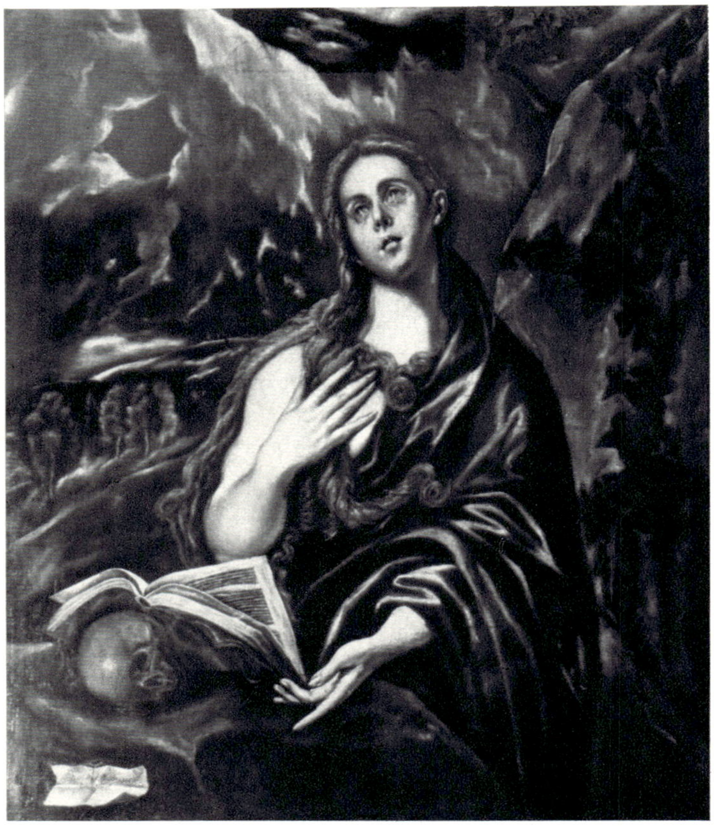
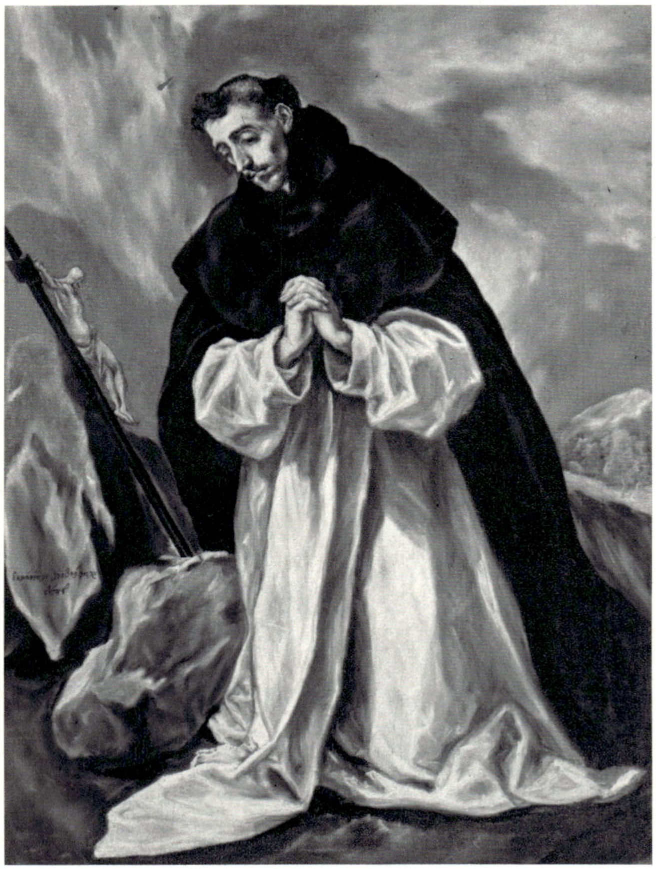
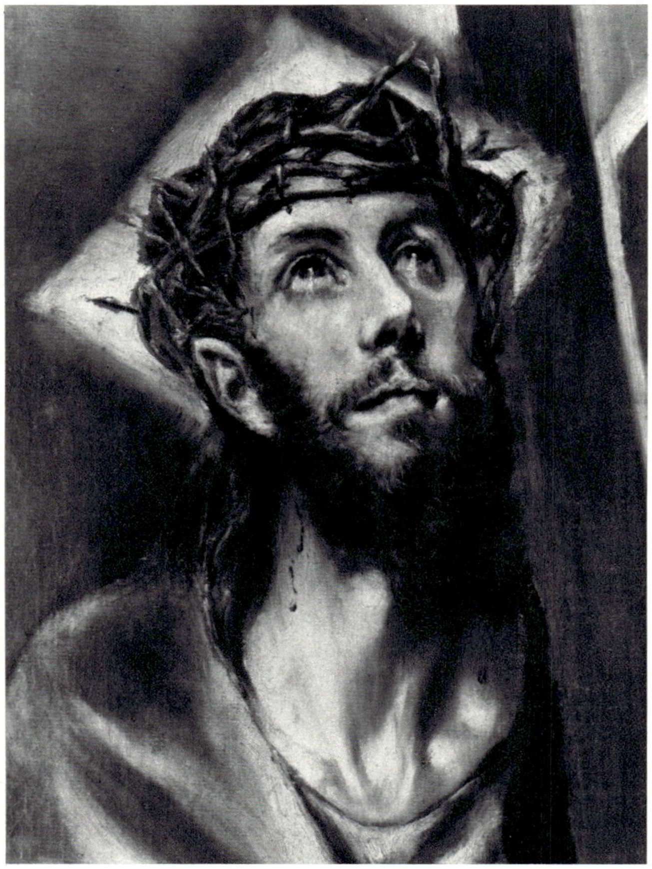

Fig. 218. St. Sebastian, 1603-1607. Bucharest, Royal Palace. Cat. No. 194.
Fig. 219. The Penitent Magdalen, 1603-1607. Bilbao, Valdés Collection. Cat. No. 195.
Fig. 220. St. Dominic in prayer, 1603-1607. Toledo, Sacristy of the Cathedral. Cat. No. 196.
Fig. 221. Christ carrying the cross, 1603-1607. Madrid, Prado. Cat. No. 199.

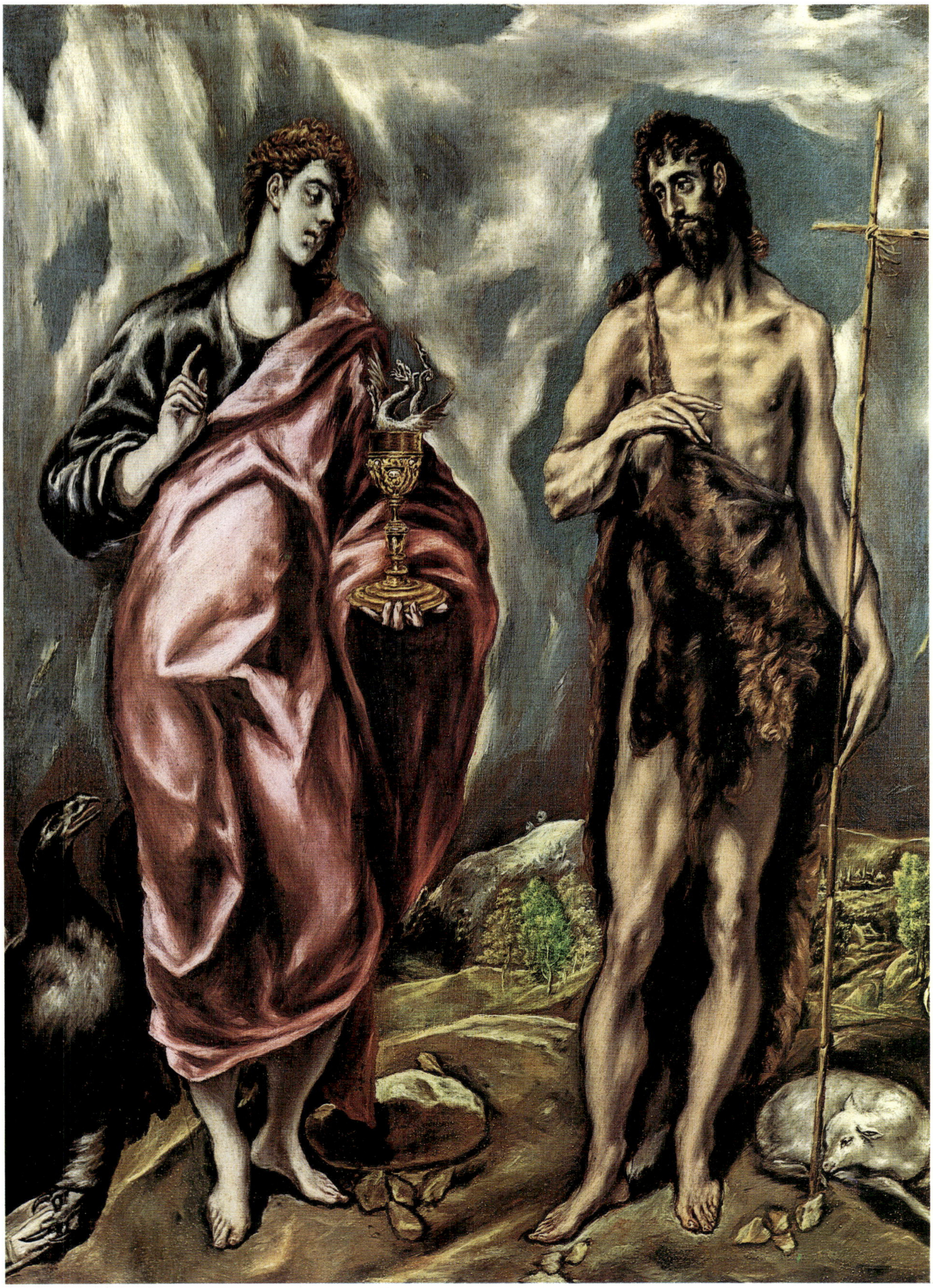

Fig. 222. St. John the Baptist and St. John the Evangelist, 1603-1607. Toledo, Santa Cruz Museum. Cat. No. 202.

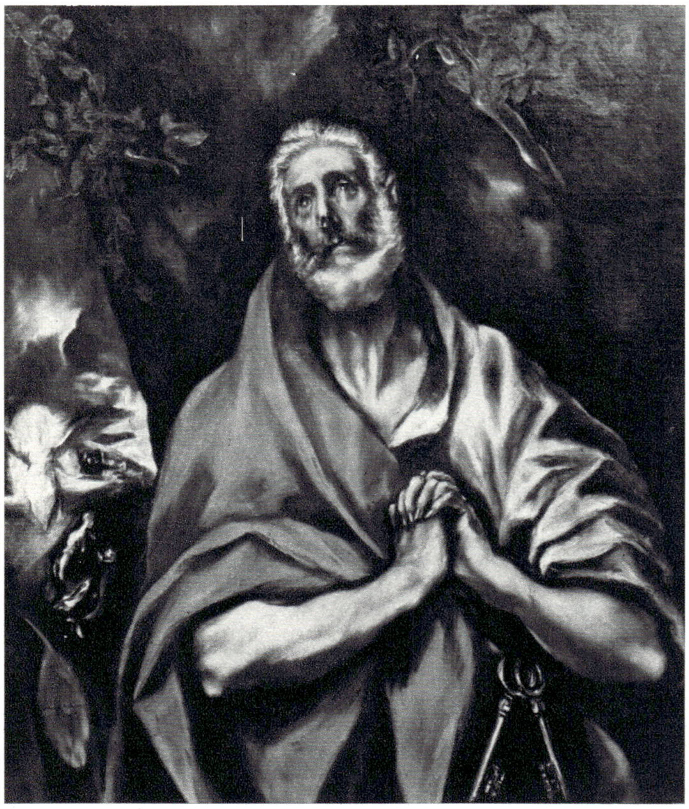

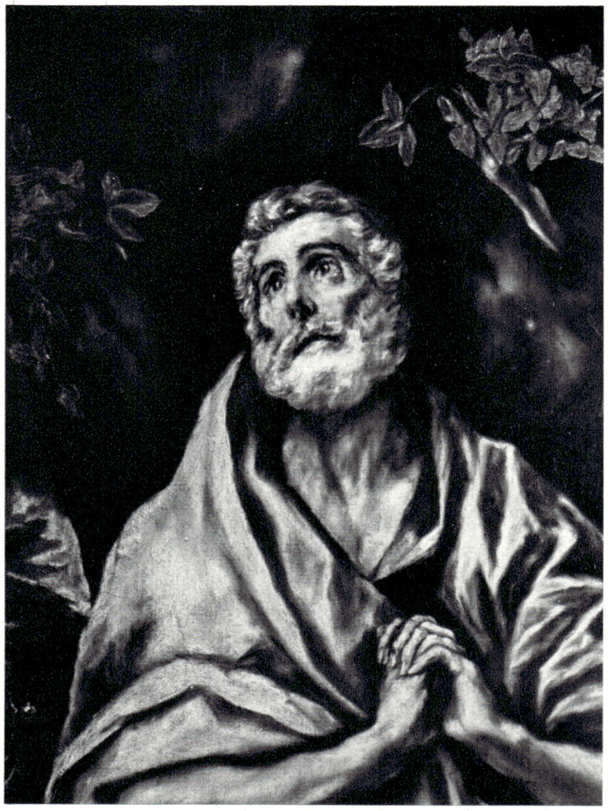

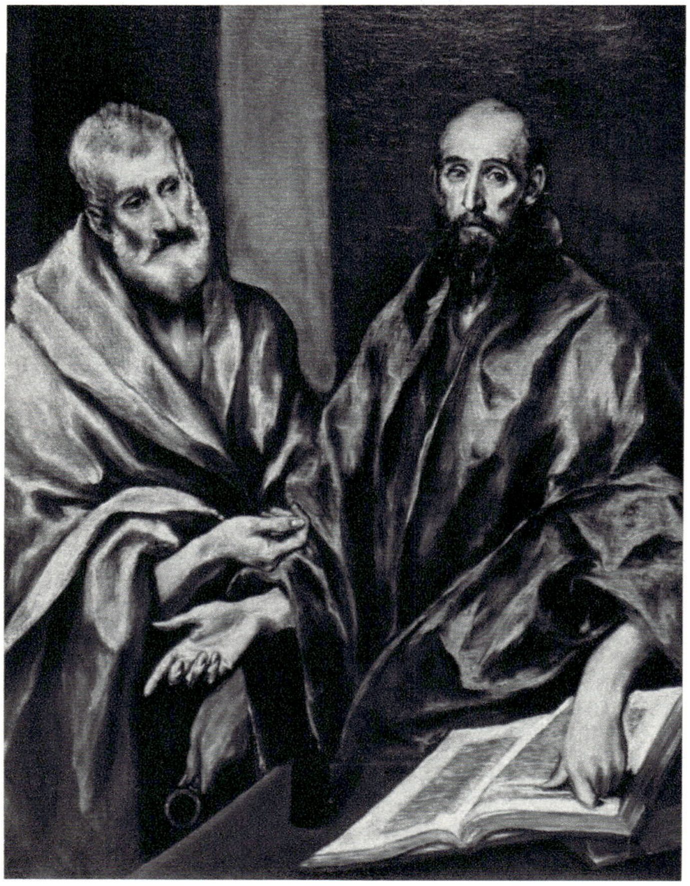

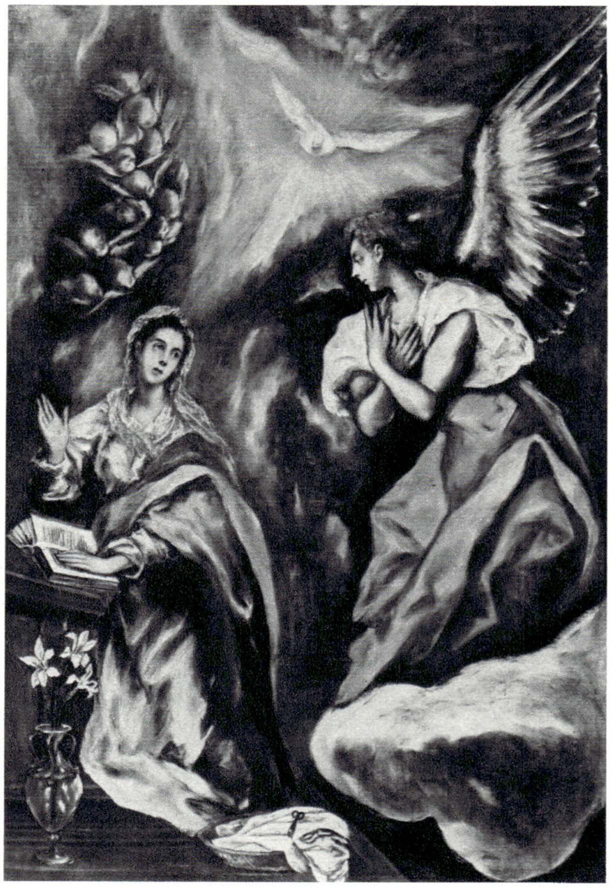

Fig. 223. St. Peter in tears, 1603-1607. Toledo, Hospital de San Juan Bautista de Afuera. Cat. No. 203.
Fig. 224. St. Peter in tears, 1603-1607. Oslo, Kunstmuseum. Cat. No. 204.
Fig. 225. St. Peter and St. Paul, 1603-1607. Stockholm, Museum. Cat. No. 207.
Fig. 226. The Annunciation, 1603-1607. Sigüenza, Cathedral. Cat. No. 208.

(Cat 197) and in the Boston Museum *(Cat 198).* A stormy sky, with intense lights and a latent dynamism, forms the background to the figure. There are minor differences of execution between the three works and minimal variations in typology; one might say that the one in the Contini-Bonacossi Collection is the most naturalistic, while that in the Boston Museum is the most dramatic. The lights are magnificently used to give a special quality to the cloth of the habit, which reflects the bluish and violet tones of the sky, its shadows creating a violent sensation of relief. Common to the three canvases is the extraordinary sensation of rhythm that is produced by the inclination of the figure, a rhythm followed by the details of the sky, which emphasizes the effect.

We believe that the period we are now studying also includes certain works derived from earlier compositions, but with variations that affect the structure, the technique and the pictorial concept. Particularly noteworthy among them is a series of canvases on the theme of *Christ carrying the cross*, all signed works painted with sensitiveness and growing emotion *(Fig. 221 - Cat. 199, 200 & 201).* Another notable work is the elegant image of *St. John the Baptist and St. John the Evangelist (Fig. 222 - Cat. 202)*, the Baptist being identical with the figure in the painting in the De Young Museum in San Francisco *(Fig. 178).*

The pathetic image of *St. Peter in tears* also reappears in canvases of the period now under consideration. The two most outstanding are the one in the Hospital de San Juan Bautista de Afuera in Toledo *(Fig. 223 - Cat. 203)* and the one in the Oslo Kunstmuseum *(Fig. 224 - Cat. 204).* According to Wethey, this is one of El Greco's absolutely original iconographical themes, never previously used and created as an image of repentance and a symbol of confession. To repeat and emphasize the meaning of the theme the painter introduced, as López Rey has observed, the figure of Mary Magdalen in the distance, which appears according to the Mannerist formula of the contrast of figures by their size. The canvas in the Hospital shows a greater resemblance to the earlier version than does that in Oslo, in which the striking head foreshadows other images of the painter's last period. Both paintings have those astonishing lights and that special treatment of the draperies that are characteristic of the later work of the artist, ever more interested in pure plastic values. Another signed replica of an old design *(Fig. 128)* is the *St. Peter and St. Paul* in the Museum of Stockholm *(Fig. 225 - Cat. 207).* This seems to be the closest version to Diego de Astor's engraving, signed in 1608, which we shall be studying in the last chapter of this book *(Fig. 348).*

The *Annunciation* in the Cathedral of Sigüenza *(Fig. 226 - Cat. 208)* is a highly emotional painting and one that evidently derives from the one already studied which hangs in the Museum of Toledo (Ohio) *(Fig. 174).* This theme was certainly one of El Greco's favourites; the mystical implications of the dialogue between the Virgin and the archangel, under the symbol of the Holy Ghost and its light, would be enough to impel the painter to major or minor renovations of the subject, with audacities of colour and form which are simply the passionate manifestation of his lyricism. We must repeat once again that in El Greco there is undoubtedly a double personality: on the one hand, the mystic who expresses himself with his brush; on the other, the reflective artist, conscious of his own daring and very mindful of his origins. In its extreme form, the daring is always a manifestation of his fear of anonymity and of the mediocrity of mere craftsmanship. In his repetitions of themes, such as this *Annunciation*, we may see the painter's amazing facility and the way in which he modifies the composition without going too far from what he had painted previously. The distortion and the treatment of canvases as forms valid in themselves are both present here. But the purity of the Virgin's face is something quite apart from all change, although the semi-transparent veil that covers her head and shoulders is like a froth of dissolving forms.

In this later period we find new interpretations of the theme of the *Agony in the garden.* One of them, in the Valdés Collection in Bilbao *(Fig. 227 - Cat. 209)*, repeats the original model *(Fig. 186)* without great change. In others, which hang in the Cathedral of Cuenca *(Fig. 228 - Cat. 212)* and in the Museum of Buenos Aires *(Cat. 213)*, the scheme of the composition is varied. The group of sleeping apostles is brought into the foreground, just below the figure of Christ praying before the angel who is offering the cup of bitterness. On the right we see the line of soldiers and executioners led by Judas. The landscape elements are rather indications than truly naturalistic representations and the light, playing with the vivid colours, creates an atmosphere we might describe as schematic. The ample folds play an important role, as in all the painter's works, especially those of his later periods. Analysis of the details reveals great freeshness of execution within a more compressed space. The figure of Christ is more pathetic in the Cuenca canvas; the angel is an arresting figure, especially in the work at Andújar. Other versions of this theme, carried out in El Greco's workshop, repeat the same composition in different sizes.

Despite El Greco's ideas regarding the independence of art and artists, it is very probable that he sometimes had to envisage the possibility of concessions, even if only by way of experiment. This would explain the appearance in his Franciscan series of certain works which are unquestionably authentic but entirely anomalous. In some of these canvases the hand of another painter is very evident. The most notable case is that of a last representation of the kneeling figures of *St. Francis and the lay brother* praying in a cave, a work housed in the Buhler Collection in Zurich *(Fig. 230 - Cat. 214)*. This painting is a unique version, in the sense that there are no known replicas or copies. It is a painting of great quality, impressive in its intimate grandeur. Its existence was revealed some years ago, and it was then attributed to an early date in the painter's career, the radical variation of the pictorial concept being explained as an attempt by El Greco to approach the style of the Escorial painters. After considering this question, we are of the opinion that this work is later than 1605. Its quality is soft, the textures smooth and regular, the forms closed in. A similar technique may be seen in one of the best versions of the *St. Francis and the lay brother*, the one in the Prado *(Fig. 231 - Cat. 215)*. In drawing and composition, typology and chromatic range, this work is not very different from the group of canvases on the same theme studied in the previous chapter. But there is a radical change in the quality of the clothing, i.e., in the representation of its texture, which extends even to the paint itself and, therefore, to the textures of the rest of the work. The whole is more gently worked. The loose, harsh qualities and fur-like textures disappear and the cloth is represented as being lighter and softer, more supply fitted to the bodies. With this lessening of the free force of the impasto, greater importance is given to the surfaces and also to the lines of drawing, especially in the outlines. The tonal relationships however, are hardly varied, though the way in which the draperies react is different.

To explain the existence of these two paintings, the execution of which is not exactly that of El Greco, but which are of great quality in comparison with what we usually find in even the better workshop copies, we would suggest the following hypothesis: recalling that Luis Tristán (1586-1624) worked in El Greco's team from 1603 to 1607, it is possible that the surprising execution of the two works —anomalous in El Greco's own production, but excellent— was the result of an act of indulgence to his assistant on the part of the master and at the same time an experiment in the transformation of both models. If this were so, the two painters would have been collaborating in an attempt to find a style that would suit the popular taste mentioned above. Whether this was the case or not, it is undeniable that El Greco played a considerable part in both paintings; we have only to see the head of St. Francis in the first canvas to realize that the execution is the work of the same painter who did the admirable head —also in profile— in the picture in the De Young Museum. We think, therefore, that these works should not be relegated to the ranks of the workshop copies, but rather maintained among the authentic works, even admitting the influence or collaboration —both equally hypothetical— of Tristán. For there might always have been some unknown factor that led to this change. We are, after all, attempting to reconstruct an artistic career that is full of uncertainties, in a life that is shrouded in obscurity, and for this reason we do not think we should suppress any acceptable hypotheses, however rash they may seem.

We might find corroboration of our hypothesis in the existence of a version of the *Agony in the garden* —in the National Gallery in London— which is undoubtedly disconcerting. We realize that what we are about to say will be unacceptable for those critics who still refuse to admit that the ultimate secret of stylistic analysis is to be found in a profound study of the execution, the painter's "handwriting". In this painting, in effect, the artist —very gifted and quite capable of achieving a complete imitation of El Greco's formula— produced a work that is exactly the same as El Greco's as regards light, colour, form and drawing. The excellence of the painting is such that it could not have been executed by an anonymous workshop assistant, which is why we believe that it was done by Luis Tristán, this time without the least assistance from El Greco, for the execution is totally different and one

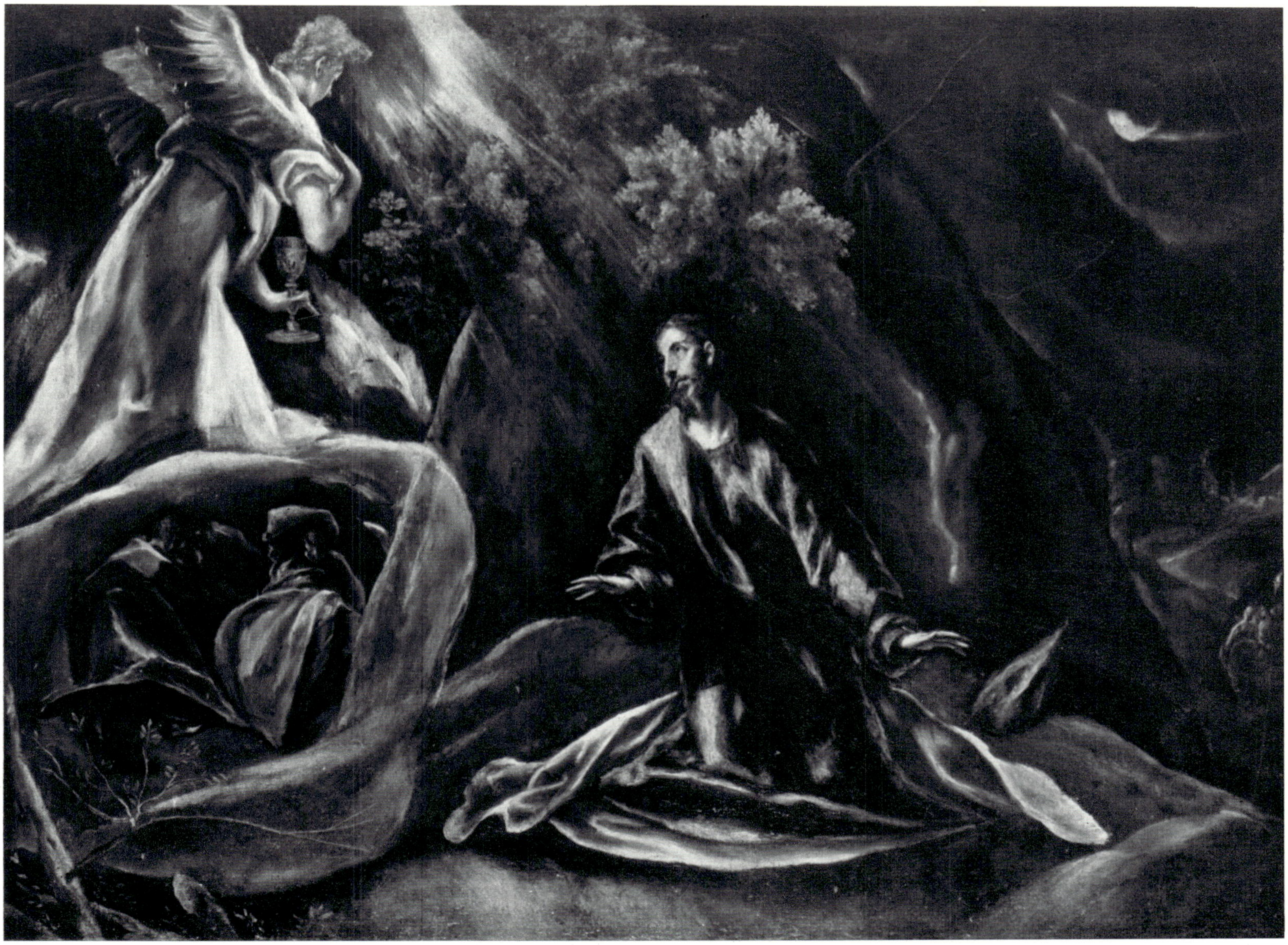

Fig. 227. The Agony in the garden, 1603-1607. Bilbao, Valdés Collection. Cat. No. 209.

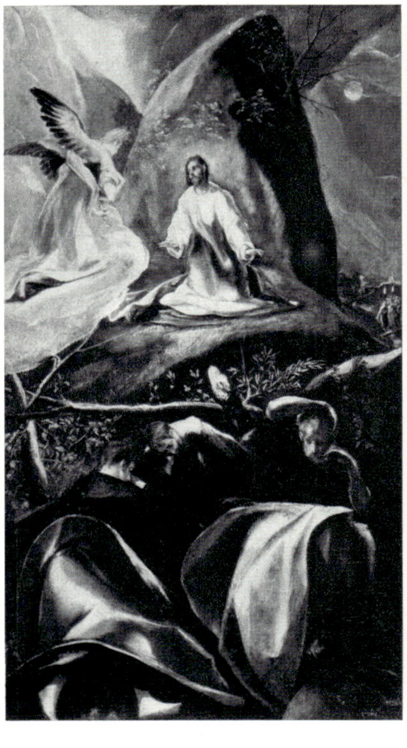

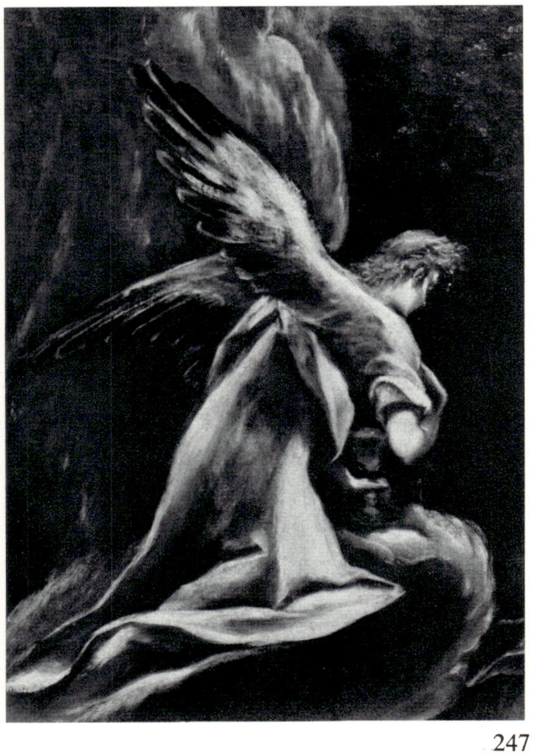

Fig. 228. The Agony in the garden, 1603-1607. Cuenca, Cathedral. Cat. No. 210.

Fig. 229. The Agony in the garden, 1603-1607. Andújar, Santa María. Cat. No. 211.

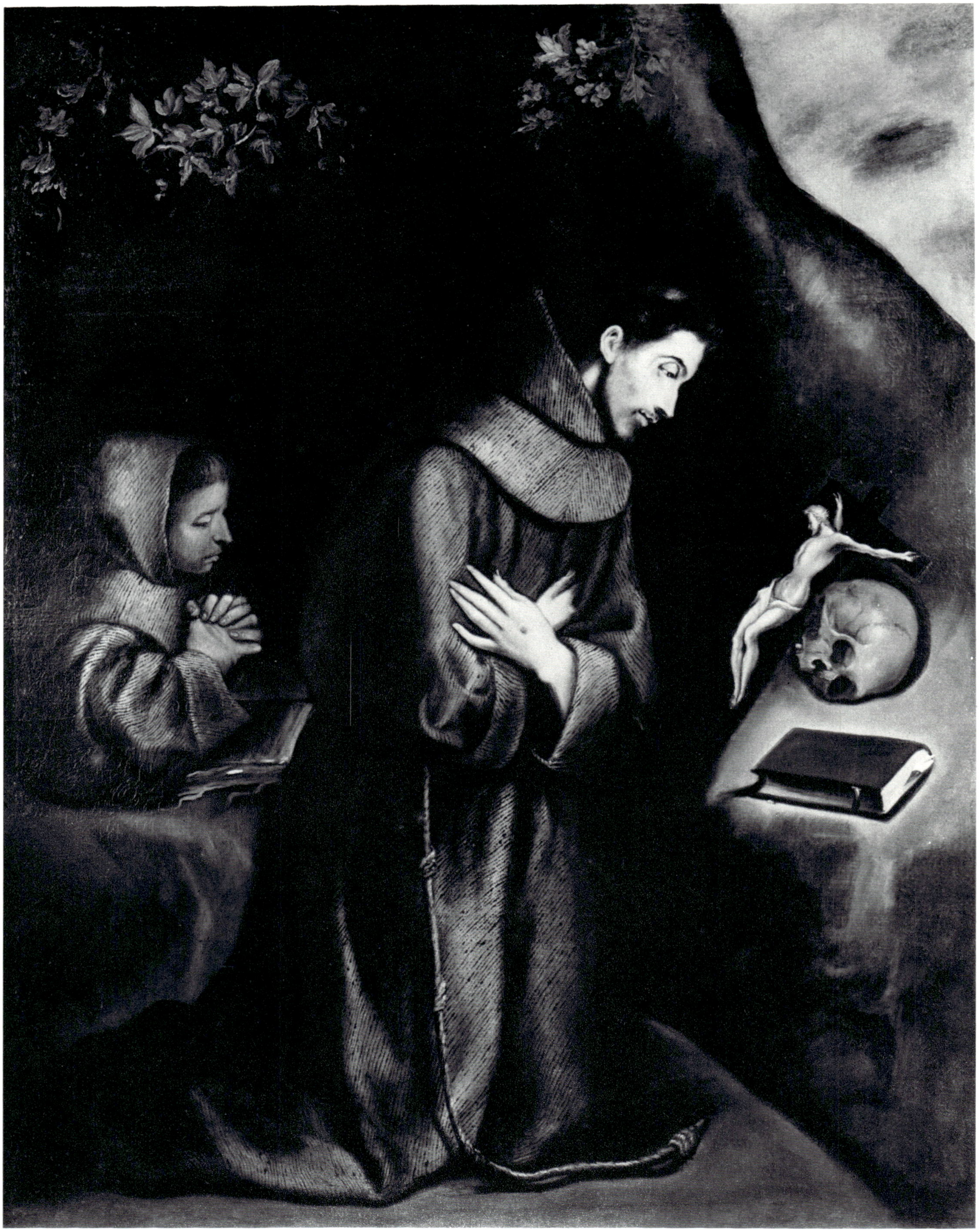

Fig. 230. St. Francis and the lay brother, 1603-1607. Zurich, Buhler Collection. Cat. No. 214.

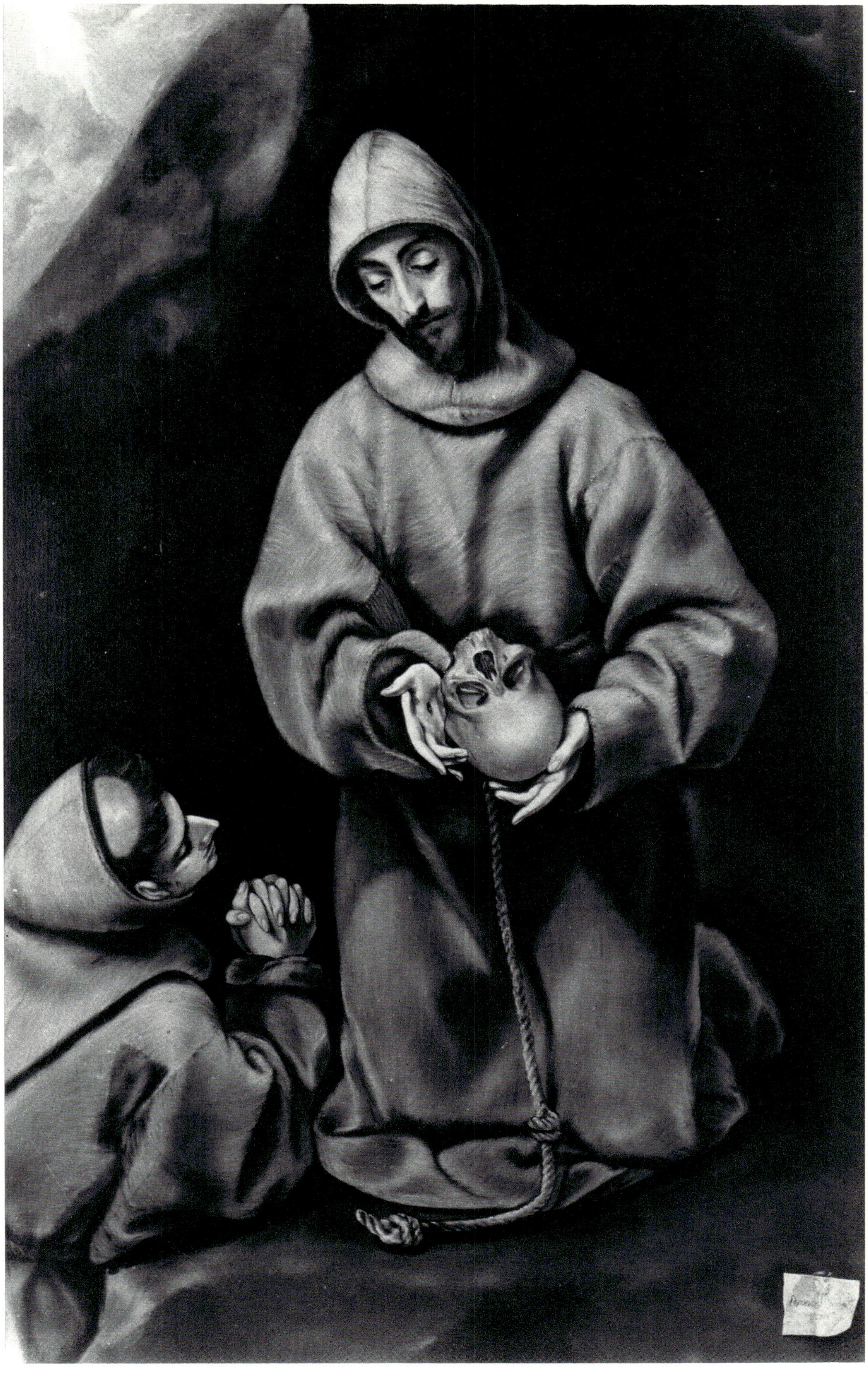

Fig. 231. St. Francis and the lay brother, 1603-1607. Madrid, Prado. Cat. No. 215.

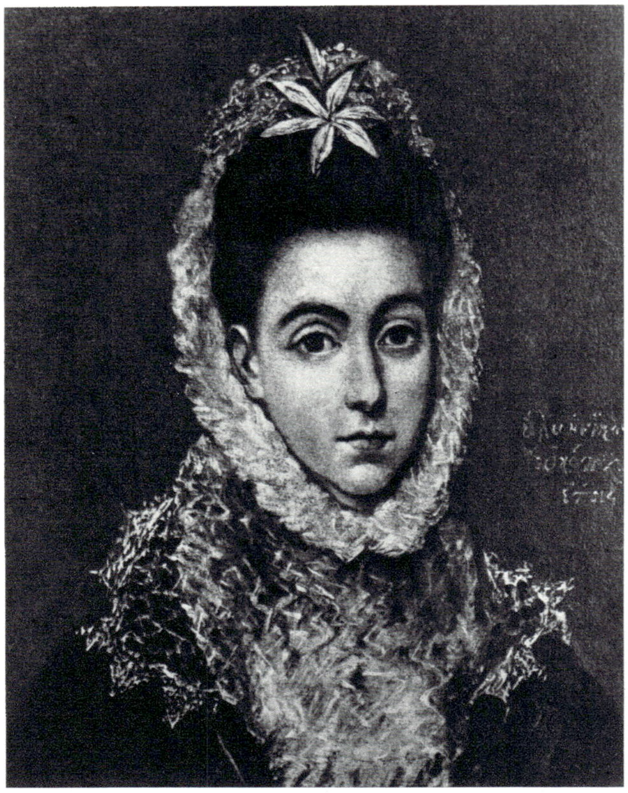

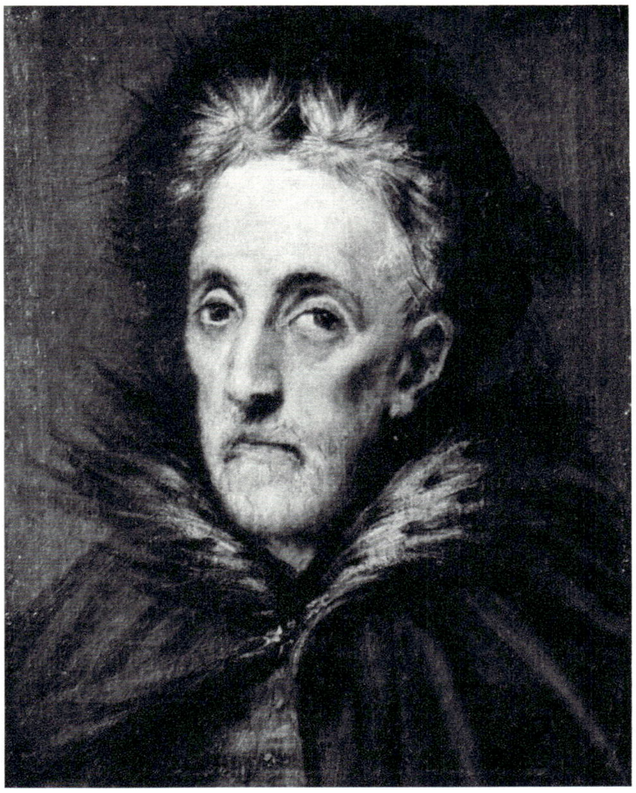

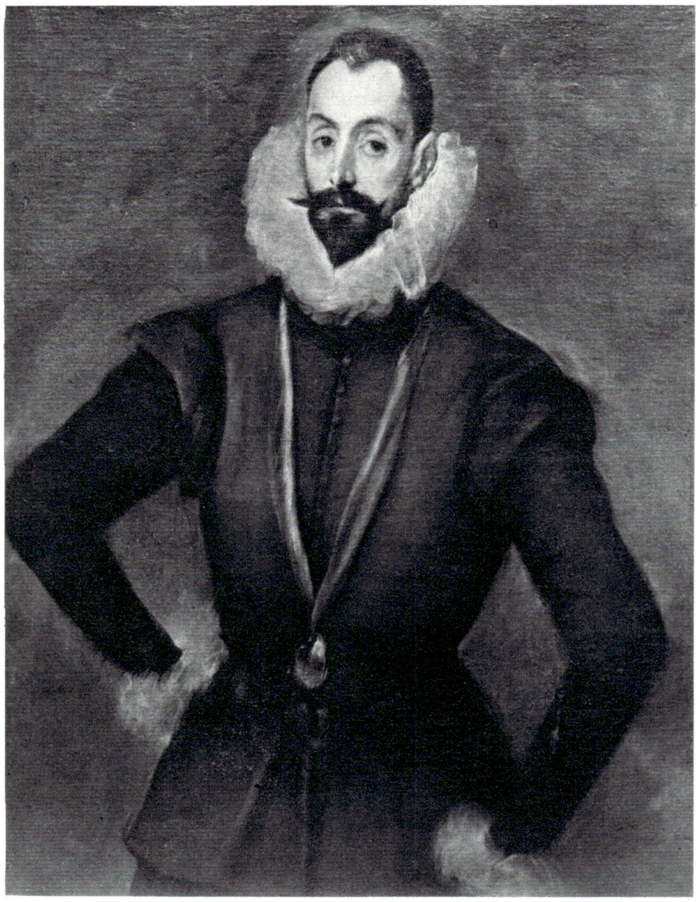

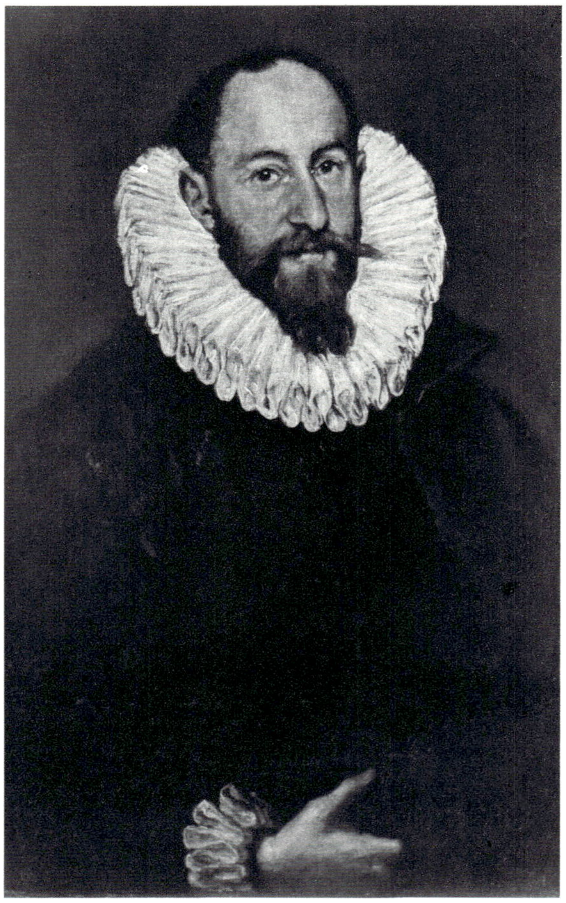

Fig. 232. Lady with a flower in her hair, 1603-1607. London, Viscount Rothermere Collection. Cat. No. 216.
Fig. 233. Portrait of an old man, 1603-1607. Florence, Contini-Bonacossi Collection. Cat. No. 217.
Fig. 234. Portrait of a gentleman, 1603-1607. Milan, private collection. Cat. No. 218.
Fig. 235. Portrait of an unknown gentleman, 1603-1607. Glasgow, Maxwell MacDonald Collection. Cat. No. 219.

can see that the hand that painted it could not have been that of the creator of the *Burial of the Conde de Orgaz*, though in all other respects it comes as near to his work as possible.

Portraits

The *Lady with a flower in her hair* in Lord Rothermere's Collection in London *(Fig. 232 - Cat. 216)* has been hypothetically identified as Alfonsa de los Morales, Jorge Manuel's first wife, on account of her apparent resemblance to the lady who appears in the *Family of Jorge Manuel*, which is studied in our last chapter among the paintings attributed to El Greco's son. If this were true, the date of this portrait, which is undoubtedly an authentic Greco, would be that of the wedding of the young couple, which, as we have said, probably took place around 1603. The sitter is a typical Castilian with a sweet, oval face, who poses with a certain indifference. Noteworthy in this portrait is the bold treatment of the fichu on the lady's head, with the flower of the title, and over her shoulders. It is a notation of zigzag lines with a rhythm that is very lively, though neither heavy nor intense, and of great originality, producing, by contrast, a heightening of the very different qualities of the flesh tints, the black hair, the dress and the neutral background, all at once. It is not a very brilliant or showy work, but one of great technical interest.

A *Portrait of an old man,* of the same date or very near it, has been supposed to be that of Manoussos, the painter's brother, who, as we have said, arrived in Toledo during the period we are studying *(Fig. 233 - Cat. 217).* Wethey does not agree with the attribution of this work to El Greco, but we believe it to be authentic, for its technique is in no way unworthy of the principles we have been setting forth, combining textural characteristics to be found in the portrait of the lady with the open brushwork of the portrait of Antonio de Covarrubias, a work which it even resembles to some extent from the psychological point of view. But it is done more quickly, almost like a sketch, though full of personality and human truth.

Then there is a *Portrait of a gentleman*, painted rather more than half-length (its present whereabouts being unknown), a work we had occasion to study directly some years ago in the Museum of Minneapolis *(Fig. 234 - Cat. 218).* It, too, seems unfinished and is not in a good state of preservation, which explains the reticence of some historians. We believe, however, that it is by El Greco and painted, moreover, during this period. There is a skill in the very simplification that even one of his closest collaborators would hardly have been able to achieve. The hands are not seen, being concealed by the evanescent cuffs. The face is typical of El Greco in typology and treatment. The suit, as one might imagine, is the most summarily executed part of the portrait.

Finally we come to another *Portrait of an unknown gentleman*, now in Pollok House, Glasgow *(Fig. 235 - Cat. 219),* a work which, unlike the preceding one, is perfectly finished and clearly realistic in intention. The sitter looks out at the viewer frankly, his right hand at his belt. His head, that of a mature man, but not an old one, stands out against his complicated ruff, the goffering of which follows that of the visible cuff. His suit is black, as usual. Just one more of those gentlemen who formed the Spain El Greco saw and succeeded in capturing for ever with his magic brushes, as skilful when he applied them to representing details of material as when he used them to make the same material disintegrate into dazzling effects of light, to give the best possible idea of the supernatural world.

VII

1608 - 1614

THE CHAPEL OF ISABEL OBALLE — THE ALTARPIECES OF THE HOSPITAL TAVERA — THE *LAOCOÖN* — *VIEW AND PLAN OF TOLEDO* — PAINTINGS OF THE LAST PERIOD — PORTRAITS.

We shall begin this closing stage in the life of El Greco by studying the pictures painted for the chapel founded by Isabel Oballe in the Church of San Vicente in Toledo. The municipal authorities commissioned El Greco to finish the altarpiece and general adornment of this chapel, begun some years before by the painter Alejandro Semyno, who died before he had properly begun. One of the members of the executive commission was Dr. Gregorio Angulo, that faithful friend and protector of El Greco who has been so frequently mentioned in this book. According to the text of the municipal decision, which figures in the minutes for December 12th 1607, it was decided to carry out a radical modification of the architectural proportions of the altarpiece already under construction, adding "four and a half feet of structure, which is over a fifth of the whole work: and thus today the structure is perfect in form and not stunted, which is the worst fault that can be found with any kind of form". An expression which faithfully reflects El Greco's own aesthetic criterion with regard to proportions and his aversion to anything on a petty scale. Alejandro Semyno had contracted to do a pictorial mural decoration, probably in tempera. But El Greco "shall do the whole in oil paints ..." and "an account of the Visitation of St. Elizabeth is to be added on the ceiling ...", "in the same way as in Illescas", since "the said Alejandro confined himself to painting some trifles on plaster, which was very ordinary and unimpressive". It was therefore agreed that, in accordance with the provisions laid down, "the said altarpiece be entrusted to the said Dominico Greco. And that in the deed signed to this effect by the said Dominico Greco he shall undertake that all the work to be done with a brush shall be done by his own hand and no other". The price agreed upon was 1,200 escudos, but this was to include the 400 escudos already received by the late Alejandro, which El Greco himself was left to recover from the guarantors. The work was to be finished in eight months as from the signing of the contract. At the end of the municipal minutes we read: "... holding Dominico Greco to be one of the most outstanding men in this art that exist in the Kingdom or outside it".

The definitive contract with the painter has not been found, but the work was carried out according to the conditions laid down in the Municipal Agreement. The carved altarpiece, which is really just a gilded frame for a large canvas depicting the *Immaculate Conception (Figs. 237, 238 & 240 - Cat. 220)*, still stood until recently in the Oballe Chapel of the church of San Vicente in Toledo, but is now in the Santa Cruz Museum of that city. The circular canvas showing the *Visitation*, painted to decorate the dome of the chapel, as we have seen in the minutes we have transcribed *(Fig. 231 - Cat. 221)*, left Spain years ago and now hangs in Dumbarton Oaks in Washington. Apparently the painter punctually honoured his commitments, as did the authorities of the city of Toledo.

In our opinion Wethey is right in identifying the theme of the altarpiece from the Oballe Chapel as a representation of the Immaculate Conception. The allegories and attributes usually accompanying such images appear in the lower part of the canvas against a desolate landscape background of Toledo, beside the superb bouquet of roses and white lilies that forms the starting-point for the wonderful spiral of angels and seraphim surrounding the Virgin. The composition tends to fill the space in the foreground as completely as possible. Some of the figures freely invade the space of others with a total lack of concern for the third dimension. The proportions have no fixed canon and the expressive feeling constantly alters the form.

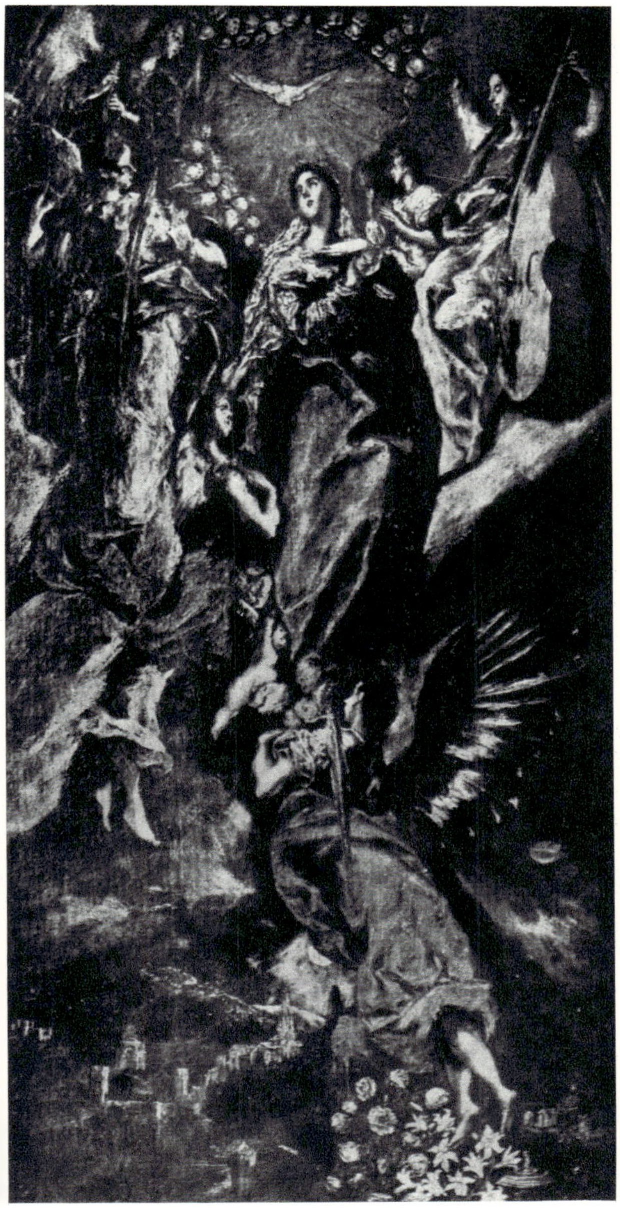

Fig. 236. The Immaculate Conception, 1607. Present whereabouts unknown. Cat. No. 222.

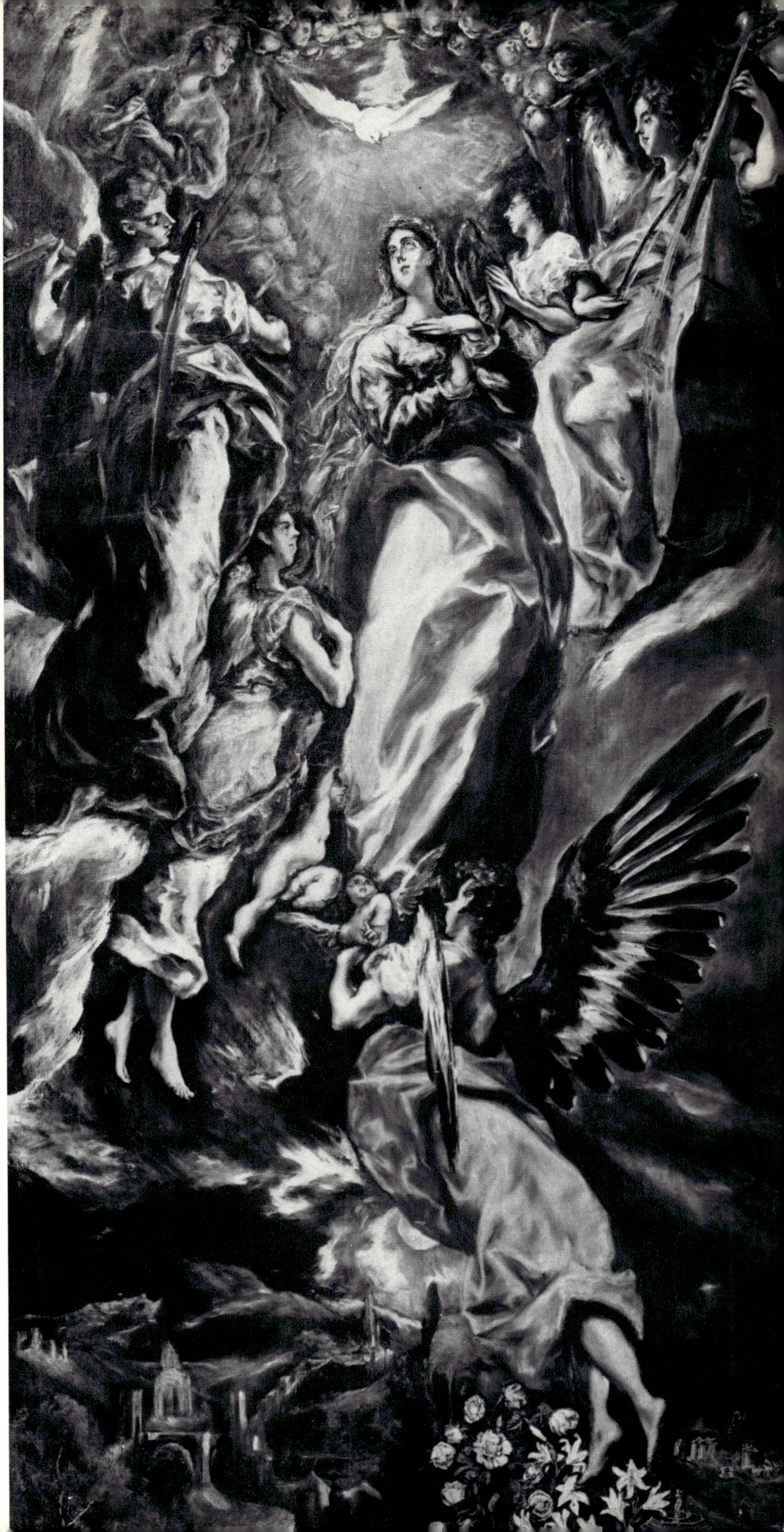

Fig. 237. The Immaculate Conception, 1607. Toledo, Santa Cruz Museum. Cat. No. 220.

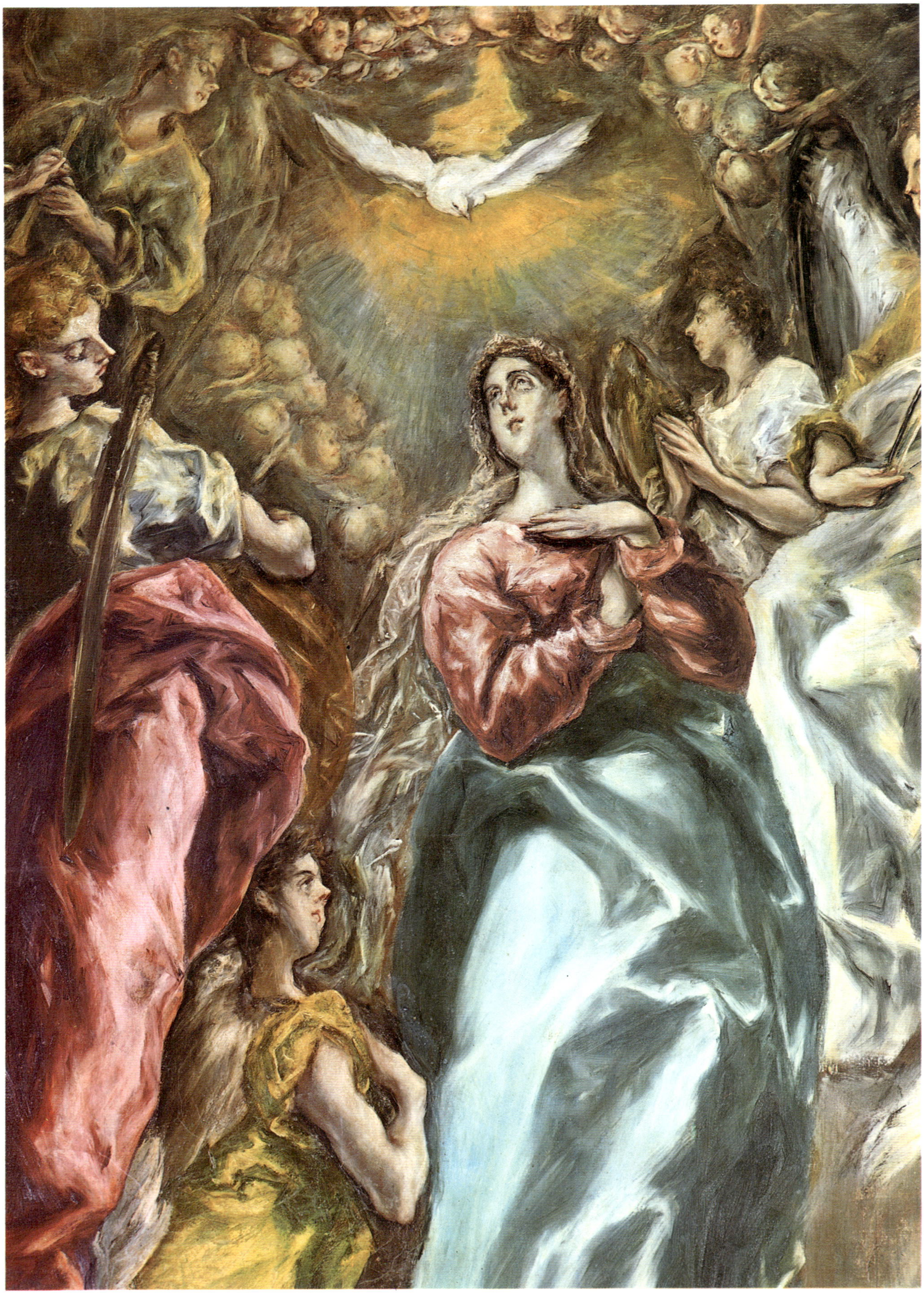

Fig. 238. Detail of figure 237.

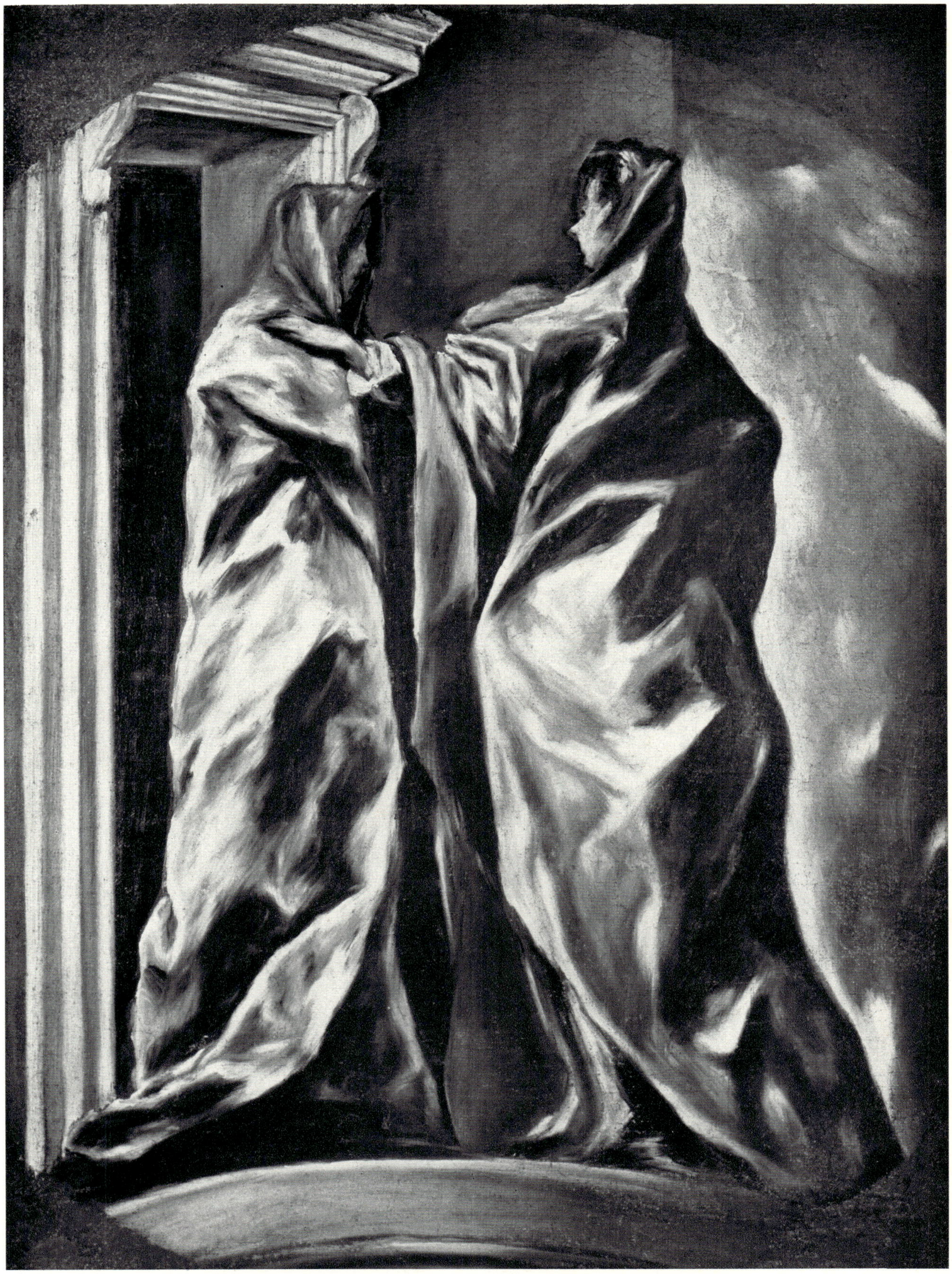

Fig. 239. The Visitation, 1607. Washington, Dumbarton Oaks. Cat. No. 221.

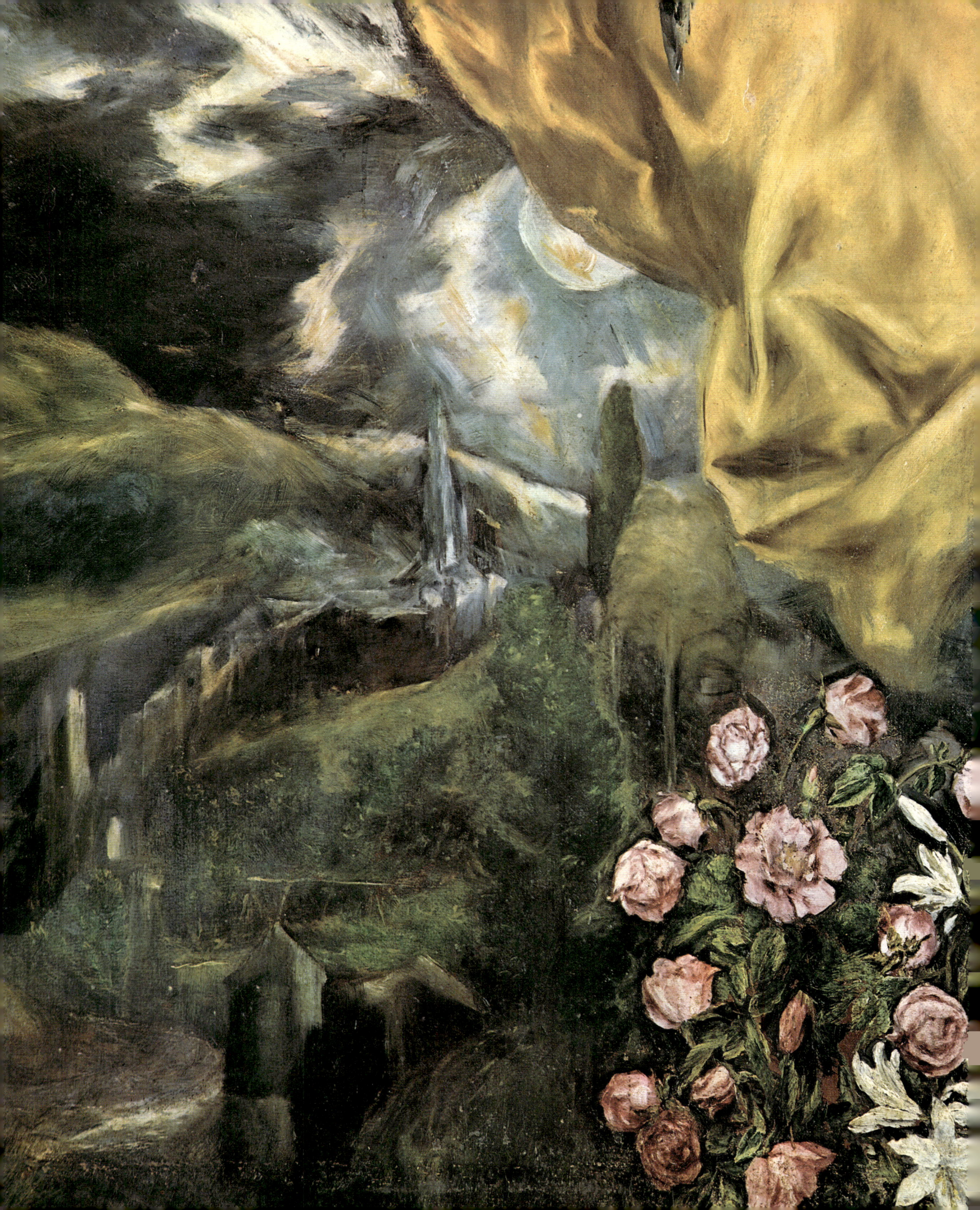

The silhouette is not of the least importance, being only perceptible when it becomes a luminous edge or a brusque border between light and shade.

The fact is that the forms are so closely bound up with the light and the colour that they almost seem to emanate from them. The essential scheme of the volumes is a really live factor in the whole, and one of such power that, despite the summary character of the forms and the total lack of details, there is never any confusion of elements. Thus the work is dominated by a deep sense of the hierarchy of the various forms, from the central and most important to those of least significance. Quite rightly, what is important is their interrelationships, not the minor characteristics of each form. Being the painter of an ideal afterlife rather than of reality, El Greco's stylistic evolution was to lead him, not to the kind of detailing that defines the specific, but always in the direction of evanescent forms, not abstract but ideal, human (since they sprang from his very soul) but with a constant flight of attraction to the beyond which is suggested by their dynamism of ascent.

The need to fill these ideal forms with something led El Greco to use a pictorial technique which would serve in itself as an interesting detail; hence the erasing of brushstrokes, the reconstitution of the sinuous curves and the repetition, even in the smallest minutiae, of the great rhythms that dominate the composition. Seen as a whole, the composition is interesting in the form and the theme, which are intimately linked. When we examine it in detail, the form is of interest because of its fluctuating, evanescent character and on account of the execution, which is untidy, almost feverish and yet at the same time very skilful. El Greco, however, never stuck to a uniform technique, and if he manipulated the material already on the surface —perhaps with a thick-bristled brush, without paint— in order to give it this flame-like quality, he only made use of this sort of dissolution where he was interested in producing such aspects. In other details —in the faces, for instance— he uses a modelling that is soft but very firm.

The clarity of the narrative appears miraculously in a world of criss-crossing brushstrokes. And this clarity is unimpaired even in the absence of colour, i.e., in black and white photographs. This is really due to his observance of the principle of hierarchy mentioned above and to the consequent use of firm modelling and of dissolution. These alternating values of intensity enable him to give relief to the form, a relief which is intensified by colour, but which already exists in the tone and strength of the form.

In few works can the action of these principles be seen so clearly as in the one we are now studying. The body of the Virgin has the rhythm needed for expressing an ascending movement. But, on the other hand, we should observe the interest in form which is especially indicated in this same body: in the draperies from the waist down, which form the true optical centre of the composition. The secondary characters are kept firmly secondary, and not by being presented out of focus —as was to be the practice of certain later painters— but by partial dissolution or by integration of the particular form of each into an ensemble which is given greater importance than any individual form. These ensembles accompany, surround and support the figure of the Virgin, without ever entering into conflict with her.

There are some incredible distortions, based on a treatment of the foreshortening that reveals astonishing virtuosity, apart from the dissolving technique. El Greco uses and exaggerates foreshortenings when they contribute to the expression of his idea and his feeling, but he dispenses with them whenever there is a danger of their impeding the heightened sense of movement. Distortion appears when the foreshortening is forced beyond the bounds of reality, as in certain angels' heads. But El Greco knows that he must give certain minimal characteristics in order to define —within this turbulent, dynamic world of his— what needs to be defined. The artist's exaltation, on the other hand, does not seem to be a question of temperament. We would say that it is the result of certain technical methods, required by an ideological principle but treated with sufficient objectiveness to make the effect of exaltation one of the artist's aims —and one that is reflected in the viewer— but never a state of mind on the painter's part.

The lyrical impulse, though it does exist, is so closely linked to the pictorial that nobody would ever dream of classifying El Greco's works, even the latest ones, as "literary". And this is because they are the result of the same intensification of the pictorial in itself. This does not mean that the painter was not attracted —and even excited— by the values of the theme or by the image, as we have insistently pointed out. The eyes of the Virgin dominate the other facial features to an unheard-of degree and there is nothing

240. Detail of figure 237.

like this for revealing the painter's inner feelings, for the eyes do indeed mirror the soul, and what is El Greco seeking but to manifest the presence of the world that lies beyond the physical?

His diehard insistence on technique and his marked interest in the value of form as pure expressiveness are factors that should always be taken into account when dealing with El Greco's paintings. There are few fragments better qualified to illustrate these assertions than the *Visitation* he painted for the upper part of the Oballe altarpiece *(Fig. 239)*, in which the theme has been given the dissolving treatment. Compare this ghostly image with Spanish Visitations of the sixteenth century, which give a delicate account of this meeting between two women who have been placed above humanity by the divine decision, but who really belong to that humanity entirely. Here we see two forms joining and about to embrace. They have one feature that differentiates them, though it is only that of intensity, and by this feature we may guess that the Virgin is the figure on the left. In all other respects they are the same: voluminous draperies given sufficient density to endow them with a tonal and chromatic value that repudiates any kind of context or detailed explanation. We should observe the painter's wisdom in giving the scene a flame-like background that harmonizes with the two great forms, which are traversed by a vigorous zigzag rhythm.

There is no reason for not supposing, on photographic evidence, that the *Immaculate Conception* that formerly belonged to José Selgas *(Fig. 236 - Cat. 222)* is an authentic work. It repeats the one in the Oballe Chapel at every point and may well have been a preparatory study for that extraordinary composition. Its present whereabouts being, however, unknown, it is impossible to give any more precise information.

The *Immaculate Conception* in the Thyssen-Bornemisza Collection *(Fig. 241 - Cat. 223)* is a work that shows great affinities with the one in the Oballe Chapel, even in the exaggerated elongation of the canon. The main difference consists in the suppression of the angels in the lower half, which is here reduced to a dream landscape, with idealized buildings and flowers in the foreground, and given an emblamatic quality. The angels bending forward on either side of the Virgin are also extremely elongated and everything about the execution shows that this work was painted during the period we are now studying.

The altarpieces of the Tavera Hospital

We will now study the part played by El Greco in the business of the altarpieces for the Hospital de San Juan Bautista in Toledo. The hospital had been founded by one of the leading figures of Charles V's reign, Cardinal Tavera, who was Rector of the University of Salamanca, Archbishop of Toledo and President of the Royal Council of Castile, and who died in 1545. El Greco's dealings with the hospital board had begun in 1595 with the commission for the Monstrance —a carved tabernacle in the shape of a little temple. This was appraised, in August of 1598, at 25,000 *reales,* which the master of his own accord reduced to 16,000; it is still kept, though incomplete, on the present high altar of the hospital church.

One of its main elements was the polychrome carved figure of *Christ*, unanimously considered to be the personal work of El Greco, which is studied in the following chapter *(Fig. 344)*. This tabernacle was to be completed in 1624, ten years after the painter's death, with sculptures of the twelve apostles carved by Jusepe Sánchez.

On November 16th of 1608, Don Pedro Salazar de Mendoza, the administrator of Cardinal Tavera's foundation, drew up a contract with El Greco and his son for the construction of an altarpiece over the high altar and two others at the sides for the magnificent church that forms the centre of the great Toledan hospital. This contract, which is not very explicit, states that the work is to be finished in five years, according to the plans presented by the two artists, including the carving and polychrome wood. This was a very important commission and one that proved to be beyond the powers of Jorge Manuel, who had become the general "manager" of the workshop in the palace of the Marqués de Villena. When El Greco died, in 1614, the great canvases that were to be the central elements of the three altarpieces were already painted and those that were to be hung in the upper parts of the side altars were prepared for painting. The work entrusted to his son, however, was far from finished. The details of this unfortunate undertaking do not fall within the scope of this book, for the ruinous and interminable series of lawsuits did not begin until after the great artist's death. Suffice it to say that the hospital board had made payments on account of the work until several years after the date stipulated for its completion. This new failure, in fact, proved a

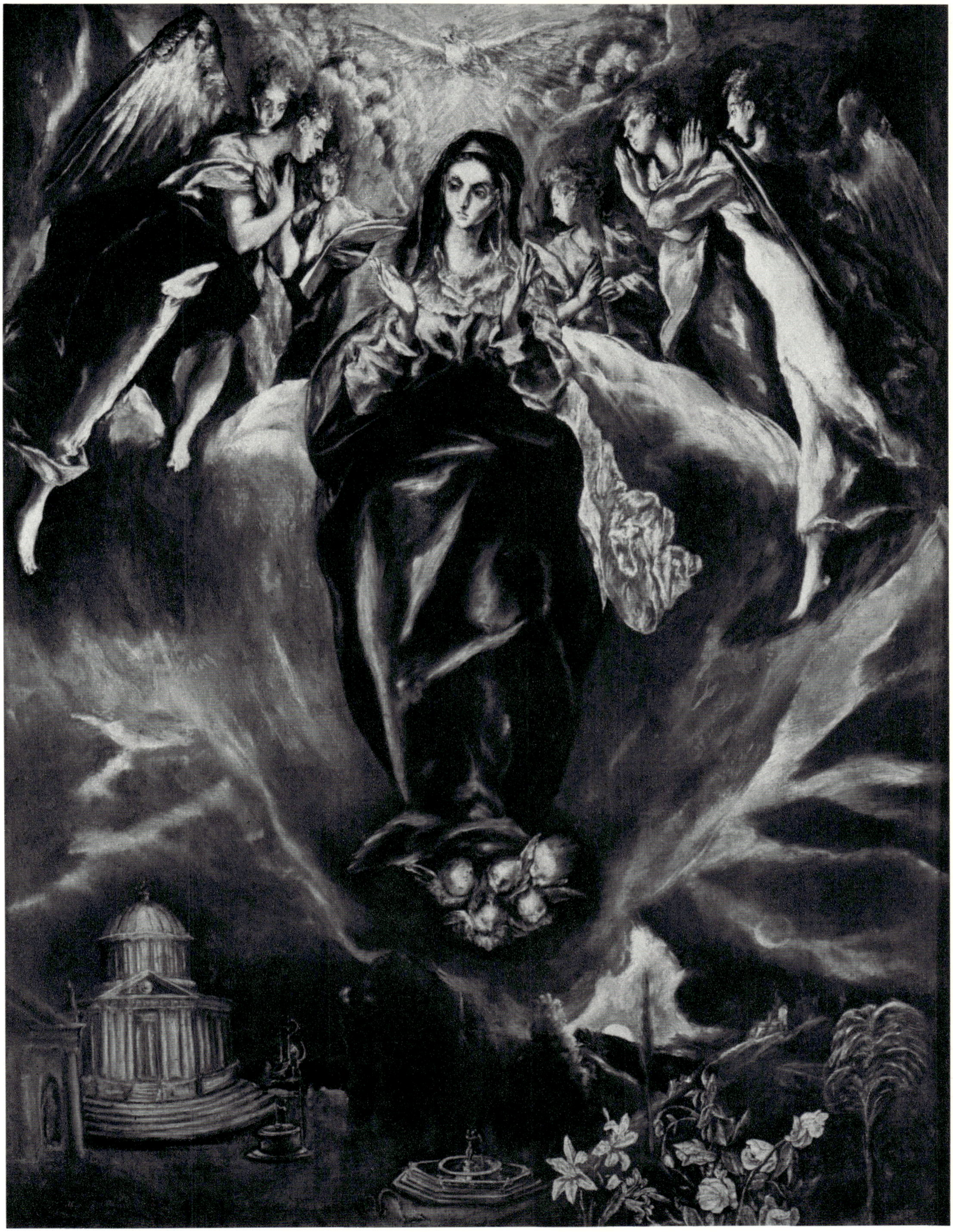

Fig. 241. The Immaculate Conception, 1607-1610. Lugano, Thyssen-Bornemisza Collection. Cat. No. 223.

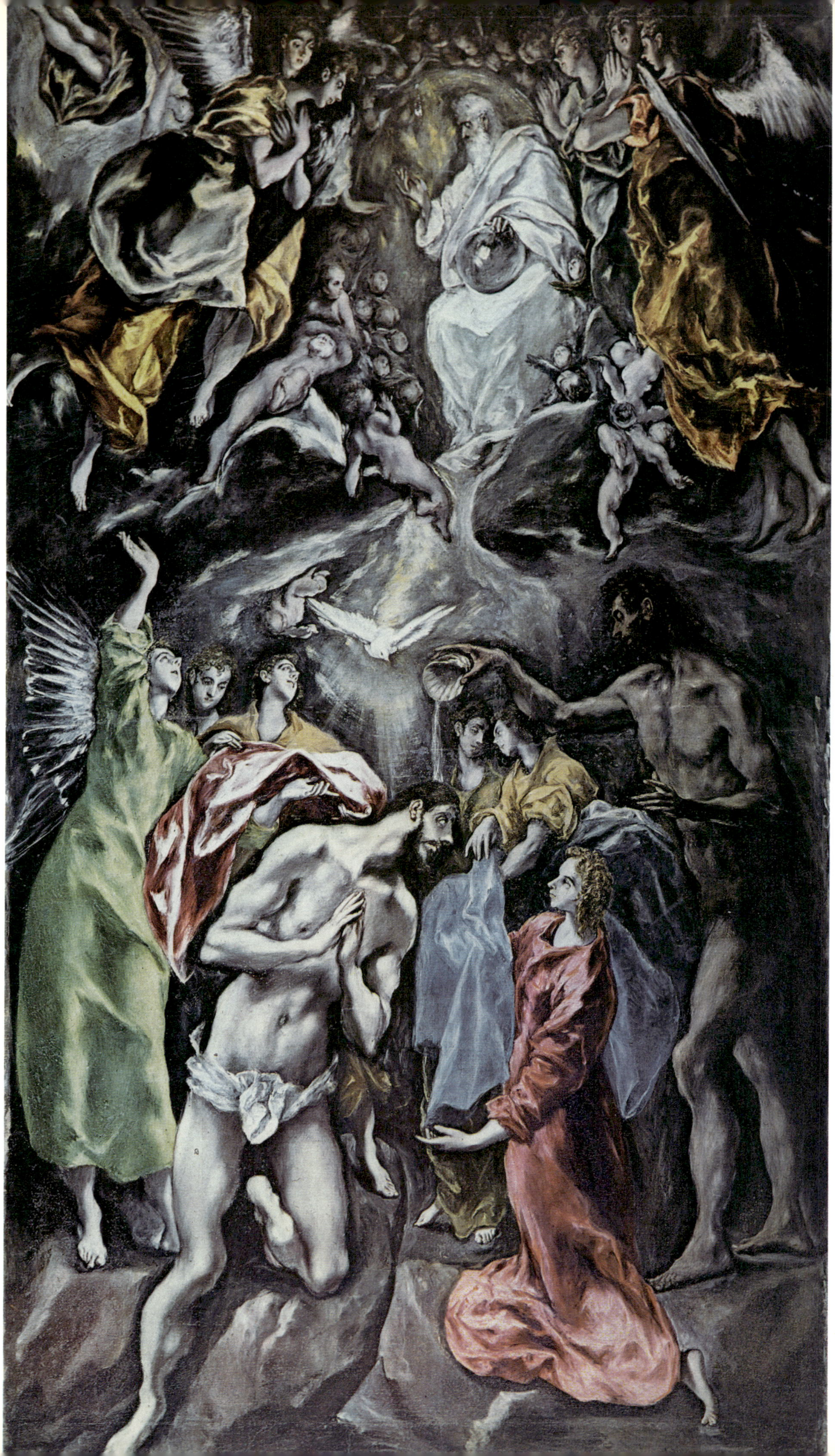

Fig. 242. The Baptism of Ch
1608-1614. Toledo, Hospital de
Juan Bautista de Afuera.
Cat. No. 224.

decisive factor in the undoing of Jorge Manuel, an unhappy story with which we are not concerned here.

The documentary data for this last period are scant enough: annual renewals of contracts and payment undertakings in connection with the rent for the premises in the Villena mansion; more loans from Dr. Gregorio Angulo; contracts signed by Jorge Manuel and payments made to him for various works, etc. Of particular interest is the fact that when Jorge Manuel signed a contract, on August 26th of 1612, for the execution of a "monument" for the community of Santo Domingo el Antiguo, he also signed his acceptance of "a vault and an altar slab" in that church for the burial of his family in perpetuity, undertaking in return to construct an altarpiece. This was the altarpiece mentioned in the previous chapter when we were studying the great *Adoration of the shepherds* now in the Prado *(Fig. 208)*. On the following 20th of November the old painter rectified the previous deed; he was then 71 years old. On March 31st of 1614, El Greco gave Jorge Manuel special powers to execute a will on his behalf. The great artist died on April 7th of the same year.

At the time of this unhappy event work on the altarpieces for the Tavera Hospital, the most important commission undertaken by El Greco in his whole career, had only just begun. In the inventory of the estate drawn up by Jorge Manuel on his father's death, we find the following items: "the main altarpiece, without the great columns or the cornice or carving or sculpture"; "the pictures for the Hospital already begun", and "two canvases prepared for the tops of the side altars". There is also "a large-sized baptism, unfinished", which San Román identifies as the one that was to be the centre of the altarpiece over the high altar. This hypothesis is confirmed by the second inventory, drawn up in 1621, in which the picture figures under the entry "the main baptism for the Hospital". This painting was probably delivered not so long after that, for according to the hospital inventory drawn up in 1624 it then hung over the altar on the Epistle side. And there it stayed until 1936.

The compositions representing *The Fifth Seal of the Apocalypse* (Metropolitan Museum, New York) and the *Annunciation* (Collection of the Banco Urquijo, Madrid) are undoubtedly those which were intended to occupy the side altarpieces. It was also San Román who proposed this identification, basing it on the inclusion of these works in Jorge Manuel's Inventory II, against the entry: "Two large sketch-portraits for the side altars of the Hospital". He mentions, too, that the study for the first of these canvases figures in Inventories I and II with the following description: "A picture of St. John the Evangelist seeing the visions of the Apocalypse, a *vara* and a third (111.5 cm.) high by two-thirds (55.8 cm.) wide".

These canvases, all that remains of the work done for the Tavera Hospital, give us the measure of El Greco's genius and of the fertility of his creation in the last years of his life. In no part of them can we see the hand of Jorge Manuel or of any other painter. The fact that they are described as unfinished works in the "Inventory of goods" drawn up on El Greco's death was probably the personal opinion of the clerk, incapable of understanding the hallucinatory character of these extraordinary paintings. It is also possible that the painter's son ordered them to be so described lest they be seized or taken from him by distraint. We should like to declare here our firm conviction that the *Baptism of Christ*, the *Annunciation* and *The Fifth Seal of the Apocalypse* are three absolutely authentic works and that El Greco considered them finished in that state in which we now see them. We do not see why certain illustrious biographers of El Greco should consider them to be works completed by Jorge Manuel in the years between the 1614 and 1621 inventories.

The *Baptism of Christ* is a typical composition in the dual aspect of the ascending dynamism of the whole ensemble and of the division of the space in the vertical sense *(Figs. 242 & 243 - Cat. 224)*. In another aspect it is also one of the compositions that betray a certain *horror vacui*, the principle of hierarchy being established by the chromatic and tonal contrasts, which also render the interplay of forms clear and harmonious with all its dynamism and meticulousness. Among the main figures that are of similar size there is also a certain differentiation, which is established by a method that is deeply primitive at bottom: that of symmetry. Thus the figure of Christ —which is also made to stand out by the colour of the flesh tints— is not opposed to that of the Baptist with a void between them, as in medieval painting, but appears almost in the centre of the lower part. The Baptist, on the right, and the angel holding Christ's robe are balanced by other figures of angels arranged on the left, the gesturing arm of the one in front making him sufficiently important to balance the Baptist perfectly. Moreover, El Greco uses the proximity of this angel's beautifully foreshortened head to those of the other two angels in order to produce a note of vivid expressiveness and clear tone, offset on the right by a pair of angels in the middle distance. We should observe, therefore, how an art so apparently —and really— fiery was at the same time meditated and executed in accordance with principles which undoubtedly owe their formalism to sixteenth-century Italy, with its interest in geometrical and admirably balanced compositions.

After an area of transition, which is not without a certain biological quality, as suggesting transit to another world, in the upper part of the picture we have the heavenly regions. Whereas the figure of Christ, in the lower part of the picture, is leaning forward from the left and, though central, is placed slightly to the side, the figure of God the Father in marvellous compensation —whether deliberate or intuitive is difficult to know— turns from the right and also occupies a position which is central but slightly to the right, so that the picture's vertical axis, at its centre, passes through the terminations of the two figures: that of Christ below and that of God the Father above. The symmetry is also observed in these heavenly regions, with the figures or heads of the angels. But what is really amazing in this painting is the relationship between the figures and the space, without the slightest harshness and with a flexibility that springs from the intimate communion of rhythm, colour and light.

The foreshortenings are treated as in other works of the painter's last period, with exaggeration and even a certain distortion; never for any "story-telling" reasons, but in order to give the composition a structure in which the slightest detail will be in consonance with the total life of the whole. The technique is that of its period: paint laid on and then smudged, with lines traced on top of it to reconstruct the half-erased form, though not always, for some of the loosely painted hands are left looking like flames. The tactile qualities are well specified, both in the principal forms and at those points of the picture that determine its rhythms; for instance, going from bottom to top and from right to left: the folds in the robe of the angel holding Christ's clothing, the head of this same angel, the body of the Saviour; the head and arm of the angel on the left; the dove of the Holy Ghost; the radiant robe of God the Father and the wing of the angel at the very top on the right. But in the intermediate areas —for there are quite precise second and third planes— form and material are left evanescent, just in order that this fluid-seeming mass may sustain the strong highlighting of the forms, which, though precisely drawn, do not contrast so strongly as to determine any dualism with the background setting. El Greco uses a subtle interplay of formal relationship in order to give a better picture of his formal world, as visionary as it was cerebral.

In the canvas representing the *Annunciation*, which was cut into two parts at the beginning of this century (the main group is in the Banco Urquijo, Madrid; the upper part, with the angel musicians, in the National Gallery of Painting in Athens), we have the same duality of spaces in the vertical sense *(Figs. 244 to 247 - Cat. 225)*. But there are some very original aspects in the two areas, which we are going to deal with separately. In the lower part, which contrasts with the spaces teeming with angels and flame-like forms of other compositions, the figure of the archangel is admirable and the qualities represented with disturbing virtuosity. Apart from skilful gradation of light and shade in the modelling, the mastery of which may be seen in the way in which the head stands out in profile against the empty background *(Fig. 246)*, the most astonishing feature is the representation of the robe, with its two contrasted qualities. The draperies, which are never hard, are used by the painter —as they had already been used by Gothic artists, but in another world of technique and sensibility— as elements of pure form. One even ends by disregarding their representational aspect and simply enjoys the vigorous brushwork, the tonal relationships and the form, which twists in and out without losing for a moment its figurative significance. That El Greco was fully conscious of the interest of these modellings —at once intense and soft, original in their scheme and profoundly eloquent as a whole— may be seen in the way in which he contrasts this angelic figure with the background, giving each character in the composition, so to speak, a space of its own in which it is completely predominant.

The figure of the Virgin, treated in accordance with the same concept and the same technique, is rendered still more beautiful by its forward movement. The modelling of the face is treated very solidly, but with visible, superimposed brushstrokes, whether to mark a highlighted point or area which reflects more light, as in the forehead, or on the contrary to sink into the shadow, as in the throat from the line of the

Fig. 243. Detail of figure

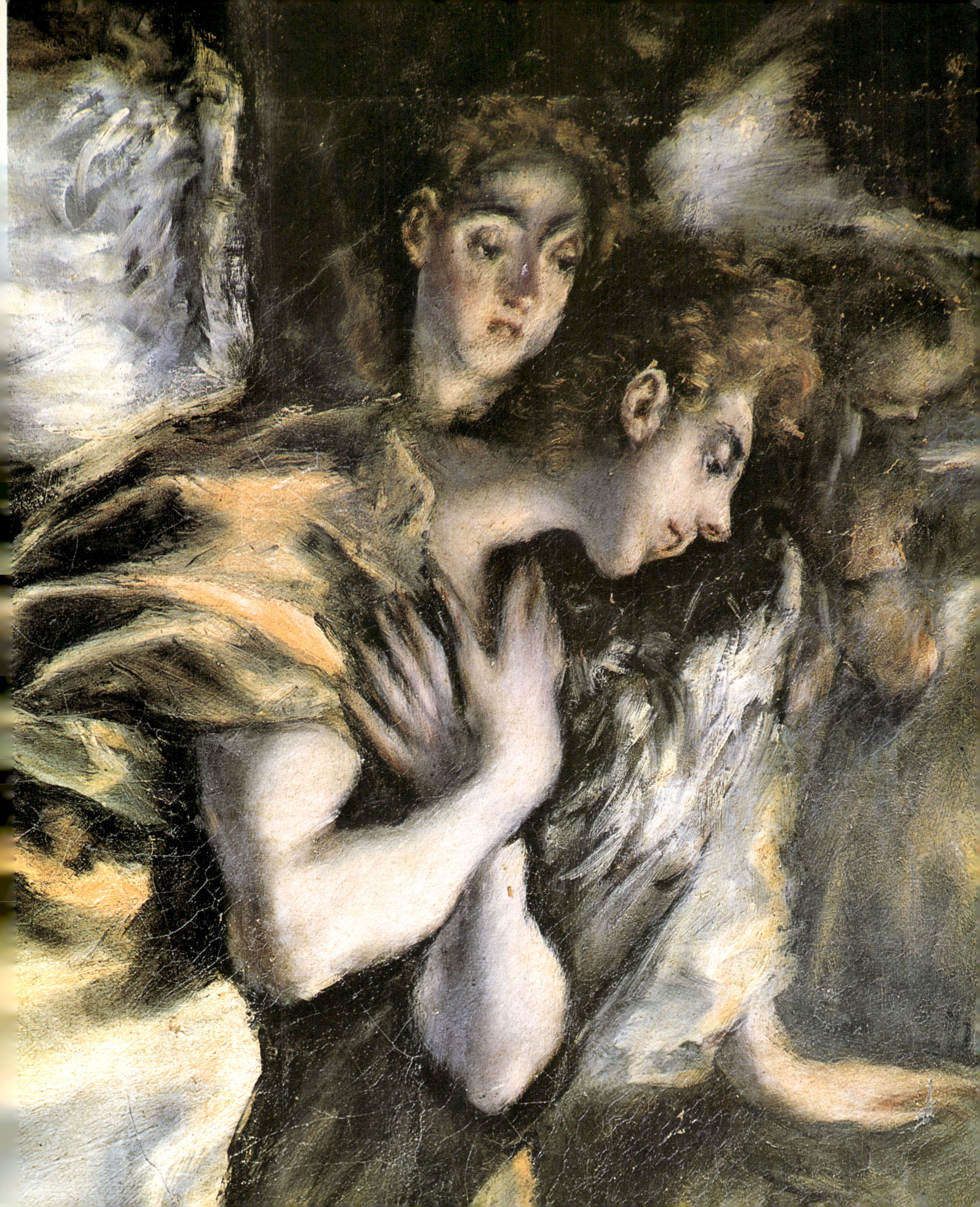

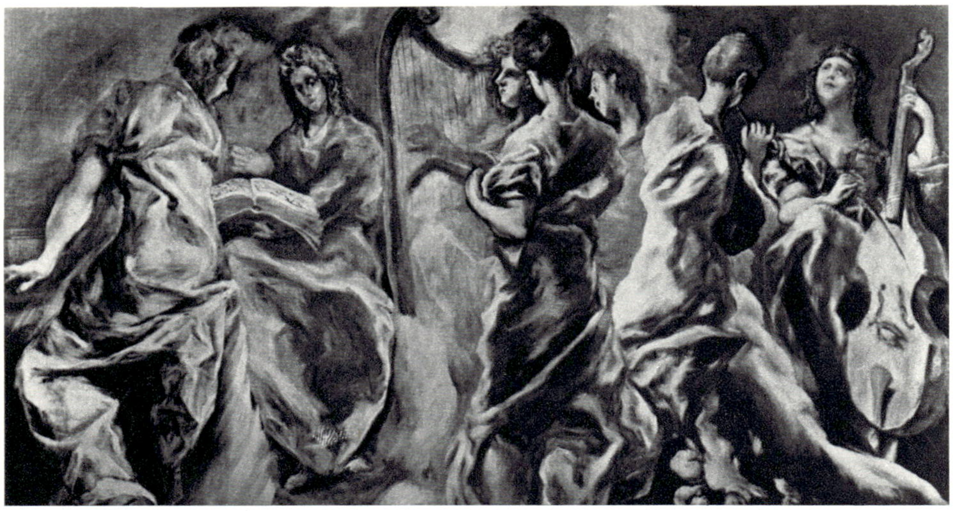

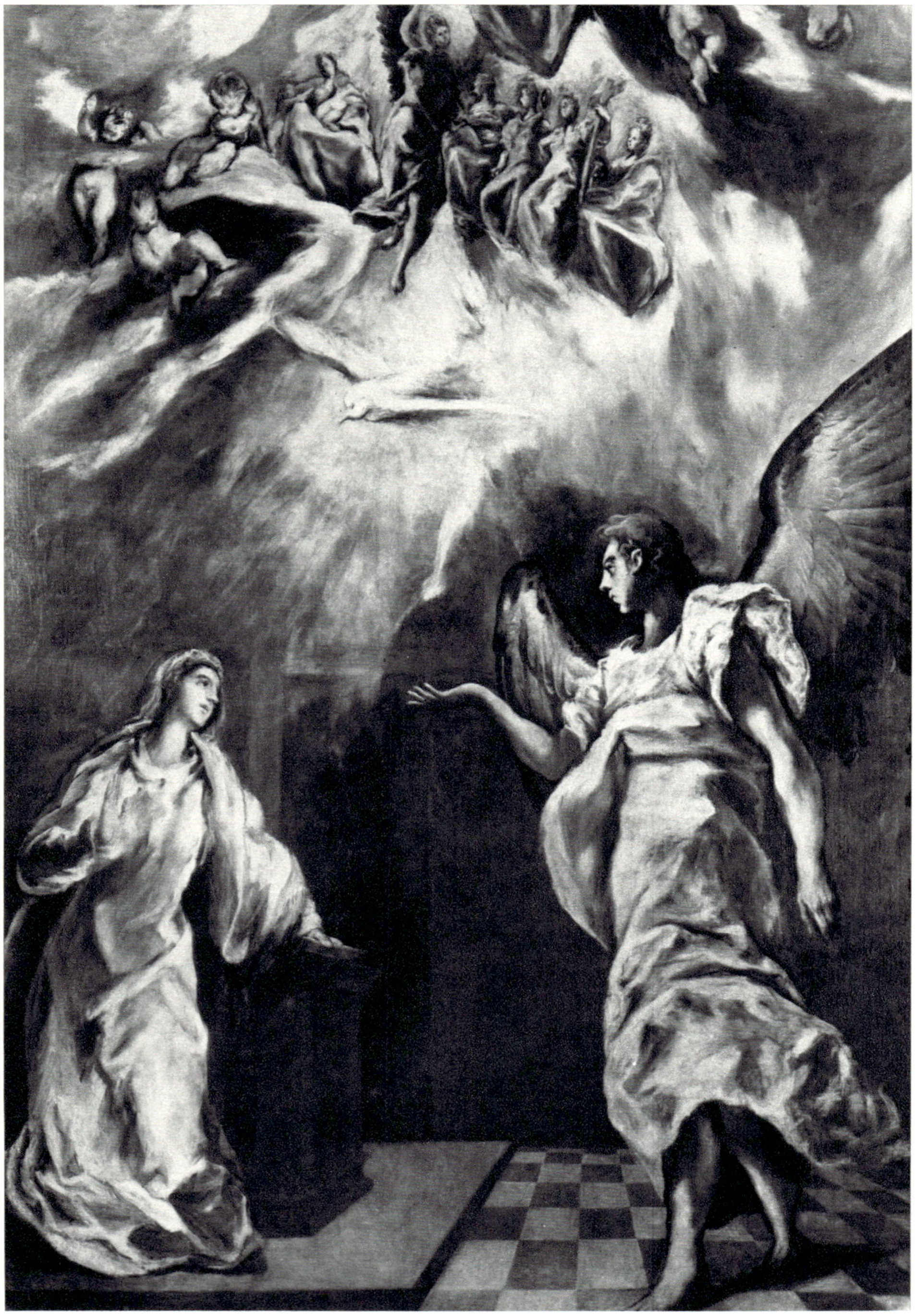

Fig. 244. The Annunciation, 1608-1614. Athens, National Gallery of Painting. Cat. No. 225.

Fig. 245. The Annunciation, 1608-1614. Madrid, Banco Urquijo. Cat. No. 225.

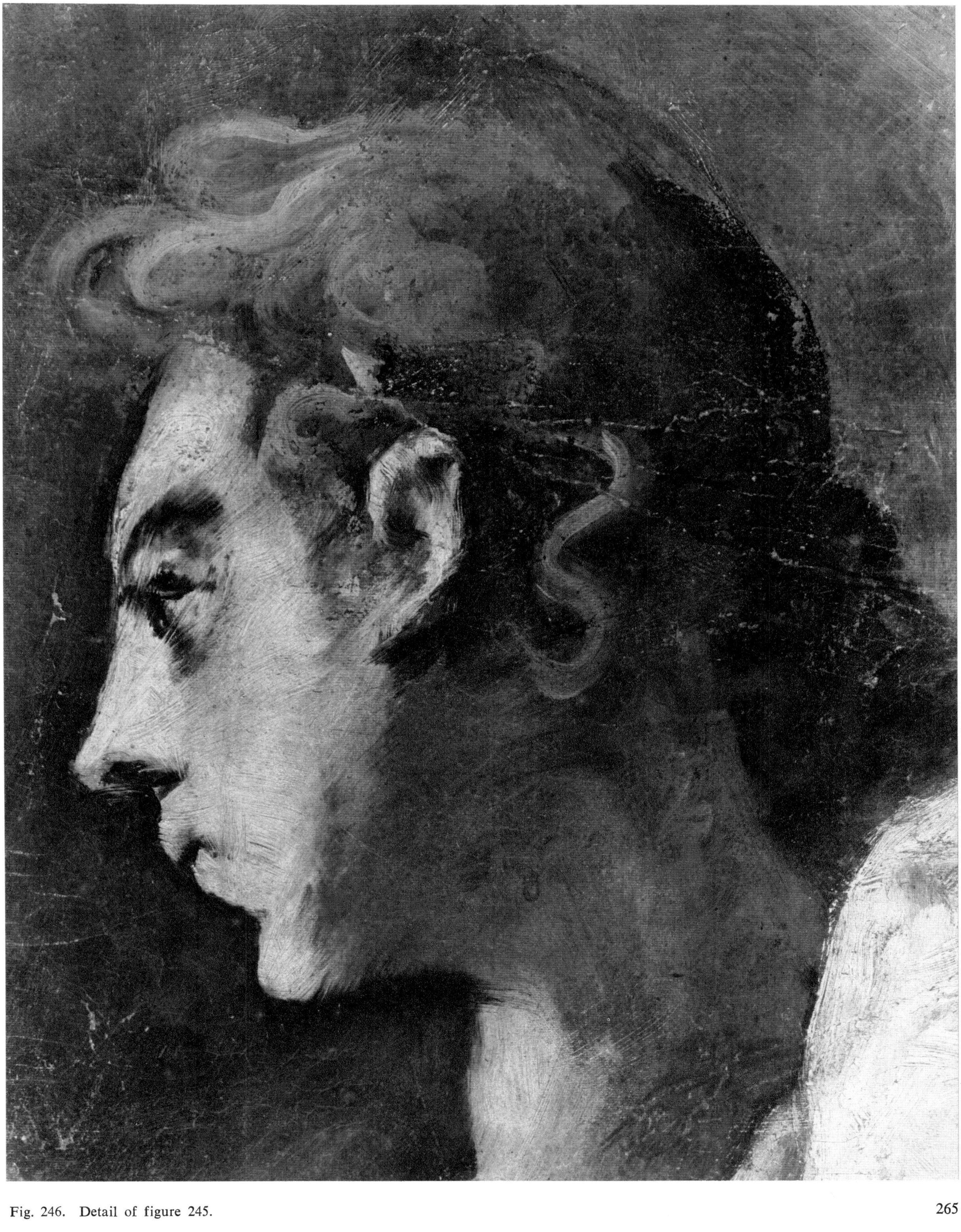

Fig. 246. Detail of figure 245.

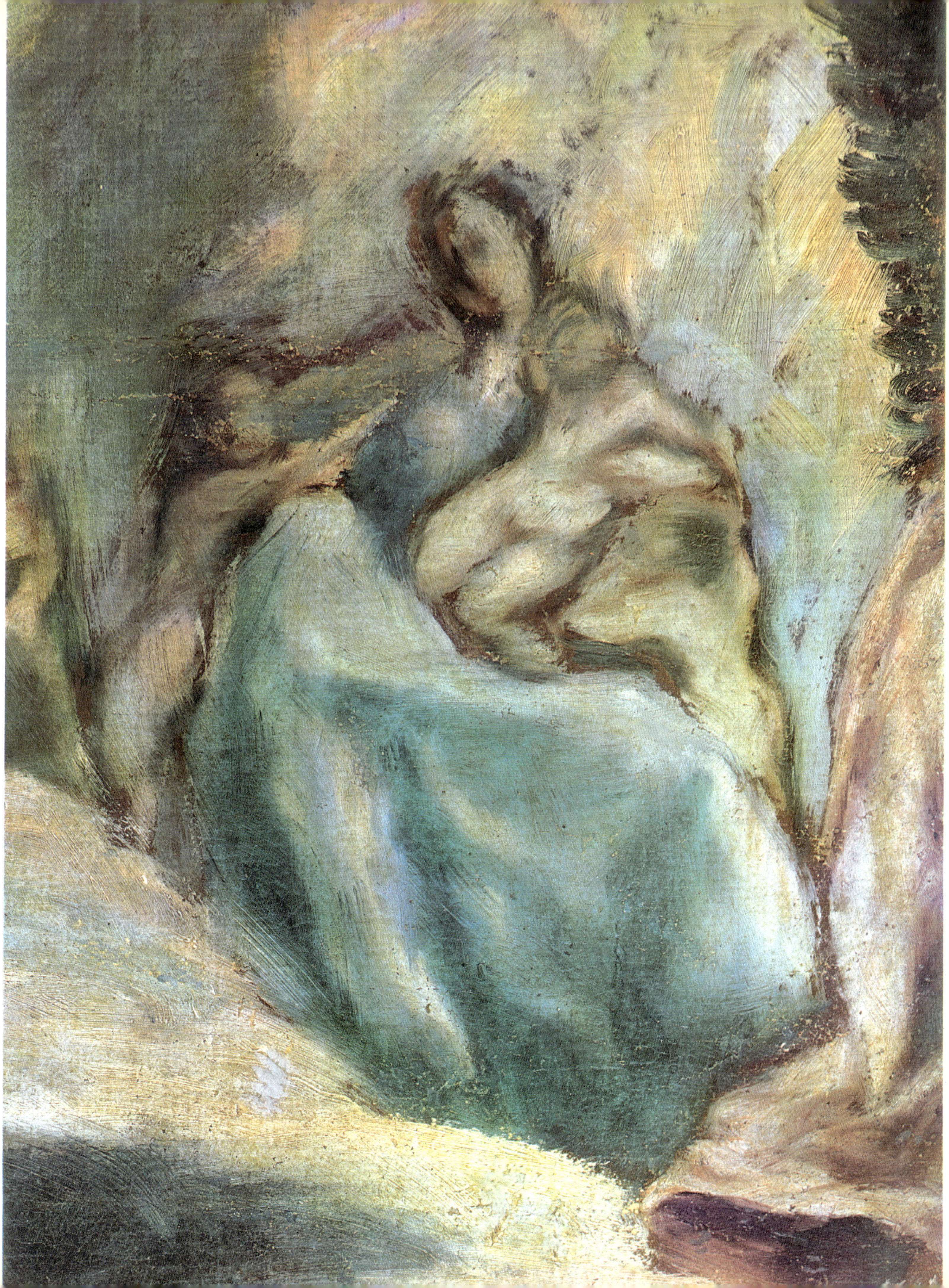

ear. The Virgin's robe and mantle are treated with the same interest in form and quality as those of the archangel, but with less precision, especially in the upper part of the figure, thanks to an intense effect of light, the source of which we find in the centre, above the figures. In this section of the great divided canvas there remained a part of the area representing the heavenly regions: an intense radiance centering on the dove of the Holy Ghost, which seems to be created out of fire. Above this we see little figures, painted in a peculiar kind of foreshortening, which would appear to represent the vision suggested to the Virgin by the words of the archangel, for she herself is depicted with the Child Jesus in her lap, surrounded by angels with various attributes *(Fig. 247)*. Though there is an evident degree of evanescence in all these figures, their lack of definition is not the result of chance or of circumstance, but of the painter's express intention. The finishing of a picture may be considered from two different points of view, that of the client and that of the artist. The client may desire —or even demand, if he insists on such clauses as have been inserted in the contract to this effect— a finish that will be more or less meticulous, but one that will, at all events, respect the principles of strict representation. The painter, on the other hand, may feel that a given area of the picture is finished, ideologically and aesthetically, though it may not be finished according to what we might call, in the widest sense of the term, academic criteria. If in his last years El Greco found any compensation for his professional failures in the country of a king who had rejected his *St. Maurice*, it was undoubtedly that of being able to paint as he wished, ignoring all rules, conventions and other people's opinions. This upper area of the *Annunciation* faithfully reflects a criterion of supreme artistic freedom which was to inspire the great experiments of twentieth-century art. The lack of definition of the figures, if we consider them properly, is in perfect agreement with their doubly oblique (upward and background) foreshortening, for this is an inner vision and the painter endeavours to evoke it as such, bringing into play all the resources of a style of painting which, after all, had to be based on the representation of real, physical beings, however much he might desire to transfer them to a plane of purely spiritual significance.

The fragment in the Athens Gallery *(Figure 244)* represents a group of angels with various musical instruments or with books of devotion. If we compare it with the upper area of the Banco Urquijo fragment, it seems more "naturalistic" —within El Greco's concept— and that is because what the painter really did in this representation of the heavenly regions was to superimpose the Virgin's "vision" and the scene that was "really" taking place in heaven during the Annunciation. We need hardly add that the technique is exactly the same as that of the picture to which it originally belonged and that the change in emphasis we have mentioned is a question of slight nuances, not a profound transition that would have destroyed the unity of a work that should never have been mutilated.

The Fifth Seal of the Apocalypse, the last of the canvases intended for the Tavera Hospital *(Figs. 248 & 249 - Cat. 226)*, is a work possessing all the characteristics of personal originality in conception and technique that distinguish El Greco's work and are accentuated in his final period, and it is, moreover, freer and more inventive in composition. As in almost all his painting, he makes no attempt to go beyond the limits of the Divine creation in order to depict what seems to him, or really is, fantastic. He displays his fantasy as an artist in the way he treats elements which in themselves have nothing strange or anomalous about them, and which are even, in comparison with the art of the Middle Ages, very much simplified. Convinced of his superhuman talent for expression through a formal medium (and not by means of weird alterations of the subject matter, such as are to be found in their most extreme form in Hieronymus Bosch), here he depicts the vision of St. John the Evangelist and gives us a sense of its intensity with no more than ten naked bodies (of men, women and children), some pieces of cloth and a dense, cloudy sky. Naturally enough, the Apostle himself —in the left foreground, with his ascetic but not emaciated young figure and his arms raised to heaven in serene violence, if we may be permitted the paradox —is the dynamic element that produces a dramatic feeling extending to every element in the composition. The bodies on the right are contorted, the little forms of the children in the air seem to be riding through the air on some strange whirlwind rather than flying. Streaks of light and dark, from left to right, are given a solidity which their rather coppery colour intensifies still further. The bodies of the group on the left are modelled like little wax figures, though their sinuous

247. Detail of figure 245.

profiles are characteristically pictorial. The blue of the Evangelist's robe, the red of his mantle spread on the ground and the mass of green against which the bodies on the right are leaning are all enclosed within the tonal force of the unleashed tempest. The true effectiveness of the colour is only represented by the warm, vivid yellow under which —for it is a kind of sweeping curtain— the naked figures on the left seem to be seeking shelter and, perhaps, by the blue of the Evangelist's robe. These complementaries and the red-green combination are, we repeat, dominated by the range of yellow ochres and purplish greys in the earth and sky. Against the green mass on the right there is a confused blue, intermingled with untidy, bristly flashes of white. This is probably intended as an allegorical representation of all the elements of the cosmos, ominously present at this fateful moment when the destroying powers that foretell the return of the Son of Man are let loose.

The composition is frankly asymmetrical. By this we mean that it has the balance of a beam scale, with the heavy weight of the great figure of St. John on the left offset by the less intense, but broader, weight of the frieze of figures gradually growing from left to right. Apart from serving to stress the counter-balancing effect, this broadening movement accompanies the rhythm of the unleashed elements, so that the force that moves them seems to originate in the very body, or at least position, of the Evangelist and move gradually towards the opposite side, at the same time moving upwards into the sky. The gestures of the upraised arms of the three figures on the right, which act as a counterpart to the gesture of St. John, are another affirmative factor of the composition, which shows yet again how, intuitively or deliberately, the turbulent genius of the old painter observed the most profound laws of that organization of forms in space that constitutes the science of pictorial composition.

A closer analysis of the details would reveal an infinity of beauties that are already apparent in a direct contemplation of the work itself or of a reproduction on a smaller scale. One instance is the way in which El Greco uses effects of light to set off, or to half-conceal, certain parts of the bodies of his figures, giving life to the form and, above all, depicting the generic and universal rather than the individual or anecdotal. Moreover, the persistence of "primitive" elements in El Greco's composition cannot be ignored. Frequently, as in Gothic paintings, the elements of his works follow parallel axes. In the present case the Evangelist's left arm is raised in a line parallel to that of the mass of fire and water rising in an intense surge above the heads of the naked group on the left. And the red of the mantle on the ground invades the space left by the figures. But this primitive scheme is radically modified by the "perpetually sinuous" character of El Greco's rhythm. If we draw a line following the feet of all the figures, we shall see that it is an S curve that gradually opens out as it advances and recedes; this line corresponds to the mass of elements, which explains the dynamic character of these latter, subjected as they are to a tremendous enclosing force.

This "Vision" has no need to display iconographic details that could have been taken from the biblical descriptions. It is enough to depict St. John representing the human race facing the supreme trial (we would say that the figures on the left are the saved and those on the right the damned, to judge by their attitudes in this final catastrophe of the world) and the unleashed fury of the elements.

The Laocoön

A work of great importance in the painter's final period is the *Laocoön* in the National Gallery in Washington *(Figs. 250 & 251 - Cat. 227).* Jorge Manuel's first inventory mentions three versions of this theme, a large one and two small ones. Inventory II includes two measuring three and a half *varas* square (2.92 m.) and another measuring one and a half by two *varas* (1.25 × 1.67 m.). These would be the same pictures, but there was probably some mistake made in the measuring, for it is to be believed that the one we are now considering would have been one of them. This canvas is the one that figures in the 1666 and 1668 inventories of the pictures in the Alcázar of Madrid. From the royal collections it made its way, through the Duke of Montpensier's collection and the international art market, to its present home in Washington. It is not only outstanding on account of its extraordinary quality, achieved at a time of life when the painter must have felt crushed by the burden of his long life of struggling and fatigue, but also because of the novelty of the subject matter and the freedom of the composition. In this work, which stands rather apart from El Greco's other paintings and acquires thereby a special interest, we may well wonder how

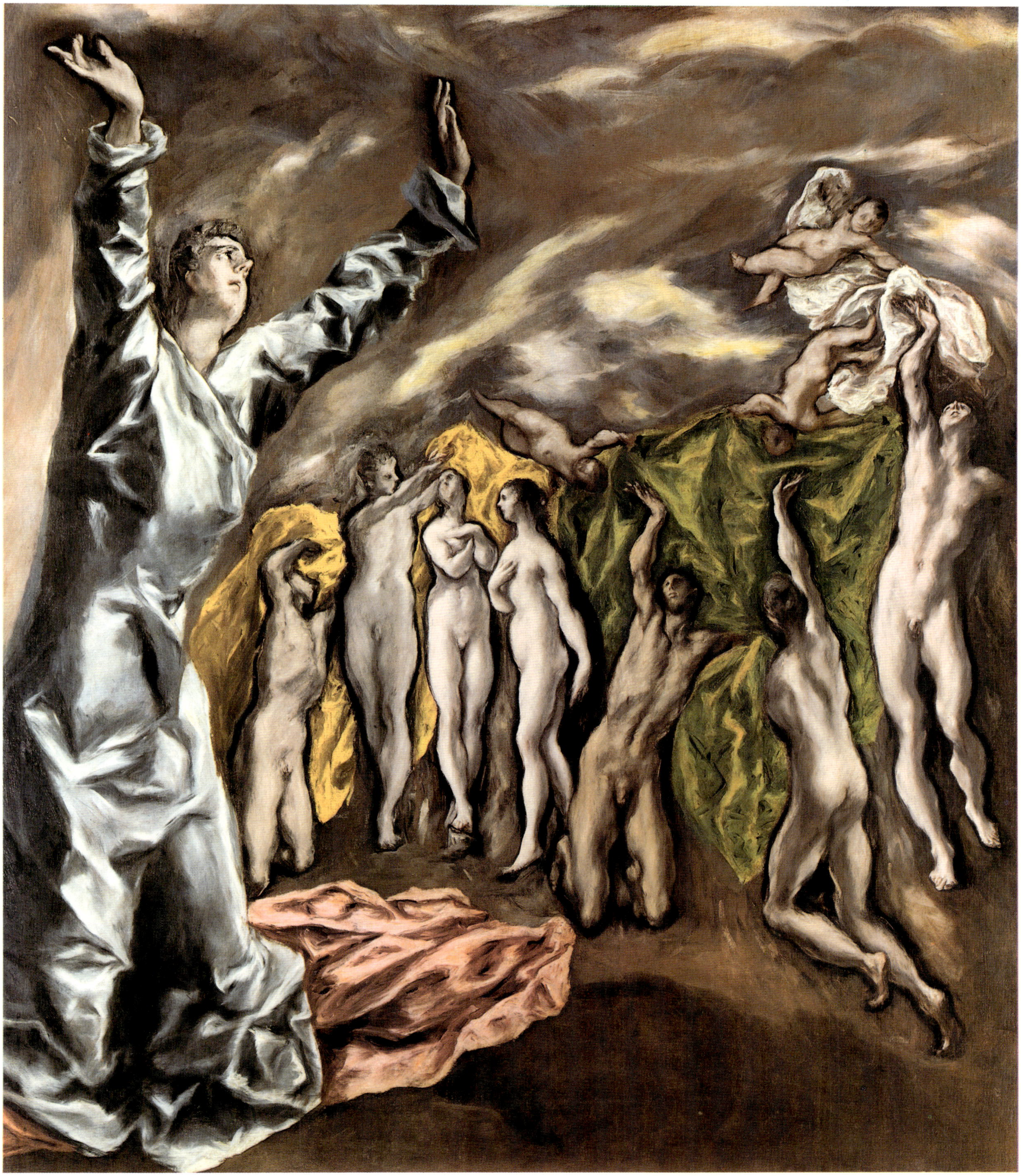

Fig. 248. The Fifth Seal of the Apocalypse, 1608-1614. New York, Metropolitan Museum. Cat. No. 226.

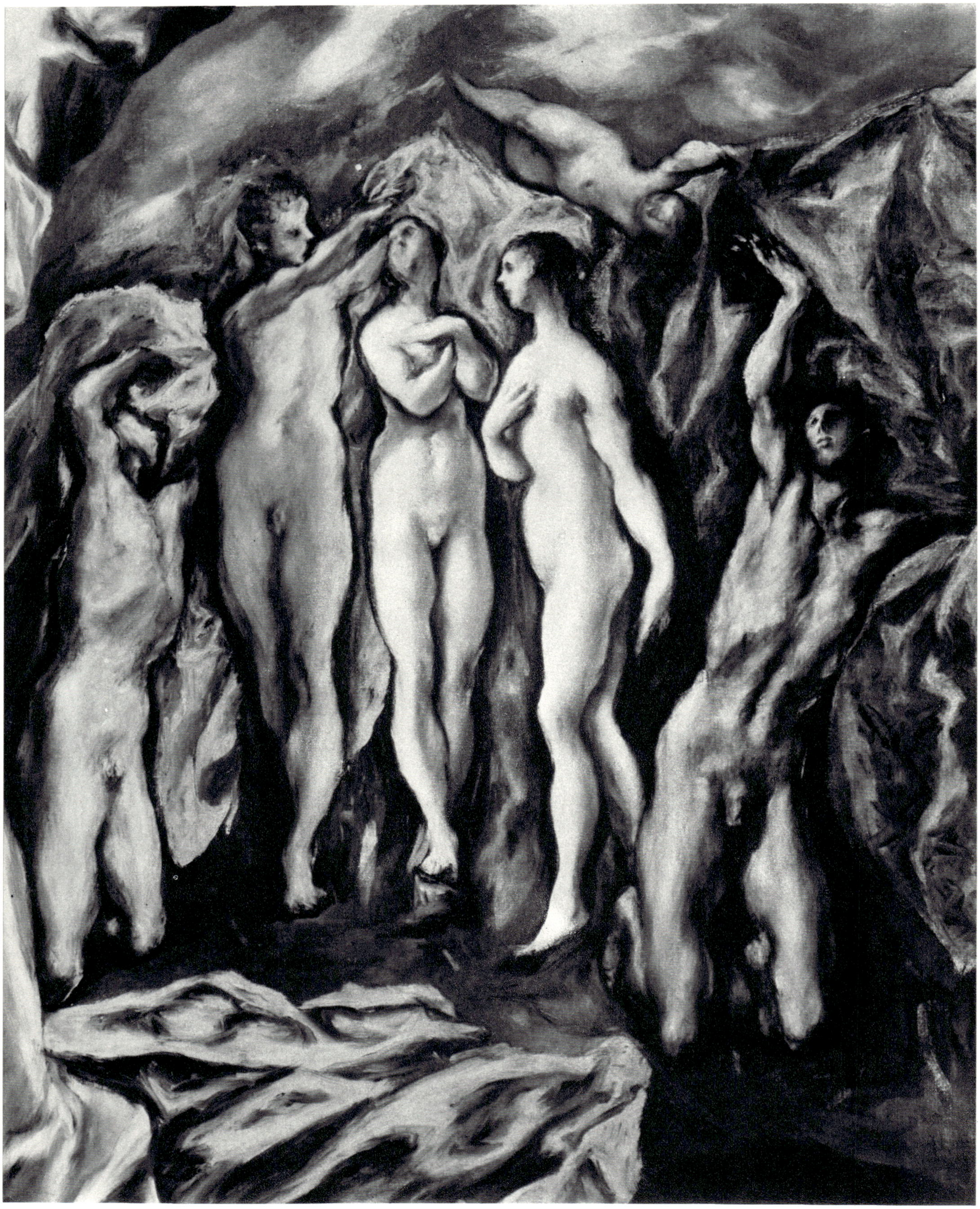

Fig. 249. Detail of figure 248.

the theme came to attract him. As in the case of Rembrandt, who at the end of his life interested himself in the theme of the prodigal son, a fact which permits us to suppose that the artist was longing to return to the bosom of God, his heavenly Father, so we might imagine that El Greco conceived the present work as a kind of symbol or allegory of the havoc wrought by evil and by the passions. Unlike the famous Hellenistic group, the three characters in the scene are separated here. One of the sons is standing on the left of the composition. The father and the other son are shown lying on the ground, the former wrestling with a great serpent and the latter apparently already dead. Three naked figures close the composition on the right and act as mysterious witnesses to the drama. The ensemble of figures is arranged rather like a frieze in the foreground, with the clear tones of the incomparable flesh tints against the dark rocks on the ground. The middle distance is occupied by a landscape view of Toledo, very freely interpreted and with few elements. The upper area of the canvas depicts a splendid sky, one of the most beautiful ever painted by the great Cretan. There is an indescribable harmony in these three horizontal areas, supported and contained by the vertical rhythms to left and right, a harmony only surpassed by the infinite beauties of the execution, so difficult to analyse. The loose execution of the painter's later years certainly prevails, but in a transfigured, triumphal form, the artist giving it a more naturalistic treatment wherever he finds it necessary, as may be seen in the two figures lying on the ground, though that distortion of the members to accentuate their serpentine, flame-like quality, which we have mentioned in connection with many earlier works, is here carried to its furthest extreme. In the serpents El Greco has an excuse for tracing arabesques in the air which complete the masterly rhythms of his figures and give new values to his drawings. As an illustration of the degree to which he "felt" this work aesthetically and treated it as a source of freedom and beauty —using the iconography as a pretext— we have the very beautiful horse that is walking, alone, towards one of the gates in the walls of Toledo. The landscape modulates its tones from a cold, whitish grey to a reddish ochre, by way of violet-tinted greys and bluish whites that reflect the intense sky. All that gesture could express, the passion we have seen gradually increasing throughout El Greco's whole development, is enormously accentuated in the painting of the apocalyptic theme studied above. But it is in the *Laocoön* that it finally attains the supreme culminating point that crowns a career so humbly begun among the "*Madonnieri*" of Crete.

View and plan of Toledo

In the year 1810 the *View and plan of Toledo,* that great oblong canvas now housed in the Greco Museum in Toledo *(Figs. 252 to 254 - Cat. 228)*, hung in the Archbishop's Palace of that city. Apparently, its first owner was Pedro Salazar de Mendoza, the administrator of the Tavera Hospital, and it is possible that it was painted expressly for him, to judge by the reference to the hospital included in the inscription the painter placed in the picture, which we quote below. In the inventory of Salazar de Mendoza's estate drawn up after his death in 1629 there are references to some "large countrysides" and to "a countryside of Toledo towards the Alcántara bridge", which was probably the picture in the Metropolitan Museum in New York which we have already studied.

The inscription, which appears in the lower right on the unfolded parchment which contains the plan of the city, reads: "I have been forced to put the Hospital of Don Joan Tavera in the form of a model, for not only did it cover the Puerta de Bisagra, but the dome or cupola rose so high that it dominated the city and so, by turning it into a model and changing its position, I thought it showed its facade more than any other part; and as for its position in the city, that is shown on the plan.

Also, in the story of Our Lady bringing the chasuble to St. Ildefonso for his adornment and in making the large figures, I have to some degree taken advantage of their being celestial bodies, as we can see in lights, which, when seen from afar, however small they may be, look large".

The composition, painted over a priming of red Sevillian ochre, like most of El Greco's later works, is a panoramic view in which the dominant feeling is horizontal. If El Greco had been seeking a dramatic sense in the *View of Toledo* already studied *(Figure 172)*, here every element is most carefully represented, with an attention to detail that does not, however, prevent the work from having an intensely pictorial character. On the other hand, the picture is improved by the recession imposed on the planes by the figures. On the left there is a figure modelled in ochre *(Fig. 254)* which, although very Mannerist in concept, is evidently an allegory of the Tagus. On the right, more to the foreground and therefore larger in size, we see a young man in green holding the parchment with the plan of Toledo *(Fig. 253)*. It is not a portrait of Jorge Manuel, for to judge by its technique this canvas must have been painted in the closing years of the painter's life, certainly later than 1610. Above all this, a little to the left of the centre and against a sky covered with clouds, we have the group of the Virgin and angels, arranged in such a way that the rhythms almost form an irregular star.

Below this group, in the middle distance and in front of the walls of the city, we may see, resting on a cloud, the Tavera Hospital, which is represented indeed as a model. On the plan the painter gave the exact position of the palace of the Marqués de Villena, in which he was then living. Despite its detailed faithfulness and the care taken in representing the walls, monuments, most important buildings and groups of houses, this picture could never be considered a minor work in the fashion of those "views of cities" which some kings commissioned from their painters at a rather later period. Throughout the work we can detect the hand of the great artist, surpassing his subject. Just as he turns a devotional image into a magnificent lyrical effusion, so he transforms this succession of buildings —perfectly articulated as regards forms and values— into a spectacle of pure art. We have only to look for a moment at the astonishing figure of the young man on the right, with the white ruff of his suit unbelievably simplified, the slightly violet flesh tints of the painter's later period and the loose execution, despite all of which the image is absolutely precise and sufficient. On the other hand, the group of heavenly figures is extraordinarily beautiful, with its yellows, blues and crimsons, pink and white contrasting with the greyish blue of the sky, a blue under which the priming can be seen everywhere. These figures give the work a sense that goes beyond pure representation.

The landscape, however, would be sufficient in itself, thanks to the viewpoint so unerringly chosen by the painter, a viewpoint that enables him to group buildings from the centre towards the left and set their clustered masses against the beautiful green undulations of the open country on the right of the composition. The execution is noteworthy for its sense of synthesis and the skilful juxtaposition of values that models the landscape in depth. But we can see that El Greco does not obey the strict limitations of aerial perspective by the lack of visual precision in the foreground, both in the figure of the young man and in the allegory of the Tagus.

Paintings of the last period

The next work we come to, which is the *Marriage of the Virgin* in the National Museum of Romania *(Fig. 255 - Cat. 229)*, may have been the preparatory study for the canvas which, according to various witnesses, hung many years ago in the right-hand altarpiece of the church of Illescas. If this were true, then this extraordinary painting would belong to the period immediately before the one we are now studying, i.e., 1603-1607. As it may also be a replica of the vanished painting, its peculiar execution has decided us to place it in this last group of original works by El Greco. It may be admitted that it is an unfinished work, but to the modern eye it lacks nothing. We may see once again a generous use of draperies as a means for creating a form that is interesting in itself, quite apart from its representative function. This can be seen in St. Joseph, but above all in the Virgin herself, whose figure is defined only by the voluminous mantle that covers her whole body and her head, letting us see no more than her face and hands. The composition is strictly symmetrical, with the priest in the centre, two male figures on the right —with St. Joseph— and two female figures on the opposite side. Of these male figures, the one between St. Joseph and the priest is possibly a self-portrait of El Greco; worth noticing is the intensity and restlessness of his gaze. To some extent the little canvas is a compendium of El Greco's audacities: rubbings, scorings, textures dissolved or intensified when the rubbing is done crosswise and against the direction of the formal axis. We may see quite clearly some separate brushstrokes in a lighter tone, the purpose of which is to draw the form, or, rather, to indicate the reflection of light. The proportions of the figures —whose heads are all at the same level— are enormously elongated, so that there is nothing in the work to contradict the painter's last style. Where this picture possibly attains its greatest intensity as regards boldness of treatment is in the figures of the women accompanying the Virgin, who

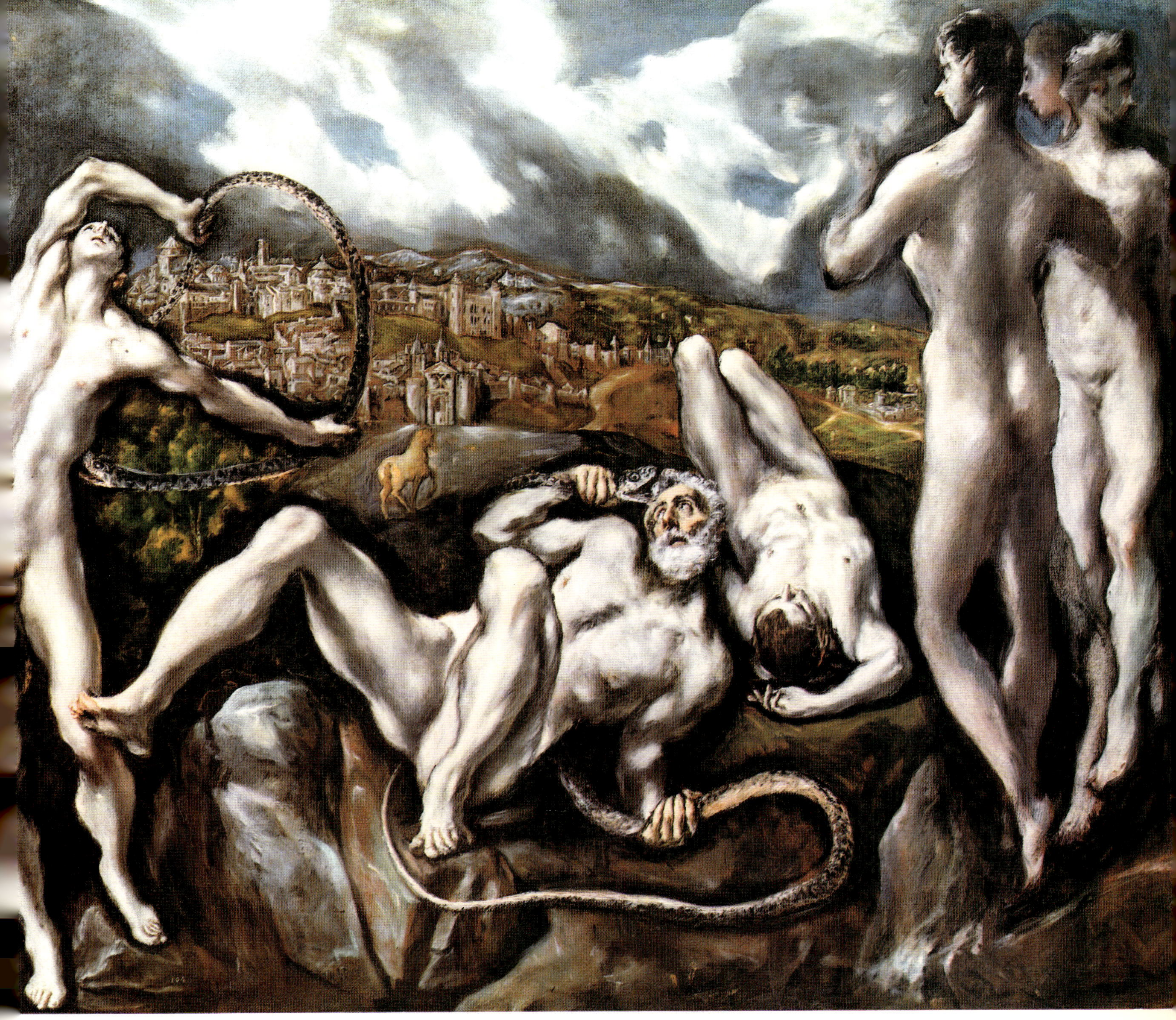

Fig. 250. Laocoön, 1608-1614. Washington, National Gallery. Cat. No. 227.

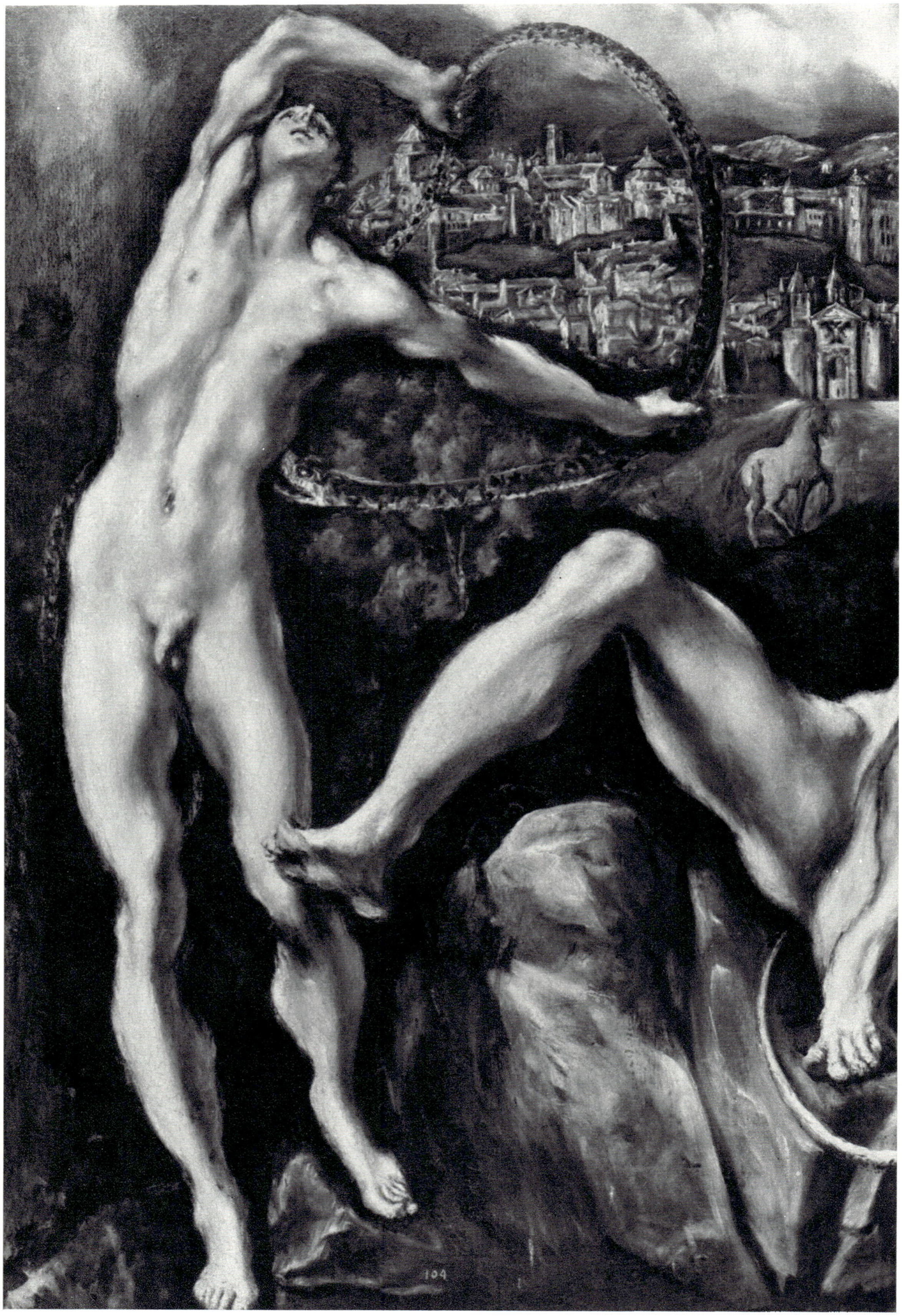

Fig. 251. Detail of figure 250.

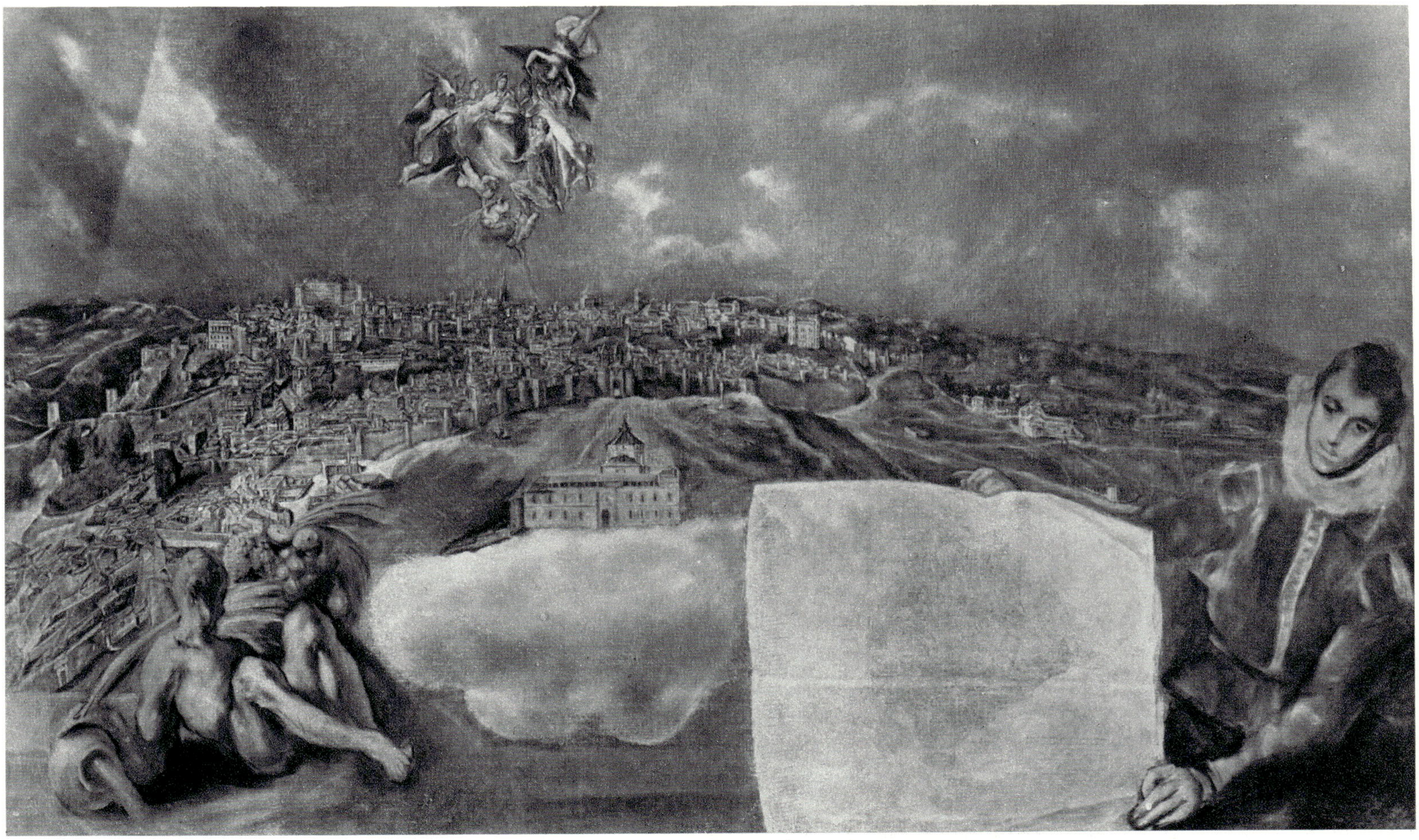

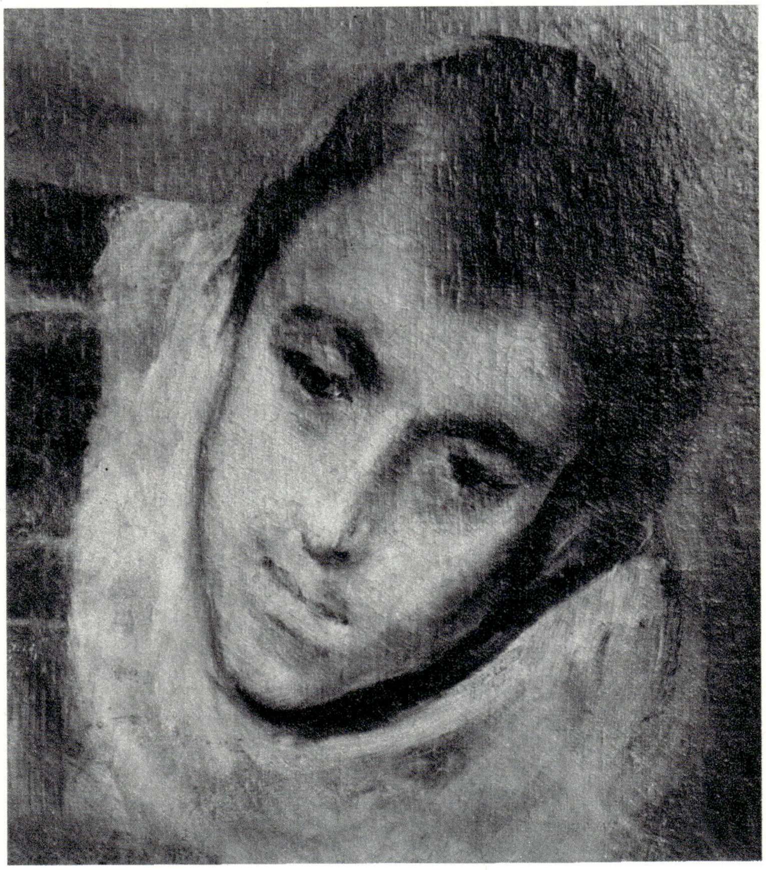

Figs. 252 & 253. View and plan of Toledo, c. 1610-1614. Toledo, Greco Museum. Cat. No. 228.

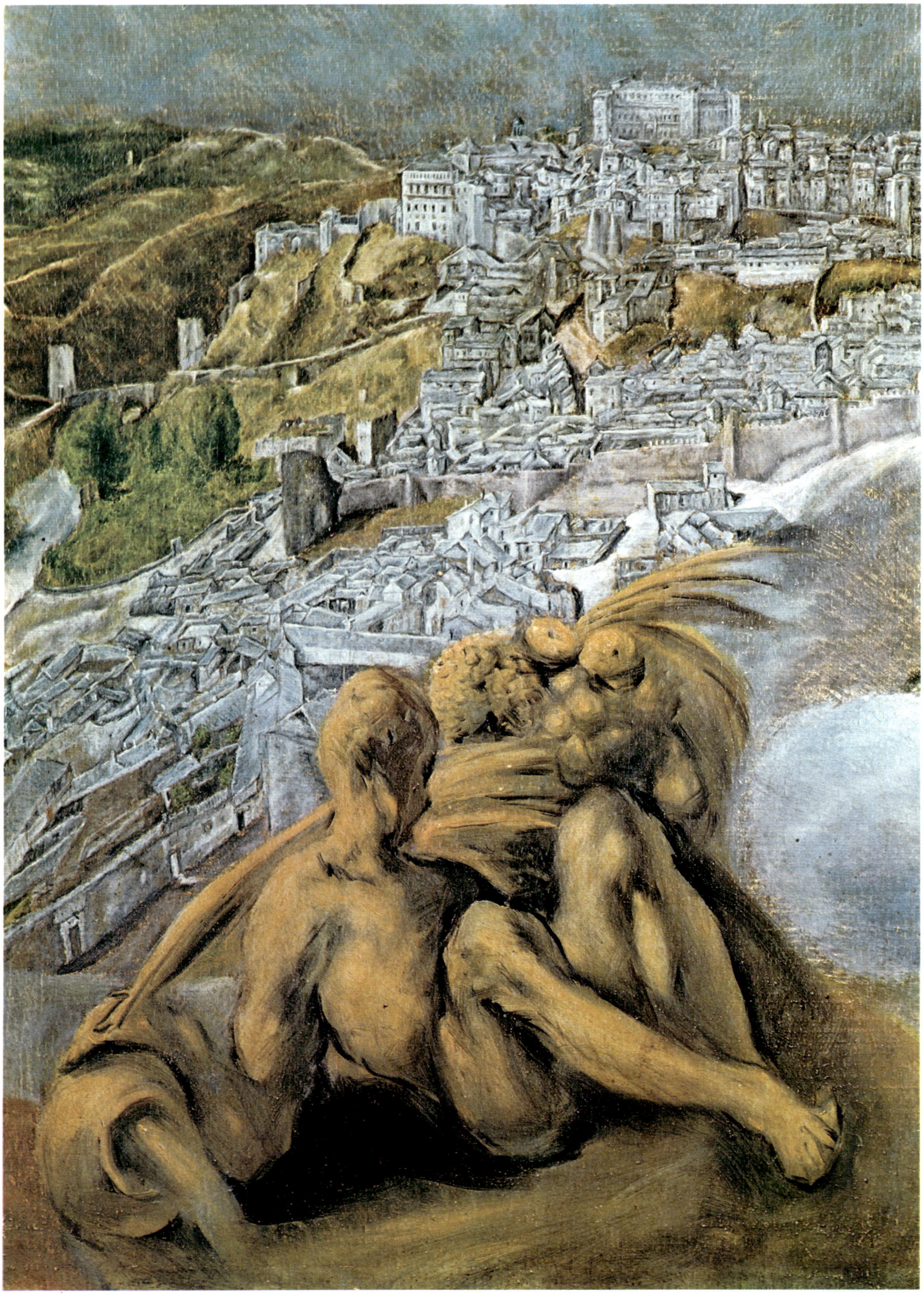

Fig. 254. Detail of figure 252.

appear to be submerged in a special penumbra. The priest is a figure of noticeably Byzantine character, though there is nothing hieratic about his attitude.

Of the *Adoration of the shepherds* in the Colegio del Patriarca in Valencia *(Fig. 119)* there are two authentic new versions extant which also belong to the period we are now studying: one of them, formerly in the collection of the Duke of Híjar, now hangs in the Metropolitan Museum in New York *(Fig. 256 - Cat. 230);* the other, which comes from the convent of Santa Clara in Daimiel (Ciudad Real), is in the Valdés Collection in Bilbao. They are works of tortured form, profoundly stylized. The gestures have become more nervous; the lights shine with unnerving force and nothing in the composition escapes their influence. There is greater boldness in this work, as we may see by simply regarding the tortured folds of the cloth on which the Infant Jesus is lying. Each of the figures, however, corresponds to the prototype we have mentioned and one would only say, perhaps, that the works represent different moments of the same scene captured by the artist. The lights change, as does their degree of proximity to the figures, and this produces alterations in the faces, although the gestures and expressions are the same. The backgrounds are not exactly the same either and the contemplation of these works, which are identical in subject matter and composition but subtly and profoundly different in reality, gives us a rather uneasy feeling. This repetition of a theme by El Greco is as far as it could be from any commercialized facility. It is simply a restatement by the artist of themes which really aroused his passionate interest and before which his feelings as an artist —and, we might say, as a man— could not remain unmoved.

Possibly we should also assign to this final period of the artist a new iconographical theme: *Christ in the house of Simon*, of which two authentic versions with variations are known to us, one in the Oscar B. Cintas Foundation in New York *(Cat. 232)*, the other in the Art Institute of Chicago *(Fig. 257 - Cat. 231)*. The composition of the group is the same in both, the figures being seated in a circle at a round table. But in the second picture mentioned we can see objects on the table, while a markedly architectural background seems to indicate a passing nostalgia for Italy. In their simplicity these architectural forms in fairly neutral tones of ochre provide a suitable background for the scene, in which the vivid colours of the clothing stand out: pink, red, yellow, green, greenish blue and orange ochre, all contrasting with the white of the tablecloth.

In the first version the table is absolutely bare and the background a blank wall. The ceiling is enlivened by the geometrical structure of a great lamp, but this hardly stands out at all against the upper background. In both versions, which were undoubtedly executed within a very short time of each other, the distortions are considerably heightened, though this does not affect the pictorial quality in the least. That is why we do not accept the opinion of those critics who assign both canvases to Jorge Manuel, arguing that he must have copied an original by his father which is now lost. Perhaps the execution of the background in the two works may be the work of the painter-architect, by now no longer so young. Its neutral treatment and smooth execution would seem to confirm this assertion. But the inner agitation, conveyed by the expressionism of gesture and drapery, that moves these figures is absolutely typical of El Greco himself. The man in the right foreground is a very close copy of the one in other compositions. As we have already remarked, El Greco often created new ensembles with elements taken from his own works, a tendency that was gradually accentuated with the years.

We are still left with a final residue of paintings done by El Greco, who in these last years of his existence continued his ceaseless quest for new themes, without ceasing to repeat —and to renew— his old favourites. Of special interest among these is the last version of the *Christ cleansing the Temple*, which hangs in the church of San Ginés in Madrid *(Figs. 258 & 259 - Cat. 233)*. In essentials it is not much different from the versions derived from the design in the Frick Collection *(Fig. 187)*, but the setting is different and there are some new characters: a naked child and a woman with upraised arms, whose gesture echoes that of one of the angels holding the Saviour's robe in the *Baptism of Christ* in the Tavera Hospital *(Fig. 242)*. The great central arch of earlier versions has been replaced by an architectural composition of greater height, making this version vertical, while the previous ones were oblong. It is interesting to notice that the background reproduces with curious fidelity the essentials of the high altar in the centre of the Illescas ensemble. The relief depicting the Sacrifice of Abraham has disappeared in this version and the scene of the expulsion of Adam and Eve from Paradise now appears on the base of a great nude statue of a young man whose identification is uncertain *(Fig. 259)*. Soehner has pointed out that the reliquary in the central niche, between the Ionic columns, is reminiscent of that of Martín Ramírez, the founder of the chapel of San José in Toledo, which houses one of the most important ensembles by El Greco. The execution is rather looser than in the earlier versions.

We believe that some new designs in El Greco's iconography belong to the same period. One of them is a *Virgin and Child* of which there is only one extant version, in the collection of the Marquesa de Campo Real in Madrid *(Fig. 260 - Cat. 234)*, despite the fact that two copies of this theme appear in Jorge Manuel's second inventory. The Virgin in this work wears an anguished expression, which is infrequent in El Greco's Marian iconography, as though she were thinking of the future Passion of her Son, whom she is caressing with her long hands. The face is foreshortened and seems distorted. The modelling of the mantle that covers her head and shoulders is astounding in technique, colour and tone. The figures stand out against one of El Greco's typical cloudy skies.

We now come to an admirable *St. Veronica*, which is in a private collection in Buenos Aires *(Fig. 261 - Cat. 235)*. As will be remembered, this subject had been treated by the painter several times during his early years in Spain. In this composition there are aspects that differ from the earlier versions: St. Veronica is shown full-face, looking out at the viewer with large, pathetic eyes. She is holding the cloth well open, slightly above waist level. The face of Christ is very similar to those on the earlier cloths, though rather thinner and with greater contrasts of tone. This picture is extremely dramatic, with its jagged rhythms and ragged textures, and there is also a quality in the execution that absolutely obliges us to consider the painting authentic. The face and hands are admirable.

Another new design is that of the *Apparition of the Virgin and Child to St. Hyacinth*, which appears in two canvases: in the Rochester Museum *(Cat. 237)* and in the Barnes Foundation in Merion, Pennsylvania *(Fig. 262 - Cat. 236)*. In this case it seems very probable that El Greco by now fast approaching the end of his life, copied the scheme of the composition from an engraving of a picture by Ludovico Carracci dated in 1594. Needless to say, he transformed this theme into an authentic "Greco", giving it not only the chromatic and formal characteristics that are typical of his work, apart from the execution, but also the emotion that had been growing increasingly dominant in his religious work since his arrival in Spain and especially in the second half of that period. Judging by the size of the two canvasses in question, it seems possible that the first was the sketch for the execution of the second.

We must now mention an excellent *St. Catherine of Alexandria*, represented in two canvases which repeat the same model with variations. One of these is in Topsfield, Massachusetts *(Cat. 238)*, the other on the international art market *(Fig. 263 - Cat. 239)*. The saint's face expresses a certain rather haughty dignity, which is made more specific by the crown. In her right hand she is holding the two-handed sword which is her attribute, while in the other hand she bears the palm of her martyrdom. The figure is depicted in a sort of zigzag distortion and the execution follows the same rhythm even in the slightest stroke of the brush, except in some velvety areas painted with a very fine finish, which, however, is never smooth. The lines of the thick brush can be seen all over the surface and we find in these works all the technical resources that are usual in El Greco, and on which we have already commented.

The original composition on the theme of the *Birth of the Virgin*, which formerly belonged to a Barcelona collection and now hangs in the Bührle Foundation in Zurich *(Fig. 264 - Cat. 240)*, is not considered by Wethey to be an authentic work. This little canvas, which looks more like a sketch than a definitive version, has such a wealth of forms and nuances, such acute vivacity in the figures that go to make it up, that it could hardly have been the unaided work of one of El Greco's pupils and still less that of his son, Jorge Manuel. In our opinion there is an absolute affinity between these diminutive figures and the ones in the upper part of the *Annunciation* painted for the Tavera Hospital *(Fig. 244)*.

An image of *St. Sebastian* which has been cut into two halves, the upper part being in the Prado and the lower in the Arenaza Collection in Madrid *(Figs. 265 to 267 - Cat. 241)*, is a faithful replica of the partial version already studied, which belonged to the Royal Collection of Romania *(Fig. 218)*. But the execution is different, with more intense contrasts and more abrupt modelling. The head is one of the most daring and beautiful examples of that facial deformation —distortion, in fact— that gives such character to the images created by the great painter in these closing

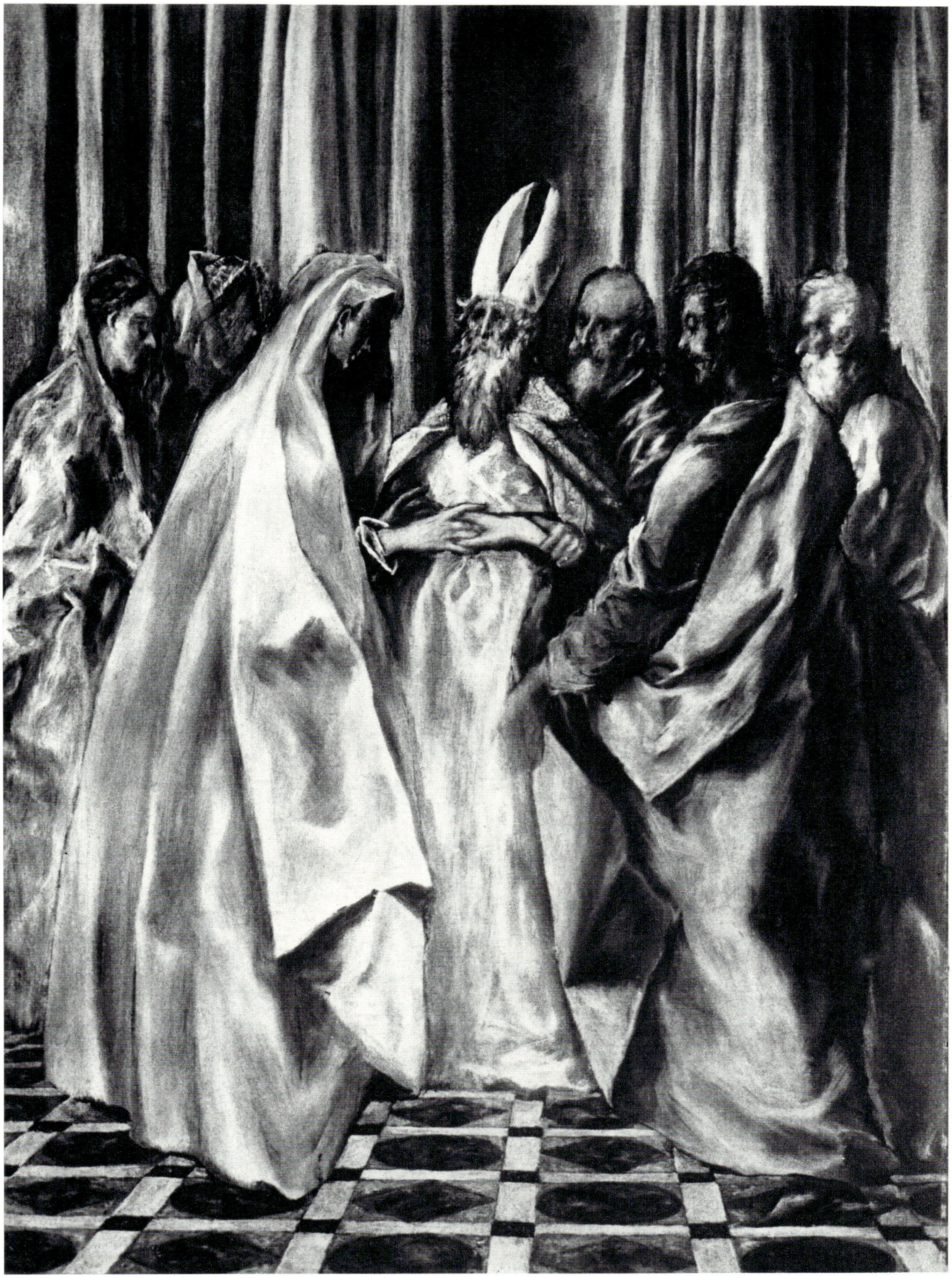

Fig. 255. The Marriage of the Virgin, 1608-1614. Bucharest, National Museum of Romania. Cat. No. 229.

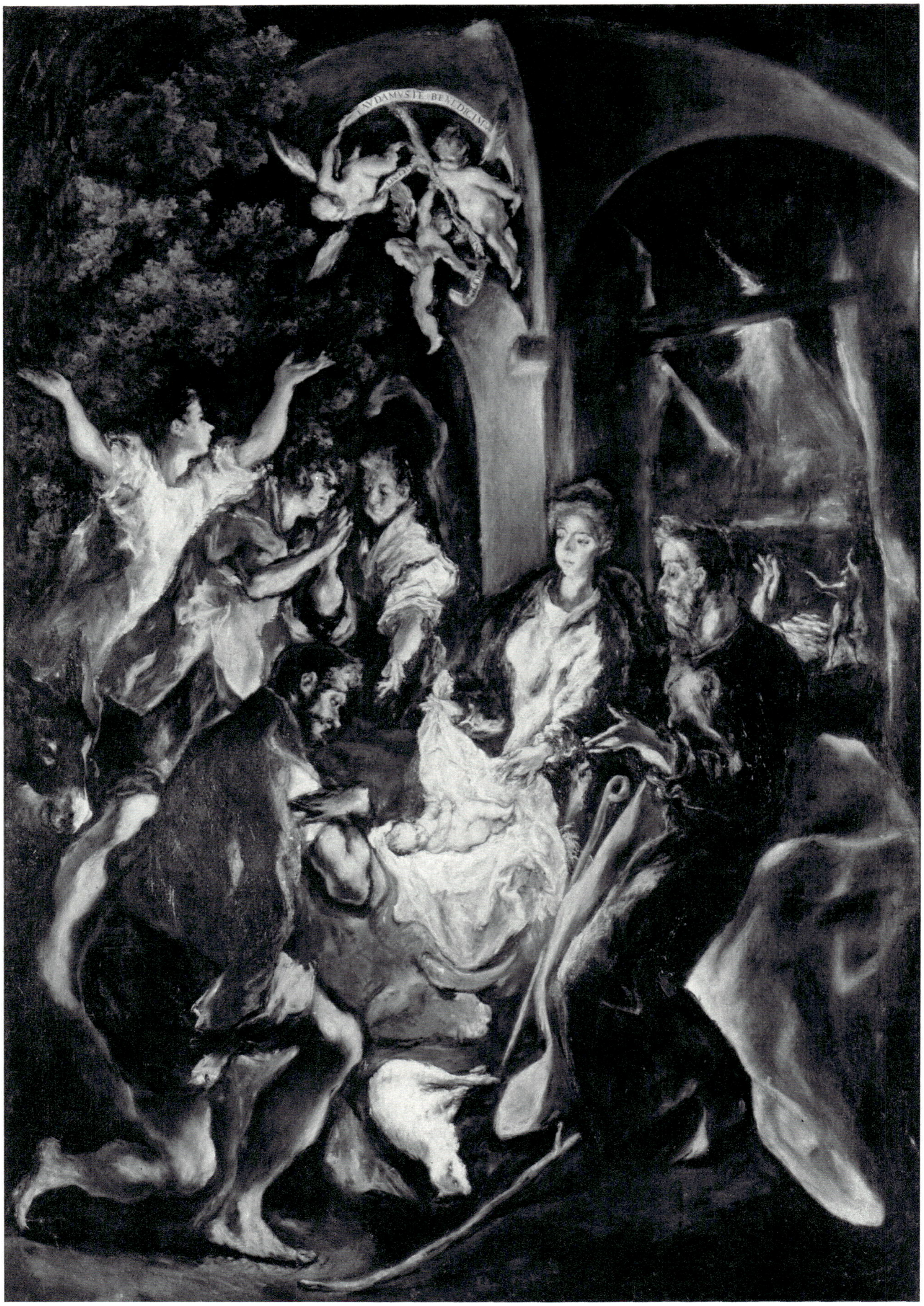

Fig. 256. The Adoration of the shepherds, 1603-1608. New York, Metropolitan Museum. Cat. No. 230.

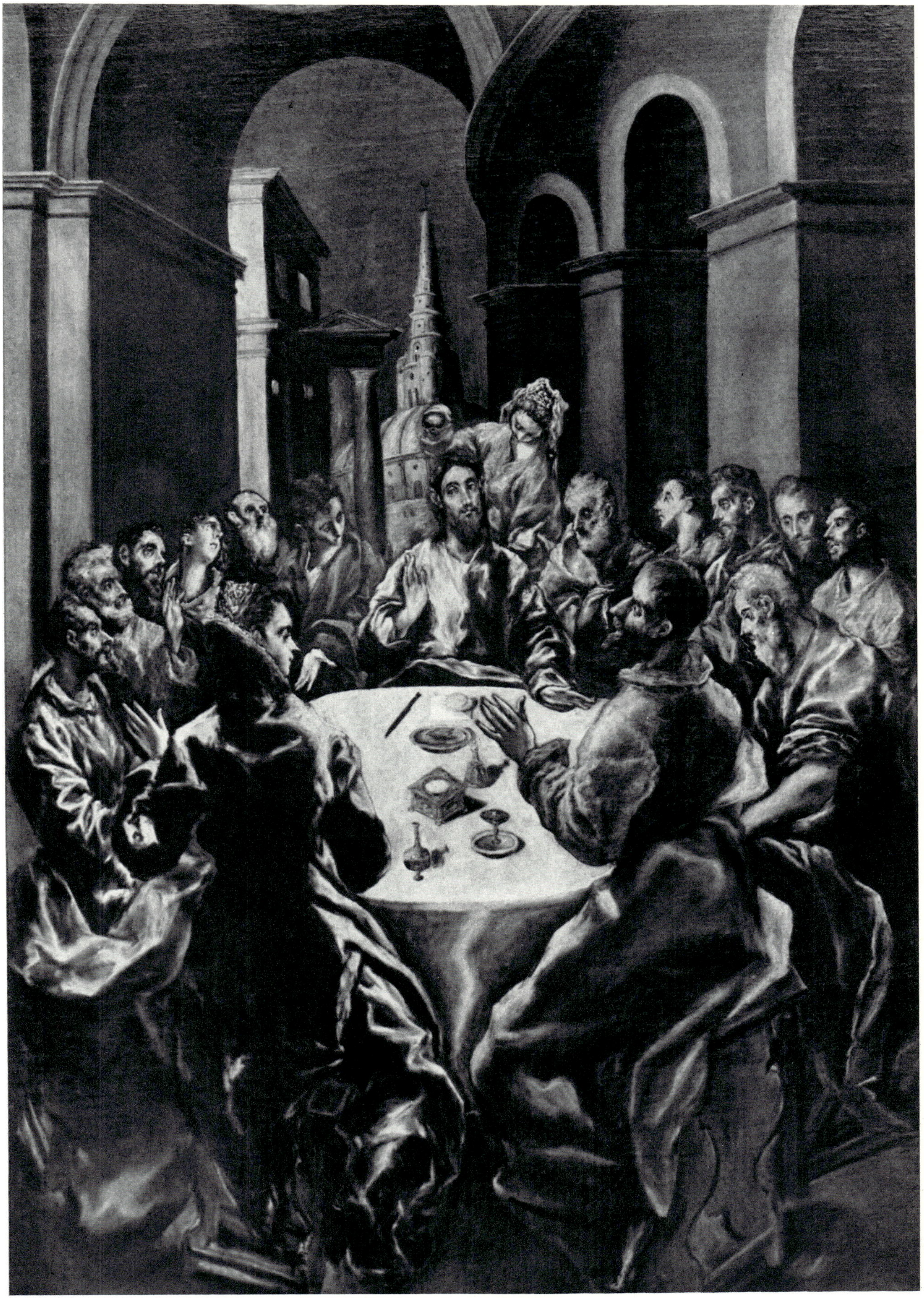

Fig. 257. Christ in the house of Simon, 1608-1614. Chicago, Art Institute. Cat. No. 231.

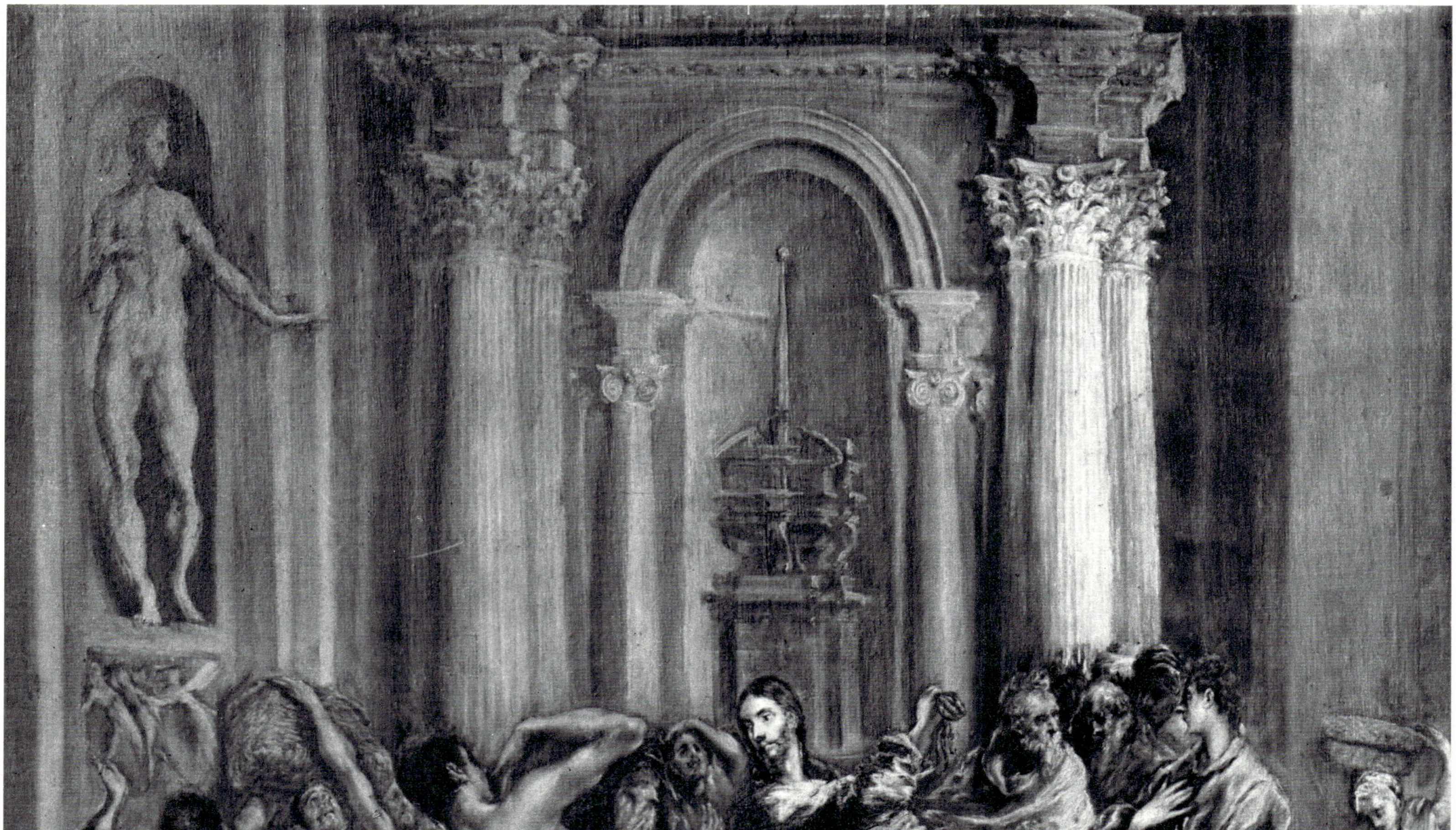

Fig. 258. Christ cleansing the Temple, 1608-1614. Madrid, Church of San Ginés. Cat. No. 233.

years of his life. Beneath the background of clouds, dense and shaded with strange reflections, we have a last, spectral version of the landscape of Toledo. The chiaroscuro is arranged here with miraculous skill, creating an atmosphere that is at once naturalistic and magical.

This study of El Greco's works in his last years rules out any decline in his powers, nor can we find in them the trace of a precarious state of physical health. On the contrary, it would seem that his inner life revives with prodigious new springs of youth and strength which enable him to attain the heights of his genius, not only in the expressionistic visions to which he was most readily led by his temperament, but also —and just as much— in portraits of implacable objectiveness.

Portraits

We will begin our study of El Greco's last portraits by discussing that of *Jerónimo Ceballos* in the Prado, which already belonged to the collections of the Spanish Crown in the seventeenth century *(Figure 268 - Cat. 242)*. Once again the great visionary shows his capacity for the realism of an incomparable confrontation. Nothing in this work betrays the age of the artist, who was nearly seventy, for the painting seems to have been done at the very height of his strength and ease. As we have already said, however, his last works are the culmination of all that went before, though this culmination was brought about rather in a line that we might call expressionistic —with works like the *Laocoön*— than in the realms of realism.

In its vivid realism —by which we mean the direct sensation of life conveyed— the superb picture of *Fray Hortensio Paravicino* is one of the finest portraits ever painted by El Greco *(Fig. 269 - Cat. 243)*. At one time (1724) it belonged to the Duke of Arcos; at the beginning of the present century it was acquired by the Boston Museum, where it hangs today. The sitter, a humanist and poet, dedicated some of his poems to El Greco. One of them includes the famous phrase: "Greece gave him life and brushes/ Toledo a better homeland where he begins/to achieve with death eternities." In another he speaks of the excellence of the portrait El Greco had painted of him, most probably the one we are now studying. Normally El Greco painted his sitters in a certain state of inner tension, contained and introspective. Without losing sight of the sitter's psychology, he tended to paint the general spirit of his age, or at least what it seems to us to have been. But in this portrait of Paravicino he paints the Trinitarian monk as if in a conversational attitude, looking attentively at the person he is speaking to, in this case the artist. His latent expression reveals an open spirit, very unlike that of the inquisitors or prelates of the time. The monk is sitting at his ease, as we can see in the excellently painted arms and hands. As for the colour, we are confronted once more by those unusual harmonies to which El Greco has accustomed us. The monk's habit is white —with the blue and red cross— and dark brown, while the back of his chair is a bluish black. But the ochre of the wall in the background harmonizes all the tonalities, which are not subjected to any marked effect of light.

The impressive canvas that represents *Cardinal Juan Pardo de Tavera* (1472-1545) is linked with the portrait attributed to Alonso Berruguete and with a death mask taken from the prelate's body, both of which are kept in the hospital that bears his name *(Fig. 270 - Cat. 244)*. This work was probably painted around 1608, when El Greco was just starting to work on the great commission he had received from Pedro Salazar de Mendoza, the administrator of the hospital. A portrait of Cardinal Tavera is mentioned in the inventory of Mendoza's estate, drawn up after his death in 1629. The work now before us is probably the one in this inventory, since it is still in the hospital today.

The colour is brilliant and the structure recalls that of the *St. Jerome* in the Frick Collection *(Figure 133)*, with superb qualities in the sitter's clothing and a face with a dramatic expression that undoubtedly comes from the sources on which the painter based this work, particularly the death mask, which would probably have had a considerable impact on El Greco's sensibility. It is a bloodless face, rather that of an invalid than of an ascetic. The contrasts of textures are perfect and are heightened by the differences of colour. The sitter, placed against a smooth, dark background, gives us the impression of being yet another archetype of the Spain of that age, which to some extent justifies all the clichés that have been coined in this respect. The execution is perfect in the sharp face, the hand that is visible and the brilliant purple of the robes.

We now come to another of El Greco's great portraits, that of an unidentified *Trinitarian monk*, which was formerly in the collection of the Marqués de la Torrecilla and now hangs in the Nelson Gallery in Kansas City *(Fig. 271 - Cat. 245)*. This must be a very late work, most probably done in the painter's last years. Its technique and structures recall those seen in the figures of the *View and plan of Toledo (Fig. 252)*, but the evanescence and dissolution of detail combine to produce a formidable portrait. A rather stout figure, with his head covered by the cowl of his cloak, he is shown sitting in the same chair as Fray Hortensio Paravicino. There is a certain lightness in the background that sets off the tones of the flesh tints, contrasting with the darkness of the cloak, which covers the white habit but leaves it visible from the level of the breast, with the same blue and red cross of the Trinitarian Order. This is also a direct, realistic and human portrait, in which the interest in the capturing of the real model prevails over any other consideration. What might look like distortion in the hands is really rather simplification, for El Greco is already confident that his brush, in depicting the exterior of a form, will also give presence to the inner structure. The same occurs, though with greater truth and intensity, in the face. The modelling has an irregular execution that is not always blended, but certain irregularities in the impasto only serve to give more life to the detail they affect, as is the case, for instance, with the right eye and eyelids or with the outline of the face on the same side.

The portrait in the Musée de Picardie shows us a middle-aged gentleman, rather stout and with black hair and beard *(Fig. 272 - Cat. 246)*. Under the name of Herrera this picture figured in the gallery of the Ursáis family of Seville, to whom it belonged until 1872, when it was sold in Paris. It is a curious fact that it should have been the portraits that first attracted the attention of the world's collectors to El Greco. This portrait may possibly be the one that figures with the name of Dr. Soria de Herrera in Jorge Manuel's second inventory. It is of later date than 1610. We may observe an evident preoccupation with the likeness and the modelling, which is magnificent in the face, but which in the hands, above all in the left hand, is extraordinarily deformed and inexplicably soft. The structure of these hands, which has no precedents in El Greco's work, suggests the intervention of Jorge Manuel. It reappears in the portrait of García Ibáñez Múgica de Bracamonte, which is studied below. The very dark background causes the body almost to melt into it, but on the other hand it sets off the sitter's head very strongly. The look is admirably painted and the work as a whole, while less direct and beautiful than the portrait of Paravicino, is not without a profound humanity. The technique is softer than that of the portraits painted during the middle period.

The portrait of *Canon Bosio* has been identified by the inscription in the book: "Bosius Canonici" *(Fig. 273 - Cat. 247)*. This work was probably painted some time after 1610 and is treated in accordance with El Greco's more usual concepts, in half-length against a smooth background, the hands being visible resting on a large open book. The sitter belongs absolutely to that gallery of hispanic types bequeathed by the great Cretan. This is an elderly man, with white hair and beard and a hard look, a man one guesses to be very upright but inclined to fanaticism rather than to comprehension or tolerance. His clothing, with a fur-lined coat thrown open at the throat, is as superbly painted as the head. The hands are less intense and their modelling shows a tendency to that out-of-focus character sometimes to be found in El Greco's detailing.

Finally we come to the portrait of *García Ibáñez Múgica de Bracamonte*, which hangs in the Cathedral of Avila and which, despite the contrary opinion of Wethey, we consider to be an original Greco *(Fig. 274 - Cat. 248)*. We need only observe the similarity of the hands to those of the previous portraits, especially that which may represent Soria de Herrera *(Fig. 272)*. The sitter seems to be frozen, as it were, in his pose, with his narrow white collar separating his sharp face from the black mass of his clothing. His right hand is placed on his breast and his left on a table beside his biretta. The background has vertical rhythms alluding to structures of the background wall. The work is in a poor state of preservation, but it does permit stylistic analysis which, in our opinion, strengthens the case for its attribution to El Greco. All the details indicate that it is a later work, probably done very near the end of the painter's life. It is impossible to see any special interest in his model on his part and the portrait is painted in rather routine fashion.

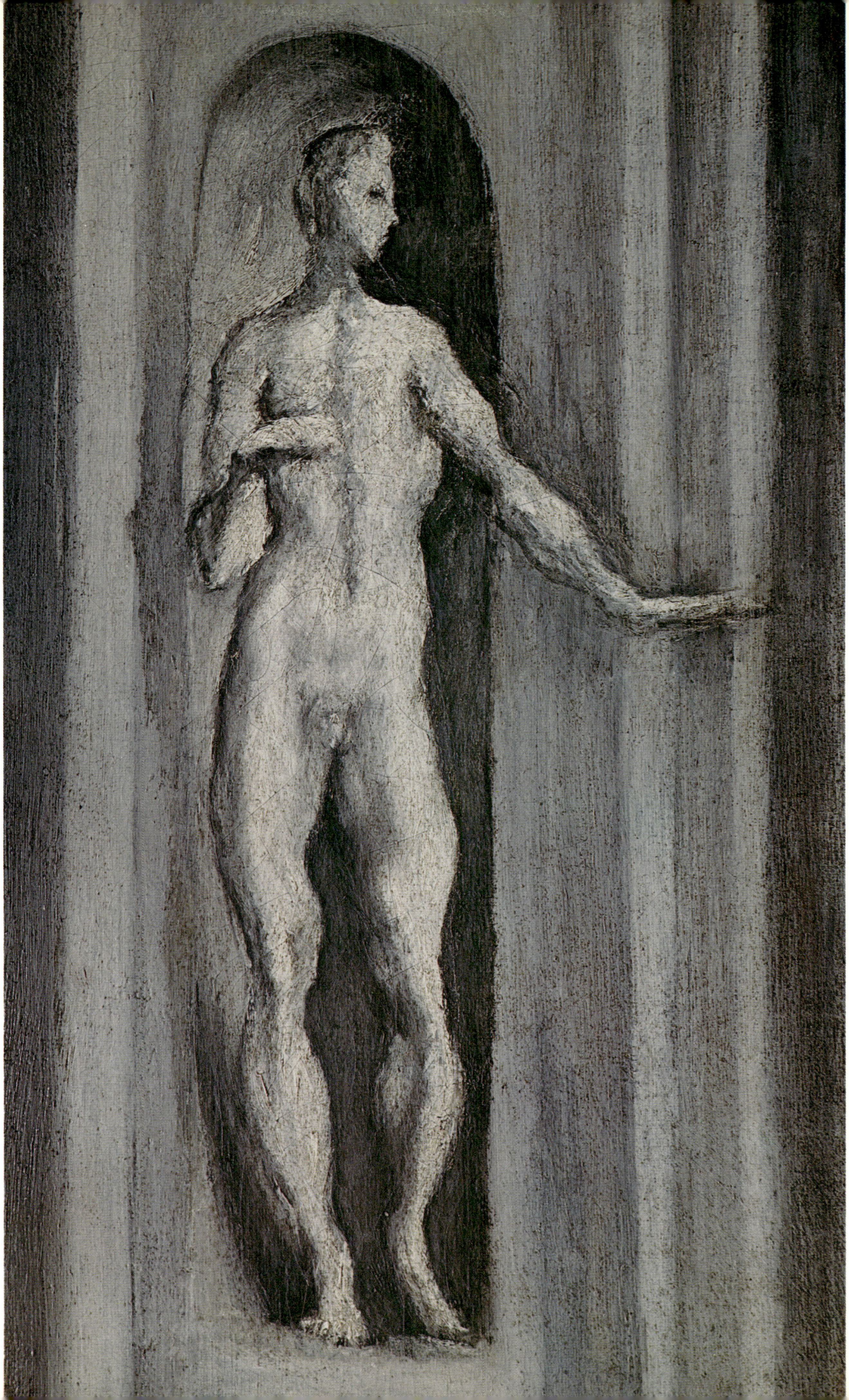

Fig. 259.
Detail of figure 258.

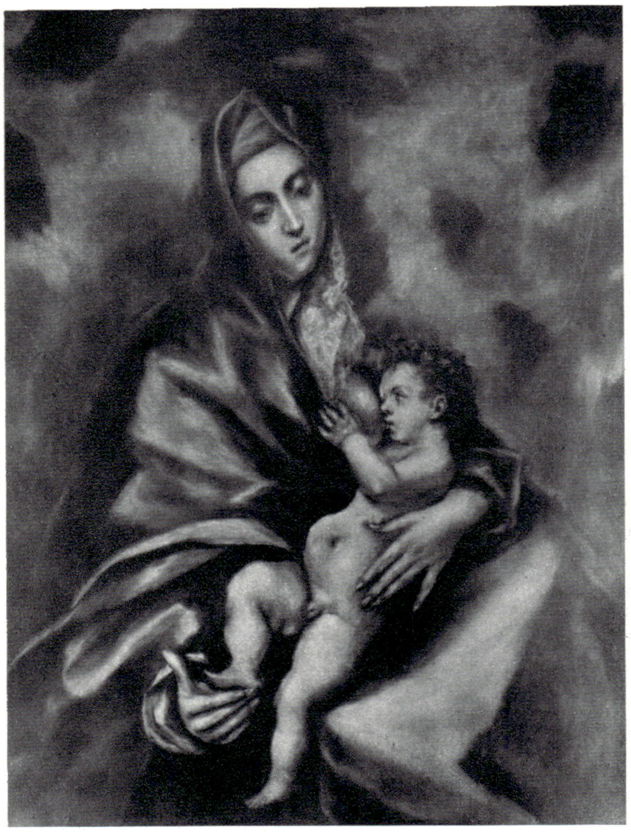

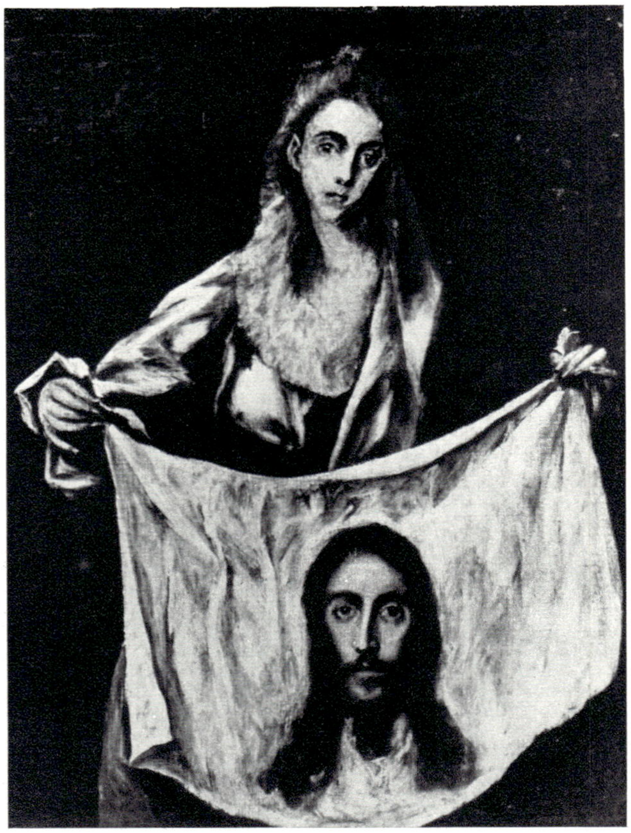

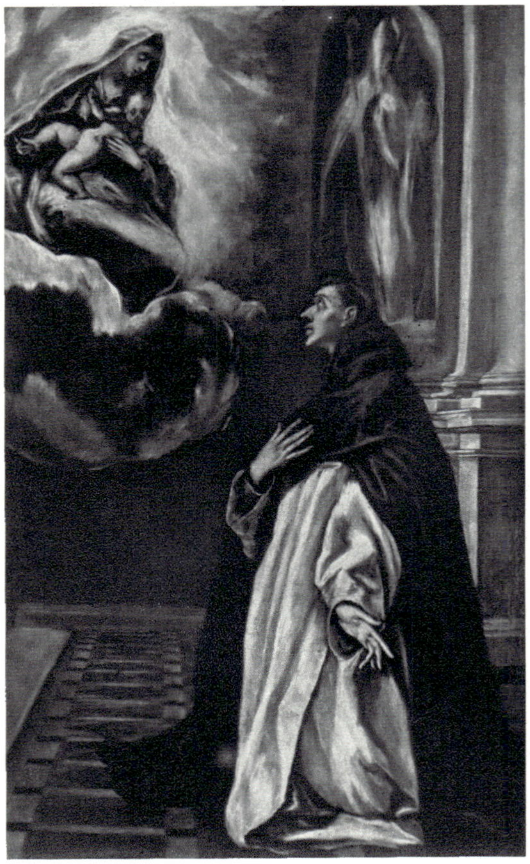

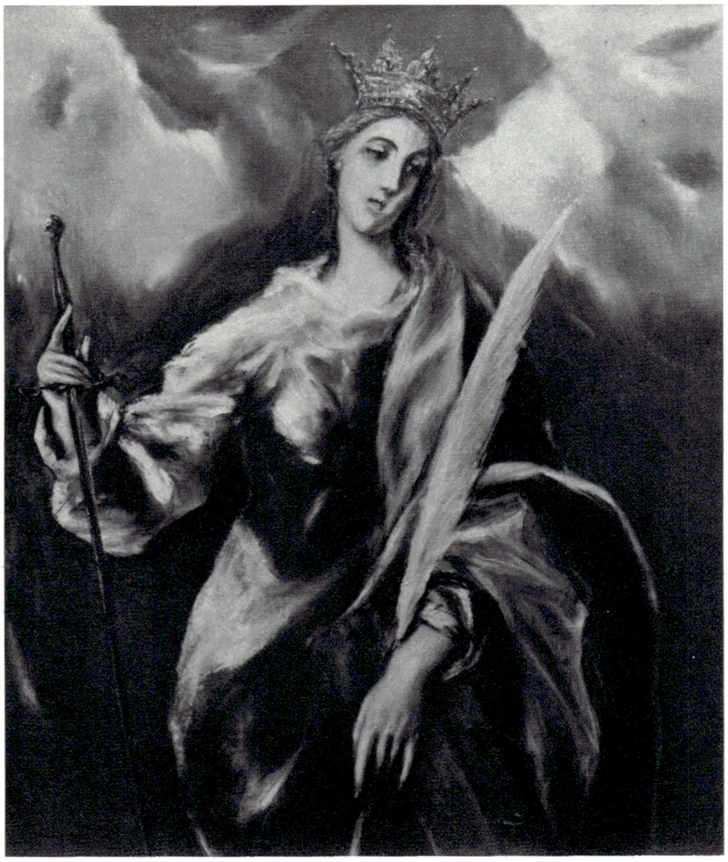

Fig. 260. Virgin and Child, 1608-1614. Madrid, Marquesa de Campo Real Collection. Cat. No. 234.
Fig. 261. St. Veronica, 1608-1614. Buenos Aires, B. del Carril Collection. Cat. No. 235.
Fig. 262. The Apparition of the Virgin and Child to St. Hyacinth, 1608-1614. Merion, Barnes Foundation. Cat. No. 236.
Fig. 263. St. Catherine of Alexandria, 1608-1614. New York, at dealer's. Cat. No. 239.

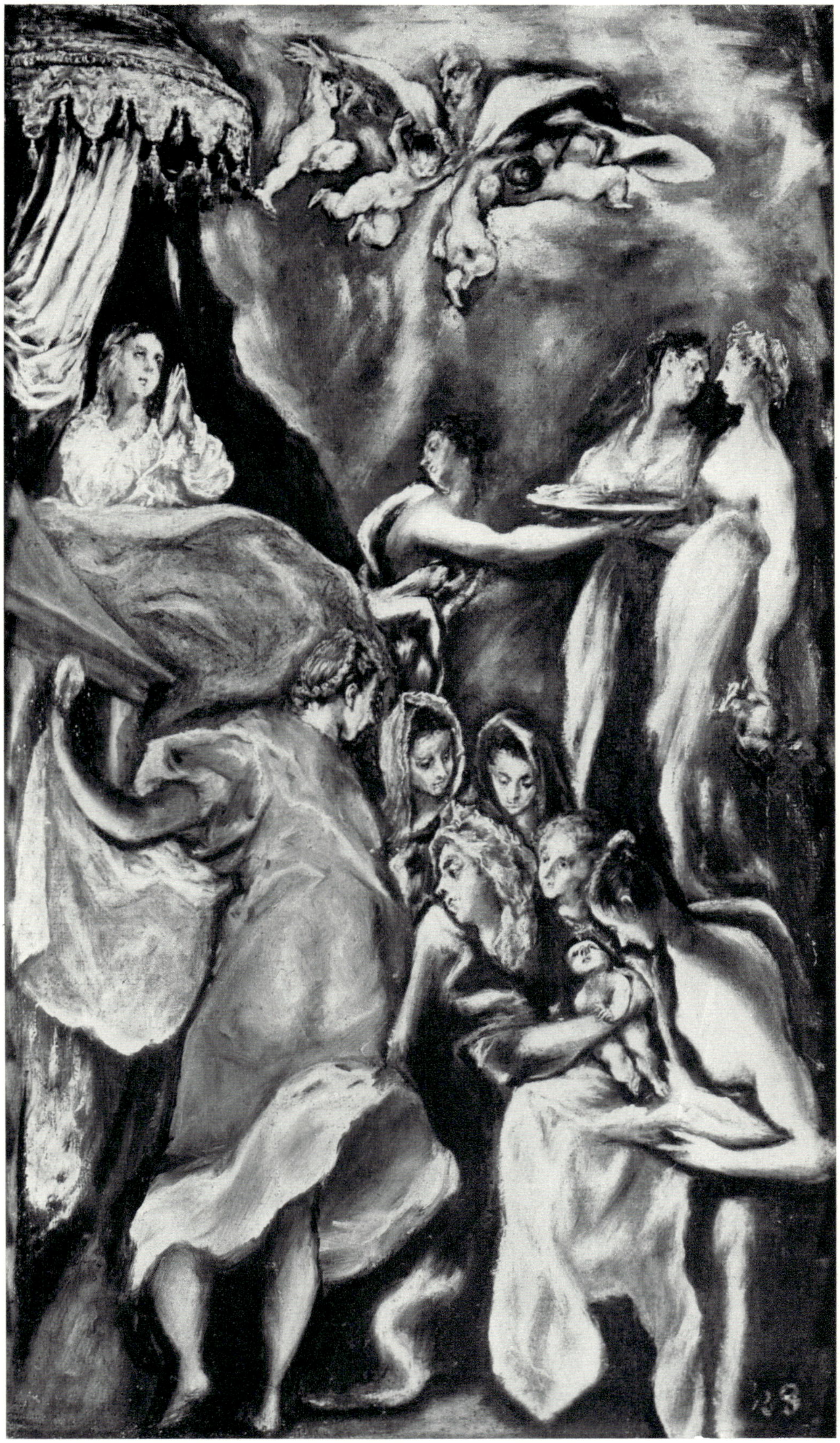

Fig. 264. The Birth of the Virgin, 1608-1614.
Zurich, Emil G. Bührle Collection.
Cat. No. 240.

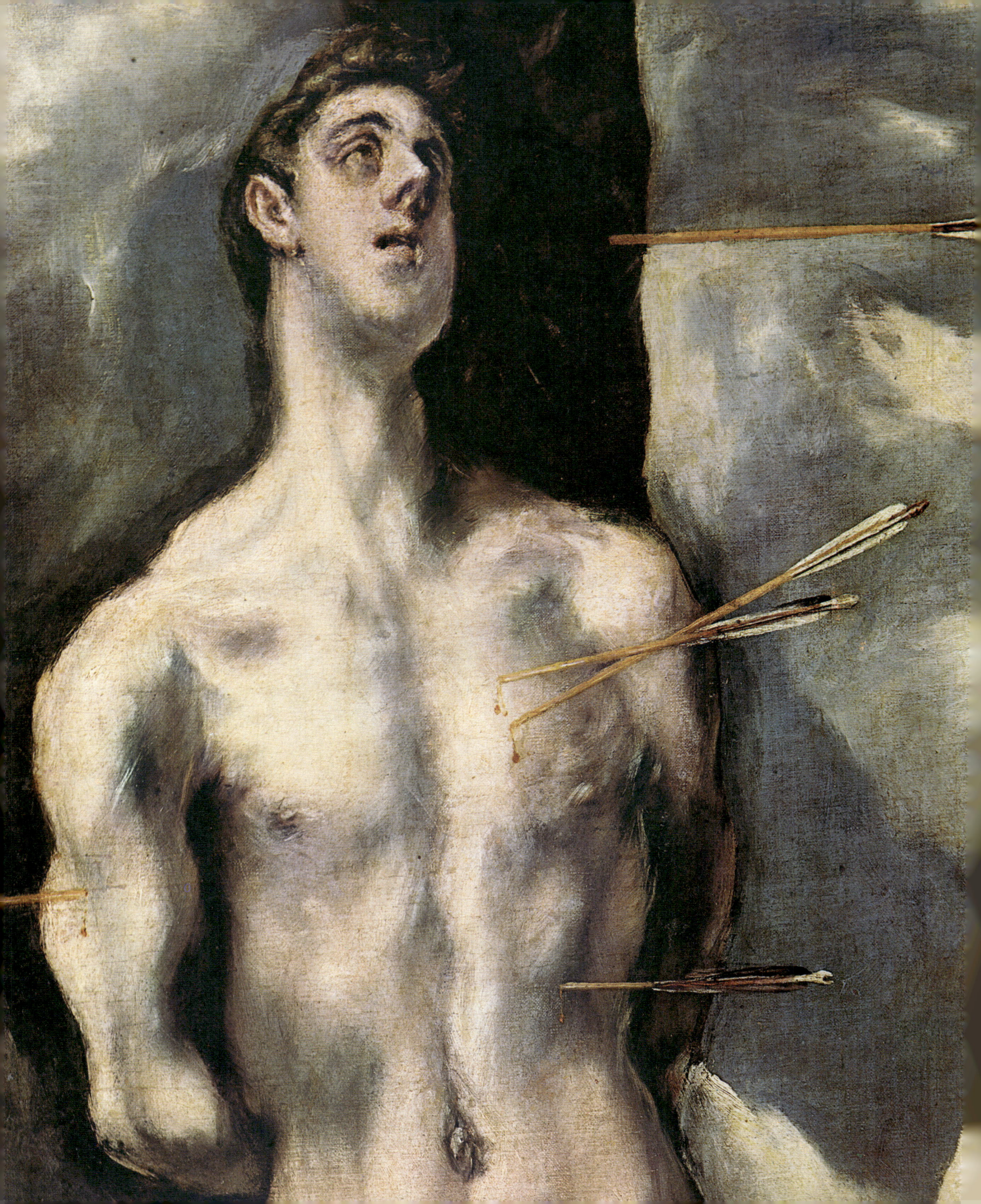

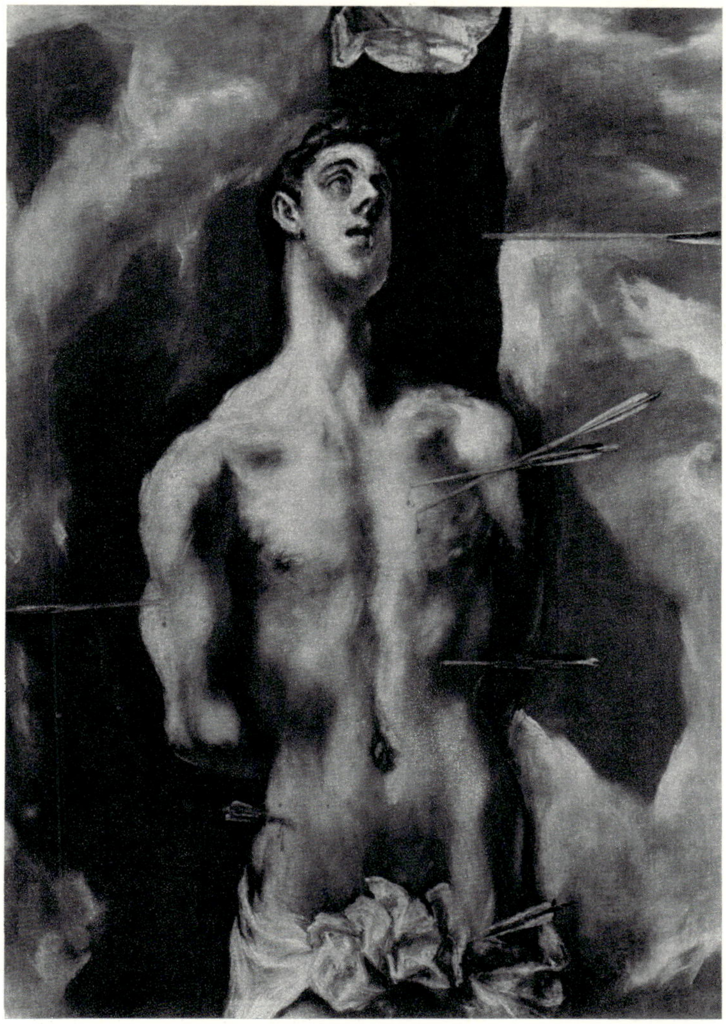

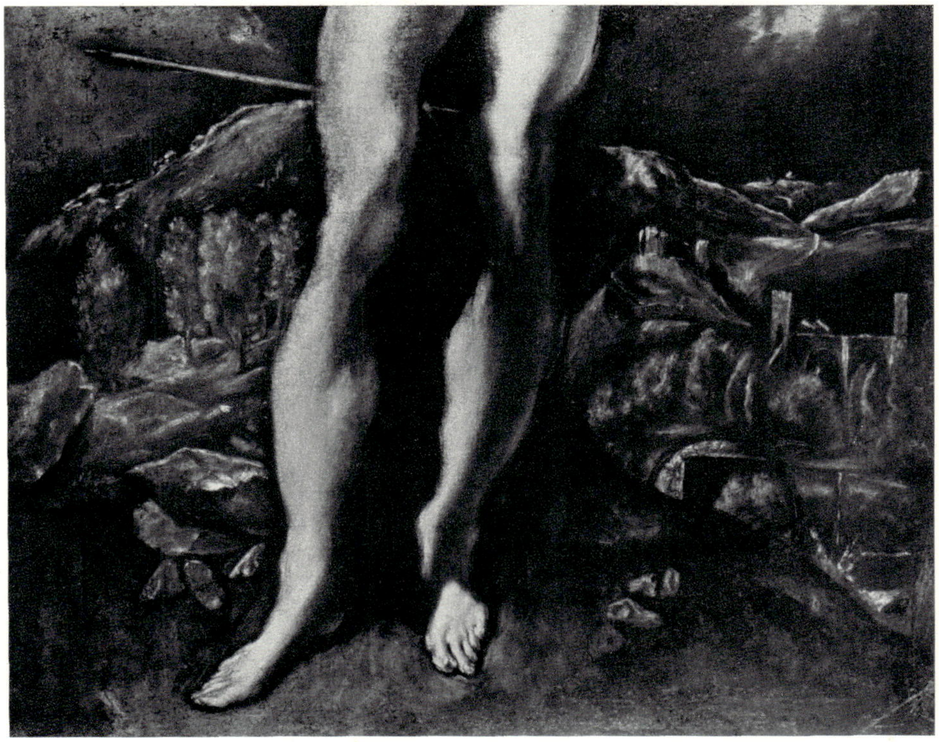

Figs. 265 & 266. St. Sebastian, 1608-1614. Madrid, Prado. Cat. No. 241.
Fig. 267. St. Sebastian, 1608-1614. Madrid, Arenaza Collection. Cat. No. 241.

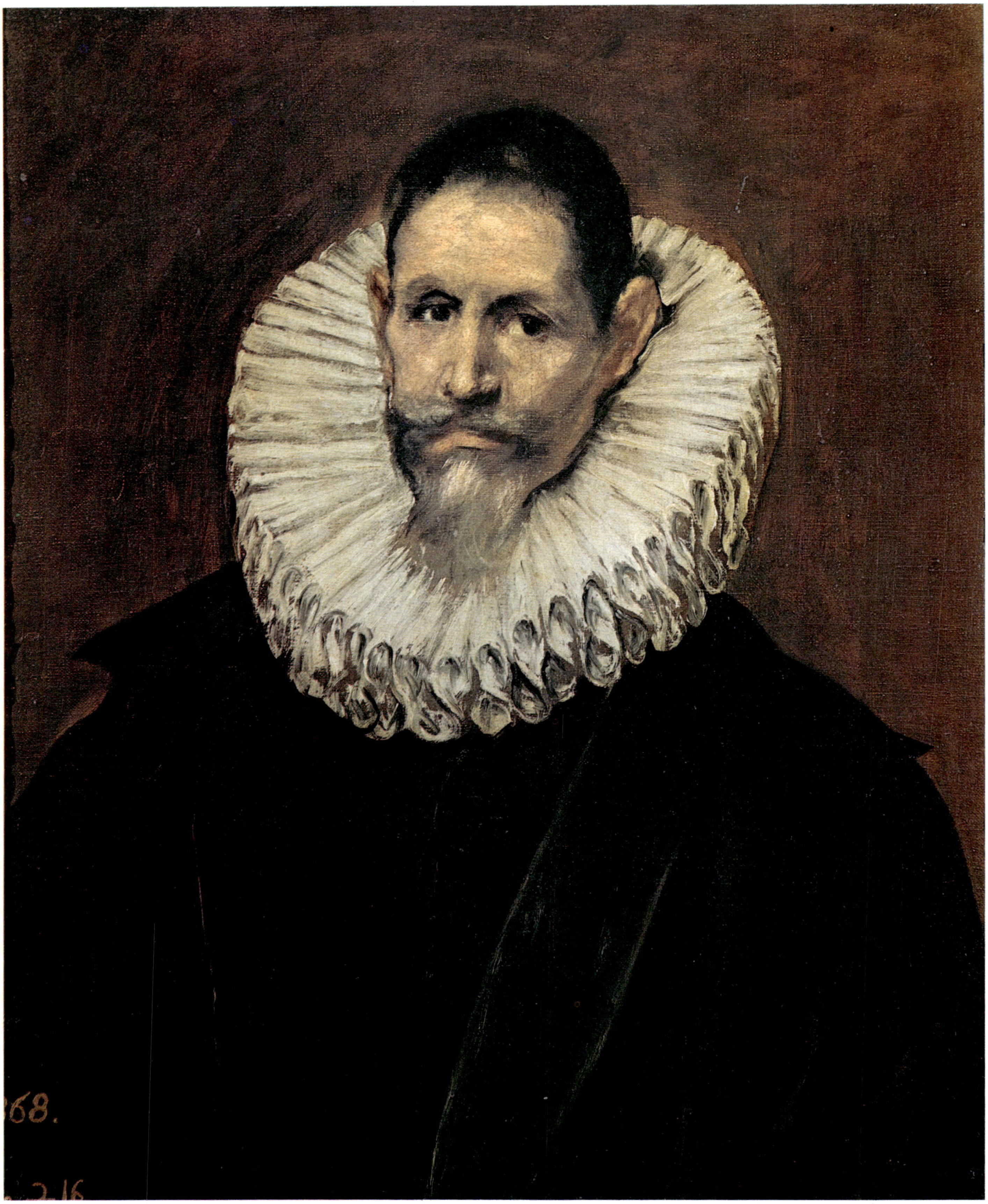

Fig. 268. Jerónimo de Ceballos, 1608-1614. Madrid, Prado. Cat. No. 242.

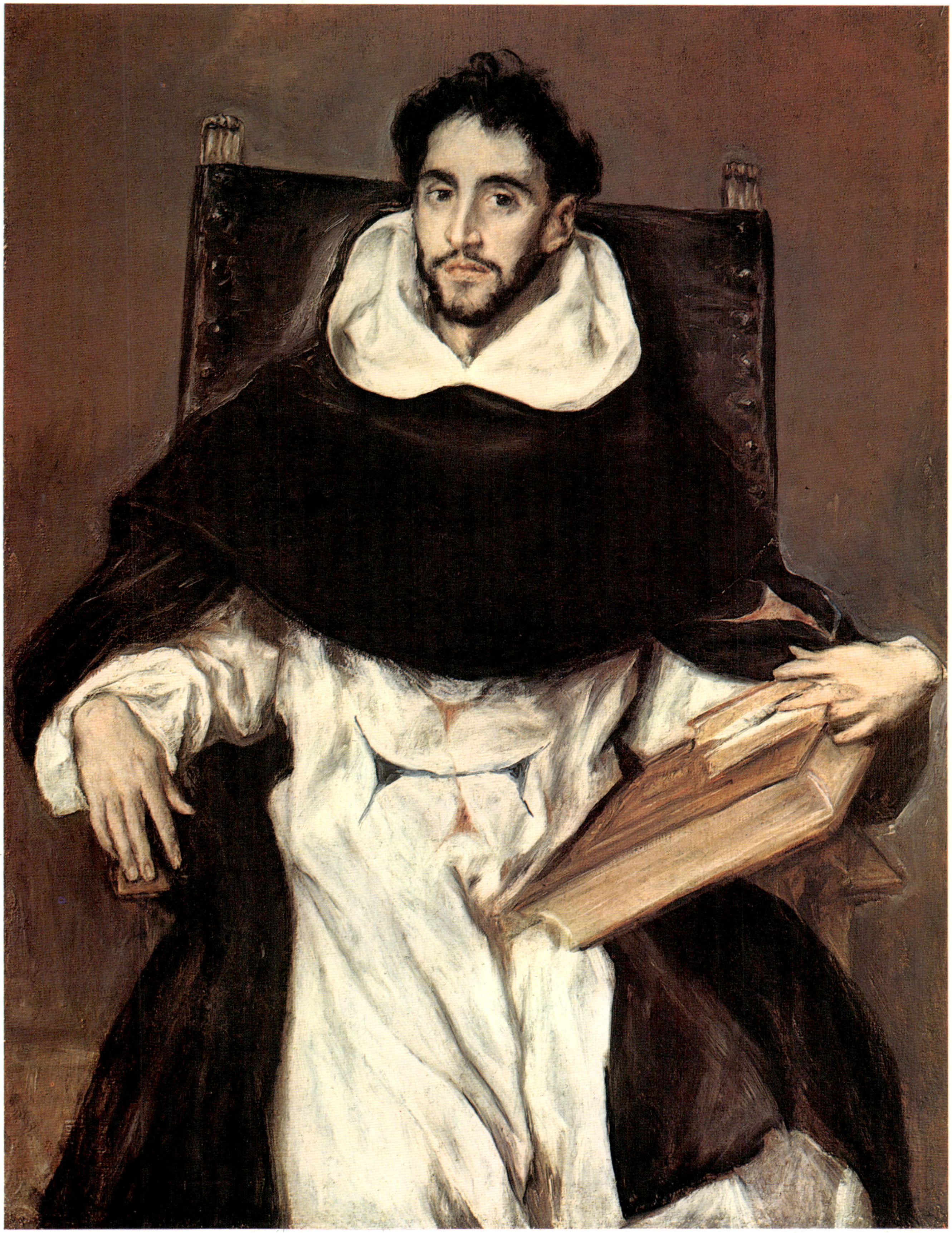

Fig. 269. Fray Hortensio Félix Paravicino, c. 1610. Boston, Museum of Fine Arts. Cat. No. 243.

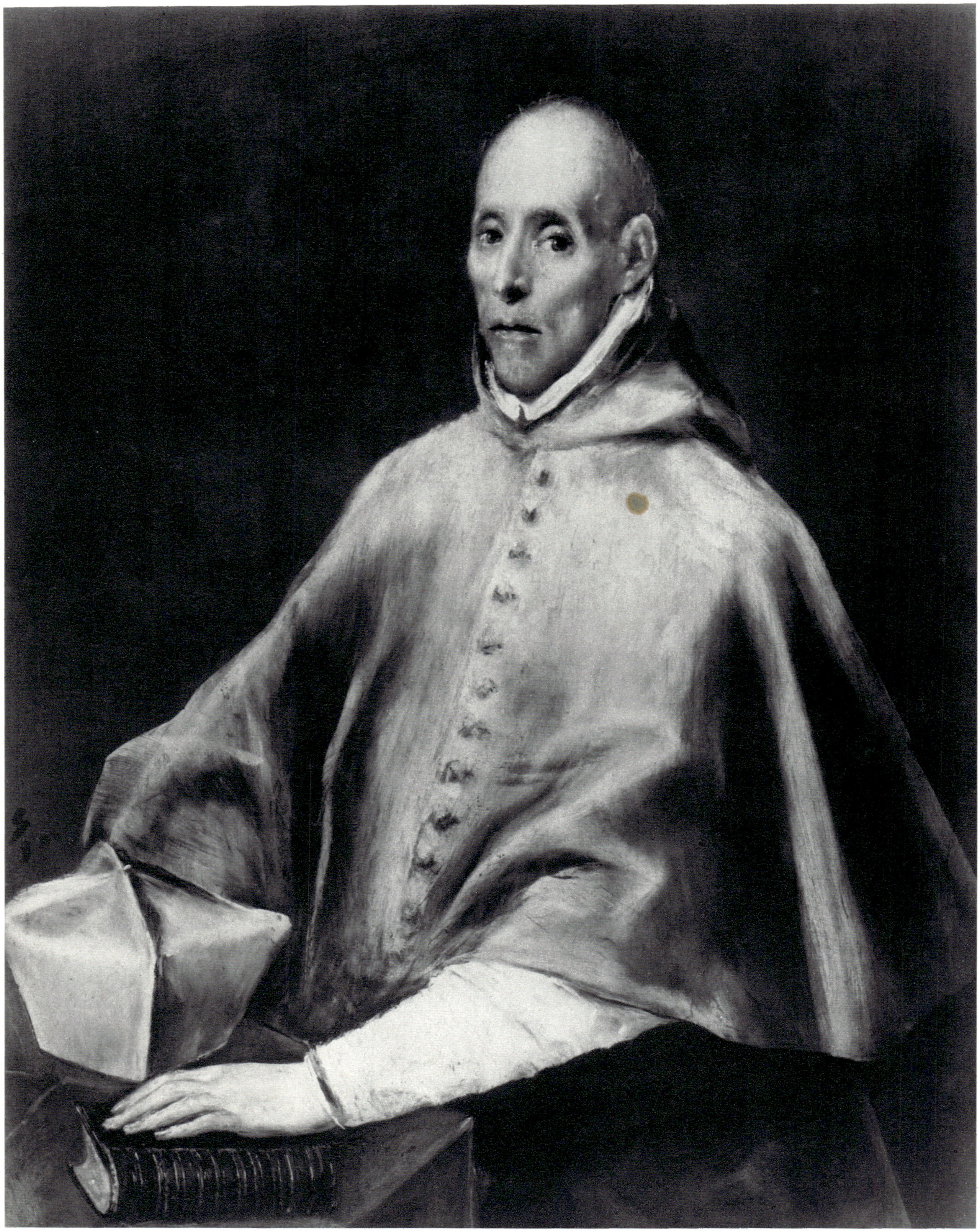

Fig. 270. Cardinal Juan de Tavera, c. 1608. Toledo, Hospital de San Juan Bautista de Afuera. Cat. No. 244.

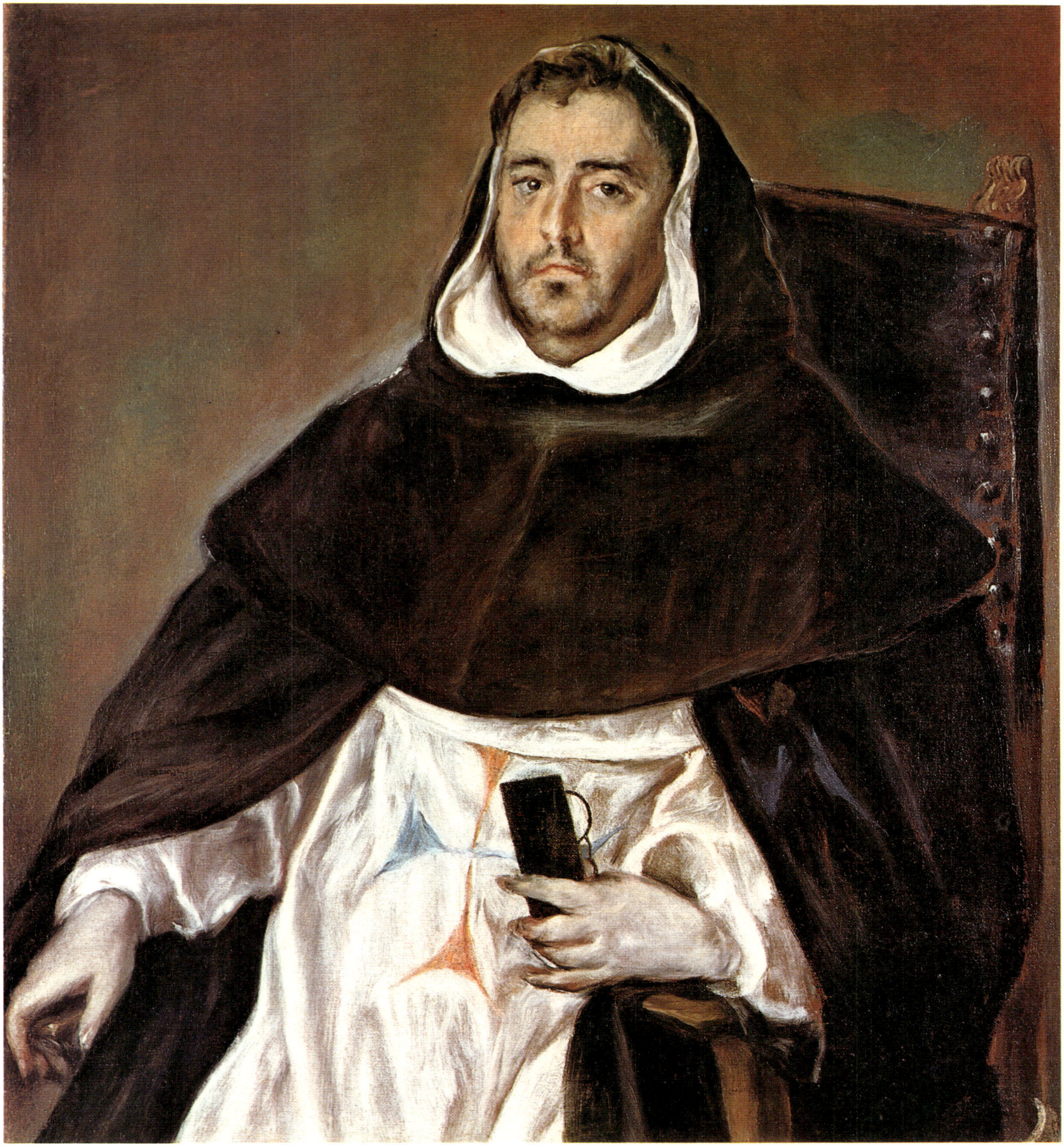

Fig. 271. A Trinitarian monk, 1610-1614. Kansas City, William Rockhill Nelson Gallery of Art. Cat. No. **245**.

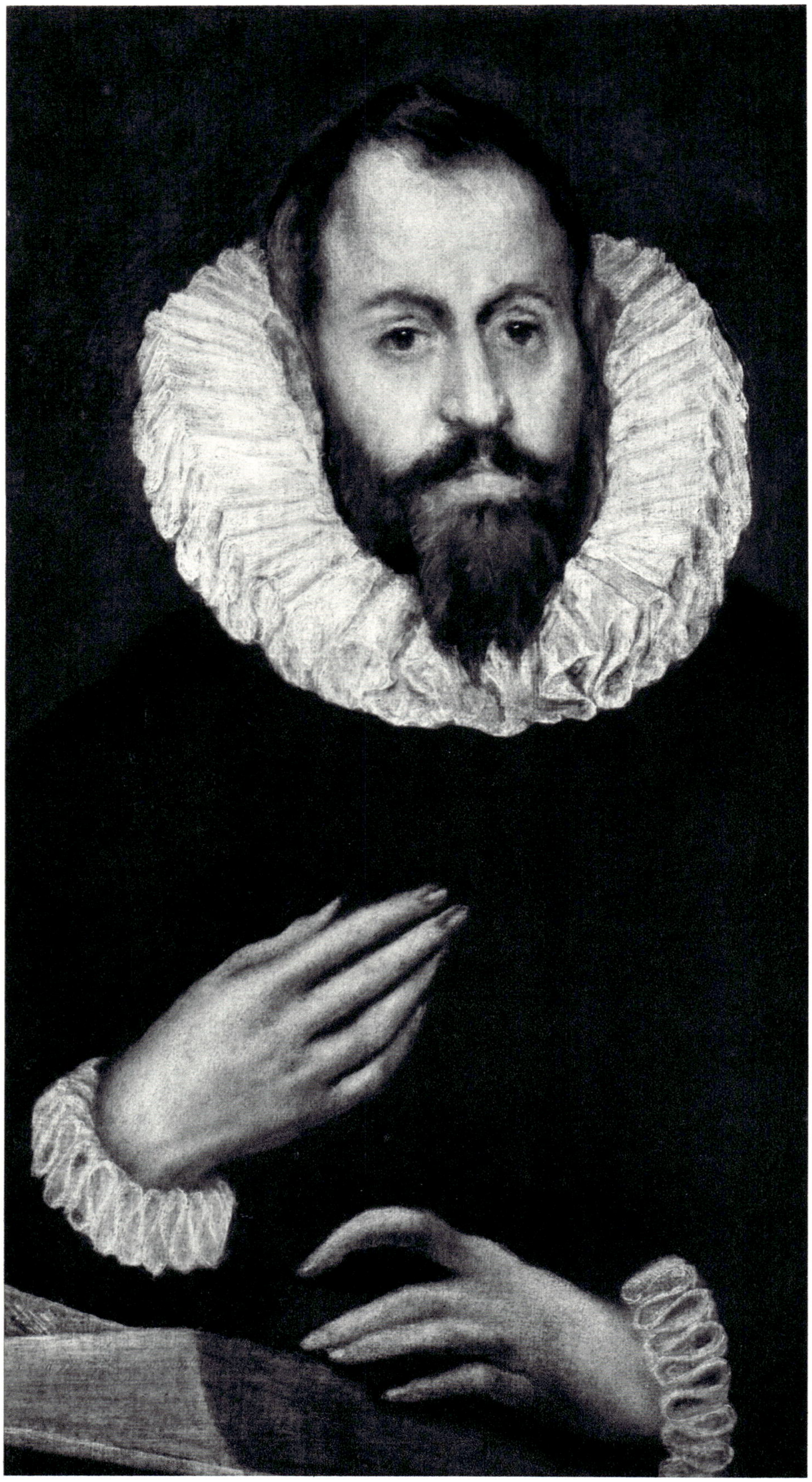

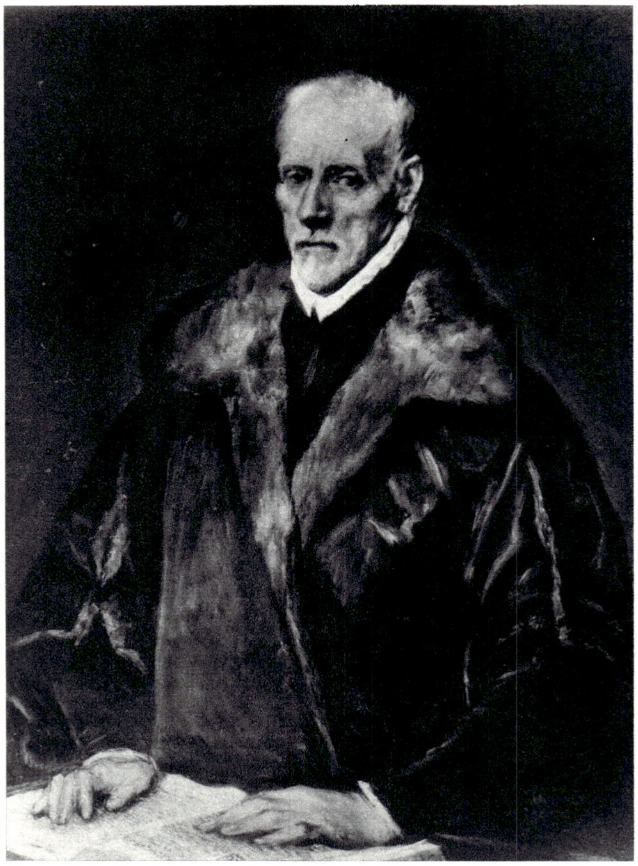

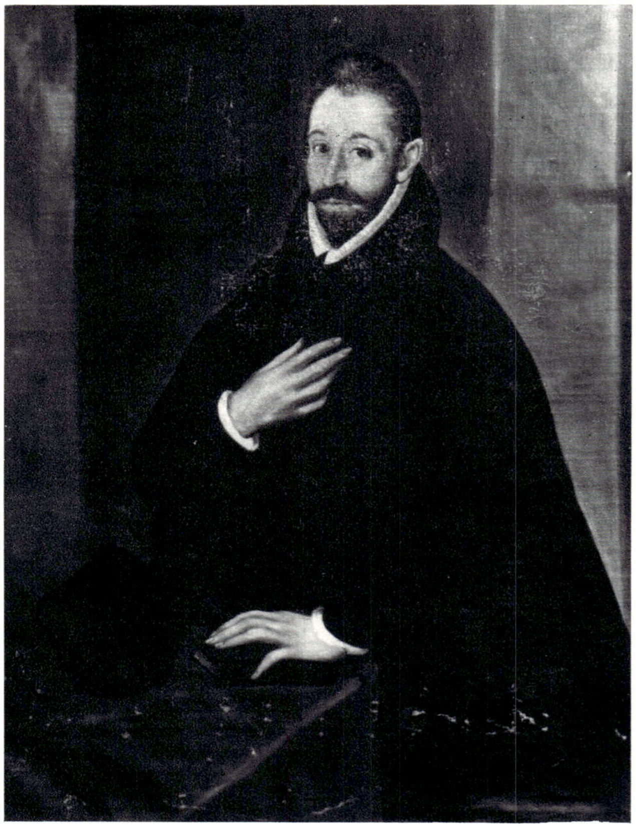

Fig. 272. Portrait of an unknown gentleman, 1610-1614. Amiens, Musée de Picardie. Cat. No. 246.
Fig. 273. Canon Bosio, 1610-1614. Sinaia, Royal Palace. Cat. No. 247.
Fig. 274. García Ibáñez Múgica de Bracamonte, 1610-1614. Avila, Cathedral. Cat. No. 248

VIII

1615

THE DEATH OF EL GRECO — THOUGHTS ON THE CORPUS OF HIS PAINTINGS — SKETCHES IN EL GRECO'S WORK — THE "APOSTLE" SERIES — DRAWINGS ATTRIBUTED TO EL GRECO — WORKSHOP PAINTINGS AFTER LOST ORIGINALS — EL GRECO AS A SCULPTOR — THE ENGRAVINGS OF DIEGO DE ASTOR — NOTES ON JORGE MANUEL THEOTOCÓPULI — EL GRECO'S PHYSICAL LIKENESS — THE INVENTORIES OF EL GRECO'S ESTATE.

As we said in the preceding chapter, El Greco died on April 7th 1614. At the time of his death he was living in what were known as the "houses" of the Marqués de Villena, that rambling building which had been one of the finest mansions in the city of Toledo and in which El Greco had taken several spacious apartments for his workshop and his living quarters. In the "Book of burials" of Santo Tomé, his parish church, we read: "On the seventh of ... Dominico Greco died, intestate. He received the Sacraments. He was buried in Santo Domingo el Antiguo and donated candles". In fact, the powers of attorney given to his son seven days before were as valid as any will. In this document, first published by San Román, the executors appointed —apart from his son— were his first friend in Toledo, Don Luis de Castilla, and Fray Domingo Banegas, a monk of the monastery of San Pedro Mártir. The funeral was a fairly ceremonious affair —though less so than he deserved— and Góngora and Paravicino dedicated sonnets to the catafalque that held his mortal remains.

Jorge Manuel inherited the property and the debts of his father, and between April 12th and July 7th of the same year the inventory of which we give an extract —with commentaries— at the end of this chapter was drawn up. This inventory confirms what was written by Jusepe Martínez: that "the wealth left by El Greco" consisted of his paintings and sculptures. A wealth that probably did not seem excessive at the time and one that was confined to the work the painter left in his workshop. But an immense, incalculable wealth in the present age, bearing in mind all the works scattered throughout the best museums and private collections all over the world.

Thus ended the life and work of an artist whose existence and evolution certainly seem absolutely unforeseeable, whether we recall the humble "*Madonniero*" of Crete or the young apprentice in Venice who endeavoured —in the shadow of the greatest painters of the day, especially Titian— to learn the principles that were to enable him to find himself, attain heights that he possibly dared not even dream of in his youth and create, in short, an art in which traditional and collective values are closely bound up with those of his individual personality.

But before this could be achieved —and even during the years of his greatest works, after his possibly unexpected journey to Spain and his decision to remain in the country— the great artist had to bear considerable reverses: his failure with Philip II, his lawsuits with the tight-fisted administrators of religious bodies, the mediocrity of provincial life and sometimes, almost certainly, financial difficulties, if not downright poverty.

In this book we have traced the evolution of El Greco's style and have synthesized the dominant factors of his aesthetic and technique, indicating —as far as possible in a text of such necessarily limited scope as this— the progressive transformation of his concept of form and emotion and not forgetting anything that may possibly be deduced from his creative procedures. The results obtained may be considered valid as an account of his life and work in essentials, but the mysteries remain latent and they appear whenever we attempt to establish the specific dimensions of the corpus of his work and that of his circle. This problem, of course, is not exclusive to the great Cretan, for others of the greatest artists —Velázquez,

Rembrandt, Goya— are surrounded by similar aureoles of uncertainty, thanks to their need to systematize their production in workshops, to the works of professional copyists who collaborated with the masters for social or economic reasons and to their hosts of plagiarists.

The corpus of El Greco's paintings really consists of the works we have dealt with in this book and a considerable number of canvases painted in his workshop, under his supervision and according to original sketches of his. There are over three hundred canvases not included in our catalogue which are admitted in other books, in museums and collections as authentic Grecos. This exclusion is not the result of any kind of precautionary measure against unknown elements, for we have given very close consideration to each of these cases —not that this means we consider our own judgment infallible either. This task of discrimination is a very difficult and delicate one and should be faced boldly and dispassionately by the analytical historian. The work of separating the authentic Grecos and the paintings produced by the assistants in his workshop, who achieved some almost perfect imitations, is complicated by the fact that many works that are not completely authentic are signed by El Greco himself, who put his name to them as chief of the workshop.

Naturally, such works were produced with the same materials and the same or a very similar technique and followed, moreover, the sketches painted by the master himself, which were the prototypes for the subject matter. El Greco organized his workshop in Toledo for production on what we might call two distinct "levels". The important commissions and the *modelli* were personally painted by him in their entirety; simultaneously he engaged in the production of canvases of somewhat smaller size, with an iconography conditioned by the fashions in popular devotion. In these latter works El Greco took some hand himself, but it would be his assistants —among them his son, Jorge Manuel— that did most of the work. It was as if he had combined the methods observed in Titian's studio with the methodical and not very ambitious working system of the painters of Byzantine icons, among whom his early apprenticeship had begun.

Among his assistants we have already mentioned Francisco Preboste, who probably came from Italy with El Greco; his son, Jorge Manuel, who certainly started in the workshop around 1590, and Luis Tristán, who worked there from 1603 to 1607. It is thought that another of the painter's assistants may have been Pedro Orrente, who, as was mentioned in Chapter VI, lived in Toledo for some time and was on friendly terms with El Greco's family. But there may have been other assistants whose names are unknown to us, for very few of the indentures drawn up during the period in which El Greco lived in Toledo have come down to us.

When organized in this way, the production of a workshop evidently cannot maintain the quality of the master's own works. Hence the "quality" and perfection, quite as much as —or more than— the stylistic features (which can be copied), are important data for the historian to consider when confronted with an "unknown factor"— that is to say, with one of the artist's *probable* works. Everybody knows of that multitude of collectors each of whom believes himself the possessor of an authentic work, when the truth is that all he has is a product of the workshop, an old copy or, worst of all, one of the modern imitations that have invaded the international art market.

But let us return to El Greco's own point of view. This organization of the workshop's production, dividing it into works entirely his own, paintings by assistants with the help of the master and works done completely by assistants, allowed a flexibility of price that was well adapted to the spirit of the age in a country never known for its inclination to pay its artists well. This had already been the reason for the organization that prevailed in medieval workshops. It would be a mistake to believe that traditions like that of the medieval workshop, which answered a profound socio-economic need, were going to vanish as if by magic with the advent of the great artists, who were rather long in coming, anyway, in the Spanish Renaissance. Besides, it should not be forgotten that quite the contrary circumstances —i.e., wealth, good prices and commissions galore— sometimes gave rise to similar situations; in the seventeenth century the great fortune and gifts of Rubens obliged him to employ collaborators to avoid breaking faith with his patrons, albeit that the great artist of Flemish Baroque did so on a much higher level than El Greco and certainly to a much greater extent, though perhaps not quite so much as has been supposed in the past.

Sketches in El Greco's work

Throughout the preceding pages we have indicated those canvases that El Greco may have painted as first versions of their subjects, as sketches for large-scale works or to be used as models by the assistants in his workshop. These sketches always possess that absolute spontaneity that leaves no doubt about a given version of a theme being the first one. The beauty of these works is extraordinary. Not too many have come down to us, unfortunately, but there are certainly enough to give us a clear idea of El Greco's way of working. The sketches are usually fairly large in size and thus the technique is not noticeably simplified. The larger works derived from them show very few variations in the secondary details and follow the compositions of the sketches quite closely. Their existence in El Greco's establishment is perfectly documented, for in a passage from Pacheco's *Treatise on Painting* we read: "Dominico Greco showed me, in the year 1611, a closet full of clay models by his own hand, intended for use in his works. And also, which transcends all admiration, the originals of everything he had painted in his life, painted in oil on smaller canvasses, in a room which his son showed me on his instructions. What will all those vain, weakly painters say to this, if they do not drop dead on hearing of such examples?" This means that Pacheco appreciated, not only the painter's art but also his methodical system of work, which enabled him to keep the image of whatever he had to give up when he sold the definitive works. Pacheco's exclamation would seem to imply that the systematic execution and preservation of *modelli* was by no means common in those days.

We must now mention once more a question of the greatest importance. Faced with the problem of placing undocumented canvases in their right position in the chronological sequence of El Greco's work, and with no more to go on than what is revealed by their style, the art historian is always assailed by a certain amount of worrisome hesitation. He must give a more or less specific date, or at least indicate the limits of the period during which the work may have been painted, and this decision, despite the fact that it has been reached after infinite consideration, has only the value of a working hypothesis. To form some idea of the difficulties this entails, we need only consider the disparity of the opinions uttered and published regarding the dates of these undocumented works. As we have said before, the chronological problem, already complicated, is still further obscured by the collaboration of the assistants. With regard to this aspect, the decision finally taken by the historian is of still greater importance and any error on this point is very serious indeed. The task of distinguishing between a truly authentic work and a workshop copy sometimes —not always, fortunately— goes beyond the bounds of human possibilities.

The "Apostle" series

The foregoing reflections are of particular interest when we attempt to find correct dates for a very numerous group of works produced by El Greco and his assistants to a limited sequence of designs. We mean the so-called "Apostle" series, the special characteristics of which have led us to study them briefly as a kind of tail-piece to the works done in the last decade of the great painter's life *(Figs. 275 to 331 - Cat. 249 to 312).* They consist of various series of canvases, of uniform size, with the image of Christ and the individual representation of each of the twelve apostles. In theory they should be sets of thirteen pictures each, and in some cases this is so, but the chance inclusion of other saints spoils the iconographical uniformity in some of the series. Three uniform and almost complete "Apostle" series are still extant: the one from the monastery of San Pelayo in Oviedo, now in the Collection of the Marqués de San Feliz; the one in the Cathedral of Toledo and the one in the Greco Museum, which originally hung in the Hospital de Santiago in the same city. Among the incomplete and dispersed "Apostle" series are the one found in Almadrones (Guadalajara) in 1936, the one formerly in the López Cepero Collection in Sevilla and the one, acquired in Toledo, which was for many years in the possession of the dealer Arteche in Madrid. There are also other representations of apostles which, to go by their iconography, format and other characteristics, are canvases from still other "Apostle" series in which most of the set has been lost. We know that Jorge Manuel lent an "Apostle" series to the Tavera Hospital in Toledo in 1622-1623, and that on his death his heirs sold it to Andrés Martínez Calvo, one of the priests of the hospital. Ponz mentions two "Apostle" series now lost: one of them in the convent of the "Baronesses" in Madrid, which he attributes to El Greco;

the other in the sacristy of the church of Santa Leocadia in Toledo, though this one he attributes to Tristán. It thus proves difficult to present a complete catalogue of the paintings that make up a group of such interest from the point of view of their subject matter. It should not be forgotten that to discover the present whereabouts of any of these pictures is a virtually impossible task, which prevents us from carrying out an absolutely satisfactory study.

As far as the chronology and the internal organization of this iconographical group are concerned, our point of view is the following. The Arteche series has half-length figures on small canvases, which we think El Greco painted as his first designs, possibly between 1603 and 1608. Observe, therefore, how late in his life this theme appeared. We have only been able to study three of the originals from this series. Some of the little canvases are signed, with the Greek initials *delta* and *theta*. The execution is rapid, but very delicate, as in all these original sketches.

The Oviedo series, also with half-length figures, is virtually the same as the preceding one but twice the size, and seems to have been painted at the same time. We are of the opinion that the hand of El Greco himself can be detected in some of the canvases in this series. Most of them are signed with the Greek initials. The execution of this series was also very rapid and not particularly careful.

The series in the Cathedral of Toledo is a complete one. It, too, uses the same designs as in the Arteche series, but the figures are knee-length. Executed with ardour and passion, we consider them to have been done around 1608. They are larger than those of the Oviedo series and most of them seem to be authentic works by El Greco himself.

The series in the Greco Museum seems to us to have been painted at or about the same time as the one in the cathedral. If we compare the execution of these two series, there are some images that would seem to be of later date in the cathedral series; in others, however, the reverse appears to be the case. On the whole, the series in the Greco Museum is the more interesting; the greater intensity with which it is painted gives it a more truly authentic air. None of the canvases in either of these two series is signed or initialled.

The Almadrones series, which is incomplete and dispersed, is also a half-length "Apostle" series. The canvases are of similar size to those in the Oviedo series. The technique seems to be later than in any of the other series and they were probably done in the painter's last years. The images, though based on the designs in the Arteche series, show some appreciable changes. El Greco himselft was probably responsible for the greater part of these canvases.

The López Cepero series, which is also incomplete and has been scattered all over the world, and in which the canvases are rather smaller than in the preceding series, likewise shows some variations vis-à-vis the prototypes in the Arteche series. It is very similar to the one from Almadrones and is not by El Greco himself. It seems rather the work of Tristán, which leads us to suspect that it may be the series mentioned by Ponz as hanging in the sacristy of Santa Leocadia in Toledo. It is possible that Tristán, with some help from El Greco himself, was also responsible for the series, similar in format and technique, which is headed by the *Christ* in the Galleria Parmeggiani in Reggio Emilia and also includes the *St. Luke* in the Museum of Rosario (Argentina), the *St. Andrew* in Budapest, the *St. Paul* in St. Louis (Missouri), the *St. James the Great* in New College, Oxford, and others.

As we have said before, there are also isolated pictures of apostles, of different sizes and painted in different periods, though always within the chronological limits we have set for the series dealt with above (1603-1614). Notable among them are the *St. John* in the Prado *(Fig. 279)*, the *Christ* in the National Gallery of Scotland *(Fig. 277)*, the *St. James the Less* in the Museum of Basle *(Fig. 322)* and the *St. Luke* in the Hispanic Society, New York *(Fig. 296)*.

To undertake the stylistic analysis of all the works included in the general category of "Apostle" series would be impracticable and repetitive. After following the artist's evolution step by step through his whole career, we know quite well how El Greco painted in the last years of his life, and these figures of apostles are certainly no exception to the norm for this period. But they did give him a reason for attempting, as if in one last, supreme effort, to capture what we might call the sacred eloquence of the faces and hands of the men who spread the faith of Christ throughout the world. In their concentration of subject matter —which limits the imaginative factor so brilliantly apparent in, for instance, the *Laocoön*— these ideal portraits are the culmination of El Greco's art in the representation of saints and sacred figures. The typological variety changes, not only from one design to the next, but

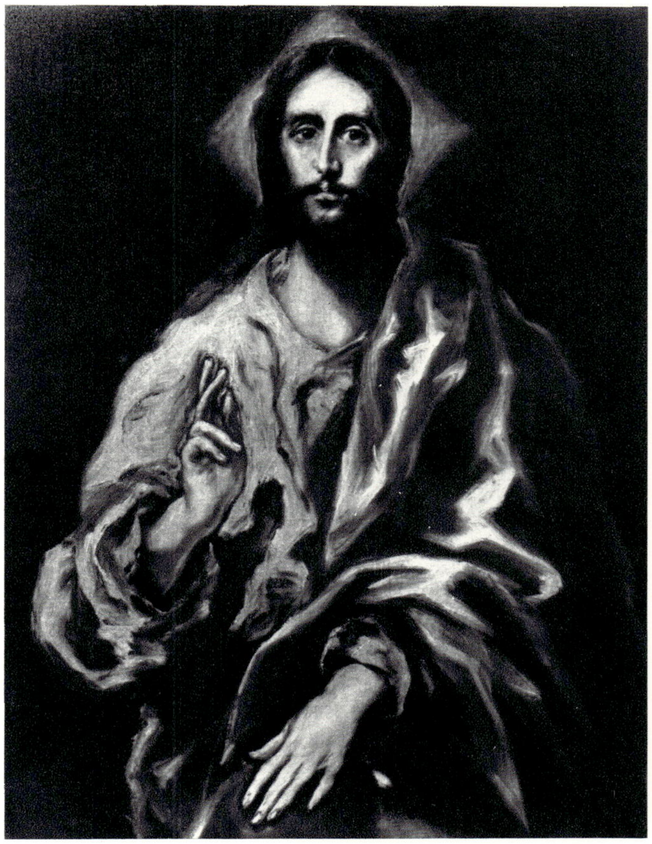
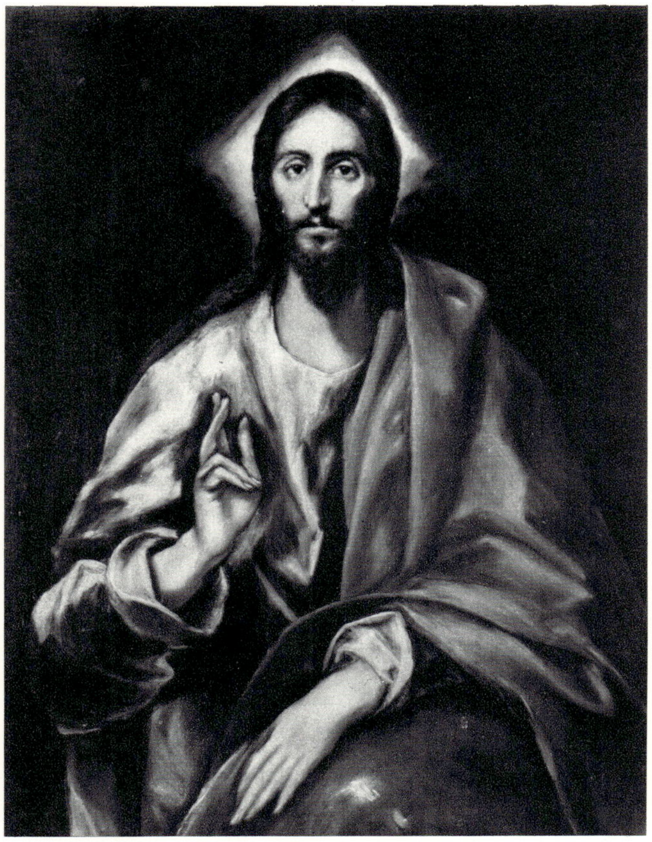
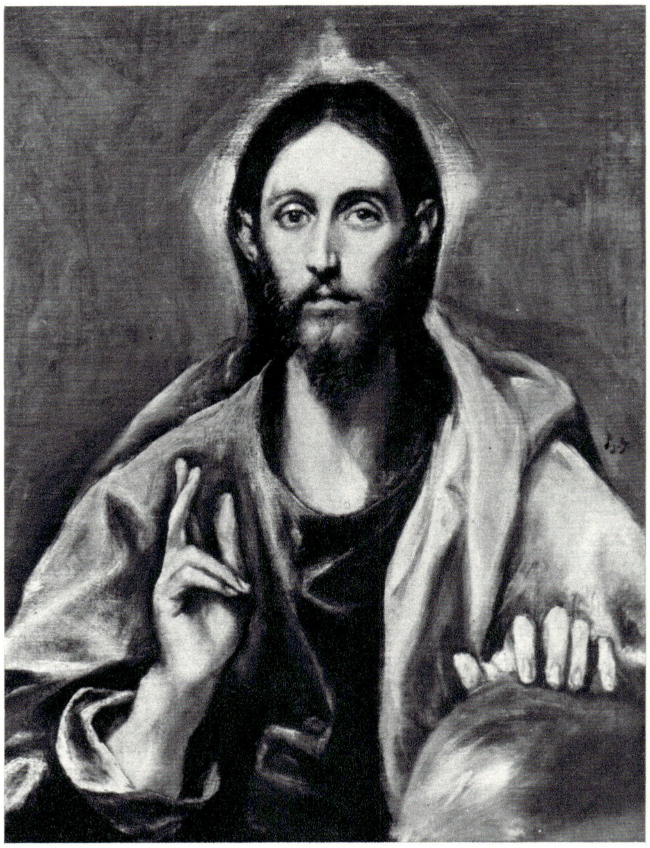
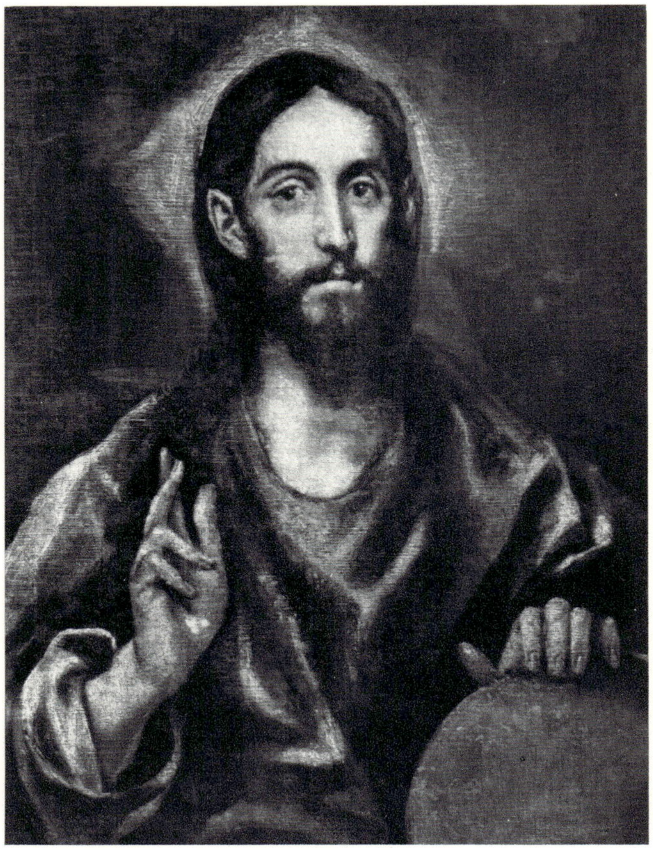

CHRIST

Fig. 275. Cathedral of Toledo. Cat. No. 270.

Fig. 276. Greco Museum. Cat. No. 283.

Fig. 277. National Gallery of Scotland. Cat. No. 305.

Fig. 278. Almadrones. Cat. No. 296.

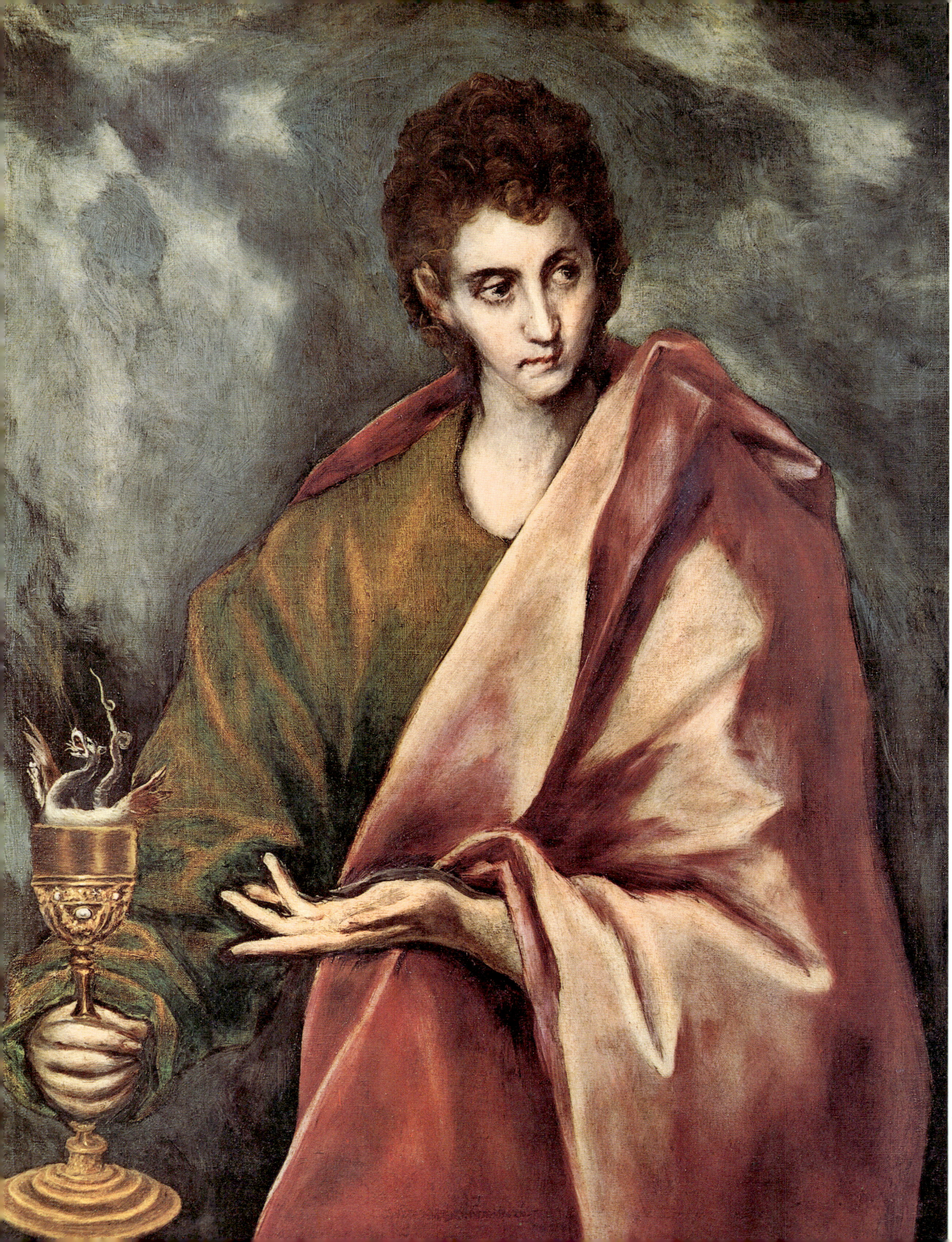

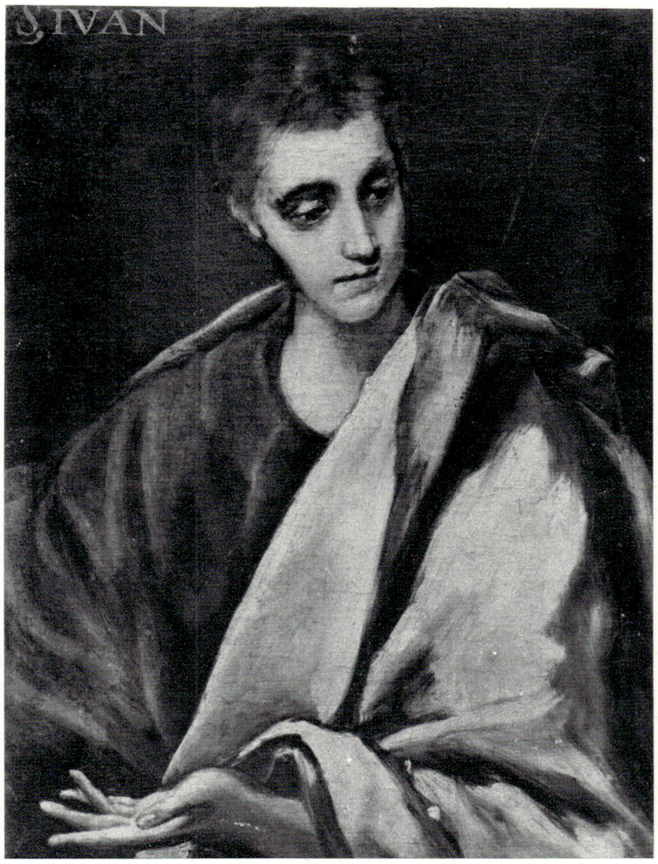

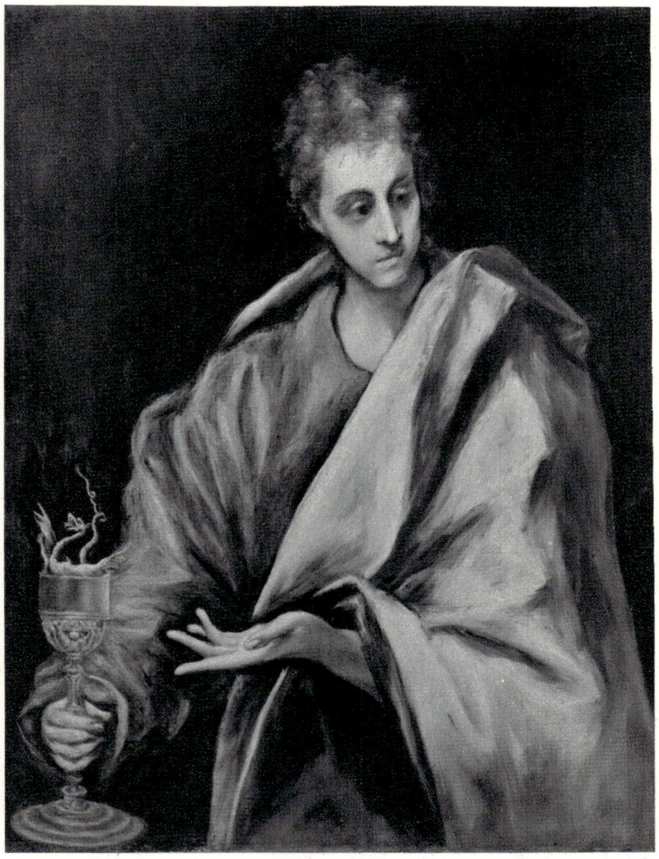

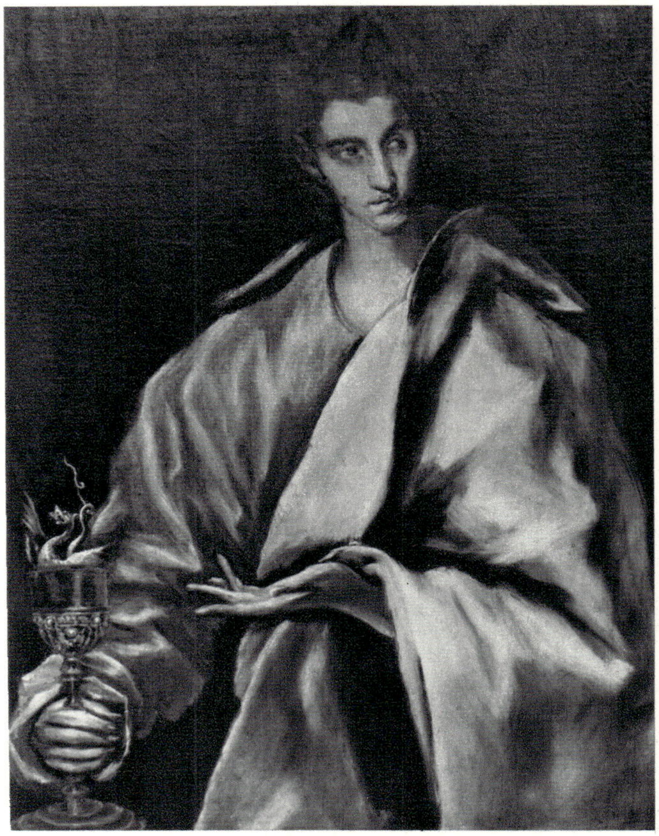

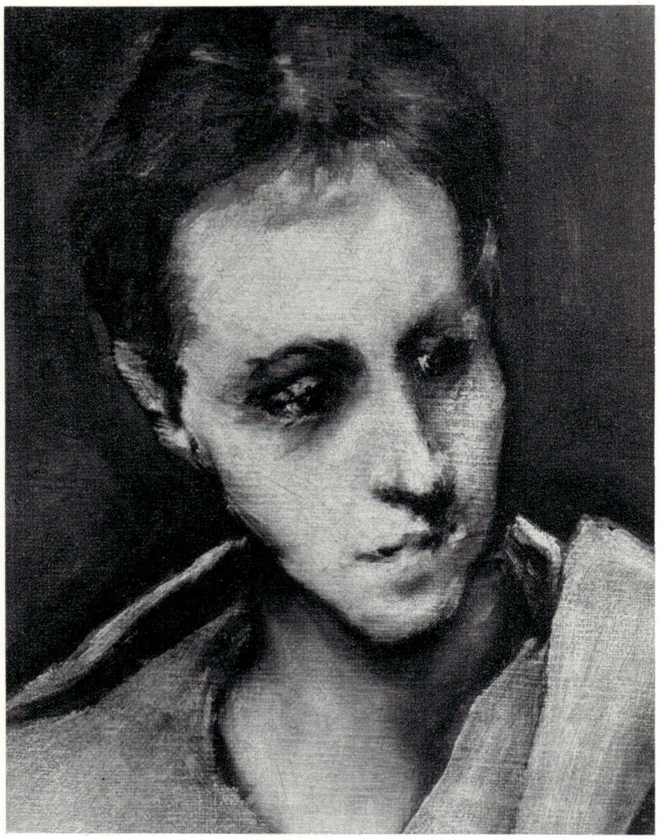

ST. JOHN THE EVANGELIST

Fig. 279. Prado. Cat. No. 306.

Fig. 280. Marqués de San Feliz. Cat. No. 258.

Fig. 281. Cathedral of Toledo. Cat. No. 271.

Fig. 282. Greco Museum. Cat. No. 284.

Fig. 283. Almadrones Cat. No. 297.

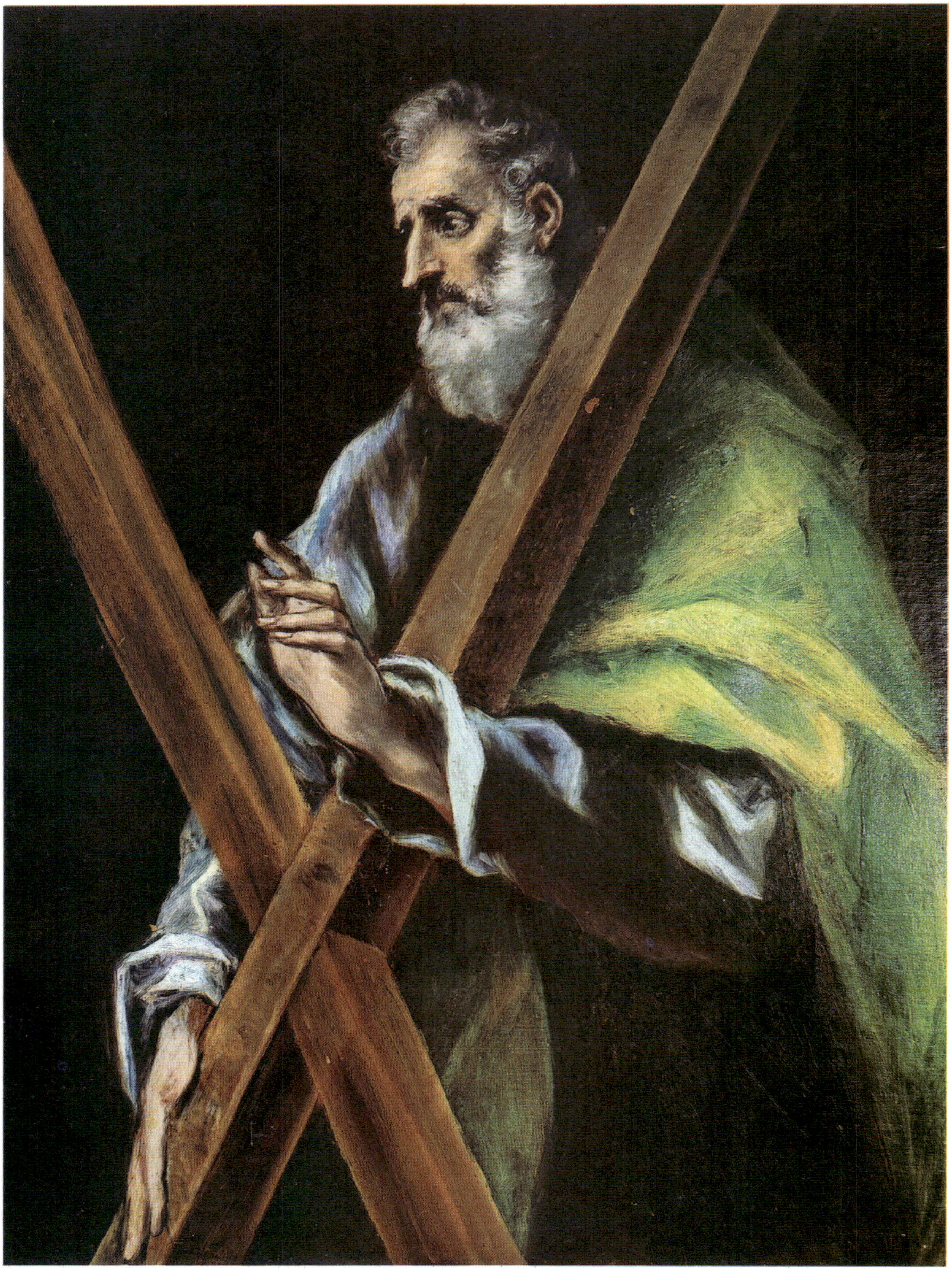

ST. ANDREW
Fig. 284. Cathedral of Toledo. Cat. No. 272.

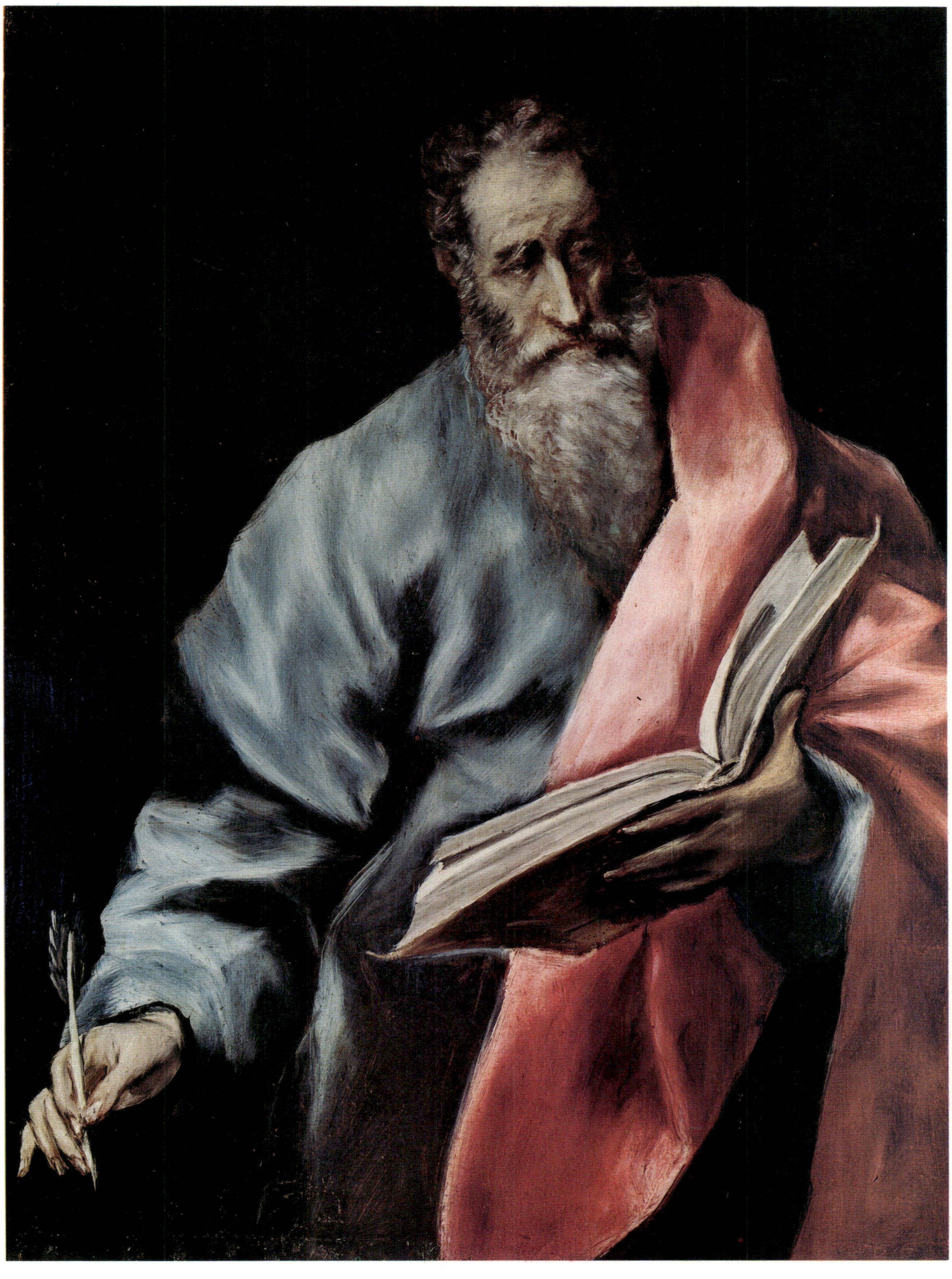

ST. MATTHEW
Fig. 285. Cathedral of Toledo. Cat. No. 273.

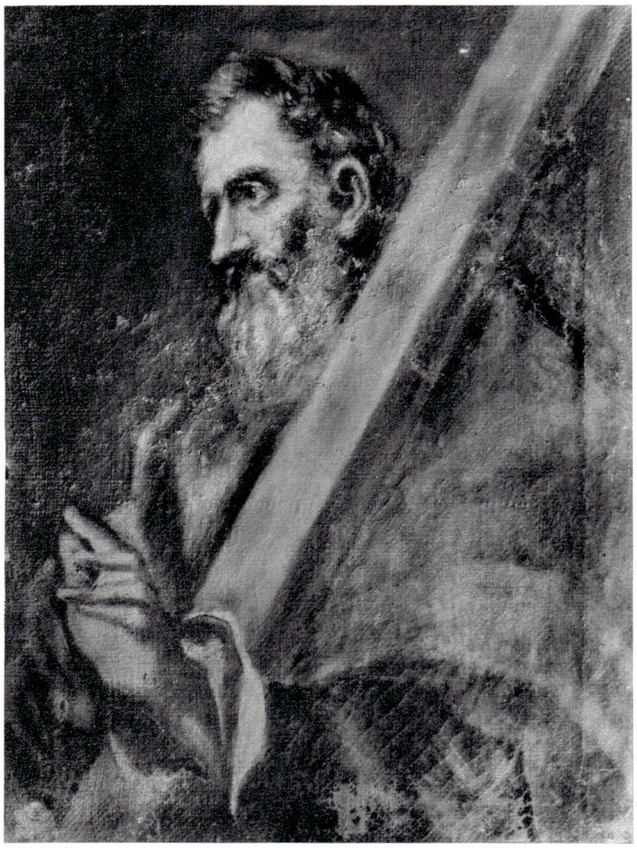
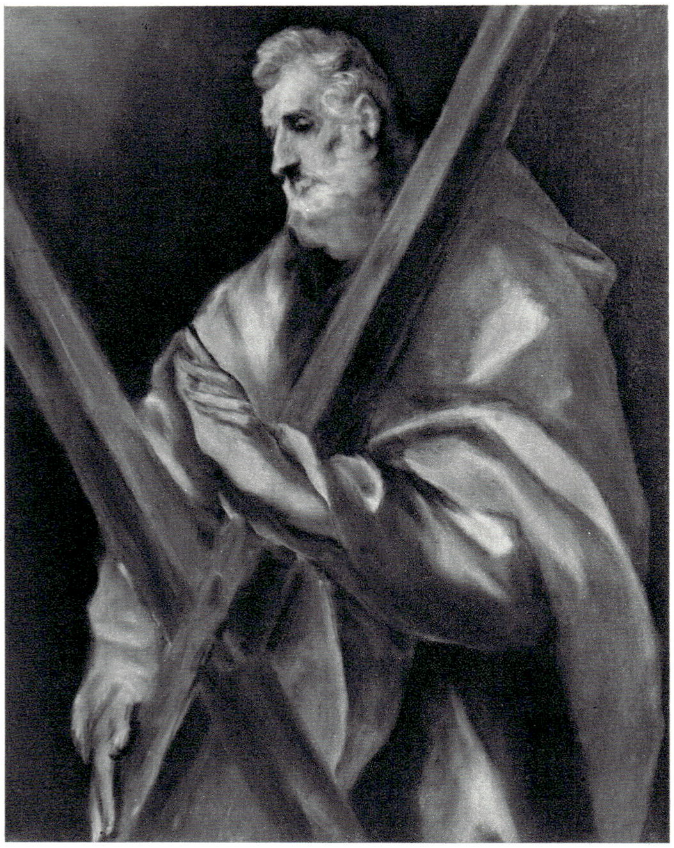
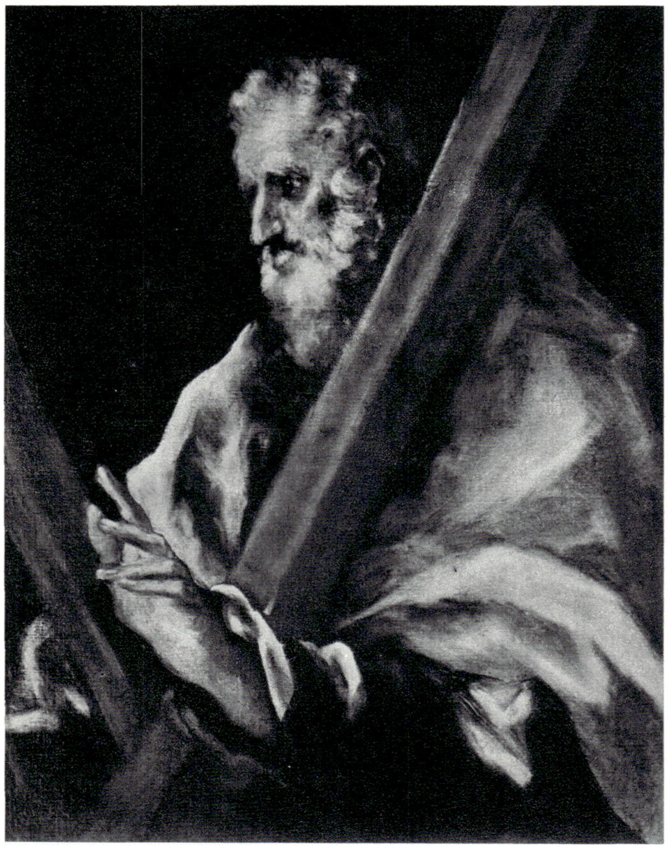
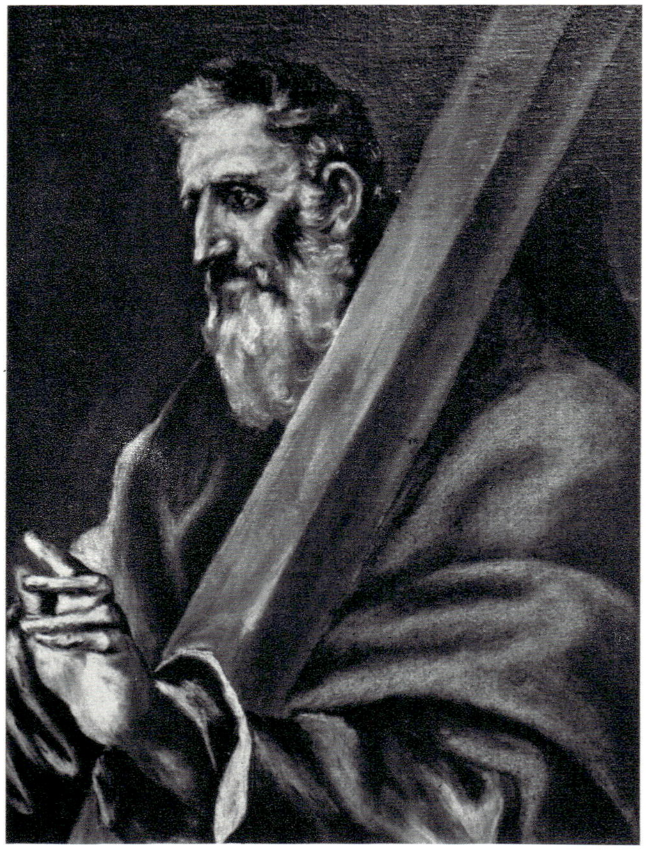

ST. ANDREW

Fig. 286. Arteche. Cat. No. 249.
Fig. 287. Greco Museum. Cat. No. 285.
Fig. 288. Almadrones. Cat. No. 298.
Fig. 289. Rhode Island. Cat. No. 307.

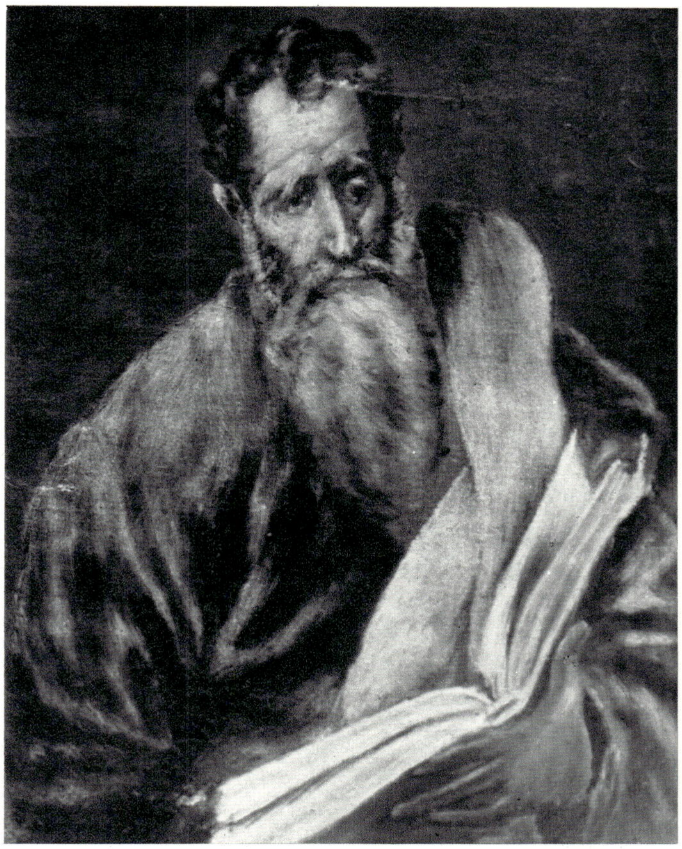

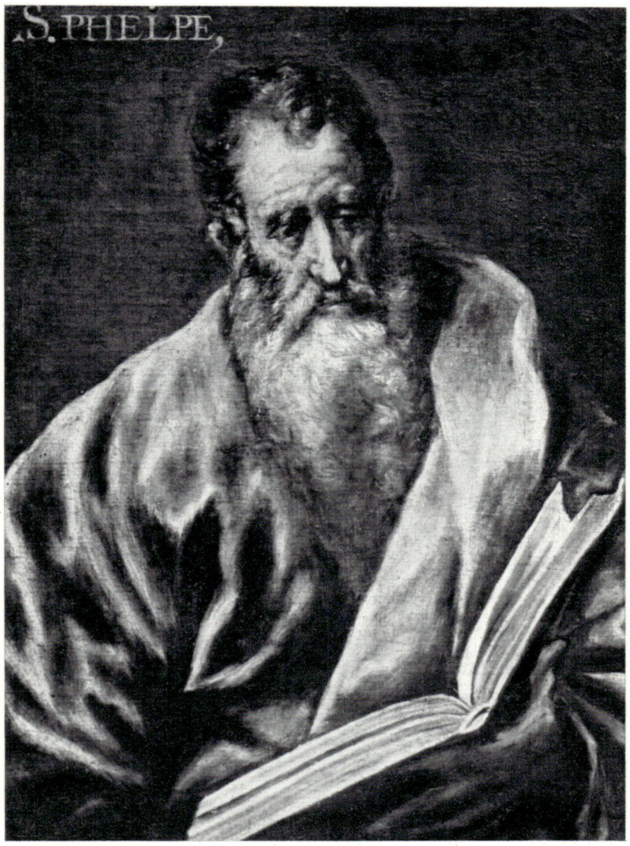

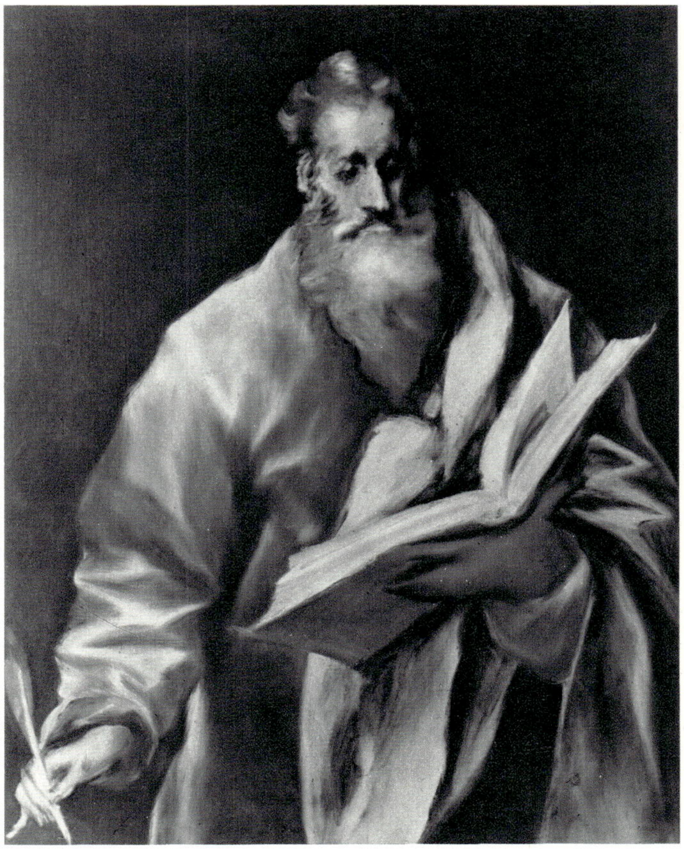

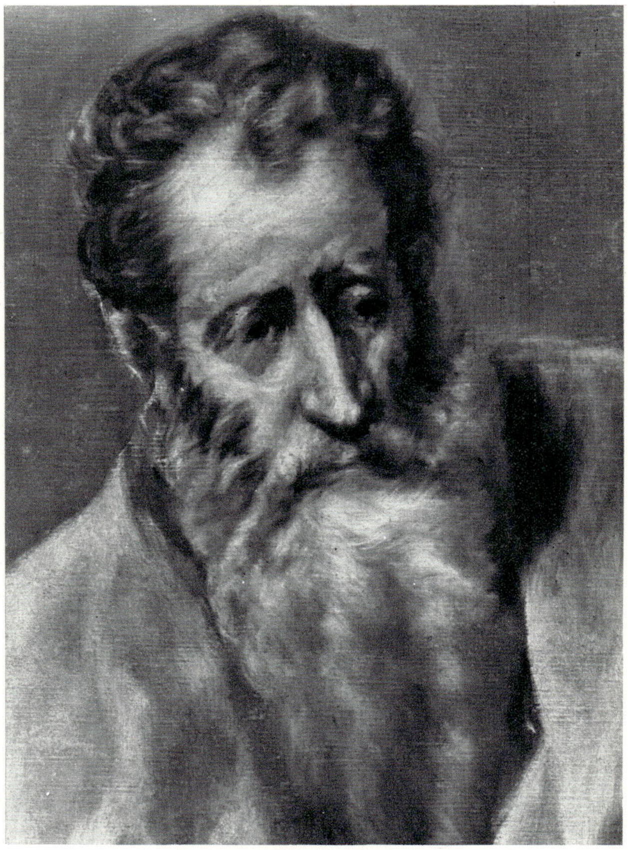

ST. MATTHEW

Fig. 290. Arteche. Cat. No. 250.
Fig. 291. Marqués de San Feliz. Cat. No. 260.
Fig. 292. Greco Museum. Cat. No. 286.
Fig. 293. Almadrones. Cat. No. 299.

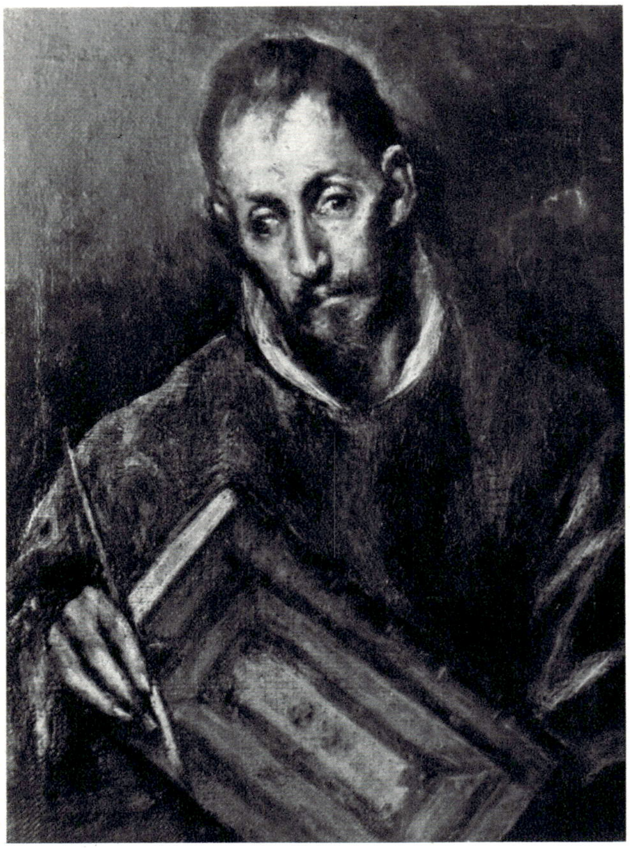

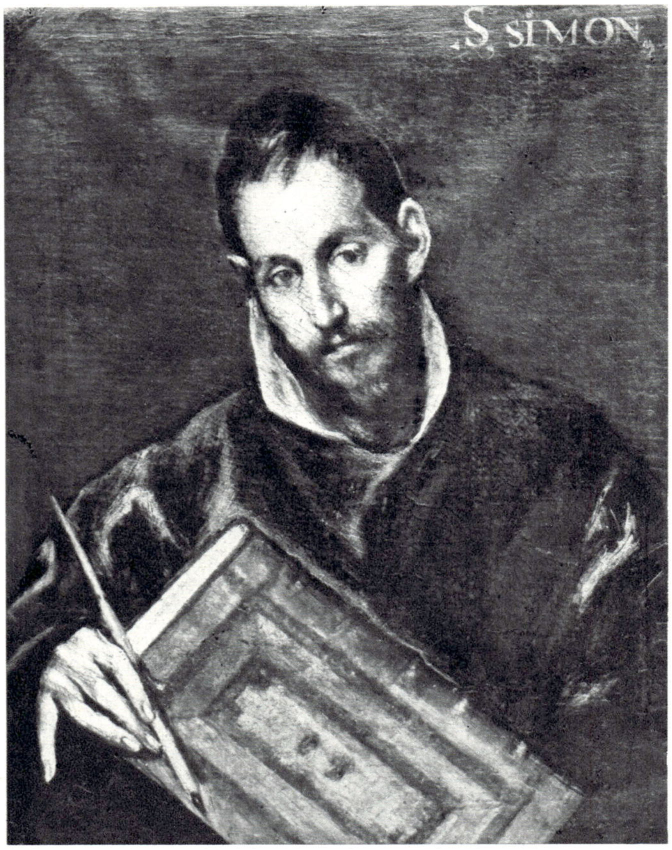

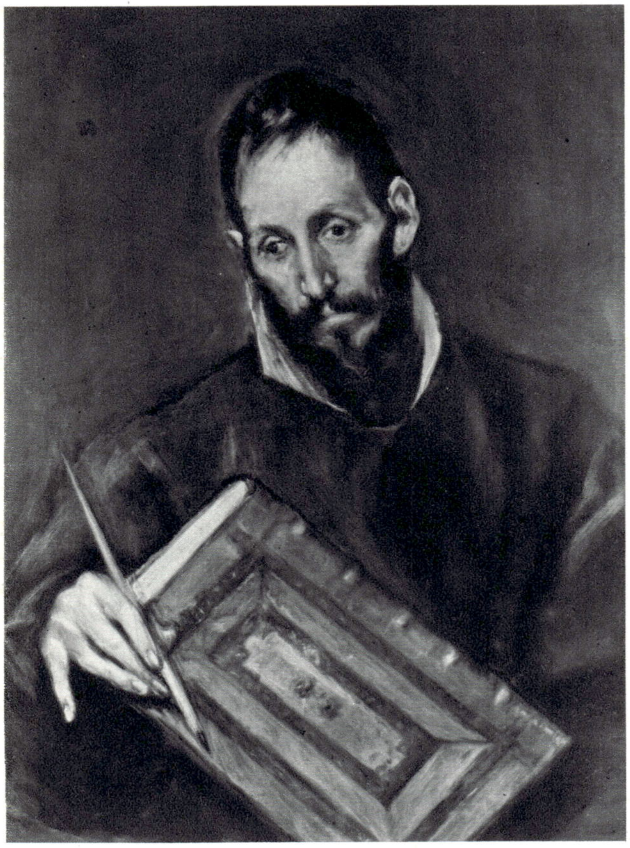

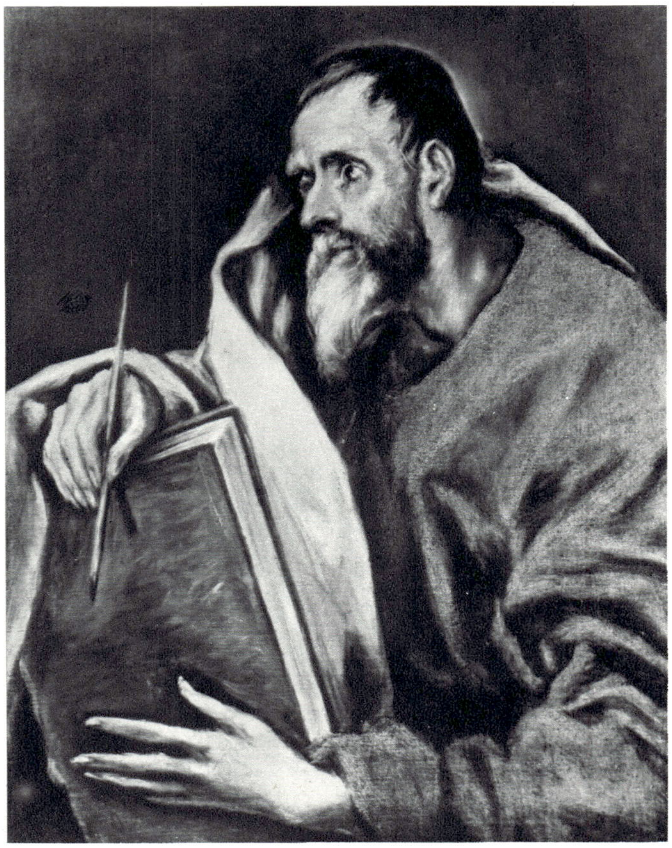

ST. LUKE

Fig. 294. Arteche. Cat. No. 251.
Fig. 295. Marqués de San Feliz. Cat. No. 261.
Fig. 296. Hispanic Society. Cat. No. 308.
Fig. 297. Almadrones. Cat. No. 300.

ST. LUKE
Fig. 298. Cathedral of Toledo. Cat. No.

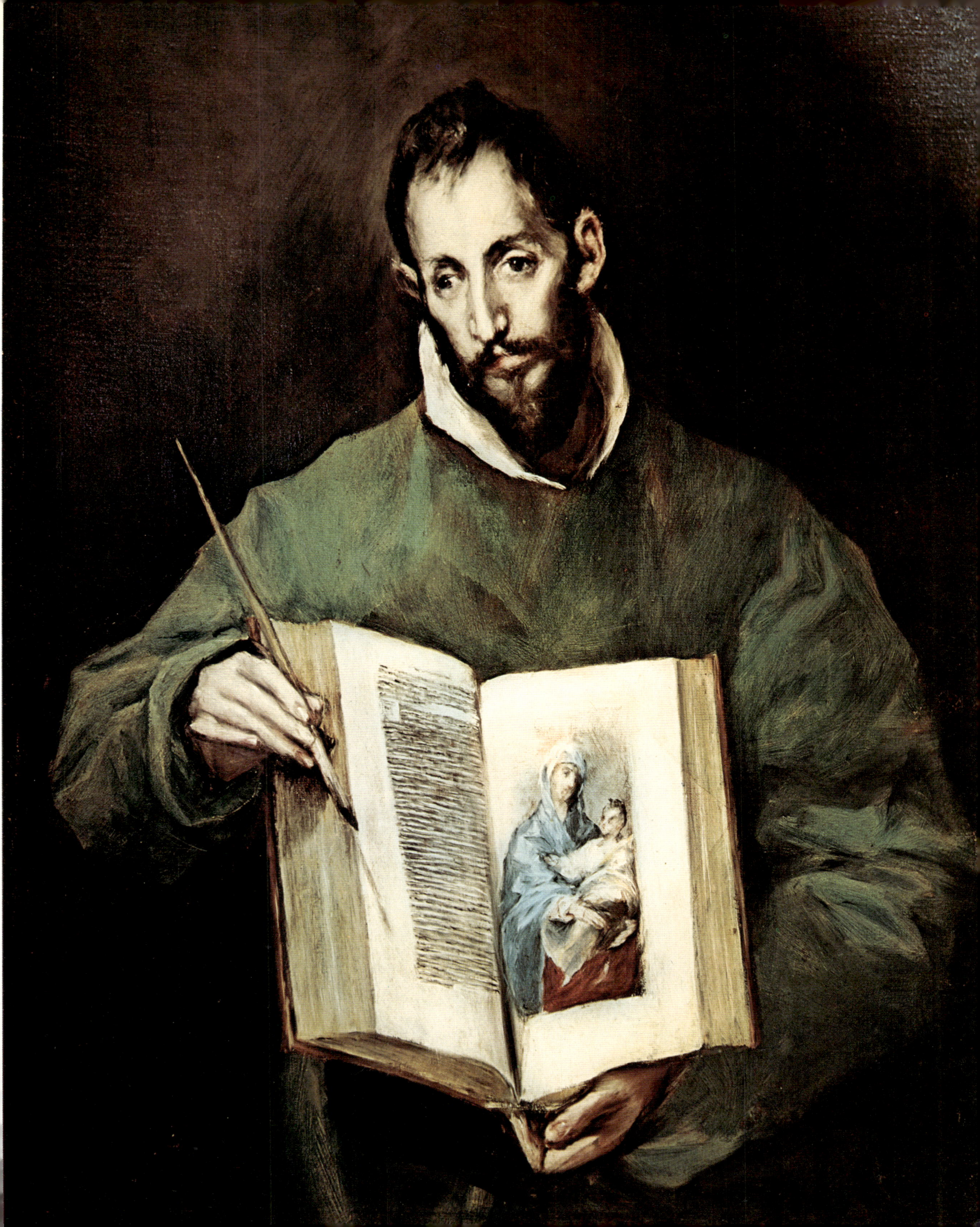

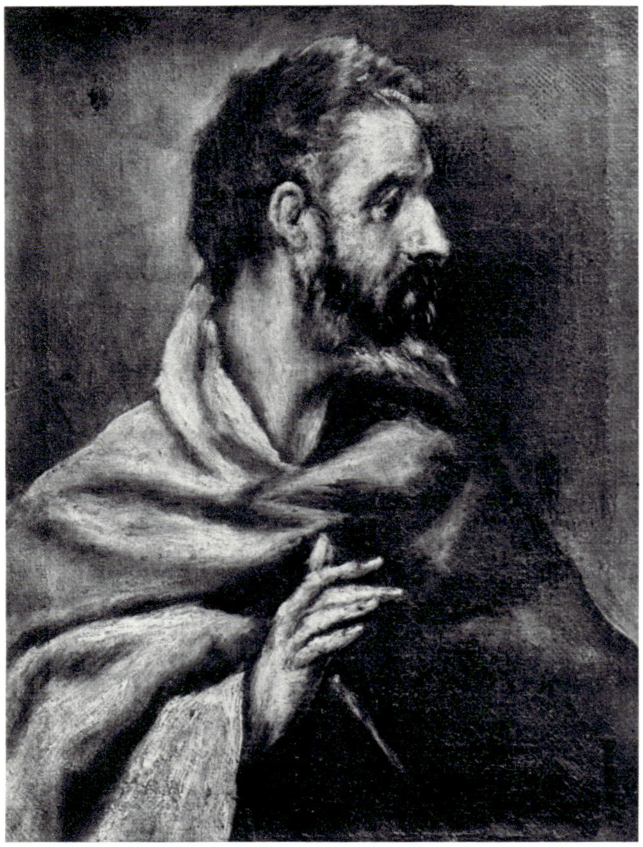

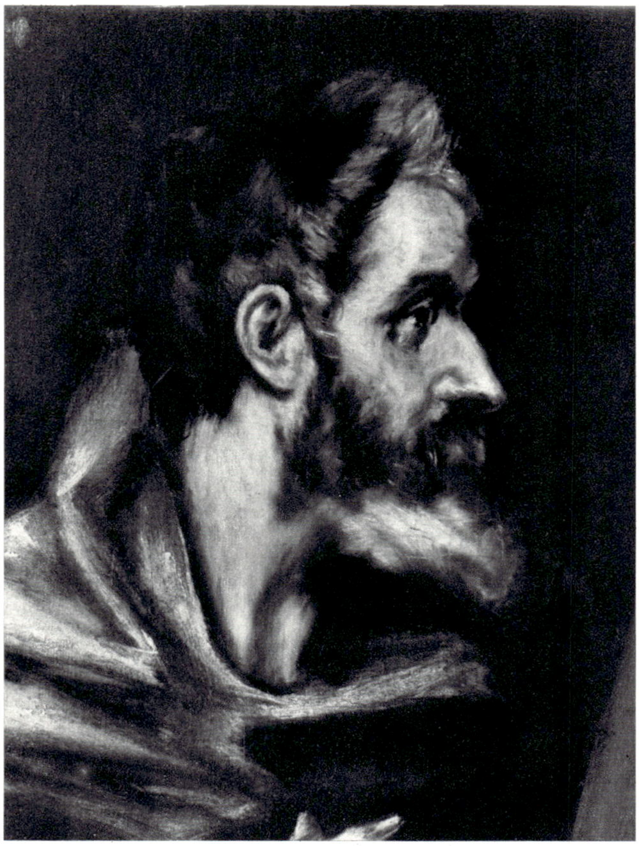

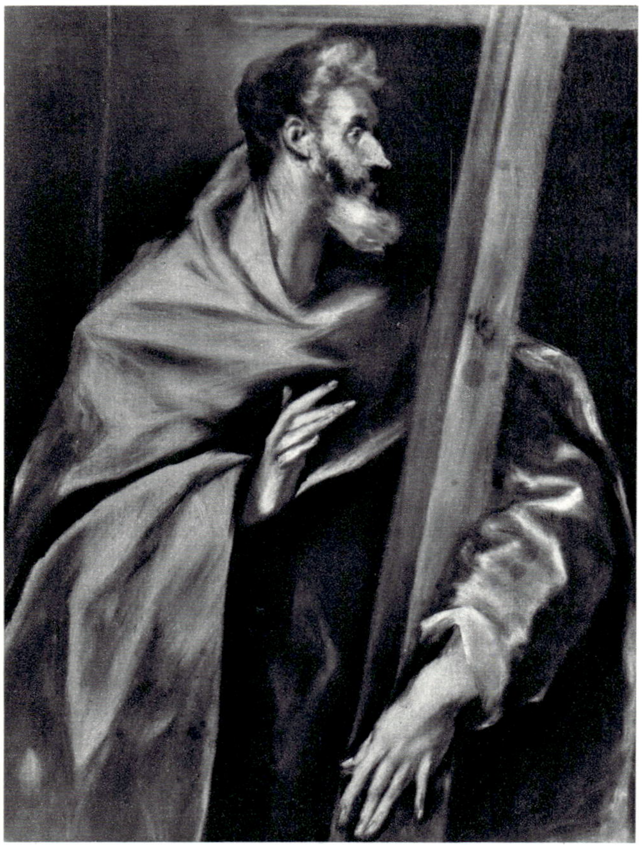

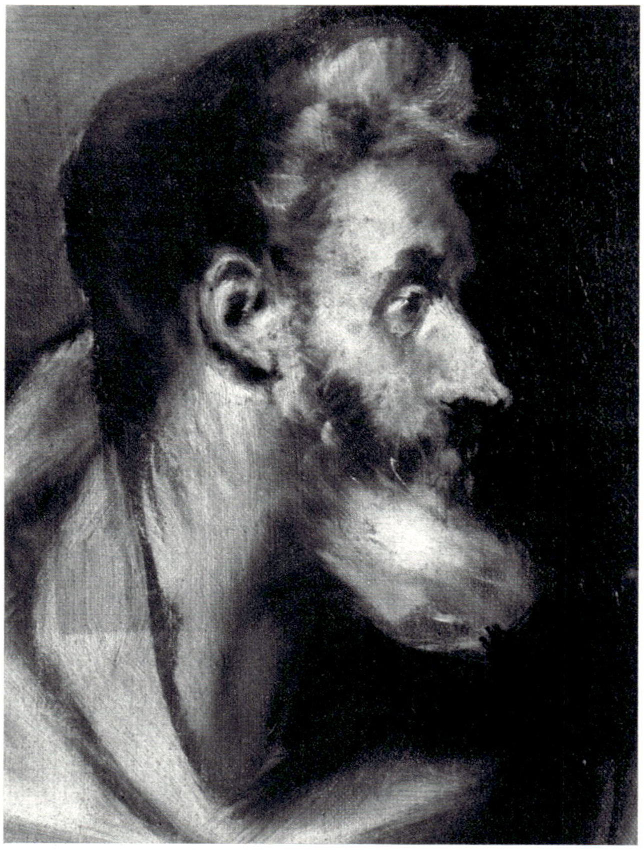

ST. PHILIP

Fig. 299. Arteche. Cat. No. 252.

Fig. 300. Cathedral of Toledo. Cat. No. 275.

Figs. 301 & 302. Greco Museum. Cat. No. 287.

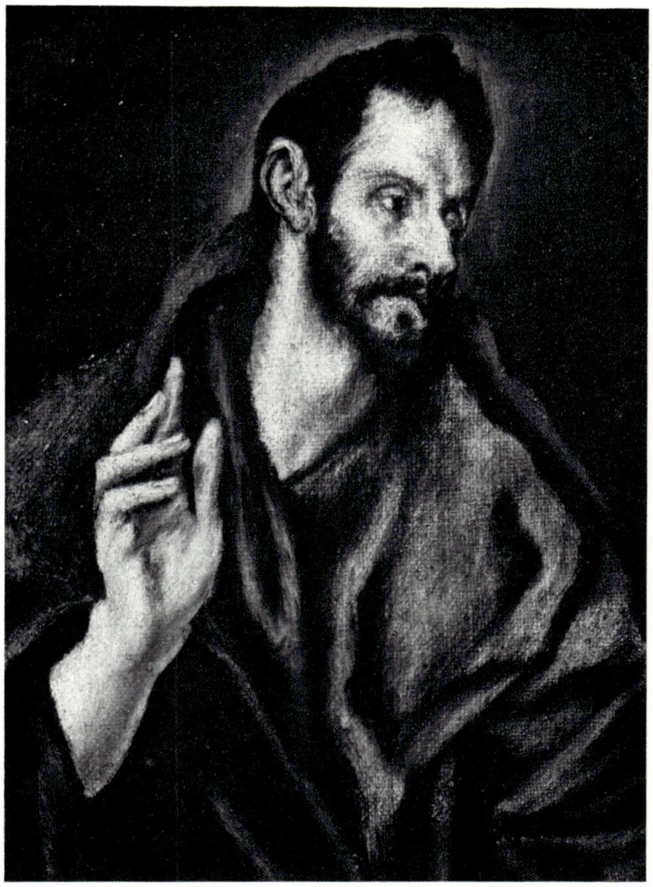
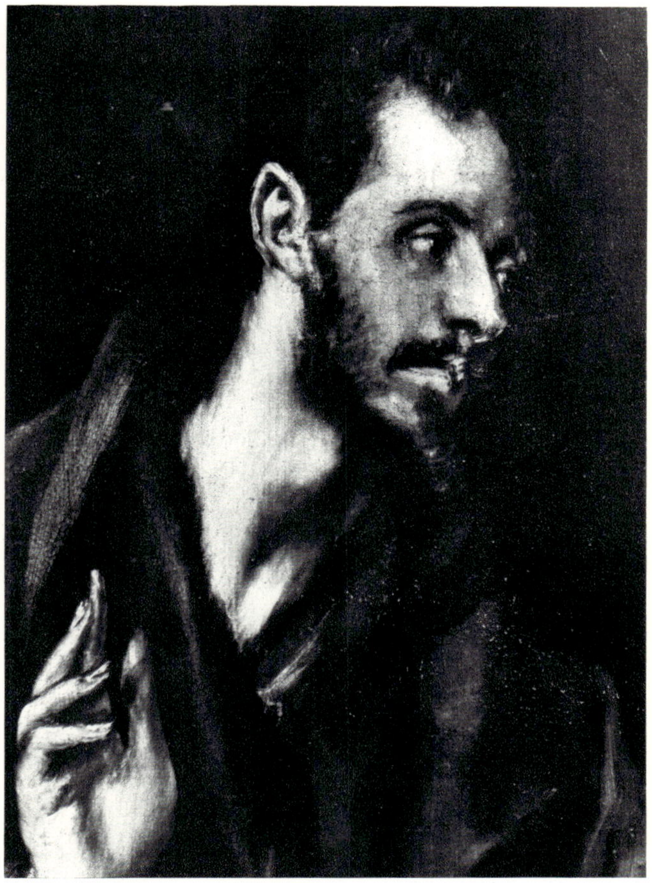
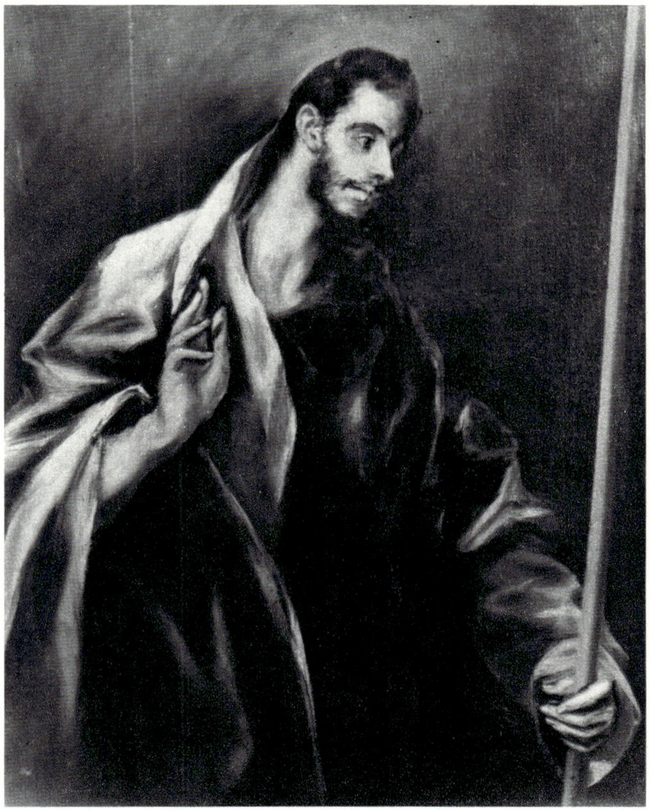
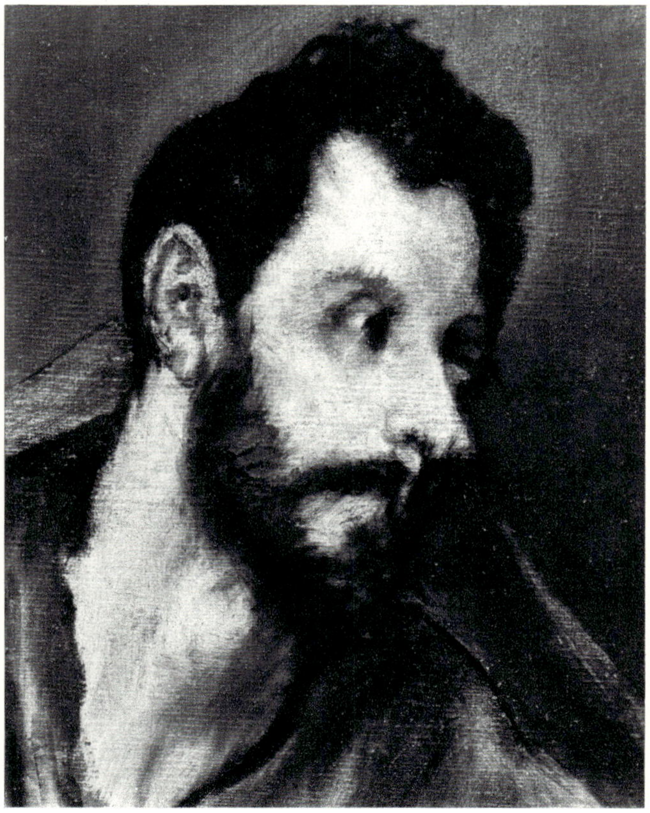

ST. THOMAS

Fig. 303. Arteche. Cat. No. 253.
Fig. 304. Cathedral of Toledo. Cat. No. 276.
Fig. 305. Greco Museum. Cat. No. 288.
Fig. 306. Almadrones. Cat. No. 301.

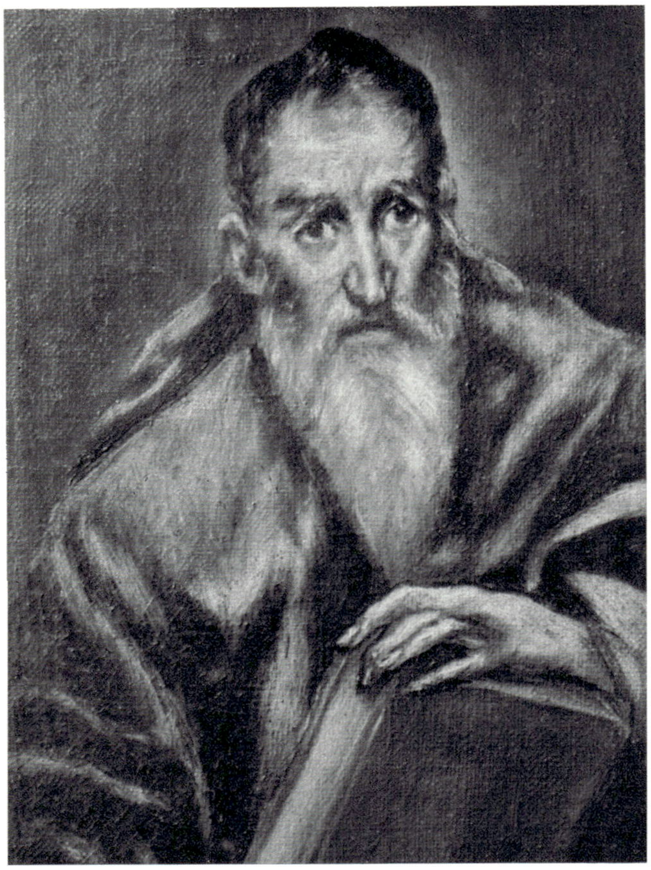

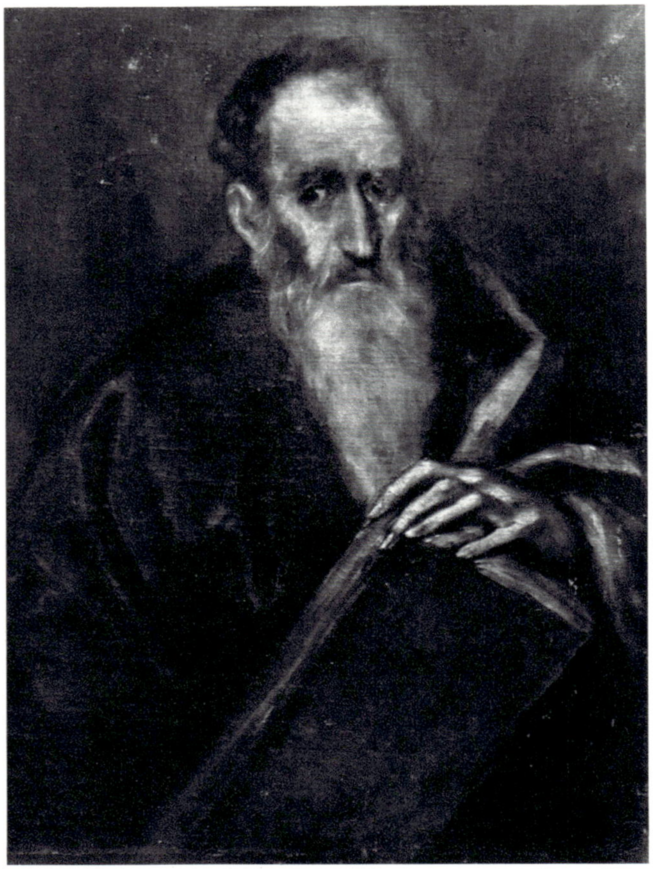

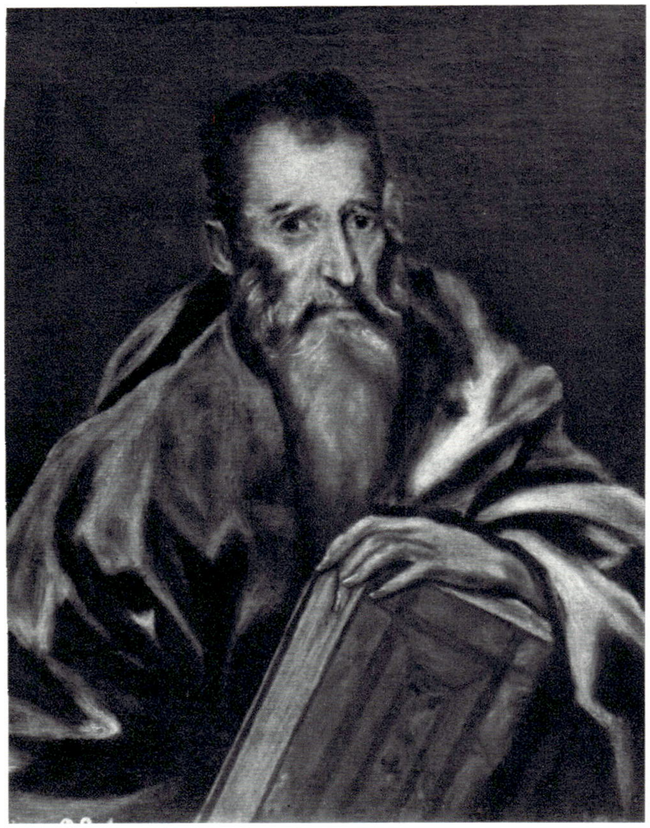

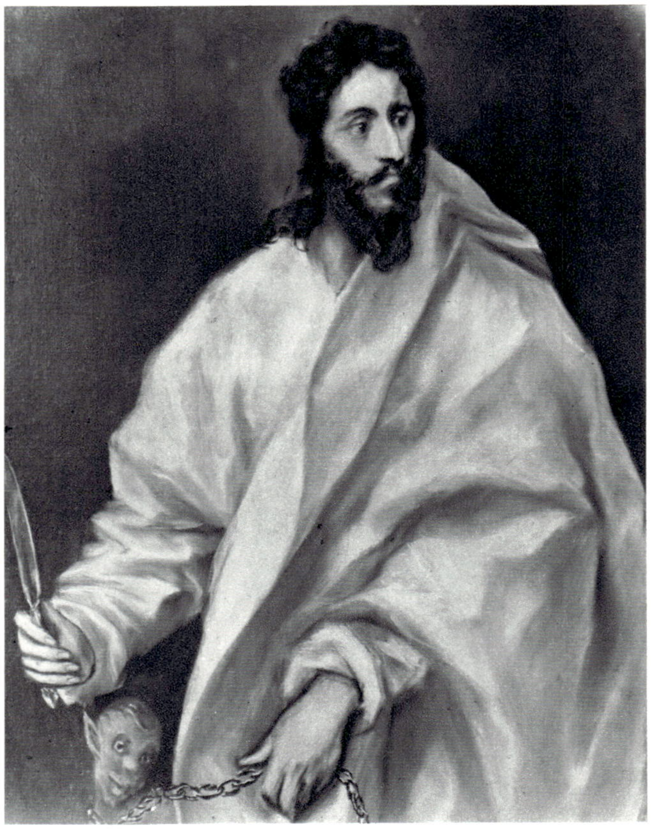

ST. BARTHOLOMEW

Fig. 307. Arteche. Cat. No. 254.
Fig. 308. Santa Cruz Museum.
Fig. 309. Prado Museum.
Fig. 310. Greco Museum. Cat. No. 289.

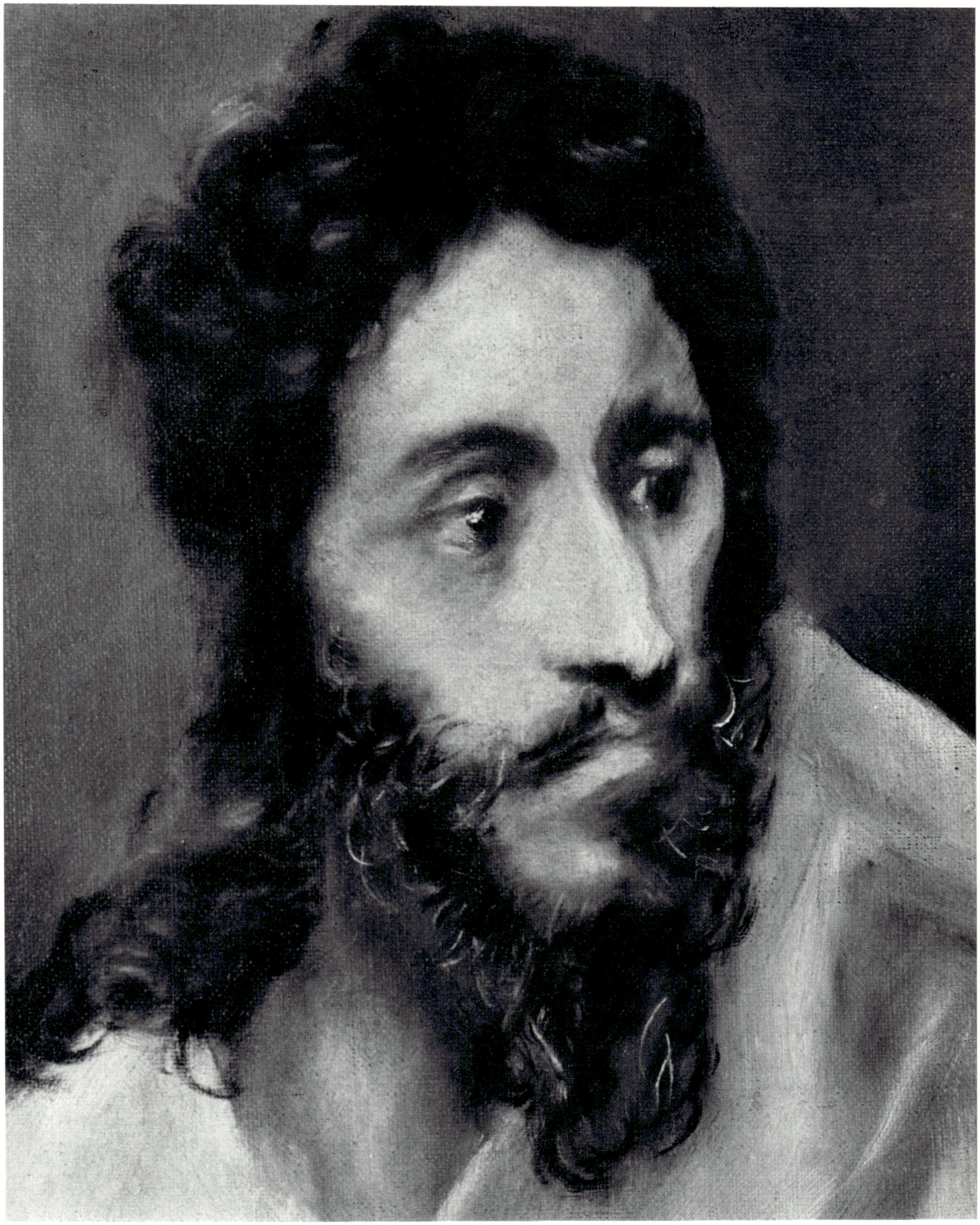

ST. BARTHOLOMEW
Fig. 311. Greco Museum. Cat. No. 289.

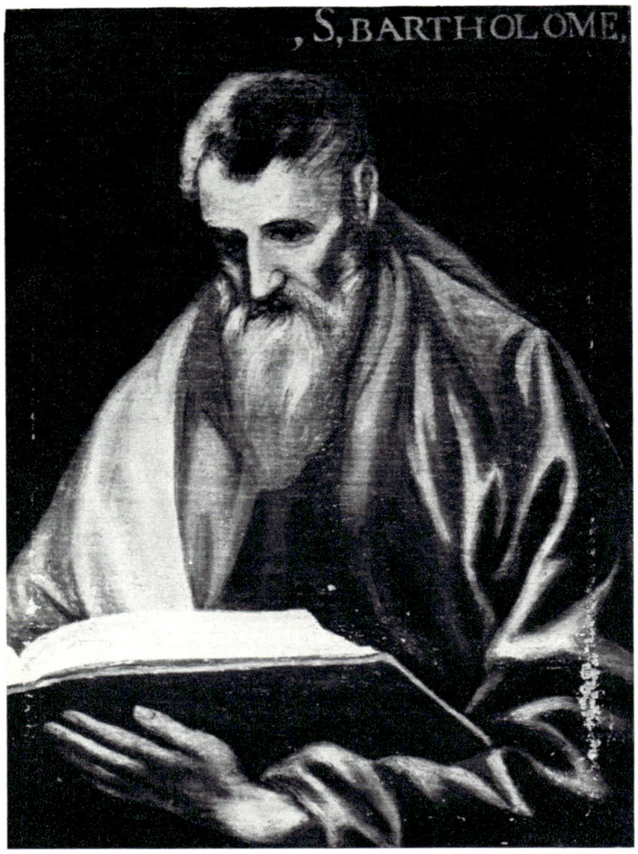

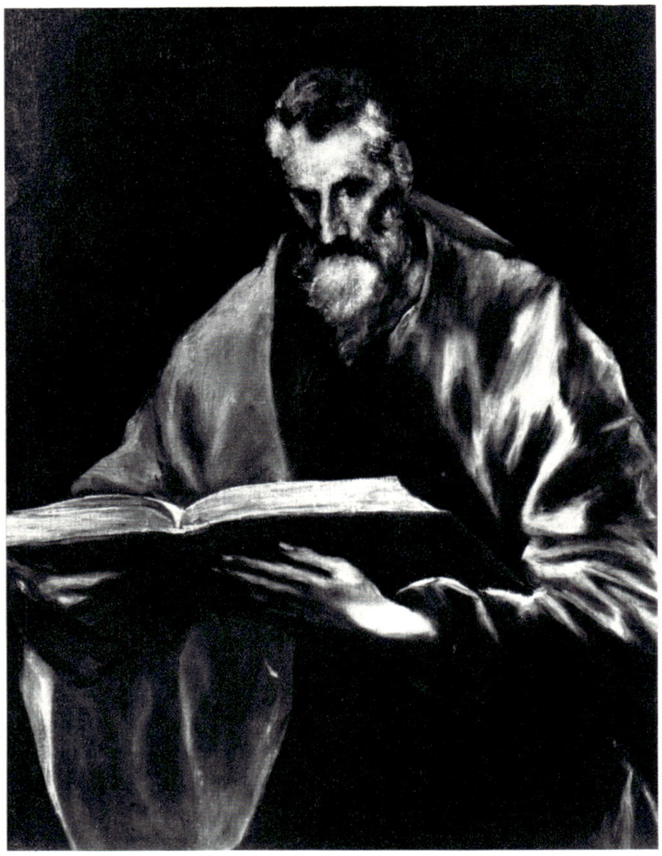

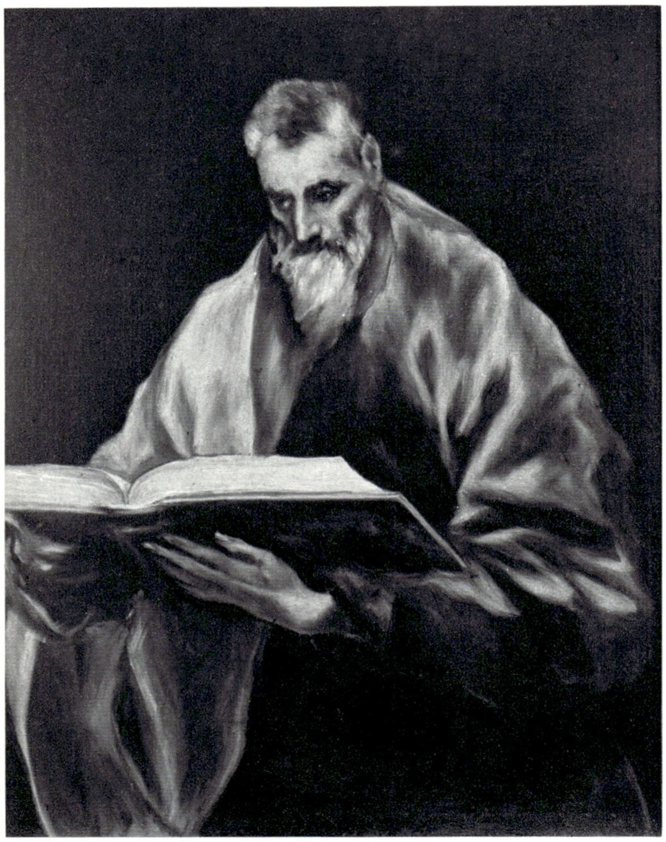

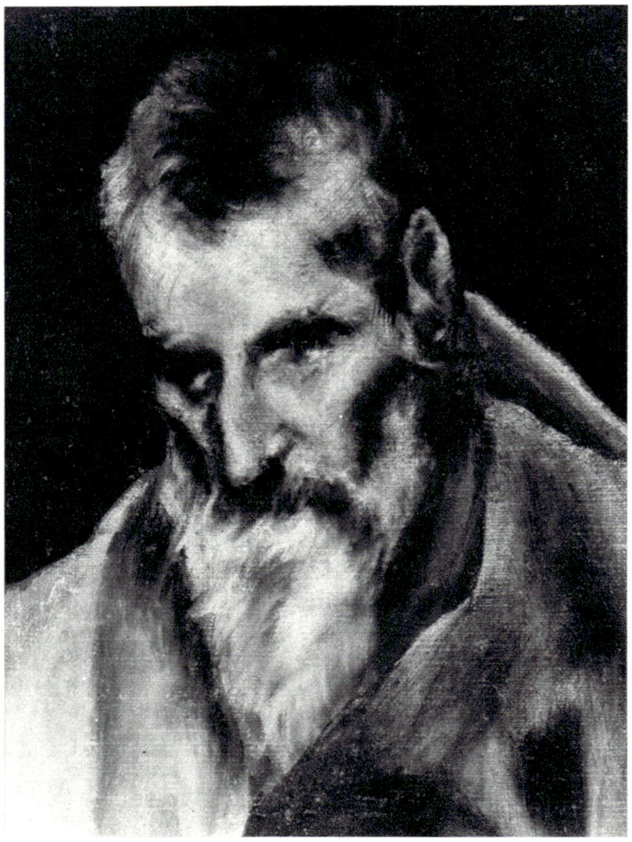

ST. SIMON

Fig. 312. Marqués de San Feliz. Cat. No. 264.

Fig. 313. Cathedral of Toledo. Cat. No. 277.

Fig. 314. Greco Museum. Cat. No. 290.

Fig. 315. Almadrones. Cat. No. 302.

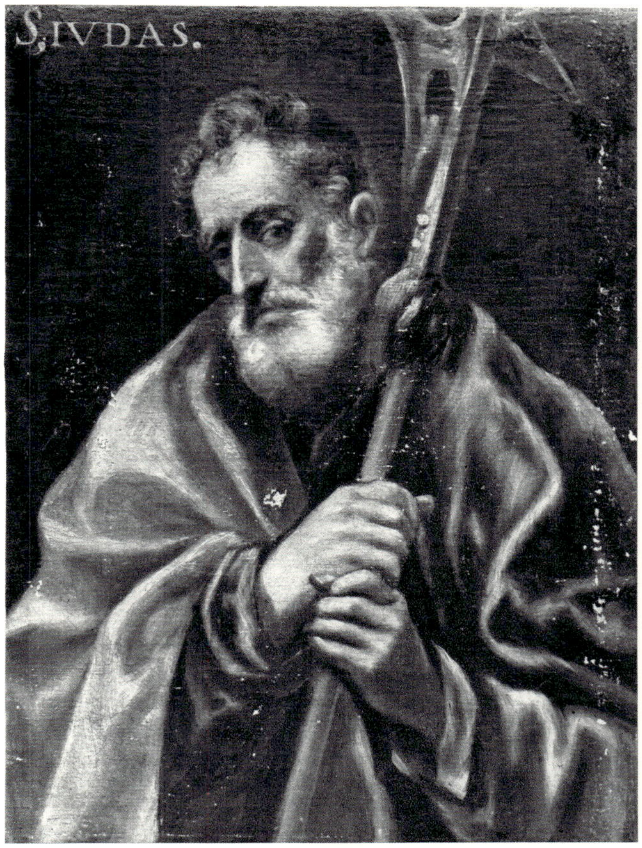

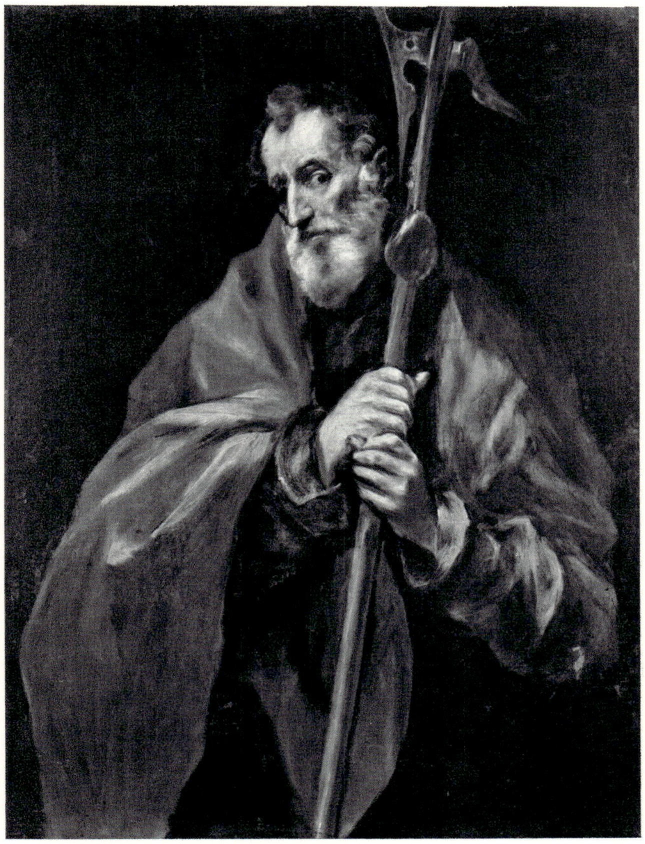
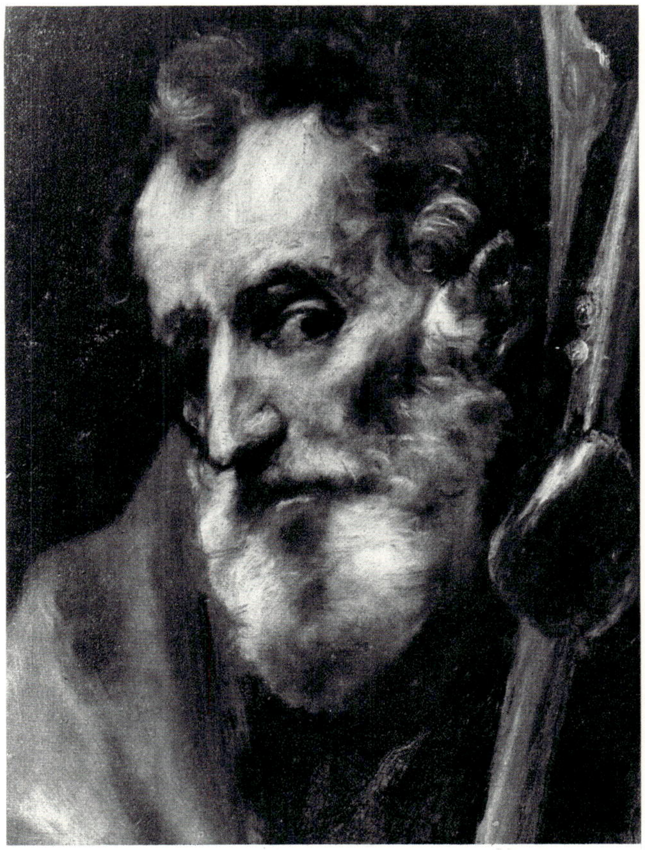
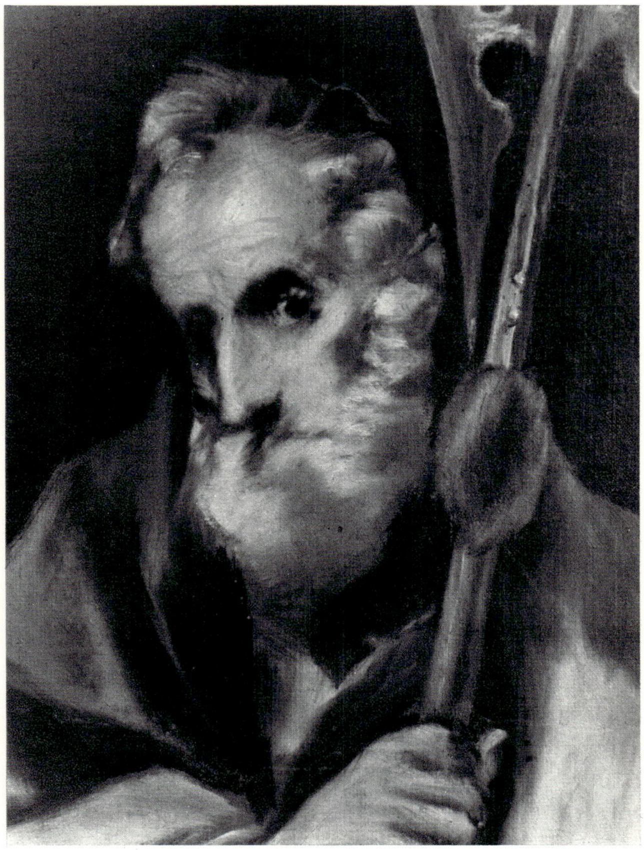

ST. JUDE

Fig. 316. Marqués de San Feliz. Cat. No. 265.
Figs. 317 & 318. Cathedral of Toledo. Cat. No. 278.
Fig. 319. Greco Museum. Cat. No. 291.

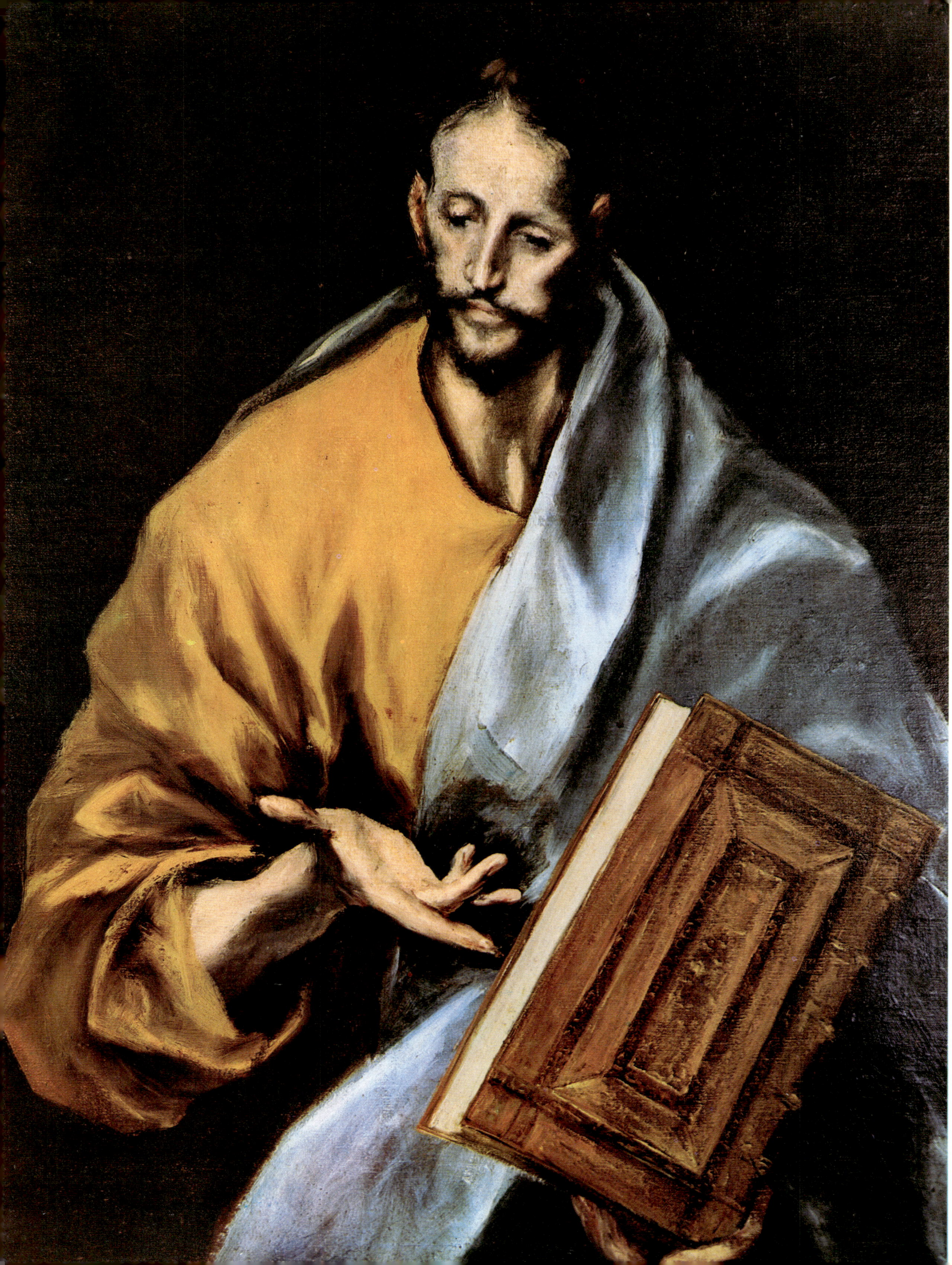

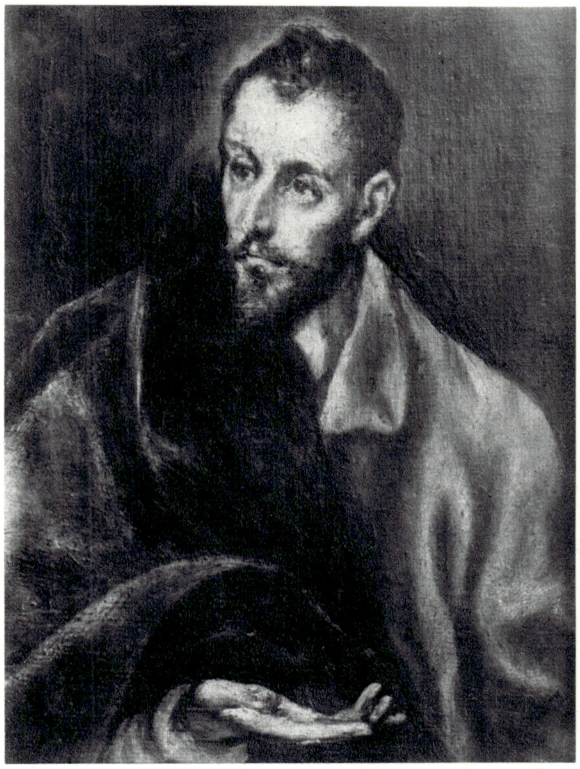

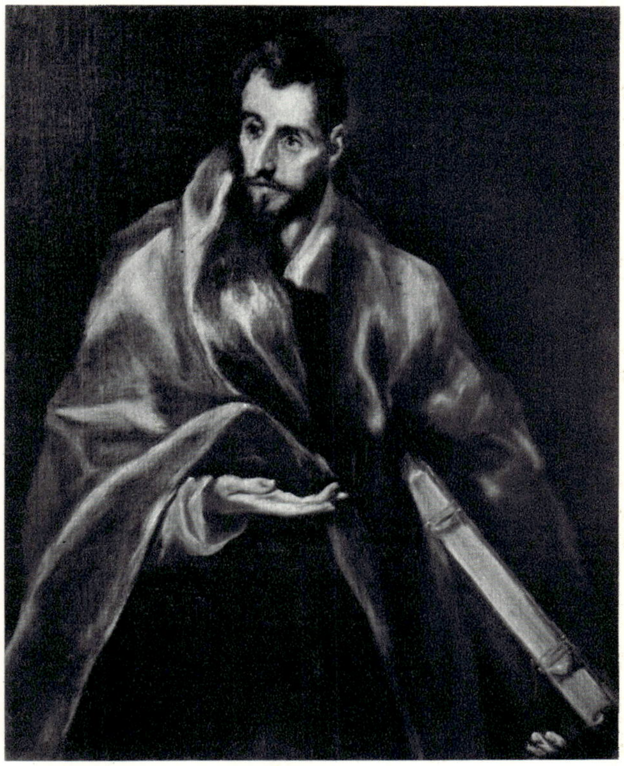

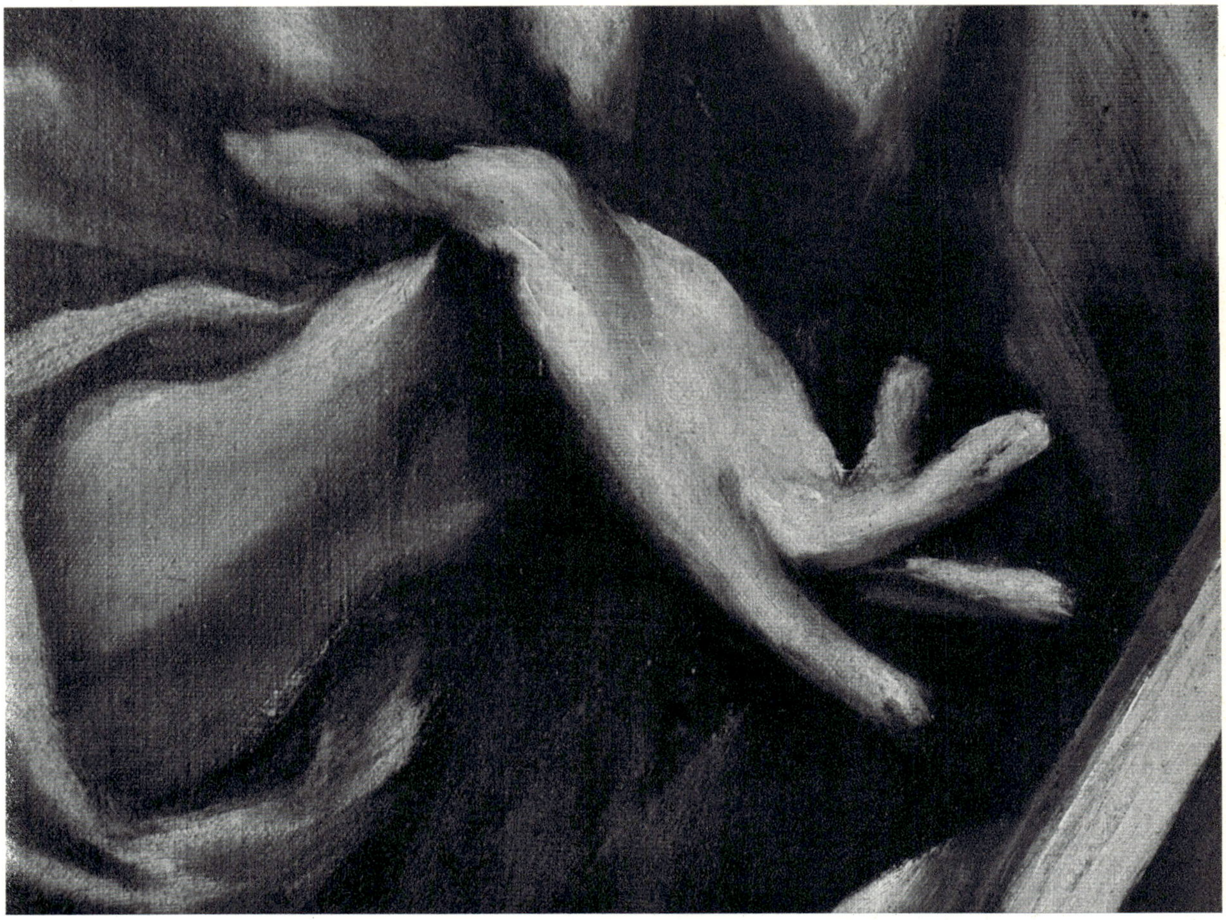

ST. JAMES THE LESS

Fig. 320. Cathedral of Toledo. Cat. No. 279.
Fig. 321. Arteche. Cat. No. 255.
Fig. 322. Basle Museum. Cat. No. 309.
Fig. 323. Greco Museum. Cat. No. 292.

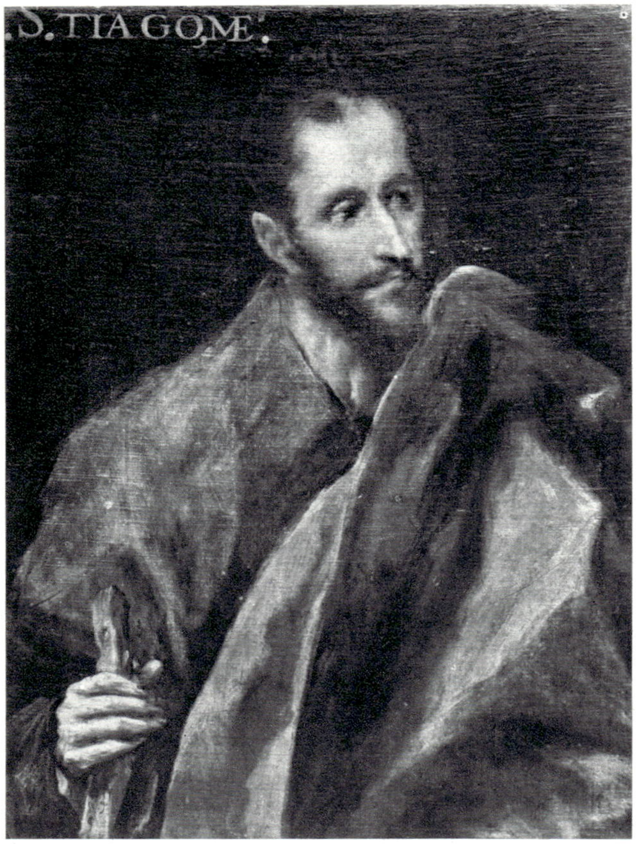

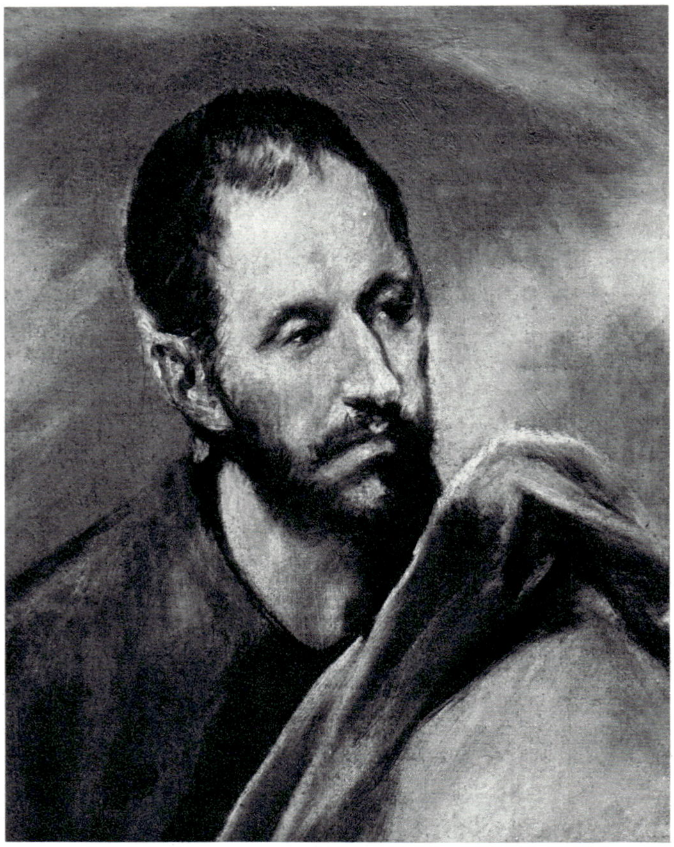

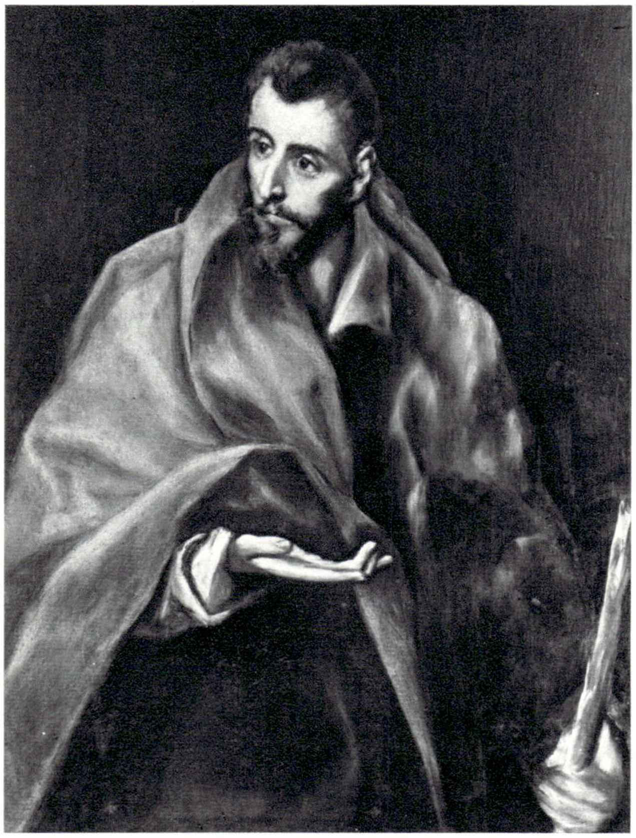

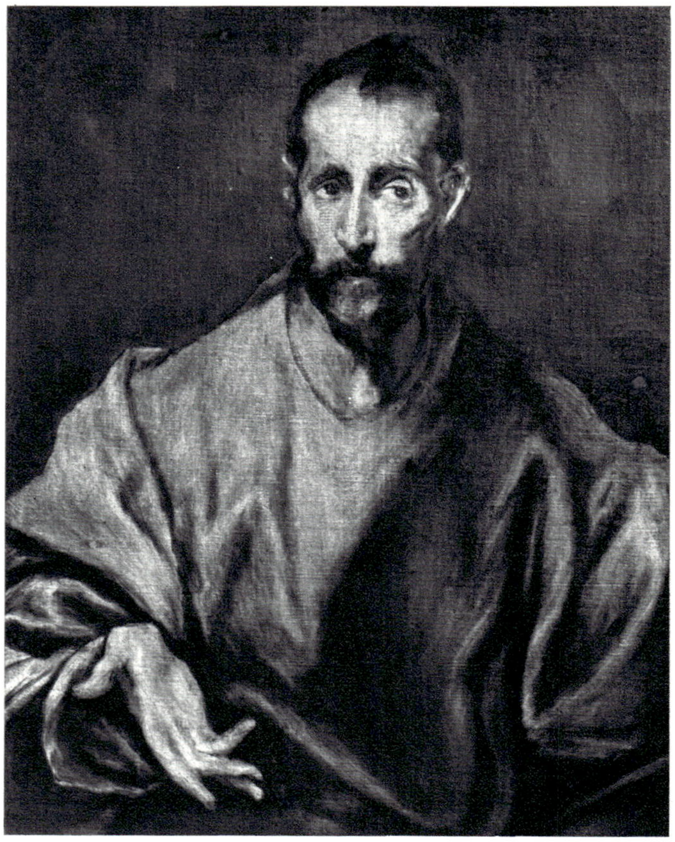

ST. JAMES THE GREAT

Fig. 324. Marqués de San Feliz. Cat. No. 266.

Fig. 325. Budapest Museum. Cat. No. 310.

Fig. 326. Greco Museum. Cat. No. 293.

Fig. 327. Almadrones. Cat. No. 303.

also —within each design, i.e., each image of the same saint— from one series to another. Sometimes these variations are the result of the execution, of the painter's greater or lesser exaltation, but there are also, as we have said, true changes in the very fashion in which the saint is depicted.

Being the oldest, the pictures in the Arteche series are the most restrained, though the freedom of execution is extraordinary and the beauty attained in this by the painter rivals that to be found in the drawing and the colour. We can see that the psychology of each character was deeply and penetratingly studied and that the attitude, the position of the head, the look and the twist of the lips were all El Greco needed to show the inner life that animated his subject. The figures in the Oviedo series, as has already been remarked, are practically the same as those in the preceding one. As is always the case with El Greco, however, although the composition, approach, drawing and colour are identical, the diversity of the execution is enough to change the whole background of the image, apart from the change inherent in the larger format of the works in this series. In this series we cannot exclude the possibility that other hands than El Greco's collaborated in the painting.

When we come to the two great central series —those in the Cathedral of Toledo and the Greco Museum, respectively— we find a tendency, apart from extending the figure to knee-length, to give a more monumental quality to the draperies. What might be considered the remains of an analytical concept disappear entirely and the synthetic vision of the image becomes absolutely predominant. The drawing traces great arabesques with the main outlines and inner lines. The colour is intensified spiritually rather than physically, while at the same time the distortions and simplifications increase.The painter contents himself with suggesting the form, without truly representing it; this is the case, for instance, with the right hand of the *St. Andrew* in the Greco Museum *(Figure 287)*, and even more so in the tremendous hand supporting a huge open book in the picture of *St. Simon* in the same museum *(Fig. 314)*. There is practically no drawing, but only a form that is —paradoxically— formless, but which, thanks to El Greco's miraculous technique, succeeds perfectly in presenting the necessary effect. It should be pointed out that these distortions still have a double origin. If on the one hand they may be called expressionistic, with all the voluntary distortion implied in that concept, on the other they are the very first signs of a vision that was not to have its full impact until some centuries later. El Greco blurs those forms that "should not be seen", or, at least, should hardly be noticeable. He uses another kind of expressionism —abrupt strokes, abbreviated modelling— in the faces, as we may see in the Greco Museum *St. Simon*.

A visionary monumental quality and a skilfully achieved harmony of arabesque, form and colour are predominant, nevertheless, and the distortions feature as devices of appreciable —and very considerable— value, but subordinated to the need to create forms that will not go too far beyond what can be conceived by the viewer. It is in the representations of Christ that we find the greatest care in preserving these values, though expressionism never ceases to make itself felt, more or less subtly. An example of this is the *Christ* in the Cathedral of Toledo *(Fig. 275)*. The face is very pure and follows the earlier designs to which the painter was always faithful; in the hands there is hardly any distortion, but the sinuosities of the draperies —twisting one way in the robe and in another in the mantle— are a proof of the need to alter the "classic" values of the texture, form and surface tension of the material represented.

Sometimes it is the simplification that produces an anomalous effect. Thus, if we compare the different images of St. James the Great, following the order of the series established above, we shall see that the right hand that stretches out horizontally, somewhat above waist level, is progressively simplified and takes on a kind of phantasmagorical quality *(Figs. 324 to 327)*. A similar increase in simplification —which at the same time partially destroys the form— may be observed in comparing the *St. Thomas* in the Cathedral of Toledo with that in the Greco Museum, while a comparison between the versions of *St. Philip* in the same two series will show us what great differences of pictorial expression the painter was able to achieve, though maintaining the same scheme of motif, composition, colour and drawing, simply by the execution.

Finally, in the Almadrones series we can see a more psychically profound insight in his expressionism. The technique is considerably modified and nobody would say, looking at the *St. James the Great* of this series, that it was painted at the beginning of the seventeenth century. There is an evident prefiguring of Van Gogh in some respects: in the independence of the lines of drawing with regard to the modelling, the fixed expresion of the character and the morphology of his head. It is interesting to compare the face of St. John the Evangelist in this series with that in the Cathedral of Toledo. If this latter seemed distorted, what can we say of the harlequin-like countenance —rubbed, whitish, at once stubborn and hallucinated— of the picture in Fort Worth? Some of the images in the Greco Museum were already coming close to this way of treating the form; the *St. Jude*, for instance, apart from its extremely daring simplification and distortion, is very strange from the psychological point of view. El Greco's last lesson would appear to be that mysticism borders on the loss of the rational sense. What else could these faces express? The image, in other words, is an absolutely ductile medium for showing the inner movements of the spirit, which is just what expressionism preaches.

In this late period of his life, the sublimation of El Greco's creative process is combined with the utmost ill-fortune. Those who accepted his works on account of the fervour aroused by his great creations —without in the least comprehending the real magnitude of his genius —now felt quite capable of attacking them when they were presented in conjunction with the pathetic structural settings of Jorge Manuel. The implacable and tenacious reaction of the board of the Hospital of Illescas was to deal a serious blow to the ambitious organization of the young architect-painter, even leading to criticism and rejection of El Greco's own work.

The great painter himself evidently attempted to give greater efficacy to his son's plans for expansion by increasing the staff of assistants in his workshop and consequently the production of copies of his originals. To the works dealt with in this chapter must be added a considerable amount of workshop paintings which the purposes and brevity of the present study do not permit us to mention here. We would recommend the reader, if he wishes to learn more about the importance and volume of the copies executed during this period, to consult the second part of the excellent catalogue published by Wethey. Even though, in our opinion, this eminent American professor is sometimes too severe in his judgments, relegating to the workshop some canvases which, we are absolutely convinced, are authentic Grecos, the number of works he mentions is sufficient to justify consulting his work. We should like to record once more our sincere admiration for the great work done by Wethey, which extends to the denunciation of quite a number of forgeries.

Drawings attributed to El Greco

Trained as he was in the Venetian school, it is quite probable that El Greco prepared his compositions with sketches and drawings done on paper. The inventory of his estate drawn up in 1614 mentions an item of a hundred and fifty drawings, which have become two hundred and fifty in the second inventory, drawn up in 1621. There are very few drawings extant that can be attributed to El Greco with any certainty. Such data as we have, indeed, are not enough to permit any categorical judgment to be made. The most convincing identifications so far are the following:

A pencil drawing *(Fig. 332)* reproducing Michelangelo's sculpture *Day*, which figures on the Medici tombs. According to Kehrer, the model for this vigorous drawing might have been a plaster cast of the sculpture which Alessandro Vittoria mentions in 1563 as being in Tintoretto's studio. The attribution of the drawing is based upon the inscription "Domenico Greco", in handwriting that Baumeister attributes to Vasari (d. 1574).

In the National Library in Madrid there is a sketch *(Fig. 333)* that is obviously connected with the *St. John the Evangelist* in Santo Domingo el Antiguo *(Fig. 60)*. It is done in pencil, is vigorous in execution and is quite convincing despite its poor state of preservation.

The most interesting of the sketches attributed to the great Cretan was a pen-and-ink drawing, with touches of wash and white pencil, which was destroyed in the fire at the Jovellanos Institute in Gijón *(Fig. 334)*. It may have been a preparatory study for the *Agony in the garden* that we reproduce in *Fig. 186*.

Other possible original drawings are the two sketches of the two Sts. John in Santo Domingo el Antiguo, which are now in the Stirling Collection in Keir, and a *St. John the Evangelist* in the Wildenstein Collection.

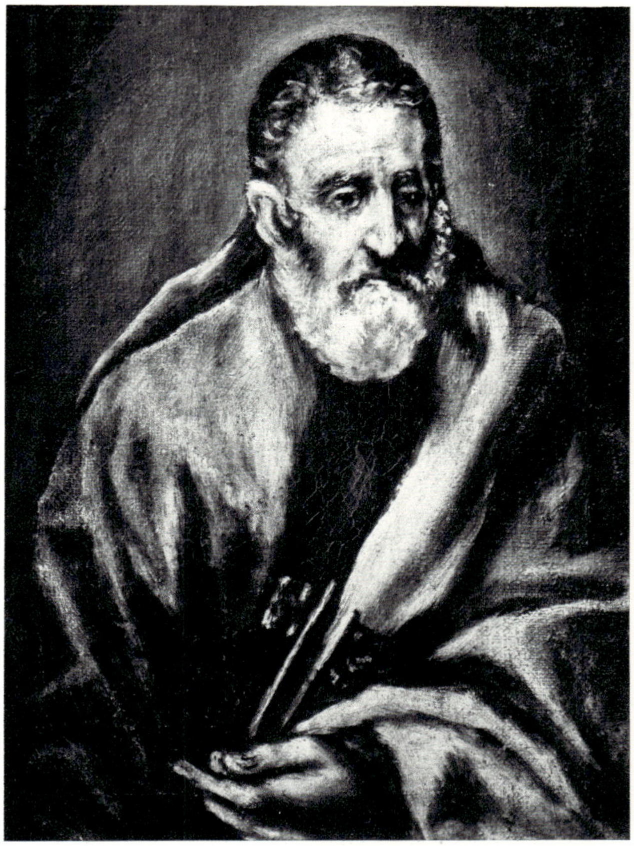
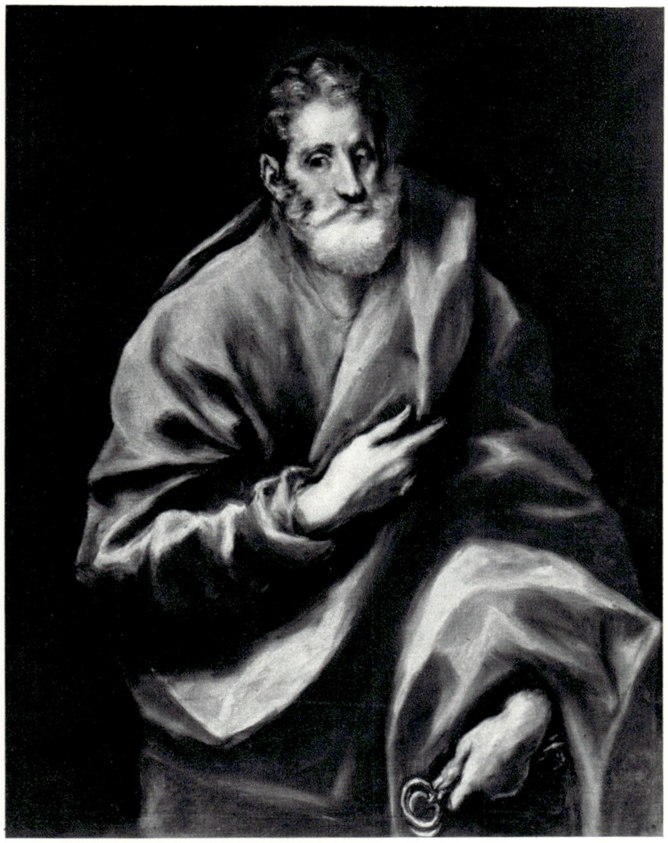
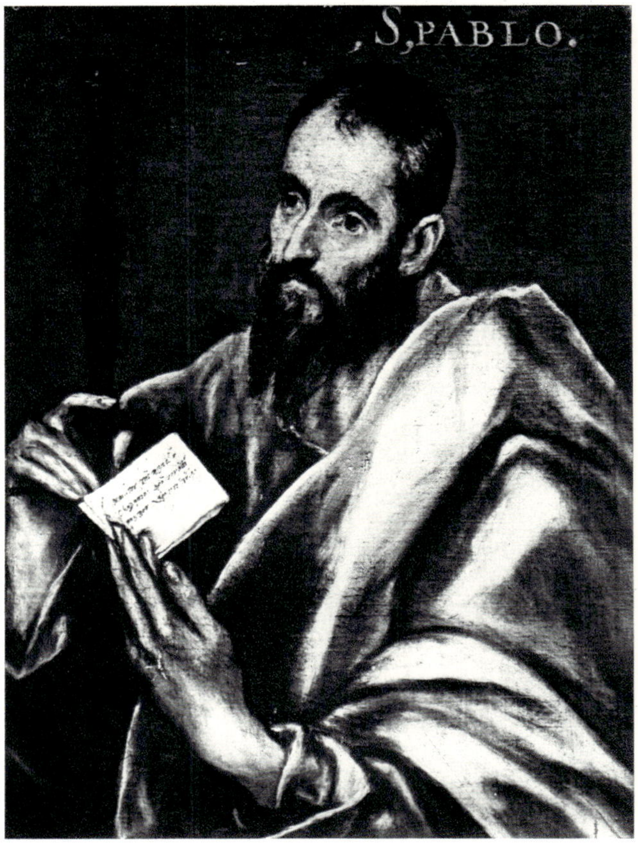

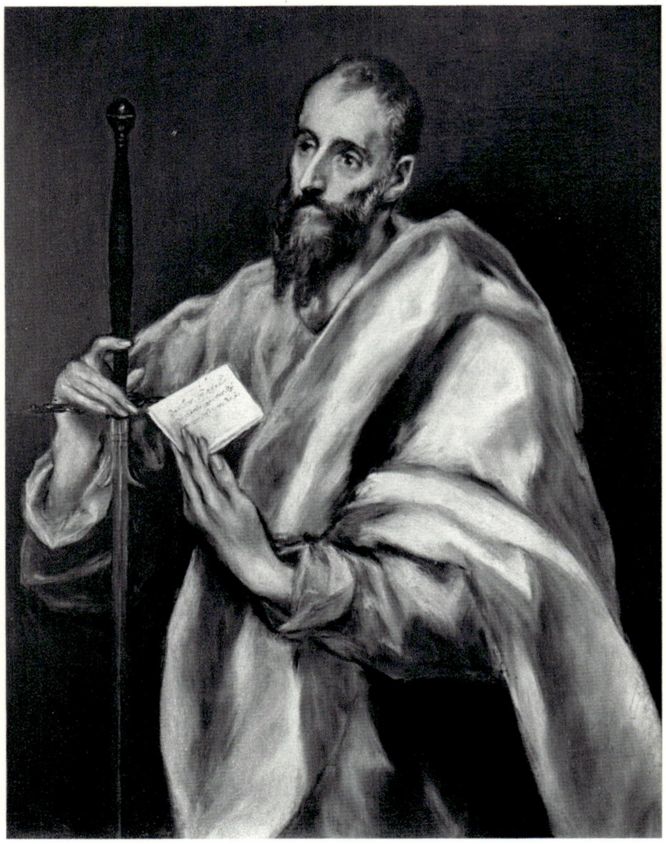

ST. PETER

Fig. 328. Arteche. Cat. No. 256.

Fig. 329. Greco Museum. Cat. No. 294.

ST. PAUL

Fig. 330. Marqués de San Feliz. Cat. No. 269.

Fig. 331. Greco Museum. Cat. No. 295.

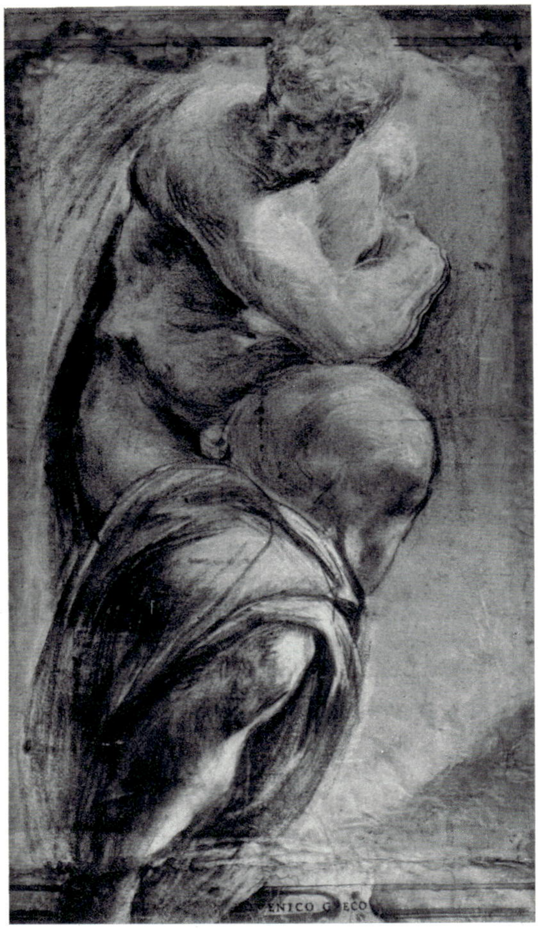

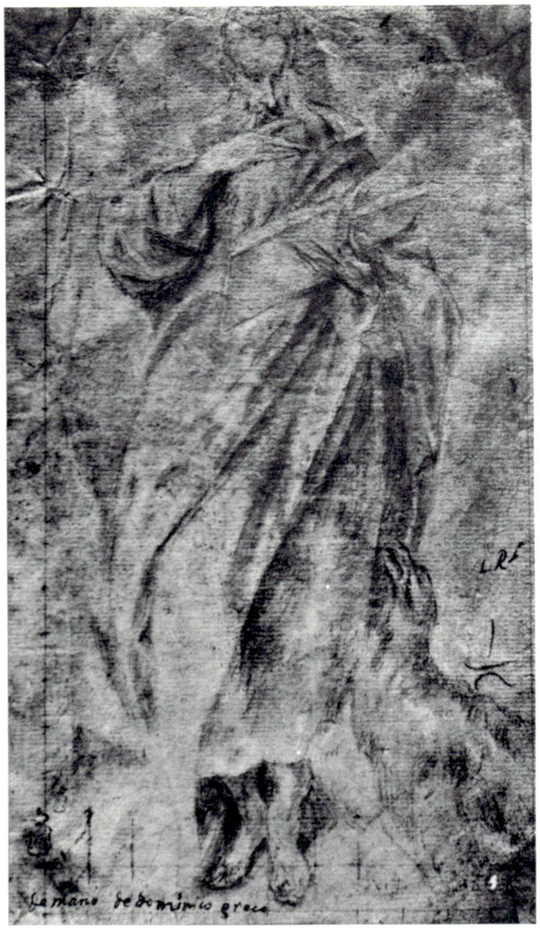

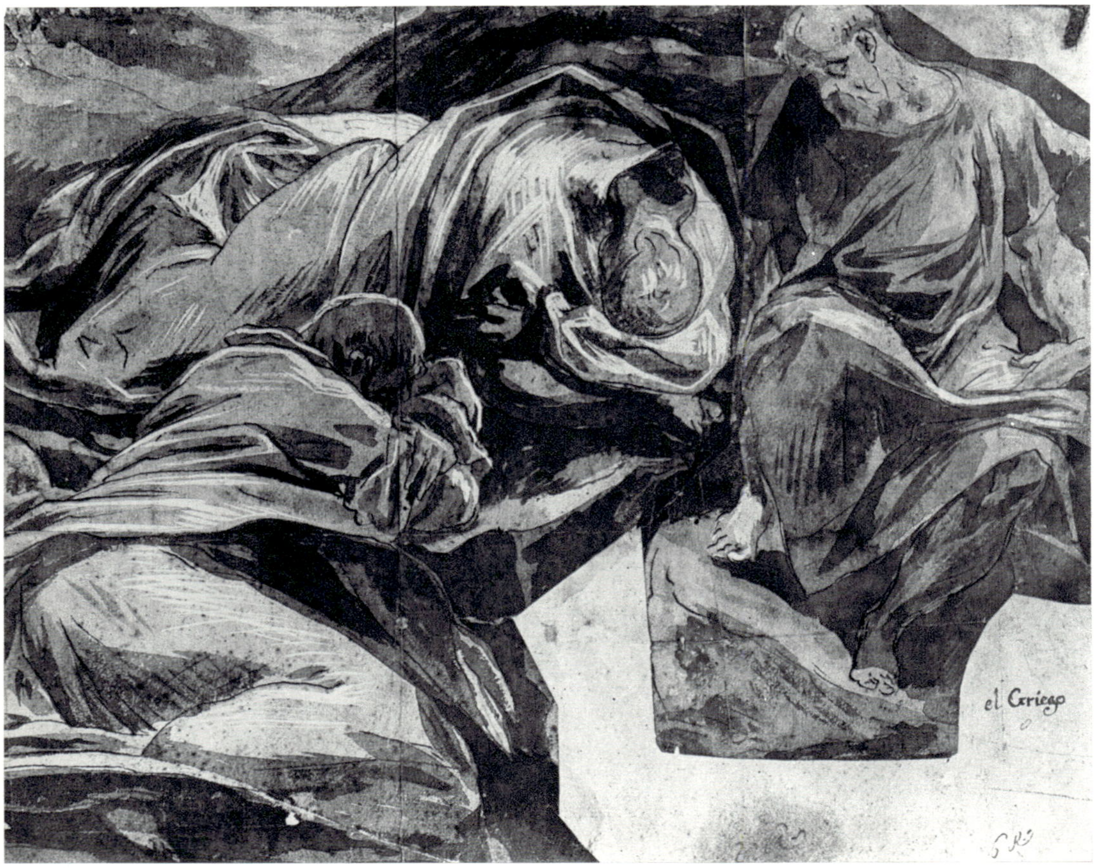

Fig. 332. Day. Pencil drawing (602 x 348 mm.). Munich, Graphische Sammlung.
Fig. 333. St. John the Evangelist. Pencil drawing (255 x 155 mm.). Madrid, National Library.
Fig. 334. Apostles at the agony in the garden. Pen-and-ink drawing. (Destroyed).

Workshop paintings after lost originals

There are still some paintings that correspond to designs different from all those studied in this book. There can be no doubt that they belong to El Greco's typological sequence, but their execution cannot be attributed to him —whether because the execution itself is different or because the quality is simply not good enough. They are, therefore, workshop paintings, some of them appearing in several versions, but none with the brilliant brushwork of the master himself.

There is no need to harp on the difficulty of establishing a dividing line between El Greco's own paintings and those from his workshop, particularly when the painter took some hand in them. There is a lot of work still to be done before any definitive classification can be made, and this will not be feasible until all the works can be studied in suitable conditions, which is practically impossible if we remember that it would entail the proper cleaning of all the known works, their direct examination in good light and the obtaining of series of photographs of whole works and details.

While awaiting the coincidence of all these circumstances, which we would imagine to be Utopian, we will confine ourselves to completing our text with this series of works which, at least, reveal the existence of some lost originals. The first of these workshop paintings is an image of *The Virgin Mary* in the Harris Collection in England *(Fig. 335),* showing the Virgin in bust length with her hands clasped, a work in which we can see the great efforts made by the copyist to reproduce El Greco's qualities on his canvas. The drawing of the face, though fairly correct, is far from possessing the beauty and the emotion of the authentic works. The *St. Jerome in penitence* in the National Gallery of Scotland is a work that is close enough to those we have considered above to be by Tristán. We are acquainted with several versions of this theme. Remembering that El Greco's versions always show absolute fidelity to the original designs, we believe that in this case the original must have been painted some time around 1600. The saint is represented half-length and naked to the waist, at which level he is wrapped in an ample pinkish-crimson mantle. There is a rocky background, not very carefully worked, which resembles those in the pictures of St. Francis, but the opening in the upper left lets more light in, which gives the work a lighter and more highly-coloured range than in the pictures of the saint of Assisi. In the foreground we see the still-life that usually appeared in pictures of hermit saints. The drawing dominates the anatomy, a system of fluctuating serpentine forms that accentuates all the natural curves, within the limitations set by a virile and ascetic torso. The white hair and beard frame an interesting face, skilfully treated as an expressive type *(Fig. 336).*

A picture of *St. Dominic in penitence (Fig. 337)* is of particular interest, since the painter took as his model the print engraved by Diego de Astor *(Fig. 349)* instead of using an original Greco which undoubtedly existed. The background is harshly schematic, as are the folds of the habit. Logically enough, the beautiful rhythms that would have existed in the original have remained intact.

Still extant are various images of *Christ on the Cross*, undoubtedly painted in El Greco's workshop, in which the obvious divergencies from the authentic works on the same subject indicate the existence of other Greco designs. One of them is the beautiful *Calvary* in the Museum of Athens *(Fig. 338).* It is interesting that the same model should appear in the canvas that hangs in the parish church of Martín Muñoz de las Posadas, in the province of Segovia. In this latter painting, which is difficult to judge properly since it has been altered by extremely bad restoration, a cleric appears as a donor and this cleric has been identified as Andrés Núñez, the priest who commissioned El Greco to paint the *Burial of the Conde de Orgaz*. This identification is based on one of the clauses in the priest's will, drawn up in 1603, in which he bequeaths to the church of Navalperal del Campo "a picture of a Christ... in which is the portrait of the aforesaid Andrés Núñez, and which is a painting by Dominico Griego and one of great value ... and ... a picture with an image of Our Lady by the hand of Dominico Griego ...". Apparently, when the village of Navalperal was depopulated in 1834 all the effects of its church were transferred to that of Martín Muñoz de las Posadas.

Another version, in the Johnson Collection, Philadelphia *(Fig. 341),* shows the Virgin and St. John standing at the foot of the cross, on the left, and on the opposite side a landscape background of Toledo with little figures. The background is dark and dramatic and the flesh tints stand out with all the force of sculpture. The distortion of the legs, which is fairly intense, is very different from that practised by El

Greco; the work, however, is not without quality. The other version, which is in the Museum of Cincinnati, has no secondary characters, but only —at the foot of the cross and behind it— a great landscape of Toledo, or, rather, some of its buildings quite near the foreground and some little figures on foot and on horseback *(Fig. 342)*. The background is as dramatic as in the preceding work, but with larger openings where the light is streaked with dense clouds. Though in rather different fashion, the distortion in this version is also principally in the legs of the crucified Christ, everything else in the picture being quite correct.

The high quality of these canvases confirms the redoubtable powers of imitation that El Greco succeeded in instilling into his assistants. At first glance —i.e., before making a detailed analysis— they seem to be by El Greco himself, and certainly they are works of considerable pictorial quality, but they do not possess the finesse or the subtleties and liberties of execution habitually practised by the great painter by irrepressible instinct.

El Greco as a sculptor

The passage from Pacheco that we have already quoted, referring to his visit to El Greco's workshop in 1611, mentions the little clay and wax models used by the painter in the preparation of his compositions. A group of these is mentioned in the 1614 and 1621 inventories. San Román, taking the text of the contracts as his authority, reached the conclusion that El Greco never executed with his own hands the carved images included in some of his altarpieces, but confined himself to providing the sculptor with drawings and models for them. As we have said, the sculptures for the high altar of Santo Domingo el Antiguo are the work of Monegro, who followed the painter's original models.

Wethey admits direct participation by El Greco in the following pieces of sculpture: the polychromed high relief representing *The Miracle of St. Ildefonso* in the Cathedral of Toledo, all that remains of the sumptuous frame for the *Espolio*, which was done between 1585 and 1587 *(Fig. 343)*, the beautiful polychromed figure of *The Risen Christ*, which crowned the tabernacle of the high altar in the church of the Tavera Hospital *(Fig. 344)*, and the images that figured in the altarpiece and decoration of the high altar chapel in the church of the Hospital of Illescas, unfortunately destroyed in 1936 *(Fig. 345)*.

The engravings of Diego de Astor

Remembering the methods that obtained in the great workshops and studios of Venice and Rome, El Greco tried to find in engravings another medium for the expansion and popularization of his work. It should be recalled that engravings really became, in the sixteenth and seventeenth centuries, the most efficient vehicle for a more universal knowledge of the great masterpieces of art, for were it not for them only literary descriptions could give any account of such works. The printed sheet made its way into the homes of different social classes; painters used them as iconographical models, while magnates and the rich in general acquired them systematically to form collections. One instance of this is the immense collection amassed in the Escorial by Philip II. About 1605, then, El Greco requested the services of the Toledo engraver Diego de Astor for the reproduction of some of his works *(Figs. 346 to 349)*. All that remains today is the scant evidence of four prints engraved after original paintings by El Greco, all of them signed by Diego de Astor and dated. The *Adoration of the shepherds*, which is a reproduction of the canvas in the Museum of Valencia, is dated in 1605; the theme, so often repeated by El Greco, of *St. Francis and the lay brother*, in 1606; the *St. Dominic*, after the workshop painting that hangs in the Santa Cruz Museum in Toledo, is also dated in 1606. One of the versions of the *St. Peter and St. Paul* is dated in 1608. Other prints must have been done, for the 1621 inventory mentions twelve plates, besides "a hundred prints done at home". It must be admitted that El Greco made a good choice. Astor was an excellent craftsman, skilled in the technique of engraving, which he managed with virtuosity and fluency, and capable of feeling emotion when faced with the originals he copied, an emotion he transmitted to his plates. Sometimes the drawing slightly exaggerates El Greco's distortions, or so it seems on account of the lack of lights and chromatic reflections to correct the form in the optical impression. This may be seen in the *Adoration of the shepherds,* particularly in the wonderful figure of the shepherd in the right foreground. On the whole, he achieves an astonishing fidelity to El Greco's originals, not only in the form but also in the spirit. We also know that his engravings in turn inspired copies, as in the case of a *St. Dominic in penitence* already studied which hangs in the Santa Cruz Museum, Toledo,

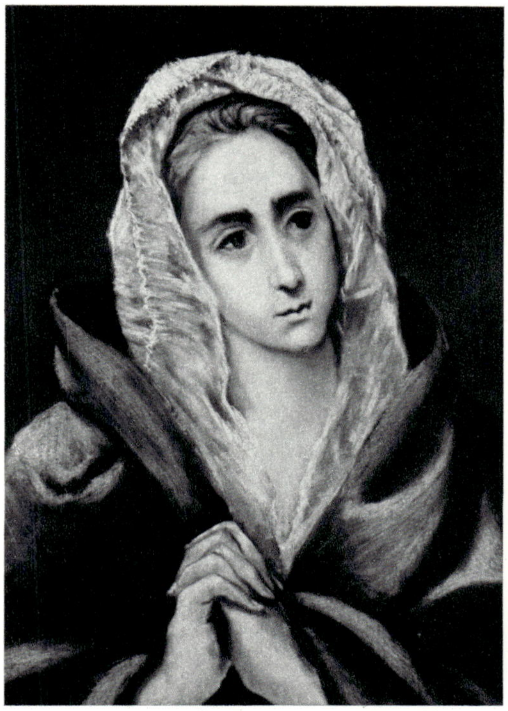

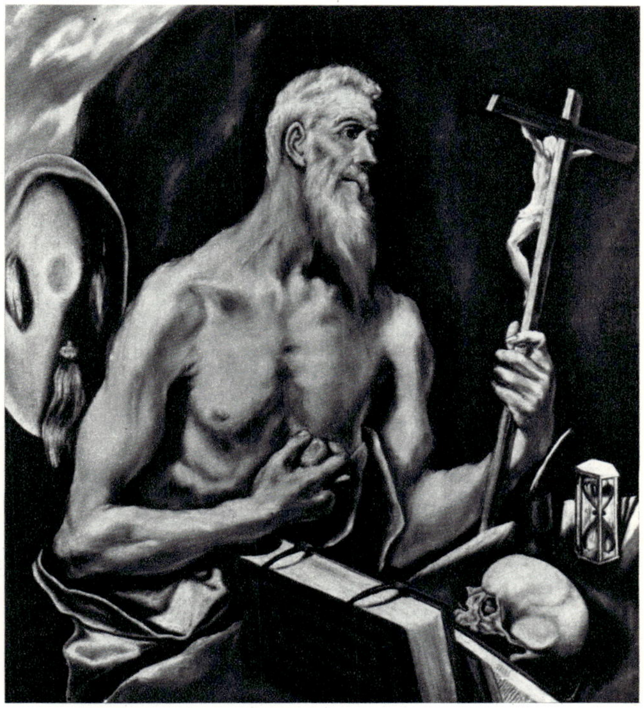

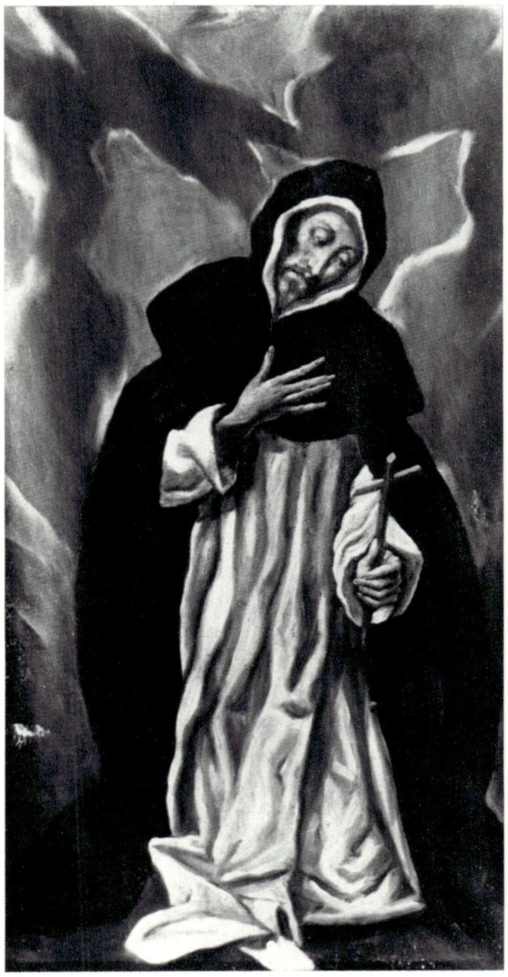

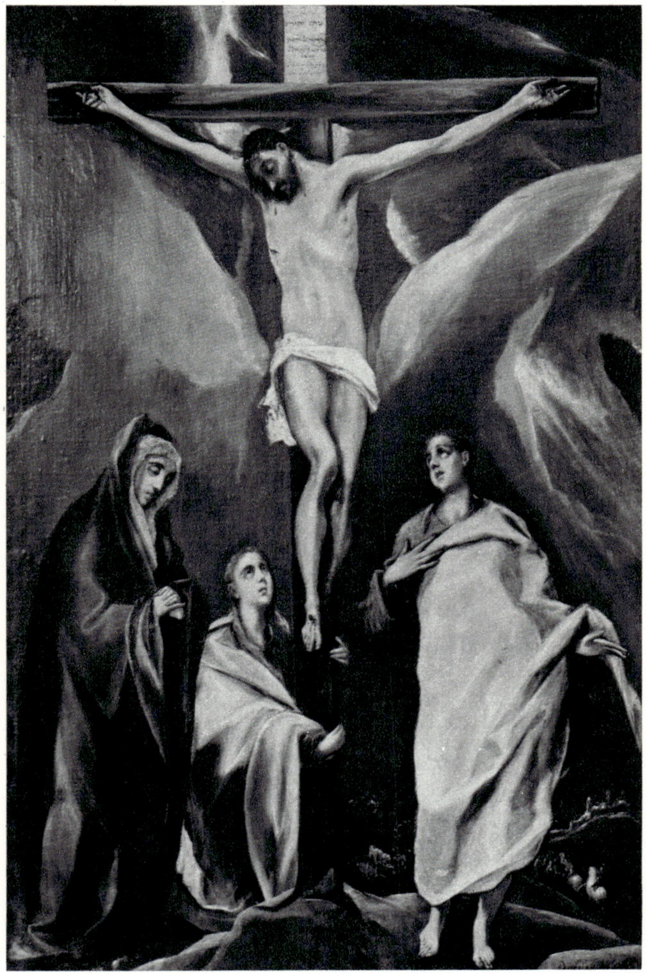

Fig. 335. The Virgin Mary. England, Harris Collection.
Fig. 336. St. Jerome. National Gallery of Scotland.
Fig. 337. St. Dominic. Toledo, Santa Cruz Museum.
Fig. 338. The Crucifixion. Museum of Athens.

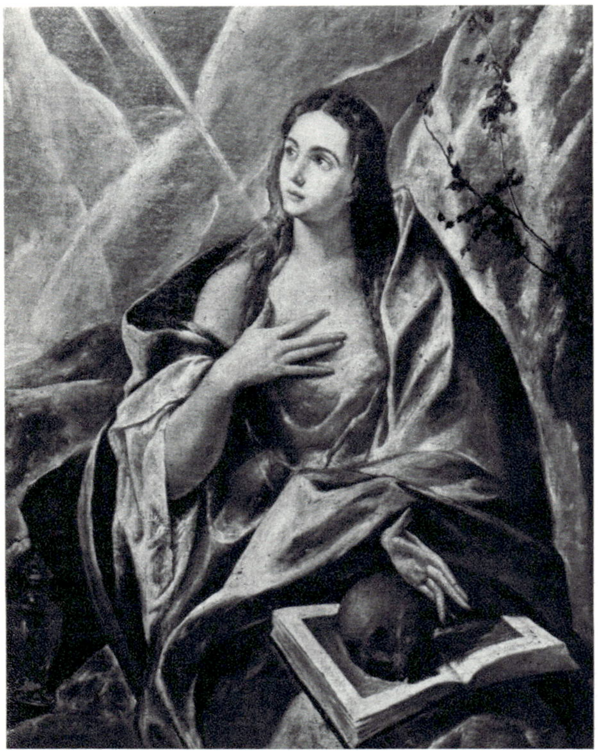

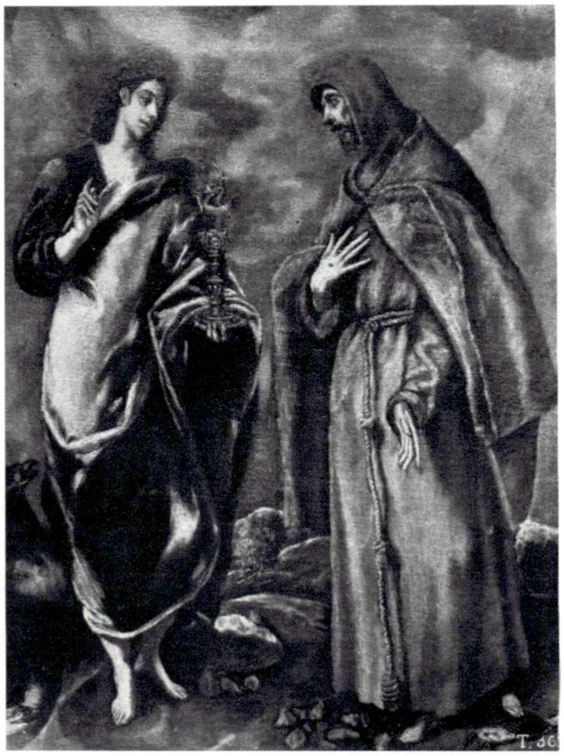

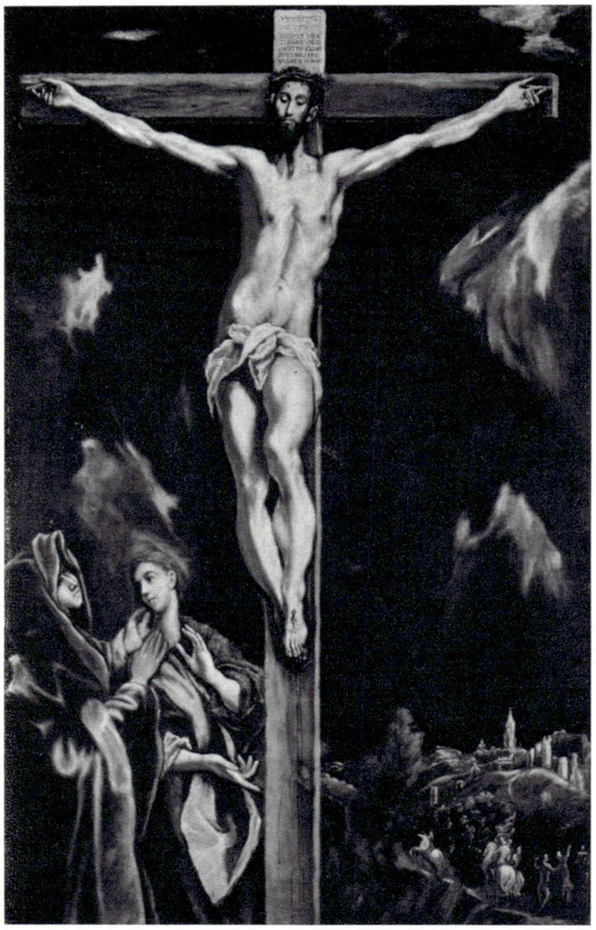

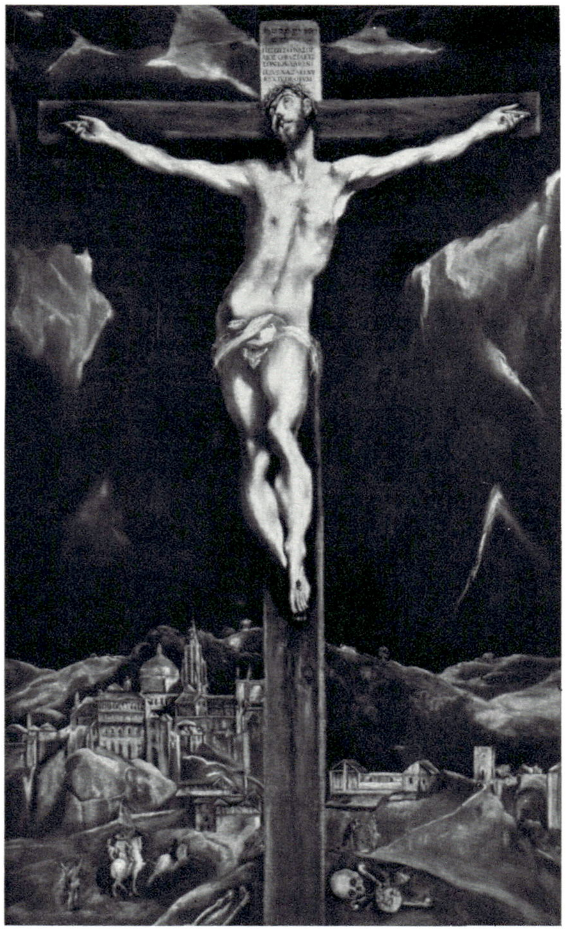

Fig. 339. St. Mary Magdalen. Barcelona, Sala Collection.
Fig. 340. St. John and St. Francis. Madrid, Prado.
Fig. 341. The Crucifixion. Philadelphia, Johnson Collection.
Fig. 342. Christ on the cross. Cincinnati, Art Museum.

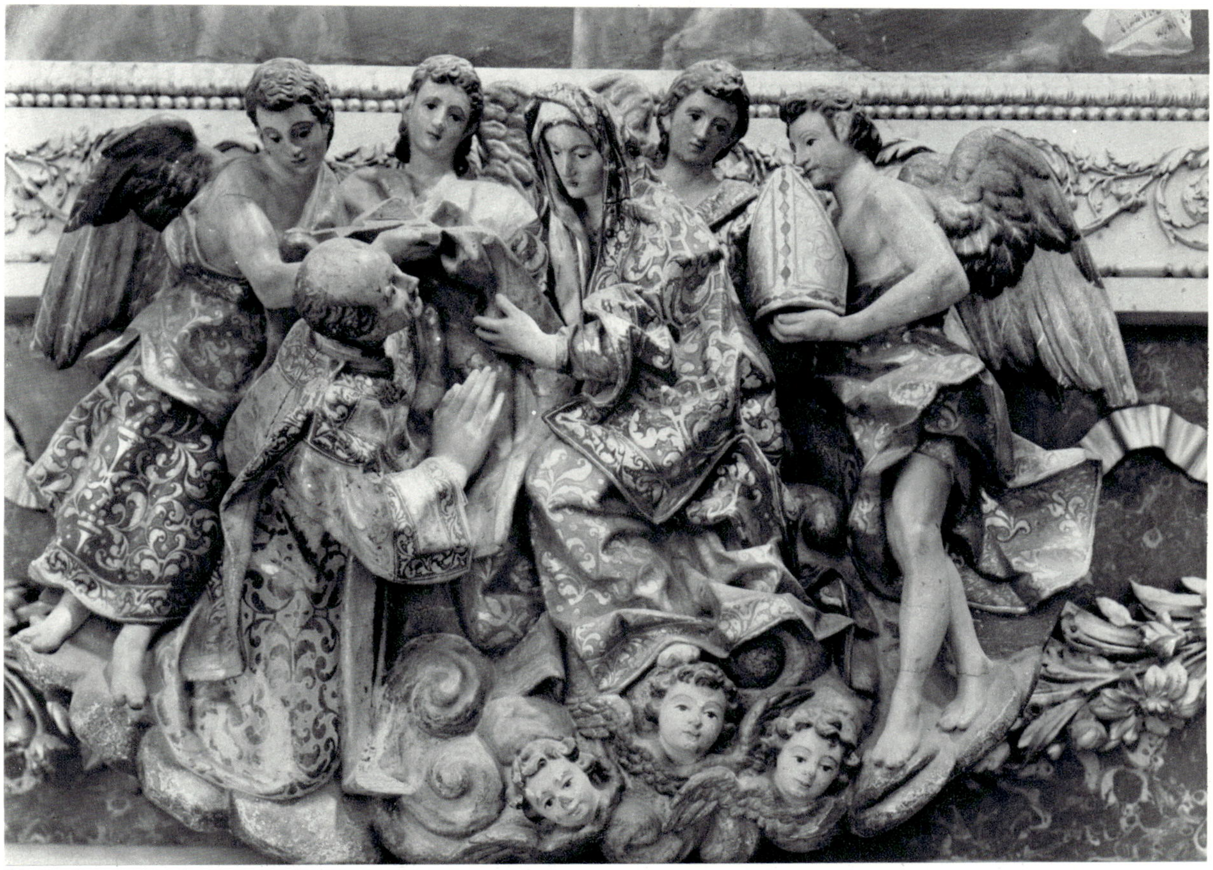

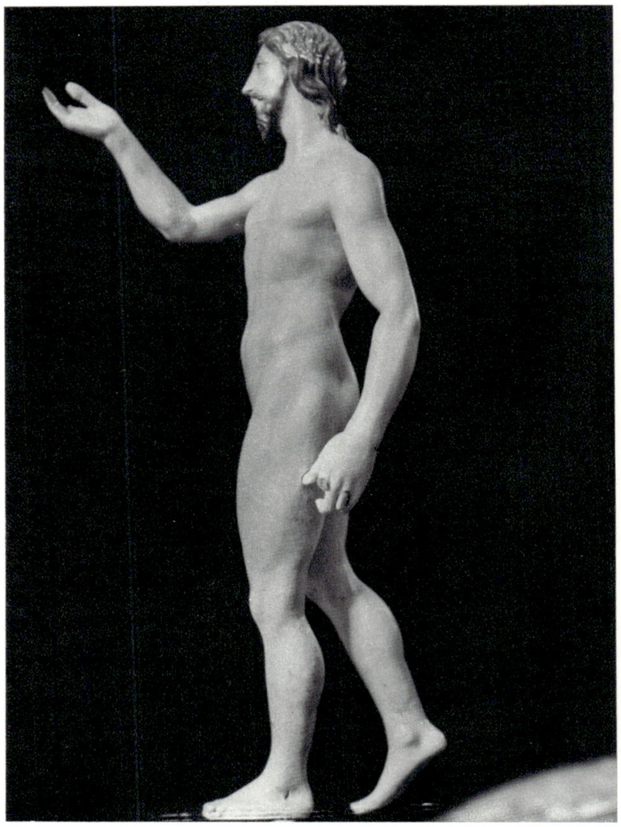

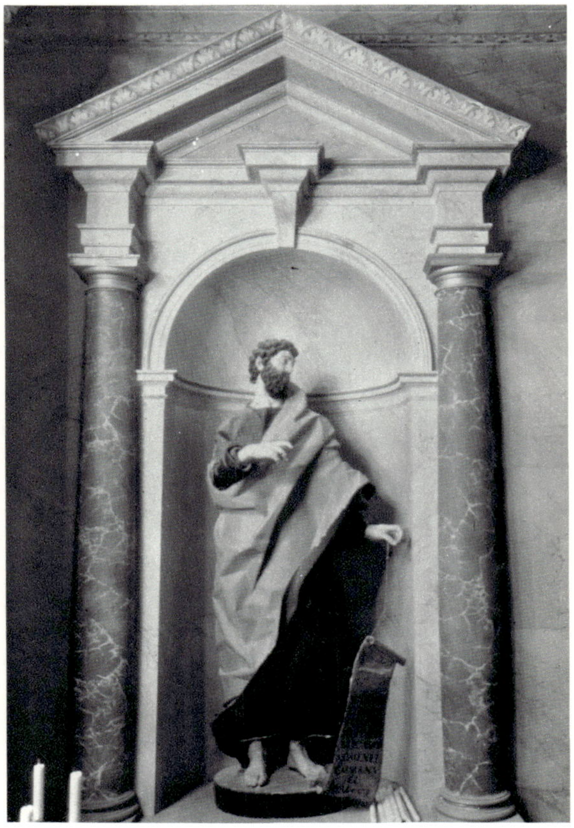

SCULPTURES

Fig. 343. The Miracle of St. Ildefonso. Cathedral of Toledo.
Fig. 344. The Risen Christ. Toledo, Hospital Tavera.
Fig. 345. Isaiah. Illescas, Hospital.

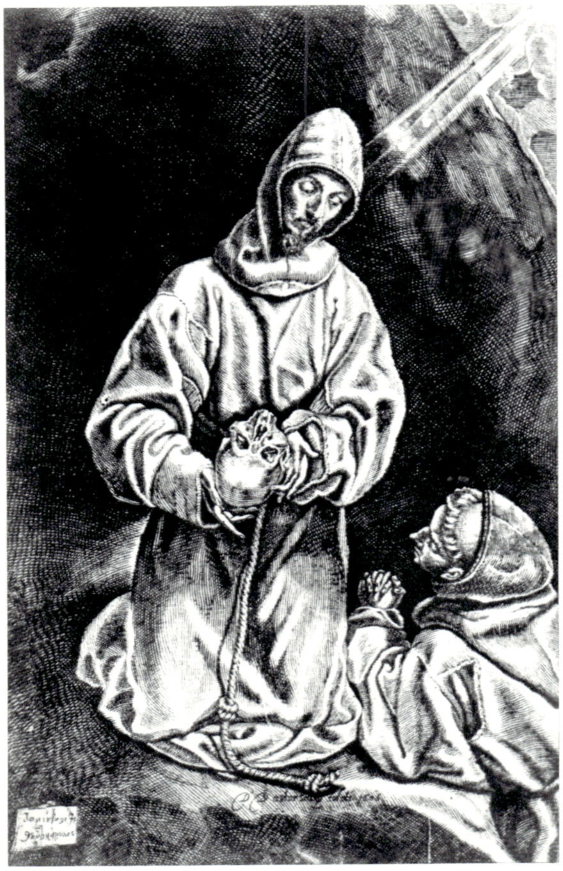

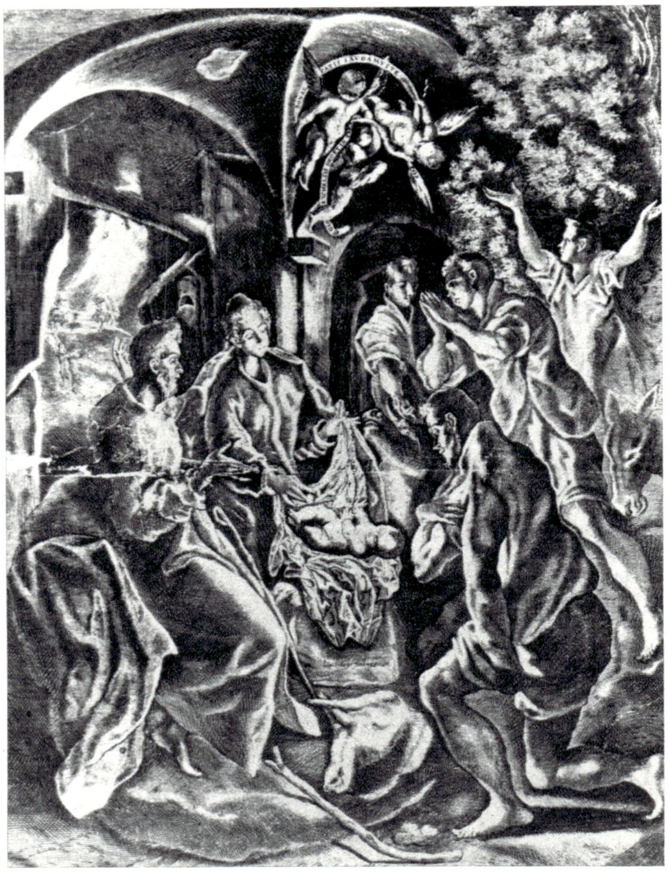

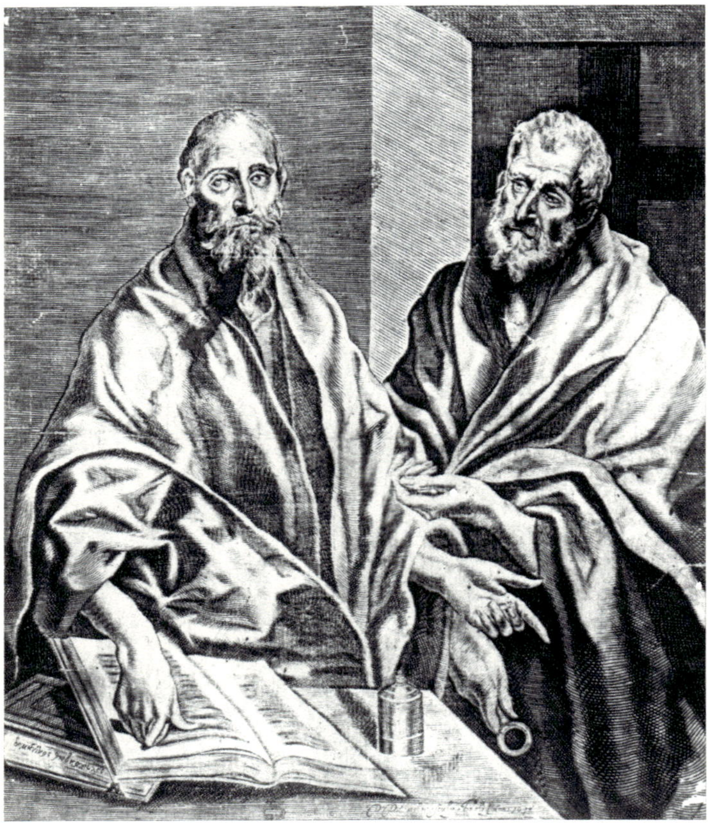

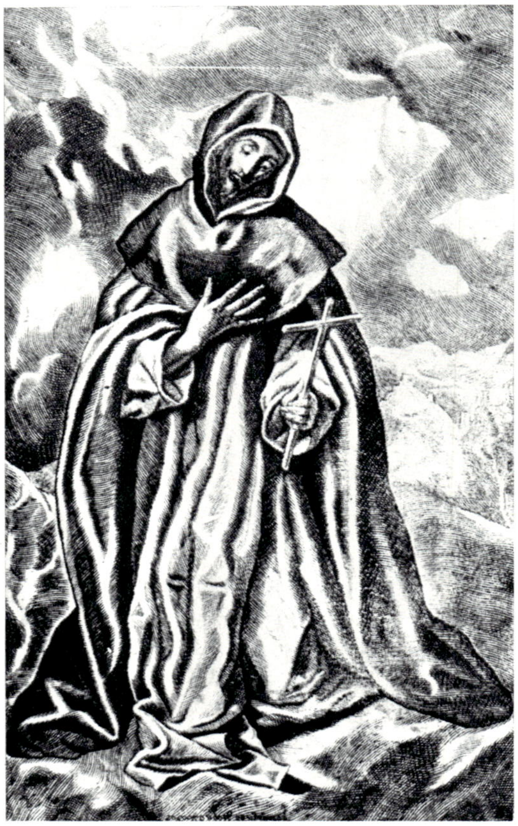

Figs. 346, 347, 348 & 349. Engravings by Diego de Astor after works by El Greco.

and derives, as we have said, from an engraving by Astor and not directly from El Greco's prototype *(Fig. 337)*.

Unfortunately for the artist, the expedients to which he resorted in order to expand his workshop, increase his sales and secure an economic success that he never fully obtained entailed two serious difficulties: he himself was already advanced in years and embittered by his frequent problems and reverses, while his son, Jorge Manuel, added to his scant artistic gifts a spirit that was undoubtedly rather fanciful and not sufficiently aware of its limitations.

Notes on Jorge Manuel Theotocópuli

The story of the life of El Greco's only son has been gradually unfolded throughout the preceding chapters. As we have said, his Christian names derived from those of his grandfather, Jorghi, and his uncle, Manoussos, who ended his days in Toledo. Most probably to save trouble in documents and social life, he changed the name Theotokópoulos, never altered in any of his father's signatures or documents, to the easier, Italianized form of Theotocópuli.

We have already recorded the little that is known of his mother, Jerónima de las Cuevas, who was El Greco's wife within a few months of the painter's arrival in Toledo and before he decided to settle there for good *(Fig. 78)*.

From various pieces of evidence, the first being that of the inscription on the handkerchief of the young Jorge Manuel who appears in the *Burial of the Conde de Orgaz (Fig. 106)*, we know that he was born in 1578. From two other portraits of him painted by his father we are acquainted with his physical appearance. The first of these, which is in the Museum of Seville *(Fig. 196)*, was perhaps painted on the occasion of his first marriage, at the age of twenty-five, and the other figures in the painting of *Our Lady of Charity* in the Illescas Hospital *(Fig. 199)*, which was painted shortly after that.

Jorge Manuel is the typical son of a genius; he learned his profession at his father's side, but he was a mediocre artist and, to judge by his life and work, he did not inherit El Greco's human disposition either. He did not confine himself to learning technical principles, so that his father's style had a disastrous influence on him and prevented him from developing whatever personality he might have had.

Around 1603 he married Alfonsa de los Morales. Their first child was christened on March 24th of 1604 and Dr. Gregorio Angulo, that unfailing prop of the family economy, was his godfather. This boy was christened Gabriel de los Morales, thus entirely eliminating his grandfather's surname. He entered the Augustinian Order in 1622. The young couple always lived with Jorge Manuel's father in the home-cum-workshop in the Villena mansion. The *Family portrait* in the Pitcairn Collection *(Fig. 352)* is thought to represent Alfonsa de los Morales with the little Gabriel, accompanied by a young maidservant and a woman of a certain age, this last being hypothetically identified as Jerónima de las Cuevas.

As from 1603, Jorge Manuel's name appears on the contracts and he also signs contracts on his own account for works of architecture and decoration. Thus, on September 17th 1603, he signed a contract for the construction of an altarpiece for the hermitage of Our Lady of the Meadow, in Talavera de la Reina, a work which never got beyond the project stage. In 1605 the Council of Toledo presented him with a silver dish for the planning and supervision of certain restorations in the "Play-House". In 1606 he signed the contract for an altarpiece intended for the chapel of the Ubeda family in the church of San Ginés in Toledo; in the contract we may read that this altarpiece was to include "a living Christ on the Cross, with St. John and Our Lady ... signed by El Greco and a countryside on the other side, by the same hand".

On November 7th of 1606 he engaged to construct the main and side altarpieces for San Martín de Montalbán. In May of the following year his father gave him ample legal powers "that he may accept on his own account and mine or on mine alone, as he sees fit, any work in connection with altarpieces, paintings and architecture". There is a remarkably large number of documents concerning Jorge Manuel's activities, and this is not the place for examining or analysing them. But there is one altarpiece that must be mentioned: the one in honour of St. Mary Magdalen, which, according to the contract drawn up in 1607, he executed on his own account in association with the sculptor Giraldo de Merlo for the parish church of Titulcia, in the province of Toledo. This work still exists and is a key element in determining the characteristics of his style.

As we have seen, on March 31st 1614 he was empowered to draw up a will on behalf of his father, who died on the following 7th of April. Between April 12th and July 7th, Jorge Manuel drew up the first inventory of the estate he had inherited, which includes the list of the paintings kept in the Villena mansion.

The story of Jorge Manuel continues with the unfortunate affair of the altarpieces for the Tavera Hospital, which, after El Greco's death, became a complete disaster. The son worked on the project at intervals for the rest of his life and in 1625 he transformed the altarpiece for the high altar, which had been designed by his father, into the structure we see there today. The altarpiece was placed in position before Jorge Manuel's death. He gave up his work as a painter almost completely —as is shown by the very few works of his preserved— and continued working as an architect and decorator.

In 1618 he finished the façade of the Town Hall of Toledo, which had been begun according to plans by Juan de Herrera. This brought him the honorary title of "Chief master of works to the Town Council", which he received in 1621. In the same year he was commissioned, with Luis Tristán, to construct the funeral catafalque in honour of Philip III.

He also continued to supervise the work on the grandiose chapel known as the Ochavo in the Cathedral of Toledo, a work begun in 1595 by Nicolás de Vergara. Between 1628 and 1631 he constructed the dome of the Mozarabic chapel, in his capacity as "Chief master of works to the Cathedral".

A lawsuit with the community of Santo Domingo el Antiguo, over the construction of the monument that was to be erected for Holy Week, cost Jorge Manuel the cancellation of his rights to the family vault acquired by his father in 1612. In 1619 he acquired another in the church of San Torcuato and on it he constructed an altar with the canvas copied from his father's *St. Maurice (Fig. 353).* Apparently, he transferred his father's remains to the new vault and was later buried there himself. Unfortunately, the church of San Torcuato was destroyed and with it were lost the remains of El Greco and his son.

In 1621, Alfonsa having died, he contracted a second marriage with Gregoria de Guzmán, a widow who apparently had means of her own. On the occasion of this new marriage Jorge Manuel drew up a new inventory of his estate. This document complements the one drawn up in 1614 and explains many of its terms, for it gives the measurements of the canvases. It also includes an important note referring to El Greco's library. Of this new union the first to be born were two girls, Claudia and María. In 1629 his second son was born and was christened Jorge, the godfather this time being the painter Pedro Orrente. A few days later the child's mother died; her will is still preserved. Jorge Manuel was married once more, this time to Isabel Villegas. He died on March 29th 1631, at the age of fifty-three and completely ruined. Philip IV granted his widow a pension of 2 *reales* a day for life.

We still have sufficient works to acquaint us with Jorge Manuel's mediocrity as a painter and that lack of character we mentioned above. The signed copy of the *Espolio* that hangs in the Prado *(Fig. 350)* must be an early work. It is a careful painting, with every detail properly placed, and we may see that he made an effort to give the form strength, but it has neither the quality nor the beauty of material, colour and expression that shine so brightly in the great original. A comparison of the details makes the whole composition seem even worse.

The compositions for the Titulcia altarpiece, being independent of El Greco's models, have to some extent another effect *(Fig. 351).* On account of the differences of opinion that arose, the canvases were not finally delivered until after 1621. They are works that derive from El Greco, but the Mannerist content is accentuated and the brilliant genius of the master's discoveries is lost. But we can see quite clearly in these paintings the collaboration of another artist, with a completely opposed style. According to Miss Trapier, author of the only biography of El Greco's son that exists, this other artist may have been a Fleming called Jan de Haesten, who was the brother-in-law of Giraldo de Merlo. The only canvas in this work that remains in its original place is the composition that crowns it, the theme of which is the *Assumption of Mary Magdalen.* All the figures are totally derived from El Greco.

Two copies of works by El Greco attributed to Jorge Manuel are that of the *Burial of the Conde de Orgaz* (in the Prado) and that of the *St. Maurice (Fig. 353).* Both reveal a synthesis of the conditions mentioned in connection with the previous works.

Also by Jorge Manuel —and it is his best picture— is the *Family portrait* mentioned above *(Fig. 352).* Might it not be a copy of one done by his father? Were it not for the existence of the compositions in Titulcia, we might suggest the hypothesis that

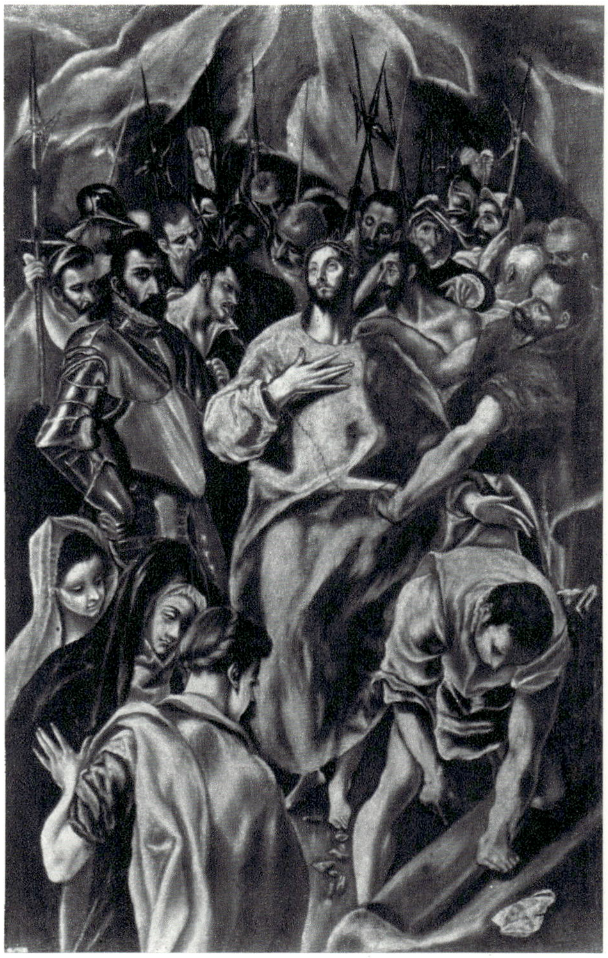

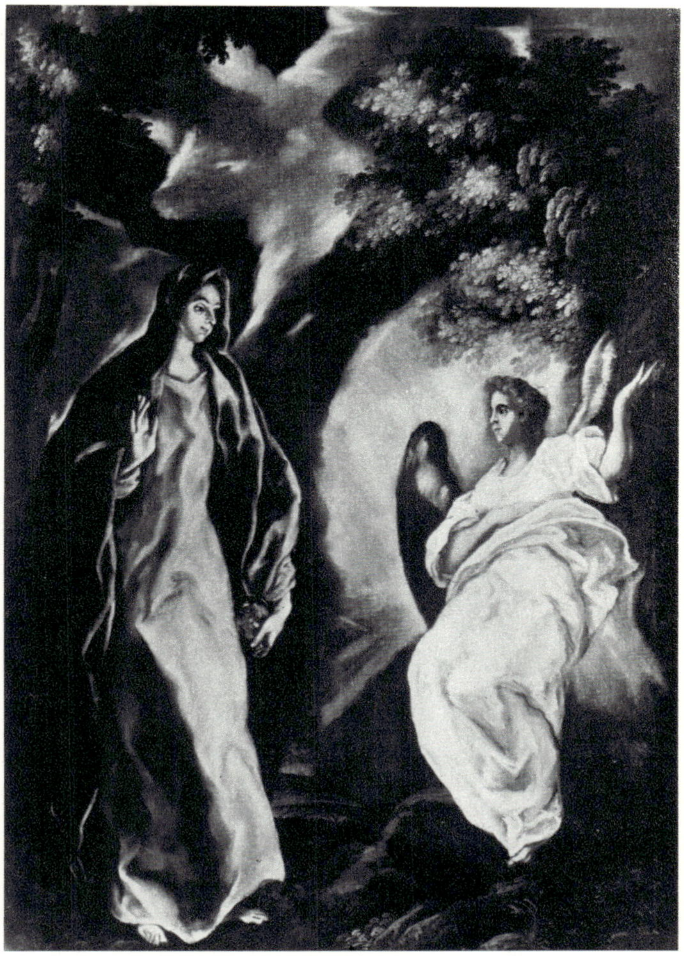

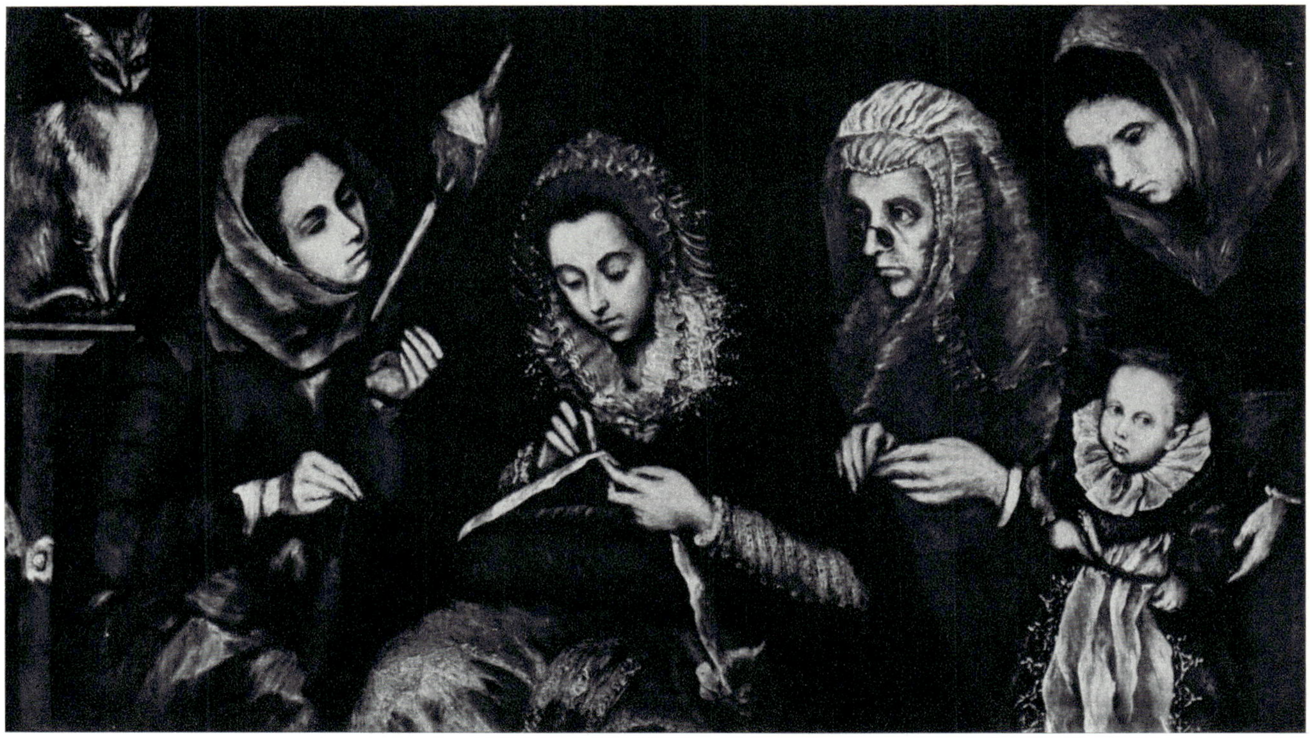

WORKS BY JORGE MANUEL

Fig. 350. Espolio. Madrid, Prado.

Fig. 351. The Apparition of the angel to St. Mary Magdalen. Venice, Papisil Collection.

Fig. 352. El Greco's family. Bryn Athyn (Pennsylvania), T. Pitcairn Collection.

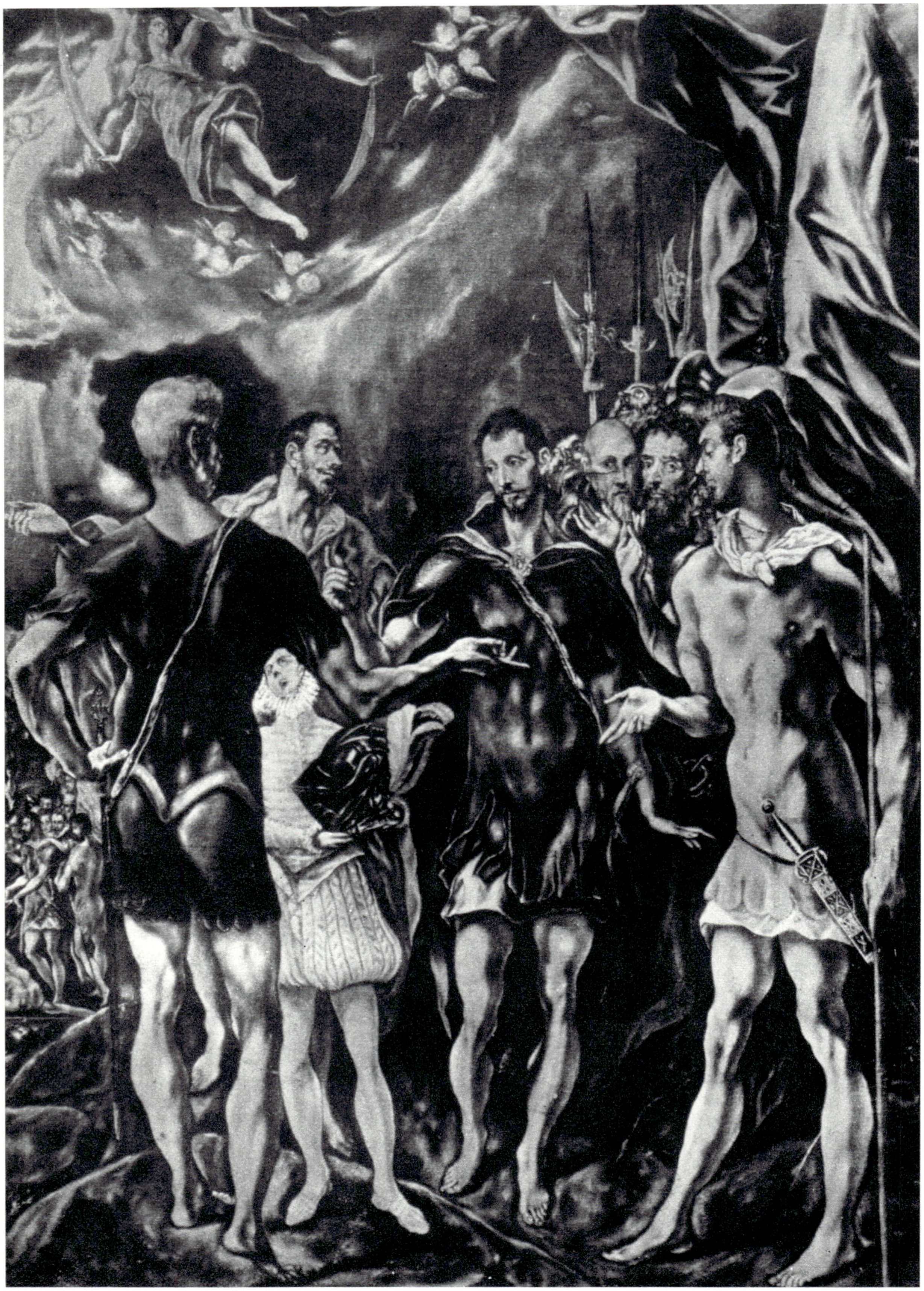

WORKS BY JORGE MANUEL

Fig. 353. The Martyrdom of St. Maurice. Formerly in the Church of San Torcuato, Toledo.

the *Family portrait* turned out better because it was an original composition. But we have seen in the Titulcia pictures that the lack of his father's influence certainly did not help Jorge Manuel to produce great paintings. The truth is that he was almost obliged to be a painter, for it is possible that when he was still a boy, and one without any particular vocation, his father guided his steps in the direction of art with the idea of having an asistant with whom it would be easy to cooperate. The *Family portrait* is a work with a certain sense of realism, a painting that is already clearly of the seventeenth century and one that is well-drawn, despite a rather hieratic character.

El Greco's physical likeness

Now that we have followed, step by step, the vicissitudes of our painter in life and art, we may be justified in wondering what El Greco looked like physically. We could easily indulge in conjectures and suppose that, since he belonged to a Mediterranean race, he was a man of swarthy complexion and felt at ease in Spain just because he found there a greater racial kinship with himself than in Venice, where blonde opulence was the rule. But it is not a question of confining ourselves to conjectures.

Some of the heads that appear in the canvases of the great Cretan painter have been indicated as possible self-portraits of El Greco, but none exists that can be classified as such by unquestionable documentation. We will therefore close this book by dealing with those suppositions that seem most likely.

The young man in black with a white ruff who appears behind the bare torsos on the left of the *Christ healing the blind man* in Parma *(Fig. 22)* is chronologically the first of these supposed self-portraits. There would also be another self-portrait from the Italian period if we admitted that the fourth figure in the foreground of the *Cleansing of the Temple* in Minneapolis *(Fig. 13)* was a representation of the artist himself. But, as has already been pointed out, other hypotheses have been advanced.

There seems to be a more plausible case for some of these "self-portraits" among the works painted in Spain. First we have the bearded head that we see behind the character of the title in the *Martyrdom of St. Maurice* in *Fig. 81*. We also have the fair-bearded gentleman looking out at the viewer from the central section of the funeral *cortège* of the Conde de Orgaz *(Fig. 105)*, though the beard would contradict our initial hypothesis as to the Cretan's appearance. The old man with the pointed black beard who is second on the right in the upper part of the *Pentecost* in the Prado *(Fig. 213)* might be another image of the artist. Possibly we may also include in the list a figure who appears on the right in the *Marriage of the Virgin* in the National Museum of Romania *(Fig. 255)*.

Any comment on such identifications is pure literary speculation, but there is one notable fact that we should not forget. In Jorge Manuel's canvas in *Fig. 353*, which is a copy of the *St. Maurice* in the Escorial, the above-mentioned man, who is seen behind the figure of the centurion, was changed to an old man with a white beard, whose resemblance to the old man already discussed in the *Pentecost* is indisputable. Is this, then, the portrait of El Greco?

We should recall that this canvas was hung by Jorge Manuel above the altar built over the second vault of the Theotokópoulos family, in the church of San Torcuato in Toledo, all of which seems to make an affirmative answer to our question fairly reasonable. And so we may accept the fact that the still-young man in El Greco's *St. Maurice* and the old one in the *Pentecost* are self-portraits of the artist painted at very different stages in his life. In the second of these two canvases he placed himself among the blessed apostles of Christ, so that there are thirteen instead of twelve. To himself, as to them, he awarded the tongue of fire of the Holy Ghost. And he certainly deserved it, as an immortal painter and man.

The inventories of El Greco's estate

At various points in the text of the present book we have mentioned the inventories of the goods and possessions of El Greco and his son, which were discovered and published by F. de B. San Román and are now kept in the register office of Toledo. They were drawn up by Jorge Manuel himself: the first in 1614, a few days after his father's death, and the second in 1621, in arranging his marriage to his second wife, Gregoria de Guzmán, "that the goods that I bring to this marriage may be known ...".

These documents are of particular importance on account of the list of painted canvases that forms the part of both, apart from the brief mention of drawings and of prints "done at home". The lists of the furniture and fittings reflect the modest style of living of the Theotokópoulos family in the decrepit old mansion of the Marqués de Villena. The scantiness of the household equipment forms a strong contrast to the importance of the library. This latter was chiefly devoted to books on architecture and geometric perspective, in Italian and Greek; but it also contained works of mathematics, history and literature. The second inventory, more complete than the first, includes five manuscripts on architecture, one of them illustrated with drawings, which in San Román's opinion might well be the "original texts by El Greco" mentioned by Pacheco in the account of his visit to the great painter, to which we have referred briefly in the preceding pages — though this, of course, can be no more than conjecture.

We give below the list of the paintings just as they figure in the 1621 inventory. It may be supposed that most of them would have been the sketches "of everything El Greco had painted in his life", as Pacheco admiringly tells us in the passage to which we have just referred. We have put asterisks against the works included in the 1614 inventory and have given numbers from our catalogue to those titles that very probably correspond to pictures still preserved.

FINISHED PICTURES

N.B. The Spanish word "vara" (or "bara", as it was usually spelt in El Greco's time), which is commonly translated as "rod", is the linear measurement used throughout this inventory. 1 *vara* is the equivalent of 83.59 centimetres (32.9 inches).

1 First, a descent of the Holy Ghost, four *varas* high by two and two-thirds wide

2 a picture of the angel Saint Gabriel bearing the message to Zachariah, with a portrait of a Hieronymite friar below, which is over three *varas* high and a *vara* and two-thirds wide *

3 A St. Sebastian, two and a half *varas* high by a *vara* and a third wide *(Cat. No. 241)*

4 A St. John the Baptist, of the same size

5 A St. Francis with his companion fallen, measuring three *varas* and two-thirds high by a *vara* and two-thirds wide

6 A picture with three saints, who are St. Andrew, St. John the Baptist and St. Francis, measuring a *vara* and a third high and a *vara* and two-thirds wide *

7 A little picture framed in black, with St. John the Evangelist and St. Francis, measuring a little more than half a *vara* *

8 another little picture with its black frame, of when Christ expelled the Jews from the temple, two-thirds high by three-quarters wide *

9 another little picture with the same frame, of Our Lady with the infant in her arms, measuring half a *vara* high by one-third wide *

10 A Christ on the cross, one *vara* high by two-thirds wide *

11 A nativity, a *vara* and a third high by two-thirds wide * *(Catalogue No. 141)*

12 A St. Francis with the skull, two *varas* high by a *vara* and a quarter wide, with its gilded frame *

13 A disrobing, measuring one *vara* high by over a half wide, with a gilded frame *

14 An agony in the garden, with gilded frame, measuring a *vara* and a quarter high by three-quarters wide *

15 A St. Ildefonso in cardinal's robes writing, a *vara* and a third high by almost a *vara* wide, with gilded frame *

16 An image, with its sleeping Child, St. Anne, St. Joseph and St. John the Baptist, and a gilded frame, almost half a *vara* wide and two-thirds high * *(Cat. No. 147)*

17 A coronation of Our Lady, a *vara* and a sixth high by over three-quarters wide, with gilded frame *

18 A Christ on the cross of the same size, with St. John and Mary and the Magdalene at the foot of the cross, and a gilded frame

19 A St. Peter weeping, almost a *vara* square, with gilded frame *

20 An expulsion of the Jews from the temple, two-thirds wide by half a *vara* high * *(Cat. No. 170)*

21 A St. Francis with his companion with his back turned, a *vara* and a quarter high by three-quarters wide *

22 An incarnation, a *vara* and a third high by a *vara* less a sixth wide * *(Cat. No. 136)*

23 A St. Francis kneeling, three-quarters of a *vara* high by two-thirds wide *

24 An expulsion of the Jews from the temple, a *vara* and a third high by a little more than a *vara* and two-thirds long, and it is the original * *(Cat. No. 14)*

25 A St. Dominic kneeling, three-quarters high by two-thirds wide *

26 A coronation of Our Lady, a *vara* and a third high by a *vara* and a quarter wide * *(Cat. No. 77)*

27 A St. Peter standing, two *varas* and two-thirds high by a *vara* and a third wide, the upper part circular * *(Cat. No. 192)*

28 A St. Ildefonso, of the same height, length and execution * *(Cat. No. 193)*

29 A Christ on the cross, two and a half *varas* high by a *vara* and a third wide, with St. John and Our Lady on one side *

30 An agony in the garden, on a panel with a black frame, half a *vara* long by a third high *

31 A St. Francis in half-length, two-thirds high by one *vara* wide *

32 A St. Joseph, a *vara* and a quarter high by two-thirds wide *(Cat. No. 132)*

33 A St. Francis with companion, of the same height and width

34 A descent of the Holy Ghost, a *vara* and a third high by two-thirds wide *

35 A St. Francis in half-length, two-thirds high by half a *vara* wide

36 Another St. Francis in half-length, with his crucifix, half a *vara* high by over a third wide *

37 A St. Hyacinth, a *vara* and a quarter high by three-quarters wide * *(Cat. No. 237)*

38 A St. Peter weeping, three-quarters high by two-thirds wide *

39 A Mary Magdalene with her crucifix and a skull, of the same height and width

40 A coronation of Our Lady, one *vara* long by two-thirds high

41 A Laocoön, two *varas* long by a *vara* and two-thirds high * *(Cat. No. 227)*

42 A St. Hyacinth, three *varas* high by a *vara* and two-thirds wide *

43 A St. Paul, a *vara* and a third wide by two *varas* and two-thirds high * *(Cat. No. 61)*

44 A nativity, a *vara* and two-thirds high by a *vara* and a third wide * *(Cat. No. 84)*

45 A nativity, two-thirds of a *vara* square, in a black frame *

46 A St. Francis, two-thirds high by half a *vara* wide, in half-length with a crucifix, framed in black *

47 A St. Sebastian, three-quarters high by almost half a *vara* wide, with a black frame *

48 A St. James, with the same height, width and frame *

49 An incarnation, with the same height, width and frame *

50 A Nativity, two-thirds high by half a *vara* wide, in a black frame *

51 A canvas of St. John the Evangelist seeing the visions of the apocalypse, a *vara* and a third high by two-thirds wide * *(Sketch for Cat. No. 226)*

52 an incarnation of the same height and width * *(Sketch for Cat. No. 225)*

53 An image in the heavens, with the Infant and some angels and seraphim and below them St. Agnes and St. Martina, a *vara* and a quarter high by three-quarters wide * *(Sketch for Cat. No. 134)*

54 Another image which is the same in everything * *(Sketch for Cat. No. 135)*

55 an image of the suckling, two-thirds square more or less *

56 another image with the sleeping Infant, of the same size *

57 An image of charity, with some portraits under the mantle, three-quarters and two-thirds in height and width * *(Sketch for Cat. No. 181)*

58 A St. Catherine of Sienna, of the same height and width *(possibly Cat. No. 238)*

59 A nativity of Our Lady, two-thirds high by a third wide * *(Cat. No. 240)*

60 another canvas the same in every particular

61 A baptism, a *vara* and a third high by two-thirds wide * *(Cat. No. 139)*

62 A resurrection of the same height and width *

63 An image with the Infant, half a *vara* high by a little over a third wide *

64 A St. Francis with the skull, three-quarters high by half a *vara* wide

65 A St. Catherine, half a *vara* square more or less *(Cat. No. 239)*

66 An incarnation, with a black frame, a *vara* high by three-quarters wide *

67 A St. Peter standing, a *vara* and a third high by three-quarters (three-quarters, *written over)* wide, I mean three-quarters * *(Sketch for Cat. No. 192)*

68 A St. Ildefonso, of the same size * *(Sketch for Cat. No. 193)*

69 A St. Sebastian, three-quarters high by half a *vara* wide *(The same as No. 47)*

70 A baptism, a *vara* and a third high by two-thirds wide *(The same as No. 61)*

71 A Christ on the cross, a *vara* and a quarter high by three-quarters

72 A nativity, of the same height and width * *(Cat. No. 189)*

92 A canvas of the [arches] *(see 86-87)*

93 A canvas of the burial of St. Thomas *(This may be the one in the Prado)*

94 Another canvas of the glory of St. Thomas *(A vanished pair to the preceding entry)*

95 A royal coat of arms

SKETCHES

73 An Angel giving the message of the resurrection to Mary Magdalen, a *vara* and two-thirds high by a *vara* and a quarter wide

74 A coronation of Our Lady, of almost the same length and width *

75 An incarnation, a *vara* and a half high by a *vara* and a quarter wide

76 An agony in the garden, two *varas* and a third by a *vara* and a third wide

77 A martyrdom of St. Stephen, two *varas* high by a *vara* and a quarter wide

78 A martyrdom of St. Peter Martyr

79 An image with St. Lawrence and other saints

80 An image with St. Joseph and St. Elizabeth, a *vara* and a third long by a little more than a *vara* high *

81 A sketched portrait of a child

82 A descent from the cross, two *varas* and two-thirds square

83 A circumcision, two *varas* and two-thirds high by a *vara* and two-thirds wide

84 An Our Lady giving the chasuble to St. Ildefonso, a *vara* and a quarter square

85 A large canvas of a fable

86 A large canvas in black and white, of the arches

87 A large canvas, of the arches, imitating bronze, of when St. Leocadia came out of the sepulchre *(This entry and the preceding one would be elements from the triumphal arches erected in 1587 on the occasion of the relics of St. Leocadia being brought to Toledo)*

88 A coronation of Our Lady, two *varas* and a third high by a *vara* and a third wide

89 A baptism, a *vara* and a third long by a *vara* and a sixth high

90 A wedding of Our Lady, a *vara* wide by a *vara* and a quarter high *(Cat. No. 229)*

91 A sketched portrait of a woman

FINISHED WORKS

96 A veronica, a *vara* high by three-quarters wide * *(Cat. No. 235)*

97 A head of Christ with the cross, two-thirds of a *vara* square *

98 a St. Francis, two-thirds high by half a *vara* wide

99 A boy blowing out a candle, measuring almost one *vara*

100 Another boy blowing out a candle, of the same length

101 A St. Francis whose companion's back is turned, and a gilded frame, a *vara* and a third high by almost a *vara* wide

102 A Mary Magdalen weeping, three-quarters high by two-thirds wide *

103 A Saviour, of the same width and height *

104 Another Saviour, in the same fashion

105 A presentation of Our Lady in the temple, half a *vara* high by a little more than a third wide

106 Another presentation, one *vara* wide by a *vara* and a quarter high

107 A St. Francis in half-length, measuring half a *vara* square

108 A little picture with two saints, who are St. John the Evangelist and St. James, two-thirds long by over half a *vara* high, in a black frame

109 A nativity, a *vara* and a third high by three-quarters wide *

110 A St. Francis whose companion's back is turned, a *vara* and a quarter high by two-thirds wide

111 A Christ on the cross, in a black frame, a *vara* and a sixth high by three-quarters wide *

112 An image of Our Lady with the Infant and St. Joseph and Mary, a *vara* and a half high by a *vara* and a quarter wide

113, 114 } two apostles, a *vara,* by a *vara* and a quarter each

115 A St. Francis, measuring a *vara* high by three-quarters wide

116 A portrait of Don Luis de Córdoba

117 A portrait of Soria de Herrera

118 A portrait of Pacheco the Hieronymite

119 another portrait of a Hieronymite friar

120 Another sketched portrait of Avila de Uera

121 A risen Christ appearing to Mary Magdalen in the garden, a *vara* and a half high by a *vara* and a sixth wide

122 An angel at the sepulchre giving the message to Mary Magdalen, of the same size

123 A Pharisee's banquet, of the same size

124 A banquet of Lazarus and Martha, of the same size

125 Another banquet of Lazarus and Martha, different, and of the same size

126 An assumption of Mary Magdalen, a *vara* and two-thirds high by a *vara* and a third wide

127 A Saviour, in a black frame, a *vara* and a third by a *vara* and a sixth *

128 A St. Bernardino, a *vara* and a third high by three-quarters wide *(Sketch for Cat. No. 180)*

129 A canvas with the two St. Johns, two *varas* and a third high by a *vara* and a third wide *

130 A canvas with St. Peter and St. Paul in half-length, a *vara* and a half high by a *vara* and a quarter wide *

131 A St. Jerome as Cardinal, measuring a *vara* by a *vara* and a third *

132 A Christ on the cross, two *varas* high by a *vara* and a quarter wide

133 A St. Sebastian, of the same size

134 An image of the Conception, measuring a *vara* by a *vara* and a quarter

135 Another image of the Conception, measuring a *vara* and a quarter by three-quarters *

136 A Mary Magdalen, measuring a *vara* and a third by a *vara* and a quarter *

137, 138 } Two countrysides of Toledo, a *vara* and a third square *

139 An agony in the garden, measuring a *vara* and a quarter *

140, 141 Two canvases of St. Peter and St. Andrew, a *vara* and a third high by two-thirds wide

142 An image with the Infant and St. Joseph and a Mary, measuring a *vara* and two-thirds by a *vara* and a third

143 A risen Christ, two *varas* and a third high by a *vara* and a third wide

144 A St. Simon, measuring a *vara* by a *vara* and a quarter *

SKETCHES

145 A St. Jerome naked, measuring two *varas* high by a *vara* and a quarter wide *(Cat. No. 153)*

146, 147, 148 } Three canvases of countrysides

FINISHED WORKS

161 Thirteen pictures in black and white, with the twelve apostles and Christ, three-quarters high by two-thirds wide * *(This may have been the Apostle series in the collection of the Marqués de San Feliz)*

162 A St. Jerome as Cardinal, of the same size, with a gilded frame *

163 A Mary Magdalen weeping, of the same size, with a black frame

164 An apostle, of the same size

165 A St. Jude in a circle, measuring three-quarters

166 A St. Francis, of the same size

167 An angel St. Gabriel with Zachariah, measuring a *vara* and two-thirds *

168 A St. Augustine, measuring a *vara* high by half a *vara* wide *

169 A St. Veronica, measuring a *vara* by a *vara* and a quarter

170 A St. Martin on a horse, measuring a *vara* and a third by three-quarters *

171 A St. Bartholomew, measuring a *vara* and a quarter

172 A canvas of T[oled]o, two *varas* long by a *vara* and a quarter high *

173 A St. Jerome naked, measuring a *vara* by a *vara* and a quarter

174 A St. Francis in half-length, of the same size

175 An image of the Conception, measuring a *vara* and a third by three-quarters

176 An agony in the garden, measuring a *vara* and a third by almost a *vara*

177 A Christ on the cross, with angels, St. John, Mary, and the Magdalen, measuring a *vara* and a third by almost a *vara* *

178 A large canvas of the baptism, fourteen feet high and seven feet wide

179 A large Laocoön, three *varas* and a half square *

180 Another Laocoön, of almost the same size

181. A picture of Our Lady, St. Joseph and the two children, of the same size as the Laocoön

183 Two large sketched pictures for the side altars of the hospital * *(Cat. No. 225 and Cat. No. 226)*

184 the principal baptism in the hospital * *(Cat. No. 224)*

188 four canvases of the arches *(See No. 87)*

189 a portrait of my F[athe]r, with its frame decorated

209 twenty unfinished portraits

212 Three unfinished canvases of countrysides

213 A St. Martin, measuring two *varas* and a third high by a *vara* and a quarter wide

214 A St. Maurice, measuring a *vara* and a third high by a *vara* and a sixth wide *
Thirty-four unfinished canvases
Thirty primed canvases

215 A St. Hyacinth, measuring two *varas* high by a *vara* and a quarter wide

216 A Christ on the cross, of the same size

217 An expulsion of the Jews from the temple, two *varas* less a quarter long by a *vara* and a third high *

Forty panels of wood, unpainted

A hundred prints, by various artists

Another hundred prints, done at home

Three books of prints

Two hundred and fifty black-and-white drawings of historical subjects and other drawings of models

A hundred and thirty designs

A hundred plaster models

Another hundred in clay and wax

CATALOGUE

1. ST. LUKE PAINTING THE VIRGIN

Fig. 1
Signed: CHEÌR DOMÉNIKOU
Oil on panel. 0.42 × 0.33 m.
D. Sisilianos Collection, Athens ; Benaki Museum, Athens

BIBL. — Camón, 1 ; Wethey, X-400

2. THE ADORATION OF THE MAGI

Fig. 2
Oil on canvas. 0.40 × 0.45 m.
Benaki Museum, Athens

BIBL. — Camón, 62 ; Wethey, X-1

3. TRIPTYCH

Figs. 5 & 6
Signed: CHEÌR DOMÉNIKOU
Oil on panels.
Central panel: 0.37 × 0.238 m. Side panels: 0.24 × 0.18 m.
T. Obizzi del Catajo Collection, Venice ; Galleria Estense, Modena

BIBL. — Camón, 2 ; Wethey, X-154

4. THE ADORATION OF THE SHEPHERDS

Fig. 3
El Greco (?)
Oil on canvas. 1.14 × 1.04 m.
Duke of Buccleuch and Queensberry Collection, Kettering, England

BIBL. — Wethey, 24

5. THE ADORATION OF THE SHEPHERDS

Fig. 4
El Greco (?)
Oil on panel. 0.25 × 0.17 m.
G. Broglio Collection, Paris

BIBL. — Wethey, X-10

6. VIEW OF MOUNT SINAI

Fig. 7
El Greco (?)
Oil on panel. 0.41 × 0.47 m.
It has been suggested that this painting may be the one described in the catalogue of Fulvio Orsini's collection in Rome: "Quadro corniciato di noce con un paese del Monte Sinai di mano d'un Greco scolaro di Titiano".
Collections: Levi, Venice ; Baron Hatvany, Budapest

BIBL. — Mayer, 318 ; Camón, 698 ; Wethey, X-157

7. CHRIST IN THE HOUSE OF MARTHA AND MARY

Fig. 8
El Greco (?)
Oil on panel. 0.33 × 0.38 m.
Italico Brass Collection, Venice ; present whereabouts unknown
BIBL. — Mayer, 44 ; Camón, 78 ; Wethey, X-48

8. CHRIST CLEANSING THE TEMPLE

Figs. 9-11
Before 1570
Signed: DOMÉNIKOS THEOTOKÓPOULOS KRÈS
Oil on panel. 0.65 × 0.83 m.
J. C. Robinson Collection, London ; National Gallery, Washington

BIBL. — Cossío, 349 ; Mayer, 49 ; Camón, 82 ; Wethey, 104

9. PIETÀ

Fig. 15
Before 1570
Signed: DOMÉNIKOS THEOTOKÓPOULOS (EPOÍEI ?)
Oil on panel. 0.29 × 0.20 m.
Collections: Chéramy, Paris ; John G. Johnson, Philadelphia

BIBL. — Cossío, 295 ; Mayer, 101a ; Camón, 199 ; Wethey, 101

10. ST. FRANCIS RECEIVING THE STIGMATA

Fig. 17
Before 1570
Signed: DOMÉNIKOS THEOTOKÓPOULOS EPOÍEI
Oil on panel. 0.29 × 0.21 m.
Collections: Pedro Salazar de Mendoza, Toledo ; Antonio Zuloaga, Geneva

BIBL. — Cossío, 326 ; Mayer, 228 ; Camón, 539 ; Wethey, 208

11. ST. FRANCIS RECEIVING THE STIGMATA

Before 1570
Signed: DOMÉNIKOS THEOTOKÓPOULOS EPOÍEI
Oil on panel. 0.29 × 0.20 m.
Monsignor degli Oddi Collection, Perugia ; Istituto Suor Orsola Benincasa, Naples

BIBL. — Wethey, 209

12. THE FLIGHT INTO EGYPT
Fig. 18
Before 1570
Oil on panel. 0.17 × 0.21 m.
Collections: Gaspar Méndez de Haro; Baron Robert von Hirsch, Basle

BIBL. — Cossío, 31; Mayer, 24; Camón, 68; Wethey, 83

13. CHRIST HEALING THE BLIND MAN
Figs. 19 & 20
Before 1570
Oil on panel. 0.66 × 0.84 m.
Bought in Venice in 1741; Dresden Museum.

BIBL. — Cossío, 2; Mayer, 41; Camón, 79; Wethey, 61

14. CHRIST CLEANSING THE TEMPLE
Figs. 12-14
1570-1575
Signed: DOMÉNIKOS THEOTOKÓPOULOS EPOÍEI
Oil on canvas. 1.17 × 1.50 m.
Duke of Buckingham Collection, York House; Institute of Arts, Minneapolis

BIBL. — Cossío, 348; Mayer, 50; Camón, 84; Wethey, 105

15. PIETÀ
Fig. 16
1570-1575
Oil on canvas. 0.66 × 0.48 m.
Luis Navas Collection, Madrid; Hispanic Society, New York

BIBL. — Cossío, 323; Mayer, 101; Camón, 200; Wethey, 102

16. CHRIST HEALING THE BLIND MAN
Figs. 21 & 22
1570-1575
Signed: DOMÉNIKOS THEOTOKÓPOULOS EPOÍEI
Oil on canvas. 0.50 × 0.61 m.
Farnese Inventory, Palazzo del Giardino, Parma; Parma Museum

BIBL. — Cossío, 354; Mayer, 42; Camón, 80; Wethey, 62

17. CHRIST HEALING THE BLIND MAN
Fig. 23
1570-1575
Oil on canvas. 1.20 × 1.46 m.
Collections: William Rennie, London; Charles B. Wrightsman, New York

BIBL. — Wethey, 63

18. THE ANNUNCIATION
Fig. 24
1570-1575
Oil on panel. 0.26 × 0,19 m.
Concepción Parody Collection, Madrid; Prado Museum, Madrid

BIBL. — Cossío, 56; Mayer, 4; Camón, 24; Wethey, 38

19. THE ANNUNCIATION
Figs. 26 & 27
1570-1575
Oil on canvas. 1.17 × 0.98 m.
Collections: Principe Corsini, Florence; Contini-Bonacossi, Florence

BIBL. — Camón, 22; Wethey, 37

20. THE ANNUNCIATION
Fig. 25
1570-1575
Signed: DOMÉNIKOS THEOTOSKÓPOLI (sic)
Oil on canvas. 1.07 × 0.93 m.
Collections: A. Beruete, Madrid; Julio Muñoz, Barcelona

BIBL. — Camón, 23; Wethey, 39

21. CHRIST ON THE CROSS
Fig. 28
1570-1575
Oil on panel. 0.28 ×0.19 m.
Collections: Rafael García Palencia, Madrid; Gregorio Marañón, Madrid

BIBL. — Wethey, X-66

22. BOY LIGHTING A CANDLE
Fig. 29
1570-1575
Oil on canvas. 0.59 × 0.51 m.
Palazzo Farnese, Rome; Capodimonte Museum, Naples

BIBL. — Cossío, 356; Mayer, 310; Camón, 682; Wethey, 122

23. BOY LIGHTING A CANDLE
Fig. 30
1570-1575
Signed: DOMÉNIKOS THEO (the rest is effaced)
Oil on canvas. 0.61 × 0.51 m.
Private collection, Germany; Charles S. Payson, Manhasset (New York)

BIBL. — Mayer, 309; Camón, 681; Wethey, 121

24. GENRE SCENE
Fig. 31
1570-1575
Oil on canvas. 0.50 × 0.64 m.
Sale in London, 1927; V. von Watsdorf Collection, Rio de Janeiro

BIBL. — Camón, 683; Wethey, 124

25. GIULIO CLOVIO
Figs. 32 & 33
c. 1570
Signed: DOMÉNIKOS THEOTOKÓPOULOS KRÈS EPOÍEI
Oil on canvas. 0.58 × 0.86 m.
Fulvio Orsini Collection, Palazzo Farnese, Rome (inventoried in 1600); Capodimonte Museum, Naples

BIBL. — Cossío, 357; Mayer, 323; Camón, 709; Wethey, 134

26. GIOVANNI BATTISTA PORTA

Fig. 34
1570-1575
Signed: DOMÉNIKOS THEOTOKÓPOULOS
Oil on canvas. 1.16 × 0.98 m.
Sale in Antwerp, 1641 ; National Gallery, Copenhagen

BIBL. — Mayer, 340a ; Camón, 708 ; Wethey, 154

27. VICENZO ANASTAGI

Fig. 35
c. 1575
Signed: DOMÉNIKOS THEOTOKÓPOULOS EPOÍEI
Oil on canvas. 1.88 × 1.26 m.
Collections: William Coningham, London ; Frick Collection, New York

BIBL. — Cossío, 445 ; Mayer, 319 ; Camón, 710 & 780 ; Wethey, 130

28. THE ADORATION OF THE NAME OF JESUS

Fig. 36
1576-1579
Signed: DOMÉNIKOS THEOTOKÓPOULOS KRÈS EPOÍEI
Oil on panel. 0.58 × 0.35 m.
Gaspar Méndez de Haro Collection (inventoried in 1687) ; National Gallery, London

BIBL. — Cossío, 337 ; Mayer, 123a ; Camón, 261 ; Wethey, 116

29. THE ADORATION OF THE NAME OF JESUS

Figs. 37-39
1576-1579
Signed: doménikos theotokópoulos krès e'poíei
Oil on canvas. 1.40 × 1.10 m.
Monastery of the Escorial

BIBL. — Cossío, 45 ; Mayer, 123 ; Camón, 262 ; Wethey, 117

30. ST. SEBASTIAN

Figs. 40-42
1576-1579
Signed: DOMÉNIKOS THEOTOKÓPOULOS EPOÍEI
Oil on canvas. 1.91 × 1.52 m.
Sacristy of the Cathedral of Palencia

BIBL. — Cossío, 158 ; Mayer, 300 ; Camón, 535 ; Wethey, 279

31. CRUCIFIXION WITH TWO DONORS

Figs. 43 & 44
1576-1579
Signed: DOMÉNIKOS THEOTOKÓPOLIS (sic) (EPOÍEI illegible)
Oil on canvas. 2.50 × 1.80 m.
Convent of the Jerónimas de la Reina, Toledo ; Louvre Museum, Paris

BIBL. — Cossío, 336 ; Mayer, 87 ; Camón, 168 ; Wethey, 74

32. KNIGHT TAKING AN OATH

Fig. 45
1576-1579
Signed: DOMÉNIKOS THEOTOKÓPOULOS EPOÍEI
Oil on canvas. 0.81 × 0.86 m.
Royal collections ; Prado Museum, Madrid

BIBL. — Cossío, 72 ; Mayer, 345 ; Camón, 723 ; Wethey, 145

33. THE PENITENT MAGDALEN

Fig. 46
1576-1579
Signed: CHÈIR DOMÉNIKOU
Oil on canvas. 1.07 × 1.02 m.
The English College, Valladolid ; Art Museum, Worcester (Massachusetts)

BIBL. — Cossío, 275 ; Mayer, 293a ; Camón, 451 ; Wethey, 259

34. THE SUDARY OF ST. VERONICA

Fig. 47
1576-1579
Signed: DOMÉNIKOS THEOTOKÓPOULOS EPOÍEI
Oil on canvas. 0.51 × 0.66 m.
Collections: E. Parés, Paris ; Basil Goulandris, New York

BIBL. — Mayer, 70 ; Camón, 145 ; Wethey, 284

35. ST. FRANCIS IN ECSTASY

Fig. 48
1576-1579
Signed: DOMÉNIKOS THEOTOKÓPOULOS EPOÍEI
Oil on canvas. 0.87 × 0.60 m.
Collections: Henri Rouart, Paris (19th century) ; private collection, New York

BIBL. — Camón, 541 ; Wethey, 214

36. ST. FRANCIS IN ECSTASY

1576-1579
Oil on canvas. 0.89 × 0.57 m.
Portilla Collection, Madrid ; Lázaro Galdeano Foundation, Madrid

BIBL. — Cossío, 109 ; Mayer, 275 ; Camón, 543 ; Wethey, 213

37. ST. ANTHONY OF PADUA

Fig. 49
1576-1579
Signed: CHÈIR DOMÉNIKOU
Oil on canvas. 1.04 × 0.79 m.
Museo Nacional de la Trinidad, Madrid ; Prado Museum, Madrid

BIBL. — Cossío, 66 ; Mayer, 217 ; Camón, 474 ; Wethey, 198

38. ST. VERONICA

Fig. 50
1576-1579
Oil on canvas. 0.84 × 0.91 m.
Santa Leocadia, Toledo ; Santa Cruz Museum, Toledo

BIBL. — Cossío, 251 ; Mayer, 67 ; Camón, 138 ; Wethey, 283

39. ST. VERONICA

Fig. 51
1576-1579
Signed: CHÈIR DOMÉNIKOU
Oil on canvas. 1.05 × 1.08 m.
Santo Domingo el Antiguo, Toledo ; María Luisa Caturla Collection, Madrid

BIBL. — Cossío, 235 ; Mayer, 66 ; Camón, 137 ; Wethey, 282

40. ST. LAWRENCE'S VISION OF THE VIRGIN

Fig. 52
1576-1579
Oil on canvas. 1.19 × 1.02 m.
Rodrigo de Castro (d. 1600) Collection ; Piarist Fathers, Monforte de Lemos (Lugo)

BIBL. — Mayer, 291 ; Camón, 519 ; Wethey, 255

41. THE ASSUMPTION

Figs. 54-56
1577
Signed: doménikos theotokópoulos Krès ó deíxas, 1577
Oil on canvas. 4.01 × 2.29 m.
Santo Domingo el Antiguo, Toledo ; Art Institute, Chicago

BIBL. — Cossío, 279 ; Mayer, 114 ; Camón, 3 ; Wethey, 1

42. THE TRINITY

Figs. 57 & 58
1577-1579
Oil on canvas. 3.00 × 1.78 m.
Santo Domingo el Antiguo, Toledo ; Prado Museum, Madrid

BIBL. — Cossío, 57 ; Mayer, 108 ; Camón, 4 ; Wethey, 2

43. ST. JOHN THE BAPTIST

Fig. 59
1577-1579
Oil on canvas. 2.12 × 0.78 m.
Santo Domingo el Antiguo, Toledo

BIBL. — Cossío, 230 ; Mayer, 188 ; Camón, 5 ; Wethey, 5

44. ST. JOHN THE EVANGELIST

Fig. 60
1577-1579
Oil on canvas. 2.12 × 0.78 m.
Santo Domingo el Antiguo, Toledo

BIBL. — Cossío, 229 ; Mayer, 187 ; Camón, 6 ; Wethey, 6

45. SUDARY WITH THE HOLY FACE

Fig. 61
1577-1579
Oil on canvas. 0.71 × 0.54 m.
Parish Church, Móstoles ; Prado Museum, Madrid

BIBL. — Cossío, 144 ; Mayer, 69 ; Camón, 144 ; Wethey, 285

46. SUDARY WITH THE HOLY FACE

Fig. 62
1577-1579
Oil on wood. Oval, 0.76 × 0.55 m.
Santo Domingo el Antiguo, Toledo ; Juan March Servera Collection, Madrid

BIBL. — Cossío, 231 ; Mayer, 68 ; Camón, 9 ; Wethey, 6A

47. ST. BERNARD

Fig. 63
1577-1579
Oil on canvas. 1.13 × 0.75 m.
Santo Domingo el Antiguo, Toledo ; present whereabouts unknown

BIBL. — Cossío, 293 ; Mayer, 220 ; Camón, 8 ; Wethey, 4

48. ST. BENEDICT

Fig. 64
1577-1579
Oil on canvas. 1.16 × 0.81 m.
Santo Domingo el Antiguo, Toledo ; Prado Museum, Madrid

BIBL. — Cossío, 62 ; Mayer, 219 ; Camón, 7 ; Wethey, 3

49. THE ADORATION OF THE SHEPHERDS

Figs. 65 & 66
1577-1579
Oil on canvas. 2.10 × 1.28 m.
Santo Domingo el Antiguo, Toledo ; Emilio Botín Sanz Collection, Santander

BIBL. — Cossío, 233 ; Mayer, 16 ; Camón, 11 ; Wethey, 7

50. THE RESURRECTION

Figs. 67 & 68
1577-1579
Oil on canvas. 2.10 × 1.28 m.
Santo Domingo el Antiguo, Toledo

BIBL. — Cossío, 234 ; Mayer, 104 ; Camón, 10 ; Wethey, 8

51. THE ESPOLIO (DISROBING OF CHRIST)

Figs. 69-73
1577-1579
Signed: doménikos theoto...krès ep...
Oil on canvas. 2.85 × 1.73 m.
Sacristy of the Cathedral of Toledo

BIBL. — Cossío, 210 ; Mayer, 71 ; Camón, 151 ; Wethey, 78

52. THE ESPOLIO (DISROBING OF CHRIST)

Fig. 74
c. 1577
Signed: doménikos theoto/krès
Tempera on panel. 0.55 × 0.33 m.
Collections: Gaspar Méndez de Haro ; Viscount Bearsted, Upton House, Upton Downs

BIBL. — Cossío, 294 ; Mayer, 73 ; Camón, 150 ; Wethey, 80
This is a companion piece to the *Adoration of the Name of Jesus* in the National Gallery, London (Fig. 36 - Cat. 28)

53. THE ESPOLIO (DISROBING OF CHRIST)
Figs. 75 & 76
c. 1577
Signed: doménikos theoto/krès ep.
Tempera on panel. 0.56 × 0.32 m.
Collections: Sebastián de Borbón (?); Contini-Bonacossi, Florence

BIBL. — Cossío, 355; Mayer, 72; Camón, 148; Wethey, 81

54. THE ESPOLIO (DISROBING OF CHRIST)
1580-1585
Oil on panel. 0.72 × 0.44 m.
Collections: Manfrin, Venice; Hugo Moser, New York

BIBL. — Mayer, 72a; Camón, 147 & 149; Wethey, 82

55. PORTRAIT OF A LADY (JERÓNIMA DE LAS CUEVAS?)
Fig. 77
1577-1579
Oil on paper. 0.058 × 0.043 m.
Collections: Rómulo Bosch, Barcelona; Julio Muñoz, Barcelona

BIBL. — Camón, 789; Wethey, X-204

56. LADY IN A FUR WRAP (JERÓNIMA DE LAS CUEVAS?)
Fig. 78
1577-1579
Oil on canvas. 0.62 × 0.5 m.
Collections: Serafín García de la Huerta, Madrid; Maxwell MacDonald, Pollok House, Glasgow

BIBL. — Cossío, 346; Mayer, 350; Camón, 716; Wethey, 148

57. THE MARTYRDOM OF ST. MAURICE
Figs. 79-83
1580-1582
Signed: doménikos theotokópoulos krès epoíei
Oil on canvas. 4.48 × 3.01 m.
Monastery of the Escorial

BIBL. — Cossío, 44; Mayer, 126; Camón, 530; Wethey, 265

58. STUDY FOR THE HEAD OF ST. MAURICE
Fig. 84
c. 1580
Oil on canvas. 0.26 × 0.20 m.
Collections: Antonio Vives, Madrid; W. van Horne, Montreal

BIBL. — Cossío, 10; Mayer, 174; Camón, 270; Wethey, X-424

59. THE APPARITION OF THE VIRGIN TO ST. JOHN
Figs. 85 & 86
1580-1586
Signed: doménikos theotokópoulos epoíei
Oil on canvas. 2.36 × 1.18 m.
San Román, Toledo; Santa Cruz Museum, Toledo

BIBL. — Mayer, 121; Camón, 250; Wethey, 91

60. THE PENITENT MAGDALEN
Fig. 87
1579-1586
Oil on canvas. 1.04 × 0.85 m.
Collections: Martínez Lechón, Seville; William Rockhill Nelson Gallery of Art, Kansas City

BIBL. — Cossío, 391; Camón, 454; Wethey, 260
In the Museum of Bilbao (No. 118) there is a small panel (0.29 × 0.24 m.) with a representation of St. Mary Magdalen which is virtually the same as No. 60 of this Catalogue. It is very probably the preparatory study for the picture in the Kansas City Museum.

61. ST. PAUL
Fig. 88
1579-1586
Signed: doménikos theotokópoulos epoíei
Oil on canvas. 1.18 × 0.91 m.
Parish Church, Iraeta (Azpeitia); Marquesa de Narros, Madrid

BIBL. — Camón, 374; Wethey, 267

62. HEAD OF CHRIST
Fig. 89
1579-1586
Oil on canvas. 0.50 × 0.39 m.
Private collection, Madrid; McNay Art Institute, San Antonio (Texas)

BIBL. — Mayer, 131; Camón, 112 & 198; Wethey, 48

63. ST. FRANCIS IN ECSTASY
Fig. 90
1579-1586
Oil on canvas. 0.90 × 0.80 m.
Parish Church, Santa Olalla (Toledo); present whereabouts unknown

BIBL. — Wethey, X-280

64. ST. FRANCIS AND THE LAY BROTHER
Fig. 91
1579-1586
Oil on canvas. 0.26 × 0.18 m.
Alejandro Pidal Collection, Madrid; present whereabouts unknown

BIBL. — Cossío, 124; Mayer, 250; Camón, 617; Wethey, X-338

65. ST. FRANCIS AND THE LAY BROTHER
Fig. 93
1579-1586
Signed: doménikos theotokópoulos epoíei
Oil on canvas. 1.55 × 1 m.
Collection of Bishop Rodrigo de Castro; Piarist Fathers, Monforte de Lemos (Lugo)

BIBL. — Cossío, 143; Mayer, 254; Camón, 622; Wethey, X-321

66. ST. FRANCIS RECEIVING THE STIGMATA

Fig. 92
1579-1586
Oil on canvas. 0.43 × 0.34 m.
Milicua Collection, Barcelona; present whereabouts unknown

67. ST. FRANCIS RECEIVING THE STIGMATA

Fig. 94
1579-1586
Signed: doménikos theotokópolis (sic) epoíei
Oil on canvas. 1.08 × 0.83 m.
Collections: Dalborgo de Primo, Madrid; Marqués de Pidal, Madrid

BIBL. — Cossío, 121; Mayer, 234; Camón, 548; Wethey, 210

68. ST. FRANCIS RECEIVING THE STIGMATA

1579-1586
Oil on canvas. 0.57 × 0.44 m. (fragment)
Laureano Jado Collection, Bilbao; Museum of Bilbao

BIBL. — Cossío, 33; Mayer, 239; Camón, 556; Wethey, X-266

69. THE HOLY FAMILY

Fig. 95
1579-1586
Oil on canvas. 1.06 × 0.88 m.
Conde de Oñate Collection; Hispanic Society, New York

BIBL. — Cossío, 308; Mayer, 25; Camón, 238; Wethey, 84

70. ST. PETER IN TEARS

Fig. 96
1579-1586
Signed: doménikos theotokópolis (sic) epoíei
Oil on canvas. 1.06 × 0.88 m.
Condesa de Quinto Collection; Bowes Museum, Barnard Castle

BIBL. — Mayer, 202; Camón, 433; Wethey, 269

71. A GENTLEMAN OF THE HOUSE OF LEIVA

Fig. 97
1579-1586
Oil on canvas. 0.88 × 0.69 m.
Cathedral of Valladolid; Museum of Fine Arts, Montreal

BIBL. — Cossío, 9; Mayer, 341; Camón, 724; Wethey, 150

72. ST. ALOYSIUS GONZAGA (?)

Fig. 98
1579-1586
Oil on canvas. 0.74 × 0.57 m.
Collections: Pablo Bosch, Madrid; Converse, Santa Barbara (California)

BIBL. — Cossío, 324; Mayer, 328; Camón, 726 & 727; Wethey, 195

73. HEAD OF AN OLD MAN

Fig. 99
1579-1586
Oil on canvas. 0.59 × 0.46 m.
Marqués de Heredia Collection, Madrid; Metropolitan Museum, New York

BIBL. — Cossío, 89; Mayer, 329; Camón, 733; Wethey, 156

74. RODRIGO DE LA FUENTE

Fig. 100
1579-1586
Signed: Doménikos theotokópolis (sic) epoíei
Oil on canvas. 0.93 × 0.84 m.
Alcázar Collection, Madrid (inventoried in 1666 and 1686); Prado Museum, Madrid

BIBL. — Cossío, 73; Mayer, 327; Camón, 725; Wethey, 149

75. THE BURIAL OF THE CONDE DE ORGAZ

Figs. 101-108
1586
Signed: doménikos theotokópolis (sic) epoíei, año 1578
Oil on canvas. 4.80 × 3.60 m.
Santo Tomé, Toledo

BIBL. — Cossío, 260; Mayer, 130; Camón, 676; Wethey, 123

76. THE CORONATION OF THE VIRGIN

Fig. 109
1591-1592
Signed: doménikos theotokópoulos krès
Oil on canvas. 1.05 × 0.80 m.
Parish Church, Talavera la Vieja; Santa Cruz Museum, Toledo

BIBL. — Mayer, 118; Camón, 12 & 258; Wethey, 9

77. THE CORONATION OF THE VIRGIN

Fig. 110
1591
Signed: doménikos theotokó (poulos?)
Oil on canvas. 0.90 × 1.00 m.
Miguel Borondo Collection, Madrid; Prado Museum, Madrid

BIBL. — Cossío, 92; Mayer, 119; Camón, 255; Wethey, 72

78. ST. ANDREW

Fig. 112
1591-1592
Oil on canvas. 1.26 × 0.46 m.
Parish Church, Talavera la Vieja; Santa Cruz Museum, Toledo

BIBL. — Camón, 12 & 402; Wethey, 10

79. ST. PETER

Fig. 111
1591-1592
Oil on canvas. 1.25 × 0.46 m.
Parish Church, Talavera la Vieja; Santa Cruz Museum, Toledo

BIBL. — Camón,12; Wethey, 11

80. ST. LOUIS OF FRANCE
Fig. 113
1587-1597
Oil on canvas. 1.17 × 0.95 m.
Condesa de Quinto Collection ; Louvre Museum, Paris
BIBL. — Cossío, 292 ; Mayer, 292 ; Camón, 520 ; Wethey, 256

81. ST. PETER AND ST. PAUL
Fig. 114
1587-1597
Oil on canvas. 1.20 × 0.92 m.
José Cañaveral Collection, Madrid ; Art Museum of Catalonia, Barcelona
BIBL. — Mayer, 197 ; Camón, 424 ; Wethey, 276

82. THE HOLY FAMILY WITH ST. ANNE
Figs. 115 & 116
1587-1597
Oil on canvas. 1.27 × 1.06 m.
Presented to the Hospital de San Juan Bautista by Teresa Aguilera, before 1631 ; Hospital de San Juan Bautista de Afuera, Toledo
BIBL. — Cossío, 246 ; Mayer, 26 ; Camón, 236 ; Wethey, 85

83. PIETÀ
Figs. 117 & 118
1587-1597
Signed: doménikos theotokópolis (sic)
Oil on canvas. 1.20 × 1.45 m.
Evariste Fouret Sale, Paris (1863) ; Stavros Niarchos Collection, Paris
BIBL. — Mayer, 102 ; Camón, 203 ; Wethey, 103

84. THE ADORATION OF THE SHEPHERDS
Fig. 119
1587-1597
Oil on canvas. 1.41 × 1.11 m.
Inventory of the estate of the Blessed Juan de Ribera (Valencia 1611) ; Colegio del Patriarca, Valencia
BIBL. — Cossío, 270 ; Mayer, 18 ; Camón, 58 ; Wethey, 26
Composition engraved by Diego de Astor in 1605 (Fig. 349)

85. THE HOLY FAMILY WITH THE MAGDALEN
Fig. 120
1587-1597
Oil on canvas. 1.31 × 1 m.
Convento de Esquivías, Torrejón de Velasco (Toledo) ; Museum of Art, Cleveland, Ohio
BIBL. — Cossío, 310 ; Mayer, 27 ; Camón, 241 ; Wethey, 86

86. ST. FRANCIS RECEIVING THE STIGMATA
Fig. 121
1587-1597
This work has been cut, so that the signature is incomplete
Oil on canvas. 1.07 × 0.87 m.
Monastery of the Escorial
BIBL. — Cossío, 46 ; Mayer, 232 ; Camón, 595 ; Wethey, 211

87. ST. FRANCIS RECEIVING THE STIGMATA
1587-1597
Signed: doménikos theotokópoulos epoíei
Oil on canvas. 1.02 × 0.97 m.
Marcello Massarenti Collection, Rome ; Walters Art Gallery, Baltimore
BIBL. — Camón, 607 ; Wethey, 212

88. ST. FRANCIS IN MEDITATION
1587-1597
Signed: doménikos theotokópoulos
Oil on canvas. 1.16 × 1.02 m.
Ceballos Collection, Madrid ; Joselyn Art Museum, Omaha, Nebraska
BIBL. — Camón, 606 ; Wethey, 222

89. ST. FRANCIS IN MEDITATION
Fig. 122
1587-1597
Signed: doménikos theotokópolis (sic) epoíei
Oil on canvas. 1.03 × 0.87 m.
Collections: Marqués de Castro Serna, Madrid ; Federico Torelló, Barcelona
BIBL. — Cossío, 97 ; Mayer, 259 ; Camón, 558 ; Wethey, 223

90. ST. FRANCIS IN MEDITATION
Fig. 123
1587-1597
Oil on canvas. 1.03 × 0.87 m.
Montesinos Collection, Valencia

91. ST. FRANCIS IN MEDITATION
1587-1597
Oil on canvas. 1.05 × 0.87 m.
Parish Church, Burguillos (1908) ; Marqués de Santa María de Silvela y Castañar Collection, Madrid
BIBL. — Cossío, 38 ; Mayer, 261 ; Camón, 563 ; Wethey, 224

92. ST. FRANCIS RECEIVING THE STIGMATA
Fig. 124
1587-1597
Signed: doménikos theotokópolis (sic) epoíei
Oil on canvas. 2.03 × 1.25 m.
Hospital de Nuestra Señora del Carmen, Cadiz
BIBL. — Cossío, 39 ; Camón, 643 ; Wethey, 231

93. ST. FRANCIS RECEIVING THE STIGMATA
1587-1597
Signed: doménikos theotokópoulos epoíei
Oil on canvas. 1.39 × 1.48 m.
Cerralbo Museum, Madrid
BIBL. — Cossío, 100 ; Mayer, 229 ; Camón, 644 ; Wethey, 232

94. ST. FRANCIS KNEELING IN MEDITATION

Fig. 125
1587-1597
Signed: doménikos theotokópolis (sic) epoíei
Oil on canvas. 1.05 × 0.86 m.
Carmelite Convent, Cuerva (Toledo), to which it was presented by the sister of Cardinal Niño de Guevara; Museum of Fine Arts, Bilbao

BIBL. — Camón, 570; Wethey, 221

95. ST. DOMINIC IN PRAYER

Fig. 126
1587-1597
Signed: doménikos theotokópo [effaced] epoíei
Oil on canvas. 1.18 × 0.86 m.
Collections: A. Sanz Bremón, Valencia; Jaime Urquijo Chacón, Madrid

BIBL. — Cossío, 273; Mayer, 223; Camón, 492; Wethey, 203

96. ST. DOMINIC IN PRAYER IN HIS CELL

Fig. 127
1587-1597
Signed: doménikos theotokópoulos epoíei
Oil on canvas. 0.57 × 0.57 m.
Collections: Ricardo Traumann, Madrid; John Nicholas Brown, Newport (Rhode Island)

BIBL. — Mayer, 222; Camón, 489; Wethey, 207

97. ST. PETER AND ST. PAUL

Fig. 128
1587-1597
Signed: doménikos theotokópoulos epoíei
Oil on canvas. 1.21 × 1.05 m.
General Durnowo Collection, Leningrad; Hermitage Museum, Leningrad

BIBL. — Mayer, 198; Camón, 425; Wethey, 278

98. HEAD OF CHRIST

Fig. 129
1587-1597
Signed: doménikos theotokópoli (sic) epoíei
Oil on canvas. 0.61 × 0.46 m.
Condesa de Quinto Sale, Paris 1862; Prague Museum

BIBL. — Camón, 114; Wethey, 47

99. MATER DOLOROSA

Fig. 130
1587-1597
Signed: doménikos theotokópoulos epoíei
Oil on canvas. 0.52 × 0.36 m.
Sir Charles Robinson Collection, London; Strasbourg Museum

BIBL. — Cossío, 3; Mayer, 83; Camón, 216; Wethey, 97

100. ST. ANDREW AND ST. FRANCIS

Figs. 131 & 132
1587-1597
Signed: doménikos theotokópolis (sic) epoíei
Oil on canvas. 1.67 × 1.13 m.
Duke of Abrantes Collection (before 1676); Prado Museum, Madrid

BIBL. — Camón, 423; Wethey,197

101. ST. JEROME AS A CARDINAL

Fig. 133
1587-1597
Signed: doménikos theotokópoulos epoíei
Oil on canvas. 1.11 × 0.96 m.
Cathedral of Valladolid (?); Frick Collection, New York

BIBL. — Cossío, 286; Mayer, 278; Camón, 503; Wethey, 240

102. ST. JEROME AS A CARDINAL

1587-1597
Oil on canvas. 1.08 × 0.87 m.
Collections: Marqués del Arco, Madrid; Lehman, New York

BIBL. — Cossío, 85; Mayer, 277; Camón, 502; Wethey, 241

103. ST. JEROME AS A CARDINAL

1587-1597
Oil on canvas. 0.65 × 0.54 m.
Conde de Adanero y de Castro Serna Collection, Madrid

BIBL. — Cossío, 96; Camón, 507; Wethey, 242

104. ST. JEROME AS A CARDINAL

1587-1597
Signed: doménikos theotokópoulos (fragmentary)
Oil on canvas. 0.59 × 0.48 m.
Lord Northwick Collection, Cheltenham; National Gallery, London

BIBL. — Cossío, 341; Mayer, 279; Camón, 506; Wethey, 243

105. ST. JEROME AS A CARDINAL

1587-1597
Oil on canvas. 0.30 × 0.24 m.
E. Mélida Collection, Madrid; Musée Bonnat, Bayonne

BIBL. — Cossío, 287; Mayer, 280; Camón, 505; Wethey, 244

106. CHRIST CARRYING THE CROSS

Fig. 134
1587-1597
Signed: doménikos theotokópoulos epoíei
Oil on canvas. 1.05 × 0.67 m.
Miguel Borondo Collection, Madrid; Art Museum of Catalonia, Barcelona

BIBL. — Cossío, 88; Mayer, 62; Camón, 118; Wethey, 54

107. CHRIST CARRYING THE CROSS
1587-1597
Signed: doménikos theotokópoulos epoíei
Oil on canvas. 1.05 × 0.79 m.
Condesa de Quinto Sale, Paris 1862 ; Lehman Collection, New York

BIBL. — Cossío, 338 ; Camón, 126 ; Wethey, 50

108. CHRIST CARRYING THE CROSS
1587-1597
Signed.
Oil on canvas. 0.81 × 0.59 m.
Lucas Moreno Collection, Paris ; National Museum of Decorative Art, Buenos Aires

BIBL. — Mayer, 61 ; Camón, 119 ; Wethey, 52

109. CHRIST CARRYING THE CROSS
1587-1597
Signed: doménikos the (otokópoulos) epoíei
Oil on canvas. 0.48 × 0.38 m. (this work has been cut down)
La Merced, Huete (Cuenca) ; Cathedral of Cuenca

BIBL. — Mayer, 62a ; Camón, 124 ; Wethey, 53

110. CHRIST CARRYING THE CROSS
1587-1597
Remains of a signature
Oil on canvas. 1.15 × 0.71 m.
Royal Palace, Sinaia (Romania)

BIBL. — Cossío, 362 ; Camón, 123 ; Wethey, 55

111. CHRIST CARRYING THE CROSS
Figs. 135 & 136
1587-1597
Signed: doménikos theotokópoli (sic) epoíei
Oil on canvas. 0.63 × 0.52 m.
Etienne Arago Collection, Paris ; Oscar B. Cintas Foundation, Brooklyn Museum, New York

BIBL. — Camón, 115 ; Wethey, 59A

112. CHRIST CARRYING THE CROSS
1587-1597
Signed: doménikos theotokópoulos epoíei
Oil on canvas. 0.66 × 0.53 m.
Collections: A. Imbert, Rome ; Thyssen-Bornemisza, Lugano

BIBL. — Mayer, 59 ; Camón, 116 ; Wethey, 59

113. CHRIST SAYING FAREWELL TO HIS MOTHER
Fig. 137
1587-1597
Oil on canvas. 0.24 × 0.21 m.
Royal Palace, Sinaia (Romania)

BIBL. — Cossío, 365 ; Mayer, 48a ; Camón, 212 ; Wethey, 71

114. CHRIST SAYING FAREWELL TO HIS MOTHER
1587-1597
Oil on canvas. 1.09 × 0.99 m.
Sacristy of San Pablo, Toledo ; R. E. Danielson Collection, Groton (Massachusetts)

BIBL. — Cossío, 259 ; Mayer, 48 ; Camón, 211 & 215 ; Wethey, 70

115. CHRIST SAYING FAREWELL TO HIS MOTHER
Fig. 138
1587-1597
Oil on canvas. 1.31 × 0.83 m.
San Vicente, Toledo ; Santa Cruz Museum, Toledo
BIBL. — Cossío, 591 ; Mayer, 47 ; Camón, 210 ; Wethey, X-69

116. THE PENITENT MAGDALEN
Fig. 139
1587-1597
Signed: doménikos theotokópoulos epoíei
Oil on canvas. 1.09 × 0.96 m.
At dealer's, Paris 1894 ; Cau Ferrat Museum, Sitges (Barcelona)

BIBL. — Cossío, 183 ; Mayer, 295 ; Camón, 453 ; Wethey, 263

117. CHRIST ON THE CROSS
Fig. 140
1587-1597
Oil on canvas. 1.93 × 1.16 m. (this work has been cut down)
Salesas Nuevas, Madrid ; Museum of Art, Cleveland, Ohio

BIBL. — Cossío, 81 ; Camón, 178 ; Wethey, 68

118. CHRIST ON THE CROSS
Fig. 141
1587-1597
Oil on canvas. 1.78 × 1.04 m.
Collections: Condesa de Aguila ; Marqués de Motilla, Seville

BIBL. — Cossío, 179 ; Camón, 170 ; Wethey, 66

119. CHRIST ON THE CROSS
Fig. 142
1587-1597
This work bears the initials *delta theta*
Oil on canvas. 0.64 × 0.37 m.
Church of San Nicolás, Toledo ; Santa Cruz Museum, Toledo

BIBL. — Cossío, 258 ; Mayer, 98 ; Camón, 174 ; Wethey, X-53

120. CHRIST ON THE CROSS
Fig. 143
1587-1597
Signed: doménikos theotokópoulos epoíei
Oil on canvas. 0.95 × 0.61 m.
Bernheim Jeune Collection, Paris 1926 ; Wildenstein Galleries, New York

BIBL. — Mayer, 96 ; Camón, 175 ; Wethey, X-50

121. THE ESPOLIO (DISROBING OF CHRIST)
Fig. 144
1587-1597
Oil on canvas. 1.65 × 0.99 m.
López Cepero Collection, Seville; Alte Pinakothek, Munich

BIBL. — Cossío, 344; Mayer, 77; Camón, 152; Wethey, 79

122. THE ESPOLIO (DISROBING OF CHRIST)
Fig. 145
1587-1597
Oil on canvas. 1.36 × 1.62 m.
Marqués de la Cenia Collection, Marratxi (Majorca); private collection

BIBL. — Cossío, 141; Mayer, 80; Camón, 159; Wethey, X-94

123. JULIÁN ROMERO DE LAS AZAÑAS AND ST. JULIAN
Fig. 146
1587-1597
Oil on canvas. 2.07 × 1.27 m.
Marqués de Lugros Collection, Alcalá la Real; Prado Museum, Madrid

BIBL. — Cossío, 304; Mayer, 337; Camón, 734; Wethey, 155

124. PORTRAIT OF A YOUNG GENTLEMAN
Fig. 147
1587-1597
Signed: doménikos theotokópoulos epoíei
Oil on canvas. 0.64 × 0.51 m.
Royal Collection; Prado Museum, Madrid

BIBL. — Cossío, 77; Mayer, 346; Camón, 742; Wethey, 144

125. PORTRAIT OF AN UNKNOWN GENTLEMAN
Fig. 148
1587-1597
Oil on canvas. 0.66 × 0.55 m.
Royal Collection; Prado Museum, Madrid

BIBL. — Cossío, 75; Mayer, 343; Camón, 730; Wethey, 142

126. RODRIGO VÁZQUEZ
Fig. 149
1587-1597
Oil on canvas. 0.59 × 0.42 m. (this work has been cut down)
In the Real Alcázar of Madrid; Prado Museum, Madrid

BIBL. — Cossío, 76; Mayer, 340; Camón, 728; Wethey, X-197

127. PORTRAIT OF AN ELDERLY GENTLEMAN
Fig. 150
1587-1597
Signed: doménikos theotokópoli (sic) epoíei
Oil on canvas. 0.46 × 0.43 m.
In the Real Alcázar of Madrid; Prado Museum, Madrid

BIBL. — Cossío, 74; Mayer, 344; Camón, 738; Wethey, 139

128. GENRE SCENE
Fig. 151
1587-1597
Signed: doménikos theotokópoulos epoíei
Oil on canvas. 0.65 × 0.90 m.
Collections: J. L. Bensusan, London; Earl of Harewood, London

BIBL. — Cossío, 343; Mayer, 304; Camón, 685; Wethey, 125

129. GENRE SCENE
Figs. 152 & 153
1587-1597
Oil on canvas. 0.66 × 0.88 m.
Collections: Féret, Paris; Mark Oliver, Edgerston Tofts, Jedburgh (Scotland)

BIBL. — Cossío, 296; Mayer, 305; Camón, 689 & 692; Wethey, 126

130. THE CORONATION OF THE VIRGIN
Fig. 155
1597-1599
Oil on canvas. 1.20 × 1.47 m.
Church of San José, Toledo

BIBL. — Cossío, 240; Mayer, 118A; Camón, 257; Wethey, 16

131. ST. JAMES THE GREAT AS A PILGRIM
Fig. 156
1597-1599
Oil on canvas. 0.43 × 0.37 m.
Carmen Mendieta Collection, Madrid; Hispanic Society, New York

BIBL. — Cossío, 110; Mayer, 180; Camón, 385; Wethey, 239

132. ST. JOSEPH AND THE INFANT CHRIST
Figs. 157 & 158
1597-1599
Signed: doménikos theotokópoulos epoíei
Oil on canvas. 1.09 × 0.56 m.
La Magdalena, Toledo; Santa Cruz Museum, Toledo

BIBL. — Cossío, 252; Mayer, 37; Camón, 269; Wethey, 254
Sketch for the central canvas in the altarpiece of the Church of San José in Toledo (Cat. 133)

133. ST. JOSEPH AND THE INFANT CHRIST
Fig. 159
1597-1599
Signed: doménikos theotokópoulos epoíei
Oil on canvas. 2.89 × 1.47 m.
Church of San José, Toledo

BIBL. — Cossío, 239; Mayer, 36; Camón, 268; Wethey, 15

134. VIRGIN AND CHILD WITH ST. MARTINA AND ST. AGNES
Figs. 160 & 161
1597-1599
This work bears the initials *delta theta*
Oil on canvas. 1.93 × 1.03 m.
Church of San José, Toledo; National Gallery, Washington

BIBL. — Cossío, 241; Mayer, 35; Camón, 227; Wethey, 17

135. ST. MARTIN AND THE BEGGAR
Fig. 162
1597-1599
Signed: doménikos theotokópoulos epoíei
Oil on canvas. 1.93 × 1.03 m.
Church of San José, Toledo; National Gallery, Washington
BIBL. — Cossío, 242 ; Mayer, 297 ; Camón, 522 ; Wethey, 18

136. THE ANNUNCIATION
Figs. 163 & 165
1597-1600
Oil on canvas. 1.14 × 0.67 m.
Collections: Pascual, Barcelona; Thyssen-Bornemisza, Lugano
BIBL. — Camón, 36 ; Wethey, 40
Sketch for the central canvas in the altarpiece of the Colegio de Doña María de Aragón (Cat. 138)

137. THE ANNUNCIATION
1597-1600
Oil on canvas. 1.10 × 0.65 m.
Condesa de Quinto Sale, Paris 1862 (?); Museum of Fine Arts, Bilbao
BIBL. — Mayer, 12 ; Camón, 33 ; Wethey, 41

138. THE ANNUNCIATION
Figs. 164 & 166
1597-1600
Signed: doménikos theotokópoulos epoíei
Oil on canvas. 3.15 × 1.74 m.
Colegio de Doña María de Aragón, Madrid; Balaguer Museum, Villanueva y Geltrú (Barcelona)
BIBL. — Cossío, 276 ; Mayer, 11 ; Camón, 25 ; Wethey, 13

139. THE BAPTISM OF CHRIST
Fig. 167
1597-1600
Oil on canvas. 1.11 × 0.47 m.
Private collection, Sicily; Galleria Nazionale, Rome
BIBL. — Mayer, 39 ; Camón, 70 ; Wethey, 45

140. THE BAPTISM OF CHRIST
Figs. 168 & 169
1597-1600
Signed: doménikos theotokópoulos epoíei
Oil on canvas. 3.50 × 1.44 m.
Colegio de Doña María de Aragón, Madrid; Prado Museum, Madrid
BIBL. — Cossío, 59 ; Mayer, 38 ; Camón, 69 ; Wethey, 14

141. THE ADORATION OF THE SHEPHERDS
Fig. 170
1597-1600
Oil on canvas. 1.11 × 0.47 m.
Private collection, Sicily; Galleria Nazionale, Rome
BIBL. — Mayer, 17; Camón, 52; Wethey, 25

142. THE ADORATION OF THE SHEPHERDS
Fig. 171
1597-1600
Signed: doménikos theotokópoulos epoíei
Oil on canvas. 3.46 × 1.37 m.
Colegio de Doña María de Aragón, Madrid; National Museum of Romania, Bucharest
BIBL. — Cossío, 360 ; Mayer, 16a ; Camón, 51 ; Wethey, 12

143. VIEW OF TOLEDO
Figs. 172 & 173
Before 1597
Signed: doménikos theotokópoulos epoíei
Oil on canvas. 1.21 × 1.09 m.
Condesa de Añover y Castañeda Collection; Metropolitan Museum, New York
BIBL. — Cossío, 83 & 403 ; Mayer, 315 ; Camón, 699 ; Wethey, 129

144. THE ANNUNCIATION
Fig. 174
1597-1603
Oil on canvas. 1.28 × 0.84 m.
S. Baron Collection, Paris 1908; Museum of Toledo (Ohio)
BIBL. — Cossío, 301 & 370 ; Mayer, 7 ; Camón, 29 & 41 ; Wethey, 42

145. THE ANNUNCIATION
1597-1603
Oil on canvas. 0.91 × 0.67 m.
Sale Baron Taylor (?), Paris (1880); Museum of Fine Arts, Budapest
BIBL. — Mayer, 6 ; Camón, 28 ; Wethey, 42A

146. THE ANNUNCIATION
1597-1603
Oil on canvas. 1.09 × 0.80 m.
Collections: Dalborgo de Primo, Madrid; Soichiro Ohara, Kurashiki (Japan)
BIBL. — Cossío, 123 ; Mayer, 8 ; Camón, 31 ; Wethey, 42B

147. THE HOLY FAMILY WITH ST. ANNE AND THE INFANT BAPTIST
Fig. 175
1597-1603
Oil on canvas. 0.52 × 0.33 m.
Carlos Beistegui Collection, Paris; National Gallery, Washington
BIBL. — Mayer, 31 ; Camón, 242 & 245 ; Wethey, 88

148. VIRGIN AND CHILD WITH ST. ANNE
Fig. 176
1597-1603
Signed: doménikos theotokópoulos epoíei
Oil on canvas. 1.78 × 1.05 m.
Hospitalillo de Santa Ana, Toledo; Santa Cruz Museum, Toledo
BIBL. — Cossío, 227 ; Mayer, 32 ; Camón, 235 ; Wethey, 93

149. THE HOLY FAMILY WITH ST. ANNE AND THE INFANT BAPTIST
1597-1603
Signed: doménikos theotokópoulos epoíei
Oil on canvas. 1.07 × 0.69 m.
Museo de la Trinidad, Madrid ; Prado Museum, Madrid
BIBL. — Cossío, 63 ; Mayer, 30 ; Camón, 237 ; Wethey, 87

150. THE VIRGIN AND CHILD WITH ST. ANNE
Fig. 177
1597-1603
Oil on canvas. 0.90 × 0.80 m.
Private collection, Scotland (?) ; Wadsworth Atheneum, Hartford (Connecticut)
BIBL. — Camón, 247 ; Wethey, 94

151. ST. JOHN THE BAPTIST
Fig. 178
1597-1603
Signed: doménikos theotokópolis (sic) epoíei
Oil on canvas. 1.11 × 0.66 m.
Discalced Carmelites, Malagón (Ciudad Real) ; M. H. de Young Memorial Museum, San Francisco
BIBL. — Camón, 409 & 410 ; Wethey, 250

152. ST. JOHN THE BAPTIST
1597-1603
Signed: doménikos theotokópoulos epoíei
Oil on canvas. 1.05 × 0.64 m.
Condesa de Ripalda Collection, Valencia ; Provincial Museum, Valencia
BIBL. — Camón, 412 ; Wethey, 251

153. ST. JEROME IN PENITENCE
Fig. 179
1597-1603
Oil on canvas. 1.68 × 1.10 m.
Felipe de la Rica Collection, Madrid ; National Gallery, Washington
BIBL. — Cossío, 113 ; Mayer, 281 ; Camón, 516 ; Wethey, 249

154. ST. FRANCIS AND THE LAY BROTHER
Fig. 180
1597-1603
Signed: doménikos theotokópoulos epoíei
Oil on canvas. 1.68 × 1.03 m.
Parish Church, Nambroca (Toledo) ; National Gallery of Canada, Ottawa
BIBL. — Camón, 554 & 632 ; Wethey, 225

155. ST. FRANCIS AND THE LAY BROTHER
1597-1603
Signed: doménikos theotokópoulos epoíei
Oil on canvas. 1.55 × 1 m.
Collections: Duke of Frías ; Max G. Bollag, Zurich (on loan to the Kunstmuseum of Berne, 1961)
BIBL. — Mayer, 247 ; Camón, 619 ; Wethey, 226

156. ST. FRANCIS AND THE LAY BROTHER
1597-1603
Signed: doménikos theotokópoulos epoíei (partially effaced)
Oil on canvas. 1.22 × 0.80 m.
Barnes Foundation, Merion, Pennsylvania
BIBL. — Wethey, 230A
It seems likely that this picture is the one that was in the Colegio de Doncellas Nobles in Toledo (Cossío, 236, plate 102)

157. ST. FRANCIS AND THE LAY BROTHER
1597-1603
Oil on canvas. 0.50 × 0.38 m.
Simonsen Collection, São Paulo

158. ST. FRANCIS IN ECSTASY
Fig. 181
1597-1603
Oil on canvas. 0.50 × 0.40 m.
Collections: Lucas de Montoya, Toledo (18th century) ; Fernández Araoz, Madrid
BIBL. — Cossío, 228 ; Camón, 656 ; Wethey, 216

159. ST. FRANCIS IN ECSTASY
1597-1603
Signed: doménikos theotokópoulos epoíei
Oil on canvas. 1.00 × 0.89 m.
Collections: Valeriano Salvatierra, Toledo ; C. Blanco Soler, Madrid
BIBL. — Cossío, 128 ; Mayer, 262 ; Camón, 655 ; Wethey, 215

160. ST. FRANCIS IN ECSTASY
Fig. 182
1597-1603
Oil on canvas. 0.75 × 0.57 m.
Musée des Beaux-Arts, Pau
BIBL. — Camón, 647 ; Wethey, 217

161. ST. FRANCIS IN ECSTASY
1597-1603
Oil on canvas. 0.60 × 0.48 m.
Dr. Miquel Collection, Barcelona

162. ST. FRANCIS IN ECSTASY
1597-1603
Oil on canvas. 1.10 × 0.87 m.
Chapel of San José, Toledo ; Conde de Guendulain y del Vado Collection, Toledo
BIBL. — Cossío, 243 ; Mayer, 232a ; Camón, 659 ; Wethey, 218

163. ST. FRANCIS KNEELING IN MEDITATION
1597-1603
Signed: doménikos theotokópoulos epoíei
Oil on canvas. 1.47 × 1.05 m.
Private collection, France ; M. H. de Young Memorial Museum, San Francisco
BIBL. — Wethey, 219

164. ST. FRANCIS KEELING IN MEDITATION
1597-1603
Signed: doménikos theotokópoulos (epoíei) (effaced)
Oil on canvas. 0.93 × 0.74 m.
Clemente de Velasco Collection, Madrid ; Art Institute, Chicago

BIBL. — Cossío, 139 ; Mayer, 267 ; Camón, 578 & 580 ; Wethey, 220

165. ST. AUGUSTINE
Fig. 183
1597-1603
Oil on canvas. 1.40 × 0.56 m.
San Nicolás, Toledo (it formed part of the altarpiece of St. Barbara) ; Santa Cruz Museum, Toledo

BIBL. — Cossío, 254 ; Mayer, 218 ; Camón, 473 ; Wethey, 199

166. ALLEGORY OF THE CAMALDOLITE ORDER
Fig. 184
1597-1603
Oil on canvas. 1.24 × 0.90 m.
Guillermo de Osma Collection, Madrid ; Instituto de Valencia de Don Juan, Madrid

BIBL. — Cossío, 118 ; Camón, 673 ; Wethey, 119

167. ALLEGORY OF THE CAMALDOLITE ORDER
1597-1603
Oil on canvas. 1.38 × 1.08 m.
Colegio del Patriarca, Valencia

BIBL. — Camón, 674 ; Wethey, 118

168. ST. JAMES THE GREAT AS A PILGRIM
Fig. 185
1597-1603
Oil on canvas. 1.23 × 0.70 m.
San Nicolás, Toledo (it formed part of the altarpiece of St. Barbara) ; Santa Cruz Museum, Toledo

BIBL. — Cossío, 255 ; Mayer, 181a ; Camón, 382 ; Wethey, 236

169. THE AGONY IN THE GARDEN
Fig. 186
1597-1603
Signed: doménikos theotokópoulos krès epoíei
Oil on canvas. 1.02 × 1.14 m.
Cacho Collection, Madrid ; Museum of Toledo (Ohio)

BIBL. — Mayer, 55 ; Camón, 109 ; Wethey, 29

170. CHRIST CLEANSING THE TEMPLE
Fig. 187
1597-1603
Oil on canvas. 0.42 × 0.53 m.
Infante Don Antonio de Borbón Collection (?) ; Frick Collection, New York

BIBL. — Cossío, 87 ; Mayer, 51 ; Camón, 97 ; Wethey, 106

171. CHRIST CLEANSING THE TEMPLE
Figs. 188 & 189
1597-1603
Oil on canvas. 1.07 × 1.24 m.
Collections: Dolores Alonso, San Sebastián ; J. L. Várez, San Sebastián

BIBL. — Cossío, 163 ; Camón, 91 ; Wethey, 109

172. CHRIST CLEANSING THE TEMPLE
Fig. 190
1597-1603
Oil on canvas. 1.06 × 1.30 m.
J. C. Robinson Collection ; National Gallery, London

BIBL. — Cossío, 342 ; Mayer, 53 ; Camón, 86 ; Wethey, 108

173. CARDINAL FERNANDO NIÑO DE GUEVARA
Fig. 191
c. 1600
Signed: doménikos theotokópoulos epoíei
Oil on canvas. 1.71 × 1.08 m.
San Pablo, Toledo (?) ; Metropolitan Museum, New York

BIBL. — Cossío, 283 ; Mayer, 331 ; Camón, 762 ; Wethey, 152

174. DIEGO DE COVARRUBIAS
Fig. 192
1597-1603
Remains of a signature
Oil on canvas. 0.67 × 0.55 m.
Pedro Salazar de Mendoza Collection, Toledo ; Greco Museum, Toledo

BIBL. — Cossío, 190 ; Mayer, 326 ; Camón, 758 ; Wethey, 137

175. ANTONIO DE COVARRUBIAS
Fig. 193
1597-1603
Signed: doménikos theotokópoulos epoíei
Oil on canvas. 0.67 × 0.55 m.
Pedro Salazar de Mendoza Collection, Toledo ; House of El Greco, Toledo

BIBL. — Cossío, 191 ; Mayer, 325 ; Camón, 756 ; Wethey, 136

176. ANTONIO DE COVARRUBIAS
Fig. 194
1597-1603
Signed: doménikos theotokópoulos epoíei
Oil on canvas. 0.65 × 0.52 m.
Archbishop's Palace, Toledo ; Louvre Museum, Paris

BIBL. — Cossío, 207 ; Mayer, 324 ; Camón, 757 ; Wethey, 135

177. PORTRAIT OF AN UNKNOWN GENTLEMAN
Fig. 195
1597-1603
Signed: doménikos theotokópoulos epoíei
Oil on canvas. 0.64 × 0.51 m.
Royal Collection ; Prado Museum, Madrid

BIBL. — Cossío, 78 ; Mayer, 347 ; Camón, 743 ; Wethey, 143

178. THE DUKE OF BENAVENTE
1597-1603. Uncertain identification
Oil on canvas. 1.01 × 0.76 m.
Musée Bonnat, Bayonne

BIBL. — Cossío, 288 ; Mayer, 321 ; Camón, 744 ; Wethey, 131

179. JORGE MANUEL THEOTOCOPULI
Fig. 196
c. 1603
Signed: doménikos theotokópoulos epoíei
Oil on canvas. 0.81 × 0.56 m.
Serafín García de la Huerta Collection, Madrid ; Provincial Museum, Seville

BIBL. — Cossío, 164 ; Mayer, 342 ; Camón, 749 ; Wethey, 158

180. ST. BERNARDINO
Fig. 197
c. 1603
Signed: doménikos theotokópoulos epoíei
Oil on canvas. 2.69 × 1.44 m.
Colegio de San Bernardino, Toledo ; Greco Museum, Toledo

BIBL. — Cossío, 68 ; Mayer, 221 ; Camón, 475 ; Wethey, 200

181. OUR LADY OF CHARITY
Figs. 198 & 199
1603-1605
Oil on canvas. 1.84 × 1.24 m.
Hospital de la Caridad, Illescas

BIBL. — Cossío, 49 ; Mayer, 112 ; Camón, 13 ; Wethey, 21

182. THE ANNUNCIATION
Fig. 200
1603-1605
Signed: doménikos theotokópoulos epoíei
Oil on (circular) canvas. Diameter 1.28 m.
Hospital de la Caridad, Illescas

BIBL. — Cossío, 52 ; Mayer, 9a ; Camón, 17 ; Wethey, 19

183. THE NATIVITY
Figs. 201 & 202
1603-1605
Signed: doménikos theotokópoulos epoíei
Oil on (circular) canvas. Diameter 1.28 m.
Hospital de la Caridad, Illescas

BIBL. — Cossío, 51 ; Mayer, 20a ; Camón, 16 ; Wethey, 22

184. THE CORONATION OF THE VIRGIN
Fig. 204
1603-1605
Oil on (oval) canvas. 0.57 × 0.74 m.
Collections: Julius Böhler, Munich ; Max Epstein, Chicago

BIBL. — Camón, 256 ; Wethey, 73

185. THE CORONATION OF THE VIRGIN
Figs. 203 & 205
1603-1605
Oil on canvas. 1.63 × 2.20 m.
Hospital de la Caridad, Illescas

BIBL. — Cossío, 50 ; Mayer, 120 ; Camón, 15 ; Wethey, 20

186. ST. ILDEFONSO
Fig. 206
1603-1605
Signed: doménikos theotokópoulos epoíei
Oil on canvas. 1.87 × 1.02 m.
Hospital de la Caridad, Illescas

BIBL. — Cossío, 48 ; Mayer, 286 ; Camón, 494 ; Wethey, 23

187. THE CRUCIFIXION
Fig. 207
1603-1607
Signed: doménicos theotokó (?) epoíei
Oil on canvas. 3.12 × 1.69 m.
San Ildefonso, Toledo ; Prado Museum, Madrid

BIBL. — Cossío, 60 ; Mayer, 88 ; Camón, 182 ; Wethey, 75

188. THE ADORATION OF THE SHEPHERDS
Figs. 208 & 209
1603-1607
Oil on canvas. 3.20 × 1.80 m.
Santo Domingo el Antiguo, Toledo ; Prado Museum, Madrid

BIBL. — Cossío, 232 ; Mayer, 21 ; Camón, 53 ; Wethey, 28

189. THE ADORATION OF THE SHEPHERDS
Figs. 210 & 211
1603-1607
Oil on canvas. 1.11 × 0.65 m.
Marqués del Arco Collection, Madrid ; Metropolitan Museum, New York

BIBL. — Cossío, 86 ; Mayer, 21a ; Camón, 57 ; Wethey, X-7

190. THE RESURRECTION
Fig. 212
1603-1607
Signed: doménikos theotokópoulos epoíei
Oil on canvas. 2.75 × 1.27 m.
Nuestra Señora de Atocha, Madrid ; Prado Museum, Madrid

BIBL. — Cossío, 61 & 402 ; Mayer, 105 & 106 ; Camón, 204 & 207 ; Wethey, 111

191. PENTECOST

Figs. 213 & 214
1603-1607
Signed: doménikos theotokópoulos epoíei
Oil on canvas. 2.75 × 1.27 m.
Museo Nacional de la Trinidad, Madrid; Prado Museum, Madrid

BIBL. — Cossío, 67; Mayer, 109; Camón, 208; Wethey, 100

192. ST. PETER

Figs. 215 & 216
1603-1607
Oil on canvas. 2.07 × 1.05 m.
San Vicente, Toledo; Monastery of the Escorial

BIBL. — Cossío, 43; Mayer, 201; Camón, 430; Wethey, 274

193. ST. ILDEFONSO

Fig. 217
1603-1607
Oil on canvas. 2.22 × 1.05 m.
San Vicente, Toledo; Monastery of the Escorial

BIBL. — Cossío, 42; Mayer, 288; Camón, 496; Wethey, 275

194. ST. SEBASTIAN

Fig. 218
1603-1607
Oil on (oval) canvas. 0.89 × 0.68 m.
Royal Palace, Bucharest

BIBL. — Cossío, 367; Mayer, 301; Camón, 536; Wethey, 280

195. THE PENITENT MAGDALEN

Fig. 219
1603-1607
Signed: doménikos theotokópoulos epoíei
Oil on canvas. 1.18 × 1.05 m.
Félix Valdés Izaguirre Collection, Bilbao

BIBL. — Camón, 471; Wethey, 264

196. ST. DOMINIC IN PRAYER

Fig. 220
1603-1607
Signed: doménikos theotokópoulos epoíei
Oil on canvas. 1.20 × 0.88 m.
Sacristy of the Cathedral of Toledo

BIBL. — Cossío, 225; Mayer, 224; Camón, 484; Wethey, 204

197. ST. DOMINIC IN PRAYER

1603-1607
Oil on canvas. 0.73 × 0.57 m.
Collections: Marqués de Aldama, Madrid; Contini-Bonacossi, Florence

BIBL. — Camón, 483; Wethey, 206

198. ST. DOMINIC IN PRAYER

1603-1607
Oil on canvas. 1.05 × 0.83 m.
Signed: doménikos theotokópoulos epoíei
J. F. Millet Collection, Fontainebleau; Museum of Fine Arts, Boston

BIBL. — Cossío, 298; Mayer, 225; Camón, 485; Wethey, 205

199. CHRIST CARRYING THE CROSS

Fig. 221
1603-1607
Signed: doménikos theotokó (poulos?) epoíei
Oil on canvas. 1.08 × 0.78 m.
San Hermenegildo, Madrid; Prado Museum, Madrid

BIBL. — Cossío, 70; Mayer, 63; Camón, 122; Wethey, 56

200. CHRIST CARRYING THE CROSS

1603-1607
Signed: doménikos theotokópoulos epoíei
Oil on canvas. 0.94 × 0.78 m.
San Esteban, Olot (Gerona)

BIBL. — Cossío, 145; Mayer, 65a; Camón, 127; Wethey, 57

201. CHRIST CARRYING THE CROSS

1603-1607
Signed: doménikos theotokó (?)
Oil on canvas. 1.01 × 0.8 m.
Cofradía del Santo Cristo de los Milagros, El Bonillo; Parish Church of Santa Catalina, El Bonillo (Albacete)

BIBL. — Camón, 121; Wethey, 58

202. ST. JOHN THE BAPTIST AND ST. JOHN THE EVANGELIST

Fig. 222
1603-1607
Oil on canvas. 1.10 × 0.87 m.
Sanctuary of San Ildefonso, Toledo; Santa Cruz Museum, Toledo

BIBL. — Cossío, 249; Mayer, 193; Camón, 418; Wethey, 252

203. ST. PETER IN TEARS

Fig. 223
1603-1607
Signed: doménikos theotokópoulos epoíei
Oil on canvas. 1.02 × 0.84 m.
Hospital de San Juan Bautista de Afuera, Toledo

BIBL. — Cossío, 245; Mayer, 207; Camón, 438; Wethey, 273

204. ST. PETER IN TEARS

Fig. 224
1603-1607
Signed: doménikos theotokópoulos epoíei
Oil on canvas. 1.02 × 0.80 m.
Cabot y Rovira Collection, Barcelona; Kunstmuseum, Oslo

BIBL. — Cossío, 371; Mayer, 206; Camón, 440 & 445; Wethey 272

205. ST. PETER IN TEARS
1603-1607
Oil on canvas. 0.94 × 0.76 m.
G. de Guillén García Collection, Barcelona; Phillips Memorial Gallery, Washington
BIBL. — Cossío, 15 & 316; Mayer, 208 & 209; Camón, 437 & 449; Wethey, 271

206. ST. PETER IN TEARS
1603-1607
Signed: doménikos theotokópoulos epoíei
Oil on canvas. 1.22 × 1.02 m.
José María de Zavala Collection, Vitoria; Fine Arts Gallery, San Diego, California
BIBL. — Cossío, 277; Mayer, 210a; Camón, 444; Wethey, 270

207. ST. PETER AND ST. PAUL
Fig. 225
1603-1607
Oil on canvas. 1.23 × 0.92 m.
Vizcondesa de San Javier Collection, Madrid; Stockholm Museum
BIBL. — Cossío, 120; Mayer, 199; Camón, 426 & 427; Wethey, 277

208. THE ANNUNCIATION
Fig. 226
1603-1607
Oil on canvas. 1.52 × 0.99 m.
Cathedral of Sigüenza
BIBL. — Cossío, 181; Mayer, 10a; Camón, 35; Wethey, 43

209. THE AGONY IN THE GARDEN
Fig. 227
1603-1607
Oil on canvas. 1.00 × 1.43 m.
Santa Teresa, San Sebastián; Félix Valdés Izaguirre Collection, Bilbao
BIBL. — Camón, 111; Wethey, 31

210. THE AGONY IN THE GARDEN
Fig. 228
1603-1607
Signed: doménikos theotokópolis [sic] epoíei
Oil on canvas. 0.86 × 0.50 m.
Parish Church, Pedroñeras; Cathedral of Cuenca
BIBL. — Camón, 101; Wethey, 34

211. THE AGONY IN THE GARDEN
Fig. 229
1603-1607
Signed: doménikos theotokópoulos epoíei. Del Griego de Toledo
Oil on canvas. 1.69 × 1.12 m.
Santa María, Andújar
BIBL. — Camón, 103; Wethey, 32

212. THE AGONY IN THE GARDEN
1603-1607
Signed: doménikos theotokópoulos epoíei
Oil on canvas. 1.70 × 1.13 m.
Cathedral of Sigüenza (?); Museum of Fine Arts, Budapest
BIBL. — Mayer, 56; Camón, 99; Wethey, 33

213. THE AGONY IN THE GARDEN
1603-1607
Oil on canvas. 1.10 × 0.76 m.
A. Pidal Collection, Madrid; National Museum of Fine Arts, Buenos Aires
BIBL. — Mayer, 56a; Camón, 105 & 107; Wethey, 35

214. ST. FRANCIS AND THE LAY BROTHER
Fig. 230
1603-1607
Oil on canvas. 1.70 × 1.40 m.
Buhler Collection, Zurich

215. ST. FRANCIS AND THE LAY BROTHER
Fig. 231
1603-1607
Oil on canvas. 1.52 × 1.13 m.
Prado Museum, Madrid

216. LADY WITH A FLOWER IN HER HAIR
Fig. 232
1603-1607
Signed: doménikos theotokópolis [sic] epoíei
Oil on canvas. 0.50 × 0.42 m.
Collections: General Meade; Viscount Rothermere, Warwick House, London
BIBL. — Cossío, 339; Mayer, 352; Camón, 717; Wethey, 147

217. PORTRAIT OF AN OLD MAN
Fig. 233
1603-1607
Oil on canvas. 0.47 × 0.39 m.
Collections: Private collection, Bologna; Contini-Bonacossi, Florence
BIBL. — Mayer, 347c; Camón, 748; Wethey, X-196

218. PORTRAIT OF A GENTLEMAN
Fig. 234
1603-1607
Oil on canvas. 1.08 × 0.86 m.
Collections: Miguel Borondo, Madrid; private collection, Milan
BIBL. — Mayer, 346c; Camón, 755; Wethey, X-175

219. PORTRAIT OF AN UNKNOWN GENTLEMAN

Fig. 235
1603-1607
Signed: doménikos theoto (?) epoíei
Oil on canvas. 0.74 × 0.47 m.
Spanish Gallery of the Louvre, Paris; Maxwell MacDonald Collection, Glasgow

BIBL. — Cossío, 347 ; Mayer, 347b ; Camón, 747 ; Wethey, 141

220. THE IMMACULATE CONCEPTION

Figs. 237, 238 & 240
Commissioned in 1607
Signed: doménikos theotokópolis (sic) epoíei
Oil on canvas. 3.47 × 1.74 m.
Chapel of Isabel de Oballe, San Vicente; Santa Cruz Museum, Toledo

BIBL. — Cossío, 261 ; Mayer, 115 ; Camón, 252 ; Wethey, 89

221. THE VISITATION

Fig. 239
Commissioned in 1607
Oil on (oval) canvas. 0.97 × 0.71 m.
Chapel of Isabel de Oballe, San Vicente; Dumbarton Oaks, Washington

BIBL. — Camón, 47 ; Wethey, 115

222. THE IMMACULATE CONCEPTION

Fig. 236
1607. It is probably the preparatory study for the *Immaculate Conception* in the Oballe chapel (Cat. 220).
Oil on canvas. 1.09 × 0.57 m.
Selgas Collection, El Pito, Cudillero (Asturias); present whereabouts unknown

BIBL. — Camón, 253 ; Wethey, 90

223. THE IMMACULATE CONCEPTION

Fig. 241
1607-1610
Oil on canvas. 1.08 × 0.82 m.
Private collection, Cadiz; Thyssen-Bornemisza Collection, Lugano

BIBL. — Cossío, 115 ; Mayer, 117 ; Camón, 251 ; Wethey, 92

224. THE BAPTISM OF CHRIST

Figs. 242 & 243
1608-1614
Oil on canvas. 3.30 × 2.11 m.
Hospital de San Juan Bautista de Afuera, Toledo

BIBL. — Cossío, 244 ; Mayer, 40 ; Camón, 71 ; Wethey, 46

225. THE ANNUNCIATION

Figs 244 to 247
1608-1614
This work has been cut down, probably towards the end of the 19th century
Upper part: *Angel Concert*
Oil on canvas. 1.12 × 2.05 m.
Collections: Marqués de Castro Serna, Madrid; National Gallery of Painting, Athens

BIBL. — Cossío, 387 ; Mayer, 13b ; Camón, 39 ; Wethey, 44b

Lower part: *Annunciation*
Oil on canvas. 2.94 × 2.09 m.
Banco Urquijo, Madrid

BIBL. — Cossío, 136 ; Mayer, 13a ; Camón, 38 ; Wethey, 44a

226. THE FIFTH SEAL OF THE APOCALYPSE

Figs. 248 & 249
1608-1614
Oil on canvas. 2.25 × 1.93 m.
Hospital de San Juan Bautista de Afuera, Toledo; Metropolitan Museum, New York

BIBL. — Cossío, 327 ; Mayer, 122 ; Camón, 266 ; Wethey, 120

227. LAOCOÖN

Figs. 250 & 251
1608-1614
Oil on canvas. 1.42 × 1.93 m.
Alcázar Collection, Madrid; National Gallery, Washington

BIBL. — Cossío, 162 ; Mayer, 311 ; Camón, 696 ; Wethey, 127

228. VIEW AND PLAN OF TOLEDO

Figs. 252-254.
c. 1610-1614
Oil on canvas. 1.32 × 2.28 m.
Pedro Salazar de Mendoza Collection, Toledo; Greco Museum, Toledo

BIBL. — Cossío, 205 ; Mayer, 314 ; Camón, 700 ; Wethey, 128

229. THE MARRIAGE OF THE VIRGIN

Fig. 255
1608-1614
Oil on canvas. 1.10 × 0.83 m.
Condesa de Quinto Collection, Madrid; National Museum of Romania, Bucharest

BIBL. — Cossío, 361 ; Mayer, 14 ; Camón, 19 ; Wethey, 96

230. THE ADORATION OF THE SHEPHERDS

Fig. 256
1603-1608
Oil on canvas. 1.64 × 1.07 m.
Duke of Híjar Collection, Madrid; Metropolitan Museum, New York

BIBL. — Cossío, 282 ; Mayer, 19 ; Camón, 54 ; Wethey, 27

231. CHRIST IN THE HOUSE OF SIMON
Fig. 257
1608-1614
Oil on canvas. 1.43 × 1.00 m.
Guinea Collection, Bilbao; Art Institute, Chicago
BIBL. — Cossío, 325; Mayer, 46a; Camón, 77; Wethey, 65

232. CHRIST IN THE HOUSE OF SIMON
1608-1614
Oil on canvas. 1.50 × 1.04 m.
Collections: José de Madrazo; Oscar B. Cintas Foundation, New York
BIBL. — Cossío, 314 & 441; Mayer, 46; Camón, 76; Wethey, 64

233. CHRIST CLEANSING THE TEMPLE
Figs. 258 & 259
1608-1614
Oil on canvas. 1.06 × 1.04 m.
Cofradía del Santísimo Sacramento, Church of San Ginés, Madrid
BIBL. — Mayer, 54; Camón, 89; Wethey, 110

234. VIRGIN AND CHILD
Fig. 260
1608-1614
Oil on canvas. 0.90 × 0.71 m.
Collections: Marqués de Perinat, Madrid; Marquesa de Campo Real, Madrid
BIBL. — Mayer, 33; Camón, 230; Wethey, 95

235. ST. VERONICA
Fig. 261
1608-1614
Oil on canvas. 1.12 × 0.83 m.
Collections: José Casado del Alisal, Madrid; Bonifacio del Carril, Buenos Aires
BIBL. — Cossío, 358; Mayer, 67b; Camón, 139 & 140; Wethey, X-459

236. THE APPARITION OF THE VIRGIN AND CHILD TO ST. HYACINTH
Fig. 262
1608-1614
Oil on canvas. 1.58 × 0.98 m.
Condesa de Quinto Collection; Barnes Foundation, Merion, Pennsylvania
BIBL. — Mayer, 227; Camón, 498 & 500; Wethey, 234

237. THE APPARITION OF THE VIRGIN AND CHILD TO ST. HYACINTH
1608-1614
Oil on canvas. 0.99 × 0.61 m.
Henri Rouart Collection; Memorial Art Gallery, Rochester, New York
BIBL. — Mayer, 227a; Camón, 490 & 497; Wethey, 233

238. ST. CATHERINE OF ALEXANDRIA
1608-1614
Illegible and fragmentary signature in Greek italics
Oil on canvas. 0.90 × 0.61 m.
Collections: Marqués de Alós, Barcelona; William A. Coolidge, Topsfield, Massachusetts
BIBL. — Cossío, 17; Camón, 481; Wethey, 201

239. ST. CATHERINE OF ALEXANDRIA
Fig. 263
1608-1614
Signed: doménikos theotokópoulos epoíei
Oil on canvas. 0.57 × 0.48 m.
José Núñez del Prado Collection, Madrid; at dealer's, New York
BIBL. — Mayer, 289; Camón, 477; Wethey, 202

240. THE BIRTH OF THE VIRGIN
Fig. 264
1608-1614
Oil on canvas. 0.62 × 0.36 m.
Collections: Marqués de Alós; Emil G. Bührle, Zurich
BIBL. — Cossío, 18; Camón, 18; Wethey, X-33

241. ST. SEBASTIAN
Figs. 265-267
1608-1614
This work has been cut in two
Upper part: Oil on canvas. 1.15 × 0.85 m.
Marqués de la Vega Inclán Collection, Madrid; Prado Museum, Madrid
BIBL. — Cossío, 265; Mayer, 302; Camón, 537; Wethey, 281
Lower part: Oil on canvas. 0.86 × 1.05 m.
Collections: Marqués de la Vega Inclán, Madrid; Arenaza, Madrid

242. JERÓNIMO DE CEBALLOS
Fig. 268
1608-1614
Oil on canvas. 0.64 × 0.54 m.
Royal Collection; Prado Museum, Madrid
BIBL. — Cossío, 79; Mayer, 322; Camón, 741; Wethey, 133

243. FRAY HORTENSIO FÉLIX PARAVICINO
Fig. 269
c. 1610
Signed: doménikos theotokópoulos epoíei
Oil on canvas. 1.13 × 0.86 m.
Duke of Arcos Collection, Madrid; Museum of Fine Arts, Boston
BIBL. — Cossío, 278; Mayer, 335a; Camón, 751; Wethey, 153

244. CARDINAL JUAN DE TAVERA
Fig. 270
c. 1608
Signed: doménikos theotokópoulos epoíei
Oil on canvas. 1.03 × 0.82 m.
Pedro Salazar de Mendoza Collection, Toledo; Hospital de San Juan Bautista de Afuera, Toledo
BIBL. — Cossío, 247; Mayer, 339; Camón, 763; Wethey, 157

245. A TRINITARIAN MONK
Fig. 271
1610-1614
Signed: doménikos theotokópoulos epoíei
Oil on canvas. 0.93 × 0.84 m.
Marqués de la Torrecilla Collection, Madrid; William Rockhill Nelson Gallery of Art, Kansas City
BIBL. — Cossío, 134; Mayer, 349; Camón, 754; Wethey, 159

246. PORTRAIT OF AN UNKNOWN GENTLEMAN
Fig. 272
1610-1614
Oil on canvas. 0.79 × 0.64 m.
Possibly the portrait of Dr. Soria de Herrera
Ursáis Collection, Seville; Musée de Picardie, Amiens
BIBL. — Mayer, 346a; Camón, 746 & 768; Wethey, 140

247. CANON BOSIO
Fig. 273
1610-1614
Oil on canvas. 1.16 × 0.86 m.
Collections: Condesa de Quinto; Royal Palace, Sinaia (Romania)
BIBL. — Cossío, 359; Mayer, 347a; Camón, 760; Wethey, 132

248. GARCÍA IBÁÑEZ MÚGICA DE BRACAMONTE
Fig. 274
1610-1614
Oil on canvas. 1.20 × 1.00 m.
Museum of the Cathedral of Avila
BIBL. — Cossío, 14; Mayer, 334; Camón, 729; Wethey, X-169

THE ARTECHE APOSTLE SERIES

A series purchased in Toledo by the Madrid dealer Arteche and now scattered in several collections.

All in oil on canvas, 0.36 × 0.26 m., some of them being signed with initials in Greek italics.

Probably the first of the Apostle series
1603-1608

249. ST. ANDREW
Fig. 286
Plandiura Collection, Barcelona
BIBL. — Camón, 351 & 396; Wethey, X-236

250. ST. MATTHEW
Fig. 290
Museum of Fine Arts, Bilbao
BIBL. — Cossío, 35; Camón, 353 & 405; Wethey, X-421

251. ST. LUKE
Fig. 294
Vda. de Arias Collection, Zaragoza
BIBL. — Camón, 349; Wethey, X-398

252. ST. PHILIP
Fig. 299
Present whereabouts unknown
BIBL. — Camón, 388; Wethey, X-450

253. ST. THOMAS
Fig. 303
Present whereabouts unknown
BIBL. — Cossío, 28; Mayer, 214; Camón, 355 & 389; Wethey, X-457

254. ST. BARTHOLOMEW
Fig. 307
Present whereabouts unknown
BIBL. — Cossío, 132; Camón, 356; Wethey, X-242

255. ST. JAMES THE LESS
Fig. 321
Vda. de Arias Collection, Zaragoza
BIBL. — Camón, 350; Wethey, X-363

256. ST. PETER
Fig. 328
Present whereabouts unknown

257. ST. PAUL
Present whereabouts unknown
BIBL. — Cossío, 29; Mayer, 195; Camón, 352 & 354; Wethey, X-429

THE MARQUÉS DE SAN FELIZ APOSTLE SERIES

A series from the monastery of San Pelayo in Oviedo, now in the palace of the Marqués de San Feliz in Oviedo.

All in oil on canvas, 0.70 × 0.53 m., deriving from the Arteche series, some of them with incorrect inscriptions.

Some of these paintings are signed with Greek initials.
1603-1608

258. ST. JOHN THE EVANGELIST
Fig. 280
BIBL. — Cossío, 150; Mayer, 139; Camón, 315; Wethey, X-210

259. ST. ANDREW

BIBL. — Cossío, 148 ; Mayer, 137 ; Camón, 313 ; Wethey, X-207

260. ST. MATTHEW

Fig. 291
Erroneously inscribed "St Philip"

BIBL. — Cossío, 151 ; Mayer, 140 ; Camón, 316 ; Wethey, X-213

261. ST. LUKE

Fig. 295
Erroneously inscribed "St Simon"

BIBL. — Cossío, 156 ; Mayer, 145 ; Camón, 321 (?) ; Wethey, X-212

262. ST. PHILIP

Erroneously inscribed "St Matthew"
Signed with Greek initials

BIBL. — Cossío, 153 ; Mayer, 142 ; Camón, 318 ; Wethey, X-216

263. ST. THOMAS

Signed with Greek initials

BIBL. — Cossío, 154 ; Mayer, 143 ; Camón, 319 ; Wethey, X-218

264. ST. SIMON

Fig. 312
Erroneously inscribed "St Bartholomew"

BIBL. — Cossío, 152 ; Mayer, 141 ; Camón, 317 ; Wethey, X-217

265. ST. JUDE

Fig. 316

BIBL. — Cossío, 157 ; Mayer, 146 ; Camón, 322 ; Wethey, X-211

266. ST. JAMES THE GREAT

Fig. 324

Signed with Greek initials

BIBL. — Cossío, 149 ; Mayer, 138 ; Camón, 314 ; Wethey, X-208

267. ST. JAMES THE LESS

Signed with Greek initials

BIBL. — Cossío, 155 ; Mayer, 144 ; Camón, 320 ; Wethey, X-209

268. ST. PETER

BIBL. — Cossío, 146 ; Mayer, 135 ; Camón, 311 ; Wethey, X-215

269. ST. PAUL

Fig. 330
Signed with Greek initials

BIBL. — Cossío, 147 ; Mayer, 136 ; Camón, 312 ; Wethey, X-214

THE APOSTLE SERIES IN THE CATHEDRAL OF TOLEDO

Complete series
Oil on canvas. 1 × 0.76 m.
Works by the hand of El Greco
1608-1614

270. CHRIST
Fig. 275
BIBL. — Cossío, 211 ; Mayer, 148 ; Camón, 272 ; Wethey, 160

271. ST. JOHN THE EVANGELIST
Fig. 281
BIBL. — Cossío, 216 ; Mayer, 153 ; Camón, 277 ; Wethey, 164

272. ST. ANDREW
Fig. 284
BIBL. — Cossío, 214 ; Mayer, 151 ; Camón, 275 ; Wethey, 161

273. ST. MATTHEW
Fig. 285
BIBL. — Cossío, 220 ; Mayer, 157 ; Camón, 281 ; Wethey, 167

274. ST. LUKE
Fig. 298
BIBL. — Cossío, 215 ; Mayer, 155 ; Camón, 279 ; Wethey, 166

275. ST. PHILIP
Fig. 300
BIBL. — Cossío, 217 ; Mayer, 154 ; Camón, 278 ; Wethey, 170

276. ST. THOMAS
Fig. 304
BIBL. — Cossío, 219 ; Mayer, 156 ; Camón, 280 ; Wethey, 172

277. ST. SIMON
Fig. 313
Erroneously inscribed "St Mark"
BIBL. — Cossío, 223 ; Mayer, 160 ; Camón, 284 ; Wethey, 171

278. ST. JUDE
Figs. 317 & 318
BIBL. — Cossío, 222 ; Mayer, 159 ; Camón, 283 ; Wethey, 165

279. ST. JAMES THE LESS
Fig. 320
BIBL. — Cossío, 221 ; Mayer, 158 ; Camón, 282 ; Wethey, 163

280. ST. JAMES THE GREAT
BIBL. — Cossío, 218 ; Mayer, 152 ; Camón, 276 ; Wethey, 162

281. ST. PETER
BIBL. — Cossío, 212 ; Mayer, 149 ; Camón, 273 ; Wethey, 169

282. ST. PAUL
BIBL. — Cossío, 213 ; Mayer, 150 ; Camón, 274 ; Wethey, 168

THE APOSTLE SERIES IN THE GRECO MUSEUM

From the Hospital de Santiago, Toledo
Oil on canvas. 0.97 × 0.77 m.
1608-1614

283. CHRIST
Fig. 276
BIBL. — Cossío, 204 ; Mayer, 161 ; Camón, 294 ; Wethey, 173

284. ST. JOHN THE EVANGELIST
Fig. 282
BIBL. — Cossío, 195 ; Mayer, 166 ; Camón, 299 ; Wethey, 178

285. ST. ANDREW
Fig. 287
BIBL. — Cossío, 193 ; Mayer, 164 ; Camón, 297 ; Wethey, 174

286. ST. MATTHEW
Fig. 292
BIBL. — Cossío, 196 ; Mayer, 168 ; Camón, 301 ; Wethey, 180

287. ST. PHILIP
Figs. 301 & 302
BIBL. — Cossío, 201 ; Mayer, 167 ; Camón, 300 ; Wethey, 183

288. ST. THOMAS
Fig. 305
BIBL. — Cossío, 198 ; Mayer, 169 ; Camón, 302 ; Wethey, 185

289. ST. BARTHOLOMEW
Figs. 310 & 311
BIBL. — Cossío, 202 ; Mayer, 170 ; Camón, 303 ; Wethey, 175

290. ST. SIMON
Fig. 314
BIBL. — Cossío, 200 ; Mayer, 173 ; Camón, 306 ; Wethey, 184

291. ST. JUDE
Fig. 319
BIBL. — Cossío, 197 ; Mayer, 172 ; Camón, 305 ; Wethey, 179

292. ST. JAMES THE LESS
Fig. 323
BIBL. — Cossío, 199 ; Mayer, 171 ; Camón, 304 ; Wethey, 177

293. ST. JAMES THE GREAT
Fig. 326
BIBL. — Cossío, 194 ; Mayer, 165 ; Camón, 298 ; Wethey, 176

294. ST. PETER
Fig. 329
BIBL. — Cossío, 192 ; Mayer, 162 ; Camón, 295 ; Wethey, 182

295. ST. PAUL
Fig. 331
Signed: doménikos theotokópoulos epoíei
BIBL. — Cossío, 203 ; Mayer, 163 ; Camón, 296 ; Wethey, 181

THE ALMADRONES APOSTLE SERIES

Found in 1936 in the Parish Church of Almadrones (Guadalajara)
Oil on canvas. 0.72 × 0.55 m.
1610-1614

296. CHRIST
Fig. 278
Prado Museum, Madrid
BIBL. — Camón, 286 ; Wethey, 186

297. ST. JOHN THE EVANGELIST
Fig. 283
Signed with Greek initials
Kimbell Art Foundation, Fort Worth, Texas
BIBL. — Camón, 287 ; Wethey, 189

298. ST. ANDREW
Fig. 288
Signed with Greek initials
County Museum, Los Angeles
BIBL. — Wethey, 187

299. ST. MATTHEW
Fig. 293
Signed with Greek initials
Clowes Foundation, Indianapolis
BIBL. — Camón, 291 ; Wethey, 191

300. ST. LUKE
Fig. 297
Signed with Greek initials
Clowes Foundation, Indianapolis
BIBL. — Camón, 289 ; Wethey, 190

301. ST. THOMAS
Fig. 306
Signed with Greek initials
Prado Museum, Madrid
BIBL. — Camón, 290 ; Wethey, 194

302. ST. SIMON
Fig. 315
Signed with Greek initials
Clowes Foundation, Indianapolis
BIBL. — Camón, 293 ; Wethey, 193

303. ST. JAMES THE GREAT
Fig. 327
Signed with Greek initials
Prado Museum, Madrid
BIBL. — Camón, 288 ; Wethey, 188

304. ST. PAUL
Prado Museum, Madrid
BIBL. — Camón, 292 ; Wethey, 192

PAINTINGS FROM OTHER APOSTLE SERIES OF UNKNOWN ORIGIN

305. CHRIST
Fig. 277
Oil on canvas. 0.72 × 0.57 m.
Signed with Greek initials
Juan de Ibarra Collection, Madrid ; National Gallery of Scotland, Edinburgh
BIBL. — Cossío, 107 ; Mayer, 133 ; Camón, 337 ; Wethey, 133

306. ST. JOHN THE EVANGELIST
Fig. 279
Oil on canvas. 0.90 × 0.77 m.
César Cabañas Collection, Madrid ; Prado Museum, Madrid
BIBL. — Cossío, 94 ; Mayer, 185 ; Camón, 343 ; Wethey, 253

307. ST. ANDREW
Fig. 289
Oil on canvas. 0.74 × 0.57 m.
Núñez del Prado Collection, Córdoba ; Rhode Island School of Design, Providence
BIBL. — Cossío, 41 ; Mayer, 177 ; Camón, 395 & 397 ; Wethey, X-235

308. ST. LUKE
Fig. 296
Signed: doménikos theotokópoulos
Oil on canvas. 0.71 × 0.535 m.
Condesa de Añover y Castañeda Collection, Madrid ; Hispanic Society, New York
BIBL. — Cossío, 82 ; Mayer, 213 ; Camón, 342 ; Wethey, 257

309. ST. JAMES THE LESS
Fig. 322
Oil on canvas. 1.03 × 0.83 m.
Dr. Félix Schlayer Collection, Madrid ; Basle Museum
BIBL. — Mayer, 179 ; Camón, 344 ; Wethey, X-362

310. ST. JAMES THE GREAT
Fig. 325
Oil on canvas. 0.50 × 0.43 m.
Marqués de la Vega Inclán Collection, Madrid ; Museum of Fine Arts, Budapest
BIBL. — Mayer, 182a ; Camón, 340 ; Wethey, X-370

311. ST. PETER
Oil on canvas. 0.71 × 0.55 m.
Jesús Lacuadra Collection, Valencia ; Palace of the Legion of Honor, San Francisco, California
BIBL. — Cossío, 392-394 ; Mayer, 200 ; Camón, 360, 363 and 366 ; Wethey, 268

312. ST. PAUL
Signed with Greek initials
Oil on canvas. 0.70 × 0.56 m.
Jesús Lacuadra Collection, Valencia ; City Art Museum, St. Louis, Missouri
BIBL. — Cossío, 274 ; Mayer, 196 ; Camón, 338 and 360 ; Wethey, 266

BIBLIOGRAPHY

Amador de los Ríos, Rodrigo: "Ruinas del palacio de Villena", in *Revista de archivos, bibliotecas y museos* IV, 1900, pp. 137-139.

Azcárate, José María de: "La iconografía de "el Expolio" del Greco", in *Archivo Español de Arte* XVIII, 1955, pp. 189-197.

Busuiocenau, A.: *Les tableaux du Greco de la collection royale de Roumanie.* Brussels, 1937.

Camón Aznar, J.: *Dominico Greco.* Madrid, 1950 ; 2nd edition, 1970.

Ceán Bermúdez, J. A.: *Diccionario histórico de los más ilustres profesores de las bellas artes en España.* Madrid, 1800.

Cedillo, Conde de: "Martín Muñoz de las Posadas", in *Boletín de la Sociedad Española de Excursiones* 38, 1936, p. 237.

Cossío, Manuel B..: *El Greco.* Madrid, 1908.

El Greco. Exhibition organized by the *Gazette des Beaux-Arts.* Paris, 1937.

El Greco (introduction by Ludwig Goldschneider). New York, Oxford University Press, 1938.

Frati, Tiziana: *L'opera completa del Greco.* Milan, 1969.

Gaya Nuño, J. A.: *La pintura española fuera de España.* Madrid, 1958.

Gómez Menor, J.: "En torno a la figura de Jerónima de las Cuevas (Un nuevo autógrafo del Greco)", in *Arte Español* XXV, 1963-1967, pp. 96-103.

Gómez-Moreno, Manuel: *El Greco. El entierro del Conde de Orgaz.* Barcelona, 1943.

Gómez-Moreno, Manuel: *El Greco (Dominico Theotocópuli).* Barcelona, 1943.

Gómez-Moreno, María Elena: "La casa del Greco", in *Mundo Hispánico* 173, 1962, pp. 37-49.

Harris, Enriqueta: *El Greco. The Purification of the Temple in the National Gallery.* London, Lund, Humphries [n.d.].

Kehrer, Hugo: *Greco als Gestalt des Manierismus.* Munich, 1939.

López Rey, José: "El Greco's Baroque Light and Form", in *Gazette des Beaux-Arts* XXIV, 1943, pp. 73-84.

Mancini, G.: *Considerazione sulla pittura.* Critical edition by A. Marucchi (2 vols.). Rome, 1956-57, p. XV.

Martín González, Juan José: "El Greco arquitecto", in *Goya* 26, 1958, pp. 86-88.

Martínez, Jusepe: *Discursos practicables del nobilísimo arte de la pintura.* Madrid, 1866.

Mélida, José Ramón: "El arte antiguo y el Greco", in *Boletín de la Sociedad Española de Excursiones* XXIII, 1915, pp. 89-103.

Mayer, August L.: *El Greco.* Munich, 1926.

Mayer, August L.: *El Greco.* Berlin, 1931.

Mayer, August L.: "Una obra juvenil del Greco", in *Archivo Español de Arte y Arqueología* XI, 1935, pp. 205-207.

Mayer, August L.: "Notas sobre la iconografía sagrada en las obras del Greco", in *Archivo Español de Arte* XIV, 1940-41, pp. 164-168.

Mertzios, Constantino D.: "Colección de los libros del notario de Creta Miguel Marás (1538-1578)". Paper presented at the First International Conference on Crete, 1961.

Nolhac, Pierre de: "Les collections de Fulvio Orsini", in *Gazette des Beaux-Arts* III période, XXIX, 1884, p. 433.

Pacheco, Francisco: *Arte de la Pintura* (edited by F. J. Sánchez Cantón). Madrid, 1956.

Palomino, Antonio: *El Parnaso español pintoresco laureado con las vidas de los pintores estatuarios eminentes españoles* (third volume of the author's *Museo pictórico y escala óptica*). Madrid, 1724. (Republished by M. Aguilar, Madrid, 1947.)

Pallucchini, Rodolfo: *Il polittico del Greco della R. Galleria Estense alla formazione dell'artista.* Rome, 1937.

Parro, Sisto Ramón: *Toledo en la mano.* Toledo, 1857.

POLERO: *Catálogo de los cuadros del monasterio de San Lorenzo.* Madrid, 1857.

PONZ, ANTONIO: *Viaje de España.* Madrid, 1772-1794. (Republished by M. Aguilar, Madrid, 1947.)

RAMÍREZ DE ARELLANO, R.: *Catálogo de artífices que trabajaron en Toledo.* Toledo, 1920.

RUTTER, FRANK: *El Greco.* London, 1930.

SALAS, X. DE: *Miguel Angel y el Greco.* Real Academia de Bellas Artes de San Fernando. Madrid, 1967.

SALAS, X. DE: "Un exemplaire des "vies" de Vassari annoté par le Greco", in *Gazette des Beaux-Arts* LXIX, 1967, pp. 177-180.

SAN ROMÁN, FRANCISCO DE BORJA: *El Greco en Toledo.* Toledo, 1910.

SAN ROMÁN, FRANCISCO DE BORJA: "De la vida del Greco", in *Archivo Español de Arte y Arqueología* III, 1927, pp. 139-195, 275-339.

SAN ROMÁN, FRANCISCO DE BORJA: "Documentos del Greco referentes a los cuadros de Santo Domingo el Antiguo", in *Archivo Español de Arte y Arqueología* X, 1934, pp. 1-13.

SÁNCHEZ CANTÓN, F. J.: *Fuentes literarias para la historia del arte español.* Madrid, 1923-1941 (P. Francisco de los Santos: «Descripción breve del monasterio de S. Lorenzo el Real del Escorial», II, pp. 247, 293).

SÁNCHEZ CANTÓN, F. J.: "La mujer de los cuadros del Greco", in *Escorial, revista de cultura y letras* I, 1942, p. 15.

SIGÜENZA, PADRE: *Historia de la orden de San Jerónimo.* Madrid, 1595-1605.

SOEHNER, HALLDOR: "Der Stand der Greco-Forschung", in *Zeitschrift für Kunstgeschichte* XIX, 1596, pp. 47-75.

SOEHNER, HALLDOR: "Greco in Spanien. Teil I", in *Müncher Jahrbuch der bildenden Kunst,* third series, VIII, 1957, pp. 123-194 ; Teil II-III *ibid.,* IX-X, 1958-1959, pp. 147-242 ; Teil IV, *ibid.,* XI, 1960, pp. 173-217.

SOEHNER, HALLDOR: *Una obra maestra del Greco: La capilla de San José de Toledo.* Madrid, 1961.

SORIA, MARTÍN S.: "Greco's Italian Period", in *Arte veneta* VIII, 1954, pp. 212-221.

STIRLING-MAXWELL, SIR WILLIAM: *Annals of the artists of Spain.* 1848.

TORMO MONZÓ, ELÍAS: "El homenaje español al Greco en Creta su patria", in *Boletín de la Sociedad Española de Excursiones* XLII, 1934, pp. 243-290.

TRAPIER, E. DU GUÉ: "The son of El Greco", in *Notes Hispanic* III, 1943, pp. 1-47.

TRAPIER, E. DU GUÉ: *El Greco, early years in Toledo.* New York, Hispanic Society, 1958.

TRAPIER, E. DU GUÉ: "El Greco in the Farnese Palace, Rome", in *Gazette des Beaux-Arts* LI, 1958, pp. 73-90.

VALLENTIN, ANTONINA: *El Greco.* Garden City, 1955.

VINIEGRA, S.: *Exposición de las obras del Greco* (catalogue). Museo Nacional de Pintura. Madrid, 1902.

WATERHOUSE, E. K.: "El Greco's Italian Period", in *Art Studies* VIII, 1930, pp. 61-88.

WETHEY, HAROLD E.: *El Greco and his school.* Princeton, 1962.

WETHEY, HAROLD E.: *El Greco y su escuela.* Madrid, 1967.

WILLUMSEN, J. F.: *La jeunesse du peintre El Greco.* Paris, 1927. 2 volumes.

ZARCO CUEVAS, J.: *Pintores españoles en San Lorenzo el Real de El Escorial.* Madrid, 1931.

ZARCO DEL VALLE: "Documentos inéditos para la historia de las Bellas Artes en España", in *Colección de documentos inéditos* LV, 1870, pp. 604-605.

ZERVOS, CHRISTIAN: *Les œuvres du Greco en Espagne.* Paris, 1939.

INDEXES

GEOGRAPHICAL INDEX

INDEX OF WORKS AND NAMES